THE WORLD OF
TIME INC.

PREVIOUS VOLUMES

TIME INC.
The Intimate History of a Publishing Enterprise
Volume One: 1923–1941
by ROBERT T. ELSON
(1968)

THE WORLD OF TIME INC.
The Intimate History of a Publishing Enterprise
Volume Two: 1941–1960
by ROBERT T. ELSON
(1973)

THE WORLD OF
TIME INC.

The Intimate History of a

Changing Enterprise

Volume Three: 1960-1980

BY CURTIS PRENDERGAST

WITH GEOFFREY COLVIN

Edited by Robert Lubar

New York ATHENEUM *1986*

Copyright © 1986 by Time Inc.
All rights reserved
Library of Congress catalog card number 68-16868
ISBN 0-689-11315-3
Published simultaneously in Canada by Collier Macmillan Canada, Inc.
Composition by P & M Typesetting, Inc., Waterbury, Connecticut
Manufactured by Fairfield Graphics, Fairfield, Pennsylvania
Designed by Harry Ford
First Edition

Acknowledgments

THIS VOLUME of the Time Inc. history relies—as did the two preceding volumes—on both the corporate record and the personal accounts of the Time Inc. staff, past and present, who participated in the events chronicled herein. Many were interviewed; all gave freely of their time, and the regret is that more of them could not be cited by name. Their assistance, though, is gratefully acknowledged.

Basic research for this volume, including most of the interviewing and all the searching through the voluminous corporate files was done by researchers Raïssa Silverman and Marta Dorion, who contributed also to the text. Jane Furth joined later in the research and checking operation, as did Valerine Marchant and Mary Fernandez, experienced Time Inc. researchers all.

Leo McCarthy of the *Fortune* art staff designed the picture spreads. Copy editing was done by Mary Grace, a *Fortune* veteran, and Ricki Tarlow, formerly of Time-Life Books and *Time*. Assisting in the picture rescarch were Colleen Murphy and Kim Dramer-Pannell, both of whom also handled copy processing. Indexing for this volume was the work of Louise Hedberg.

As head of the corporate archives, Elaine Felsher, who worked also on the previous volume of the Time Inc. history, lent valuable help. Assistance came also from the staffs of the Time Inc. library, particularly the index section.

The writing was a joint effort. Geoffrey Colvin, of *Fortune's* board of editors, wrote a number of the chapters, and, continuing the tradition of the previous volumes, it was a former managing editor of *Fortune*—in this instance, Robert Lubar—who edited the text. Casting an eye overall on the project was Ralph Graves, who in his long Time Inc. career was managing editor of *Life*, associate publisher of *Time* and editorial director of Time Inc.

CURTIS PRENDERGAST

Contents

Contents

Illustrations

ix

x

Michael Fuchs
Winston Cox
Philip Kunhardt Jr. and Charles Whittingham   Hugh Patrick Brown
Leon Jaroff   Hugh Patrick Brown
Richard Stolley and Patricia Ryan   Nancy Kessler
Reginald Brack Jr.   Bachrach
Richard Durrell and
   Christopher Meigher III   Raeanne Rubenstein/Telephoto
William Rukeyser   John Marmaras/Woodfin Camp and Associates
Marshall Loeb
Time Inc. directors, 1979   Henry Groskinsky
Henry Grunwald   Nancy Kessler
Richard Munro and Ralph Davidson   Ted Thai

Prologue

S IX DECADES separate Time Inc. of the 1980s from the publishing enterprise launched with the creation of *Time*, The Weekly News-Magazine. From the $85,675 that Henry R. Luce and Briton Hadden borrowed from their Yale classmates and family friends—and others willing to take a chance on an idea—corporate assets have swelled to over $2.5 billion, annual revenues to over $3 billion. From the small crew who squeezed into three taxis to take copy to the printer's and see *Time*'s first issue to press, the company has grown to some 20,000 employees worldwide, handling a wide range of corporate activities. Time Inc. has become the world's largest magazine publisher, the U.S.'s largest direct-mail book publisher, operator of the country's largest pay television network and a major owner of cable TV systems, among other varied interests.

The previous volumes of the Time Inc. corporate history have recounted events up to 1960. This volume carries the story forward into the early 1980s. The earlier volumes were subtitled, "The Intimate History of a Publishing Enterprise." The change of subtitle in the current volume is significant. During the first two-thirds of Time Inc.'s existence, its business was principally the production of magazines, although by the mid-1950s diversification into other fields had begun. That diversification accelerated greatly in the succeeding two decades. Not only did Time Inc. expand its interests in television, book publishing and pulp and paper manufacture, but it went into newspapers, educational systems, films, marketing services and, most importantly, into the building materials and paperboard container industries through a corporate merger—later reversed. With that reversal, Time Inc. returned largely to the communications field, where its interests are in entertainment as well as information, in video as well as publishing.

In another important respect this volume differs from its predecessors. It was appropriate for them to tell the story largely in terms of one individual, Harry Luce, who assumed principal direction of the company after the death of his partner in 1929. For Luce, to all intents and purposes, *was* Time Inc. He set the editorial tone, made the crucial business decisions, spoke for the company to the world, attracted to himself the attacks and criticisms to which Time Inc. was subjected—indeed, he personified what caused it to be admired, or disliked, by the public.

Luce's death in 1967 removed the man, but not his influence. Although he had passed the mantle of editor-in-chief to his deputy, Hedley Donovan, three years earlier, Luce was to the end a powerful presence in the company. Donovan recalled an observation made by a onetime *Fortune* colleague, the economist John Kenneth Galbraith, that while employees of most other companies, when they went to lunch together, talked about money or sex or sports or the stock market, the Time Inc. people talked about Luce. He was "an inexhaustible source of stories, jokes, anecdotes, quotations," said Donovan, who considered this to be "a very good aspect of leadership."

Of the many aspects of Luce's legacy to Time Inc., perhaps the most frequently cited is the separation of editorial and publishing functions—known around the company as the separation of "church" and "state." Designed to keep editorial judgments untainted by commercial considerations, the separation doctrine acquired under him almost sacred status, even if profaned sometimes in actual practice. Also surviving Luce is the belief he held that publishing should fulfill a purpose, this purpose being not simply to prosper but to educate—"to inform, to awaken, to edify, to persuade," as a close friend of his, *Life* editorialist John K. Jessup, phrased it. Luce was contemptuous of the give-the-people-what-they-want theory of publishing, considering it a formula for mediocrity if not worse: an abdication of the editor-publisher's responsibility. His aim was to make what interested and concerned him of interest and concern to the readers. Out of this came a corporate approach to magazine creation that Andrew Heiskell, who was chairman from 1960 to 1980, once put this way: "A publication depends on a great idea, not on there being a market out there. Obviously, there's a relationship . . . but you start with an idea, rather than trying to get an idea which goes with that market."

The top officers who ran Time Inc. during the 1960s, and in some cases through the 1970s, had been handpicked by Luce. A generation younger than he, they had worked directly with him, usually on one or more of the original magazines—*Time, Fortune* and *Life*. The generation that succeeded them had, for the most part, only a fleeting acquaintance with Luce, but had grown up with the company. Those on the business side had usually climbed the ladder from advertising sales or circulation to assistant publisher and publisher, then to a corporate vice presidency. Few upper-level executives were recruited from the outside, and the earlier managers who made the long climb often seemed like gifted amateurs, capable of doing any job. Like Luce, they tended to rely on intuition and inspiration. In the middle to late 1970s, this began to change. Sharp young business school graduates began working up through the ranks, bringing with them a concern for "return on equity" and similar corporate performance criteria. Time Inc. became more structured, more bureaucratized; much of its entrepreneurial informality was lost.

Both old- and new-style managers were expansion minded, however. Luce was too, but he was wary of distractions that might lead to the neglect of Time Inc.'s main business, which was publishing. A good deal of this book is taken up with the tales, happy and sad, of schemes for enlarging Time Inc.'s scope and thrust. Results of these endeavors have been mixed. Time Inc.'s publishing resources were unable to save the Washington *Star*, but the company was able to secure for itself a powerful and lucrative position in cable television, in contrast to earlier frustrations in broadcast television. Meanwhile, in the field where it was most experienced—the creation of new magazines—Time Inc. scored one spectacular triumph, *People*; one robust success, *Money*; one modest winner, the monthly *Life*; one problem magazine, *Discover*; and one disaster, *TV-Cable Week*.

If Luce had lived to observe the resurgent contribution of the magazines to Time Inc.'s present prosperity, in spite of all the efforts to diversify out of publishing, he would doubtless have relished the irony of the situation. He might have been more reserved in his reaction to the editorial voice of the magazines. Present-day editors share Luce's belief that the mission of journalists is to report the truth as they see it and not to strive for the phantom goal of "objectivity." But they have seen their primary function as clarification and explanation rather than exhortation. Time Inc.'s tone of voice has moderated. The stridency and partisanship that used to infuriate critics have vanished.

One company characteristic of Luce's day has not changed. In publishing, and now video, where important segments of the corporate assets tend to be off the books and wandering the hallways, Time Inc. has remained remarkably successful in attracting and holding good people. Various reasons have been advanced, including the generous material benefits the company offers. But to many on the staff, the larger attraction at Time Inc. is stimulus. A *Fortune* veteran, reminiscing about his days on the magazine, could have been speaking of any of the Time Inc. publications when he wrote, "The whole place was charged with energy; ideas bounced around like balls in a Ping-Pong tournament."

It can be fairly stated that ideas were still bouncing around as the company entered its seventh decade.

THE WORLD OF
TIME INC.

CHAPTER

I

A Management
"Just Itching to Expand"

"**S**TRATEGY" WAS A WORD widely, not to say constantly, heard among Time Inc. executives in the early 1980s. Vice presidents, publishers, other officers, task forces, outside consultants—all were massively engaged in strategic planning. In the company's earlier years, this activity had been carried on instinctively and casually. Now an attempt was made to put it on a systematic, even quasi-scientific basis, undergirded by marketing and statistical studies, enhanced with computer projections, graphics and charts.

Another widely heard word was "process," referring to the ways and means of managing the company. New or revised tables of organization, new lines of responsibility, new business groupings and new ways of dealing with personnel—henceforth known as "human resources"—were being developed throughout. This reflected not only a new, deliberately more professional management, a growing, increasingly complex company and a necessary concern for how Wall Street regarded corporate performance. It also reflected a serious, almost grimly determined attempt to understand the several marketplaces in which Time Inc. did business and to grasp the trends in the communications field, for instance the dizzying ups and downs of cable and pay television, and the new computer-based technologies which were revolutionizing magazine publishing. The

3

aim was both defensive and aggressive—to avoid costly mistakes; to seek out opportunities, including acquisitions; to get a firmer hold on the future.

Despite all the new names and faces in the company, despite some new jargon and some new ideas, it was all in a well-established Time Inc. tradition, at least in the sense that from the start, the company knew it could not stand still. Luce's report to the stockholders for 1923, Time Inc.'s first full year in business, stated that plainly. As treasurer, Luce summarized Time Inc.'s financial results for the year and then indicated the corporate intent. "Deficit for operations for the period was $39,454.16. Accounts payable were $9,569.03. Liquid assets were . . . $36,532.78. Although the Company is thus in very sound financial condition, it is recommended that no preferred stock dividend . . . be paid during 1924. The money should be used for expansion."

Luce's recommendaton was recalled, many years later, in a speech to the Time Inc. staff by his closest living business associate from those early days, Roy Larsen, who had come to *Time* in 1922 as the yet-unpublished magazine's first circulation manager, and remained to succeed Luce as the company's president. In his talk Larsen traced the company's growth since Luce's first financial accounting to the board, which coupled the declaration of an operating loss with plans for expansion. "Now that might sound like the neatest trick of the century—using money derived from a $39,000 deficit for expansion. But it is not as tricky as it sounds," Larsen observed, going on to explain how Time Inc., small as it then was, still found the money to grow on—from prepaid subscription income:

By the end of 1923 we had all learned that there is a kind of bonus inherent in the magazine publishing business. If you concentrate your circulation efforts on subscriptions, your readers pay you for the magazines in advance. So, if you are expansion minded, and confident of your ability to deliver the magazine you have sold, there is money that can be used for expansion. The kind of expansion we had in mind, of course, was the development of *Time* . . . But that did not hold us back from expanding in other directions at the same time.

In 1924 Time Inc. earned its first profit—$674.15. But the first profit that had any meaning at all came in 1928, when we showed a net of $125,000. And that was when we started to use "the money . . . for expansion" in earnest. A good part of that

4

1928 profit, if not all of it, went into work on a new magazine, to be called *Fortune*.

By 1930 Time Inc.'s net profit was up to more than $800,000. So we promptly set about pouring almost half of that into letting a wider world know about *Time* through the radio *March of Time* in 1931. And the next year we bought *Architectural Forum* for something like $100,000.

And so it went on and on . . . Our combined net profits for 1935 and 1936 . . . were around $5 million. And that is just about the amount of money that was spent over a two-year period on our next major magazine expansion—getting *Life* under way . . .

What all this spells out to me is a corporate philosophy—not just Time Inc.'s corporate philosophy, but that of any truly vital business organization. The healthy corporation, like the healthy human organism, has an inner drive to strengthen itself and to create new cells in the compulsion to continue its growth.

By 1960—the base point for this installment of the corporate chronicle—the compulsion for growth had already carried Time Inc. beyond magazine publishing, and into pulp and paper manufacturing, broadcast station ownership and the beginnings of book publishing on a major scale. In magazines, Time Inc. was preeminent. Together, *Time*, the weekly *Life*, *Fortune*, *Sports Illustrated*, *Architectural Forum* and *House & Home* sold more than 10.7 million copies in the U.S.; the international editions of *Time* and *Life* another 1,330,000 in some 150 foreign countries. Of every dollar spent in the U.S. on general magazine advertising, the Time Inc. publications received 33 cents. *Life* by itself took 17 cents. Corporate assets had grown to $230,585,000. On revenues of $287,121,000, pretax income had reached $16,903,000 (after taxes, $9,303,000). With a 9.7 percent return on invested capital, Time Inc. represented the median performance for the publishing companies on the *Fortune* list of the 500 leading U.S. industrial firms, on which Time Inc. ranked 177th. The staff had grown to 5,650 people. Of these, nearly 200 were employed full time in the company's 19 editorial and publishing offices abroad. The Time Inc. magazines' impact on publishing had been worldwide. *Time* had spawned such imitators as *Newsweek* in the U.S., *Der Spiegel* in Germany, *L'Express* in France. *Life* had been the inspiration for *Paris-Match*, *Der Stern* in Germany, *Epoca* in Italy, *O Cruzeiro* in Brazil.

Yet, for all its size, Time Inc. remained even then something of a family business. Luce's presence was very much felt, although he was physically less in evidence. From 1953 to 1956, while his wife, Clare Boothe Luce, was ambassador to Italy, Luce had been in Rome, "pouring the tea," as he put it. Not quite: he kept in constant touch with New York, returned home frequently, and was intimately involved in the planning for *Sports Illustrated*, which was launched during that time. (Luce said later that it was his experience of seeing Italians in Rome absorbed, at every free moment, in reading a sports paper that confirmed him in his judgment that Time Inc. should launch its own sports magazine.) When he was at his winter home in Phoenix, he kept up a constant stream of memos—story suggestions, exhortations to his editors or publishers, comments on the state of the nation and every aspect of Time Inc's business. Every major decision went up to Luce, as founder, editor-in-chief and the company's principal stockholder. Together, he and Larsen and a small group of relatives and old colleagues held effective control of Time Inc.'s nearly 2 million outstanding shares of stock.

The dominance of this small group was mirrored in the composition of Time Inc.'s management, which had remained very stable—almost static. Larsen had been president for 22 years; the company's elder statesman (apart from Luce), Larsen had imbued Time Inc. with much of his own personal warmth. Chairman for 18 years had been Luce's brother-in-law, Maurice T. Moore, a genial Texan (hence his nickname, Tex) who as senior partner in Cravath, Swaine & Moore was also the corporate counsel, and additionally Luce's personal attorney. Of the dozen directors on the Time Inc. board, to whom a 13th was added in 1960, 11 were either company officers, longtime associates or friends. Financial direction of the company was under Charles L. Stillman, then 56, treasurer since 1930 and executive vice president since 1948. Overall supervision of advertising was the responsibility of executive vice president Howard Black, 63, who had been with Time Inc. since 1924. At the two principal magazines, younger men were in charge, but both had been in position for well over a decade. James A. Linen III, 47, had been *Time*'s publisher since 1945, and Andrew Heiskell, 44, had been publisher of *Life* since 1946.

It was an informally administered company, more structured than in earlier decades, but still far less rigid than many other companies of comparable size. Lines of authority ran confusingly down from Luce and Larsen, power not always relating to title. Luce, although editor-in-chief, was not an officer of the company; annually, the Time

Inc. board went through the charade of "reappointing" him to his position. Over the years, management had taken a certain pride in its amateurism, in being, as Larsen once put it, "journalists and communicators by vocation . . . businessmen mostly by necessity." A cocky corporate self-confidence prevailed that Time Inc. could handle anything it turned its hand to—not always true, as events proved.

Curiously, despite its free-spending habits and cavalier attitude toward budgets, which made it difficult for Time Inc. to do anything cheaply, the company was fiscally conservative and had always hedged against the possibility that one of its magazines might fail. Thus the prepaid subscription money that had been used to finance expansion was always carried on the books as a liability, an obligation to be fulfilled, and not taken as income until the magazines were actually delivered. Magazine start-up costs had not been capitalized. These practices reduced reported earnings but enhanced stability.

Publishing, primarily magazine publishing, still overwhelmingly dominated Time Inc.'s business in 1960, accounting that year for just under 90 percent of revenues, 56 percent of pretax income. Only in the mid-1950s had nonpublishing activities begun to make a rising contribution to corporate income.

This profitable diversification had been spurred, in part, by *Life*'s voracious appetite for paper, which made Time Inc. one of the country's largest private users of paper. Time Inc. never operated its own presses, but contracted out its printing, thus avoiding the trap that the Curtis Publishing Company had fallen into: the *Saturday Evening Post*, the *Ladies' Home Journal* and the other Curtis publications had become hostages, in effect, to Curtis's investment in the printing facilities required to produce them. Time Inc. did, however, have a stake in advancing both printing and papermaking techniques. In the aftermath of World War II, the company had been worried about the adequacy of presses and coated paper to feed *Life*'s anticipated needs. The company sought to invent its way out of the problem, setting up its own technological research laboratory in the Springdale section of Stamford, Connecticut. The Springdale lab made important contributions to machine coating of paper, platemaking and ink making, printing-press manufacture, drying and folding procedures. Eventually developments within the industry caught up with Springdale, but meanwhile it had, in 1950, fostered creation of Printing Developments Incorporated (PDI) to market. Springdale's most commercially attractive products—notably an offset printing plate and an electronic scanner used in separations for four-color printing. A small business, PDI earned $187,000 in 1960 on revenues of $2,133,000.

Life's paper chase meanwhile had led to two larger ventures. One was the construction, jointly with the Crown Zellerbach Corporation, of a $33 million paper mill at St. Francisville, Louisiana, for the production of magazine stock. This eventually turned out to be a failure. In contrast, Time Inc.'s other papermaking venture was hugely successful. This was the East Texas Pulp and Paper Company at Evadale, near Beaumont. Eastex, as the subsidiary was soon to be formally renamed, never produced any magazine paper as such; its pulp was better suited for kraft paper and the manufacture of paperboard containers. But Eastex functioned efficiently as a hedge against rising paper prices generally, and on its own netted $3,202,000 in 1960 on revenues of $26,498,000—providing 19 percent of Time Inc.'s total pretax profit.

The other major segment of Time Inc.'s nonpublishing interests was broadcasting. As television fastened its grip on American life, the company began to yearn for an important role in it. During the 1950s, Time Inc. bought TV and radio properties with the aim of widening its broadcasting experience. The four stations that Time Inc. held in 1960 were contributing 18 percent of corporate pretax earnings—$3,028,000 on revenues of $10,589,000.

Included in Time Inc.'s assets were extensive real estate holdings. In 1960 the company moved into the new Time & Life Building, an $83 million, 48-story structure in New York's Rockefeller Center, which Luce said "spoke eloquently of the future" of Time Inc. The company's move was important for the future of New York City as well, in extending Rockefeller Center westward to embrace a formerly seedy area of Sixth Avenue—or Avenue of the Americas, as it is known to non-New Yorkers. Thus a whole new segment of midtown Manhattan was opened to large-scale commercial development. Time & Life Buildings were located also in Chicago, on North Michigan Avenue, housing the magazines' subscription services; in London, on New Bond Street; plans were under way for buildings in Paris and Amsterdam.

Among Time Inc.'s smaller interests was the Family Publications Service, a nationwide magazine subscription sales agency that served other publishers as well as Time Inc. Improbably, in 1961 the company also found itself part owner of a shopping center, built on land owned by Time Inc.'s Denver station KLZ.

Luce would have preferred this expansion to be more closely related to publishing. As Stillman recalled, "Harry fought everything. He never liked anything to take away from the primary mission of the company. But he would take the money." He initially opposed Eastex and agreed to buying the broadcasting stations only after decreeing, as one editor interpreted Luce's dictum, "that we not try to improve the breed."

Around Luce, however, were associates who felt the company had to develop alternative sources of income as protection against the vagaries of publishing. Foremost among the expansionists was Stillman, who had come to Time Inc. in 1928 and had been arguing the case for diversification almost incessantly since then: "Who would have gone to work for a company as young as we were if we weren't growing? A company where there were no expanding opportunities? We had to be doing something besides publishing." An engaging combination of fey personality and steel-trap financial mind, Stillman had been proved right in a succession of investments culminating in the Eastex venture, which he engineered and ran thereafter.

That nonpublishing money had arrived fortuitously, as far as the corporate profit and loss statement was concerned. Over the decade of the 1950s, Time Inc.'s operating profit margin had fallen by about half, and since 1957 magazine income had dipped appreciably. Some of this was due to a severe recession midway in President Eisenhower's second term; more, however, was because of the illness that had suddenly overtaken *Life*. With a circulation of 6,746,000 in 1960, it topped all weeklies, and was second only to the monthly *Reader's Digest*. Throughout the 1950s *Life* had accounted for over half the corporate revenues, and its leverage on profits was huge. In 1956, on 4,654 pages of advertising, the magazine's pretax income soared to an all-time high of more than $17 million, nearly 70 percent of corporate earnings. Within three years, though, advertising sales had dropped by a thousand pages and *Life*'s profits disappeared. In 1960, *Life* went further in the red, losing $1,176,000 on revenues of just over $138 million.

Time, although hit too by the recession—its advertising revenues fell 27 percent in a single year, 1958—was recovering. Its position as the leading newsweekly remained unchallenged. *Time*'s 2,511,000 domestic circulation was nearly double that of *Newsweek*, and its $51,144,000 in advertising revenue, in 1960, was greater than *Newsweek*'s and *U.S. News & World Report*'s combined. On revenues of

$52,897,800, *Time*'s pretax earnings that year were just under $8 million, about half the company's total. *Time*'s international editions, circulating 590,000 abroad, earned another $2,047,000.

Fortune, although crowded by new or revived older competitors—*Business Week* had just passed it in circulation—was doing well at the proportionately lower revenue and income levels that applied to monthly, as compared with weekly, magazine publishing. With a circulation of 335,694, *Fortune* earned $2,083,000 in 1960 on revenues of $12,646,700. Time Inc.'s other two monthlies, *Architectural Forum* and *House & Home*, remained in chronic deficit. For both these trade magazines, the time was approaching to decide whether to continue publication.

Sports Illustrated's position was special. It was still in the red after six years, with cumulative losses through 1959 totaling $27,648,000, yet the magazine was in no real danger of being folded. Some members of Time Inc.'s board of directors protested the losses, but too much corporate pride was riding on *SI*. Like *Time* and *Life*, it had pioneered a new field of journalism, "providing sport with a respectable literature [and thus having] given it a higher, rather than a lower, common denominator," as Larsen declared in a 1960 speech to the *SI* staff. The company's faith in *SI*'s future was strong; encouragingly, the magazine was edging closer to breakeven. Since its launching in 1954, circulation had nearly doubled to 935,000, losses over the same period had fallen steadily, to $2,156,000 in 1960 on revenues of $16,037,000, and further improvements were forecast for 1961.

Magazine publishing, it was sometimes observed, differed from other businesses in that the product had to be sold twice—once to the reader, again to the advertiser. In Time Inc. there was an added managerial complication, which Luce touched on in a 1963 lecture at the Columbia University Graduate School of Business:

> The one thing which is unusual about Time Inc. is that we have to combine the practice of journalism with all—*all* the aspects of any other business organization . . . Furthermore—and this is our proudest boast—journalism has top priority. Journalism and all its demands for freedom and responsibility. So, then, the most interesting thing about our company is how we set up a management which is required to produce a profit and yet has no control over our essential product, the editorial content of our magazines.

Luce was only slightly overstating his case. Subject only to normal

10

budgetary constraints—the duty not to spend wildly, at least without reason—the editorial side in every Time Inc. magazine operated independently of the publishing side. To varying degrees, this editorial autonomy could be found in other publications; in the glory days of the *Saturday Evening Post* under George Horace Lorimer's editorship, the story was told of a lobbying group that called on the *Post*'s principal owner, Cyrus H.K. Curtis, and was told to go see Lorimer—he, Curtis, was only the proprietor. But in Time Inc. the division between the separate but coequal hierarchies—church, or editorial, on the one hand, and publishing, or state, on the other— was both wider in practice and more openly enshrined as a matter of corporate policy. Editors occasionally made the transition to the publishing side, being, as it was said, defrocked in the process. And publishers could, and often did—especially in times of circulation or advertising difficulties—make their displeasure with editorial performance plain. There were frequent wrangles over cover selections also. But the governing factor remained: the managing editor did not answer to the publisher. There were two parallel lines of authority, one running up through the editorial echelons to the editor-in-chief, the other through the publishers to the chairman and president. Disputes, when they occurred, were settled at the top.

During Luce's lifetime the church-state distinction tended to be blurred by the fact that he was also the principal stockholder; the pope, so to speak, had sufficient troops for any temporal battle. Luce's determination to preserve that separation beyond his own tenure was made plain, however, in the sweeping managerial changes he initiated, starting in late 1958. He began by choosing as his own successor a man with the weight to hold the editor-in-chief's position in balance with a strong and vigorous publishing crew.

That choice was Hedley Donovan, who had been for six years the managing editor of *Fortune*. At 45, he was impressive both physically and personally—a tall, big-boned Minnesotan, with a deep rumbling voice and an understated wit, whose reserved manner reminded one *Fortune* editor of "a Supreme Court justice trying to suppress a puckish sense of humor." Luce was a passionate talker; Donovan, in contrast, used silence as a weapon; he was "the kind of man who could make a solemn observation about an issue and then wait for his guest to talk himself into a pitfall," as the same *Fortune* associate put it. Donovan and Luce were intellectually close, however, sharing many of the same economic views, moderately conservative politics, rather stern moral values and missionary attitudes toward journalism. In the view of Luce's elder son, Henry

(Hank) Luce III, it was Donovan's "thoughtfulness about the broad issues" that was the determining factor in his father's choice.

In conversations with Donovan, Luce had broached the proposition of his becoming editorial director, with the understanding that "not right away, in a few years," Donovan would take over as editor-in-chief. Thus was that function in the dual hierarchy to be institutionalized. Several months later, in July 1959, Donovan's appointment as Luce's deputy was announced.

In April 1960 came state's turn. *Time* publisher Linen was appointed to succeed Larsen as president, while *Life* publisher Heiskell took Moore's place as board chairman. Vice president David W. Brumbaugh, 51, who had been in charge of production, distribution and subscription services, succeeded Stillman, with the title of executive vice president and treasurer. Larsen became chairman of the board of directors' executive committee; Stillman, chairman of the finance committee. Moore remained a director and the company's chief counsel.

These changes triggered a number of others. Howard Black became senior vice president, also retaining his seat on the board. Vice president Arnold Carlson, 53, former controller, became assistant to the new president. Vice president Bernard Barnes, 51, became corporate secretary. Charles L. Gleason Jr., 41, formerly budgets and projects manager, became assistant secretary and assistant controller, under controller John Harvey.

There was an element of quirkiness in the Linen and Heiskell appointments. Neither man was designated the company's chief executive, in title or function. Time Inc.'s separation of powers was thus carried a step beyond church and state; state now had two heads instead of one. In later days, this arrangement likewise became a target of criticism from outside members of the board of directors, but as Linen remarked, "You've got to remember that in all those years Luce was the final authority on both sides. While he was alive and active, you really didn't have two camps . . . If anyone was chief executive officer at Time Inc., it was Luce." And in a general way, the separate responsibilities of the new president and the new chairman were understood. In Heiskell's recollection, "Jim [Linen] was supposed to deal more with day-to-day affairs and I was supposed to deal more with planning and long-range things."

The division of responsibilities suited the personalities. Linen and Heiskell made a complementary pair. Linen, a stocky 5 feet 10 inches, outgoing, enthusiastic, hyperactive—"with an adrenal gland

12

as big as a baseball," one friend said—was a matchless salesman, difficult to turn aside, impossible to put down. He was to supply much of Time Inc.'s drive over the years immediately ahead.

Heiskell, standing a towering 6 feet 5½ inches, was a less hurried sort, more contemplative. Like Luce, he had grown up an expatriate. Educated in Europe, Heiskell functioned gracefully in three languages and had immense presence, together with a deceptively nonchalant managerial style. "The board was rather surprised that I seemed to know more about Pablo Picasso than Peter Drucker," Heiskell said. But it was Heiskell who supplied the executive solidity and continuity that carried Time Inc. through the troubled corporate times of the late 1960s and early 1970s—probably the most difficult years since Time Inc.'s founding—and into the even greater growth period that followed.

Linen had joined *Time* in 1934, fresh out of Williams College, where he had become fascinated with Byzantine history. His job choice was influenced by the fact that his grandfather, a businessman in Scranton, Pennsylvania, had helped finance the religious mission of Luce's father in China. Linen was taken on as a CBOB (college boy office boy), one of several young college men who were hired for a year, during which they were supposed to find a niche for themselves in the company or leave. Linen's hopes of becoming a writer were dashed when he flunked a writing test, but he turned out to have spectacular sales talent. Sent to Detroit, Linen "called on every smokestack . . . , sold more accounts in Michigan than have ever been sold before or since," Howard Black remembered. In 1940 Linen became advertising manager of *Life*; that year *Life*, then just four years old, took advertising leadership away from the long-established *Saturday Evening Post*.

Linen spent the war years with the Office of War Information, much of the time directing psychological warfare in his old area of historical interest, the eastern Mediterranean. It was during OWI service overseas that he began assembling his "Linen network" of acquaintances throughout the world. One was Greece's exiled Princess Frederika, later Queen, whom Linen used to take out in Cairo for evenings of dining and dancing. Another was Gamal Abdel Nasser, then teaching at Egypt's Royal Military Academy. By the time his OWI duty ended, Linen was running U.S. propaganda services for the entire Mediterranean. In September 1945, he returned not to his old job in *Life* advertising sales, as he had hoped to do, but to a happy surprise Luce and Larsen had cooked up in his absence: he was to take over "the best job with the company, the best job in

13

publishing," as Linen viewed it—publisher of *Time*.

Heiskell's rise in the company had been just as rapid. Born in Naples of American parents who had come from West Virginia to Capri on their honeymoon and stayed on in Europe, Heiskell spent the first 19 years of his life moving around Italy, Germany, Austria, Switzerland and France; Heiskell's father, an artist by inclination, eventually turned to business, becoming European representative for the Commercial Cable Company, an ITT subsidiary. Heiskell got his baccalaureate from the Sorbonne in 1933, remaining in France to teach mathematics and geology at the Ecole du Montcel, where he had attended secondary school. The cosmopolitan background gave Heiskell not only language fluency but easy social adaptability. It did not, he observed, give him "the idealized view of the U.S." that Luce brought from his missionary upbringing in China.

In 1935 he enrolled at the Harvard Business School, but left after a year. From a reporter's job on the New York *Herald-Tribune* at $25 a week, he soon switched to the newly founded *Life* at $40. Heiskell covered medicine and science, wrote about the first experiments in nuclear fission ("a little blip on the screen; I had no idea of its great significance"), and also began poking around *Life*'s publishing offices, where his inquisitiveness as "one of the few editors who asked how a publication makes money" greatly impressed Larsen, then *Life* publisher. In 1939, Larsen made Heiskell the magazine's assistant general manager.

Recruited for editorial duty when war broke out in Europe, Heiskell got to Paris in time for the fall of France ("Seeing a nation crumble before your eyes is extraordinary, especially when you were brought up in it and rather loved it"). Back with *Life* in New York, with Larsen serving as both *Life* publisher and company president, Heiskell became "a sort of semipublisher." In January 1946, at 30 "and looking younger," as a trade magazine reported, he was given the publisher's title formally.

As the company's two dominant publishers, Linen and Heiskell were the obvious choices for the two top corporate posts. So was Brumbaugh as the top financial officer. With Stillman's growing involvement with Eastex, Brumbaugh had been handling many of the treasurer's duties. "The casting director's image of a corporate accountant—squarish, neat, bespectacled, soft-spoken," as he was once described—Brumbaugh was the first CPA in the company's executive ranks, and one of its first Harvard Business School graduates. Born in Virginia, Brumbaugh had gone to Roanoke College

14

and then Harvard; in 1933, Stillman hired him to head the company's then all-woman bookkeeping department. With some forays into production and distribution, Brumbaugh spent his entire career on the financial side of Time Inc., where he inaugurated the company's first long-term planning operation and helped to shape its first employee profit-sharing plan.

Brumbaugh also represented Time Inc. in long tussles with the government over postal rates. In 1956 the Post Office Department tried to get Brumbaugh over to its side, offering to make him first assistant postmaster general. Brumbaugh declined. But his presentations in Washington of Time Inc.'s system of using zoned cities to speed magazine deliveries influenced the Post Office Department's development of ZIP codes, a fact recognized in a special merit award to the company from the department in 1965. Around the Time & Life Building, Brumbaugh was sometimes referred to as Mr. Zip.

"A management which will match the great opportunities of the future," Luce heralded his new appointments in announcing them in April 1960. The press release proclaimed: "Younger men of proven ability take over positions of leadership." The appointments did more than bring in a new generation, which in the key positions averaged ten to 15 years younger than the old. Essentially, they committed the company to vigorous expansion, beyond publishing, on a scale greater and wider than before. A management "just itching for places to expand" is the way one insider described the new group.

It is impossible, in retrospect, to believe that Luce and Larsen did not realize this perfectly well. Hank Luce said of his father: "He didn't want to hold the new management back. He became, with great wisdom I think, interested in having them create. He had an incredibly strong sense of history and the fact that this company would have to have a future without him. He worked on encouraging them to have ideas."

On taking over as president, Linen set himself the objective of doubling Time Inc.'s business—to "make Time Inc. a half-billion-dollar company." It took only six years to achieve. Heiskell, by his own later reckoning, was less driven by the idea of growth per se than Linen. But both men were in agreement that Time Inc. should diversify, that the international field was particularly promising and that the company should work more at asserting business leadership. "Taking our place in American industry was important," Linen said.

15

"We didn't occupy the position, as a leading communications company, that we thought we should." As magazine publishers, both he and Heiskell had devoted much time to public service, particularly in urban affairs, and as corporate chiefs they did even more.

Circumstances put Linen largely in charge during his and the new management's first year. Inconveniently for Heiskell, his appointment as chairman presented him with a domestic dilemma. He was then married to his second wife, the actress Madeleine Carroll, who was born in England and wanted to live in Europe. At one point Heiskell had liked the idea too; before he was offered the chairman's post he had suggested to Luce and Larsen that he leave *Life* and become Time Inc.'s senior representative abroad. Now, as chairman, Heiskell took off for a long leave in Europe. Partly he hoped to settle the transatlantic disagreement with his wife (he did not succeed; they separated and were divorced in 1965). Partly he wanted to begin surveying Time Inc.'s opportunities abroad.

Coincidentally, it simplified matters for Linen in New York. Recalled Heiskell:

> I realized what a problem this kind of dual appointment [presented]. An awful lot of managers around this company wouldn't know who to look to directly for decisions. And if they started playing games or felt they had to check everything out with two people this wouldn't make sense. So as part of starting my career and trying to solve my personal problem I went around the world to see what there was [abroad] for Time Inc.

For the incoming crew, there hardly could have been a better time to take over. Or so it seemed. The U.S. was entering the "soaring '60s"—those years when the millions of children born during the postwar baby boom would become young adults, eager to buy and with money to spend. Declared *Fortune*, in an editorial written by Donovan, his last as managing editor before becoming Time Inc. editorial director:

> Today, with the [1958] recession well behind us, confidence in the economic future of the U.S. is probably higher than at any time for 30 years. One would have to go back to the Roaring Twenties, or a great deal further back—to the innocent optimism of the 19th-century U.S.—to find a time when Americans were so nearly unanimous in their belief that the country is bound to grow.

The predictions were slightly premature. The decade started slowly, with a mild recession at the end of 1960 continuing into autumn 1961. *Life* that year suffered its third straight loss and *Time*'s net also dropped. Corporate pretax income was down about 10 percent.

Nonetheless, a buoyant mood pervaded the company. In May 1960, Stillman, in his new capacity as finance chairman, had dropped on management an especially bullish appraisal of the corporate future, prepared by an independent financial analyst. Despite publishing's currently declining profitability, Time Inc.'s long-term prospects were excellent and the stock a sleeper, he suggested. "The present may be an unusually good time to invest."

The buoyant mood was reflected in Luce's remarks at an executive dinner for the new management in May 1961. "While there is no way of measuring these things, either at the Harvard Business School or elsewhere, I would say that rarely in the history of organizations does it happen that so many right men are in the right spots as is now the case in Time Inc. Should I now, for modesty's sake, exclude myself from that sweeping encomium? Well, I don't. I include myself in!" Luce began, warmly. Then he reverted to the familiar themes of publishing and profit. Time Inc.'s profit ratio was still too low, he declared: "We are and we will always be primarily in the publishing business . . . I emphasize [this] not only because that is our vocation but also to assert my belief that there is lots of money in them thar publishing hills."

CHAPTER
2

"I Read That Damn Magazine..."

FROM THE BEGINNING, Henry Luce listed himself on the masthead of the Time Inc. magazines as editor, later as editor-in-chief. But circumstances during the company's early years had forced Luce to devote much of his attention to the business side. His partner, Briton Hadden, hated business and showed it during his brief tenure as publisher of *Time*. Then Hadden died in 1929, and Luce had to take over everything. It was another decade before he worked his way back fully to the editorial side. In 1939, as war began in Europe, Luce resigned as corporate president in favor of Roy Larsen, and in 1942, after the U.S. entered the war, he gave up the chairmanship as well, retaining only the title of editor-in-chief.

"I thought the editor's job was so important—even more important than ordinarily—that I should give my full attention to it. I was all the more inclined to do so because I was fortunate enough to have a longtime partner in Roy Larsen . . . a great publisher," Luce told a television interviewer in 1961, on the occasion of *Life*'s 25th birthday. "I have continued as editor-in-chief because the world crisis was by no means resolved in 1945 and 1946. The other reason for remaining editor-in-chief, of course, is because I like it."

In February 1958, at the winter home in Phoenix, Arizona, that he and his wife had bought after their return from Italy the year before, Luce suffered a heart attack—a pulmonary embolism that put him on a regimen of anticoagulant drugs for the remaining nine years of his life. His illness was officially described as pneumonia. Only the family, Larsen and a very few other old Time Inc. associates knew what had actually happened.

Luce had always been vigorous, trimmer looking than many of his younger executives, and he was hardly slowed by illness. Though slightly deaf, he was still not much inclined to wear a hearing aid. He smoked as much as ever, appropriating any pack of cigarettes within reach. He continued to drink moderately. But on doctor's orders, he was spending more time in Phoenix's warmer, drier air. He also exercised more. The Luces' house bordered the golf course of the Biltmore Estates, and had a heated pool where they regularly went swimming before lunch. Writer John Kobler, who visited them in the course of preparing a *Saturday Evening Post* profile on Luce (later made into a book), described the ritual: "Both wearing bathing caps, they would enter at the shallow end and slowly side-stroke up and down, conversing gravely as they swam."* Afternoons, Luce usually played nine holes of golf, his caddy often lending a hand to improve his lies.

If Luce was a less familiar figure around the Time & Life Building, his presence as editor-in-chief—and, as always, final arbiter of the major corporate decisions—was still felt. His memos, dashed off in longhand on yellow pads and transcribed by his secretary (Luce never typed), continued to flow—story suggestions, exhortations to his editors and publishers, complaints, compliments, random ruminations, observations on the state of the world and every aspect of Time Inc.'s business.

In Phoenix he worked at a desk in his bedroom, sharing a secretary with his wife to handle his correspondence and keeping in constant contact with New York by letter, memo and telephone. In New York he kept his usual six-day work week and presided at the weekly managing editors' lunches. These were command performances attended not only by managing editors but by one or two of their senior lieutenants as well. Luce sometimes just wanted to talk, or bloviate, as he called it—sometimes to recount observations from his travels or books he had read, more often to argue out editorial positions. The sessions could turn into monologues, as Luce cerebrated audibly in abrupt, stop-and-start sentences. As *Time* commented after his death:

He loved dialectic exchange, and often shifted his own position

Luce: His Time, Life and Fortune (Doubleday, 1968).

in midsentence, to the consternation of novice listeners . . . For Luce would often come to a dead stop in his torrent of words, while he thought out the next phase of his argument, and into such 30-second silences many a tyro editor or visitor blundered, thinking it was his turn to talk at last. The fate of such rushers-in was painful to behold: they could be as far as two or three sentences into their rebuttals when Harry would find in his mind what he had been looking for, and pick up exactly where he had left off—talking through their lines as though they had never been spoken.

His schedule of outside speaking engagements with academic, business and church groups remained full. During his travels around the U.S. and abroad, he dropped in on the Time-Life news bureaus—visits that could be frightening, not because of Luce's personal demands but because of the factual interrogations he put the reporters through. Again, *Time*'s description:

> Luce's curiosity was insatiable . . . Correspondents, notified that H.R.L. was about to appear in their territory, frequently gave themselves cram courses of vital statistics about the area to cope with his barrage of queries. The ride from the airport [with Luce] was legendary, and many a correspondent prepared himself by making the run a couple of times with a guide—only to have Harry ask him about some distant ruin he had failed to notice.
>
> He was a ruthless enemy of small talk—it bored him, and he made little effort to hide the fact. To forestall chitchat, his most effective weapon was the wild-swinging question. Many a correspondent and editor sitting with him at dinner has been hit by some such query as: "Do you think Los Angeles makes any sense?" After a visitation from Luce, one correspondent reported that he was left "intellectually black and blue."

In March 1960, Luce made his last managing editorial appointment on *Time*. Roy Alexander, who had been in the chair since December 1949, was given the emeritus title of editor. Assistant managing editor Otto Fuerbringer, 49, was named managing editor. Succeeding Fuerbringer as assistant managing editor was senior editor Thomas Griffith, 44.

Although Fuerbringer's appointment had been a foregone conclusion for several years, it had not been easy for Luce to suggest to Alexander that it was time to step down; at 61, he was within a year

20

of Luce's own age. To ease the transition, Luce took Alexander with him on a long tour of Europe and the Far East. Luce returned to New York in May, just as the U.S. presidential primaries were ending. Richard M. Nixon's nomination as the Republican candidate was virtually certain; John F. Kennedy's as candidate of the Democrats was somewhat less so, but still likely.

In the two preceding presidential contests Luce had been deeply involved, and his Republican position clearly indicated in the enthusiastic coverage that his magazines, *Time*, in particular, had given to Dwight Eisenhower—and the contrasting treatment given his Democratic opponent, Adlai Stevenson. The 1960 campaign found Luce less openly committed. This reflected some mellowing on his part, but also his growing sensitivity to accusations of bias—a sore spot that Luce's newly appointed deputy, editorial director Hedley Donovan, was touching on in conversations with Luce.

"It was a terrible bother to Harry because he thought *Time* deserved to be better regarded by academics and intellectuals," Donovan recalled. "I shared with Harry the idea that there was no such thing as strictly objective journalism, but there were obvious degrees of fairness and attention to the other side," Donovan added. "I felt *Time* was rather deficient in this. He rather reluctantly agreed that perhaps this was so." The period ahead, therefore, was to be something of a test.

Luce's personal fondness for Kennedy was plain. The Democratic candidate was the son of his old friend Joseph Patrick Kennedy, and it was at the father's request in 1940, when the elder Kennedy was American ambassador in London, that Luce had written the foreword for Jack Kennedy's book on Britain's unpreparedness, *Why England Slept*. More than friendship moved Luce to oblige. He was genuinely impressed, he said, by the son's "careful scholarship . . . the qualities of mind and involvement in public affairs that he displayed in this book."

Kennedy had first appeared on *Time*'s cover in December 1957, as he was beginning his drive for the 1960 Democratic nomination. The exposure the cover story offered his candidacy gratified Kennedy enormously and he telephoned Marshall Berges, the *Time* correspondent involved, in the middle of the night to express his pleasure. The gesture was typical; more than most politicians, Kennedy understood the workings of the press, and he was particularly interested in Time Inc.'s operations. "[Kennedy] was always fascinated by the whole structure," recalled correspondent Hugh Sidey, who

21

covered Kennedy's campaign for *Time*. "He knew the editors by name, knew which ones were the ones that put the magazine to bed." He could even, Kennedy claimed, detect differences in *Time*'s tone from one issue to the next, depending on who was top-editing the political stories in New York that week.

With Kennedy, as with other politicians, it was television that would soon command primary attention. But during the 1960 campaign he had considered *Time*'s role crucial as the most influential of the newsweeklies, often more important than the daily newspapers. His travels as Senator had confirmed this, he told Sidey. "I read that damn magazine . . . And I don't care where I've been in the world—I go into the ambassador's office and he says, 'As I was reading in *Time* . . . ' "

Joe Kennedy was Luce's dinner guest in New York the night his son accepted the Democratic presidential nomination in Los Angeles. Together the two fathers watched the televised speech. In a note to himself, Luce recorded his impressions of the candidate:

> The man—one of America's great success stories. Cheers . . .
> Put the man and the platform together [and] the whole
> becomes a stirring prospect. The man is no visionary, no "can-
> didate for martyrdom." He is a tough fellow but educated, with
> a good and even beautiful mind.

The next month, Kennedy came to lunch at Time Inc. with Luce and a dozen or so *Time*, *Life* and *Fortune* editors. The affair went swimmingly. One incident stuck in Luce's mind for years after. "Before the conversation got going, I said to Jack, apropos something: 'Of course you haven't read it, but you may have heard of the new 600-page biography of [President] McKinley . . . ' Jack broke in: 'What makes you think I haven't read it?' I said, 'You just couldn't have had time.' Jack: 'You forget the kind of life I've been leading—traveling on airplanes.' That left me even more amazed. After campaigning for 15 hours a day, he climbs bone-tired into an airplane—and settles down with 600 pages on McKinley!"

Kennedy's respect for Luce, despite their political differences, was obvious. At Hyannis Port the next day, Kennedy told his friend Arthur M. Schlesinger Jr.:*

> I like Luce. He is like a cricket, always chirping away. After

*A Thousand Days (Houghton Mifflin Company, 1965), p. 63.

all, he made a lot of money through his own individual enterprise so he naturally thinks that individual enterprise can do anything. I don't mind people like that. They have earned the right to talk that way . . . My father is the same way. But what I can't stand are all the people around Luce who automatically agree with everything he has to say.

Would Luce, after years of Republican constancy, switch and support the Democratic candidate? Some political commentators thought it possible. *Time* had no editorial page; it was in *Life* that Luce's position would be announced, and in an unsigned editorial in the August 15 issue, dashed off in evident enjoyment of the situation, Luce addressed himself to the question:

> Soon after the Democratic convention the *Wall Street Journal* published an item saying that the editor-in-chief of *Life* might come out for Kennedy. The item was not wholly untrue; the paper had merely indulged in the popular exercise known as leaping to conclusions. *Life* readers wrote in to say in effect: "Say it ain't so." So the editor-in-chief said it wasn't so.
>
> Then last week an enterprising newspaperman discovered that the first book written by Jack Kennedy carried a foreword by Henry R. Luce, then and now editor-in-chief of *Life* . . . The newspaperman wanted to know if Mr. Luce still admired Jack Kennedy. Accordingly, *Life* issued the following statement:
>
> Mr. Luce is proud of having written the foreword to the book Jack Kennedy wrote in 1940 when he was 23 years old. Since then Senator Kennedy has justified Mr. Luce's high opinion of his ability. There is another man of that same generation who has done more for the nation and the world—Richard M. Nixon. Mr. Luce has admired Mr. Nixon since he first entered public life in 1946.

Intended or not, the editorial's result was to compound the confusion, with some newspapers taking Luce's statement as a declaration for Nixon. This required another statement in *Life* as follows:

> Mr. Luce has in no sense of the word come out for Richard M. Nixon for President and neither has any of the Time Inc. publications. Mr. Luce has the highest regard for the two candidates, both of whom he has known for a long time.
>
> In a presidential campaign, it is a matter of minor, though

reasonable, interest as to what editorial voices come out for whom.

Life, on its editorial page, will come out either for Nixon or for Kennedy . . . and for whatever interest it may be, *Life* will express its views not later than early October.

On *Time*, meanwhile, there had been a medical emergency that injected an additional note of uncertainty into the situation. This was the sudden illness of the new managing editor, Otto Fuerbringer. Working late one night a few weeks after the Republican convention, Fuerbringer was struck suddenly by what was first diagnosed as a cerebral aneurysm. Subsequent diagnoses were inconclusive, but Fuerbringer was out of action until January; in his absence assistant managing editor Tom Griffith took over. As Griffith moved temporarily into command, the question arose: how would this affect *Time*'s campaign coverage? For Luce, in his way of deliberately pairing opposites, had put in the magazine's two top positions men of differing political sympathies, differing temperaments.

"The managing editor of a Time Inc. magazine," Luce once remarked in a speech, "comes as close as anything in America to being a czar." Fuerbringer met those specifications. Tall, ramrod straight, jet-haired, he was a commanding figure—to some on the *Time* staff, intimidating. Appearance, together with his Germanic background and managerial style, gave rise to published stories later that the staff called Fuerbringer the Iron Chancellor. Some colleagues had never heard him called that until they read it elsewhere, but the description was apt enough. Fuerbringer was a strong, shrewd editorial executive, not easily crossed. He had a notably sharp news sense, a solid, Midwestern feel for the country; he was quick to spot trends. His politics and Luce's coincided; so did their views on advocacy journalism. Donovan, who did not always agree with Fuerbringer, felt that "Otto was probably Harry's ideal managing editor."

Like Luce, Fuerbringer came from a family of clergymen. His grandfather, a Lutheran pastor, left Germany in 1839, seeking religious opportunities on the American frontier, and helped found Concordia Theological Seminary, now in St. Louis, over which Fuerbringer's father and brother, Lutheran pastors also, subsequently presided. Fuerbringer attended Harvard on a scholarship, was president of the daily *Crimson* and broke into newspapering on the St. Louis *Post-Dispatch* in 1932. From reporting Boy Scout troop activities, Fuerbringer graduated to covering city hall and the state legislature, wrote book reviews, started an art column for the paper and, on the side, freelanced for the *Saturday Evening Post*. In 1942, Alexander, who had once been assistant city editor at the *Post-Dispatch*, recruited Fuerbringer for *Time*. (The company's *Post-Dispatch* mafia, as it was called, was growing. Already on hand, in addition to Alexander, were Sidney James, then *Time*'s Los Angeles bureau chief, and *Time* writer Ernest Havemann, afterward with *Life*. A later arrival from St. Louis was Lawrence Laybourne, who was to complete his 30 years with Time Inc. as a vice president and director of corporate affairs in Washington.)

It was a depleted and overworked wartime staff that Fuerbringer joined on *Time*, and the competition for promotion to senior editor devised by T.S. Matthews, then managing editor, was ferocious. Six writers were pitted against one another in a race for openings. Fuerbringer survived to become senior editor for *Time*'s lead section, National Affairs, and in 1951 assistant managing editor. In that position, he sat in frequently for Alexander and so it was no surprise when Luce broke the news to him in characteristically abrupt fashion: "I daresay you've often thought about being managing editor . . . Well, you are."

Griffith too had joined *Time* as a writer during the war and, like Fuerbringer, had survived the senior editorial ordeal. A onetime police reporter and assistant city editor on the Seattle *Times*, later a Nieman Fellow at Harvard, Griffith first edited *Time*'s back-of-the-book sections, then succeeded Fuerbringer as senior editor in National Affairs—the "bloody angle" where most of *Time*'s political battles were fought. Griffith edited there during the tumultuous years of the Hiss-Chambers trial, the rise of Senator Joseph McCarthy, the Korean War and President Harry Truman's recall of General Douglas MacArthur. During this period Griffith had gained a reputation among outside critics of *Time*'s performance as a "house liberal"—a tag he resented because it suggested "a favored, or tolerated, status I never had."* Indeed, in July 1951, in the aftermath of a bitter intramural dispute over *Time*'s treatment of the Truman-MacArthur controversy (the magazine favored the General), he had been asked to switch to the less politically contentious Foreign News department. He retained Luce's professional respect and personal friendship, however. For Griffith's outspoken criticism of what he considered *Time*'s journalistic lapses, Luce took to calling him (borrowing the British parliamentary term) *Time*'s "loyal opposition."

*Thomas Griffith: *How True: A Skeptic's Guide to Believing the News.* (An Atlantic Monthly Press Book. Little, Brown and Company, 1974), p. 77.

Now, as he sat temporarily in the managing editor's chair, Griffith faced some suspicion from committed Nixon supporters on *Time*'s staff; one accused him of intending to put out a pro-Kennedy *Time*. Griffith was admittedly for Kennedy, "though not passionately, and certainly not for Nixon," but "determined that our coverage . . . be as fair to both sides as I could make it."

> There were office cynics who were sure that I'd soon have to get smart: I think they were right that in the old days such even-handedness would not have been tolerated. My own attitude was that if Luce wanted partisanship, *he'd* have to raise the subject with me . . .
>
> The first week . . . all the stories came to me bland and salt-free, with Nixon and Kennedy getting equal space (as on many newspapers) whether or not each had equally made news. Louis Banks, the National Affairs editor, and I agreed this seemed too namby-pamby for *Time*. People would expect us to declare whether Nixon or Kennedy had won each televised debate . . . But since *Time* also had to overcome its past reputation . . . our fairness had to be explicit, and so [I] made it my own business to see that in each week's issue the magazine touched four bases. In its coverage it had to record the best thing that might be said about the performance of either Nixon and Kennedy, and also the worst about each one, to assure the reader that we were not shading the news . . .
>
> As for Luce, he would drop by my office to talk over the campaign with all the delight he always got from politics, but he never made suggestions or wanted to see stories in advance, and only after the last issue before the election went to press did he call me to say how pleased he had been, and ordered me to send a message to the staff saying that the real winner of the election was *Time*, the Weekly Newsmagazine.*

Looking back, Luce acknowledged that "we were always going to be for Nixon" in the long run. In this he was not alone; Larsen, Donovan, Alexander all concurred in the consensus that was developing in Time Inc. for Nixon. In September, Donovan cast up a balance sheet:

As to the men themselves, Kennedy wins on:

*Griffith: *How True*, pp. 107–108.

Eloquence (which can be very useful in the presidency).

Grace, style . . .

They're both tough but I think maybe Kennedy is the . . . more aggressive. This could be of some importance in the Cold War.

Against Kennedy, in the "character" department, I would say that he is:

Cynical in his out-promisings.

Too remote (by temperament, not . . . money)

Along with his aggressiveness, maybe inseparable from it, Kennedy is quite a gambler. This could also be important in the Cold War.

So I also end up "giving Nixon the nod" in character. I think . . . (after acknowledging the things Kennedy has an edge in) that Nixon is a man of broader sympathies, more responsible, more judicious.

Time Inc.'s support for Nixon was formally declared in a two-part *Life* editorial published in mid-October. The endorsement was decidedly lukewarm. In an interview for the Kennedy Library in 1965, Luce explained the dilemma that he and *Life*'s chief editorial writer, Jack Jessup, faced as the October date approached:

Up to the day that Jack Jessup was to start getting to his typewriter and writing the pro-Nixon endorsement . . . Nixon had not really established himself as clearly superior to Jack Kennedy from our point of view in the foreign policy area. So we decided . . . [that] all Jessup would write that week was the endorsement of Nixon on domestic policy grounds . . . We thought another week would go by and Nixon might sharpen the foreign policy argument.

A week went by and Nixon hadn't done any better so we were in kind of a hole . . . [but] we couldn't very well go against him . . . Well, having said (a) we had to say (b), ending up with an endorsement of Nixon.

Luce seemed prepared for Nixon's defeat. Several days after the *Life* endorsement, and ten days before the voting, he was already jotting down ideas for *Life* articles in the event of a Kennedy victory. "Journalistically, it will be exciting" with Kennedy in the White House, he judged. "It will shake up the country and . . . be good for Free Enterprise in the following sense . . . businessmen and others will have to fight like hell for their cause . . ." And finally, "it will be a pleasure to have the majority [of] intellectuals riding high politically."

Four days after the election, Donovan wrote Luce appraising Time Inc.'s position with the new administration:

> It occurs to me . . . that Time Inc. might have a lot more influence on Kennedy than it had on Eisenhower. Partly the difference between a 300,000 plurality [it was actually 119,000] and a 9,000,000 plurality [Eisenhower's margin over Stevenson in 1956], partly because Time Inc. is in no way committed to, or to be taken for granted by, the new administration.

Certainly the President-elect was watching closely what the magazines were saying about him. On *Time*, Fuerbringer returned to the managing editorship fully recovered from his illness. Kennedy thought he could detect a difference in *Time*'s attitude and told Sidey as much. Getting off the press plane one night, Sidey found Kennedy on the tarmac, leafing through the pages of *Time* under the lights of an automobile, muttering complaints. "This goddamned magazine is just awful, just awful." Finally, only half joking: "Sidey, you failed me. You assured me that man was at death's door."

Kennedy's inaugural in January 1961 began a period of extraordinary presidential domination of the news. As *Time* wrote, 19 months into his regime, "No U.S. President has been more copiously reported by the U.S. press than John F. Kennedy. Nor has any President paid more attention to newsmen—or kept more constantly in mind the uses of the press."

Recalled Fuerbringer: "It was one of the liveliest presidencies to cover and more fun and more interesting than any other," but a presidency, also, "where Kennedy took all praise as his due and reacted with anger to any criticisms." That was to prove a pattern in his relations with Time Inc. in the years ahead.

Directing Washington reporting for Time Inc. was John L. Steele, 43, an alumnus of Chicago's City News Bureau and the United Press, who had come to *Time* in 1953 after a Nieman Fellowship. He had covered Congress and the Eisenhower White House before becoming bureau chief in 1958. After the campaign, Sidey took over the White House beat for *Time*. A fourth-generation Iowa newspaperman who learned his trade on a country weekly founded by his great-grandfather, Sidey, 33, combined an easy manner with a folksy wit. He and Kennedy had hit it off well on the campaign trail,

and the friendship continued; from it *Time* got White House reporting of an intimate anecdotal style that Sidey subsequently carried
over into his successful column for *Life* (and later for *Time*), "The
Presidency."

Kennedy continued to cultivate Luce and Time Inc. In December
1960, in his last piece of outside writing printed before becoming
President, he contributed an article to *Sports Illustrated* on fitness.
In January, Luce and his wife were guests of Kennedy's parents at
the inauguration in Washington, riding to the festivities that night in
a chartered bus (with younger brother Edward M. Kennedy, the
Luces reported, leading the passengers in group singing). In February, at Luce's request, Kennedy filmed a congratulatory message for
Life on its 25th birthday, to be broadcast as part of an NBC network
television spectacular celebrating the anniversary. In March, Kennedy used *Life*'s Spanish-language edition to deliver another message, to Latin America, explaining his projected hemispheric aid
program, the Alliance for Progress.

By Luce's count, he had some dozen White House meetings with
Kennedy during his brief presidency. In most, the two men were
alone together. The give-and-take was spirited. Luce later recalled:

> [The President] would . . . give me the needle, and the question
> then was just how sharp a needle I could, with due deference,
> return. One of his gambits was to exaggerate my Republicanism
> and leave me with the alternative of defending Republican stu-
> pidity or seeming to desert that unhappy party . . . I thoroughly
> enjoyed all my conversations with the President—except one.

The exception was a session that occurred after *Time*, in September
1962, had spoofed the marital tangles of Jacqueline Kennedy's sister, Lee, and her husband, Prince Stanislaus Radziwill. Reported
Time: "Radziwill, 48, was once married to shipping heiress Grace
Kolin, who last year married the Earl of Dudley, who was formerly
married to Laura Charteris, who is now married to U.S. Socialite
Michael Canfield, who was the first husband of Lee Bouvier, who
since March 19, 1959, has been married to Prince Stanislaus Radziwill." Describing the uncomfortable session that followed, Luce
wrote:

> The President was bitter as he pointed out the hurt feelings that
> would be caused by this story. Like other laymen when their

feelings are hurt, the President had no conception of what masses of material most of the press throws into the wastebasket because of our editors' judgment that feelings will be hurt without adequate journalistic reason. But even this bad half-hour was somehow got out of—thanks to the President's urbanity.

The encounter may have been even rougher than the editor-in-chief later admitted. Sidey remembered Luce emerging from the White House quite shaken and saying, "I think I need a drink," and in a letter afterward to a friend Luce wrote:

> Two weeks ago I got into a real bind with the President of the United States and still don't know how I'm coming out of it. The fascinating thing is that when you get into a private ruckus with one Kennedy, you get involved with the whole blinking clan—including selected O'Learys, O'Brien, etc.

For reasons that he stated later, quite openly, to Luce, Kennedy regarded anything *Time* said with particular concern. At the President's request, an early copy of *Time* went by special messenger from the printer's to the White House every Sunday night—"usually before I got it," Luce observed—and by the following day Time Inc.'s Washington bureau usually had the presidential verdict. Luce was gratified by the attention: "Now any editor . . . what he's out to do mainly is to interest readers to the point where they become regular and careful readers, and President Kennedy was . . . So that there was this very close relationship stemming from the fact that, first of all, the President read *Time.*"

Like Luce, Fuerbringer relished political jousting through the columns of the magazine; *Time* was, in his view, "at its best when dueling with—I wouldn't say opposing—the President of the United States." The first serious tilt came with the Bay of Pigs invasion and its aftermath.

The invasion story was one that both *Time* and *Life* had been onto well in advance. Since the summer and fall of 1960, it had been an open secret in the bars of Miami that Cuban exiles were being recruited for action against Fidel Castro. In January 1961, *Time* published a revealing account of actual military preparations—an eyewitness report from a Guatemalan training site, where *Time* correspondent Harvey Rosenhouse had slipped in to watch through binoculars as supplies were unloaded from unmarked aircraft and Cuban commandos drilled under the eyes of a CIA agent known as

Mr. B. By April, *Time* writer Sam Halper and *Life*'s Kenneth Gouldthorpe, who had both been in the Sierra Maestra with Castro and had kept in contact with disillusioned Fidelistas since then, had much of the story in hand. Halper had the invasion area and probable date, together with an independent military appraisal of the operation's chances of success, which were deemed almost zero. Tipped also by Sidey in Washington, who had advance word from the President's brother Robert, *Time* faced a dilemma as the actual invasion began: the operation bridged *Time*'s editorial closing on Saturday and the magazine's appearance on the newsstands Tuesday. In the end *Time* carried only a carefully worded story under the headline "Toward D-Day," reporting Saturday's preparatory air strikes against Cuban military airfields. The following week the coverage was detailed—and unsparing in its exposition of the seeds of disaster.

Nor did Kennedy ask to be spared. "I fully expected to get my head kicked off," he confided to Sidey a few weeks later. "We f-----up." But the President was stung by the press criticism he was getting, and his wrath led to a notable encounter with Luce.

He took the occasion of a White House gathering in July—a lunch honoring Nationalist Chinese Premier Chen Cheng, to which Luce was invited—to berate *Time*'s editor-in-chief personally. Luce had asked for a "private ten minutes" with the President after lunch, to argue Time Inc.'s case against proposed postal rate increases, but the encounter turned into something quite different. Luce's version of the meeting, as recorded in a memo for the files:

The President made it clear that he was more concerned by what *Time* said about him than by the utterances of any other publication or commentator in the land. *Time*, he allowed, had by far the greatest influence on the "swing opinion" that decided elections and influenced public attitudes on important issues—both at home and abroad (i.e., he meant foreign opinion, as well).

So Kennedy was angry because *Time* had been unfair to him. How, when? H.R.L. wanted to know. During the campaign? No—*Time* was "magnificent" in its campaign reporting. Well, then, during Cabinet appointment? No, that was all right. Well, when? Ever since Cuba. So, said Luce, what should *Time not* have said about Cuba? The President rejoined that he was willing to take his beating about Cuba per se, but *Time* had given him a raw deal about almost everything else he had done since then.

And Kennedy understood that his rough treatment was perpetrated by those editors in the Time & Life Building who "lived in Greenwich and ate at '21'."

H.R.L. brought the President up sharp, asked if Kennedy meant that the Washington staff was intimating to the White House that their reporting was twisted in New York? Kennedy quickly denied this—but repeated that he knew about the sequestered, commuting editors—and particularly Fuerbringer.

H.R.L. suggested that the President invite Managing Editor Fuerbringer to see him and talk it all over—adding a friendly warning that J.F.K. be well prepared on his facts and figures before taking Fuerbringer on.

"The parting was cordial," Luce reported, but the results of the meeting were inconclusive. At Luce's request, his executive assistant Albert L. (Bill) Furth surveyed *Time*'s treatment of Kennedy over four months, from April to August 1961. Independent in his judgment, often critical of *Time*, Furth was, on this occasion, only mildly disapproving. While "*Time* had not always been fair to the President," he concluded, "the lapses from fairness do not add up to an 'attack.' "

At the end of August, the presidential anger exploded again, detonated this time by a major article in *Fortune* by Charles J.V. Murphy. The article, which led off the magazine's September 1961 issue and was excerpted simultaneously in *Time*, was a painstaking dissection of the Bay of Pigs failure. Murphy was one of Time Inc.'s most experienced Washington hands, a colonel in the Air Force reserve, with excellent CIA and military intelligence contacts, and his indictment of the Cuban operation was brutal: "an American Suez . . . an utter fiasco . . . wholly self-inflicted." The article backed up its indictment with detailed citations of wrong decisions or failed will.

Most crucial, Murphy contended, was Kennedy's refusal to furnish, until too late, the U.S. military assistance that some of the planners had "taken for granted." Under pressure from his political advisers, Kennedy ruled that U.S. air power would not be on call at any time, according to Murphy. Moreover, preliminary air strikes by American B-26s flown by Cuban exiles would be strictly limited: the first, two days before the invasion; the second, on the Monday morning, April 17, of the actual landings. However, on Sunday night, even as the exile brigade's invasion fleet crept toward the Cuban shore, Secretary of State Dean Rusk, acting for the President, called off this second air strike, and Kennedy himself refused a CIA plea that the aircraft carrier on station nearby should provide jet air cover instead. On Monday, Kennedy again changed his mind, authorizing the Cuban exiles' B-26s to attack, but only a small force could be scratched together. On Tuesday night, with the expedition now at the point of no return, Kennedy finally ordered Navy air support, but this could not prevent "the melancholy end" of the affair.

Fortune had braced for trouble as the article neared publication. One of Murphy's Washington sources, to whom he had shown a prepublication draft, asked: "Do you want to raise the roof, Charlie?" "No," Murphy replied, "just lift a few nails." Luce, reading the draft copy, had a similar reaction. "For Harry, the story couldn't have come at a worse time, just when he was trying to make peace with Kennedy," Murphy said. Luce's first impulse was to hold the piece for an easier moment. This story, however, could not be stalled. *Fortune* was up against its deadline; the magazine had nothing "in the bank" (in reserve) to replace Murphy's story, managing editor Duncan Norton-Taylor informed Luce. With some rewriting, some cushioning of the thrusts at Kennedy, the story went back up to Luce, who gave the go-ahead. Murphy was in the Far East, on loan to *Life* to do a profile on Chiang Kai-shek, when the storm broke.

In a televised press conference, Kennedy denounced Murphy's version of the events; privately, in the Oval Office, in a tirade directed at John Steele, Kennedy excoriated the article as "the lousiest, most inaccurate job I've ever seen . . . shockingly inaccurate and completely wrong. Printing it in *Fortune* is one thing, but I can't understand the editors of *Time* picking it up and running it. *Time* is supposed to be a newsmagazine. This thing is five months old." The President then handed Steele a 17-point rebuttal prepared by General Maxwell Taylor, formerly U.S. Army Chief of Staff, now Kennedy's personal military adviser. Kennedy asked that Taylor's report be shown Luce, and two weeks later Taylor came to New York to discuss it further.

The confrontation with General Taylor, which Kennedy specifically asked Luce to keep confidential, took place in Luce's office; lunch followed. Accompanying Luce were Donovan, Norton-Taylor and Murphy, who had been summoned home by telephone from his Far East assignment—"there was mention of a bomb, or something," he wryly recalled. Murphy prepared point-by-point replies to the presidential challenge of his reporting.

Luce entered the meeting in a conciliatory mood, inclined to cede in the interests of peace with the President. He stiffened as it became plain that Murphy's account was essentially correct. Two dates were in error and as Luce said afterward, "Murphy got the wrong flattop." The Navy carrier involved in the operation was the *Essex*, not the *Boxer*. But otherwise, Luce reflected, "when we got all through with analyzing those 17 points—I'm not sure we didn't stop after about 12 of them—Taylor, in effect, threw in his hand and said, by his tone and attitude more than by anything he said, that it was evident the critique of the article was not substantiated." Donovan closed the subject, Norton-Taylor remembered, "by standing up and booming, 'Well, I think that the President owes *Fortune* an apology.' "

Needless to say, none was forthcoming. Time Inc.'s relations with the White House nevertheless eased somewhat. For its 1961 Man of the Year cover, *Time* chose Kennedy. The cover story was favorable; Kennedy had already shown qualities of leadership that, *Time* observed, "may yet make him a great President." *Life*'s editorial that week took a similar line.

The next month, however, there was another blowup. The provocation was trivial: a *Time* story reported that the President had appeared in a "specially posed" cover for *Gentlemen's Quarterly*, a men's fashion magazine. Outraged at appearing to be clothes-conscious, Kennedy denied that he "posed" for *GQ*. As his anger mounted, *Time*'s correspondent Sidey was hastily summoned from the White House pressroom to the Oval Office for a presidential tongue-lashing. By coincidence, Colonel John Glenn had just been hauled from his space capsule in the Atlantic Ocean after his pioneering orbital flight, and the White House was contacting Glenn by radio-telephone just as Kennedy began berating Sidey for the sins of *Time*'s editors. Thereupon ensued the comic spectacle of the President swiveling from Sidey to Glenn, shouting his anger to the one, his congratulations to the other, listening for the astronaut's far-off reply, then turning back to resume his tirade against *Time*.

In September 1962, as a consequence of the Radziwill incident mentioned earlier, Luce once more attempted to mollify Kennedy, promising that he and Donovan would undertake "a careful review of the course which *Time* has pursued." After reviewing "some 80 or 90 stories that had something important to say about [the Kennedy] administration," Donovan stated in a memo to Luce:

I don't see how anybody can conclude that *Time* is "against Kennedy whatever he does." *Time* has criticized Kennedy for some things, praised him for others—would anybody except the most rabid campaign orator do otherwise? . . . *Time*'s 1962 coverage of Kennedy began with a Man of the Year story . . . It was the kind of story that caused some of my Republican friends to ask, not for the first time, "When are you guys gonna stop being a propaganda sheet for the Kennedys?"

Donovan thought Luce could "speak to the President with great satisfaction of *Time*'s coverage of his administration. It has been penetrating, independent, principled."

The political jousting between Kennedy and *Time* abruptly halted in October 1962. The Cuban missile crisis was at hand. U-2 overflights had confirmed the presence of Soviet medium-range missiles on the island, and on Monday night, October 22, Kennedy delivered a televised ultimatum to Khrushchev: withdraw the missiles or else. The next morning the President sought out Luce to give him and Fuerbringer a private briefing, and inferentially, to seek their support.

Kennedy's summons to Luce caught the editor-in-chief at the airport in Chicago. He had just come from a Time Inc. reception for automobile executives in Detroit. Late the following afternoon, Luce and Fuerbringer met with Kennedy at the White House. In a quiet, intense session Kennedy outlined the military contingencies he faced, including possible Soviet retaliation against Berlin. "My recollection of the 40 minutes when the three of us sat together is that hardly a word was said," Luce wrote later. "That, of course, was not the case. Words were spoken. Mostly they were in contemplation of that cloud that hangs over our century—atomic war."

Luce recalled: "I think when I came in . . . [Kennedy] said with a smile, 'Well, you've been very interested in Cuba for a long time.' I replied, 'Not just Cuba, the global situation.' And then . . . when we left . . . the President said, 'Well, you have been the strongest advocate of vigorous action in Cuba—and you were right.' " Luce continued:

Otto and I were certainly not wrong in understanding the heavy emphasis J.F.K. put on the imminent possibility of invasion . . . He *did* have it in mind—he damn well did . . . Over the past 18 months since the Bay of Pigs, on the half dozen times when I had seen the President, I had advocated blockade and not invasion. *His* argumentative attitude toward me was that it was a choice between invasion and nothing—i.e., nothing in a military way. He kept putting it up to me: "Are you for or against invasion?" My reply was invariably that I would not be drawn into that corner. I was *not* for invasion; I was *for* blockade. (Explicitly so stated in *Life* editorials.) But I also always added that, of course, a blockade would have to be backed up by a readiness to invade . . .

The President kept repeating, "Berlin . . . Berlin . . . Berlin." He had been reiterating the same emphasis to me for over a year. My attitude was not to be impressed by this Berlin talk. Berlin or no Berlin, we had to do something about Cuba. And if there was going to be a Berlin crisis, all the more necessary to have disposed of the Cuba menace. But, of course, on this October 24 meeting I didn't make that point . . . The President was taking firm action—so there was no occasion for argument.

Life *Seeks a Formula for Survival*

L IFE'S PREDICAMENT CONTINUED to dwarf all other corporate worries in the early 1960s. The giant picture weekly was like a beached whale; the effort to get it afloat again was to command more attention, over a longer period of time, than any problem in the company's history.

The revenue flow from *Life* remained enormous as the 1960s began, despite the steady fall in advertising page sales. Reading *Life*'s three-year budget projections in December 1959, Luce wrote publisher Heiskell: "Lump together 1960, 1961 and 1962 and you have a gross business of about $500 million. That is a huge sum and maybe it's just too damn big for any one magazine to handle. But as a business proposition, such a gross should yield a profit of at least $75 million."

Truth was, *Life* had reached or exceeded Luce's target of 15 percent return on revenue only during the wartime years of the early 1940s. In 1956, when *Life*'s profit reached its all-time high, the pretax return was only 12.5 percent. Then had come *Life*'s disastrous downward slide, culminating in the 1959 loss—the first since 1938, when *Life* was still trying to cope with the huge audience it had suddenly found for itself. In the intervening two decades, *Life* had attained a position that was special—not only in the company but also in the magazine business. A veteran *Time* editor who later worked on *Life* wrote:*

> *Life*, with its success, gathered around itself a high-spirited staff, full of talent, cocksure of itself, and to those of us on *Time* magazine, riding the same elevators to a different floor, enviably glamorous. Starlets, not yet able to get nationwide attention on television talk shows, would do anything to get on the big cover of *Life* . . . Studios would delay release of their films if *Life* would promise them a spread; Broadway musical producers assembled their casts in full costume for expensive "photo call" rehearsals in hopes of coverage. *Life*'s attention was just as important to major political figures, and to generals in wartime, who gave its photographers, artists and correspondents special status. Margaret Bourke-White witnessed the German shelling of Moscow from the rooftop of the American embassy, and Harry Hopkins was happy to be the courier who took her pictures back to New York. *Life* was king, and flung its money around as only a new rich Arab king would. Even occasional attempts to economize were apologetic: there was *waste-waste*, which was to be deplored, but *useful-waste* was shooting 100 frames instead of ten, if doing so produced one great picture. *Life* opened its checkbooks to get the best pictures, the biggest memoirs. Once in 1958 when the *Saturday Evening Post* signed up the commander of the first submarine journey beneath the North Pole, managing editor [Edward K.] Thompson gathered every reporter and photographer he could find or fly to England to throw a party for the entire submarine crew on its arrival there, and in one night of booze-fueled interviewing of everyone present, got the whole story before the *Post* could.

To what extent *Life*'s fall into deficit was caused by television was arguable, and remained so to the end. As the average family's TV viewing hours increased, there was clearly less time left for magazine reading; there were other and growing demands on leisure time, as well, in the increasingly affluent American society. In picture coverage of the news, though, the competition to *Life* was not yet as formidable as it would shortly become. The networks' evening news shows ran only 15 minutes, and only 340,000 American households had color receivers. Satellite broadcasting had not yet begun

*Griffith: *How True*, p. 141.

38

to bring pictures from abroad. Television had to deal with the same physical handicaps of time and distance as did *Life*. Bulky cameras and sound and lighting equipment further limited TV's reportorial capabilities.

Television's impact on advertising was easier to gauge. Offering large, albeit undiscriminating, audiences at relatively low unit cost, TV was becoming increasingly attractive to the mass merchandisers who for years had been *Life*'s mainstay. Television was the hot new advertising medium; along Madison Avenue, it was in TV that careers were now being made. And more money also, in agency billings. "*Life*'s basic competitive problem in relation to its past and its future advertising performance . . . is television," *Life* advertising director Clay Buckhout informed management in July 1959. "Our biggest classifications are pretty much the same as television's— food, toiletries, tobacco, drugs." There were, Buckhout added, "33 advertisers who spent over $4 million each to buy television time . . . last year. All but one of these ran in *Life*, spending $37 million in our pages; but they spent $380 million in network television and $139 million in spot [local] television."

At the moment, however, it was the internecine competition in the mass-circulation magazine field that focused corporate attention. In the so-called numbers game, the *Reader's Digest* was in first place, selling 12 million copies a month in late 1959. But with monthly publication and a smaller page size, the *Digest* was in a somewhat different category from the others. *Life* regarded as its main competitors the weekly *Saturday Evening Post* and the fortnightly *Look*, each with a circulation of about 6 million. In 1959 *Life* still topped everybody in ad revenues. To retain leadership, it had, in early 1959, decided to increase circulation in stages to 7 million by reducing prices to their lowest level in more than a decade. Newsstand copies came down from 25 cents to the weird (but testproven) figure of 19 cents. Subscriptions were lowered by a dollar to $5.95 a year, with a 32-week trial offer at $2.98, or about 9⅓ cents a copy; this strategy would ultimately prove disastrous.

Editorially, *Life* claimed superiority over both *Look* and the *Post*. With due allowance for corporate pride, the claim could be supported—certainly in the magazine's grandly conceived, lavishly produced series on such subjects as "The World We Live In," "The Epic of Man," "The World's Great Religions," and others that no mass-circulation magazine except *Life* had attempted. Nor could the competition match the depth of talent in *Life*'s editorial staff of some 275 persons, the extent of its worldwide news coverage, and the technical excellence and speed of *Life*'s news delivery. By in-house estimate, *Life*'s $10 million editorial budget was double the *Post*'s, quadruple *Look*'s.

Even though *Life*'s profits had been declining, there was as yet no corporate hesitation at spending heavily when journalistic opportunity arose, as it had in 1959 when the National Aeronautics and Space Administration selected the first seven Mercury astronauts and the rights to their personal stories came up for sale. "I thought men in space and the idea of Americans going to the moon was the biggest story around and that *Life* should somehow be identified with it," said managing editor Ed Thompson, who oversaw *Life*'s winning $500,000 bid.

The job of producing *Life*, Luce once remarked, was like "putting on a Broadway show every week," and Thompson ran it as a one-man show. A Midwestern newsman who joined *Life* a year after it was founded, he was, by 1960, in his 11th year as managing editor. Every picture, every layout had to meet his approval. He ruled by grumping commands in a mumble that tended to get lost somewhere behind his ever-present well-chewed cigar. The staff admired him enormously; the exploits they performed to meet his demands were the subject of much fond reminiscing afterward. As much as any man, he set the *Life* tone. Questioning *Life*'s spending habits, Luce once asked Thompson if he could "lop a million dollars off the top." Thompson was quoted as replying, "Harry, I could lop a million off the bottom—for rent, light, heat, mandatory raises, that kind of thing. But I couldn't spare the top million. That's gambling money."*

Life's reputation for profligacy was deserved; legend magnified it. The magazine harbored some of the company's most creative expense-account artists. C.D. (for Charles Douglas) Jackson, Heiskell's successor as publisher, knew whereof he spoke when he told a staff gathering he knew there had been many a mink coat put on the company tab—"hair by hair." Yet for all the dogsleds imaginatively hired and airplanes legitimately chartered to cover the big news breaks, *Life*'s editorial expenses were not as extravagant as the legend. Then at about 7 percent of revenue, they were proportionately lower than *Time*'s. The outlays that really mattered were for printing, circulation promotion and distribution.

*Dora Jane Hamblin: *That Was the LIFE* (W.W. Norton & Company, 1977), p. 187.

It was the cost of getting subscribers and newsstand buyers that Heiskell examined most closely in a study of *Life*'s economics he completed in January 1960. This was one of his last chores as *Life* publisher before he went upstairs to become corporate chairman. The study was prompted by a query from Luce. *Life*'s price reductions, instituted along with the circulation increases, had not brought the reader response Luce anticipated, and just before Christmas 1959 he wrote Heiskell, wondering if *Life*'s editorial formula was to blame.

> Around the office we seem to think *Life* has been producing good issues. And I gather "friends" give us good marks. But how *strong* (not how big) is our circulation? Maybe we can tell better in the spring. But I certainly don't want to go after 6,800,000 with the feeling that 20 percent of it is forced. *That* way is surely trouble.

Replying to Luce's question, Heiskell pinpointed rising circulation costs as the main reason for *Life*'s declining profitability. *Life*'s $23,875,000 expenditure on maintaining circulation was triple in percentage terms, quadruple in actual dollars, what it had been ten years earlier. The reason was largely *Life*'s shift from high-profit newsstand sales to low-profit subscriptions. Heiskell pointed out that "we had a net income from newsstand in 1950 . . . of over $9 million. In 1960, the newsstand net will be zero." To get new subscribers and hold old ones, *Life* would be sending out 82 million pieces of mail in 1960, at significantly higher unit costs than in 1950.

In April and May, Luce's newly appointed deputy, editorial director Hedley Donovan, spent six weeks on *Life*. "The most discouraging thing about the *Life* situation," he reported afterward, "is that the magazine is so good." Nevertheless, Donovan called for "a substantial (corporate) appropriation, money and bodies, for an examination of the concept of the mass magazine, i.e., of Time Inc.'s biggest product, in the kind of economy and society the U.S. has arrived at." Could *Life* be maintained as "a viable product for some years to come"? Donovan saw various possible answers:

> Yes. This just happens to be a sort of sticky period . . .
>
> Yes, though it won't be easy. There are a lot of factors working against the mass magazine, and it will take a sort of permanent *tour de force* to pull it off, but Time Inc. has the people who can do that . . .

No. Therefore, *Life* must get ready to appeal more deeply to fewer (relatively) people . . .

No. *Life* should spin off two, three, four magazines of specialized appeal. Like *the* Living magazine; *the* Culture magazine; and what else? . . . The parent publication should become the 10 cents news-and-fun picture magazine for 10 million people?

Another two years passed before either the *Life* research study or experimentation with specialized editorial supplements got under way. Luce in the interim returned to the *Life* editorial review he had broached earlier with Heiskell. Luce admitted he had been stalling, "partly because of laziness." But he was now being pushed to it; Heiskell, for one, remained sharply critical of *Life*'s editorial performance. "The thoughts of others plus my own bring me to the conclusion that *Life* requires a new prospectus," Luce announced, noting that this would be the first charter for *Life* since its original prospectus in 1936.

"Harry's mind being what it was, he felt nothing was valid unless underpinned by a theory," Heiskell once remarked of Luce, and the 27 typewritten pages of cerebration that Luce produced, under the title *"Life*: A New Prospectus for the Sixties," aptly demonstrated this. Full of sonorous rhetoric, perplexing as a guide to editorial policy, Luce's proposal was that *Life* needed more than a new editorial formula, it needed a new statement of purpose:

So what would be the purpose of *Life* in the Sixties? My answer: *Life* is and shall be designed to be the magazine of national purpose. In his first statement as President-Elect, Jack Kennedy called for "A Supreme National Effort." Amen. *Life* has called for just that . . .

The national purpose, as seen by the Editor-in-Chief, and for which he sees the need of a great magazine, can be summarized under two heads:

1) Win the Cold War.
2) Create a better America . . .

This certainly does not mean that the magazine I envision would be a series of preachments about national purpose . . . What I am saying is that *Life*, dedicated to helping bring about a great humane civilization, shall be:

A great Magazine of Art.
A great Magazine of Science.

42

A great Magazine of Religion.
A great Magazine of Politics (grand scale) . . .
A great Magazine of Economics (dull word!) . . .
A great Magazine of History—for you cannot build a civiliza-
tion without a deep and personal sense of history . . .

Luce conceded it would be a long slog to the realization of that purpose in actual magazine format:

> Looms now the question of Formula. How do we put all this
> together? . . . Formula! Yes, there's much sweating to be done
> about formula—just how to use, week after week, each of the
> 60 precious million-dollar pages (and half pages) to convey the
> throb and stir of these great themes . . .
>
>   This is magazine-making at its highest and most skill-demand-
> ing level.

In December, managing editor Thompson and art director Charles
Tudor were detached to start thinking about the "new *Life*." Staff
contributions were also invited.

If an injection of cheer had been needed on the publishing side,
C.D. Jackson, the new publisher appointed in 1960, was the man to
supply it. "I never saw such delightedly sustained ebullience . . .
such high optimism, the way he projected the expectation that
things were always going to work out," a publishing colleague said
of him. Jackson was, indeed, one of Time Inc.'s sunniest personalities—a witty, engaging man, as much diplomat and politician as
publishing executive, with acquaintances worldwide. People everywhere were always asking to be remembered "to my friend C.D."
He had the look of a boulevardier—tall, trim, dapper, given to
chuckling delightedly at his own jokes, which he could pull off as
easily in French and Italian as in English. Educated in Switzerland,
then at Princeton, Jackson had joined Time Inc. in 1931 as Luce's
personal assistant, becoming successively general manager of *Life*,
corporate vice president, managing director of Time-Life International, and publisher of *Fortune*. On leave from the company, Jackson had organized the prewar Council for Democracy to promote
American support for Britain, and later helped direct psychological
warfare for General Eisenhower in North Africa and Europe; after
the war, Jackson had headed the committee that set up Radio Free
Europe. In 1953 he had taken a one-year leave to go to the White

43

House as Eisenhower's special assistant for international affairs and Cold War planning.

Not long after assuming the duties of *Life* publisher, Jackson chose *Time*'s James R. Shepley, former chief of domestic correspondents, as his assistant publisher. Jackson also named a new general manager of *Life*, Arthur W. Keylor, to succeed Robert Elson, who went back to the editorial side as Time-Life bureau chief in London. Jackson's immediate aim, in taking over as publisher, was to lower *Life*'s breakeven point, measured in the number of advertising pages necessary to cover expenses and show a profit. Obviously, breakeven could be lowered either by reducing costs or by raising ad rates. Paper costs had already been trimmed slightly by cutting the basic weight of *Life*'s cover stock. Under Jackson, personnel cuts also began; some 70 people were lopped off the editorial and publishing staffs. Expecting resistance on the editorial side, Jackson was pleasantly surprised to find Thompson "incredibly . . . most cooperative. Being a complete dictator himself, what he needs, and most readily accepts, is an order. The order is 25 editorial people and $1 million," Jackson reported to Heiskell. The subsequent cuts included the first major reduction in photographic staff since *Life*'s founding. A number of veteran photographers were shifted from a salaried to a contract basis.

Life's advertising rates confronted the publisher with a tougher problem. These had nearly doubled between 1950 and 1960, the result of both increased circulation and increased cost-per-thousand (CPM) rates—the unit price *Life* charged the advertiser for each thousand of paid circulation. At $4.52 *Life*'s CPM was lower than *Time*'s but was consistently higher than that of its direct competitors: for example, *Look*'s was $4.29. To justify the difference, *Life* asserted its superiority as an advertising medium. Its readership per copy was claimed to be higher, its subscribers better educated, more urban, more white collar, more numerous in the better income and age brackets.

Nonetheless, advertiser resistance was building as prices went up. With another loss year ahead—1960 advertising sales ended up 200 pages below 1959's—the *Life* salesmen winced as new rate increases were announced for September. Jackson conveyed the advertising staff's distress in a note to Luce. "I hope never to have a defeatist attitude about *Life*, but I do think that after two and a half decades of steady ad rate progressions, we have finally reached the point where the absolute—not the relative—cost of a page in *Life* has become such a serious factor that it can overshadow the many other factors involved in an enthusiastic, effective and sympathetic sales campaign." To which Luce penciled in the margin: "Agreed." For 1961, accordingly, *Life*'s advertising rates were frozen, and circulation was held at 6.7 million.

Life celebrated its silver anniversary in March 1961 with a 90-minute television spectacular on NBC. As a prelude, the magazine's 1960 year-end double issue was devoted to a nostalgic review of its own history. A gatefold cover reproduced more than a hundred covers from past issues; inside was a selection of memorable *Life* photography, from the satiny pin-up picture of Rita Hayworth, Hollywood's "Love Goddess Personified," to Robert Capa's unforgettable Spanish Civil War shot of a Loyalist soldier snapped at the moment of his death on a stony hillside. The issue was a "jackpot" success, Jackson reported. The following month came the Kennedy inaugural issue, a complete sellout.

The progress in editorial revisions Thompson and Tudor had been making meanwhile pleased Luce. "I think we've about got it—the New *Life*," Luce wrote jubilantly, in mid-April. Six weeks later the first issue, dated June 2, 1961, came off the presses.

One immediately noticeable change was in the cover design. No longer was the picture display constrained by a red border across the bottom of the page; the cover photo now bled to the edges—showing, in the initial issue, Fidel Castro in full oratorical fury, flanked by a cover billing announcing the first part of a new series entitled "The Crisis in Our Hemisphere." Inside, the most striking innovation was the "banking" or clustering of advertising pages to open up larger edit "wells" in which the picture stories could run unbroken by advertisements. Editorial innovations included the Article of the Week, in which Shana Alexander, *Life*'s first woman staff writer, sympathetically chronicled singer Judy Garland's troubles and triumphs. Inaugurating a new Better Living department were seven pages on the fashions, food and furniture of California patio life, including floor plans for an economical patio-style home billed as *Life*'s House of the Month.

Eight weeks after the editorial revisions, Jackson assessed subscriber reaction. "Enormously satisfying to me, as a publisher," Jackson claimed in the July 28 issue, citing "mail sacks full of letters" and words of praise from such figures as Carl Sandburg, Arthur Godfrey and Richard Nixon. In truth, however, *Life* was experiencing a familiar publishing phenomenon: format changes were upsetting to readers, and their response ran more negative than positive. For Luce, personally, the most negative was a letter from Raymond Rubicam of Young & Rubicam, one of Luce's and *Life*'s oldest friends in the advertising business. "*Life*, 'new' or old, seems to me to have no sense of direction," Rubicam wrote. " 'Stentorian' is the word for *Life*. Every picture a blast . . . Why not try getting human?"

Floored, Luce picked himself up to reply:

WOW! SOCK! . . .

Yours of September 25 is so overpowering that it seems literally impossible to answer.

When I was in a British boarding school in China, boys were flogged more or less regularly and even though they were all over tears, they were supposed to straighten themselves up and say, "Thank you, Sir."

So I could say "thank you"; and indeed I do. For in using the word "stentorian" you gave me just the word I needed (and hadn't thought of) . . . The "stentorian" noise will be screened out—without any lessening of the message.

I will say just this: *Life* has made up its mind as to what kind of magazine it intends to be. And I think this make-up-its-mindness will soon become evident.

Negative was the word for Madison Avenue's reaction to the banking of advertisements. Although *Vogue*, *Harper's Bazaar* and the New York *Times* Magazine, all featuring fashion advertising, did it regularly, the clustering was clearly not welcomed by *Life*'s package-goods accounts.

"Much of the past month has been spent putting out fires started by the new *Life* format," advertising director Buckhout informed Jackson in July. "On that score, the *Reader's Digest* is saying, 'We started out banking ads and learned the hard way that we were wrong. Now *Life* is making the same mistake.' " Within a few months, publishing considerations were prevailing over editorial, and some of the larger ad banks were being broken up—necessarily at a cost to *Life*'s picture display.

To Jackson's distress, it was just at that point that further trouble loomed on the advertising front, provoked by a 30-line item in the Newsfronts section of *Life*'s September 1 issue. It was an excellent example of how a tiny and genuinely unimportant story can cause big trouble. The offending article dealt with the Christian Anti-Communism Crusade led by Frederick C. Schwarz, an Australian-born physician and "evangelist gone secular," who, *Life* said, "preaches doomsday by Communism in 1973 unless every American starts distrusting his neighbor as a possible Communist or 'comsymp' [Communist sympathizer]." There was a barrage of protest mail and alarms from *Life*'s advertising sales office in Los Angeles, where it was feared that some important advertisers sympathetic to Schwarz's crusade might withdraw their business from the magazine.

Life had erred in one respect. Schwarz had not explicitly urged Americans to distrust their neighbors; that was a paraphrase, and *Life* acknowledged its mistake in the September 22 Letters column. But the next month Jackson went beyond this, flying to California to make amends before 10,000 people gathered in the Hollywood Bowl for "Hollywood's Answer to Communism." Joining Schwarz on the platform, Jackson declared it was his "great privilege . . . to align *Life* magazine in a very personal way with a number of stalwart fighters" against communism. "Like all dedicated men, [Dr. Schwarz] will be subjected to oversimplified misinterpretation. Regretfully, my own magazine recently published such an oversimplified misinterpretation," Jackson said, adding, "I am profoundly sorry." Reverberations from the incident continued for months. Luce, questioned at a Los Angeles news conference, mixed defense of Jackson as one of the U.S.'s "most experienced experts . . . on ideological warfare" with a mild disavowal. The Hollywood Bowl speech was "entirely Jackson's own idea," Luce said. He also managed to deflect the wrath of the liberal Episcopal Bishop of California, James Pike, who challenged the editor-in-chief to state "where *Life* magazine really stands" on Schwarz's "Christian" crusade. Taking time two days before Christmas to write Pike a long and thoughtful letter, Luce declared: "I regard all manifestations of McCarthyism, Birchism or historic American 'know-nothingism' with repugnance—and, at least on Sundays, with some modicum of compassion."

In July 1961, Thompson's long reign as managing editor ended. George P. Hunt was named to succeed him. Thompson was named editor—a new post. "Why an editor?" wrote Luce. "In any place except Time Inc. this question would be superfluous to the point of being silly. Here, for various reasons, the post of 'managing editor' has become the prestigious post. But the world's greatest magazine ought not to be the prisoner of local custom." Instead, Luce proposed that authority be split, with an editor to hold "broad responsibility for the quality of *Life*," and a managing editor to "direct the week-to-week production of the magazine, and to supervise the editorial staff."

Thompson agreed that *Life* probably needed two men at the top. "Or at least one and a half, or one and five-eighths," as he said later. Over the years, producing the weekly magazine had grown into a huge juggling act, with myriad picture and text projects in various stages of planning, execution or completion; parts of three separate issues could be running on the presses simultaneously. Nonetheless, Thompson was "kind of shook up," as he wrote Luce, when his appointment was announced. With reason. While Thompson knew Luce's intent, he had questions about the editor's role, and Luce's memo suggested that the editor-in-chief would discuss these with him first. Instead, it was from Hunt that Thompson learned Luce had already gone ahead and made the change. Hunt described the circumstances:

> One day Luce called me up to his office and told me he'd like me to be the next managing editor, effective the following Monday. He had taken me out to lunches at the St. Regis and elsewhere and we had discussed the magazine. That day it was short and sweet.
>
> I expected there'd be a memo or something around. I expected to hear from Thompson but I waited and I heard nothing . . . I thought, I've got to tell him, so I went in and said, "Ed, I've been tapped."
>
> "Tapped for what?" Ed asked.
>
> "Tapped to take your place."
>
> "You can take over the magazine's close," he said. "I'm going home." Later that night we talked on the phone. He thanked me . . . But Luce was a real coward about Ed . . . just couldn't face him.

The new editorial tandem did not work out as Luce intended, nor as Thompson hoped. Thompson remained editor of *Life*'s editorial page, general counsel to Luce on many matters concerning *Life* and overseer of *Life*'s contractual arrangements with the astronauts and such outside contributors as Richard Nixon, Douglas MacArthur and Stalin's daughter Svetlana, all of whose memoirs appeared during Thompson's tenure as editor.

But as "inspector general" of *Life*'s journalistic performance, as Thompson understood his assigned role, he inevitably came in conflict with Hunt. The relationship was not easy for either man. In 1967 Thompson retired from *Life* and began a second successful career as founding editor and publisher of *Smithsonian* magazine.

Hunt, who was 42 when he took over from Thompson, was one of Time Inc.'s sizable contingent of ex-Marines—a tall, powerfully built man, looking more like a professional football player than the artist he had originally set out to be. As an Amherst undergraduate, he had spent a couple of summers studying at the Pennsylvania Academy of Fine Arts, and also made the art student's pilgrimage to Paris; afterward, he studied with Guy Pène du Bois in New York. Back in the U.S. and needing a job, Hunt was hired by *Fortune* as an office boy, later moved to *Life* as an art researcher. In 1941 he joined the Marines, coming out in 1946 as a captain, with a Silver Star for valor on New Britain and the Navy Cross for leading a bloody assault on Peleliu from which only 78 out of 235 men in Hunt's company emerged alive. In *Coral Comes High*, published in 1946 by Harper & Brothers, Hunt gave a vivid account of the Peleliu battle; in "Honorable Discharge," written for the September 1947 issue of *Fortune* and later also published as a book, Hunt picked up on the survivors' postwar experiences. Joining *Life* as co-editor in the art department, Hunt became successively military affairs editor, news bureau correspondent in Chicago and Washington, and then assistant managing editor, in charge of *Life*'s back-of-the-book departments.

Hunt's appointment as managing editor triggered other changes. Assistant managing editor Philip H. Wootton Jr. moved up to executive editor. Assistant managing editor Hugh Moffett, an earthy newsman of the Chicago school, took charge of the combined foreign and domestic news departments. Two new assistant managing editors were named: former articles editor Ralph Graves, to supervise *Life* text; and the veteran *Life* correspondent Roy Rowan, to supervise photographic operations, assisted by senior editor Richard Pollard. Philip B. Kunhardt Jr., previously assistant picture editor, was named a senior editor and took over Hunt's back-of-the-book responsibilities, but without the promotion to assistant managing editor that the job merited; against Hunt's wishes, Luce withheld the title from Kunhardt for a year, arguing that the leap was too much. As his art director, Hunt named the 20-year *Life* veteran, Bernard Quint, a temperamental and gifted man who had been associate art director under Thompson and Charles Tudor.

Hunt brought to *Life* a different style of editing. He was warm, emotional, impulsive, given to large enthusiasms, fond of citing military maxims: *Life* should "seize the high ground and hold it"; *Life* stories should "move within forceful distance of their subject." If Thompson, as one colleague remarked, used "a kind of psychological acupuncture" to get results, Hunt liked to sweep the staff along with his own infectious confidence. Recalled *Life*'s longtime copy editor, Joseph Kastner:

> George was more of a consensus editor [than Thompson]. He was very much the Marine captain—morale of the troops was very important to him. He would urge a sort of "Uncle Sam Needs You" idea, whereas Ed Thompson was more the kind who'd say: "Uncle Sam doesn't need you. What makes you think you're good enough to work for *Life*?"
>
> But the men were exactly alike in that they both wanted their own way.

Hunt's way, as he put it himself, was a magazine that "pronounced with more showmanship," and he considered as a compliment the half-joking remark Luce once made to him: "George, you're a god-damned sensationalist."

Under Hunt, *Life*'s focus remained the news. But the emphasis changed from photographic narrative to pictorial dramatization—frequently a single picture spread across two pages—capturing what Hunt called "the frozen moment." Six months into Hunt's regime, *Life* promotion director Richard Coffey summed up the new approach for the advertising sales staff's guidance:

> The most noticeable aspect of the editor's visual presentation is a flair for . . . and a pronounced use of the *big* photograph. Never in my memory have so many double-truck pictures been used in visual effect with so little accompanying . . . caption [material] . . . More often our lead stories tend not to be of the "hard news" variety . . . Instead George views the role of *Life* as a "communicator" of emotion, of beauty, of humanity and events.

A *Life* editor later recounted how Hunt handled the bombing of a black church in Birmingham, Alabama, in September 1963. When he was brought a particularly poignant picture of one victim, a little girl blinded in the blast, "We knew how George would react. He took one look at that picture and said, 'That's it. It says it all.' *Life* ran it as a double-truck in Newsfronts and that was it. It made a big statement."

Multipage spectacular projects, known as blockbusters, also became more frequent, as did special issues devoted entirely to a single subject. In 1962 there were four such issues—on money, on California, on food and on America's "takeover generation" of rising young leaders in business, politics, the arts and sciences—in addition to the customary year-end double issue.

As an economy measure—although actually, the savings proved small—*Life*'s news service operations were reorganized a few months after Hunt became managing editor. *Life* correspondents and photographers, previously scattered among 28 Time-Life bureaus around the world, were regrouped independently of *Time* in six regional bureaus under regional editors. A seventh *Life* bureau, in Moscow, was opened in 1964, following the publication of a *Life* special issue on the U.S.S.R. entitled "A Long Visit with the Soviet People."

The new bureau deployments—"massing our teams so they could operate as a unit," as Hunt said—fitted the magazine's changed approach: fewer stories played larger and with more splash. In 1962, economic necessity forced another change in operating style. That March, *Life*'s editorial close was moved back from Friday to Wednesday night; the press run was scheduled to begin on Thursday to save on printing costs and speed up distribution. The move, distancing *Life* from the week's news, upset the editors at the time. Afterward, they conceded that few major stories had actually been lost (the magazine was reopened for the assassinations of President Kennedy and, in 1968, of Martin Luther King Jr.; and the deaths of the three astronauts killed in a launch-pad accident in 1967). The result, in any case, was to move the editorial frenzy to midweek and give the staff quieter, more civilized weekends.

Paradoxically, as *Life*'s picture display got larger, the magazine's word content also increased, with signed columns, signed reviews, more bylined pieces generally throughout the magazine. Part of this had begun with the 1961 redesign. Pictures alongside partial-page advertisements had always posed layout problems for *Life*; the magazine's first managing editor, John Shaw Billings, once remarked that the only suitable picture for a vertical half-page was a one-legged man on a mountain—a picture that Billings had, in fact, managed to find. To deal with partial pages in the "new" *Life* format, short text pieces were used instead. Under Hunt, the expansion of text went further. Counting wordage in 1964, he found that it had more than tripled since 1960, from an average of 7,000 words per issue to some 23,000; bylines had also just about tripled.

This "overthrow of anonymity," as Hunt called it, broke sharply with *Life* tradition. Previously, only major articles had been bylined; now, *Life* was regularly running signed film, theater, book and other reviews. In March 1964, a series of biweekly columns, "The View

51

From Here," by former *Life* articles editor Loudon Wainwright began on a trial basis. In the fall of 1964, Shana Alexander began writing another column, "The Feminine Eye," to run alternately with Wainwright's. In 1966 came a third *Life* column, running weekly, Sidey's "The Presidency."

Another innovation for *Life* was the establishment of an investigative reporting team. Like many of his generation, Hunt had been greatly influenced by the autobiography of the turn-of-the-century muckraker Lincoln Steffens, and he wanted to kindle some of the same spirit on *Life*. Fortuitously, Time Inc. had a man for the assignment already on the staff, in the person of William Lambert, a *Time* correspondent in the Los Angeles bureau who earlier, as a reporter for the Portland *Oregonian*, had won a Pulitzer Prize for exposing labor racketeering in the Northwest. In 1963 *Life* brought Lambert to New York, assured him of special handling of his files (and his expense accounts) to mask his sources, and gave him freedom to dip where and when he wanted.

In November came the first big results: a two-part series by Lambert and *Life* staff writer Keith Wheeler on the financial dealings of Lyndon Johnson's protégé, former Senate majority secretary Bobby Baker. In August 1964 another two-part series by Lambert and Wheeler uncovered Lyndon Johnson's Texas path to enormous personal wealth. Later it would be Lambert's exposé of U.S. Supreme Court Justice Abe Fortas's private financial dealings that led to Fortas's resignation from the court. Sandy Smith, a former Chicago *Tribune* reporter, joined *Life*'s investigative team in 1967, and soon did a notable job on organized crime. *Life* had become a maker, as well as reporter, of the news.

At the end of his first year as managing editor, Hunt assembled *Life*'s editorial staff for dinner in New York's Sheraton East Hotel. The Hunt Ball, as the gathering was immediately dubbed, was the first in an annual series of *Life* dinners—exuberant affairs for the most part, sometimes turning quite rowdy. On this inaugural occasion, in June 1962, Hunt had reassurances to offer the group. *Life*'s economic "compression" was over, he reported, and "despite the scuttlebutt you may hear whispered within and without the Time & Life Building, *Life* is still the biggest and strongest single unit in the entire publishing world." (The scuttlebutt apparently had spread as far as London, where the *Times*, in April, asked its New York correspondent to query C.D. Jackson about a rumor that *Life* was going out of business.)

Life was, in fact, heading for a modest 1962 profit of just over $1.4 million, a return of barely 1 percent on revenues but welcome nonetheless after three consecutive years of loss. Although *Life*'s new advertising director, James Dunn, who had succeeded Buckhout in July 1961, reported page sales down again, rate increases based on increased circulation raised advertising revenues 6.5 percent. Meanwhile, the breakeven point had been reduced sharply through internal economies and what assistant publisher Shepley wryly called "fiscal methodology"—partly, by crediting *Life* with some revenue from the newly established Time Inc. book operation, which drew heavily on *Life*'s subscriber lists for mail-order sales (see chapter 4). *Life*'s own circulation continued to pose problems, however. "The plain fact is that the circulation director is meeting the 7 million guarantee to advertisers in the second half of 1962 only with considerable difficulty," Shepley reported.

It was at this point that the battle of the mass magazines took another sudden turn. Abandoning the circulation race it had set out to win at all costs only three years earler, *Life* announced it was holding its rate base for the next year at 1962's figure of 7 million. *Look* moved into the lead, announcing a circulation increase to 7.4 million in June 1963. The *Saturday Evening Post* fell further behind with 6.5 million.

For the *Post*, it was the beginning of the end. In 1961, the magazine had been editorially restyled, as had *Life*, but more drastically. The *Post*'s abandonment of its familiar homey format offended old readers without winning new advertisers. That year the *Post* lost $3 million, and the parent Curtis Publishing Company went into the red for the first time since its founding in 1891. In the spring of 1962 there was a corporate upheaval. The board dismissed the company's longtime president and installed in his place the flamboyant one-eyed advertising man, Matthew J. Culligan, whose first task at Curtis became a search for additional cash to keep the company afloat. Rumors circulated that the *Post* might have to go biweekly to survive.

The fortnightly *Look*, however, continued to press *Life*. While its advertising revenues were only half of *Life*'s, because of less frequent publication, they were growing at a faster rate. Between the two magazines, the fight turned quite nasty. *Look* belittled the "doddering" *Life*; *Life* publicly charged that *Look*'s circulation was being fed from the cemetery, not only with subscribers from the defunct *Collier*'s but also from *Capper's Farmer*, which had died in 1960. When its circulation finally passed *Life*'s, *Look* trumpeted its new promotional theme: "*Look* Is Bigger Than *Life*."

Life's pullback from the circulation race was not as abrupt a decision as it seemed. The realization had been growing that circulation increases could not be sustained indefinitely. What finally clinched matters was *Life*'s budgeting for 1963, which showed an increase in circulation costs of nearly $2.5 million to more than $27 million, even at the 7 million rate base.

In abandoning "firstism," as it was called around the shop, the corporate aim was to upgrade *Life* circulation further, emphasizing its quality in an "upper brow" promotion campaign with advertisers. To support the theme of *Life*'s quality and selectivity, circulation pricing policy was also reversed. The annual subscription rate was raised to $6.75. After some hesitation, the newsstand price, which had been rounded upward to 20 cents when the new editorial format was introduced in 1961, was pushed further up to the 1958 level of 25 cents. *Look* was already at 25 cents and making capital of its higher newsstand price in its advertising promotion.

Not everyone on the *Life* staff was convinced that the magazine's new sales pitch, class vs. mass, would impress Madison Avenue. "For one thing, many of our big money advertisers simply don't care about *Life* being so upscale," warned marketing director Richard Ostheimer. Still, there was general agreement with a statement Luce made in a strategy session on promotional tactics: "Let's promote what we have and forget what we haven't got."

Doubts persisted, however, that the magazine had yet found a new place for itself. The uncertainties struck C.D. Jackson keenly on his return in August 1962 from a world tour. From the perspective of a quarter-century of association with *Life*, the publisher wrote Luce:

> *Life* was born, brought up, housed, fed, clothed and indoctrinated as a *monopoly*. *Life* did not plan it that way. It just turned out that way, and it was wonderful. That monopoly no longer exists . . .
>
> I do not believe we can either edit ourselves or promote ourselves or sell ourselves into a restoration of that monopoly with our present formula. Besides, I believe that our monopoly hangover is in for further jolts. I felt an ominous shiver during

my trip when I read all about Telstar in *Time*. What I read was the warning of instant color TV simultaneously all over the world. That was when I got really excited over Wootton's proposal.

The proposal that Jackson referred to was to publish editorial supplements to *Life* to suit particular groups of readers, as first suggested a couple of years earlier by executive editor Phil Wootton. Originally Luce was cool to the idea of *Life* supplements; better to improve *Life* as it was—"the big *Life*," as he called it. By mid-1962, however, the editor-in-chief was willing to listen further.

Wootton, who later went on to help direct the corporate research program, had the distinction of being *Life*'s only working cowboy, spending summer vacations punching cattle on a friend's ranch in Colorado; but it was the horseless-carriage parallel that he drew in putting his proposal to Luce. He recalled that one-choice option Henry Ford used to offer buyers of his model T: "You can have any color car you want so long as it's black." Observed Wootton: "With *Life* we are turning out a single unvaried product (like the hypothetical Ford sedan) which we expect the whole country to buy." Wootton proposed getting away from "our one-model magazine" by offering additional pages on special subjects, stapled into the regular *Life* on a regular schedule—a science supplement one week, travel the next, entertainment the following—which subscribers could choose for an additional few dollars per year over the basic subscription price.

By late fall 1962, two supplements had been dummied. One, on science, was devoted largely to an exposition of radio astronomy, *Life* science writing at its lucid best, handsomely illustrated. The other, on travel, featured the touristic and archaeological attractions of Mexico's Yucatan peninsula and the bucolic pleasures of a Sunday on the Marne River outside Paris.

Then, in December, an unexpected opportunity to try a different approach to supplements suddenly presented itself. Just before Christmas, New York's nine major dailies were hit by a printers' strike. The strike was two weeks old when *Life* dropped 900,000 copies of a special New York edition onto the city's newsstands. It happened to be the one week in the year that the regular *Life* (because of the year-end double issue) did not appear; the New York edition was put together in six days and squeezed into a gap in *Life*'s printing schedule. It was a complete 72-page magazine offering local and world news, from death on the New York City streets to Christmas by the Berlin Wall, plus other picture and text spreads on art, entertainment, fashion and business. The editorial was an ode, on a verse of Walt Whitman's, to the "Mettlesome, Mad, Extravagant City." Text pieces included a "Lament with Love" for New York's disappearing landmarks and a whimsical look at how New Yorkers were filling the newspaperless void in their lives. There were also seven pages of hastily sold advertising.

All in all, it was a nimble performance and gave *Life* a springboard start into the 12-page special New York sections that continued as *Life* returned to its regular weekly schedule and the newspaper strike dragged on into 1963. Circulated only in the metropolitan area, *Life*'s New York Extra, as it was labeled, offered readers a bonus of local coverage—investigative stories, for instance, that were too New York-oriented for the national edition to use—plus all the rest of the regular magazine. Advertising sold at a premium and closed on a fast schedule almost like a newspaper. The morale of the edition's small staff ran high; there was talk of trying similar editions in Chicago and Los Angeles.

It was during this time that the study of *Life*'s problems in relation to the general situation of mass-circulation magazines—the R & D project proposed by Donovan in 1960—finally got under way. To direct it, Donovan assigned two *Time* men, senior editor Henry Grunwald and general manager Rhett Austell. Their report, completed in June 1963, conceded that Time Inc. was several years late in researching television's impact on *Life*; *Look* now seemed to have adapted better as an entertainment complement to TV and the *Reader's Digest* seemed more widely accepted as an information complement than *Life*.

The current experiments with editorial specialization—"new editions based on subscribers' demographic characteristics"—were worth "thorough investigation," they felt. Only mildly optimistic about *Life*'s future, Grunwald and Austell recommended that it try to build "a new, dynamic relationship with its audience." This was primarily an editorial task, in their view. "In addition to being a picture magazine," *Life* had to consider itself "an idea magazine." *Life*, they said, "must be more precise in its aim. It should reach higher, at a more educated, knowledgeable and worldly reader . . . not necessarily by being more highbrow . . . but by being smart, exciting and sophisticated. Both in selection and treatment of topics, it should go deeper . . . reach for the extra question, the unexpected angle." Meanwhile, *Life* should not increase circulation, nor push

56

its advertising rates further above the competition until some "unique, new marketing value could . . . enable it to charge more."

Both of *Life*'s editorial experiments were, in fact, up for corporate decision at that point. Neither appeared to offer the answer to the magazine's problems. In March the New York newspaper strike had ended, but even before this, newsstand sales of *Life*'s New York edition had begun to fall. Advertising also slowed. Meanwhile, mail testing of the specialized supplements began, using a list of 500,000 *Life* subscribers, who were offered a choice among the travel and science supplements and a third, called "Show World," devoted to entertainment, at prices ranging from $1.50 to $2.50. The travel supplement aroused some interest. Otherwise the results were a jumble, illustrating the vagaries of mail-order selling. "I am afraid it is the old old story of giving the customer a choice, which creates confusion, resulting in the wastebasket instead of an order," Jackson wrote Luce. Nonetheless, he was for taking a plunge.

In late June an executive dinner was convened to settle the question. Luce, who presided, went around the table taking a vote. Sentiment favored testing regional editions of *Life* a little longer. The New York edition was given another six months, until Christmas 1963, to demonstrate whether it could "approximately" pay its way. On the topical supplements, Jackson argued spiritedly in favor, but the vote was against. After the dinner Larsen drew Wootton aside to explain his opposition: "Look, the fact that you offer this says— by implication—that the basic *Life* is inadequate. I cannot support this." (That was not the last word on the subject, however. In 1970 the *Life* supplements came up again briefly for corporate consideration, but by then *Life* itself was near the end.) The New York Extra did not last out even its allotted time. In October, with revenue still falling short of covering the $100,000 monthly in added editorial costs, the edition was killed.

In early 1963, Luce personally committed *Life* to the largest editorial purchase in its history. Hunt learned of the transaction by way of an order—the only direct order to publish anything, he said, that he ever got from Luce. "Luce called me up and said, 'George, I want you to run Douglas MacArthur's memoirs. He wants precisely what we paid Churchill—a million dollars.' " (Actually, *Life* had paid $750,000 in 1947 for the magazine rights to Churchill's war memoirs.) Harold McGraw, president of the McGraw-Hill Book Co., who bought the MacArthur book rights from Time Inc., had a different story: that MacArthur named no figure, but did make one stipulation—that *Life* pay him more than it had Truman, who got $600,000 in 1953 for his account of his presidency.

"Never in my 40 years as an editor has there been anything to exceed in importance this publishing event," Luce said at a press conference in August, announcing the acquisition. MacArthur's reminiscences would "rank with the greatest historical writings of any age," Luce predicted. The financial terms were not disclosed; in fact, MacArthur took $900,000, the other $100,000 going directly, at his instructions, to his longtime military aide, Major General Courtney Whitney. As a publishing property, the old soldier's story certainly did not match Luce's advance billing, and there were editing problems when it was discovered that MacArthur had refreshed his memory with borrowings from other authors. Events diminished the book's value further. With MacArthur's death in April 1964, reader interest waned. Three installments had been published in *Life* by then; Luce had promised MacArthur nine. In July, after four additional installments, the series ended.

More valuable as a publishing property, but causing more contractual problems at that point, were the rights that *Life* had acquired to the personal stories of the astronauts in the U.S. space program. In 1962, the National Aeronautics and Space Administration had begun to select the nine Project Gemini astronauts who would join the original Mercury seven in two-man flights preparatory to a final ascent to the moon. Once again, as it had when the first Mercury contract was signed, the issue arose of "commercialization" of the space program, and the position *Life* had bought within it.

NASA's position had been ambivalent. "The story of what the Mercury astronauts do belongs to the public. It cannot be sold by anyone to anyone," a NASA policy statement declared when the *Life* contract was made; nonetheless it had already permitted the astronauts to negotiate, through their agent, for sale of their "personal" stories. For these *Life* had agreed to pay up to $71,000 per man through completion of Project Mercury. This included also their families' personal stories.

Life mobilized a task force for space coverage. It included, in the early days, staff writer Loudon Wainwright (who figured subsequently in Tom Wolfe's *The Right Stuff**), military affairs editor John Dille, science editor Albert Rosenfeld and other staffers. *Life* photographer Ralph Morse, who had begun following the astronauts

*Farrar, Straus & Giroux, Inc., 1979.

even before the *Life* contract was worked out, did most of the photography, becoming not only a close personal friend of the fliers and their wives and children, but also a sort of unofficial photographic adviser to the space program. Wainwright wrote of Morse: "When special [photographic] equipment was needed to get the shot, he designed and built it . . . On numerous occasions he was able to suggest to the flight directors and astronauts how to take photographs to improve their own record of the flights. He all but became a member of this select group of pilots . . . "*

For all that, it was never an easy matter for *Life* to maintain exclusivity under its contract. The line between official and personal information remained a fine one, and the magazine found itself in constant dispute with NASA officials, even with the astronauts themselves. And other publications had challenged the deal from the start.

With criticism mounting, Alfred Friendly, managing editor of the Washington *Post*, on behalf of the American Society of Newspaper Editors, examined the first article *Life* ran under the contract. This was the cover story in the September 14, 1959, issue, running 18 pages. It included the astronauts' bylined personal declarations; that much was exclusive to *Life*. But the bulk of the story, including eight pages of color, was devoted to the astronauts' training, showing them practicing with the space capsules' control mechanisms, being whirled in centrifuges to experience the G-forces they would encounter in liftoff, learning other maneuvers of space flight.

Friendly, delivering his judgment in the ASNE bulletin, remained opposed to the *Life* contract. But the result in print, he conceded, was a story that was "more complete, more interesting and better presented than stories on Project Mercury presented elsewhere . . . [*Life*] appears to have done it by the expenditure of money, manpower, space, brains and imagination rather than by favored . . . treatment." NASA chief James Webb praised *Life* for "waking up the country to the space program."

Life and the astronauts both did well in the Mercury deal. There was continuing worldwide interest in the astronauts' experiences; from the sale of subsidiary rights to their stories, *Life* eventually recovered about $400,000 of its $500,000 outlay. But whether the Kennedy administration would allow a replay, in the case of Project Gemini, was uncertain. In April 1962, NASA officials drafted a declaration "not to support contractual arrangements of the *Life* magazine variety in the future." In September, NASA policy

LIFE In Space (Time-Life Books, 1983), pp. 6–7.

changed to allow for a Gemini contract. Anticipating criticism, Vice President Johnson—delegated by Kennedy to oversee the matter—privately sought *Life*'s guidance. Thompson supplied a talking brief—on plain paper, without indication of authorship—for the administration to use in explaining itself.

Thompson outlined a defense of the previous contract from the astronauts' viewpoint: the *Life* money was "insurance" for their families, *Life* had shielded them from "the thousands of requests . . . which would have been impossible to accommodate" and as "engineers as well as fliers," they could be sure *Life*'s handling of their story was "infinitely more thorough, more accurate . . . than any other." Thompson offered *Life*'s own defense as well:

> Everyone—including newspapers, wire services, syndicates, TV, radio, magazines, book publishers—had a chance to bid and either refused to bid or bid too low . . . *Life* carefully explained the solid, technical aspects of this program from the beginning and it was only when the spectacular, sensational aspects began to occur that the clamor became loud.

Prices escalated in the renewed bidding. For contracts covering 16 astronauts—the Gemini nine plus the Mercury seven—*Life* was prepared to go to $1 million. Field Enterprises, publishers of the World Book encyclopedia and the Chicago *Sun-Times*, among other interests, was ready to go higher. A joint deal was worked out; for all rights worldwide, Field Enterprises would pay $3.2 million, or $25,000 per year per man, over the eight years of Project Gemini and the still tentative Project Apollo moon shot to follow. For United States and Canadian magazine rights, *Life* would, in turn, pay Field $800,000.

The $3.2 million figure caused a furor. Newspapers editorialized against the arrangement; the Senate Space Committee began inquiries; NASA backed away from its earlier endorsement. Briefly, contract negotiations were suspended.

In the interim, Time Inc. reconsidered its position. Former *Time* editor Roy Alexander, asked by Donovan to look into matters, reported back in June 1963. Although "the whole idea of checkbook journalism" was bothersome to Alexander, he felt *Life* had no choice. It was already too far down the road to turn back; its readers expected "high performance in coverage of astronautics, and this is a muscular leg up in achieving that." Also, there was the competitive threat:

The certainty that if *Life* pulled out, someone would pop in. *Satevepost*, if it could talk the banks out of the money. Perhaps *New York Times*. Perhaps, a long shot, *Look* . . . Where *would* we be without the contract . . . when the first astronauts get back from the moon, to figure week to week in the news?

On balance, Alexander concluded: "I should say, 'Execute.' " In September *Life* did, in a joint arrangement with Field Enterprises, running for four years (but renewable) with annual payments scaled back to $16,250 for each astronaut, of which *Life*'s share was $6,250, for a total of $100,000. In 1967, Field let its option lapse. *Life* dropped out three years later with an announcement that "with the completion of the first landings on the moon, *Life* has finished the story it set out to tell." An internal *Life* memo, for management's guidance, was more candid. "The real reason for dropping the contract: lack of [continued] interest in the first-person stories."

The increasingly hard fight that *Life* found itself in during the mid-1960s, as it attempted to hold its position against television, was recalled by one *Life* bureau chief: "When the networks went to half-hour news [programs] and equipment was miniaturized so that they didn't need all those lights and could carry their cameras everywhere, the competition became very serious. They had a story on the evening news before we could do anything." Battle footage from Vietnam was coming directly into American homes every night. With satellite transmissions, moreover, this living-room war, as it was often called, was becoming a war in the instant color that C.D. Jackson earlier had predicted and feared.

Reflecting both viewer demand and advertiser support, the networks had gone from 15-minute to half-hour news shows in the fall of 1963. A few months before, largely as a result of the Austell-Grunwald research study of mass magazines, there had been another round of editorial and publishing introspection on *Life*. Luce took the occasion to pen a note of self-criticism. "On looking over my major effort at 're-thinking *Life*' in 1960-61, I don't think it was much good," he wrote. "For one thing, it may have left the impression that *Life* was no longer to be, or to be considered, primarily a picture magazine. Insofar as I said that, I should now like to reverse myself . . . Picture magazine *Life* inevitably is and must be."

But within that definition, Luce felt, "*Life* needs to generate more enthusiasm and more addiction among more people. It does not need more circulation; it needs more response from the 30 million people it already reaches." Luce engaged Donovan and Hunt in several days of intensive discussion, out of which came a reaffirmation of *Life*'s charter as a picture newsweekly. "About this business of defining *Life*, and what doesn't belong in *Life*," the editor-in-chief noted, "the ordering principle should be *news*."

That principle was emphasized in the editorial budget approved later that year. To counter TV, and to further outdistance *Life*'s slower print rivals, *Life* in the coming year would have 100 pages—subsequently upped to 150 pages—of "crash" or fast-closing current news color. This would be in addition to the allocations for color essays, historical series and other regular *Life* color features.

The crash color allowance was put to good use throughout 1964 and was renewed just in time for a bravura display in the February 5, 1965, issue: a color cover and 21 pages of inside color on the funeral of Sir Winston Churchill, photographed in London on Saturday, delivered to *Life* readers in the U.S. the following Monday. The coup was made possible only by taking *Life*'s operations aloft in a chartered jetliner converted into a photographic laboratory and editorial office, and there, in the eight hours of flying time between London and Chicago, carrying out *Life*'s entire editorial process—processing the film, selecting the pictures, laying out the pages, writing captions, text and headlines, editing, checking and fitting the copy—all to be ready for the printer on arrival. For the Editors' Note prefacing that issue of the magazine, Hunt wrote this in-flight account:

> We are 33,000 feet up in the sky, traveling at 600 mph . . . [in a] DC-8 chartered from Seaboard World Airlines, fitted out as a flying editorial office to carry 40 busily working members of *Life*'s staff. In the forward part of the plane is a photo laboratory in which, at this moment, six technicians are developing 70 rolls of color film taken of the service and ceremonies. Moving aft inside this airborne city room are layout tables and light boxes, where color transparencies already developed are being sorted out and arranged so that they tell the story of the memorable event our 17 photographers covered in London. Then, more tables for editors, typists, reporters, a small but complete library (including *Debrett's Peerage*, ten volumes of Churchill's works, a copy of *Henry V*). Scattered through the seats filling up the rest of the plane, the writers are clattering away on their typewriters . . . The concentration is furious, and only your

voice raised over the sound of jets or your pencil slipping when the plane dips reminds you that this is not the Time & Life Building on a busy closing night. A cheer comes from the forward area just behind the lab. The pilot has sent back word that instead of expected snow at Chicago the weather is clear!

Life's picture coverage was poignant, unforgettable: Churchill's coffin lying in state in Westminster, the slow funeral procession through Whitehall and into St. Paul's, then a last voyage down the Thames and finally, at Waterloo station, in a brief glow of afternoon sunshine, the coffin being marched aboard the funeral train for the trip to its final resting place.

For Hunt, it was further proof that *Life* could hold its own by offering a dimension that TV could not. He commented later: "TV hadn't killed the [still] photo. TV did well in bringing war into the living rooms. We certainly brought in memorable sights for them too . . . the Kennedy assassination and the funeral, the Bay of Pigs, the Vietnam War, the dogs chasing blacks all over [Southern cities] and Churchill . . . Permanence is what photographs and paintings are. The TV set represents the fleeting moment. You can see the great photos in *Life* forever, and that was what it was all about."

Ill with cancer, C.D. Jackson left the *Life* publisher's post in February 1964 for lighter duties on the corporate staff (he died seven months later, aged 62). His successor was Time-Life Books publisher Jerome S. Hardy.

Life that year seemed on the mend. The long drop in advertising page sales ended; the *Life* division's pretax profit was $4,460,000, its best showing in six years. Circulation also strengthened. With net paid averaging 250,000 over the 7 million circulation guaranteed to advertisers, the argument began again: should *Life* raise its rate base and, with it, advertising rates?

Corporate management was at first opposed, preferring to cash in on *Life*'s improved circulation income at present levels. But in April 1965, a new circulation guarantee of 7.2 million vs. the fortnightly *Look*'s 7.4 million was announced. Page sales held steady despite the resultant advertising price hike, and *Life*'s pretax income rose to $6,082,000 on revenues of $158,016,000.

That was still a very low profit ratio. No less worrisome was the continuing decline in *Life*'s share of general magazine advertising revenues, from 16.3 percent in 1964 to 15.5 percent in 1965 (compared with just under 20 percent in 1956). *Look*'s share and that of the *Saturday Evening Post* were likewise declining—in the *Post*'s case dangerously so, threatening the whole Curtis Publishing Company.

The *Post*'s condition raised the question: If the magazine went under, who would get its outstanding subscriptions? At Linen's request, *Life* associate publisher Art Keylor ran a comparison of the likely advertising benefits, to *Life* and to *Look*, of a million added names from the *Post*'s list. In May, Keylor reported that "a swing of $30 million . . . doesn't seem wildly improbable"—he meant the difference between the $10 million in advertising that *Life* could gain with the *Post* names, and the $20 million it might lose if they went to *Look*. In August the publisher's office began considering the price *Life* might pay—for what proved the worst buy the magazine ever made.

4

Journalism in Hard Covers

IT SEEMED A CURIOUS WAY to publish books, and the author who was engaged by *Life* in early 1960 to write a book about Russia—the first volume in a projected series to be called the Life World Library—asked for a weekend to consider the proposition. The author, Charles W. Thayer, knew his subject well; he had served in the American embassy in Moscow, spoke Russian and had already published a witty account of his diplomatic experiences with the Soviets during World War II, entitled *Bears in the Caviar*.* But *Life*'s publishing plans gave him pause. The Life World Library books were being sold before they were written, in fact even before their authors were named. Moreover, Thayer was being asked to compress Russian history, Russian politics, the look and feel of the country into 28,000 words, ten chapters—all to be finished, edited and ready for printing by mid-July, only three months away.

Over the weekend Thayer consulted his brother-in-law, Charles E. Bohlen, a former ambassador to the Soviet Union. Bohlen's advice was to go ahead, produce a manuscript and let *Life* worry about the rest. Thayer retired to an office in the Time & Life Building with a stack of yellow legal pads and began churning out the required wordage. There were champagne toasts when advance

---

*J.B. Lippincott Company, 1951.

orders for the still unfinished book passed the 100,000 mark. Completed on schedule, *Russia* went out in September 1960 to 232,000 buyers who had, by then, signed up for the series.

In December came the second in the Life World Library series, *France*, for which the noted British historian D. W. Brogan flew to New York to dictate the text, with researchers filling in the details that escaped Brogan's encyclopedic memory. Thereafter followed books on Italy, Britain, Japan and other countries—34 titles over the next six years. The 32nd volume, on the United States, was the combined work of nine European writers, with a foreword by Luce. Other series, on nature, science and American history were meanwhile being created and mailed to 40,000 buyers a month.

Much copied since, these multivolume series were a publishing innovation: books produced like magazines, using magazine editorial techniques, published on a regular schedule like magazines and distributed by mail, using a combination of magazine subscription and book-club sales methods. "Journalism in hard covers," their creators called the books.

The *Life* book department's early runaway success could not have come at a more opportune moment for Time Inc., doing much to compensate for the troubles its magazine parent was then encountering. By 1961, income from the Time Inc. book division (as it shortly became) almost exactly covered the losses suffered by *Life*, and the following year, when *Life* had gone into the black again, the book division's earnings were triple the magazine's. The books venture was, indeed, the company's most immediately successful publishing enterprise since *Life* itself, a quarter-century earlier. Within the first two years, the volume of books business nearly quadrupled, from $5.5 million to $19.6 million, and leapt another $10 million in each of the two years following—"a gusher that suddenly burst from the ground," as one editor put it.

Like most magazine publishers, Time Inc. had dabbled in book publishing before. Since 1931, when Knopf brought out a collection of stories on successful companies under the title *Fortune's Favorites*, a hundred books had evolved from material that appeared first in one of the magazines. But it was not until *Life*'s *Picture History of World War II*, in 1950, that the company published under its own imprint a volume not derived from a magazine article. The *Picture History* sold 645,000 copies, largely by mail order, and netted $1,495,900. In 1955 *The World We Live In*, a one-volume compilation of a *Life* magazine series on the physical and biological history of the earth, earned nearly twice as much. Two years later, *The World's Great Religions*, also based on a *Life* series, was a comparable success.

Along the way there were failures and overlapping efforts by the various magazines. In 1957 *Sports Illustrated* overpriced, at $5, a book of golf lessons by Ben Hogan and lost $214,000. *Three Hundred Years of American Painting*, put out by *Time* in 1957, lost $341,000 and raised doubts about the market for an art book *Life* was independently planning. Still, with *Life*'s latest, a two-volume illustrated abridgment of Winston Churchill's war memoirs, total Time Inc. book sales over the decade netted a profit of $5.5 million.*

From within the company, there were periodic proposals that by tapping Time Inc.'s abundant editorial resources even more books could be generated. This opinion was shared by Jerome S. Hardy, a vice president at the publishing firm of Doubleday & Co., whom Time Inc. consulted. Individually, *Life*'s major book projects were already grossing more than the entire annual operations of some established book-publishing houses, Hardy pointed out. In October 1959 the *Life* division was given management's approval to pursue "a vigorous book program." Hardy was hired to direct it—one of the first senior Time Inc. executives ever to be recruited from the outside. Named as Hardy's counterpart on the editorial side was Norman P. Ross, a *Life* associate editor and former correspondent. Although his only previous book experience had been editing the Churchill abridgment, Ross proved a fortuitous choice.

Hardy, then 41, had been in charge of Doubleday's book-club operations and he arrived at Time Inc. with a reputation, well deserved, for expertise in mail-order selling. "Jerry could sell elephants to the Pentagon," a Time Inc. colleague concluded, after watching him in action. Personable and articulate, Hardy had a long background in the arts of persuasion. After graduating from the University of Maryland, where he edited the college humor magazine, he had spent some time learning to fly before going into public relations for the automobile industry in Washington. During his wartime service, he wrote Army Air Force flight safety manuals, then knocked around Latin America as a freelance publicist before joining Doubleday as a promotion writer. He was a fast man at the typewriter; in one year he wrote dust-jacket copy for 500 books. Later he was appointed Doubleday's advertising director.

*The six-volume memoirs had been excerpted in *Life* from 1948 to 1953.

At Time Inc., the pairing of Hardy and Ross was in the nature of a corporate blind date. The two men had barely met when they were put in charge and asked to make a success of *Life*'s newly authorized book program, and Heiskell had added his own encouraging send-off: "If it doesn't work, one or both of you will have to go." The warning was unnecessary. The two men meshed perfectly. Hardy had editorial feel as well as sales flair; Ross, in the words of one editorial associate, was "an idea man, an organizer, an extremely astute promoter."

A large and friendly man, Ross, 39 in 1960, was a Phi Beta Kappa and summa cum laude graduate (in American history) from Brown University and had spent two semesters at the Harvard Business School. But he was not inclined toward business and in 1947, after Navy service as an aviation ordnance officer, he joined the *Life* research staff, becoming successively a writer, an editor in the education and religion departments, and, in 1957, the magazine's chief correspondent in London. Ross had long been interested in visual presentations; as a boy he started his own signboard company and as a high school student in Newtonville, Massachusetts, had produced a *Life*-style picture album of a national Boy Scout jamboree. Later he worked briefly in documentary films. Ross's organizational skills, demonstrated in the production of the illustrated Churchill volumes, greatly impressed Heiskell.

Heiskell's instructions as Hardy and Ross began work in December 1959 were, in Hardy's recollection, cheerfully brief: "Put us in the book business, make money and don't do anything to embarrass us." Subsequently Heiskell was more explicit, giving Hardy a target of $5 million in sales and $1 million in profits for 1961, and five times those amounts by 1965. Hardy, for his part, aimed at creating an "on-going, on-growing" book business. The individual books published earlier by *Life* were, he observed, "very interesting, almost awesomely successful projects but they were not in any sense a continuing business, because although *The World We Live In* sold something like $5 million worth of books in one year, it sold almost zero [actually under $200,000] the next, and there was no other book published to take its place. There was no forward momentum."

The publishing program to provide that momentum was worked out in the somewhat unlikely surroundings of a country inn, Stonehenge, in Ridgefield, Connecticut, where Hardy had suggested they meet once a week to escape the interruptions of the New York office. "Norm agreed instantly and we settled on a few ground

68

rules," Hardy recalled:

> Every trip to Stonehenge had only one agenda item and if that
> agenda item got completed by noon we went home. If it was
> still open at the end of the day it was the agenda item for the
> next week until it was disposed of. That had the marvelous
> quality of allowing us to tackle the problem without somebody
> saying, "Well, it's five minutes to four; we've got to have a
> decision. Let's not break this meeting up without a decision."

Every Monday, over the succeeding months, the two men walked
the country roads around Stonehenge and, as the weather warmed,
swam in the pool, tossing pebbles and diving to retrieve them as
they mulled over publishing projects. Many years afterward, Ross
still remembered where various ideas jelled—for the science series,
on a tree stump; a reading program of paperback reprints, in the
swimming pool; textbook publishing, on a walk along a damp, leaf-
strewn road fronting a firehouse. Later, others on the Time-Life
Books staff joined Hardy and Ross at Stonehenge. (In a nostalgic
tribute to the inn's role in the early development of Books, its name
was given to a subsidiary created in 1979 to publish the works of
outside authors and editorial packagers: Stonehenge Press.)

From the Stonehenge sessions, a three-phase publishing strategy
emerged. It called for expanding existing book operations—essentially, the production of single volumes, including both reprints of
earlier successes and new books compiled from articles appearing in
the Time Inc. magazines—while simultaneously exploiting the mail-
order potential of series publication on the Life World Library
model; and, finally, for probing unrelated publishing areas such as
textbooks, encyclopedias, correspondence courses, legal and technical books.

The publication of single volumes continued intermittently over
the following years; 1961 saw the appearance of the *Life Pictorial
Atlas of the World*, a collaboration with Rand McNally that was up
to then the company's most ambitious single book project. But
attention was focused primarily on the production of books in series.
Here there were both editorial and publishing advantages. Writers,
designers, researchers could be assembled to carry a series through
several years; with single volumes, editorial production was an inter-
mittent, stop-and-go affair. More important, the book series offered
multiple sales for a single selling expense, as had the book clubs
Hardy supervised at Doubleday.

For the *Life* series, Hardy proposed adapting book-club sales terminology: book buyers would be known as "subscribers" rather than "members"; otherwise the approach was the same. "Since book clubs have no terminus—when you become a member you're a member until you say, 'Stop, that's enough'—it struck me that we didn't want to lose that ingredient, so we devised what came to be known as the open-end subscription. It went on for no specific length of time, but would continue until you said, 'Stop!' " In effect, the series, consisting of a dozen or more volumes in all, was to be a big-ticket item sold in small increments. "Not unlike selling refrigerators through the mail," one editor observed.

Initial test mailings of the *Life* subscriber lists produced astonishing results. Selling by mail customarily works on minuscule percentages; sometimes less than a 2 percent return is considered good enough to go ahead, and there are infinite variations in the circumstances of an offer, including such extraneous factors as climate and season, that affect response. For instance, April, income-tax time, is not considered the best month for a mailing. It was in April 1960, though, that the first test mailing for the Life World Library went out. The illustrated sales brochure set a pattern that was followed successfully through this and subsequent series. It showed the as yet unwritten books spread open for display as if already completed, with precomposed text on the open pages that buyers could, by squinting, actually read. The response to the Life World Library brochures exceeded all expectations, reaching 2 percent within days, then 3, then 5, and by about the sixth week, an incredible 7.74 percent. In his years at Doubleday, Hardy had never seen anything like it. "Nor did I ever meet anybody who had," he said.

The test, however, had involved a predisposed group of *Life* book purchasers, and one rule of mail-order selling is that previous buyers are more likely to respond than nonbuyers—"the more the more," as Heiskell phrased it. Hedging against an expected smaller response from a full-scale mailing, Hardy informed Heiskell that the Life World Library could make money with a 4 percent response. But a second mailing, at the end of June, to a general list of 3 million names, got an overall return of 7 percent again (nearly 14 percent in Canada). The book operation found itself sitting on a quarter of a million orders. Confidently, Hardy predicted that the operation would be in the black by year's end. It was, earning a 1960 pretax profit of just over $750,000.

In January 1961 the *Life* book department was detached from the parent magazine and given separate corporate identity as the Time

Inc. book division, with Hardy as publisher and Ross as editor. John Watters, 40, assistant to *Life*'s advertising director, was named general manager to supervise the new division's business and production operations. John D. McSweeney, 34, *Time*'s assistant business manager, became the book division's business manager. Also joining the new division as assistant to the publisher was Hardy's former secretary at Doubleday, Joan Lanning (known as Joan Manley after her remarriage). At Time Inc., Mrs. Manley rose steadily, to become the executive overseeing book-publishing operations and the company's first female vice president.

The series books were aimed at a general, not an expert, audience— "the Ford dealer in Wichita and his family," as Ross frequently put it, suggesting the age range of the intended readership as well. A prospectus drafted when the World Library series was already in production outlined the "basic proposition . . . part journalistic hunch, part article of faith in a great opportunity" that underlay the editorial approach:

> The book division believes there is not only a market but a hunger in the U.S., and possibly abroad, for books shaped to these precepts. It believes that despite issuance of some 14,000 new nonfiction titles in a year by the book-publishing industry, the general reader is not satisfied. It believes that while the scholar and the specialist are well served today, the busy, intelligent layman is generally neglected . . . Busy, intelligent laymen actually comprise a class-mass audience, reachable by a new kind of book . . . both comprehensive and concise—a combined quality whose appeal has been proven by our magazines . . .
>
> So that it may communicate the most possible within workable limits of the reader's time and patience, this new kind of book is made bilingual: it speaks the language of words and the language of pictures. It is not a conventional "illustrated" book, in which pictures are inserted as pictorial footnotes to a fully developed manuscript. It is rather a duet of word and picture in roughly equal parts, orchestrated from the start, each voice given the role best suited to it, both voices blending in counterpoint.

For all the violin music, the description of the books was accurate enough. *Time*-sized, they had pictorial covers and used color generously inside; *Life*-style photographic essays alternated with chapters

71

of text and carried the narrative line forward visually, making for an easily accessible volume, inviting to both quick skimmers and leisurely readers. Illustrations were sometimes very elaborately achieved; for instance, for the *Imperial Rome* volume in a later series, Great Ages of Man, Caesar's siege of Avaricum was staged in miniature, with scale-model armies of Gauls and Romans, then photographed for 13 pages including a pull-out.* Over the years, Time-Life Books won numerous awards for graphic excellence.

Expensive to produce—editorial costs averaged $103,000 per title for the World Library and nearly double that for the science series launched three years later—the books were, because of economies of scale, attractively priced. The first series sold at $2.95 per volume, the second at $3.95. A more lavishly illustrated Time-Life Library of Art sold originally for $5.95 per volume. (Inflation later raised all prices.)

Like the Time Inc. magazines, the books were the product of so-called group journalism, the collaborative research, writing and editing process that applied throughout Time Inc. Ross added consulting editors—experts in the field, usually academics, brought in at the planning stage and consulted as the books were being written. It was a controversial innovation, leading inevitably to tensions between the series editors and writers and researchers and the academic experts; some unholy rows ensued. Ross felt, however, that the pairing—"a marriage of journalism and scholarship"—lent authority to the books' content, felicity and clarity to the text.

Also in keeping with magazine procedures, there was heavy text editing in all the Time Inc. books; authors' drafts were sometimes substantially rewritten. The editing assured the overall unity of the various series, but it also made for bruised feelings on the part of outside writers unused to company practice in this regard; some refused to undergo the ordeal a second time. The Time Inc. checking process—word by word scrutiny of the text for factual accuracy—was likewise infuriating to outsiders, particularly to academics unaccustomed to having their facts questioned by publishing houses.

Breaking with book-publishing tradition, Hardy and Ross decided to pay outside authors by fee instead of by royalty. "Since we were going to invent the books and they would be books that could be written by any one of a number of people," Hardy explained, "a flat fee made a lot more sense than continuing royalties. We said to ourselves: 'Let's find the right guy to write the book and let's pay

*The original is on display in the museum at the United States Military Academy at West Point.

him more than he's ever made on a book before, so that the question really never comes up.' "

In fact, fees did become a question. Thayer asked for $15,000 for his book on Russia and settled for $10,000, a figure that became more or less standard for the early books.

In the fall of 1960, after the series-opening volume on Russia had rolled off the presses, Hardy and Ross, "on a powerful hunch," flew out to the Crawfordsville, Indiana, bindery "to which we had entrusted our book, our jobs and our future," to watch the first copies being assembled and bound. They toured the assembly line, observing the folded pages coming from one direction and the stiff-backed covers from another, to be mated, glued, pressed together, inserted into cardboard cartons, labeled and packed into mailbags for loading onto waiting railway cars. With each book, along with the bill, went a welcoming letter.

Some 20 mail sacks of books had already been loaded when Hardy suggested to Ross, "Let's see what one of these is going to look like to the customer when it reaches his house." Taking a carton from the assembly line, he ripped it open and shook out the book. A dozen of its pages, front and back, were glued together. At random, they opened other cartons. Again, the same problem of "squeeze out"—excess glue forced out around the pages during the binding. The volumes were "useless, worthless," Hardy recalled. "We would have sent out a quarter-million books and they would have all come back." The assembly line was stopped, the mail sacks unloaded and some 8,000 faulty books destroyed before binding recommenced. It was a close call. The bungle could have doomed the entire project at birth.

With the third Life World Library volume, *Italy*, which appeared in February 1961, the books began coming out at two-month intervals. In August 1961 the Life Nature Library was launched on a similar schedule; it continued for 25 volumes. The Time Reading Program, soft-cover reprints of outstanding modern fiction and nonfiction issued bimonthly in a package of three or four volumes (the selections were made by Max Gissen, former editor of *Time*'s book review section), began in April 1962. In February 1963 the 12-volume Life History of the United States began, followed in July by the Life Science Library, which ran for 26 volumes. Foreign sales began in 1961 with translation of the Life World Library into ten languages; translation of the other series books followed. The following year Time-Life International, the company's international publishing division, established a book department of its own to produce and sell Time-Life Books' creations abroad. John Snedaker, TLI's London general manager, was put in charge. By the end of the decade, foreign sales accounted for nearly a quarter of Time-Life Books' revenue—but, because of fragmentation of the market, only a small part of the total profits.

Along "Cardboard Alley," as editorial staffers dubbed the book division's hastily partitioned offices, a frantic scramble began to gather staff and meet production deadlines. From an original *Life* contingent of three—Ross, research chief Beatrice T. Dobie and *Life* associate editor Oliver Allen, who edited the Life World Library—the editorial staff grew within two years to 73 people. William Jay Gold, former articles editor of *Life*, more recently at *Fortune*, was recruited as copy director and Edward A. Hamilton, who had left *Life* to become a graphics consultant, returned to become the book division's first staff art director. At the elevator one day, Ross chanced upon another *Life* alumnus, former assistant managing editor Maitland Edey, and enlisted him to organize and edit the projected Nature Library.

Looking back 20 years afterward on his experience as a series editor, Edey recalled the travails:

> That first year was utter hell. We worked ten- and 12-hour days, often six days a week. I went to work in December 1960. I was presented with a schedule that called for completing the first book in the Nature series by June or July 1961 and another every two months thereafter—a far cry from the later practice of scheduling the first book two or more years down the road. I was given Martha Turner [later Goolrick], a *Life* reporter, as chief researcher and George McCue [who later organized the Life Science Library] as an assistant. The designer was Paul Jensen, a wacky but wonderful man who could draw, paint, do lettering, make layouts—all in hit-or-miss fashion, and that's how we functioned at first: hit or miss.
>
> By blind luck . . . I found men to write the first two books: Leonard Engel [a writer on scientific and medical subjects with a special expertise in oceanography] who wrote *The Sea*, and Peter Farb [a naturalist and freelance writer] who wrote *The Forest*. If they had not produced as they did, the Life Nature Library would never have gotten off the ground, for the five or

six books that followed from other authors were uniformly terrible, and had to be largely rewritten in the office . . .

The pressure of getting out the first Nature book . . . was
nothing to that caused by the second, the third and the fourth.
It was astonishing how their due dates galloped forward. I
learned that I had to have a project person working ahead on
each of two books while I struggled with laying out, editing and
closing the current one. That way, we could get one book to
press, gasp, pull ourselves together for a couple of days and
then look to see how editor A was doing on the next one, and
with luck take a moment to confer with editor B. Of course,
the instant I got A's book, he went to work on book C, and so
on, leapfrogging with never a letup . . .

Theoretically, we had access to front-office help. But the division was off to such a spectacular start that both Ross and
Hardy were caught by surprise and engulfed by horrendous
problems of their own . . . getting paper, printing capacity,
storage and working out a reliable bimonthly delivery service of
books that were going out to buyers in the hundreds of thousands. This meant that we series editors *had* to get our books
out on schedule. If we missed, bingo—a million or two dollars
in sales down the drain, plus a sense right at the start, on the
part of the new subscriber, that we weren't reliable publishers.

There was no less pressure on writers to meet deadlines. On one
notable occasion in 1962, a gap in the World Library schedule
loomed threateningly when the author of a projected volume on
tropical Africa could not produce on time. A volume on Israel was
hurriedly substituted instead; British journalist Robert St. John flew
to Israel and turned out the text in three weeks.

The *Pictorial Atlas* was an editorial headache despite its financial
success. Featuring sumptuous *Life* color and striking perspective
views of a geophysical model of the earth as seen from outer space,
the volume had been heavily promoted as a "new kind of book . . .
completely unlike any existing atlas." But from the day a secretary
lost the draft of a prospectus carefully crafted by Ross, the project
was beset by mishaps. The most dismaying was the discovery by
researchers, too late to make changes in the printing plates, that
there were errors on the maps and in the gazetteer, or index of geographical place names. A savage New York *Times* review of the
completed volume by the noted mapmaker Richard Edes Harrison,

formerly a cartographer for *Time* and *Fortune*, compounded the project's woes. Luce was upset enough to suggest that Time Inc. might now "set out to produce the world's best Atlas, to be sold at whatever price necessary, e.g., $100 or even $150," with buyers of the old volumes offered full cash credit toward purchase of the new one. This suggestion, however, was not taken up.

There were some other embarrassments, as well as outright failures. In 1961 *The Sports Illustrated Book of Bridge*, a collection of magazine columns by Charles Goren, showed some of the diagramed bridge hands with the suits reversed; disaster was averted only by mustering an army of "little old ladies," as Ross called them, to paste corrections onto the printed pages. The following year, a *Life Guide to Paris*, produced in association with American Express as the pilot volume in a planned series of travel guides, sold so poorly that the whole guidebook project was abandoned. The *Life Book of Christmas*, a three-volume book and record set issued in 1963 and, as part of a marketing experiment, sold in supermarkets, did poorly. Moreover, the phonograph record in some sets did not contain Christmas music at all but rather bawdy ballads, entitled *Knockers Up*, sung by a Chicago nightclub singer. A distraught letter from a Florida pastor who had assembled his flock to read the book and listen to the music first alerted Time Inc. to the awful fact that a substitution had been made—perhaps deliberately by a disgruntled worker at the factory.

"The Mount Everest of the book-publishing industry is the general reference encyclopedia. Just because it's there, it commands our attention," Ross wrote Donovan in October 1961, adding that "ever since we got into the book business, Jerry Hardy and I have known it would be difficult to evade the [encyclopedia] question indefinitely." In 1962 a study group headed by *Time*'s ex-managing editor Roy Alexander found strong editorial arguments for "the first general encyclopedia done from the ground up in our generation."

Less encouraging were the findings on the publishing side. To put an encyclopedia into production required a five- to ten-year gestation period, during which costs could run to a couple of million dollars yearly; so William Benton, board chairman of Encyclopaedia Britannica, informed his friend and Phoenix neighbor Harry Luce in a personal letter. Even as editorial experimentation continued, Ross came around to the belief that the publishing opportunity did not warrant the effort. In December 1962 he and Hardy joined in recommending that Time Inc. drop the encyclopedia. Luce, reluctant from the start, needed no urging.

Concurrent with the encyclopedia project was a move into educational publishing, which had considerable corporate push behind it—particularly from Larsen. He was past president of Harvard's Board of Overseers and incumbent chairman of the Fund for the Advancement of Education. Since handing over the Time Inc. presidency to Linen in 1960 he had been devoting much of his time to arousing support for the advancement of public education. He had also had his assistant, former *Architectural Forum* managing editor and *Fortune* assistant managing editor Edgar P. Smith, scouting textbook publishing firms for possible acquisition. By early 1961, Smith's search turned up one likely prospect: the Silver Burdett Company of Morristown, New Jersey.

Founded in Boston in 1885 on assets consisting largely of some second-hand printing plates for a teacher-training music course, Silver Burdett had grown to be one of the better regarded medium-sized U.S. textbook houses, grossing in 1961 a respectable but not remarkable $7.6 million in sales, on which it made a profit of $137,000. Its books were used by schools in all 50 states and most countries abroad. Its top managers were nearing retirement age. They stalled when Time Inc. first approached them, but by that fall Hardy was in active negotiations with them.

Simultaneously, Ross made an editor's pitch to Time Inc. management, once again extolling the benefits of marrying journalism to education. In a January 1962 memorandum entitled "The Remaking of American Education: Challenge and Opportunity for Time Inc.," he proposed that the company, as a publisher and broadcaster long engaged in popular education, should now engage itself in formal education through textbook publishing:

> As teacher at large to the public, [Time Inc.] has long been committed to the very philosophy that the high priests of formal education only *now* have adopted as their own—the belief that the pursuit of intellectual excellence should be the central and overriding goal of education in a democratic society. Moreover, in our own dialogue with the public week in and week out, we have demonstrated the viability of intellectual excellence as a hallmark of mass communication . . . Let us not underestimate our talent for interpretation on the magazine page; it may have unimaginable consequences on the schoolbook page.

77

In March 1962 the agreement to purchase Silver Burdett was announced. It was Time Inc.'s first acquisition using stock. The price was 85,000 shares, then worth $6 million over the counter, 22 times Silver Burdett's 1961 earnings.

Silver Burdett remained a wholly owned Time Inc. subsidiary for nearly four years, until January 1966, when it was merged into the General Learning Corporation, the joint venture that Time Inc. entered with the General Electric Company (see chapter 13). Over those years Time Inc. invested an additional $3.3 million in Silver Burdett, enlarged its editorial and sales staff, expanded its book lists and built a 7 million-volume book distribution center in Indianapolis. Silver Burdett began school distribution of the World and Nature series, and the *Life* photographic essay technique was introduced into Silver Burdett school texts, starting with an eighth-grade American history book published in 1963. Drawing on the Time Inc. news files, Silver Burdett and the book division began joint publication of a weekly world-events wall chart for classroom use. Because certain state legislatures required teaching of the Soviet system, the book division in 1963 produced *The Meaning of Communism*, with text by *Life* staff writer William J. Miller, in association with Henry L. Roberts of the Russian Institute at Columbia University and Marshall D. Shulman of Harvard's Russian Research Center.

But the school market was not one where Time Inc. found itself comfortable. Sales methods, the intricacies and the politics of obtaining textbook acceptance from state and local school boards were "different from anything we had ever encountered before," the company's senior financial officer, Charles Stillman, remarked later. "We didn't like what we found."

As a business, educational publishing proved modestly profitable. During Time Inc.'s tenure, Silver Burdett revenues nearly doubled, to $15 million, but increased editorial outlays and production costs cut into earnings, which rose to a peak of more than $1 million in 1964, then fell back.

Most of Silver Burdett's business was concentrated in the "elhi," or elementary and high school, field. On its own, separately from Silver Burdett, the book division had also been investigating the peripheral areas—preschool materials and college texts. In 1963 it took on Jerome Bruner, a noted psychologist and director of Harvard's Center for Cognitive Studies, as educational adviser. The following year, a study of college textbook publishing was made by Ezra Bowen, the division's educational research and development director; it revealed a situation analogous to that in the encyclopedia field, of evident editorial opportunity but uncertain publishing prospects.

The pace of production for the book division's principal stock in trade—the series books—was accelerating meanwhile. In 1964 a new volume for one series or another was coming off the bindery line every ten working days; within two years the pace would be up to one new volume every seven working days. By 1964 the Life World Library had 402,000 subscribers; the Nature Library 428,000; the Science Library 421,000. The cultural series, Great Ages of Man, was launched in April 1965 with a book entitled *Classical Greece*; 160,000 subscribers signed up, and the series ran to 21 volumes. The Time-Life Library of Art was also in preparation; launched in April 1966 with *The World of Michelangelo*, it ran to 28 volumes.

Subscriber demand did not seem to flag. The symptoms of "list fatigue"—a chronic problem in mail-order selling resulting from repeated mailings to the same names—were not yet evident. Some on the editorial side felt that the pressure to maintain the flow of books led sometimes to a proliferation of titles beyond the useful life of a series. The World Library eventually devoted one volume to the River Plate countries of South America, another to the Andean republics. The Nature Library was subdivided regionally as well as biologically and geologically. There were office jokes, Ross recollected, about creating World Library volumes on "North Vietnam, East" and "North Vietnam, West." However, the fact that buyers continued to be interested was in itself tribute to the editors' ingenuity, since, as Ross pointed out, the presold subscribers were free to quit at any point simply by returning the book—thus terminating their subscription.

Only one series tested well and sold poorly, marring the book division's string of early successes. This was the International Book Society, launched in June 1964 to market large, expensive, lavishly illustrated volumes produced by European and Japanese publishers—so-called coffee-table books—to American subscribers. The scheme proved to be misconceived. The first volume, *Life* photographer Dmitri Kessel's *Splendors of Christendom*, weighing eight pounds and costing the then fancy price of $20, was well received. The next, *Picasso: Women*, was not, and more buyers dropped out as succeeding offerings—*Great Tapestries*, *The Voyages of Ulysses*, and *Japanese Temples*—strayed further from the subscribers' individual fields of interest. A consistent money-loser for Time Inc., IBS was abandoned in 1967.

79

In 1964 Time Inc.'s book sales totaled 9.4 million volumes in the U.S. and Canada, another 2 million abroad (plus 3 million copies of an official guide to the 1964 New York World's Fair, a losing publishing proposition undertaken largely as a civic service). The main business—Time-Life Books—was soundly profitable. Start-up costs for most of the series were recovered by the fourth volume. On a 1964 gross of $39.6 million, the book division earned $6.3 million.

For the Books staff, it was a happy, disordered, exhilarating time, despite the pressures they were working under; morale was high. At the start, the division had been a convenient place for the magazines to unload excess staff—"for editorial redemption," as Ross put it. But the situation had changed. Recalled Edey, who in 1965 became executive editor under Ross: "People in other divisions of the company began to realize that Time-Life Books was booming, and *good* ones, of their own accord, began applying for places . . . I became accustomed to meeting old *Life* friends in the halls and hearing: 'Thank God you people are doing well; you could be the salvation of this company. Do you have a job for me?' "

In February 1964, Hardy left the book division to become publisher of *Life*. He was succeeded by Rhett Austell, formerly general manager of *Time*. In January 1966, Norman Ross moved to an executive post at General Learning, and Maitland Edey took his place as editor.

Hardy was hesitant about taking the *Life* job; the magazine's circulation and advertising troubles made it a very tough assignment. The *Life* offer was put to Hardy at lunch with Linen and Heiskell. "I can't tell you," Hardy said, recalling the conversation, "whether I said or just thought, 'I wish you hadn't asked, but since you did, I guess I have to say yes' . . . That was a job no self-respecting publisher of books or anything else could turn down. That was *the* big job in the publishing world. So it had been for years."

Henry Luce and presidential candidate John Kennedy, at the Time & Life Building on August 5, 1960. Left to right: John Jessup, Luce, Otto Fuerbringer, Kennedy, Joseph Kastner, Thomas Griffith, James Keogh. Partially hidden: Albert (Bill) Furth, Roy Alexander.

Roy Larsen, president of Time Inc. 1939-60.
He retired as vice chairman in 1979 after
56 years with the company.

Hedley Donovan, editor-in-chief 1964-79.

© 1960 Esquire

ED DAHLIN

"He's getting his last-minute instructions from Life"

James Shepley, *Time* publisher 1967-69 and
Time Inc. president 1969-80 at a board meeting
in Wyoming, June 1981.

Andrew Heiskell,
chairman of the board
1960-80.

…nes Linen, *Time* publisher 1945-60 and Time Inc. president 1960-69, with David Brumbaugh,
…cutive vice president and treasurer 1960-68 and chairman of the finance committee 1969-71.

Charles Bear, corporate secretary 1971-84, group vice president 1972-84.

Henry Luce III, publisher *Fortune* 1968-69, *Time* 1969-72, vice presid corporate planning 1972-80.

Richard McKeough guided vario elements of Time Inc.'s financial activities for 30 years.

Rhett Austell, publisher Time-Life Books 1964-69, vice president responsible for books, films, broadcast and cable TV 1969-74.

Edgar Baker, managing director Time-Life International 1952-65, director corporate development 1966-69.

Arthur Keylor, group vice
president–magazines 1972-80,
with his successor, Kelso Sutton.

Charles Stillman, corporate treasurer
1930-60, chairman of the finance
committee 1960-68. He retired in 1971
after 42 years with the company.

Board of directors meeting. November 17, 1966, on board a Canadian Pacific train between Montreal and Ottawa. Clockwise: Hedley Donovan, David Brumbaugh, Samuel Meek, Charles Stillman, Roy Larsen, Frank Pace Jr., Gaylord Freeman Jr., Andrew Heiskell, Maurice (Tex) Moore, Bernard Barnes.

Bernhard Auer, *Time* publisher 1960-67, group vice president– magazines 1969-72.

John Watters, SAMI president 1972-80 and chairman 1981-82.

ston Pullen Jr., president
ne-Life Broadcast 1961-69.

Charles Gleason Jr., personnel
director 1965-72.

William Trent Jr. headed
affirmative action program
1964-75.

Lyndon Johnson and Henry Luce, May 1963.

Overseas Beacheads

Time Inc. was the first American firm to move into international publishing on a large scale, with overseas editions first of *Time*, then of *Life*. In Luce's view, the move was an imperative, dictated as much by considerations of national interest as by publishing opportunity. Speaking in September 1965 at the 20th anniversary of Time-Life International, the corporate branch that reigned over all foreign activities, Luce described its origins in almost missionary terms: "TLI was started in 1945 because the U.S. was literally the only power in the world capable of restoring some of the continuities of civilization . . . It is this towering uniqueness of power and influence [of the U.S.] that is . . . the factual premise—the existential premise for the assumption that Time Inc. should do things in the international world." For Luce, the magazines' international editions were a "tool" of tremendous importance—"something that the leading people all over the world can read: one common account of what is going on in the world."

The 1960 managerial changes had brought in a new corporate leadership even more inclined, by both temperament and wartime experience, toward international ventures. Linen saw Time Inc. eventually doing a third of its business outside the U.S.; Heiskell's first preference, as chairman, was to devote himself to promoting the company's European interests. Together with Edgar R. Baker, the managing director of TLI, they formed an executive trio determined to expand considerably on the overseas publishing base established earlier.

Thus Time Inc.'s global thrust was no peripheral gesture; it was a central mission, amply and enthusiastically nurtured by top management. Yet in the end it turned out to be mostly grand hopes dashed by the realities of operating in foreign environments.

In November 1960, the cornerstone was laid in Paris for Time Inc.'s second headquarters building in Europe—the one in London had opened in 1953—a $6 million structure at the corner of the avenue Matignon and the rue Rabelais, a block from Charles de Gaulle's presidential palace. The cornerstone ceremony was a celebrity affair, presided over by Heiskell with his customary bilingual aplomb; it was also the occasion for reiterated predictions of a greatly enlarged Time Inc. future abroad.

By then, TLI was investigating a number of new publishing proposals: joint ventures with foreign publishers to introduce new general interest magazines, foreign language derivatives of *Fortune*, acquisition of existing magazines, foreign syndication of *Time* and *Life* material.

"Through a combination of growth of our present magazines and expansion into new fields," Baker declared, "our purpose is to turn TLI into a $100 million annual business during the 1960s"—a fourfold increase over the decade. Heiskell was slightly more restrained. Writing a corporate colleague from Paris, as he began to survey European publishing possibilities, Heiskell conceded: "I must be truthful in saying . . . that I don't know exactly how we are going to develop the second $50 million of volume." Nonetheless he felt that in forward planning "the most important opportunity for Time Inc. not to miss is . . . in the foreign field." He was particularly bullish about the overseas television potential, where, he noted, the company was "late—very late—in attempting any expansion plans" and must now make "the maximum effort to establish as many beachheads as possible."

Luce was evidently upset by the speed of these moves; Larsen perhaps even more so. From surviving correspondence of that period, glimpses emerge of the two older men urging caution on their younger corporate successors. After the Paris building ceremonies, Heiskell had gone on in early 1961 to scout prospects in the Far East. In New Delhi he received a letter from Baker in New York reporting on his discussions with Linen and others to devise "strategy and techniques for getting some of the new ideas through Harry, Roy [Larsen] and the board." Wrote Baker: "As Jim [Linen] will explain, Harry has become increasingly concerned with the demand that might be made on him and Hedley [Donovan] on the editorial side of some of the new projects, and Roy, as you know, is greatly concerned about anything that he considers to be diverting in money or talent from the main job on *Life*."

From Sydney, Heiskell dropped a handwritten letter to Linen: "I should tell you how grateful I am to you for having kept H.R.L. and R.E.L. in check during these months. If we are to have a $100 million operation abroad, it's not going to be done by everyone sitting at home." In Australia, Heiskell had discussions about television; he then went to Japan, where TLI was examining a Tokyo publisher's proposals for a Japanese-language version of *Fortune*.

Heiskell returned to New York for the annual stockholders' meeting that April, at which he reported on his European and Asian travels. In those areas, in both the broadcasting and publishing fields, Heiskell said, "we feel pretty optimistic about our possibilities." Later that year he went off to survey prospects in Latin America.

The circumstances of TLI's birth and growth in the immediate postwar period and the special problems it had to deal with—blocked currencies, travel restrictions, slow and erratic transport facilities, as well as censorship, confiscation or banning of the magazines—had put the division into a separate world from the rest of the company. By the time TLI was finally disbanded in 1968 and its activities reabsorbed into the parent publishing divisions, it had a staff of nearly 900, mainly non-Americans, posted in 16 countries around the globe. Under its first managing director, C.D. Jackson, and his successor, Ed Baker, TLI had something of the aspect of a colonial empire. Its headquarters spread in New York, just below the executive floor of the Time & Life Building, was the most lavish of any corporate division, resembling the state reception rooms at some foreign ministry. In this opulent setting, Baker operated in highly personal, uninhibited style.

A prodigy in finance, Baker had come to Time Inc. in late 1944 after service with the Lend-Lease Administration. As deputy to Jackson in TLI's early days, he had done most of the division's legwork abroad, devising currency exchange arrangements for repatriating Time Inc.'s foreign publishing revenues. For example, TLI used blocked yen to buy Tokyo real estate, which was later sold to the U.S. government for an embassy residence (another scheme, proposed but never carried out, involved using blocked guilders to buy Dutch cheese for import into the U.S.). In 1949, when he took over as TLI's managing director, Baker was, at 28, the youngest of Time Inc.'s divisional executives, and possibly the only acknowledged Democrat among them.

For the TLI staff, life with Baker was both exhilarating and exhausting. Tall and rather fleshy, he operated at a frenetic pace. Heiskell, speaking after Baker's death from hepatitis in 1969, at 48, described his office habits: "Ed could listen to a ball game on the radio, disagree loudly with the umpire, read the afternoon mail, carry on a three-way overseas conversation and dictate to his secretary—all at once." Traveling abroad, he was no more relaxed. His wife recalled that railway journeys with him in Europe were punctuated at every stop by his jumping off to check the *Time* and *Life* displays on station newsstands. Once, during the partition troubles in India, when TLI's local distributor, a Hindu, balked at going into Calcutta's Moslem area, Baker went in personally with a truck to load magazines and bring them out of the warehouse.

The stimulating atmosphere at TLI and the personalities of Baker, and Jackson before him, helped in the recruiting of some notably capable people; from the TLI ranks were to come several leading corporate figures, among them Ralph P. Davidson, later to be chairman of Time Inc.; Charles B. Bear, eventually the company's chief administrative officer; Richard B. McKeough, future chief financial officer.

Lending great distinction and their own personal flair as well to Time Inc.'s overseas operations were the non-Americans who had been attracted to the TLI staff. In London, as chairman of TLI's British subsidiary, Time-Life International, Ltd., was Christopher Sinclair, O.B.E., M.C., who joined TLI in 1958 after 22 years of distinguished service with the British army. Until shortly before his retirement from Time Inc. in 1979, Sinclair was also a member of the royal household's elite honor guard, Her Majesty's Bodyguard, the Honourable Corps of Gentlemen at Arms. Heading U.K. advertising sales and later succeeding Sinclair was Robert Edward John (Robin) Compton, an Etonian and veteran of the Coldstream Guards, whose extra-publishing activities included restoring and tending one of England's stately homes, Newby Hall, the family's 17th century mansion in Yorkshire. Also in London, directing *Life International*'s European advertising, was Charles Florman, son of the founder of Swedish Air Lines (the cornerstone of SAS); Florman later turned his sales talents to building a large European business for *Fortune*.

To head TLI's Düsseldorf sales office, opened in 1957, Baker recruited Egenolf Christian Siegmund Philipp Clemens Quidotto, Baron von Berckheim. Born of a Prussian noble family, an infantry captain in the Wehrmacht on the Russian and Italian fronts, later a journalism student at Heidelberg, Chris von Berckheim ended his career with Time Inc. as European public relations director. In Milan, TLI's chief representative was Carlo Greppi, Conte di Bussero, whose father, an admiral in the Italian navy, had been an aide to the last Italian king, Victor Emmanuel III. Yasuo Kitaoka, the first head of TLI's office in Osaka, had been a kamikaze pilot in training when World War II ended.

Probably the most famous member of TLI's overseas staff, certainly the subject of most legend, was Raimund von Hofmannsthal, son of Hugo von Hofmannsthal, the Austrian poet, dramatist and librettist of several Richard Strauss operas. Working mainly out of London but roaming Europe, Raimund was nominally an advertising salesman. In fact, as former *Time* editor Tom Matthews wrote after von Hofmannsthal's death in 1974, "he served *Time* for more than 30 years as ambassador, scout, mender of fences, social mentor and guide, interpreter, defender of the faith—faith in Luce," who was, as were most who met Raimund, captivated by his pixyish charm.*

TLI, in establishing itself abroad, had brought off something of a publishing revolution. The concept of international advertising, crossing national frontiers, was not easy to sell; its effectiveness was difficult to measure. "The selling certainly wasn't done with any facts or figures," according to Ralph Davidson. Subscription selling by mail was also relatively new in many foreign markets. "Skeptics said flatly it couldn't be done," a TLI anniversary booklet recalled. "It would be demanding an impossible act of faith to ask customers to send a fairly large sum of money in advance to a company they might never have heard of for magazines they might never have seen." But the unfamiliarity of mail-order selling worked to TLI's advantage. "Thousands of people took our circular letters as private correspondence and answered courteously, even when they did not

*Married to Lady Elizabeth Paget, daughter of the Marquess of Anglesey, Raimund von Hofmannsthal had two children, named, appropriately, for characters in von Hofmannsthal-Strauss operas: Arabella, for the heroine of the opera of the same name, and Octavian, for the knight of the rose in *Der Rosenkavalier*.

subscribe." Enough did subscribe, however, to bring the combined circulation of the international editions of *Time* and *Life* to 1,334,000 by 1960. A small amount of that circulation was among U.S. troops stationed abroad; otherwise, readership of the magazines was largely non-American—an estimated 90 percent in the case of *Time*'s international editions, 96 percent in the case of *Life*'s. It was, moreover, a demonstrably elite readership, well educated, and including a high proportion of business and government leaders.

With a profit of $2,360,000 on revenues of just under $22.5 million, TLI was then accounting for a quarter of Time Inc.'s publishing income. Largest money-maker was *Time*'s Canadian edition, which in 1960 had a circulation of 226,000 and netted $1,018,000. For *Time Atlantic*, distributed to Europe, Africa and the Mideast, the figures were 174,000 and $709,000; for *Time Latin America*, 71,000 and $79,000; and for *Time Pacific*, distributed from Japan to Australia and New Zealand and westward to the Indian subcontinent, circulation was 121,000 and earnings were $283,000. The Canadian and Latin American editions each contained added pages of regional news; but apart from this, all were substantially the same in editorial content as the American edition, offering the "one common account" that Luce envisaged. Typeset in Chicago, printed from film flown to overseas printing plants, all offered reasonably fast delivery, within the same week as in the U.S.

Life's two foreign editions, *Life International* and *Life en Español,* differed more from their domestic parent. Both were amalgams of two weeks' issues of the U.S. edition, with occasional admixtures of pictures and text from the other Time Inc. publications and some original material as well. Both editions were beset with problems. Distribution was slow, mainly by surface transport. Copies arrived weeks late in some areas, the editorial content often long outdated. At best, circulation was spread thin and market penetration was shallow. Both international editions of *Life* were a harder advertising sell than *Time International*.

Life International's audience, in particular, was difficult to define. International editions editor William P. Gray, writing to Luce, described the magazine's probable readership: "Pakistani importers whose wives remain in purdah, and Swedish industrialists whose wives enjoy sun-bathing in the nude; young Japanese trying to learn English, and Cambridge students preparing for business careers in Japan . . . Aussies and Algerians, Brahmins and Brazilians, Buddhists and Billy Graham fans."

Edited during its early years almost as an afterthought to the U.S.

86

edition, *Life International* underwent an editorial upgrading in 1956 at Luce's direction. Over the next four years circulation increased nearly 30 percent, to 358,000. Advertising also improved, although annual revenues were less than those produced by a single fat pre-Christmas issue of the domestic *Life*. In 1960 *Life International* earned $406,300 on revenues of $5,339,700.

Further attempts at editorial improvement followed in late 1961 and 1962, after printing of the edition was moved from Chicago to Paris. Gray undertook a complete reexamination of *Life International*'s situation. His proposal to Luce was that the company should "end the frustrations of trying to create a magazine of equal timeliness in Berlin this week and Burma six weeks later" and concentrate instead on "readership in Europe—or more broadly, the 'Atlantic Areas.' " Luce was in agreement: "It is there, clearly . . . that [*Life International*'s] primary axis of dialogue should lie."

Life en Español, aimed at a somewhat better defined audience, faced fewer editorial problems. The edition had grown rapidly since its founding in 1953, nearly doubling its circulation in eight years to 416,000. Produced in New York by a bilingual staff, *Life en Español* was editorially vigorous, even feared, and its prestige was considerable. In 1960 every Latin American head of government except Cuba's Castro responded to a *Life en Español* poll of their attitudes toward U.S. aid. But in the fragmented Latin American market, advertising remained scanty. Only once since its founding had the edition made a small profit; in 1960 its losses were $93,300 on revenues of $3,991,500.

However, it was not south of the border where TLI was then having to devote most of its attention, but rather north, where *Time Canada* risked becoming the victim of its own success. With its combination of U.S. and international coverage, not duplicated by any Canadian magazine, together with the four pages of Canadian news that led the edition each week, *Time Canada* offered great attractions for the Canadian reader. But for Canadian nationalists, *Time*'s prominence on the Canadian publishing scene was part of a larger political problem: how to maintain the nation's identity, separate from that of its powerful southern neighbor. In a memorable line, Canada's longtime Prime Minister, Pierre Elliot Trudeau, once described his country's relationship to the U.S. as being "in some ways like sleeping with an elephant. No matter how friendly and even-tempered is the beast . . . one is affected by every twitch and grunt."

To Canadian publishers, at least, the presence of American magazines in Canada did seem elephantine. Three out of every four magazines circulating in Canada were imported; in 1959 *Time Canada* and the *Reader's Digest*, which also had a Canadian edition, together were taking more than 40 cents of every dollar spent on consumer magazine advertising in Canada.

In 1956 the Canadian government levied a 20 percent excise tax on Canadian advertising in foreign publications. Two years later, after elections that brought the Progressive Conservative government of John Diefenbaker to power, the tax was repealed. But the new Prime Minister, who had ridden into office on a "Canada First" platform, remained concerned about the political influence of American magazines in Canada. A careful reader of *Time*'s Canadian news pages, Diefenbaker erupted in a desk-pounding tirade during an interview with two Time Inc. reporters in June 1959, shouting that "*Time* is trying to tell Canada what to do [and] I won't stand for it," and reminding his visitors that the magazine was only a "guest in Canada." TLI interpreted Diefenbaker's words correctly as a warning; the next year, his government appointed a royal commission to examine Canadian publishers' problems, with an eye to protective action against their foreign competition. TLI, in a protective action of its own, designed both to improve service to Canadian subscribers and to establish *Time*'s Canadian residence, prepared to have the edition printed in Montreal.

In November 1960, the royal commission hearings opened under the chairmanship of Ottawa *Journal* editor M. Grattan O'Leary. Time Inc.'s brief to the commission emphasized *Time Canada*'s Canadian bona fides, its planned production move to Montreal, its predominantly Canadian reportorial and publishing staff (only three non-Canadians out of 32) and *Time*'s overall contribution to Canadian life: "It may be said confidently that no other journal provides as much information about Canada to as many readers throughout the world."

Luce flew up to Ottawa to testify personally. His remarks, before the commission and in a press conference afterward, made headlines. Taking a view divergent from that of his subordinates, he made no claim that *Time Canada* was a Canadian publication. Rather, it was an American magazine "that serves Canadians." Its American editorship, Luce insisted, was immaterial: "Suppose our staff was Patagonian? What do you care as long as it provides a service?"

The O'Leary commission report was published in June while Luce was traveling in Europe; his editorial assistant Bill Furth cabled him there that the Canadians had "lowered the boom on us with a bang." Without "a fair share of domestic advertising," the O'Leary report declared, "Canadian periodicals are denied competition on an equitable basis with foreign publications publishing so-called Canadian editions." To rectify matters, the commission proposed that advertising should be a tax-deductible business expense only if placed in Canadian publications. And a publication could be classified as Canadian only if it were "owned . . . by Canadian citizens . . . controlled and directed by Canadian citizens and . . . not a licensee of or otherwise substantially the same as a periodical owned or controlled outside Canada." Such publication would furthermore have to be "edited in Canada by a staff normally resident in Canada" and its "entire mechanical production must be in Canada."

The O'Leary recommendations were not legislation, but the menace was clear enough. Later that year, *Time* moved to make its Canadian residence complete, by preparing to shift editorial operations physically to Montreal. The proposal came from managing editor Fuerbringer; for support he had a report from John M. Scott, then writing on Canada for the Hemisphere section. Scott, himself a Canadian, appraised the move as "a wonderful journalistic as well as commercial opportunity." On-scene editing and writing would "sharpen the Canadian section's perception without making it any the less *Time*." Former *Time* managing editor Roy Alexander disagreed, fearing loss of the magazine's distinctive voice: "I had thought that an essential secret of success in *Time* edit was the process of unitary editing—everybody from the writing side under one roof." Despite these objections, the decision was made to go ahead.

Yet even as the *Time* editorial group of ten, including Scott as editor, moved to Montreal in the spring of 1962, nationalist pressures appeared to be dying down. Diefenbaker had suggested earlier in the year that because *Time* (as well as the *Reader's Digest*) had established itself in Canada "in good faith," he would propose for it a privileged position among foreign publications, by allowing Canadian advertisers to deduct 50 percent of the cost of advertising in *Time*—instead of none, as the commission had proposed—as business expenses on their taxes. In February 1963, Canada elected a new government under the Liberal leader, Lester Pearson, and the advertising tax legislation died. But the threat itself did not: it was to hang over *Time Canada*—sometimes heavily, other times less so—throughout the rest of the 1960s, and come to a crisis in the mid-1970s.

Offsetting the uncertainty over Time Inc.'s future in Canada were the prospects opening up elsewhere. In late 1960, Baker had assigned TLI general manager David Ryus full time to the development of new international publishing and nonpublishing projects. Coincidentally, TLI's network of overseas publishing subsidiaries was restructured for greater operating and financial flexibility. Keystone of the new structure was the company's Dutch subsidiary, Time-Life International (Nederland) N.V., based in Amsterdam. The Dutch company became the umbrella for Time Inc.'s foreign activities, grouping under it TLI's other European subsidiaries, holding publishing rights to *Time Atlantic* and *Life International* and running their advertising, circulation and direct-mail operations. Most important, Baker informed management, the Netherlands company would help shelter overseas earnings from U.S. taxation until repatriated. Thus, instead of having 48 percent of TLI's profits over the next five years available for channeling into other international ventures, Time Inc. would, under Dutch taxes only, have 90 percent left. And as a base of operations, Holland offered not only stability but "traditional friendship . . . toward American business, and specifically toward Time [Inc.]. The company's Dutch connection has, in fact, endured to the present day.

Early in 1961, TLI began negotiations on the first of its acquisition projects—for a controlling interest in the glossy French monthly *Réalités* and three associated magazines. The *Réalités* group was owned principally by its management; a minority share was held by the giant French publishing combine, Hachette. Heiskell, who because of his French background took a personal interest in the negotiations, conceded that the *Réalités* group was "long on editorial ability, short on business management," but that with the purchase Time Inc. could "establish a strategic foothold in French publishing and an entrée to other fields such as books, records and TV."

Talks went on throughout 1961. Then abruptly, when agreement seemed imminent, they broke down. By the end of January 1962, it was clear that Hachette had blocked the sale; what was not clear was whether the De Gaulle government had entered political objections to Time Inc.'s purchase.

Despite this setback, TLI continued to push for partnership ventures with other publishers. Luce had apparently been hesitant. Writing to the editor-in-chief, Baker reminded Luce that he had broached the subject with him earlier, in 1959, and "understood you to agree in principle" that in international publishing, Time Inc. had to go beyond its own magazines in order to reach "the full potential

90

of such great *domestic* markets as Germany, France, Italy and Brazil." This could only be done in partnership, Baker argued: "It would be extremely difficult for us, as Americans, to edit and publish locally from our own resources a magazine which would speak satisfactorily in their own la: guages to the people of these countries."

Baker's reasoning was persuasive. In April 1962, the Time Inc. board approved TLI's first joint venture: a general-interest monthly entitled *Panorama* to be published in Italy as "the prototype of a family of monthly magazines to be jointly produced by Time Inc. and national partners in other countries." Total investment was foreseen to be $500,000, half of it Time Inc.'s share. Breakeven was predicted within two years, a small profit in the third.

In seeking a magazine family name that would carry easily from country to country, TLI's first preference had been for *Orbis*. Then it was discovered that two other publications were already using the name, one a Swiss magazine that featured astrological advice. Bill Gray, heading a task force producing the *Orbis* dummies, offered a whimsical way out: "The most enchanting name yet suggested (for Italy) would be *Luce*, which in Italian means 'light.' It is pronounced 'loo-chay.' " From dozens of alternatives, *Panorama* was chosen.

Time Inc.'s partner in Italy was the country's largest publisher, Arnoldo Mondadori. The septuagenarian Mondadori had started as a printer's apprentice and launched his own small socialist weekly; his firm, Arnoldo Mondadori Editore, now published some 600 book titles and 18 magazines, including the picture weekly *Epoca*. At a new plant in Verona, he was printing Time-Life books as well.

The prospectus submitted to the Time Inc. board described *Panorama* as "a truly new magazine, designed to fill a clearly defined gap rather than merely compete with existing magazines." Its audience would be "the Italian man or woman who is interested in a wide spectrum of information: . . . art, sports, politics, science, economics and people." Mondadori's son Giorgio, who conducted the negotations with Time Inc., suggested that *Panorama* would not rile that audience with sex, scandal or partisan politics: "We want a peaceful political approach to life." *Panorama*, he said, would "go gaily."

Time-sized, consisting of 100 editorial pages, *Panorama* would draw on Time Inc. for three-quarters of its editorial content. The remainder would come from Mondadori. TLI was to handle international advertising sales, Mondadori all other publishing details.

"Though Time Inc. will retain control of material furnished by it," final editorial decisions would be made in Milan.

The agreed choice for editor was Nantas Salvalaggio, a longtime foreign correspondent for Rome's *Il Tempo*. Supplementing the Time Inc. staff in New York dealing with *Panorama* the company had, as resident adviser on the scene, Leo Lionni, former art director of *Fortune*. Dutch born, Italian educated, always involved with painting and design projects, Lionni was now consulting for Time Inc. and living on the Italian Riviera.

Panorama's first issue, dated October 1962, was a newsstand sellout at 280,000 copies. It was fat with advertising, including such international accounts as Singer, Pan American, IBM, Coca-Cola, Ford. Time Inc.'s and Mondadori's names figured prominently under the cover logo; the cover's color photo, of a cabaret hostess in Tokyo, was by *Life* photographer Eliot Elisofon. *Life* also contributed 14 pages of color by Dmitri Kessel on "The Glory Bernini Gave to Rome." *Time*'s contribution included color photos and text on the European Common Market. Curiosity and prepublication promotion had been important elements in *Panorama*'s initial reception; the question over the next few months would be whether editorial performance could sustain that level of reader and advertiser interest.

A month after *Panorama*'s launch in Italy, Time Inc. approved a second *Panorama*, in Argentina. The local partner here was César Civita, an Italian who with his brother Victor had fled during the Mussolini era to set up a publishing business in South America. César Civita's Editorial Abril published nine magazines including *Claudia*, Argentina's leading women's book. The Argentine *Panorama* was brought off more quickly than the Italian one; it was a smaller project with a planned investment of $350,000 divided between the two partners. Like its Italian predecessor, it bore prominent cover identification with Time-Life and made liberal use of *Life* pictures inside, but it managed to convey a distinctly local Argentine editorial flavor. The initial press run of 130,000 copies sold out in 48 hours.

In December 1962, a month after the Argentine investment had been agreed to, TLI gained board approval for a third foreign-language magazine venture: a Japanese version of *Fortune*, which had been under discussion for nearly two years with the Diamond Publishing Company of Tokyo. Entitled *President*—Pu-re-shi-den-to as it came out in the phonetic Japanese syllabary—the magazine was aimed at an elite audience of about 15,000 top executives. Initial investment was tiny, only $150,000 between the two partners, with profitability predicted in *President*'s third year. Like *Panorama*, *President* was seen by TLI as a prototype of a long line of similar magazines.

Smaller in page size than *Fortune*, with less lavish graphics, *President* was nonetheless intended to be a class magazine, in format as well as audience. In a revolutionary step for Japanese publishing, it was printed entirely on coated paper stock, breaching the Japanese magazine practice of using glossy covers but pulp paper inside. *President*'s typography raised eyebrows also: its lines of type ran horizontally rather than vertically, as do most Japanese publications, and its pages ran the opposite way—left to right—from the usual right-to-left Japanese newspaper and magazine style. Both innovations made transposition of *Fortune* layouts easier.

President's first issue, dated May 1963, carried no cover identification with Time Inc. or *Fortune* but took most of its major articles from *Fortune*. The new magazine was an immediate success. It quickly acquired a reputation as the *shacho-sans*' magazine—the bosses' book, in slangy Japanese—and circulation nearly doubled within the first five years. An advertising success from the start, *President* went into the black in 1965, a year ahead of expectation, earning $17,000 on gross sales of $469,000. By then, also, it was drawing less on *Fortune* and using more original material.

No less energetically, Time-Life Broadcast had been establishing the overseas beachheads that Heiskell had urged. Broadcast's franchise had been laid down in a 1960 management policy decision, authorizing the division to gear itself up immediately to explore investment and management opportunities in international television. The field seemed attractive in a number of ways: as a hedge against Federal Communications Commission restrictions on domestic station ownership; as a means of extending Time Inc.'s "historic interest in the communication of words, ideas and pictures"; as an outlet for "the very considerable reservoir of talent" available at Time Inc.'s domestic stations. Moreover, the broadcasting investments could be financed with the cash flow from TLI's international publishing revenues.

In February 1961, Sig Mickelson, the former president of CBS News, joined Time-Life Broadcast to assist in the overseas search, and by the end of that year the company had stakes in two ventures: a 50 percent interest in a German television production company in partnership with the DuMont Schauberg publishing group of Cologne; and a 12.5 percent interest in the Compagnie Libanaise de Télévision, operator of what was then Beirut's only TV station, broadcasting on two channels, one French and English, the other Arabic. In July 1962, Broadcast made its first Latin American television investment, an $845,000 outlay for a 30 percent share in a Rio de Janeiro station then being built by the Brazilian newspaper publisher Roberto Marinho, owner of the daily *O Globo*. Marinho planned a second station also, in São Paulo. The Brazilian constitution limited ownership of broadcasting stations to Brazilian citizens; Time Inc.'s investment therefore took the form of so-called "bricks and mortar" contracts, covering real estate and technical assistance—a legal arrangement, but one that did not shield Marinho later from attacks by his political opponents.

Some uneasiness about Broadcast's plans in Latin America was apparent among the Time Inc. board, so Heiskell drafted a written policy statement. As publisher of *Life*, Heiskell had been active in the Inter-American Press Association, formed to advance press freedom throughout the hemisphere; his policy statement on broadcasting now reflected a similar concern. He began by stating his belief that "Time Inc. can expand profitably throughout the world and at the same time serve a very useful purpose." In Latin American broadcasting, Heiskell declared,

> If you start from the fact that TV is a powerful influence on the mores and views of the people (particularly in nations where newspapers reach a relatively restricted percentage of the people) you can be sure it will play an important role—for good or bad. Left to their own resources, these stations (being independents because networks are barely existent) will tend . . . as do the weak newspapers, [to] be at best the tools of political parties and more often sell out to the far right or far left (the only groups that have money in Latin America). Just as my experience in the Inter-American Press Association has convinced me that top priority should be given to making South American papers independent by virtue of being commercially viable, so am I equally convinced that a well-run station is the first step to independence on the air. Once this status is achieved, one can then tackle, step by step, the creation of sound news programs and the use of TV as an instrument of political dialogue.

To Time Inc.'s newest director, Gaylord A. Freeman Jr. of the First National Bank of Chicago, Heiskell's answer was not wholly satisfactory. Freeman wrote:

I am so new to the company that I do not yet understand the allocation of responsibilities for the determination of the direction in which Time Inc. would like to influence the world. What philosophy does it espouse? Who sets it? Who determines its application to the question of democracy in Algeria or land reform in Peru?

Luce, although reconciled to the television investments themselves, took the occasion to reiterate a familiar caution, "namely, the extent to which efforts of this kind distract from the maximum efficiency of our main business . . . Another 100 pages [of advertising] in *Life* would yield more profit than we could hope to get from a lot of our peripheral operations."

Television investment in Latin America nevertheless continued. In October 1962, Time Inc. purchased, for $800,000, a 12.5 percent share in Producciones Argentinas de Televisión of Buenos Aires and an affiliated company, both in association with Goar Mestre, Cuba's leading broadcaster in pre-Castro days, and CBS. This association led to Time Inc.'s taking stakes in three other Mestre broadcasting enterprises in Peru, Venezuela and Panama. Probes continued elsewhere—for a pay-TV project in Britain, a television production company in Sweden, a television station in Australia and another in Hong Kong where, in 1966, for an initial $350,000 commitment, the company took a one-eighth interest in the Crown Colony's first broadcast TV system.

Symbolizing the company's growing international interests, Heiskell took the Time Inc. directors to Europe in May 1963 for their first board meeting outside the U.S. They lunched atop the new Time & Life Building in Paris with France's future president, Valéry Giscard d'Estaing (then finance minister), proceeded to London for the formal board session and then went on to inspect TLI's operation in Amsterdam. High point of the Paris social calendar, although not quite as intended, was a floating dinner party for the directors aboard an excursion boat on the Seine, to which a hundred or so prominent Parisians and their wives had been invited. Unfortunately, the Time-Life staff, although accustomed to Paris society's habit of arriving fashionably late, had not taken Luce's passion for punctuality into account. A member of Time Inc.'s Paris bureau related the sequel:

> It got to be time to sail but there must have been a couple dozen guests who still hadn't arrived. I tried to point this out to

Luce, but he wouldn't hear of it. "If we don't leave right now," he said, "I'm going to get very unpleasant." Believe me, he was that, already. I hadn't the slightest idea of how to give a nautical command in French, so I just went up to the skipper and poked him in the back and said, *"On y va"*—let's go. We took off at flank speed . . . The evening was a shambles. We'd matched guests carefully, who was deaf in which ear, whose wife spoke English and whose didn't; but all that went by the boards—empty chairs everywhere, one Time Inc. director sitting all by himself at a table. Afterwards, Larsen, bless his heart, took us out to drink and forget.

In October 1962, Bill Gray, the editor of *Life*'s international editions, died suddenly of heart disease at 53. A quiet man, he evoked intense admiration and affection from his colleagues. His successor was A.B.C. (Cal) Whipple, a veteran *Life* writer and editor.

Three months later, European advertising prospects for both *Time*'s and *Life*'s international editions were darkened by Charles de Gaulle's abrupt veto of Britain's bid to enter the Common Market. More ominous was the outlook for TLI's first joint publishing venture, then four months old. "Italian *Panorama* has run into very heavy weather," Baker reported, "mainly due to failure of the magazine editorially to meet the wants and needs of the Italian market. Circulation has dropped by almost one-half since the first issue . . . Advertising is running 50 percent below budget, reflecting agency and advertiser awareness of circulation difficulties." Baker himself was running into heavy weather—from Luce, whose original doubts about the project now erupted into sarcastic comments scribbled on the margins of a Baker memorandum explaining *Panorama*'s poor performance. Baker said there had been a misreading of the Italian market, and a new magazine concept was being created. Wrote Luce: "What *was* the misreading? . . . What *is* the new concept? . . . I'd like to meet Baker's staff of concept-creators some day."

From Rome, the Time-Life news bureau chief, R. Edward Jackson, wrote Donovan offering his editorial appraisal. *Panorama*, Jackson felt, lacked urgency and was skirting the topics Italians were talking about: "After that blinding first sale, the magazine has failed to make an impact on the Italian scene," Jackson reported. In May, after sessions in Milan with Mondadori editors, Donovan informed Luce of their agreement that "*Panorama* must take stands . . . [It] must develop a more compelling journalistic character."

As the rescue effort continued, Time Inc.'s publishing as well as

96

editorial responsibilities mounted. "At one time when I was in Milan, there were no fewer than nine Time Incers in town, all working on *Panorama* problems," Cal Whipple wrote Donovan in October. In January 1964, at Time Inc.'s urging, Leo Lionni was named editor, replacing Salvalaggio. Mondadori also appointed a new publisher. Time Inc.'s hopes rose; *Panorama*'s income did not.

In February 1965, Baker left TLI to join corporate management, and Charles Bear became TLI managing director. Bear, then 45, was a Phi Beta Kappa graduate of Grinnell College with a master's degree in international relations from the Fletcher School of Law and Diplomacy at Tufts University. He had served as an intelligence officer with the U.S. Eighth Air Force in Europe, and had come to Time Inc. in 1945. As head of TLI's Paris office in the postwar period, he managed the distribution of *Time* and *Life* in some 40 countries in Europe, North Africa and the Middle East. In this job he managed to run afoul of the Russians, who in April 1948 took him from a train at the Czech-East German border and held him incommunicado for four days (although not enamored of the sour sauerkraut soup he was fed, Bear was unharmed).

Two months after his promotion, Bear was pronouncing his discouragement with the Italian *Panorama*. Circulation was below 150,000, advertising page sales were down, joint losses were already $1,430,000 and likely to top $2 million. "We might be in our second decade of publishing before we could recoup our investment," Bear informed Linen, later labeling the whole Italian venture "a fiasco." In June, dissolution of the partnership was negotiated, with Time Inc. selling out to Mondadori for an after-tax loss of $400,000—little enough, considering the anguish. Mondadori took title to *Panorama* and continued it as a general-interest monthly.

Time Inc. also began to distance itself from *Panorama* Argentina. The Argentine venture, unlike the Italian, had been able to build on its initial success; circulation and advertising had continued to rise. Under the editorship of César Civita's son-in-law, Giorgio de Angeli, the magazine displayed a flair for investigative journalism uncommon in Argentina, turning a sharp eye on such subjects as anti-Semitism, the role of the Catholic Church, official censorship, rural poverty in the Argentine north. But in June 1965, *Panorama* published a report on American troop landings in the Dominican Republic that Time Inc. editors in New York considered "rather more anti-Yanqui than is called for, even allowing for Argentine reactions [to U.S. military intervention]." The Time-Life identifica-

97

tion was taken off the magazine's cover. In June 1968, Editorial Abril converted *Panorama* into a weekly, and Time Inc. withdrew as co-publisher, although retaining a 20 percent interest in the parent company. In 1970 the link was severed completely.

The foreign broadcasting ventures were not faring well either. Two years after the initial investment in the Beirut television station, Time Inc. sold its minority interest at a loss. The Latin American investments were souring. Only the Buenos Aires station showed a profit, earning $2,199,000 in 1966. But the following year, devaluation of the Argentine peso turned anticipated dollar returns into a loss of $331,000. The small Peruvian venture was liquidated. In Venezuela, operating losses for the Caracas station mounted, nearing $3 million by 1966. The two Brazilian stations, TV Globo in Rio and TV Paulista in São Paulo, also remained a cash drain. Meanwhile, Time Inc.'s contract with *O Globo* publisher Roberto Marinho came under investigation by two governmental commissions for possible violations of the Brazilian constitutional limitations on broadcast station ownership. The political uncertainty dragged on until 1968, ending finally with a Brazilian presidential decree validating Time Inc.'s position. Bad luck dogged the São Paulo operation, however. In July 1969, fire destroyed the station and virtually all its technical equipment. Only the station's new transmitting equipment, recently installed on a mountaintop ten miles away, survived. While Paulista technicians kept the station on the air, using makeshift facilities, Time Inc. began considering ways to disengage from the Brazilian enterprise entirely.

The following year, the company started to liquidate all its Latin American broadcast investments, which by then totaled almost $11 million. In contrast to what had gone before, the salvage operation turned out fairly well. Net losses, when the transactions were finally completed in 1972, were only about $4 million. Elsewhere also, the company withdrew, retaining only its stake in the Hong Kong station. The sole success that Time Inc. could count among its forays into foreign broadcasting, Hong Kong too was finally sold in 1982, but for a $12 million capital gain.

TLI's *Panorama* experience had reinforced Luce's skepticism about overseas publishing initiatives. In late 1964, at his behest, a corporate research study of the international publishing field was undertaken by Paris news bureau chief Curtis Prendergast and assistant corporate controller and assistant secretary Charlie Gleason. Their report, completed in June 1965, offered a generally sobering set of conclusions: foreign publishing ventures were likely to be more trouble than they were worth, and primary attention should be given to the company's own international editions.

Fortunately for TLI's P&L statement, the international editions of *Time*, as a group, were showing robust growth, accounting for most of the $4 million divisional income for 1965. Buoyed by TLI's overseas sales of Time-Life books, that figure rose another half million the next year. *Life*'s two international editions remained TLI's trouble spots. Their condition was worsening. Two years of marginal profit for *Life en Español* in 1961–62 had been followed by three of more substantial deficit. *Life International* was in a stronger position, but only relatively. A small pretax profit in 1965 turned into a $1.2 million loss in 1966.

The corporate research team studying the magazines' problems had recommended assigning the international editions their own publisher, and this step was taken in 1965. The new publisher was Lane Fortinberry, former managing director of TLI Asia. For *Life en Español,* Fortinberry favored radical surgery: reduction of its large *Life*-sized pages to something nearer conventional magazine dimensions to save production costs. The proposal ran into editorial objections and was not adopted. Instead, another idea was pursued, and a new "three-*Life*" strategy, as it was called, was announced in December 1965. The existing *Life International* would remain largely as it was, Europe-oriented and printed in Paris. But new editions would be created for Asia and for the Pacific. Competitively, the situation looked promising: nothing comparable to *Life* existed east of Suez, and it was unlikely that a national publication, even in Australia or Japan, would be created to fill the vacuum.

In July 1966, *Life Asia* was launched. It was edited in New York and printed in Tokyo, with about a quarter of its editorial content generated regionally. It was aimed at Asians and Americans living (also, at that time, fighting) in the crescent from Japan to India. Circulation averaged 160,000 the first year. *Life Australia* and *Life New Zealand* were launched in March 1967, but proved short-lived; 18 months later, with circulation failing to reach needed levels, both were folded.

Disaster struck Time Inc.'s international operations at the end of that year. Shortly before 10 o'clock on Thursday morning, December 7, 1967, smoke and flames burst from the wall of an office in the new Time & Life Building in Paris. Probably caused by faulty electrical wiring, the fire spread behind the interior paneling of the cast-concrete structure, the heat gathering in intensity until, within minutes, the three top floors were burning fiercely. Two members of Time Inc.'s French staff died: Françoise Hirou, a TLI administrative assistant, trapped in an elevator; and Jean de Wissocq, a TLI public affairs executive, found slumped in a corridor not far from the elevator where Mme. Hirou was discovered.

French newspapers speculated on the possibility of sabotage by anti-American groups, but circumstances of the fire made this highly unlikely. While the Time-Life news bureau improvised temporary offices in a nearby hotel (it was a year before the Paris staff could return to their old quarters), messages of sympathy poured in. French newspapers volunteered use of their archives, *Paris-Match* the facilities of its photo laboratory. Friends, professional associates, French officials and others wrote; subscribers also. In a spidery hand, an elderly French woman wrote to say that she had been a *Time* reader ever since some American friends had given her a subscription. For her, *Time*'s news was "perfect," its photos "marvelous" and with the magazine she could "tour the world in my armchair . . . I send you, therefore, dear *Time*, this expression of my heartfelt sympathy in hoping that you will continue the good work. *Bon courage et sursum corda!*"

As 1968 began, Time Inc. was doing a $53,406,000 business in publishing abroad, about 10 percent of total corporate revenues. But the corporate passion for overseas expansion had largely faded. Management attention was shifting back home again. In January 1968, the Time Inc. board ratified the breakup of TLI. "In the belief that we are a 'world' corporation rather than a U.S. corporation with an export division," it was announced, the international editions of *Time* and *Life* would go back to the parent magazines, TLI Books to the domestic book division. TLI managing director Bear would become Time Inc.'s vice president-international, overseeing corporate international policy abroad.

For *Time*, the consolidation meant gaining assets; for *Life*, two more liabilities.

Turning 40

IN 1963, TIME TURNED 40, the age of maturity; Luce reached 65, the age of retirement. But he was not yet ready to quit. Moreover, in May he was to be host at the biggest celebration in company history—a 40th birthday party for *Time*, to which were invited hundreds of the personalities who had been on the magazine's cover all over those years.

As rehearsal for the public party, there was a dinner for the staff in March (the actual anniversary month) at which Luce attempted, "as my offering to this family birthday," a definition of *Time* and its articles of belief. *Time*, he conceded, was an opinionated publication. "*Time* makes judgments—in nearly every paragraph—sometimes with quite a sting . . . *Time* may often seem to be arbitrary . . . whimsical, even, as they used to say, flippant. And yet through all the huge tapestry of 20th century history which *Time* has woven, there is a clear pattern of belief." Luce went on:

> The problem of belief or faith is not entirely a question of believing in certain truths that are not mechanically verifiable. It is also, at any given time in history, a question of vision . . . vision of how to live an individual life, and also a vision of how the nation is to live, and in our day, of the whole world . . .

What then does *Time* now believe? . . . *Time* believes that human life is tragic and triumphant and also comic but never, as Sartre proclaims, absurd. Tonight I shall focus on just one category—political philosophy—one category of human existence in one unique time and place—the United States. My specific subject is the American proposition . . .

By the American proposition we mean the total political philosophy of the Declaration of Independence, of the Constitution and of its evolution in the history of the United States to the present day . . . The whole of the American proposition has been epitomized [by *Fortune*] as "a word, a tendency and a method. The word is liberty, the tendency is equality, the method is constitutionalism." That is the core and essence of what *Time* believes—the proposition to which we give our loyalty and our service . . .

We used to say that *Time* is the most important magazine in America—in the world. We no longer indulge in that kind of boasting, but it is obvious that *Time* is very important in the life of this country, since several millions of our most capable citizens have a firm date with *Time* each week for their most comprehensive and serious consideration of public affairs—the *res publica* of the republic. If, therefore, the country were in a sorry and shameful state, we would have to bear a share of the blame. And if, on the contrary, the republic is strong, we can drink our birthday toast in at least a moment of reflected glory . . .

Bear in mind, that the whole concept of the American proposition requires . . . a free and responsible press . . . we are called to this service, as essential to the republic as the air we breathe . . . So—when we judge the state of the union over a cycle of years, it is not only America we judge; it is also ourselves.

In a note to Donovan beforehand, Luce had indicated his concern about the speech, and probably not everyone in his audience would have gone as far as Luce did in defining *Time*'s role in the nation's life.

There was no question, however, that *Time* was then in very robust condition. It was vigorously edited under Otto Fuerbringer's direction. It had an enthusiastic advertising, circulation and promotion staff under publisher Bernhard M. Auer. Competitively, the magazine's position was unchallenged. By in-house estimate, *Time*'s profits were ten times those of *Newsweek*, which had undergone a financial crisis and was sold to the Washington Post Company in 1961. With *Life*'s continuing inability to turn its huge revenues into substantial profit, and with *Sports Illustrated*'s continuing losses, *Time*'s importance to the overall health of the company was magnified.

The last of the six managing editors appointed personally by Luce after Hadden's death,* Fuerbringer was, in a sense, the last editor of the "old" *Time*; at the same time, his innovations pointed the magazine in the direction it would increasingly take under the editors who followed. The magazine that Fuerbringer took over in 1960 was still, and would remain, a weekly version of the newspaper of record—necessarily selective, but dealing "*briefly* with EVERY HAPPENING OF IMPORTANCE . . . according to a FIXED METHOD OF ARRANGEMENT which constitutes a complete ORGANIZATION of all the news," as the original prospectus, including capital letters and italics, had promised *Time*'s first subscribers. In Fuerbringer's view, that obligation to the reader, to touch all bases in every issue, remained in force. In late 1959, shortly before Fuerbringer was named managing editor, Luce asked him to prepare a draft "re-prospectus" defining *Time*. Fuerbringer wrote:

> "Curt, clear, complete" was *Time*'s first slogan and *Time* is still the only magazine providing a consistent, continuing summary of all the news. *Time* was founded on the principle of organizing the news by departments and it has an unspoken contract with the reader to tell the news in all those departments every week. *Time*'s editorial space has remained constant for the last 15 years, even though more and more news is available and *Time*'s news-gathering facilities have doubled. By discarding irrelevancies, by judicious selection, *Time* promises to get the week's meaningful news into manageable space (42 pages)—a budget of information that can be read in one sitting, at a time and place of the reader's choosing.

Within this formula, *Time* had evolved. *Time* style had grown up, lost the brashness of the magazine's youth. The pejorative physical

*The others were John S. Martin, 1929–33, 1936–37; John Shaw Billings, 1933–36; Manfred Gottfried, 1937–43; T.S. Matthews, 1943–49; Roy Alexander, 1949–60.

descriptions—"gnomelike," "frog-faced," "snaggle-toothed"—that had so infuriated the subjects of early *Time* stories were gone, most discarded during Matthews's editorship nearly 20 years before. But the wordplay and the puns remained: "The Wages of Spin," for a story on disc jockeys; "Pineapple Epic," for a review of James Michener's just-published novel about Hawaii. *Time*'s emphasis on telling the news through personalities had also remained largely unchanged. Almost invariably, *Time* cover stories were built around an individual. Almost all of the 1,922 covers published from *Time*'s founding up to January 1960 displayed human faces; among the exceptions were three racehorses, two dogs, five bulls (for Wall Street), one building (the Pentagon), one machine (a computer). Most covers were painted or drawn; photographs were infrequent. Slow color printing required that covers be scheduled four weeks in advance; late cover switches were rare.

Inside, the page layouts had not changed greatly. All headlines remained single-column, picture displays were conservative and four-square. The sections marched regularly from National Affairs and Foreign News at the front of the magazine to Books at the back. Seldom was a section omitted. The individual stories had lengthened beyond Luce's liking—he was forever urging his editors to be briefer. But *Time* still disposed of much in small space. Half a page, 100 lines of type, about 700 words, was considered a long story. Often, part of a column sufficed.

Also unchanged was *Time*'s system of anonymous "group" journalism—the assembly-line meshing of effort by correspondents, researchers, writers and editors that went into producing the magazine each week. Luce's dislike for the term group journalism persisted; a remark of Fuerbringer's that *Time* had invented the system moved Luce to protest: " 'Group journalism.' If I ever used that word in the old days, I soon quit it. *Time*'s method of journalism is highly organized—but a high degree of individualism has always been required—beginning with the absolutist authority of the M.E. [managing editor]."

The absolutist authority did prevail. *Time*, it was then often said, read as if written by one man, and one man—the managing editor—did pass his pencil over almost every word. The system imposed his viewpoint indelibly on the magazine. It also imposed tremendous physical pressures on the man himself, culminating on the night the magazine went to press. Fuerbringer's predecessor Roy Alexander once likened the managing editor's dual role as both executive and wordsmith to that of a factory boss who spent half his week in the front office directing the enterprise, the other half out in the back shop running a lathe.

Time's editorial production system created tensions within the staff. Stories were edited at least twice, sometimes heavily, as they passed up the chain from writer to departmental senior editor to managing editor; then, in a reverse process, back down again to the researcher for a final check of factual accuracy, to the copyreader for stylistic and syntactical review and then, in the last hours before print, to a late-duty editor who trimmed (or, sometimes, expanded) the story to fit it exactly into its allotted space.

Writers, whose names remained unknown beyond a listing in minute type on the masthead, complained of the anonymity of their labors. "If reputation is a writer's capital, *Time* staffers can never invest," a former *Time* writer once observed.* There were greater frustrations in the assembly-line process itself, in the mountains of material—correspondents' files, sometimes from half a dozen or more bureaus, researchers' notes, newspaper clips, encyclopedia references, statistical abstracts—all to be reduced within a relatively short time into a relatively few lines that would, nonetheless, be worked on further by other hands as the story moved toward publication. In a classic lament, written in an earlier decade but still applicable, one of Time Inc.'s most consistently dependable producers, Paul O'Neil, voiced the *Time* writer's discontents:

> The world knows little about him [the *Time* writer], and what it does is generally incorrect. It is true that somebody . . . sometimes grabs one of him and holds him up to the pink window of the publisher's letter for the readers to see . . . and the world is given the impression that he has just got back from Yucatan with a tan, and is going off to see Churchill as soon as he has had lunch with Lana Turner at the Stork Club.
>
> Actually, he is an anxious looking fellow with thinning hair, whose stomach has the knobby rigidity of a Mexican gourd from eating too much [lunch-counter] food. He spends his days crouching in . . . his writing hutch, like an incorrigible in solitary, fumbling with paper and hating himself. He never sees the outside world—he is forcefed by paper. Occasionally he takes a pill. Occasionally he glares wildly out the window. But mostly he sits humped over his typewriter, smoking cigarettes and throwing them on the floor and staring morosely at the wall. He is waiting for his brains to work.

*Andrew Kopkind, *New York Review of Books*, September 12, 1968, pp. 23–28.

He is a kind of word mechanic who must yank odd shaped chunks of raw fact off the overhead belt, trim it to size (often with his teeth), assemble his jig saw of conflicting information into something with a beginning, a middle and an end, bolt the whole together with adjectives, and send it through the hopper, glittering, polished . . .

Like the club fighter, whose work is that of getting his ears scrambled once a fortnight at St. Nicholas Arena, the *Time* writer has his points. He is durable and cunning. It is my contention that he is a unique and valuable fellow. I am inclined to believe that the theory of group journalism is highly overrated, and that the brigades of editors, researchers, advisers and assorted double-domers who are popularly believed to be helping the writer are actually just riding around on his back, shooting at parakeets, waving to their friends, and plucking fruit from overhanging branches while he churns unsteadily through the swamps of fact and rumor with his big, dirty feet up to the knee at every step . . .

Time's correspondents had their own problems with the system. They wrote not directly for print but rather for the information of the editors, filing copiously without too much regard for word limits or literary effects; New York would always rewrite and compress anyway. This reporting system produced the mountains of detail, color and quotes that the writers drew on to give *Time* stories their characteristic vividness. But it was also wasteful, and frustrating for the correspondents; an hour's interview with a news source could end up as a couple of lines in print, or be ignored entirely. Inescapably too, every correspondent could cite instances where the process had gone wrong despite careful checking, where detail had been skewed, emphasis misplaced—where indeed *Time* had erred. More serious were the disputes when correspondents in the field questioned the appraisal of a situation that *Time* made from New York.

Fuerbringer, in his 1959 draft re-prospectus for Luce, had defended the system:

Eyebrows have sometimes been raised on the outside as to how all this [group journalistic] collaboration can work . . . Quite obviously, *Time* believes that many minds are better than one. On occasion, *Time* has come under criticism by fellow journalists because its writers and editors in New York rewrote dispatches sent in by the correspondents. Championing "the man on the spot" as the man with the truth in his notebook, the

106

critics called this a violation of journalistic integrity. Of course, they were quite wrong. *Time* believes in "the man on the spot" and has more men on more spots than anyone except the two U.S. press services (AP and UPI). But *Time*'s correspondents know that in most instances their dispatches will be part of a larger file; even when their dispatch is the sole basis for a story, they overfile on details, knowing that the story will gain more perspective when rewritten in New York . . .

Whatever feelings it engendered, the system worked; it worked especially well under pressure. In May 1960, two months after Fuerbringer became managing editor, one of the CIA's high-altitude U-2 reconnaissance airplanes was shot down on a spying mission over the Soviet Union. With the plane's wreckage on display in Moscow, Nikita Khrushchev used the incident to break up his Paris summit meeting with President Eisenhower, General de Gaulle and British Prime Minister Harold Macmillan. News of the U-2's downing and the capture of its pilot, Francis Gary Powers, reached New York 40 hours before *Time*'s press deadline. Scrapping more than 2 million covers already printed and dated for the May 16 issue, *Time* rushed out a cover story on Powers, putting a black-and-white photo on the cover. The cover change was the fastest *Time* had made up to then. By the following year, so-called crash covers were coming one week in every three, on the average.

Time's normal routine also quickened. Planned in an earlier era as a magazine "for weekend reading," with a publication schedule fixed accordingly, *Time* had kept to the same editorial schedule for the first 32 years of its existence. Editors, writers and researchers came in on Thursday, worked on Friday, Saturday and Sunday to get the magazine to press Monday night for delivery to most of the subscribers by the following Thursday, the remainder on Friday   a work week that took its toll on staffers' social and family lives. In 1955, *Time* advanced its publication date by a day, closing on Sunday night. In 1959, as assistant managing editor, Fuerbringer had proposed moving to a Friday close, and printing on the weekend. American leisure habits had changed and weekends were now spent in other pursuits besides reading; thus, the magazine should reach readers earlier. In so doing, Fuerbringer wrote Luce, *Time* would gain a jump on *Newsweek*, which shared some press facilities with *U.S. News* and thus could not easily change printing schedules to match *Time*'s.

That proposal was not adopted. But in July 1960 a Saturday-night closing was announced, effective in September. Inauguration of the new earlier schedule found Fuerbringer away from his desk with the illness that kept him out until the following January. Further changes had to await his return. One of the first was the appointment in March 1961 of a second assistant managing editor, James Keogh, to join Tom Griffith. Then 44, Keogh was, like Fuerbringer, a Midwesterner. Born in Platte County, Nebraska, where he was brought up on a farm and attended a one-room school, Keogh had gone from Creighton University to the Omaha *World-Herald*, spending 13 years there as reporter, rewrite man, political writer and city editor before joining *Time* as a writer in 1951. In 1956, Keogh wrote *This Is Nixon*, a sympathetic biography.* That same year he was named a senior editor. As assistant managing editor, Keogh took over as Fuerbringer's principal deputy, handling covers, administration and staff recruiting. Griffith moved to top-editing the Business section and overseeing *Time*'s Canadian and Latin American editions.

Fuerbringer had moved into the managing editor's office determined not only to make *Time* newsier but also, he said, "to make it livelier, both in the stories [chosen] and in the writing." *Time*, in his view, "had gone a little flat." Now, to brighten the magazine's appearance, page layouts were opened up with larger and more striking photographic displays, and more "run-arounds"—lines of text set irregularly to fit the contours of the pictures (a trickier process in those days, with mechanical typesetting, than it is today with computer typesetting). Color pages, previously confined largely to the Art section, were used more freely throughout the magazine. In June 1963 came *Time*'s first typographic updating since early days, with the introduction of a bolder, slightly larger body type, called Times Roman.

Cover portraiture had become one of *Time*'s strongest features. A group of artists had been assembled—of whom two Russian émigrés, Boris Artzybasheff and Boris Chaliapin, were the most prolific—able to turn out likenesses of any subject, almost overnight. Fuerbringer, handling covers under Alexander's editorship, had begun varying the routine, seeking out prominent artists for special assignments: France's stark modernist Bernard Buffet was commissioned to do General de Gaulle as 1958's Man of the Year; the Mexican expressionist Rufino Tamayo to do his country's President, Adolfo Lopez Mateos. Keogh took over covers under Fuerbringer's

*G.P Putnam's Sons, 1956.

editorship, and the process continued. Pop artist Andy Warhol was commissioned to do a cover on American youth. For a cover on Marc Chagall the subject did a self-portrait. Henriette Wyeth Hurd painted a portrait of her brother, Andrew Wyeth. Cartoonists, sculptors and collage artists were also used. For a 1967 cover on the Beatles, the British caricaturist Gerald Scarfe re-created the four young musicians in molded papier-mâché. After being photographed for *Time*, the figures went on display at Madame Tussaud's famous London wax museum.

More important for *Time*'s development was the addition of new sections to the magazine. Then as now, innovations were rare; the original contents lists that Luce and Hadden drew up had proved remarkably durable. Of the 22 headings under which *Time*, at its inception, treated the news, a large majority still remained. Animals, Transport, International (a subdivision of Foreign News) and Personality (an offshoot of the People section) had come and gone. Radio, launched in 1938, became Radio & TV and finally, in 1958, evolved into Show Business, where Luce, with a print journalist's disdain, felt the coverage of television properly belonged. (In 1967, though, Television reemerged as a separate section.)

Fuerbringer made one change that dismayed some of the staff. July 1960 saw the end of the Miscellany section, a collection of bright, punny one-liners culled from the newspapers, which had run almost unchanged in format since 1923. Samples:

KIPPER OF THE FLAME. In North Haven, Conn., after dozing off while cooking a snack, Herbert Herring was smoked out of his house.

HEADS OR TAILS. In Los Angeles, at a pre-divorce hearing, Mary Lieblich received custody of the family dachshund but her husband was granted visitation rights.

Fuerbringer recalled the laments at Miscellany's demise: "People said, 'How could you do this? It's the only thing that's fun in the magazine.' I said, 'Hell, the whole magazine's going to be fun.' "

In March 1961, the two lead sections of the magazine were renamed. National Affairs became The Nation. Foreign News became The World, eliminating a parochialism that was annoying to many of *Time*'s overseas readers. In May the first new section, Modern Living, later shortened to Living, was launched, aimed at covering "every aspect of how people, and Americans in particular, live— their cars, homes, travel, play, food, fads, fashions, customs, manners." Luce was not much in favor; the section "didn't fit the [news] budget he and Brit had worked out," Fuerbringer said. Three years later, though, in January 1964, Modern Living was to produce one of *Time*'s most controversial cover stories ever, on Sex in the Sixties—a subject perhaps more controversial for the cover picture than for the text. After a long search *Time* had found, in the collection of a Durham, North Carolina, couple, a painting by the Manhattan artist John Koch entitled *Siesta*, a summery midafternoon scene of amorous languor, showing a nude man partly covered by a sheet, lying on a tousled bed, looking toward a dressing table where a nude woman sat combing her hair. *Time* was deluged with mail, newspapers took up the subject and syndicated cartoonist Bill Mauldin lampooned it.

In June 1962 came another new section, World Business, which was to report separately the growing economic importance of Europe and the Common Market, and Asia. With the World Business section, *Time* also added two more pages to its total news budget. (In 1967 the section was reabsorbed into Business.) In October 1963 the Law section was inaugurated, reviving a feature that had been part of the early *Time* but long since abandoned.

Time's next new section did more than stake out new territory for coverage; it inaugurated a new sort of editorial treatment. The *Time* publisher's letter of April 2, 1965, described the section and its intent:

> In this issue, the editors launch a major new department: the *Time* Essay. Its sights are high.
>
> Like the other sections of the magazine, Essay will treat topics in the news, but (except for the cover story) in greater detail and length. Essay will take a problem under current discussion and lay it bare. The new department will not treat a story or an issue when it is making the biggest headlines. That will be done in the appropriate section. Essay will come in later, when the problem is still far from settled but when second thoughts and greater reflection can be of particular benefit.
>
> Essay will be unlike other *Time* stories in two respects: 1) there will be little narrative quality to its prose, and 2) it will only rarely deal with personalities.

Essay was a seminal development in *Time*, presaging a discursive approach to topics both in the news and off the news that would increasingly become "*Time* style" in subsequent years under Fuerbringer's successors. The section was Fuerbringer's invention, conceived during an Asian tour, when he was away from the weekly editing chores and had gotten to "thinking about subjects that could be dealt with in greater density without any news pegs coming up. The idea was that we'd have subjects explored with experts in the field, covering most aspects of the topic so that for a time, anyway, it would be a fair summation of the matter." He saw Essay also as a way of letting the experts speak at greater length than in the often truncated quotes *Time* used in its news sections.

As for the new section's title, Fuerbringer considered Essay a "nice, old-fashioned [one] to bring back." Essay made its debut with two pages on "The U.N.: Prospects Beyond Paralysis." Succeeding weeks brought such subjects as "Viet Nam: The Right War at the Right Time"; "The New American Jew"; "The Pleasures and Pitfalls of Being in Debt"; "Bay of Pigs Revisited"; "Opera: Con Amore."

Considerable editorial dexterity was required to get the section started and, more demanding yet, to sustain it on a weekly basis. Under senior editor Henry Anatole Grunwald, Essay's first editor, some of *Time*'s most versatile writers and editors were enlisted. The principal writer at the start was Joe David Brown, a former *Time* foreign correspondent, *Saturday Evening Post* short-story writer and author of five novels, three of which were made into movies (*Paper Moon*, *Stars in My Crown*, *Kings Go Forth*). Brown's preference was for *Time*'s narrative form rather than dissertation, and he "bled" doing Essays; nonetheless he managed to turn out eight during the first six months. Another frequent contributor was senior editor Champ Clark, son of a Senator from Missouri, grandson and namesake of a famous Speaker of the House of Representatives. He lent his personal knowledge and authority to Essay's various examinations of the American political scene. The polished touch of *Time*'s longtime Religion writer Douglas Auchincloss was visible in the Essays on the American Jew and such others as "Death as a Constant Companion" and "On Not Losing One's Cool about the Young."

"The best *Time* ever had—look at the masthead," Fuerbringer said of *Time*'s editorial staff during his period as managing editor. It was a talented group, comprising veterans from the early postwar years together with a rising younger generation, many of whom went on to prominence outside Time Inc. A mainstay of the World section was Robert McLaughlin, a novelist and playwright, author of many *New Yorker* pieces and also of many of *Time*'s most memorable phrases. "His mind," McLaughlin once wrote in a cover story on General de

111

Gaulle, "is like the Louvre, filled with battle pictures in which the French are always winning." Another veteran was cinema critic Henry Bradford Darrach, whose sharp judgments and outrageous puns ("Esther Williams's pictures are generally just so much water over the dame") had delighted readers and needled Hollywood for two decades. Outstanding among the younger writers was John Elson, a second-generation Time Incer,* who, as Religion writer, produced the much-discussed April 1966 cover story, "Is God Dead?" This question, posed provocatively on *Time*'s cover, aroused nationwide debate . . . and drew some 3,500 letters to the editor—the greatest reader response to any story *Time* had ever published, up to then, and one of the greatest in the magazine's history.

There was a comparable lineup of strength on the reporting side. *Time* editors were getting files from a network of foreign and domestic news bureaus that constituted one of the largest news-gathering organizations maintained by any publisher anywhere. Growing gradually during the 1950s, the *Time* and *Life* news services had, by the early 1960s, reached a total of some 135 full-time correspondents, plus 300 part-time "stringers" and 150 others, stationed in 30 bureaus in the U.S. and abroad. Cost of the news services was around $4 million yearly—not much less than *Time* itself was spending on all the rest of its editorial operations.

The relation of the news services to *Time* was curious, however. In January 1962 the previously separate U.S. and Canadian and foreign news operations were merged into one worldwide Time-Life News Service; Richard M. Clurman, former domestic service chief, was named chief of correspondents, with John Boyle, who had headed the foreign bureaus, as his deputy. In merging the two services, Luce ended an anachronism but perpetuated an anomaly. This was the independence of the news service from *Time,* for which the correspondents did most of their reporting. Luce had always kept his own hand on the news operations, often choosing the major bureau chiefs himself; the situation remained the same after the merger. The chief of correspondents was responsible to him, as editor-in-chief, not to the managing editor of *Time.* Rivalry was inherent in this separation, and there had been clashes in the past; the strong personalities of the two men in this instance—Clurman and Fuerbringer—were to lead to more.

Clurman was a whirlwind executive—he liked to say he was first

*Son of Robert T. Elson, the author of the first two volumes of Time Inc.'s corporate history.

diagnosed for an ulcer at age nine—who was to play an important role at Time Inc. over the next decade (he took leave in 1973 to become New York City's parks commissioner). Clurman had come to *Time* from the magazine *Commentary* in 1949 as a Press writer, leaving in 1955 to become editorial director, at age 31, of the large Long Island daily, *Newsday.* He returned to Time Inc. in 1958 to go into news service administration, where he set an operating and living style that was to become legendary for its lavishness. One legend was that he always bought two first-class airplane tickets—the other seat for his briefcase. (Clurman said that actually what happened was that the Time Inc. travel department would arrange with the airlines to keep a seat empty next to him when he traveled.) But the *Time* correspondents found his leadership exhilarating. He toured the bureaus constantly, giving what one correspondent called "the journalistic equivalent of locker-room fight talks. . . . The charge that Clurman gave off ran through the whole news service. He managed to keep a whole coterie of different correspondents excited about their job."

When Clurman took over the combined news service, the bureaus were in experienced hands. In London was Bob Elson, who in his long Time Inc. career had been Washington bureau chief, assistant managing editor of *Fortune,* deputy managing editor and later general manager of *Life.* Back in Bonn, after a tour in Africa, was the indefatigable James Bell, in the view of Luce and many others Time Inc.'s outstanding reporter. In Rome was William F. McHale Jr., a deft and witty newsman who had reported also from Washington, London, Paris and Beirut; he was to die later in 1962 in a plane crash with Enrico Mattei, boss of Italy's oil industry. In Hong Kong was Stanley Karnow, later to gain distinction as a historian of the Vietnam War. Donald S. Connery, formerly bureau chief in New Delhi, held down the important Tokyo post. Heading the major U.S. bureaus were Steele in Washington and Berges in Los Angeles and, in Chicago, Murray J. Gart, a shrewd political reporter who was later to succeed Clurman as news service chief. An energetic spotter of talent, Clurman recruited numerous correspondents who were to fill important bureau posts over the succeeding years.

The vigor of Fuerbringer's editorship of Time, and the editorial innovations he was making, won the enthusiastic support of the publishing side. The magazine's publisher, Bernie Auer, was not long in the job when he wrote Luce: "I feel—and have more supporting evidence than ever—that the editors have just caught fire. I hope you agree with me that the magazine has never been better."

Auer's own background was in circulation and promotion. A Williams College man like his predecessor, Auer had come to *Time* straight out of college but his acquaintance with the publishing business went back to boyhood days. In prep school at Taft, he had sold newspaper subscriptions, and at Williams he had been both business manager of the college newspaper and campus circulation representative for *Time* and the newly founded *Life*, for which magazine he once sold a hundred subscriptions in a single afternoon. Joining *Time* in the mailroom in 1939, Auer graduated shortly to newsstand sales and then to public relations, returning to *Time*'s circulation department after wartime service with the U.S. Army's Counter Intelligence Corps in India and Burma. He was doubling as *Time*'s circulation and promotion director when, in 1960, he was named publisher. Auer was a breezy, relaxed executive with a flair for winning friends for *Time*. To deal with an industrialist who stopped advertising because *Time* had once described him, in Auer's recollection, "as a rather rude fellow who spat on the floor," Auer flew in the Time Inc. company plane to the man's Midwestern headquarters, landed on the property and announced, "Okay, I've come to let you bawl me out." *Time* regained the account. It was Auer who, with news service chief Dick Clurman, devised the highly successful *Time* news tours, in which selected groups of American business executives were taken abroad for face-to-face meetings with foreign political and military leaders. These tours were not only unique experiences for the participants but enormously productive of corporate goodwill for Time Inc.

In 1956 Auer, then circulation director, had hired a jazz band to parade around the Time & Life Building to celebrate *Time*'s passing 2 million in circulation. Since then, net paid circulation had been rising by more than 100,000 a year, surpassing 3 million in 1964. The rival newsweeklies *Newsweek* and *U.S. News* were also showing circulation increases, reflecting an apparent rekindling of American interest in public affairs, dating, in the *Time* circulation department's view, from about the time of Kennedy's inauguration. But *Time*'s innovative circulation techniques were also helping. Among them was the use of subscription cards blown loosely into the magazine's pages during binding rather than being stapled in—a *Time* first that some readers regarded as a scourge. ("I'm afraid we did unleash that on America," circulation director Putney Westerfield ruefully concluded.)

Time's circulation promotion expense, meanwhile, had declined slightly, a further indication of circulation strength. This, together with increased per-copy prices, was producing a steadily rising circulation net. Luce was not entirely in favor of charging readers more. As he wrote Auer later: "One of the significant characteristics of the popular or quasi popular press—and even of printing itself—was to make information available to as many people as possible with a minimum of 'price barrier.' " Luce admitted, though, that he couldn't argue with the policy's success.

On the advertising front, *Time* had suffered a sharp drop in page sales in 1960. In 1961, a few months behind *Newsweek*, *Time* moved to accommodate advertisers who wanted to target specific markets; it brought out its first regional advertising editions. And in 1962, under the newly-appointed advertising director, Robert C. Gordon, planning began for further advertising specialization: *Time*'s first demographic edition, sorting out subscribers by occupation—in this case the medical profession—rather than by geography. Meanwhile, in order not to push advertising rates higher until page sales caught up, *Time* slowed its circulation growth, also cutting its cost-per-thousand rate slightly. For 1963 a recovery in profits to 1960's level of just under $8 million pretax was anticipated.

Luce was pained rather than pleased. "A deeply discouraging document," he called *Time*'s 1963 budget. "Here is *Time*, the strongest magazine in the world, at the height of its strength, doing the fairly immense volume of $58 million—and unable to make a profit of more than 6 percent (after taxes)." No less than 10 percent should be *Time*'s "urgent business goal," Luce said. He was in for a pleasant surprise. That profit was coming sooner than he expected. Appropriately, *Time*'s 40th anniversary year was to be the best year yet in the magazine's history.

In Clare Boothe Luce's opinion, intimations of mortality may have spurred her husband to make *Time*'s 40th birthday the big one. Mrs. Luce recalled asking him: "People don't celebrate anniversaries except the 25th or 50th—why the 40th, Harry?" "Because I won't be here for the 50th," he had replied.

It was at a *Time* senior editors' lunch in September 1962, when the anniversary was being discussed, that the idea first popped out. Senior editor Cranston Jones suggested: Why not have a party and invite *Time* cover subjects to join in? Picked up by publisher Auer, tried out on Luce, the suggestion soon snowballed, overriding all objections of impracticality.

The first problem concerned the guest list: Who among the thousand or more from 1923 onward still living should be invited? "Though it has been our journalistic duty to take notice of some rogues and tyrants," Auer explained later, it was *Time*'s "social pleasure and host's privilege" not to have to invite all of them. Thus the winnowing began. Excluded were the infirm and overly aged, the ephemeral personalities whose fame had long since flickered out, the unfriendlies (Fidel Castro, Jimmy Hoffa) and others certain not to attend (Howard Hughes). Then a key list of 27 persons, chosen as bellwethers, was sampled. That list is lost, but General Douglas MacArthur, Thomas E. Dewey and Henry Ford II are remembered as having been on it. On their expressed willingness to attend, preparations went forward. In all, 630 cover figures were invited, by personal letter from Luce. Nearly half accepted; virtually all paid their own way to New York. Invitations went out later to several hundred other prominent people, plus Time Inc. staff.

Too complicated to arrange even in six months, the party was postponed from the actual March 3 anniversary date to Monday, May 6. The affair expanded to a long weekend of activities including a Saturday welcoming reception in New York and a Sunday-evening garden party for more than a thousand guests, with dancing, at Linen's home in Connecticut, as prelude to the black-tie dinner Monday night at the Waldorf-Astoria. The logistics occupied some 40 Time Inc. staffers and, as one said later, "would have challenged the Pentagon." Details ranged from hotel arrangements, escort and limousine service for the visitors and touchy questions of protocol for the banquet seating to such small matters as having trout for the fish course specially hatched to fit the Waldorf-Astoria's chinaware. A booklet was printed reproducing in chronological order the *Time* covers on which the guests had appeared. Heavyweight boxer Jack Dempsey, September 10, 1923, led the list.

Winston Churchill sent his regrets. So did Charles de Gaulle. Germany's Chancellor Konrad Adenauer, who in the German *Who's Who* listed his appearance as *Time* 1953 Man of the Year as one of his foreign "decorations," accepted but then was forced by "compelling political reasons" to cancel. From John Kennedy came a message in lieu of a personal appearance; brother Ted, a cover figure in his own right, attended.

Of the ex-Presidents, Herbert Hoover, 88, felt too infirm to come; Harry Truman, who had received rough treatment from *Time* during his presidency, declined with what seemed sincere regret. Eisenhower also declined, writing Luce that he and Mrs. Eisenhower had an annual party date at the Masters golf tournament in Augusta,

116

Georgia, "that we have promised ourselves never to break if we can possibly avoid it." This was a bitter disappointment to Luce after all the printed and spoken adulation he had lavished on Eisenhower. But no amount of importuning would budge the general, not even Luce's offer to send a Time Inc. plane to fly him from Augusta to New York and back the night of the party.

The dinner gathered an astonishing array, withal. A total of 1,668 people were seated in the Waldorf-Astoria ballroom and its balconies; 284 of them were *Time* cover subjects. Running from A (Mexico's ex-President Miguel Alemán) to Z (moviemaker Darryl Zanuck), they included international banker Eugene Black, cartoonist Al Capp, author John Dos Passos, former Democratic Party boss James Farley, Republican presidential hopeful Barry Goldwater, actor Rex Harrison, Olympic athlete Rafer Johnson, entertainer Danny Kaye, movie actress Gina Lollobrigida, European Common Market founder Jean Monnet, former NATO commander Lauris Norstad, baseball magnate Walter O'Malley, broadcasting pioneer William Paley, union chief Walter Reuther, polio vaccine discoverer Jonas Salk, socialist Norman Thomas, space scientist James Van Allen, former Vice President Henry Wallace, supersonic test pilot Charles Yeager. All the cover subjects were to be individually introduced. Five were lined up to speak: Vice President Johnson and Secretary of State Rusk; Francis Cardinal Spellman to deliver the invocation and Union Theological Seminary president Henry Pitney Van Dusen the benediction; theologian Paul Tillich, head of the University of Chicago School of Divinity, to deliver the principal address. Another cover subject, soprano Leontyne Price, sang a Puccini aria.

"Never in our experience have as many titans and titanesses of industry, sports, music, theater, philanthropy, politics, publishing, finance, science, medicine, government, advertising and religion taken spotlighted bows in one place," observed Geoffrey Hellman of *The New Yorker*, one of 228 journalists from 160 publications, news agencies and broadcast organizations in the U.S. and abroad who covered the affair. Added Hellman: "The religion that struck us as pervading the celebration was one of success."

It was certainly a tribute to Luce himself. He was as much a star as any of the invited celebrities who, he said, "should enjoy meeting each other face to face, as we hope they have enjoyed meeting each other in the pages of *Time*." The point of this party, Luce declared, "is the people who are here."

Felicity prevailed. Cardinal Spellman read cabled greetings from

117

one cover subject not present, Pope John XXIII. Luce toasted one guest present but never on *Time*'s cover "for a unique but very poor reason: she married the editor-in-chief." Lyndon Johnson, looking around the room, complimented Luce for "being the first publisher to select magazine cover models on a basis other than beauty." Dean Rusk, obviously enjoying membership in what he called the "special order of cover-story victims here this evening [who] share the experience of having been fully exposed," delivered a graceful tribute to *Time* journalism and its creators: "They set out 40 years ago to talk about what the news means—not in some disembodied spirit, not claiming to have some special revelation, but stepping forth frankly and boldly to tell . . . readers what the publishers and editors of this great publication themselves believed." Rusk observed that *Time*'s outspokenness had landed it—honorably—in trouble. "I suppose *Time* holds the all-time record for having been banned from more countries than any other publication of general circulation. I would suppose that in these past 40 years that is something of a medal of merit." Foreign diplomats often asked whether the editor of *Time* spoke for the U.S. government, Rusk noted. "Regularly we say, 'No, brother, shake hands; he was only speaking to you, just as he speaks to us.'"

President Kennedy's message, read aloud by Linen, was more barbed:

> Every great magazine is the lengthened shadow of its editor, and this is particularly the case with *Time* . . .
>
> *Time*, in its effort to embrace the totality of human experience, has instructed, entertained, confused and infuriated its readers for nearly half a century. Like most Americans, I do not always agree with *Time*, but I nearly always read it. And, though I am bound to think that *Time* sometimes seems to do its best to contract the political horizons of its audience, I am especially glad that it has worked so steadfastly to enlarge their intellectual and cultural horizons. This has contributed materially, I think, to the raising of standards in our nation in recent years.
>
> I hope I am not wrong in occasionally detecting these days in *Time* those more mature qualities appropriate to an institution entering its 40s—a certain mellowing of tone, a greater tolerance of human frailty, and most astonishing of all, an occasional hint of fallibility. For *Time*—congratulations!

Luce had saved a reply for this, and now delivered it. One of the great personal privileges of his job as editor-in-chief, Luce began, "is to have at least some degree of dialogue with the President of the United States," who, he hoped, would remain *Time's* No. 1 subscriber, "especially one who reads us with such very fine-combed, judicious . . . sensibilities." Then, bringing out a telegram, Luce went on, "Here is one from one of the great editors of America, Roy Roberts of the Kansas City *Star* . . . 'Just a word of caution,' says Roy Roberts, 'on this historic anniversary, from one who has been in the business even longer. Don't get too mellow.' "

It was nearly midnight when Bob Hope, the last of a relay of toast-masters who took over from Luce, finally finished introducing the guests, and it was another couple of hours before the Meyer Davis orchestra stopped playing and the last guests straggled away. The cost of the party was never precisely calculated—a quarter of a million in uninflated 1963 dollars was Linen's estimate.

Reporting the Assassination

WHEN THE THREE SHOTS WERE FIRED from the Texas School Book Depository in Dallas on November 22, 1963, it was 1:30 p.m. in New York, lunchtime on a warm and sunny Friday. The new edition of *Life* was at that moment rolling off the presses in Chicago with a cover story on Roger Staubach, the Navy football team's remarkable quarterback. *Time* was in an unusually advanced state of preparation. The Nation section was already edited, and the magazine seemed headed for an early close the next day. In one of the private dining rooms on the 47th floor of the Time & Life Building, the regular weekly managing editors' lunch was under way. Among those gathered around the table with Luce were editorial director Hedley Donovan, George Hunt and assistant managing editor Roy Rowan of *Life*, assistant managing editor Louis Banks of *Fortune*, Andre Laguerre of *Sports Illustrated* and Otto Fuerbringer of *Time*, along with three of his colleagues, assistant managing editor Tom Griffith and senior editors Champ Clark and Henry Grunwald. They were discussing the U.S. economy.

At mid-meal, the phone in the dining room rang. Fuerbringer answered. Washington bureau chief John Steele was on the line. A moment later Fuerbringer announced, "The President has been shot."

The response was a curious kind of delayed reaction, as if the news, of such enormity and so utterly unanticipated, could not immediately be grasped. For a moment Luce continued the discussion of the economy. The atmosphere soon changed as the head-waiter walked in and announced solemnly, in his understanding of an English idiom: "Gentlemen, the President is on his way out." For a moment, Fuerbringer recalled, "Nobody knew what to do—and suddenly it sank in that we had to get back to work." Most of the editors returned to their offices, leaving Luce, head in hands, sitting with Donovan. In the days that followed, as events demanded instant reactions from the magazines' editors, he stayed largely out of the editorial fray.

Life had to act the fastest. It was already past deadline; 300,000 copies with Staubach on the cover had actually been printed. By the time Hunt got back to the *Life* editorial floor, assistant publisher Jim Shepley had already ordered the presses stopped. Hunt called publisher C.D. Jackson, who came down and seated himself at Hunt's desk, checking with *Life*'s production crew on costs as preparations for remaking the magazine began. An appealing but trivial feature on debutantes would obviously have to be thrown out. The Staubach story was also tossed, as well as the Newsfronts section. In their place would go 37 pages of assassination coverage and related stories.

In ordinary circumstances, *Life* editors would edit copy and lay out stories in New York, then send everything by plane or wire to the printing plant in Chicago. But now, as was customary when pictures were coming in late, *Life* stationed editors in the printing plant and sent film directly to them. That afternoon, Roy Rowan and senior editor John Dille flew to Chicago, along with associate art director David Stech and layout man John Geist. They set up shop not far from the presses. There, for the next two days, they stayed.

Correspondents swarmed into Dallas: from Miami, bureau chiefs Edwin Reingold for *Time* and Richard Billings for *Life*, along with *Life*'s Michael Durham and David Nevin; from Chicago, *Time*'s Marsh Clark and *Life*'s Jane Scholl; and from New York, *Life* reporter Maynard Parker (later to be editor of *Newsweek*). But since most of the drama occurred in the hours immediately following the shooting, coverage fell largely to those already on the scene. At the moment of assassination *Time*'s Houston bureau chief Mark Sullivan was waiting at Kennedy's next scheduled stop, the Dallas Trade Mart. *Time* White House correspondent Hugh Sidey and *Life* Washington correspondent Thomas Flaherty were aboard one of two press buses that were 50 or 100 yards behind the motorcade as it proceeded from Love Field to the Trade Mart. *Life* photographer Arthur Rickerby was in a separate photographer's car. When the shots were fired, those in the press bus were aware only that something unexpected had happened. The bus stopped for a moment and some reporters jumped off, but Flaherty and others followed what he called "an old rule of *Life*—stay with your wheels." The bus raced on to the Trade Mart, where those aboard learned what had happened and individually made their way to Parkland Memorial Hospital. Others, Sidey among them, persuaded the bus driver to take them. Flaherty's method was to flag down a car and induce the woman behind the wheel to taxi him and a *Newsweek* reporter to Parkland.

Rickerby was there when they arrived. That morning he had taken an exceptionally vibrant color photo of the President and First Lady in the bright sunshine at Love Field, which became a memorable full page in *Life*. At the hospital he captured a stark, affecting black-and-white picture of L.B.J.'s limousine, its back door still open wide, a bouquet of roses abandoned on the seat.

Sidey was also at the hospital, but since *Time*'s deadline was still one day off, it was less urgent for him than for the newspaper and wire-service reporters to file. Phones were already in short supply; Sidey held off. He was, however, with the pack of reporters who first learned from two priests leaving the hospital that Kennedy was dead. A few minutes later, assistant press secretary Malcolm Kilduff made the official announcement to reporters in a temporary pressroom. Sidey flew to Washington that evening—as always, following the President—and filed his report from there.

At *Life*'s Los Angeles bureau, correspondent Thomas Thompson was watching the wire-service printer when the news chattered across. He shouted it out. Pacific Coast regional editor Richard B. Stolley immediately told his secretary to check plane schedules, then called New York for instructions. Assistant managing editor Hugh Moffett told him to get to Dallas if he could. Stolley and Thompson headed straight for the airport, driven by Shana Alexander. Enroute they heard that the President had died. Photographers Allan Grant and Don Cravens joined Stolley and Thompson at the airport. Aboard an airliner teeming with reporters, some sitting in the aisle, they flew to Dallas. Through the open cockpit doorway, they heard the radio: Lyndon Johnson had been sworn in as the new President.

122

In Dallas, Stolley and Thompson split up, each to accomplish on his own an astonishing journalistic coup.

Stolley headed for the Adolphus Hotel, where *Time* and *Life* had set up temporary bureaus, complete with Teletypes. There he learned a fascinating fact from stringer Patsy Swank: a man named Abraham Zapruder had taken a home movie of the assassination, and it could conceivably be valuable.

Stolley simply looked up Zapruder's number in the phone book and began dialing. No one answered. After several hours, sometime in mid-evening, Zapruder himself picked up the phone. Indeed, he had the film and it had been processed. But when Stolley proposed coming out to his house to look at it, Zapruder hesitated. He was exhausted and needed time to think; Stolley should be at his office the next morning at 9.

Zapruder, then 58, "a round man, rather short and bald, with glasses," as Stolley remembered him, owned a small company called Jennifer of Dallas that manufactured dresses. When Zapruder had arrived that Friday morning at work, in a building near the Texas School Book Depository, he had forgotten the movie camera he had intended bringing and was resigned to missing his chance to film the President. But his secretary, Lillian Rogers, who apparently had a good deal of influence over Zapruder, chided him: the President of the United States did not drive past their office every day. Zapruder returned home and fetched the camera, planning on filming from an office window. At the last minute he decided to join the crowd on Elm Street. There, standing on a concrete abutment looking down on Dealey Plaza, he panned his camera steadily as the limousine passed. He later reported that when the shots sounded, he believed they had come from behind him; yet he remained standing and kept filming, shouting, "They've killed him! They've killed him!" until the limousine disappeared beneath an underpass.

Zapruder then returned to his office "incoherent, in a state of shock," according to an employee. Harry McCormick, a reporter for the Dallas *Morning News*, had been standing near Zapruder when the assassination happened. A little later McCormick ran into an acquaintance from the Dallas office of the Secret Service, and together they went to Zapruder's office. There they helped Zapruder get the film processed and have three copies made: one for the Secret Service in Washington, one for the Secret Service in Dallas and one for Zapruder. McCormick also called his friend Holland McCombs, a veteran correspondent for *Time* and *Life* in Latin

America and Texas, who was now working on special assignments. Would *Life* want the film? It certainly would, promised McCombs on his own. Harry McCormick eventually received a $1,500 finder's fee from Time Inc.

Stolley arrived at Zapruder's office at 8 a.m. on Saturday just in time to watch the film as Zapruder showed it to law-enforcement officers. In a small, darkened room he ran the film over and over— "the most dramatic thing I ever saw," Stolley said. "He had a creaky old projector. The sound it made was incongruous with the pictures on the screen."

Then came the inevitable pounding on the door: the rest of the press had discovered Zapruder. In poured the AP, the UPI, the *Saturday Evening Post*, CBS. "They'll tear you apart," Stolley warned, and he begged Zapruder to deal with him first. Zapruder obligingly showed the other reporters the film but asked Stolley to wait in an inner office, where he chatted with Lillian Rogers. By happy coincidence they were both from downstate Illinois, and had a bushel of stories to trade. Soon Zapruder joined them, leaving behind a mob of desperately hungry journalists screaming at him not to make any deals. "He had a stricken look on his face," Stolley recalled. "Lillian calmed him down and said something to him about having grown up in the same part of Illinois as I had."

Partly because of Lillian Rogers's influence, partly because Stolley had been the first of the national press to reach him, partly because he respected *Life* and liked Stolley, Zapruder decided to ignore the mob's advice. He made a deal. Stolley had already talked to Dick Pollard, *Life* director of photography, and been authorized to spend $50,000 for print rights to the film. Zapruder's position was delicate and painful. He had deeply admired Kennedy, had been utterly undone by the assassination and insisted that he wished he had not made the film. But having made it, he realized that it was valuable and that it could ensure his family's financial security. He had obtained affidavits from the lab technicians who had developed and copied the film, swearing that no extra copies had been made— guaranteeing not only the film's integrity, important to authorities, but also its commercial value. At the same time he was tortured by visions of the film being exploited, of barkers in front of tawdry Times Square theaters urging passersby to step in and gawk at the horrid spectacle.

Stolley opened with an offer of $15,000, which quickly rose to nearly $50,000. Meanwhile, the reporters outside were telephoning the inner office to ask what was going on. As a bargaining ploy, Stolley hesitated and told Zapruder he would need permission from headquarters to go as high as $50,000. He picked up the phone. His call, however, went to *Life*'s temporary bureau at the Adolphus Hotel, where Dick Billings answered and listened, flummoxed, as Stolley pretended to ask for special authorization to offer $50,000 but no more.

That amount, plus Stolley's promise that *Life* would not sensationalize the film, satisfied Zapruder. Stolley typed out a crude contract, which both men signed. Stolley then took the original and the one remaining copy of the film and left quickly through a back door, so that the mob of reporters would not tear *him* apart.

Within a short time a courier carrying the film was aboard a plane for Chicago, where Roy Rowan and colleagues selected 31 frames and laid them out across four pages of the magazine. Although the film was in color, to push the magazine to press faster it was reproduced in black-and-white.

Later that Saturday, Stolley returned to *Life*'s office at the Adolphus, where he rejoined his Los Angeles colleague, Tommy Thompson, who was a native of Fort Worth. In those same few hours since their arrival in Dallas, Thompson had also collected a remarkable journalistic treasure, which compared in value with Stolley's own: Lee Harvey Oswald's mother, Marguerite, his wife, Marina, and their two daughters. Thompson recalled:

> I was looking around for some justification for my trip to Dallas and thought, why don't I do a backgrounder? I ran to the police station, where there were several hundred other reporters milling around. There was a rumor that they were going to bring Oswald out. My problem was to find something that would hold until next week. I saw a policeman at the soft-drink machine and in my best Fort Worth accent asked him if he knew where the police had been looking for evidence. And he said they had been out to a house at Oak Cliff.

Thompson and photographer Grant drove out to Dallas' Oak Cliff section. The house turned out to be the one where Oswald had rented a room for several weeks; they were the first reporters to find the place, the landlady informed them, pointing out Oswald's room, a tiny cubicle barren of personal effects. She said the man whom she knew as O.H. Lee didn't socialize a lot, kept pretty much to him-

125

self, but he did make occasional phone calls in what sounded to her like German. (It was, of course, Russian.) She remembered that the calls were to Irving, Texas, about ten miles away. Thompson and Grant headed for Irving. As Thompson remembered:

> In Irving we found the sheriff's dispatcher, and again in my best Texas accent I asked him if there had been any activity in town. Well, some Feds had been in earlier looking for some women. Do you know their names? No. What about an address? Well, he did know the street.

Fortunately, the street was only a few blocks long. By this time it was dark, and Thompson simply approached one of the houses that had its lights on. He was lucky. He knocked on the door and was greeted calmly by Mrs. Ruth Paine, a tall, dark woman who was the owner of the house. She said she had been expecting the press. She invited the two men in, but none of those present—several women, a man in a mechanic's uniform and some children, all watching television—paid much attention.

Mrs. Paine told Thompson that she knew Oswald, and he, excited, began asking her questions. But when he asked her if she thought Oswald could have killed the President, a corpulent woman in a nurse's uniform jumped up and shouted, "I can answer that, I'm Lee's mother." At that moment the bedroom door opened and a slight young woman with a baby in her arms emerged, speaking softly in a foreign language. And who was that? Mrs. Paine explained that it was Oswald's wife, Marina. Only then did Thompson realize what he had found.

He turned his attention to Oswald's mother, Marguerite, who immediately served notice that she wasn't going to talk for free. Asked how much she wanted, she said she wanted a lot—$2,000 would do. Thompson called George Hunt in New York, who refused to authorize the payment; the women might be implicated in a conspiracy to assassinate the President and it would not do to have them receiving large sums from *Life*. Thompson, who recalled being "terrified" that other reporters would discover his story, suggested they all go to a hotel near the Dallas jail—the Adolphus—so they could see Oswald in the morning. Marguerite agreed, but Marina wanted to wait until morning so she would not have to wake her children. Thompson, playing it nervously by ear, said he would return in the morning.

126

Next morning Thompson gathered the two Mrs. Oswalds and Marina's two children and drove them to the Adolphus, guiding them in through a freight entrance. Marguerite now appeared willing to talk for no greater remuneration than a free hotel stay, but she did not make things easy.

It was the FBI, not rival reporters, who eventually tracked Thompson down. Around midday they banged on the door. Thompson let them in and they took the Oswalds away. With what he had gathered from the Oswalds and other sources, Thompson assembled a remarkably comprehensive—and exclusive—2,000-word portrait of the assassin.

Life's coverage of the assassination also included pictures showing reaction around the world and nine pages on the career of Lyndon Johnson. Two pages were by Theodore H. White, who had been a *Time* China correspondent in the 1940s, had resigned and had returned in 1962 to work for *Life* as a contract writer. Immediately on hearing the news in New York, where he had been lunching with Jim Shepley, he flew to Washington and wrote a two-page essay on the final return of the man he had come to know intimately in the course of covering the 1960 campaign.

Not long after the sun rose Sunday morning, the team of editors and layout designers in Chicago finally closed the issue, or thought they had. A few hours later, as they sat on a plane about to take off for New York, Paul Welch of *Life*'s Chicago bureau rushed to the airport with the news that Jack Ruby had just shot Oswald. It was now impossible to make any large changes in the magazine. All that could be done was to alter the headline and the first and last paragraphs of Tommy Thompson's piece and, in 95 percent of the copies, lead the story with a Dallas *Morning News* photo of Ruby aiming point-blank at Oswald's abdomen a moment before firing.* By early afternoon the magazine was finally closed for good.

Time's handling of the assassination was more controversial—then and later. Within minutes after the adjourned lunch at which the news was received, Nation editor Champ Clark, who would be in charge of the main narrative of events, was in his office outlining coverage plans with his writers and researchers, many of them numbed by the news, at least one sobbing openly. Queries went out to the Time-Life news bureaus, after which Clark told the writers to

*Not the Pulitzer Prize-winning Dallas *Times-Herald* picture taken at the exact moment of the shooting.

go home, get some sleep and be back at 4 a.m. There were already 2 million covers printed for what had been planned as *Time*'s cover feature that week on jazz pianist Thelonius Monk; these, of course, were scrapped. Clark then went to confer with managing editor Fuerbringer on the replacement cover. At this point the arguments began. They would continue, well after that issue of *Time* was in print.

Recalled Clark: "I assumed the cover would be Kennedy, but Otto was very firm that it would be Johnson"—specifically, a realistic head-and-shoulders painting of Johnson, a faint smile on his lips, with the Great Seal of the United States painted as a burst of red, white and blue above his right shoulder.

The Johnson cover was one that *Time*, in accordance with custom—in preparation for just such an emergency—already had in hand, engraved and ready for the press. Fuerbringer himself did not much like the cover portrait, but offered several arguments for going ahead with it. First, there was a long-standing tradition that *Time* did not put dead men on its cover. The rule was not ironclad, but nearly so; the magazine should look forward rather than backward. Second, in Champ Clark's recollection, Fuerbringer "explained very clearly that there would be talk of conspiracy, and by putting Johnson on the cover it would show the continuity of government." Third, when Franklin Roosevelt had died, *Time* had put Truman on the cover. And fourth, when *Time* had broken its no-dead-man rule by putting Joseph Stalin on the cover at the time of the Soviet dictator's death, the week's issue had been a notable newsstand failure; Fuerbringer remembered that well, having written the cover story himself.

Clark and Fuerbringer also had to decide about the magazine's tone in reporting the assassination events. It was a somewhat touchy subject, since *Time* had often been critical of the Kennedy administration. Any sort of sustained criticism was obviously out of the question, coming so soon after the shock that had plunged everyone, approving or not, into despondency. On the other hand, unqualified praise of the dead President would sound hypocritical. The two editors decided to pursue—and they largely achieved—a neutral tone, though in spots they erred on both sides of their ideal.

By late Saturday night, an entirely new Nation section, 13 pages long, had been written, edited, checked and closed. The World section's lead story included foreign reaction to the assassination; the Press section looked at how it had been reported; the U.S. Business

128

section discussed its effects on the economy. The exhausted *Time* staff went home. Sunday morning, just as the magazine was about to go on the presses, Jack Ruby shot Oswald. A small group went in to make changes—a few extra paragraphs plus the photo of the shooting—which caught about 90 percent of the press run. Fuerbringer was particularly proud that a sentence could be worked into the Nation lead: "And on Commerce Street in Dallas, in an incident little noted at the time but to assume later significance, Jack Ruby silently closed down his strip-tease joint, the Carousel." *Time* appeared on newsstands and in subscribers' homes on its regular schedule.

Reaction to the assassination issues of both magazines was overwhelming. *Life* sold out within hours of its arrival at newsstands, and readers stood in line waiting for more deliveries. There were reports of copies being sold for $5, $10, $20 (the regular price was 25 cents). The next week's issue, containing pictures of the funeral in color as well as new photos, was another quick sellout. *Life* decided to combine its coverage from both issues in a special memorial edition without advertising. Again demand was huge; by January, 2,750,000 copies had been sold for 50 cents each, but bootleggers could reportedly command $10 or more. So the company ordered a fourth printing of close to 300,000 (of which 80,000 were left over), and by September 1965, Time Inc. had earned $102,000 on the special edition, which it contributed to the charity of Mrs. Kennedy's choice: the Kennedy Memorial Library.

In response to its two issues following the event plus the memorial edition, *Life* received a staggering half million pieces of mail (including orders for the memorial issue). In explaining it, one can point to the extraordinary power of *Life*'s coverage and to the important fact, sometimes lost sight of in the years since the use of videotape has become commonplace, that the Zapruder film was the only record of the assassination as it happened—the only connection to the awful, palpable reality of the event. But at least as important an explanation was the popularity of the President. Many of the letters had little to say about *Life*'s coverage; they were notes of affection for Kennedy.

Time received about 3,000 letters, most of them tributes to Kennedy. Of 777 that commented directly on *Time*'s coverage, 634 were critical. One reason: the *Time* publisher's letter, which appears at the front of every issue over the name of the publisher (Bernhard

Auer at that point) but which is always written by someone on the editorial staff—in this case, assistant managing editor Griffith. He had received word from Luce not to forget Kennedy's fascination with *Time* and the political importance he accorded its influence. By the time the magazine was being read, a few days later, the nation's mood of mourning had descended into blackness, deepened by television coverage of the funeral, and the letter sounded crassly self-serving. It read in part:

> The President had a special feeling about *Time*. In the study of his penthouse suite in the Hotel Carlyle, an alert New York *Times* reporter recently noted a white White House phone, a box of Havana cigars and that week's issue of *Time*. In Washington, the President got his copy early, and sometimes within an hour was on the phone to our White House correspondent with comments—wry, appreciative or angry—on what had been written about him. He said on several occasions that he regarded *Time* as the most important magazine in America, for it reached the kinds of people in both parties that he most wanted to influence. And when surprised, in talking to leaders abroad, by the close knowledge of some domestic U.S. event, he said that he had asked where they had learned about it, and was invariably told, "In *Time*."

Complaints from readers poured in. Wrote one: "*Time* sees fit to eulogize itself rather than the late President."

Time Inc.'s other magazines reacted to the assassination in their own way. *Sports Illustrated* ran a small item on the question of whether sports contests scheduled for that weekend should have been played (some were canceled). The following week *SI* ran a memorial piece on "The President Who Loved Sport." *Fortune*, then a monthly, had just completed printing its December issue; the January issue carried a cover story by assistant managing editor Max Ways reflecting on Johnson as man and President.

Life's connection with the assassination story did not end with the events in Dallas. Just a week later, the day after Thanksgiving, Teddy White was called from his dentist's chair by a message from Hyannis Port: Jacqueline Kennedy urgently wanted to speak with him; she had things to tell him in person. It was, once again, long past *Life*'s regular closing time, but two pages of the magazine were opened up for White. He hired a limousine to drive him from New York through a hellish rainstorm to Hyannis Port. There, late into the night, Mrs. Kennedy related her experience of the shooting and, more important, her concern for what history would record of the Kennedy administration. After she had finished, White dictated his account by telephone to two *Life* editors and a typist in New York. Probably best remembered from the article is the story Mrs. Kennedy told about her husband's favorite song, which she used to play on an old Victrola; White made one line from it the theme of his still famous essay: "Don't let it be forgot, that once there was a spot, for one brief shining moment that was known as Camelot."

The company had quickly strengthened its hold on the Zapruder film. On Sunday, the day after Stolley had purchased print rights in Dallas, C.D. Jackson viewed the film in New York and, like Zapruder himself, was both horrified and frightened that the horror might be exploited. Since it had become known that *Life* had bought only print rights, Zapruder had been hounded by movie and television producers, whom he evaded. Jackson was so upset by the film that he decided Time Inc. should buy all rights—film, broadcast, everything worldwide. Stolley and Zapruder met again on Monday, this time in the office of Zapruder's attorney, and came to terms: $100,000 plus the original $50,000 for all rights. (Zapruder immediately gave $25,000 to the widow of J.D. Tippett, the Dallas police officer Oswald had shot after the assassination.)

Time Inc. rarely used the film for any purpose, almost never granted permission for outside use and exercised neither its movie nor its broadcast rights. The original film was slightly damaged in the company photo lab, causing the loss of six frames, but a number of copies had already been made. (Nonetheless, conspiracy theorists detected profound significance in this accident.) In 1975 the company returned the original film to Zapruder's heirs (he had died of cancer in 1970), selling it to them for $1, and they in turn gave it to the National Archives. (Time Inc. risked being sued by the Zapruder heirs if it gave the film directly to the Archives.) Time Inc. kept a few copies for its own archives.

Stolley wrote a detailed account of the Zapruder film episode for *Esquire* in 1973. Five years later, Teddy White, in his journalistic memoir *In Search of History*, wrote of his post-assassination interview with Mrs. Kennedy. Not long before he died at 49, in October 1982, Tommy Thompson wrote a meticulous but fictionalized version of his encounter with Oswald's wife and mother in

131

his best-selling novel *Celebrity* ("Hurricane Mama" in that book is Marguerite Oswald).*

As time passed and controversy continued over Oswald's motivation, *Life* was occasionally able to add new details to the whole inexplicable story. From Marina and Marguerite Oswald the magazine bought a number of photographs including the famous snapshot of Oswald proudly holding the rifle he later used in the assassination; this made a cover for *Life*'s February 21, 1964, issue. *Life* also published, in its July 10, 1964, issue, excerpts from the diary Oswald had kept in Russia from October 1959 to March 1962. The diary was obtained through the good offices of Holland McCombs, and Marina Oswald had no part in the transaction, but to avoid legal problems *Life* "bought" the copyright from her for $20,000.

About the same time, *Life* was also negotiating with Gerald Ford, then a Congressman from Michigan and member of the Warren Commission. Ford was considering writing a book about Oswald and asked *Life* editor Ed Thompson's help in finding a publisher. He also offered *Life* the serial rights. Excerpts from Ford's book appeared in *Life*'s October 2, 1964, issue, concurrent with the release of the Warren Report. Nine years later, when Ford was facing Senate confirmation as Vice President, the propriety of his dealing with *Life* while still a member of the Warren Commission was challenged. Ford argued convincingly that he had leaked no information in advance of the official report, nor, in fact, had he been under obligation of secrecy.

One other assassination narrative that *Life* badly wanted to excerpt was William Manchester's book *The Death of a President*. Produced with the cooperation of the Kennedy family, relying on private Kennedy documents, the book was originally scheduled for publication after the fifth anniversary of the assassination, in November 1968. But by July 1967, a manuscript was ready. Nine Time Inc. editors and executives read the manuscript. All thought it too laudatory of John Kennedy, too disparaging of Lyndon Johnson and Texas governor John Connally. But all felt it was compelling reading—the terrible events of Dallas as the Kennedy family had experienced them—and that *Life* should have the book. *Life*'s bid of $560,000 for magazine rights, in addition to $500,000 to be spent on promotion, went in to Manchester's agent 90 minutes before the deadline, on Friday, July 29. An hour later, *Look* came in with its bid, lower than *Life*'s, but subsequently raised to top

*Doubleday & Company Inc., 1982.

it. *Life* offered to go still higher; a night and a day of telephoning followed. That Saturday afternoon, *Life* was abruptly shut out; the Manchester book went to *Look*. *Life* felt, as one editor put it, "jobbed."

Two factors counted against *Life*. One was Robert Kennedy's apparent preference for *Life*'s rival. The second, more fundamental, was *Life*'s unwillingness to name Manchester a "special editorial consultant" and cede him control over the book's presentation—layout, pictures, captions, etc.—in the magazine's pages. This *Look* would grant; *Life*, as a matter of journalistic principle, would not.

8

Into the Television Age

TELEVISION WORRIED TIME INC. —and lured it too. The first order of business for the corporate research and development department that editorial director Hedley Donovan had established in 1962 was to study "Time Inc.'s role in and about TV." Reporting in March 1963, *Time* senior editor Henry Grunwald, who produced the study, made the case for taking up television's journalistic challenge:

Before television is anything else, before it is entertainment or information or education, it is a *presence* in the house . . . before it even reaches the mind, it reaches a mood: it breaks into the routine, the daily affairs, if you will, even the loneliness, of 50 million dwellings in this country . . .

I find it a little painful to think of how little Time [Inc.] has contributed to television so far while, by contrast, in every decade since the founding of *Time* it has made a major and distinguished contribution to printed journalism—not to mention *The March of Time*'s contribution to film and radio . . . [Time Inc.] could and should be present on that odd rectangle of light and shade which exists in almost every home, and which has already influenced American politics, speech and folklore.

The company was, of course, already present on the ownership side of television's odd rectangle of light and shade. Where Time Inc. was largely absent was on the programming side, in the production of documentaries, public affairs programs and other shows for television utilizing the by-product of Time Inc. pictorial and print journalism, and the creative talents available around the magazines. Here, the experience to date had been frustrating; in fact, the frustrations were to continue for years. It was not until the 1970s that the company found a formula for dazzling success in television—of an unforeseen sort.

Time Inc. had begun a series of investments in television and associated AM and FM radio stations in 1952 with a half interest in an Albuquerque station (later sold). By 1963, the year of the R & D report, Broadcast was contributing 14 percent of the company's pretax profits—$3.5 million. Just the year before, the company had brought television holdings back up to the five-station maximum then permitted by the FCC in the commercially most valuable VHF (very high frequency) range. These stations were KLZ, Denver; WFBM, Indianapolis; WTCN, Minneapolis; WOOD, Grand Rapids; KOGO, San Diego. Located in medium-sized but growing cities, all were doing well except Minneapolis, which had lost its ABC affiliation and would be sold in 1964. Of the remaining stations, Denver was a CBS affiliate, the others NBC. After the Minneapolis sale, Time Inc. bought another NBC affiliate, KERO, a UHF (ultrahigh frequency) station with no radio service, in Bakersfield, California.

The properties were grouped as a subsidiary, Time-Life Broadcast, Inc., under Time Inc. vice president Weston C. Pullen Jr., a protégé of Stillman's, who had been instrumental in the broadcast acquisitions. Pullen was then 39, a brawny, hard-driving executive—a "have gun, will travel type," as Stillman characterized him. He had won his letter as a guard on the Princeton football team, commanded PT boats during World War II and, at Time Inc., had won some notoriety as an after-hours drummer in New York's 52nd Street jazz joints.

From the start, the stations were run as largely autonomous businesses—"kegs on their own bottoms," as Stillman put it. Local management was, as a rule, left in place. Time Inc. exercised no oversight of broadcast content either, although in the news area the company had given a helping hand by setting up a radio-TV news bureau in Washington in 1958 to provide the stations with locally oriented coverage of federal government activities. In 1961, another bureau was opened in New York to tap the Time Inc. magazine correspondents' news files. Acting as an overall broadcast consultant to Time Inc. was Denver's Hugh B. Terry, senior station manager of the broadcast group.

Station ownership had not created a captive market for Time Inc., nor did it offer much as a testing laboratory for television programming. For one thing, the stations themselves were not greatly interested; their network affiliations already supplied most of their program needs. Also, original programming was expensive. It was unlikely that Time Inc. could recoup the production costs from its own stations. Accordingly, the company looked to the larger territory beyond—syndication of programs to other stations or to the networks.

Of the early experiments, the most promising were the television documentaries being produced, under *Life*'s aegis, by Robert Drew. A former *Life* correspondent and assistant picture editor, Drew had come back from a Nieman Fellowship at Harvard in 1955 to propose a "mass-audience weekly news show in TV," adapting *Life*'s pictorial techniques for television.

Most filmed documentaries, in Drew's opinion, were "lectures with picture illustrations." He was out to capture reality, using a lightweight camera and synchronous sound equipment to record events as they occurred, instead of reconstructing them, as in conventional documentaries. Drew's first *Life* film, *Bullfight in Malaga*, was intensely dramatic, shot in blood-spattered detail by his colleague, cameraman Richard Leacock. Intended as a promotion piece for the magazine, it showed how *Life* put together a picture story photographed by Larry Burrows and James Burke on the historic duels between matadors Antonio Ordóñez and Luis Miguel Dominguín. (Ironically, both photographers later died on *Life* assignment. Burke fell from a Himalayan mountain ledge while photographing a color essay in India in 1964. Burrows was killed in the Vietnam War.)

Drew made two more films based on *Life* stories, then was moved to Time-Life Broadcast to produce full-length documentaries for sale to the networks. His first, *Primary*, which followed John Kennedy and Hubert Humphrey down the Democratic primary campaign trail in Wisconsin, won the 1960 Flaherty Award for documentary films. CBS bought his next film, *On the Pole*, which was about the Indianapolis 500 auto race. Impressed, ABC contracted with Time Inc. for four Drew documentaries to be shown under commercial sponsorship.

136

As Drew won critical acclaim, Pullen grandly predicted that Time Inc. would reap a potential $1 million annual profit from first-run showings and residual rights to the documentaries. In 1961 Time-Life Broadcast had spun Drew off on his own, as Robert Drew Associates, with Time Inc. continuing to back him with financing, equipment and sales help. But Drew's artistry came at a price. Costs could not be recovered. In 1963 Time Inc. bowed out, retaining title to the films Drew had made under its sponsorship. (Finally in 1981 they were sold to Drew, who had continued as an independent producer.)

In the early 1960s, Time-Life Broadcast continued to nurture programming within the corporation. Inevitably, thoughts turned to reviving *The March of Time*. A 13-part series was constructed of excerpts of original *MOT* footage from the 1930s and 1940s, with a narrative update by former U.S. ambassador to the United Nations Henry Cabot Lodge Jr.* But for all their vintage flavor, the films found no takers and were shelved.

The news programming effort for both radio and TV had got a boost by the assignment of Time Inc.'s most senior editorial hand, Manfred Gottfried, to the broadcast area, where he personally supervised the production of a pilot series of background reports for radio, drawing on the resources of the Time-Life News Service. The results were uneven and the series was not continued.

Attempts to adapt magazine material to television form were only marginally more successful. A *Fortune* story on the Jonathan Logan dress-manufacturing company was turned into a documentary called *$100 Million in Rags*, as the pilot of a proposed "Men of Fortune" series. It was shown as part of a Hartford, Connecticut, pay-TV experiment, then remained unwanted. On a more ambitious scale was an hour-long film, *The American Commitment: South Vietnam*, also with narration by Ambassador Lodge, which was produced as the first of a series dealing with America's global obligations. It received favorable reviews and was bought by 14 independent stations, thereby recovering about half its costs. "The networks, of course, refused to touch it," reported Edgar Smith, then a vice president of Time-Life Broadcast, in an October 1964 summary of the division's programming accomplishments.

The year before, Smith had written a grim memo to Pullen. "The

---

*As a Washington newspaperman in 1924-25, Lodge had been *Time*'s first stringer, or parttime correspondent. After running for vice president on the Republican ticket in 1960, he was hired by Luce to be an international affairs adviser to Time Inc.

137

broadcasting landscape as viewed by a newly arrived visitor from the magazine planet," Smith wrote, "appears extremely rugged—and even forbidding." He ticked off the obstacles to Time Inc.'s exploiting its journalistic resources in television programming. News-related programming was where Time Inc.'s talents lay; entertainment, occupying over 80 percent of air time, was where the television money was:

> Therefore, unless Time Inc. is prepared to engage in the production of such frothy fare as *Bonanza* and *The Beverly Hillbillies*, it must seek its programming fortunes primarily in that relatively small section of the TV industry labeled "News and Public Affairs"—and clearly posted by the networks with large signs reading: "Keep Out" . . . They not only don't think they need Time Inc.; they regard Time Inc. as potentially dangerous.

Even for the networks, Smith noted, news was a profitless proposition. In 1962, CBS, NBC and ABC together had spent $66 million on news and public affairs, running up operating deficits of $31 million.

By late 1964, a corporate consensus was emerging that Time Inc. could not succeed in its chosen area of news-related programming; the distribution roadblock was insurmountable. Some of the disappointment had been reflected in a memo circulated to Time Inc. executives by Gottfried:

> Looking at these efforts with a fresh eye . . . I believe it fair to call them a failure—that is, a failure in the sense that a military reconnaissance is a failure when it finds an enemy position is too strong to be taken . . . Several people here have ideas for changes in strategy.

A strategy change did come. It was in the form of a decision to suspend Time-Life Broadcast's own production efforts and instead enlist the collaboration of outside producers with proven TV experience. The first collaboration, with documentary filmmaker David Wolper, was another try at reactivating *The March of Time*, using the old name and some of the old techniques, but on current topics.

The initial product was a behind-the-scene view of Lyndon Johnson, entitled *Seven Days in the Life of a President*. It was syndicated to individual stations and first aired in October 1965. The critics were less than thrilled; the New York *Times* headlined its review "Time Marches On, Awkwardly." Relations soon soured between

138

the partners in the venture. The "editors of *Time* and *Life*," as they were identified in the screen credits, carped at the scripts; Wolper complained that editorial changes were running up costs. After eight weekly shows the collaboration ended. No others were tried.

Time-Life Broadcast's programming efforts, costing a little more than $2 million between 1960 and 1964, hardly dented profits. By 1965 Broadcast's pretax income was more than $5.5 million. There was concern about the stations' future, however; the FCC had proposed reducing the maximum holdings of any one owner in the top 50 markets to three stations, of which only two could be in the VHF range. Actually those changes were never carried out. But the prospect was real enough to steer Time-Life Broadcast in a new direction in television investment—toward cable TV.

Two avenues into the cable business were open. One was to own and manage the wire systems themselves: CATV, or community antenna television. The other was in supplying the programs to be transmitted by wire. CATV, first conceived as a means of transmitting television to remote areas where over-the-air signals were faint or blocked, had also caught on in other areas where viewers were finding that it offered what *Life* once described as "mirror-clear, ghostless, blizzardless, wiggleless, fadeless, unconfounded-by-airplanes-or-your-neighbor's-power-saw" television reception. As early as 1962, Eldon Campbell, manager of Time Inc.'s Indianapolis station, became concerned about proposed CATV ventures on the outer edge of his market. He had urged the company to take an interest in the new medium.

The profits in CATV were certain, once investment costs were recovered. A system functioned as a sort of utility, holding the franchise to an area. The system operator simply sat back and collected stipulated fees from his customers. But cable could also serve as a medium for any of the various pay-TV services then coming in for discussion, and this offered a new dimension. If programs could be beamed directly by wire into selected homes, then viewers could be charged for what they watched. For its supplier, pay-TV became more like a magazine, dependent on subscriber acceptance.

In his 1963 television report, Grunwald had weighed the respective virtues of the two approaches to cable. "The attractive part about CATV is that it clearly makes money and would start paying off on investment rapidly and handsomely. The less attractive part is that it is, to say the least, uncreative." Supplying programs for

139

pay-TV was more in Time Inc.'s line, another form of journalism. "Time Inc. would have the great advantage . . . not now available in conventional television, of dealing directly with the public, the only consideration being, as in the magazine business, what the public will want to pay for." Predicting that "pay television would be a reality in five years from now," Grunwald urged that Time Inc. stake out a position.

Time-Life Broadcast opted for CATV. By early 1964, it had received authorization from corporate management to explore opportunities actively, looking toward an eventual commitment of $10 million or more. An enthusiastic presentation to the Time Inc. board by Pullen in January 1965 expounded on the rewards of cable. With the directors' approval of a $5 million investment, to be ventured on buying minority interests in CATV systems, Broadcast representatives fanned out across the country scouting the opportunities. Edgar Smith headed the operation; "Edgar's Tigers," the scouts were called. By June 1965, cable investments had been made in Terre Haute, Kokomo and Marion, Indiana; Lima, Ohio; Bakersfield; and three systems in Michigan.

Meanwhile, closer to home—on Time Inc.'s own doorstep in Manhattan—a potentially more promising opportunity in cable had emerged. Rich and densely populated, New York seemed especially ripe for wired TV. The "canyon" effect of the city's skyscrapers on broadcast signals gave New Yorkers some of the worst over-the-air television reception in the country, and several firms were fighting for CATV franchises. Of these, Sterling Information Services, Ltd., a subsidiary of Sterling Communications, Inc., founded by an imaginative and aggressive entrepreneur named Charles F. Dolan, seemed to have got the jump on its competitors.

In 1961, Sterling had received authorization from the New York Board of Estimate to go into the underground ducts of the Empire City Subway Company* to bring its Teleguide service of news, shopping and sightseeing information to some 35,000 New York hotel rooms. In 1963, Sterling's authorization to wire buildings for Teleguide was extended to include most of the borough of Manhattan. The only franchise applicant yet authorized to lay cables under the New York streets, Dolan envisioned converting his closed circuit service into a full-fledged CATV system for Manhattan apartment

---

*A wholly owned subsidiary (incorporated in 1890) of the New York Telephone Co., which constructs and leases the ducts under the streets of Manhattan and the Bronx that carry the wires of the telephone company, Western Union and, more recently, the cable companies.

buildings. Beyond that lay the possibility of inaugurating pay-TV over the same system.

By early 1965, Sterling had laid 17 miles of cable. With costs expected to run $300,000 a mile, Sterling was short of capital. Dolan had refinanced once, selling a 60 percent interest to Elroy McCaw, formerly one of the owners of the Denver broadcast stations that Time Inc. had bought in 1954, and two of his associates: William Lear, developer of the Learjet, and former Secretary of the Treasury Robert Anderson.

In April, Time Inc.'s board approved a $1,250,000 investment in Sterling Information, representing a 20 percent equity. On December 31, 1965, a Solomonic division of New York's cable territory between Sterling and a competing franchise applicant cut Manhattan in two, giving Sterling "interim consent" to wire the island's southern half, including much of wealthy Park Avenue, the midtown hotel district and Wall Street. Yet desirable as Sterling's territory seemed, and demonstrable as the need for cable service was, a hole in the New York streets was literally opening at Time-Life Broadcast's feet, into which many millions more would be poured over the coming years. It was from the Manhattan venture, however, that a major profit center of Time Inc., as large as magazine publishing, was eventually to come.

CHAPTER
9
────────────────

Sports Illustrated
Goes over the Hump

STUBBORN DETERMINATION, journalistic instinct and a paternal fondness for this last of the Time Inc. magazines he personally sired help explain why Luce stuck with *Sports Illustrated* through ten straight years of losses. An encouraging trend in the numbers—the magazine's losses were falling each year, not rising—also buoyed his confidence that *SI* would eventually succeed. Even before it reached its first million circulation, Luce enjoyed challenging *SI* editors to define the shape of the magazine when it reached its second million, as he was confident it would.

Still, Luce was annoyed by the disparaging comments, inside Time Inc. and out, that he had little personal interest in or knowledge of sport—"didn't know whether you stuffed a football or blew it up," as an *SI* executive once remarked. Luce's boyhood in China, away from American sport, had put him at a disadvantage. But he was "really annoyed," Luce said, by a magazine account (incorrect) that at his first exposure to major league baseball, he had mistaken the seventh-inning stretch for the end of the game and had got up to leave. Speaking at an *SI* sales convention a few months later, Luce undertook to set the record straight.

"The point of that story was that I didn't know anything about sport, and cared even less," Luce complained. "So one night I got

to brooding about it and suddenly I began to think about the sports
I've engaged in . . . I don't mean tangentially or anything like that,
but earnestly engaged in."

I played on the senior class football team of the Hotchkiss
School. Besides class football—a very serious proposition—I
seriously engaged in the following: cricket, soccer, lacrosse,
tennis, squash, golf, swimming, gymnastics, cross-country,
yachting, croquet, riding, skeet shooting, bird shooting (quail,
duck, pheasant, grouse, woodcock), animal shooting (deer),
fishing (trout, bass, deep sea, and also one 20-foot shark).

Furthermore, *Sports Illustrated* occasionally acknowledges
the validity of indoor sports, among which I boast bridge . . .
also chess, also bezique (with Winston Churchill), also gin
rummy, dominoes, Parcheesi, Monopoly and backgammon.

Whatever Luce's prior acquaintance with sport, he had set about to
enlarge his sporting knowledge after the magazine's founding in
1954. With *SI*'s first managing editor, Sid James, and others as
guides and informants, Luce started going to as many sports events
as he could—World Series games, boxing and basketball at Madison
Square Garden and, at least once, to the racetrack near his home in
Arizona, where Luce's reportorial curiosity took him into the jockeys' steam room to watch them sweat off weight. *Life*'s Ed Thompson recalled a college basketball game, when Luce observed one
team trying to protect its lead by freezing the ball. "No good," Luce
said. "What Charlie Stillman taught me was that you can't survive
by hoarding. It's like making money. Any small boy can save
money, but you've got to spend money to make money. The team
that's ahead now is going to lose." So it did.

Time Inc. sustained pretax losses of $33,689,000, including $3,278,000
in prepublication expense, before *SI* turned the corner. The *SI* story
was the reverse of *Life*'s. Television hurt *Life*. For *SI*, television
helped create an audience.

Corporate planning for *SI* had foreseen "the emergence . . . of a
new leisure class—young, energetic, well educated, influential, anx-
ious to participate actually and vicariously in the tremendous array
of leisure-time activities available in an affluent age." Not so clearly
foreseen was the emergent growth of big-money spectator sports.
Via network television and jet air travel whisking teams across country overnight, major sports went national. And year round as well.

From the outset, *SI* had treated sport as a subject unconfined by regional boundaries or local loyalties. One veteran of the magazine's earliest days observed: "Long before television, *SI* started considering sport as of national interest. If you had a fascinating fishing story in Oregon, it was of interest to people all over the country." Television's huge audiences confirmed that anew. By 1969, as *SI*'s William Oscar Johnson wrote, even a bowling tournament could attract 13 million viewers, while the Super Bowl would find no less than "60 million citizens arranged . . . in darkened parlors, behind drawn sun-porch blinds, beneath lightless bulbs in kitchen ceilings, in a million dim basements with knotty pine nailed over cement blocks . . . bathed as one in the moon-gray glow of black-and-white cathode tubes or the ghostly green-peach of living color."

Nonetheless, *SI* had encountered difficulty in defining its editorial approach to those transfixed millions, and even greater trouble selling that approach to advertising space buyers along Madison Avenue. *SI* became a corporate problem drawing in virtually everyone from Luce and Larsen on down. In 1957, Linen, then publisher of *Time*, was assigned additionally to lend a hand at *SI*. More than once, Luce had invited editorial executives of the other Time Inc. magazines to give their critiques of *SI*'s performance. "There were more doctors trying to fix *SI* than was really good for *SI*," Heiskell recalled.

SI's initial difficulty was, as Sid James put it, the advertisers' tendency "to consider sport a mug proposition worthy of attention as an advertising medium only for sports equipment and hemorrhoid remedies." After the turn of the decade, this had been partially overcome and *SI*'s advertising base had broadened appreciably. Automotive and alcoholic beverage advertising trailed menswear at first; sporting goods, important early on, declined in relative importance; cameras, radios, toiletries, travel and insurance were growing. In hopes of paving the way to further ad diversification, *SI*'s enterprising ad sales director, Llewellyn L. (Pete) Callaway Jr., in mid-1961 persuaded the media buyer's bible, *Standard Rate & Data Service*, to list *SI* as a news as well as a sports magazine. Callaway later enlisted Allen Reffler, an energetic ad salesman from *Life*, to spark a drive for corporate advertising, up to then an untapped field for *SI*.

Still, too many of *SI*'s advertisers were not renewing. Too many sales, also, were for partial pages—"scrabbling for that *last* buck," Heiskell, not unappreciatively, described *SI*'s advertising sales effort. *Life*'s C.D. Jackson, after talking to some advertisers in California, wondered why *SI* could not break into *The New Yorker*'s monopoly of offbeat, "stylish," "fun" advertising.

On the editorial side, Donovan suggested in a memo to Luce in September 1958 that *SI* give more attention to the "sociology" of sport, "more articles where sports intersect with the rest of the reader's life: family, friends, business, money, prestige, etc." Les Girls, an informal panel of professional women assembled by Time Inc. promotion consultant and novelist (*Gentleman's Agreement*) Laura Z. Hobson, thought *SI* neglected women's interests. An outside analysis of subscription nonrenewals concluded that *SI* was not giving enough attention to major sports; but from within Time Inc., Larsen saw the problem as exactly the contrary. "If in order to get our second million, we lean toward . . . the direction of the big sports," Larsen wrote, "neither the audience we get, nor the magazine's appearance, will improve our advertising story."

Just before Christmas 1959, Luce finally decided the time had come for "a major, formal reconsideration of the *SI* formula and its execution." He asked Sid James to devote a month to the project, while Donovan sat in as *SI*'s acting managing editor. Assistant managing editor Andre Laguerre was assigned meanwhile to mock up a sample issue of the magazine as if he were in charge.

In itself, Luce's request to Laguerre was not unusual; Luce had a habit of playing off his editors against one another. In this case, more was involved. Laguerre was a favorite of Luce's, and had served for a while as his personal assistant. And it was with the understanding—at least, so Laguerre perceived it—that he would eventually take over as managing editor that he had been brought to *SI*. Now, however, Laguerre was impatient, openly discontented; only recently, he had gone to Luce asking to be transferred elsewhere in the company.

The upshot was a decision by Luce, reflecting the recommendations of Donovan and *SI* publisher Arthur R. Murphy Jr., to reshuffle the *SI* top command. Laguerre was named managing editor, effective April 1960. Sid James, whose ebullient optimism had helped sustain the magazine during its toughest time, was named publisher, succeeding Murphy. A plain-spoken Boston Irishman, Murphy had in his years at *SI* injected much of his own earthy realism into the magazine's publishing operations. He now moved up to head Time Inc.'s corporate production department.

Laguerre, then 45, born of a French father and a British mother, was an unlikely sort to be running an American sports magazine.

But he had been a baseball fan since high school days in San Francisco, where his father, a diplomat, was stationed for several years in the French consulate. Later he spent a year in London as a reporter and was working in France for British newspapers and *Paris-Soir* when war came in 1939. Drafted into the French army, he nearly drowned in the Dunkirk evacuation when his ship struck a mine. He ended up in London doing sentry duty outside General Charles de Gaulle's Free French headquarters. Taking advantage of the situation to write the General a letter suggesting that his press relations needed improvement, Corporal First Class Laguerre found himself summoned into the General's presence and commanded to take on that task himself. Laguerre ended the war as General de Gaulle's press chief.

In 1946 he came to Time Inc. as a correspondent in the Paris bureau (for a while doubling as a horse-racing columnist for the Paris *Herald-Tribune*, under the name of Eddie Snow). Luce was much taken with Laguerre—"one of the best political journalists in the world"—and in 1948 named him to head the Paris bureau. It was a time of mounting tension over France's involvement in Indochina, and at one point the French government, angered by Laguerre's reporting on French military corruption, threatened to deport him; belatedly it was discovered that Laguerre was still a French citizen and undeportable. After that episode, Luce put Laguerre on his personal staff in New York for a year, then sent him back to Europe as London bureau chief and chief European correspondent. In 1956, Luce, knowing Laguerre's "secret vice, which was an unconscionable attention to sport," made him the "surprise" offer of the *SI* assistant managing editor's job. Laguerre accepted—reluctantly, however. Luce recalled that the deal was wrapped up on a wintry walk through the Tuileries in Paris.

In a company that has harbored many strange ducks, Laguerre was certainly one of the strangest. A heavy-set, rather shambling man, seldom without a cigar, he drank his lunch and hardly slept at night, rising at 3 a.m. to edit copy in the bedroom of his Fifth Avenue apartment; an inveterate horse player, he placed bets nearly every day and, according to friends, usually won; an aloof, close-mouthed loner, he was almost unknown in the sports world his magazine covered. Laguerre shunned Time Inc.'s clubby corporate sociability, participating unwillingly even in the executive lunches where Luce assembled the Time Inc. managing editors. If Laguerre attended, he would sit wordlessly nursing a drink, refusing to be drawn into the conversation.

146

To Luce himself Laguerre could be almost insultingly blunt. No corporate history would be complete without recounting the story—possibly apocryphal, but characteristic enough of both men to be true—of Laguerre's put-down of Luce during a public affairs conference. After expounding on the state of the world as he saw it, Luce turned to Laguerre for approval: "Wouldn't you say so, Andre?" Replied Laguerre: "No, Harry, I wouldn't." Laguerre's speeches at *SI* gatherings were famously brief. "Last year," said Laguerre, at one staff Christmas party, "I was asked to say a couple of words and I said them: 'Merry Christmas.' This year I would like to expand a bit: 'Merry Christmas and hello.' "

His managerial style could be frightening. An authoritarian boss "with intentions carved in stone and zero tolerance for surprises," Laguerre was, in the description of Ezra Bowen, one of *SI*'s early staff:

> The kind that made clear not only what pleased him but what he damn well expected. You could decide for yourself whether or not he would get it. He always did because he was scary . . . He spoke perhaps once a week and with shuddering impact. For example, one day in his office . . . I found myself rattling on at great length about some special project in which I was going to send two photographers and an artist to Japan, and how I had hired a couple of authors, and how seven months hence we would run a cover and 32 inside pages. Laguerre stared stonily at me for a full minute while the ashes from a cigar tumbled in tiny gray smudges down his shirt front, and finally said with syllables like a measured thud of a death march, "You mean, that's what you're *proposing*," I said yes, right, and we shortened sail.*

But Laguerre commanded enormous respect and loyalty, and was, in his own way, approachable. Every noon he adjourned to the bar of a Chinese restaurant next to the Time & Life Building where, for several hours, he held court—a sort of king's levee in which staff complaints were aired, tales traded, story ideas floated. Every year too, during the racing season, Laguerre led an expedition to Saratoga for several days at the track and nights at poker, and back to New York in time to get the next issue of the magazine out.

Laguerre took a serious view of sport. It was "an important

Henry and Other Heroes (A *Sports Illustrated* Book. Little, Brown and Company, 1974), p. 243.

branch of human activity," he once told Luce. "Quality of achievement—physical, intellectual, aesthetic or moral—is the essence of competitive sport; this could not be said of politics, nor of many of the aspects of society with which general magazines have to deal." An editor with superb story sense, Laguerre also took a broad view of sport, encouraging his writers to look for the odd angle; during his tenure, *SI* covered the Miss America pageant and TV game shows as sporting contests, and ballet dancing as athletics of the most demanding sort.

But it was to "hard" sport that *SI* should devote its primary attention, Laguerre made plain in taking over the managing editorship. With the mockup of a sample issue that he sent up to Luce in January 1960, Laguerre also submitted a declaration of editorial intent. It dealt with the question, raised so many times already in the magazine's short life, of how to allocate editorial space between out-and-out sports coverage for the sports enthusiast and features such as bridge, food, fashion and travel that *SI* had been providing for a more general audience. Wrote Laguerre:

> My premise is that we are a news and feature magazine about sport. We have a certain "classy" view of sport—unlike, say, the average bleacher fan on Chicago's south side—which should not be reflected snobbishly or cutely, but which calls for quality of mind in our approach . . .
>
> There is a good deal of talk about the "general" factor in *SI*. Sometimes it rings as if it were somehow desirable to conceal the fact that we are a magazine about sport in the first place . . .
>
> Should there . . . be more "hard sport" and less of the other? Many readers and many of our staff would say yes. They resent it when . . . we are overloaded with fashions or the recreations of the wealthy. They share in the sport mystique; some of them regard sport as an art form, and most of them as more than recreation; there may be some immaturity in their attitude, but these people have the flame which makes any journalistic enterprise interesting, and with which we tamper at our peril.

Laguerre was ready to keep a certain proportion of general material, "because sport is a rapidly expanding interest in this country, and we ought to be ready to welcome the increasing number of converts, neophytes and mildly-generally-interested types." But, he said, "to increase the quota would be to out-general ourselves; the result might or might not be a successful magazine, but it wouldn't be a sport magazine."

Laguerre described his proposed changes as "not . . . too brusque to fit into [*SI*'s] normal evolutionary pattern." As implemented over the succeeding months, they involved eliminating some editorial fixtures while rearranging others, in the process giving picture and text play to the major news of sport, weeding out the peripherals. The magazine's photographic miscellany, entitled Wonderful World of Sport, was dropped; pictures now related more directly to the main news stories. The "wonderful world" was Luce's own phrase, but Laguerre felt it "disbars fine pictures of the grave or dramatic"—for instance, a photo of an unhorsed jockey lying in the mud was not exactly wonderful. Also dropped was a section called Events & Discoveries, four pages of discursive *New Yorker*-style commentary, including light verse and often a full-page cartoon; the half a dozen writers, among them the magazine's best and most experienced, assigned to the section could be better deployed elsewhere. Taking its place was a briefer, brighter Scorecard section. Food coverage, which by Laguerre's count had been getting a third more space in the magazine than basketball, was shrunk, as were fashion and travel.

The sum of the changes was a more cohesive magazine, more sharply focused, with a pattern that, once established, stayed virtually the same over the next two decades. That pattern consisted of a tandem of strong news leads on the week's big events; a "feature well" at the middle of the book, containing one or two in-depth takeouts on sporting subjects; then columns on individual sports; and finally, to enliven the closing pages of the magazine, a long text piece of general or sometimes offbeat interest, not tied to the current news—an extra dividend for the reader, a "bonus piece," as it came to be called.

Laguerre also reorganized *SI*'s staff structure. From *Time*, he borrowed the system of using departmental editors to supervise coverage of specific sports. Taking a leaf from *Life*, where a single copy editor polished all the text, Laguerre assigned copy supervision to his deputy, assistant managing editor Richard Johnston, whose duty it was to see that *SI* had a more or less consistent viewpoint throughout the book and maintained a high level of literary style. Johnston, a veteran United Press war correspondent who had written and reported for both *Time* and *Life* before joining *SI* in its prepublication days, was later named executive editor. Assistant managing editor John Tibby took over budgets and administration.

SI's writing staff remained lean, smaller than either of Time Inc.'s other weeklies, and as had been the case throughout *SI*'s profitless years, editorial salaries remained likewise at a lower level (not until 1966 was additional money put in the budget to give *SI* staffers an overdue boost). Expense accounts were watched "like it was Andre's own money you were spending." Yet Laguerre could tell Luce truthfully, as he did in 1963, that "morale on the editorial floor remains good. Your staff continues to be generally enthusiastic about its work and to have fun doing it." One measure was that despite raiding attempts by other publications, among them *The New Yorker* and *Saturday Evening Post*, there were few defections.

Like *Fortune*, which a quarter-century earlier had gone looking for poets to write business, *SI* had sought verbal flair before sports expertise. It gave its writers exceptional freedom, and they used it to create a unique literature of sport. When *SI* was starting out, its talent hunters were quickly disabused of the notion that the best writing in America is on the sports pages. But once in a while, the magazine's stringer system would come up with a writer of rare ability. In Texas an offbeat column on horse racing by the sports editor of the Corpus Christi *Caller*, Roy Terrell, caught *SI*'s eye and was reprinted in the second issue of the magazine. A few months later, Terrell was invited to New York to join the staff. Hired originally for his competence at hard sports reporting, Terrell displayed a flair for vivid description in sports as diverse as sailplaning and cricket, a game he managed to make not only intelligible but exciting:

> A good fast cricket bowler can deliver the ball, which is slightly smaller and harder than a baseball, and is painted red—probably so the blood won't show—at 90 miles an hour . . . The batsman, in order to stay alive . . . must possess the courage of a water buffalo, something of a buffalo's hide and the reactions of a cat.

In Terrell, *SI* had acquired the editor who eventually succeeded Laguerre at the magazine's helm. Another celebrated Texan recruit was Dan Jenkins, probably the best known of *SI* writers during Laguerre's editorship. Drawn by *SI*'s growing reputation among sports reporters ("a writer's paradise, I couldn't wait to get up there"), Jenkins, a topflight college golfer, produced in February 1965 the most famous of all *SI*'s golfing articles, a selection of "The Best 18 in America." It was in writing about football, though, that Jenkins became a celebrity in his own right, with his best-selling novel *Semi-Tough*,* a rowdy spoof of the pro game that was later made into a movie. Jenkins helped create what novelist James Michener described as *SI*'s "Texas-Oklahoma refined jock" style, and the influence he exerted on some of the writers who followed him at *SI* was enormous.

SI was attracting writers from the company's other magazines also, in contrast to an earlier day when transferring to *SI* was, as one *Time* staffer remarked derisively, "like being sold to the St. Louis Browns." From *Time*, *SI* acquired a number of talents, including the magazine's former Chicago bureau chief, Jack Olsen, whose investigative series for *SI* on the plight of black athletes later won nationwide attention, and Robert H. Boyle, a conservationist of contagious indignation, which exploded in 1964 in a long text piece on the ecological destruction of the Hudson River, followed shortly by a much quoted article, "America Down the Drain," on the general despoliation of the nation's countryside. Wrote Boyle: "America the Beautiful is becoming America the ugly, the wasted, the blasted and the blighted . . . We have, in short, become a nation of pigs. Hello pigs." Luce was among those whom Boyle infused with his rage. "Righteous indignation, even to the point of excess," said Luce of Boyle's piece. "But as Boyle got madder and madder, I got madder and madder."

Reflecting the greater depth of in-house talent that *SI* was able to call on, the magazine's use of outside writers decreased. Fortunately, though, George Plimpton's tragicomic amateur forays into professional sport continued. An *SI* contributor since 1956, Plimpton was back again in 1961, describing his self-imposed ordeal of pitching to 16 major league batters, including Mickey Mantle and Willie Mays, during the All Star Game warmups, a story that elicited a rave from Ernest Hemingway as "incredibly conceived with the chilling quality of a true nightmare . . . the dark side of Walter Mitty." In the summer of 1963, Plimpton/Mitty was at the Detroit Lions' training camp, playing quarterback and losing 20 heartbreaking yards in five embarrassing misplays; his 1964 *SI* account made a book, *Paper Lion*,† and a movie.

SI was born in a television age of black-and-white, when fewer than 5,000 households in the entire country had color TV sets. Thus *SI*, carrying an average of about nine color pages (out of a total of 48

*Atheneum, 1972.
†Harper & Row, 1965.

to 50 editorial pages) in its early issues, had offered its readers views of sport unduplicated on the tube. The magazine had made the most of its opportunity.

Both in color and black-and-white, *SI* had introduced a new kind of sports photography, borrowing heavily from the skills of *Life*. Mark Kauffman, a *Life* veteran who became one of *SI*'s first staff photographers, roamed the ballparks and football fields, shooting with a motor-driven rangefinder camera to catch the tension and speed of sports action. John Zimmerman, who had worked for both *Time* and *Life*, used his technical expertise to reveal sport from unusual perspectives, in multiple exposures and swirls of color. In *SI*'s newer generation were two precocious youngsters, Neil Leifer and Walter Iooss (pronounced yohs), who started working for *SI* while still in their teens. Leifer, an aggressive New Yorker who used to deliver delicatessen sandwiches to the *Life* photo studio and then hang around to watch the photographers at work, produced some of *SI*'s most technically innovative action shots. Iooss became known for his long-lens photography and his exceptional sensitivity; eventually he was to top even Leifer in the number of *SI* covers to his credit—well over 150.

But by the time Laguerre became managing editor, *SI*'s continuing losses had forced a sharp cutback in color pages, to about six per issue. Almost all the color, moreover, remained on a slow schedule; *SI*'s covers, for instance, were printed four weeks in advance. In the fall of 1959, *SI* managed to squeeze from its tight editorial budget an extra color page a week, eight in all, which were, for the first time in *SI*'s history, printed on a "fast" schedule—shot on the weekend for appearance on the newsstands Tuesday or Wednesday. For the entire year of 1960, 11 fast color pages were printed.

Laguerre, as managing editor, set out to get more, particularly more fast color to compete with television, where the conversion to color was proceeding rapidly—explosively, even. The battle for color continued throughout Laguerre's tenure, dominating relations between the editorial and publishing sides.

As part of the effort to improve the magazine's appearance, Laguerre had brought in a new art director, Richard Gangel, another *Life* recruit, whose elegant design work for *Life*'s illustrated edition of the Winston Churchill war memoirs had won much praise around the shop. Gangel proceeded to give *SI* something of a facelift. The layout was cleaned up. The spidery logotype on the cover was replaced with bolder, more compact lettering that gave better display to the cover picture. Eventually, the body type was changed too. Gangel also increased the use of artists to illustrate sport events, as a way of enabling readers, he said, "to look at old friends in a fresh way, the old friends being baseball, football and the rest." Thus Gangel sent the French satirical painter André François to cover ice hockey at Madison Square Garden, British cartoonist Ronald Searle to sketch baseball's spring training in Florida, Saul Steinberg to apply his penmanship to the horse races, Wayne Thiebaud to apply his pop art to tennis at Wimbledon. However, protests from New York art dealers forced Gangel to cancel plans to have the notorious art forger David Stein paint the races at Hialeah in the style of Raoul Dufy. Too many of the protesting dealers, Gangel suspected, had been stung by Stein to appreciate the joke.

It was a picture of continuing austerity that Laguerre painted for Luce in July 1961, in reporting on the progress made during the first 15 months of his editorship. "Football and baseball are the only departments in which we can afford the luxury of more than one writer—so that one can research next week's story while the other is writing this week's," Laguerre wrote. He was pleased with staff performance, though, and with *SI*'s editorial development:

> The fact that we have adhered for 15 months to a definite formula has not prevented a philosophical evolution of the magazine. This has been away from a straightforward reportorial approach to a sports event and toward an attack both broader and deeper . . . Our constant search is for ways to connect our broad concept of sport with the social scene.
>
> At the same time . . . economic "recession" and now an apparent heightening of international tension have not provided the best climate for *SI*. Another specially current dilemma is that of corruption in sport. It is not *SI*'s wish, nor is it in *SI*'s interest to concentrate on the seamy side of our subject. But neither, as news gatherers and leaders of opinion in our sector, can we ignore an aspect which I fear is greater than anything yet revealed.

In January 1962, the progressive increases in *SI*'s guaranteed rate base, which had been accomplished at a fairly steady ratio of circulation income to expense, took circulation over the million mark. "An excellent figure for selling advertising," Pete Callaway noted.

153

Laguerre was also encouraged. "My feeling is strong these days," he wrote Luce in February, "that this is the year to get over the hump." He felt that *SI* was riding a winner with its increasing coverage of pro football:

> I'm developing a strong hunch that pro football is *our* sport. We have grown with it, and each of us is a phenomenon of the times . . . It seems that our reader identifies himself more with this sport than with golf or fishing. College football is too diffuse and regionalized. Baseball in some quarters is considered old-fashioned or slightly non-U. Horse racing and winter sports have less broad appeal.
>
> *SI* evokes the most one-shot response over a big fight or a hot international sports situation, such as the Olympics. I guess this merely restates the obvious: we are at our most effective when the story transcends the sports section and becomes a national talking point . . .
>
> I believe our edit formula is right. We could not sacrifice more to general interest at this time without threatening our status as an authoritative sports magazine.

Madison Avenue's interest, however, failed to match *SI*'s growing readership. Despite Callaway's initial optimism, ad sales in the first half of 1962 fell below budget, and although *SI* finally gained 97 pages over the preceding year, the sales force had to drum up 659 pages of new business to offset the dropouts among existing accounts.

Disputes between the publishing and editorial sides flared again. That May, in an exasperated memo headed "Mortality (Why a magazine loses such a high percentage of its advertising accounts)" Callaway wrote publisher Sid James:

> *SI* is . . . a high-cost editorial product . . . a complex product to sell and promote. Nevertheless, the principle still stands that the sales staff should be selling the product produced by the editors and that product must be right . . .
>
> The sales staff is selling a concept of high quality circulation . . . members of country clubs with high incomes who live in the suburbs . . . Leaders of business and the professions who participate actively in sports. The sports are, obviously, such things as golf, tennis, sailing, etc., i.e., the fashionable sports.
>
> The covers of *Sports Illustrated* indicate the preoccupation of the editors with *spectator* sports. This is the exact opposite of

what the sales staff is selling . . . It is recognized that as a news magazine we must frequently carry the news of sports on our covers. However, since newsstand sales are only 8 percent of our circulation it is not necessary that our covers be overboard on spectator sports. A particularly horrible example of the kind of covers that make it hard for the sales staff is the [heavyweight boxer Floyd] Patterson cover on May 28th which is then followed next week by a Willie Mays [baseball] cover.

Callaway's sentiments were echoed by Larsen, who also wanted an upscale audience for *SI*, not readers of the sort who bought *Physical Culture*, published by the Macfadden company, and similar pulp fare. "Let us not make the mistake of addressing [*SI*'s] cover picture to the unwashed newsstand buyer—we don't want him—let Macfadden have him," Larsen wrote Sid James.

Nettled, Laguerre ran a count of *SI* covers over the preceding two years; it showed that the magazine had been giving the country-club set more than its due. Golf led all sports with 18 covers, baseball followed with 13, pro football only seven. Washed or unwashed, *SI* readers seemed to prefer the sweaty sports, for seven football covers were among the 13 best-selling issues during that period. Two basketball covers were also among the 13, but only one golf cover made the best-seller list.

A better indication of where *SI*'s readership lay was provided a few months later, when W.R. Simmons & Associates Research, Inc. began an audience measurement of 37 publications, based on interviews with 14,800 persons in 5,500 households across the U.S. *SI* emerged third among all magazines, with more than seven readers per copy. Adult readership was 5 million, of whom 4.2 million were men. *SI* was shown to reach one in five executives in the top income bracket, only slightly less than *Newsweek*, whose circulation was half again as big. *SI*'s male readership was to become a major talking point in subsequent years.

While the implications of the Simmons survey were being digested, there were some changes in the publishing staff. Callaway had been lured away from Time Inc. to become publisher of *Newsweek*. *SI*'s new ad sales director was Stephen E. Kelly, promoted from advertising manager. Garry Valk, assistant managing director of Time-Life International, was recruited as associate publisher; in 1965 he was to succeed James as *SI*'s publisher. A hard-driving salesman,

Valk had joined the company after Army Air Force service in Italy, where *Time*'s wartime "pony" edition had awakened his interest in publishing. Turned down when he first applied at Time Inc., Valk had returned to work his way up from a job in the mailroom.

For three years, 1961 through 1963, *SI* seemed stalled, unable to reduce losses below the $1 million level, despite gradual improvement in ad revenues reflecting the rise in page rates. Advertising sales seemed unable to break the 2,000-page barrier—*SI*'s break-even point. Spencer Earnshaw, a former *SI* ad manager in New York, Chicago and Los Angeles, recounted the problems of trying to win over the media buyers: "The excitement of the World Series, or the crowds that turned out to cheer or boo . . . cut absolutely no ice in a decision about where to spend the advertising allocation of marketing budget dollars."

The old arguments—over editorial mix and advertising sales approach—were still unresolved when, in August 1963, Heiskell stepped in. His intervention was decisive; effectively, he ended the debate. Cutting through the mass of memos with their incessant disclaimers that "it's a great magazine but . . ." Heiskell decreed the advertising strategy to be followed. His analysis put *SI*'s situation in stark, even gloomy, terms.

"We do not have, presently or potentially, a viable publishing equation," Heiskell declared. *SI* had fulfilled its editorial promise, he thought; its circulation growth was satisfactory, expenses were under control and production and editorial costs were at a nearly irreducible minimum consistent with quality. But in advertising sales, where the problem lay, "it is not just a matter of *SI* being at the bottom of [a media buyer's] list. It is that in practically every sales situation the *SI* case is relatively weak"—in apparel advertising against the New York *Times* Magazine and *The New Yorker*, in travel against *Holiday*, in the home field against *House Beautiful*, in outdoor sports against *Field and Stream* and *Yachting*, in consumer goods against the general magazines and TV. Heiskell went on to say:

> As a result of all these specialized competitive situations, *SI* has reacted imaginatively [with] individualized arguments (in terms of copy ideas, merchandising, or anything else it could dream up) somewhat unrelated to its basic advertising function . . . It must be quite obvious that this highly competent sales staff would not have become so deeply involved in "special" selling but for the fact it did not have a good general sales story . . .

156

[*SI*] should disassociate itself from the *Holiday*, *Esquire*, *National Geographic*, *Playboy* field and promote itself as one of the newsweeklies. The monthly leisure field simply doesn't supply enough potential ($) for *SI* and forces it into competitive battles it cannot win at a profit.

Afterward, Heiskell explained the proposed strategy to the Time Inc. board: "Most advertisers think of [news] weeklies as ranging from *Time* to *Business Week*. *Sports Illustrated* must make them think of one additional rung—*Sports Illustrated* . . . as an ideal medium for advertising addressed to businessmen, both as buyers of consumer goods and in their corporate capacity." Along with realigning its sales approach, Heiskell suggested that *SI* should slow its circulation growth—a move that would hold down both circulation costs and advertising rate increases.

Heiskell also asked for an editorial prospectus: "Not necessarily for publication [but] just what does Laguerre think he is doing. It could be of real help to the circulators, and maybe to the editors." Produced by assistant managing editor Jack Tibby on Laguerre's behalf, the prospectus was sent to Luce, who had it distributed to a few select Time Inc. executives for their views as to whether "changes in the magazine's declared 'formula' will be required to make it salable to the desired degree."

The prospectus, a lyrical 2,500-word essay on *SI*'s purpose—"to capture in print . . . the pleasure and joy of sport, its shine and color and movement . . . with honesty and style . . . *every week*"— suggested no changes. More important perhaps, it helped put to rest any thought that the magazine should reduce its frequency, perhaps go biweekly, to bring its publishing economics into better balance. Wrote Tibby: "Each weekend swallows the week before. *Sports Illustrated* is a weekly because of the cycle of sport itself."

Meanwhile, on the advertising front, publisher James launched a sales push called "Operation Breakthrough," aimed at boosting *SI*'s ad pages to 2,500 over the three years ahead—a more than 500-page increase, no easy target. For the campaign, an eye-catching little doodle was designed, entwining *SI*'s initials to form a dollar sign. Operation Breakthrough scored gains across the board—a 240-page increase in 1964 and another 200 pages the following year. Subscription prices were raised and *SI*'s newsstand price was brought even with *Time*'s at 35 cents. As a result, the ratio of circulation expense to income fell sharply and the increasing circulation revenues further improved the magazine's financial condition. In fact, as *SI*'s corporate boosters were quick to point out, the magazine was just about at the breakeven point.

By mid-1964—in time for *SI*'s tenth birthday—the magazine was edging into the black. In the anniversary issue, August 17, Luce pre-empted the page usually devoted to the Letter from the Publisher to write a Letter *to* the Publisher (with the "to" in color for emphasis), sending an *olé* and a bravo to James and his colleagues:

> You have achieved something so extraordinary that even among publishers its uniqueness is not fully appreciated. You have established a successful national weekly. This is a very rare occurrence. Altogether, there exist only seven general weeklies in the U.S., and of these *Sports Illustrated* is the only one founded since World War II.
>
> The years since that war have seen scores of business successes. We all know about such glamour stocks as IBM and Xerox and Litton . . . but—and I may be excused for being an extremist (hyperbolist) on this occasion—none of these industrial and commercial miracles involves such risks and difficulties as establishing a national weekly.
>
> To be sure, *Sports Illustrated* is a small business as business goes these days: its gross is only a little over $25 million and, while the net profit isn't hay, we are not yet earning the 10 percent after taxes that is a businessman's par for the course. That is for tomorrow.

SI's earnings that year were barely straw—a wispy $564,000, or only 2.4 percent, on revenues that by year's end reached $22,580,000, somewhat below the gross that Luce predicted. Nonetheless, *SI*'s breakthrough was definitive: the magazine never again went into the red. A few months later, in May 1965, James, Laguerre and the *SI* sales staff gathered to celebrate at the resort center appropriately named Carefree, Arizona, not far from Luce's home in Phoenix, where, in retirement, he was now spending more of his time. James, inviting Luce over to the party at Carefree, wrote: "Everything the figures [on *SI*'s improving financial condition] tell you is true. What the figures don't convey is the lift in spirit, determination, sophistication, confidence, etc., etc., that results from inhaling the sweet smell of success."

Luce showed up in a relaxed, expansive mood and delivered a graceful speech paying warm tribute to James and Laguerre. It was James, Luce said, who as *SI*'s first editor "had the nerve and enthusiasm to undertake what had already been proved . . . impossible."

As for James's successor, Luce said: "During my career as editor-in-chief, all those years, my main single job was to pick a managing editor or to have one in sight . . . The choice I'm proudest of, vainest of, is the choice of Andre Laguerre."

As for the magazine itself, Luce went on, "as I am no longer editor-in-chief, it is no longer my duty to read it . . . Joy for me is when *Sports Illustrated* comes around and I grab it, and say, 'Thank God I don't have to read it.' So what do I do? I spend the rest of the night reading it!"

"He Wants Me to Be Him"

"IT MUST BE LIKE being elected Moses," a friend wrote Hedley Donovan when, in April 1964, he was formally appointed by the Time Inc. board to succeed Luce as editor-in-chief. There was that aspect to Donovan's appointment: Could anyone else wear the mantle that had been Luce's own for so long? And was Luce, indeed, giving that mantle up?

In the publishing world, and outside too, it was hard to conceive of the Time Inc. magazines without Luce's name at the top of the masthead, and his departure from active editorial direction brought forth a spate of press commentary amounting almost to premature obituary notices. "Relinquishing of Editorial Control at Time Inc. by Henry Luce Marks End of Era," the New York *Times* headlined a full page devoted to the Luce-Donovan succession. The British Broadcasting Corporation revived long-discarded Timestyle to report the departure of "slim, high-domed . . . millionaire Luce" and the arrival of "younger . . . soft-spoken, easy-gaited Hedley Donovan." *Newsweek* voiced the doubts of many: "Strong emperors do not usually abdicate easily . . . Could it really be that a reign was ending?" One skeptic was former *Time* managing editor Tom Matthews, queried by *Newsweek* in London. "It's not in Luce's character to step down, any more than it is in Lord Beaverbrook's," Matthews said.

As a matter of fact, Luce had prepared for the transfer of power better than most corporate creators. As principal stockholder Luce could not, during his lifetime, let go completely; in January 1966, for instance, he intervened to block a proposed merger that would have significantly altered the corporate balance (see chapter 13). However, he had once declared, "I want everyone to get used to the idea of what they call the Lucepapers without Luce," and it was his style of having "shared authority without diluting it," in Donovan's phrase, that greatly eased Luce's transition to the advisory role he assumed after Donovan became editor-in-chief.

Writing later about his selection in 1959 of Donovan as his deputy and eventual successor, Luce said: "When, without consultation, I chose Donovan to succeed John Shaw Billings* as Editorial Director, after the post had been vacant for too long a time, I had thought that this was a brilliant stroke all my own. The first executive I met that day and asked, 'Well, what do you think?' replied, 'It was obvious . . . inevitable.' "

On some editorial floors below, the selection had not seemed so obvious. Coming from *Fortune*, never having worked anywhere else in the company, Donovan was only a name to many in Time Inc., and not a very familiar name at that. Between the *Time* and *Life* staffs there was considerable intermingling. They were chasing many of the same stories each week and at both magazines a sort of firehouse atmosphere prevailed. But *Fortune*, working to a more stately publishing rhythm, was a place apart. "Here was the fair-haired boy that nobody knew coming in to tell them how to run their show"—such was the typical reaction on *Time* and *Life* to Donovan's appointment.

Born in northern Minnesota at Brainerd, where his father was a geologist and mining engineer, Donovan grew up in Minneapolis. His sister worked there for Time Inc. in public relations. His parents were early *Time* subscribers; Donovan and his brother much admired the magazine's "saucy way" with words and tried to imitate it in letters to each other. At the University of Minnesota, Donovan wrote editorials for the campus daily, played ice hockey, made Phi Beta Kappa in his junior year and, after graduating magna cum laude, spent three years at Oxford (Hertford College) on a Rhodes scholarship, intending to become a historian. The teaching assis-

*Managing editor of *Time* (1933-37) and of *Life* (1937-44), Billings was Time Inc.'s editorial director for ten years, until his retirement in 1954.

161

tant's job he was offered at Harvard paid only $600 yearly, not enough even in mid-Depression 1937. So Donovan went instead to the Washington *Post* as a reporter at $25 a week, doing general assignment, then Congress and finally, in the year before Pearl Harbor, covering the State Department and the White House, where his position at the far edge of the arc surrounding F.D.R.'s desk did nothing to dampen Donovan's exhilaration at the experience. "If you were a very young reporter, it was flattering to have the President of the United States call you by your first name and wink at you." In January 1942, Donovan went into Naval Intelligence, emerging in November 1945 as a lieutenant commander.

Time Inc. was just then engaged in a talent search among returning servicemen; Donovan's sister, seeing mention in the company house organ, sent in his name to vice president Eric Hodgins, who was heading the search. Judged by Hodgins to be a "very good gamble" warranting a six months' trial on *Fortune*, Donovan was taken on. He found himself thrown into writing the lead article for an issue devoted entirely to the postwar housing industry. The article went through four drafts before it was considered publishable; Donovan was suffering from the new writer's tendency, as he described it afterward, of having "too much of his research showing." But he caught on quickly. In 1947 he was given *Fortune*'s Books and Ideas department to edit. Four years later, he became associate managing editor and early in 1953, when *Fortune*'s longtime managing editor, Ralph Delahaye (Del) Paine Jr., moved over to the business side as publisher, Donovan succeeded him.

At 38, Donovan was the youngest managing editor of any Time Inc. magazine. To *Fortune*, he brought a managerial style best described as no-nonsense. He was a man of notably few words—one waggish colleague called him Old Flapjaw—whose reserve tended to break down only after hours at office parties, when he became a convivial drinking companion, fond of rendering Irish ditties or the *Marseillaise* in a booming baritone. During the working day, he was a hard taskmaster, a stickler on deadlines, a stern critic of writers' copy, given to "writing a lot of questions, tough questions, in the margins," one writer remembered. "Hedley was very, very organized, extremely demanding and very tough. He had people going without sleep to produce stories for him. I remember that at the end of 1959 [when Donovan left *Fortune*] I was exhausted," another associate said. "At the same time it was fun and it was satisfying."

Self-assured, confessing once that the managing editor's job itself demanded a "certain lack of humility," Donovan was stubborn in his views—a quality Luce appreciated; he encouraged argument from his associates. (Donovan later recalled asking Luce how many arguments he, as editor-in-chief, could be expected to win. "I told him I expected to win two out of three. Harry said he'd settle for 50-50.") It was, appropriately enough, in the wake of serious argument in early 1959 over what Donovan considered improper corporate intrusion into his prerogatives as managing editor that Luce first broached the idea of Donovan's eventually becoming editor-in-chief.

The episode arose over some strong criticisms expressed to Luce and Donovan by Charlie Stillman, then executive vice president and treasurer, of a *Fortune* series on tax reform. Reading the first article in draft at Luce's request, Stillman dismissed it as "preposterous" and "presumptuous" and intimated (according to Donovan) that "any writer who held these views must be quite pink."* A couple of days later Donovan, who had refused to cede to Stillman editorially, was summoned to dine alone with Luce at the editor-in-chief's Fifth Avenue apartment. He went intending to protest Stillman's comments.

"I didn't know what Harry's agenda was, but that was on mine. I was quite unprepared for Harry's agenda," Donovan said. Afterward, Donovan met his wife at a nearby bar. "Dorothy, knowing the arguments I had been having, asked, 'Did you get fired?' And I said, 'No. He wants me to be him.' "

So it was that Luce put the editorial succession to Donovan. Donovan was taken aback. "If I had been sitting around with very close friends or my wife speculating who would be the next editor-in-chief, I would not have named myself. I guess I assumed it would be either the editor of *Time* or of *Life*. Later when I recovered from my surprise and came to think about it, of course, Roy Alexander [of *Time*] was the same age as Harry and that wouldn't have been a very good move for the future. I know Harry considered Ed [Thompson of *Life*] a great editor, but what his views about him as a successor were, I don't know."

Donovan said later that he accepted Luce's offer conditionally. As managing editor of *Fortune*, Donovan had been critical of *Time*'s politics; now, in becoming Luce's deputy, he sought—and

---

*The writer of the article was Robert Lubar, later to become *Fortune*'s managing editor.

obtained—Luce's assurance that changes would be made. Addressing a *Time* editors' meeting shortly after Luce's death, Donovan
recalled the conversations:

> Since [Luce] had asked me whether I would be editorial direc-
> tor of the company I said I wouldn't be unless, among other
> things, it was understood between him and me that *Time*'s tone
> of voice and substance on various policy questions did leave
> something to be desired; and that there was an intention on the
> part of him to fix this. Otherwise I would not want to take on
> the responsibility . . .
>
> I felt *Time* had been quite unfair in several instances to Harry
> Truman. Harry Luce agreed that this was so. I felt *Time* had
> been somewhat unfair in the first Eisenhower-Stevenson cam-
> paign. Harry had a very interesting response on that . . . He
> felt it was very important that the Democrats not become the
> permanent governing party of the United States in terms of
> political theory . . . that the public not conclude that the
> Republicans automatically equated with depression and also
> that Republicans did not automatically equate with isolation-
> ism. His formulation was that: yes, *Time* was pretty much an
> alley fighter in 1952 but he thought in good cause . . .
>
> He said maybe we shouldn't have been quite as rough on
> [Adlai] Stevenson—nice fellow and all that . . . [But] what
> actually bothered me most was what I felt was . . . the suspen-
> sion of critical judgment, as it seemed to me, in regard to the
> Eisenhower administration once it was elected . . . In the col-
> umns of *Time* [it] got away with things without needle or flick
> that practically nobody else conceivable would have.

Luce left the timing of the succession vague. "Not for tomorrow or
next week but in a few years," he told Donovan. Meanwhile Luce
would, as he phrased it, serve "a ninth term" in the job he had held
for so long. Donovan hesitated, suggesting that he and Luce both
think about it a while longer. "I had serious doubts about whether
he should commit himself before he had to. In three or four years
he might find someone else much better. But Luce was quite insis-
tent that it was settled in his mind . . . Of course in the background
of that, which I was not aware of, was how serious his illness had
been. He was much more concerned than I realized about having
some stand-by."

The appointment added much needed manpower to Luce's imme-

164

diate staff. At the time of Donovan's arrival upstairs in 1959 that staff consisted of four people: his personal assistant, vice president Allen Grover; an executive assistant for liaison with the editorial staffs, former *Fortune* executive editor Bill Furth, who also served as editorial watchdog on the magazines' performance; a researcher and special assistant, Emeline (Emmie) Nollen; and secretary Gloria Mariano. (Another secretary, not on the Time Inc. payroll, handled household matters for Luce and his wife.)

In former days Luce had kept in personal touch with the magazines by sitting in occasionally as acting managing editor. Donovan began his tenure similarly, going downstairs to sit in first at *Sports Illustrated*. He also took over the periodic page-by-page editorial appraisals to which all the magazines were subjected. Donovan's authority under Luce expanded gradually: "Luce remained very much the editor-in-chief of *Time*; I was the editor-in-chief of *Fortune* and *Sports Illustrated*; we were co-editors-in-chief of *Life*."

One of Donovan's early moves as Luce's deputy had been to expand editorial recruiting, instituting a program for hiring promising young journalists—not to fill immediate openings, but as long-chance bets for the future. "Among journalists, Time Inc. doesn't exert as strong a pull as it once did," Donovan wrote Luce in January 1961, explaining that pay differentials were narrowing and the Time Inc. magazines no longer seemed "glamorous new ventures." Additionally, Donovan warned, the company risked falling into "an age structure that is unhealthy for our sort of business: an increasing bunching of talent over 40, not enough comers in the 30s; hardly anybody at all, comers or otherwise, in the 20s." One result was a corporate allocation enabling the managing editors to take on a selected few younger talents—"Donovan scholars," as they inevitably became known—above and beyond the magazines' regular staff needs. Also on Donovan's initiative, a research and development department was established as an extension of the editor-in-chief's office.

In September 1962, Donovan was named to the Time Inc. board, the first editorial executive apart from Luce and Hadden themselves to be a corporate director. The appointment came at a moment when Luce was engaged in one of his recurrent efforts to define the editor-in-chief's function—to put on paper "the ontological necessity of the Office in the special world of Time Inc.," as he expressed it in this instance.

Prompting this particular effort of Luce's was a memo from Donovan noting, among other things, how the task of editorial overseers

165

had grown as the company's publishing activities had expanded abroad as well as at home. The new book division, only two years old, was already the company's third largest editorial operation, with a staff bigger than all but *Time* or *Life*, Donovan pointed out. Acknowledging Donovan's memo, Luce conceded that "it may be . . . we have expanded beyond the bounds of our essential philosophy. Or to put it another way, our philosophy may need to be expanded to give intellectual and moral coherence to our expanded activities." Luce continued:

> Meanwhile I shall rehearse a few basic considerations. We are in journalism for profit—and in allied activities for profit. But we stand for responsible journalism—for the responsibility of our journalism to our fellow-man, especially to our readers, and ultimately to Truth itself. This is why we have since the beginning maintained not only the "independence" of the editorial side from the "front office" but also its primacy. This is pretty well understood—even at times excessively—throughout our very large organization.
>
> For this reason the office of Editor-in-Chief is necessary for Time Inc. . . . Several corollaries follow . . . One is that there must be a basic compatibility among all Time Inc. divisions as to public policy, intellectual and other standards and other matters. The Office of Editor-in-Chief cannot be morally or intellectually schizophrenic—or at least not very.

Luce projected a "Set-up for Office of Editor-in-Chief beginning now and continuing, hopefully with only minor changes, for two years"—obviously, the time he saw remaining in his own tenure, which he had not hitherto indicated. Also historically interesting in this exchange between Donovan and Luce was their designation of a "Fourth Man" at the top echelon, one of whose purposes—"perhaps the chief purpose," according to Luce—would be "to enlarge our ability to 'THINK.' " This man, Luce said, would be *Time* senior editor Henry Grunwald. "A superb all-round journalist" who "can think—and think journalistically—that is, translate large concepts and ideas into journalistically useful forms," Luce said of the man who, some 17 years later, would become Time Inc.'s third editor-in-chief.

Grunwald, as it turned out, did not then join Luce's staff. He was detailed instead to the new R & D unit, handling its initial studies into broadcasting and mass magazines, returning afterward to *Time*. The death of Bill Furth from cancer that fall forced another change in the arrangements Luce envisaged. *Time* editor Roy Alexander temporarily took Furth's place.

At the end of 1963, the editor-in-chief's office did acquire a fourth man in the person of *Time* assistant managing editor Tom Griffith, who took on Furth's old role. Griffith's move upstairs gave Luce and Donovan a general-purpose deputy whose editorial judgment both men thought highly of. It also resolved a sticky situation on *Time*. This was, in Donovan's description, the "painful friction" between Griffith and managing editor Fuerbringer. Politically and temperamentally, Griffith was Fuerbringer's opposite; knowing it, Luce had deliberately put the two men in tandem. "Harry had set great store by this," Donovan said, but as peacemaker between the two men Donovan himself had come to a different conclusion. "It was foolish to set up somebody consciously as the opposition in management," he commented later.

Griffith stayed on with Donovan after Luce's retirement, assuming Donovan's previous functions as editorial director, but without the title. Instead, the clumsy label senior staff editor was created. (Griffith was not enchanted with the title, which in his view had "two ups and a down"—the ups being senior and editor, the down being the staff designation—but neither he nor Donovan could think of anything better. "Deputy" in the title was out; that implied succession.) In January 1968, Griffith moved to *Life* as editor. Eventually, Donovan set up a system of assigning senior editorial executives from the various magazines to temporary tours of duty in the editor-in-chief's office.

As the date of his retirement approached, Luce wrote a note to his secretary, Gloria Mariano, and his researcher, Emmie Nollen: "We three will be coming down in the world a bit—but there will be plenty to do." What he intended doing in his diminished capacity was outlined in an enclosed memo for the Time Inc. board's approval. While Donovan would assume "the full authority over, and responsibility for, all editorial activities," Luce wrote:

> My name will continue on the masthead [as editorial chairman] to indicate my close operational connection with the work of the company . . . My main, more or less continuous work would be in the nature of advice, criticism and suggestions to

167

the Editor-in-Chief and to other appropriate editors and staffers. Most of this would be done informally but it is planned that once every three months I would conduct a seminar with the top editors on important items of policy or attitude with respect to public affairs.

In his new capacity, Luce added, he would "maintain an office, with a very small secretarial and research staff, would be paid a substantial salary, and would have the travel and other facilities available to senior executives."

Luce professed to "feeling wonderful" about the transfer of power, which was formalized at a board meeting April 16, the day of the annual stockholders' meeting. But by the time of the ceremonial sequel, a staff dinner the following month at the New York Hilton, assembling Time Inc. editorial and publishing executives from around the world, Luce and Donovan both seemed "a little skittish," as their mutual assistant, Tom Griffith, remembered. "Luce and Donovan had separately written their speeches and had made no effort to learn in advance what the other would say. Fearing overlaps, or anything in one speech that the other should know about, I volunteered to read them both." One paragraph near the end of Donovan's text caught Griffith's eye. "I showed the paragraph to Harry. He read it and thanked me in the manner of a man who knew there would be a passage like that from Hedley Donovan."*

At the dinner, Luce began with a pronouncement:

Tonight [the office of editor-in-chief] is no longer a personal prerogative derived from a legendary and/or murky past. Today it becomes a very constitutional office by order of the board of directors. And from now on [it] more clearly than ever before expresses Time Inc.'s understanding of that great doctrine of freedom of the press by which we live. Freedom's correlative is responsibility. But to whom is the individual journalist responsible? To whom is the great organization of editors and publishers responsible? Not certainly to any organ of government. Not, we hope, to any vested interests, and not even to stockholders . . .

Freedom of the press is responsible only to conscience, and conscience can only be found in a man . . . We cannot evade

How True, p. 109.

the demand for a general coherence and for a clear sense of direction . . . And this must come from the Editor-in-Chief. It must come by means of his intelligence and through his conscience.

Donovan, in reply, paid a warm tribute to Luce: "The quite extraordinary fringe benefit so many of us have enjoyed in working for Time Inc. [has been] the friendship of a great man." He continued with remarks about the attitudes he felt governed Time Inc.:

One of them is simply this: we are a permanently dissatisfied company. We are not a small, weak, struggling company. We are a big, strong, struggling company. And what are we struggling about? Chiefly, we are struggling to do a better job. If we do, we are likely to get bigger and more profitable in the process, but I suggest that that was never exactly the main point about Time Inc., and is not likely to become so.

So where and how might we do a better job? Well, for one thing, that profitability I mentioned a moment ago . . . We could stand more of it—to make sure that Time Inc. careers are always the most rewarding in publishing, financially as well as intellectually; to make sure our publications have the resources to exploit new journalistic opportunities; to make sure a recession could not damage the quality of our publications; to make sure we are never afraid to tell somebody to go to hell.

"Some of our competitors, by the way, are . . . better publications than they used to be," Donovan noted. As for Time Inc.'s publications, he observed:

I think we have pretty much won that old argument about "objectivity" [in journalism] . . . We do not claim to be neutral; we do claim to be fair. But our occasional lapses hurt us among some of the very people our magazines are meant for. I have sometimes heard it said that it will be a sorry day for Time Inc. if we ever run out of enemies. I consider this such a remote danger I refuse to worry about it. We do indeed have some enemies to be proud of, and we want to keep them. We also have some unnecessary enemies whom we acquired rather carelessly.

Then Donovan reached the paragraph in his speech that Griffith had shown to Luce in advance. As spoken, the lines provoked more than a few exchanges of glances in an audience to whom the intramural political battles of the 1950s, and the magazines' reporting of the Eisenhower and Stevenson campaigns were very recent history. Declared Donovan:

> The vote of Time Inc. should never be considered to be in the pocket of any particular political leader or party. The vote of Time Inc. is an independent vote. Not an independent vote in the sense of some snooty or finicky disdain for political parties. And certainly not independent in the sense of any wishy-washy confusion as to what we believe. But independent in the sense that we are in no way beholden to any party, have no vested interest in any party as such.

Large excerpts from Donovan's speech were reprinted in the company's annual report for 1964. Rereading the words, Luce wrote Donovan: "What you had to say is even better than I remembered."

Donovan's declaration of independence came up for a test soon enough, with the 1964 presidential campaign. On the Republican side, opinion around the company, Donovan's included, leaned originally toward Pennsylvania's Governor William Scranton, whose appeal as a progressive was not diminished by the fact of a close Time Inc. family relationship—Linen's wife, Sally, was Scranton's sister.

Luce, for his part, was cool toward the candidacy of Arizona's right-wing Senator Barry Goldwater. With his deep and emotional attachment to establishing an international rule of law, Luce was especially irked by Goldwater's hostility toward the World Court. When *Fortune* assistant managing editor John Davenport, a strong Goldwater partisan, wrote Luce in mid-1963 that "if Goldwater's philosophy is lunatic, many famous men, including some editors of Time Inc., would have to take a bow," Luce brushed the argument aside. Goldwater was "innocent of legislative effort," and a pork-barreler too: "Against federal spending, his state of Arizona gets more federal funds and projects per capita than any other state, I think. Check," he wrote Davenport.

Chances that any Republican could beat Lyndon Johnson appeared slight, however. Luce came away from a White House visit in March 1964 obviously impressed. "I had lunch with the President on Monday—and enjoyed every minute of it."

Luce's cordial relations with Johnson continued throughout the spring. Johnson telephoned him at home one Sunday afternoon in May, bending Luce's ear for 40 minutes on "practically everything you can think of," asking Luce's appraisal of how he was doing. "I said he was doing just fine," Luce reported. That same month, Luce saw in Johnson's University of Michigan commencement speech calling for the creation of a "Great Society," the reprise of an idea he himself had long been advocating. Luce had used the phrase as early as 1939 (and others had before him). Johnson, for his part, was much taken with a speech Luce made at Harvard Business School two weeks later, in which Luce called on business leadership to help "build a finer civilization than the world . . . has ever known." Time Inc. correspondents who attended an off-record session with the President afterward reported that he had spent five minutes reading to them from a heavily underlined copy of Luce's Harvard address. "Excellent speech," Johnson said. "This man *knows* what we're trying to do . . . I'm going to try to get Mr. Luce down to Washington."

But inevitably, with the campaign's progress, asperity crept in. In August both *Time* and *Life* angered the President—*Time* with a somewhat unflattering cover story on Lady Bird Johnson, *Life* with a two-part series on "The Man Who Is President," detailing Johnson's rise through Texas politics to presidential power and personal affluence, during which the Johnson family had become "one of the four richest ever to occupy the White House."*

The *Life* series by staff writer Keith Wheeler and investigative reporter Bill Lambert valued the Johnson family holdings at $14 million, including an 85 percent interest in an Austin, Texas, television station that had received consistently favorable treatment from the FCC during Johnson's years in the House and Senate. The heat in Washington built as the story neared print. The President's personal attorney, Abe Fortas, telephoned *Life*, requesting an advance look, which was refused; Fortas then summoned the *Life* team to Washington "at the President's request." Wheeler, Lambert, *Life*'s Washington bureau chief Dick Stolley, articles editor David Maness and assistant managing editor Ralph Graves met at Fortas's law office, where Fortas again asked to see the *Life* story and was again refused. Graves recounted what followed:

> An hour later . . . we were summoned to the White House and sat with Johnson in the family private dining room along with Fortas and [presidential assistant] Walter Jenkins. For four hours, with scarcely a word from Fortas or Jenkins, the

*The other three, according to *Life*: the George Washingtons, the Herbert Hoovers, the John Kennedys.

President held forth to us. He knew all the people Wheeler and Lambert had been interviewing ("my enemies"), and he had a long, single-spaced typewritten report detailing the date, time, location, duration and content of the talks. He told stories (both political and scatological), he cajoled, he told us he was the "only President we had," he revealed the specific problems he was worrying about that very night. He also gave answers to every financial question that Wheeler or Lambert could think to ask. Dick Stolley, who had sat next to the President for four hours, had a sore right thigh from Johnson constantly grabbing his leg for emphasis. Johnson held us until two in the morning, when he said he was going to have a massage and read a few more reports. He finally showed us out, turning off a few lights as he went. It was a stunning show—and all in an effort to protect himself against our article.

Finally, from Johnson's principal trustee came an itemized statement of the President's holdings, which *Life* published, showing a book value of $4,160,000. (*Life*'s estimate represented current value. Later estimates of Johnson's wealth ranged as high as $20 million.)

A month after the election, Johnson, still rankling, blew up in an hour-long tirade at *Time*'s Washington bureau chief John Steele, reminiscent of Kennedy's earlier outbursts. *Time*, Johnson claimed, "twisted" facts; *Life* "took the word of some drunks in Texas against that of the President of the United States."

A month before the Republican convention, Scranton, who had been holding back on a formal declaration of candidacy, finally jumped into the presidential race. Annoyed with his delay, *Life* declared him the better man nonetheless: "We would far rather see Scranton than Goldwater as President of the United States." *Life* conceded that Scranton's chances were slim. Indeed, the main result of the *Life* editorial was to focus press attention on Luce and his wife as they arrived at the convention in San Francisco's Cow Palace—Luce's publications were for Scranton; his wife Clare was vociferously for Goldwater and ready to include Time Inc. in her indictment of the press for having made Goldwater "Mr. Republican Victim of 1964."

The press, she declared in a preconvention session with reporters, "always picks a Republican victim." *Time* and *Life* too? "I don't

172

think they've been as fair to Goldwater as they should have been," she replied. After making one of the four speeches seconding Goldwater's nomination, Mrs. Luce went on to become national co-chairman of the Citizens for Goldwater committee, whereupon one prominent commentator imagined he saw Time Inc. swinging about to conform.

The immediate cause for comment was a sidebar story in *Time*'s convention report, examining the question: "Who Are the Goldwaterites?" Picking up a phrase from the Atlanta *Constitution*, *Time* described them as neither racists nor "nuclear bomb-throwers" but rather as a "federation of the fed up"—middle-class voters "fed up with the portents of economic, social and moral decay they see across the U.S., particularly in its crime-infested cities." For James Wechsler, columnist and editorial page editor of the New York *Post*, *Time*'s convention coverage represented "an exercise in the rehabilitation of Barry Goldwater," attributable at least partly to Mrs. Luce's influence. "It is true," Wechsler added, "that Henry Luce officially abdicated high office some months ago and on the magazine's masthead, he is now listed modestly as 'editorial chairman.' But one assumes that those technically in charge are still mindful of his presence, and sensitive to the complexities of his political relationship with Mrs. Luce."

That the boss's wife influenced *Time* editors was a popular misconception. Time Inc. journalism, whatever its idiosyncrasies, did not work that way. Mrs. Luce herself set the record straight in September, at a meeting of Americans Abroad for Goldwater in France. A member of the group asked Mrs. Luce: "How can we expect to win when even your magazines say such things about Senator Goldwater?" Cabled Time-Life correspondent James Bell from Paris: "La Luce fixed her with a cold stare, said, 'Well, in the first place, they are not *my* magazines.' "

In October, in a *Life* editorial, Donovan declared Time Inc.'s position. Luce was out of the country as the time for decision approached. "I think it was so he would be out of my way," Donovan said after Luce's death. "He gave me a completely free hand. To this day I don't know whom he voted for."

Before he left, Luce was showing some reluctance to dismiss the Republican candidate entirely; at one point he was so exasperated by the New York *Times*'s anti-Goldwater editorials that he snapped in a memo to Tom Griffith: "Alas, it is not true that the press has no influence. The New York *Times* singlehandedly is driving me into the Goldwater ghetto." But Donovan was already nudging Time Inc. toward endorsement of Johnson.

He moved deliberately—his style, different from Luce's, which inclined toward impulsiveness, was one that Donovan's associates would come to know well. New in the editor-in-chief's chair, Donovan had also, in this instance, the problem of taking an independent-minded crew of managing and assistant managing editors with him. "It's not," Donovan once remarked, "something that is done by just pushing a button and telling everybody to start writing one way or the other way." Looking back, Donovan estimated that of some 15 senior editorial executives, only about three were for Goldwater.

From the Johnson partisans, there was pressure for Time Inc. to state its position sooner rather than later, so as not to be left too far behind. Reading reports of the normally Republican newspapers that were already lining up for Johnson, Ed Thompson, in charge of *Life*'s editorial page, wrote managing editor George Hunt, "I was tempted . . . to press very hard for a commitment to Johnson, editorially, fairly soon so as not to be accused of metooism by trailing Roy Roberts [of the Kansas City *Star*], Hearst, Scripps-Howard . . . (not to mention Henry Ford II). I did mention this to Hedley, who said he was tempted, too, but thought, in sum, we should stick to the schedule we had talked about in . . . positioning *Life* for its eventual endorsement of L.B.J."

The schedule was followed. In September *Life* ran a signed article by Donovan, a seven-page tussle with Goldwater's contradictory positions on a number of issues, entitled, "The Difficulty of 'Being Fair' to Goldwater." In early October came the formal endorsement of Johnson.

There were few qualifications to this first declared support for a Democratic presidential candidate in Time Inc.'s history. The President, *Life* said, had "led the country out of the deep shock of the Kennedy assassination," had given Congress leadership for "a striking record of constructive legislation" notably on civil rights and taxes, had "shown generally good judgment in foreign policy and [had] begun to find the consensus that will keep the country unified in the face of its perils and opportunities." Nor was *Life* for Johnson merely as "the lesser-evil candidate. He is a well-qualified President of the U.S." For Goldwater and "the brand of Republicanism he espouses, we do not think a landslide defeat would be unjust to either."

Donovan relayed the reaction to Luce in Tokyo. "We had at

least one satisfied reader," Donovan wrote, reporting that Johnson telephoned the day the magazine appeared "to say that he had just read that 'simply wonderful' editorial in *Life*. 'I can't tell you how much I appreciate it. All I can say is that I'm going to do my dead-level best to be worthy of it.' "

Added Donovan: "We're also beginning to get some telegrams canceling subscriptions."

The Most Rethought of All

FORTUNE WAS THE FIRST MAGAZINE that Luce had launched on his own, after Hadden's death, and in an article for the February 1965 issue, entitled "The First 35 Years of *Fortune*," Luce spoke with pardonable pride of the magazine's impact on business—and on business journalism:

> I would cite at the start the proposition on which *Fortune* was founded—that all business is vested with a public interest. And since it is [so vested] like no other capitalistic business, anywhere, ever, American business . . . is not only open to inspection by all manner of government agencies [but] is also open to the inspection of journalists, and in this *Fortune* has played a leading role.
>
> I elaborated all this once in a speech to young businessmen, when I said: "It is, I suppose, almost impossible for the younger men here to realize how radical was this proposition of inspection when I was your age. To be sure, at the beginning of this century there was a great deal of public law . . . But still . . . the bankers in Wall Street and LaSalle Street and the heads of great corporations sincerely thought of themselves as individ-

uals going about their private business, with essentially no more accountability to the public than the corner grocer or soda-pop vendor.

Journalistically, this meant that no leading banker or businessman considered that the inquiring reporter had any right to knock on his door—unless he came to write a puff story . . . The idea that the journalist should inquire after the facts was not only outrageous to the businessman, it was inconceivable. And anyway, who cared about the facts of business?

A great many cared, as was soon evident. Through the door *Fortune* opened, numerous competitors had crowded in, a proliferation of magazines, newsletters and other publications addressed to various levels and segments of the business audience.

Fortune still stood in a class by itself in the depth of its reporting and lavishness of its presentation—an expensive magazine to produce, circulating to a relatively small audience and commanding premium advertising rates. But it was being pressed hard. Not only was *Business Week* offering a larger circulation guarantee than *Fortune*'s 330,000, but the fortnightly *Forbes* was edging up. The newsweeklies, *Time* included, were beginning to compete with *Fortune* for business and corporate advertising. "Here is the basic competitive position," *Fortune* publisher Del Paine had written Luce in early 1960. "*Fortune* has the smallest circulation and by far the highest [advertising] rate per thousand in our competitive universe."

Within the company *Fortune*, then still a monthly (as it had been since its founding), ranked as a comparatively modest business. By their nature, monthly magazines were usually smaller operations than weeklies, which dipped 52 times each year into the available pool of advertising dollars. Except for 1944 and 1945, when wartime industrial advertising briefly inflated *Fortune*'s page sales, the magazine had taken 26 years to turn its first million dollar profit. Editorial pace also set *Fortune* apart. To editors and writers coming to *Fortune* from *Time* or *Life*, the monthly publishing rhythm seemed blessedly relaxed. The corporation stories on which *Fortune* had made its reputation—exhaustive company profiles that were months in preparation and could run many thousands of words in print— offered a journalistic challenge that had attracted some of Time Inc.'s best talents. Writers could, for the most part, pick their own stories; many worked mainly at home, coming in only occasionally for editorial consultations. It was an enviable life, offering exceptional independence. "We're like little corporations here," one *Fortune* writer remarked.

The contemplative ambience was deceptive, however. *Fortune*'s longer deadlines did not relieve the editorial pressure. Duncan Norton-Taylor, Donovan's successor as managing editor, who arrived at the magazine "after many breathless years of weekly sprints on *Time*," found *Fortune*'s monthly "mile run . . . no easier." And in another respect, monthly publication imposed editorial demands that the more news oriented weeklies escaped. Norton-Taylor discussed it in a 1964 speech to *Fortune*'s advertising salesmen:

> There is a hand that will pass automatically across the pages of, say, *Time* . . . It is current history writing. Congress will meet . . . satellites will go up into orbit. You can count on it. The test of a weekly editor's skill is in how closely he keeps on the heels of current events . . . But whether a monthly magazine is a journalistic success or not depends very largely on how a bemused editor decides to fill in the blanks, how well he guesses in April what's going to be hot in September.

Norton-Taylor's remarks touched on the central question then facing *Fortune* in its competitive battle. This was the question of editorial urgency: to what extent the magazine, in its present format and on a monthly publishing schedule, was imperative reading for its managerial audience. The question had been posed before, and would be posed again; in the "rethinking" process to which Luce periodically subjected his publications, *Fortune* was probably the most rethought of all.

Having pioneered its field, the early *Fortune* had staked out its own boundaries. They were quite wide. Along with examination of the structure of United States Steel, the workings of the city of Miami, the Vatican, the League of Nations and a Vermont farm, *Fortune* could, in a 1933 profile of the Duke Ellington orchestra as a business enterprise, get away with a few lines on the band's earnings, devoting the rest of the seven pages to a loving essay on the delights of jazz music. Caught up in the early New Deal ferment, *Fortune* for a while veered politically leftward; Luce pulled it back to a more conservative course without abrogating its charter to be a critic as well as a chronicler of business. Because of a postwar advertising slump, *Fortune* came under intense corporate scrutiny. There was even talk, Luce recalled, "of an 'American *Economist*' "—a *Fortune* modeled on Britain's influential weekly journal of economics and politics.

The net, finally, was a full-blown "reprospectus" produced in 1948. It asserted that *Fortune* would continue to be a monthly, handsome, with high pictorial content. But the key new factor was that *Fortune* was to be "conceived of as a magazine with a *mission*." That mission, said Luce, was to "assist in the successful development of American Business Enterprise at home and abroad." With that reorientation, *Fortune*'s editorial approach became more functional; there was expanded coverage of labor, science and technology, as well as the inauguration of an authoritative monthly analysis of business and economic trends.

In 1953, Paine, who had edited *Fortune* since 1941, became publisher. Donovan, succeeding him, continued the redirection of *Fortune* toward its readers' primary interests, producing what one of Donovan's successors later described as "a brass tacks business magazine." In 1955 *Fortune* put a new phrase into the language of business—and popular terminology—with the creation of the *Fortune* 500 listing of the largest U.S. industrial firms (the inspiration of Edgar Smith, then an assistant managing editor). During this period, *Fortune*'s profits improved markedly.

For a magazine over which he had worried so much, Luce handled changes in its top editors haphazardly. Norton-Taylor's appointment to succeed Donovan in 1959 was characteristically casual. The magazine's elders, Donovan, Bill Furth and Paine, had considered Norton-Taylor a good choice for the job, and Luce accordingly invited him to lunch at New York's St. Regis Hotel. Norton-Taylor remembered Luce downing several martinis and rambling on about everything except the magazine. Not until two weeks later when the managing editor of another magazine called to congratulate him ("Why?" Norton-Taylor asked) did he learn that he had been appointed.

A compact little bulldog of a man, quite forceful—"can be pretty tough . . . a good no-man," as Donovan described him to Luce— Norton-Taylor was then 55, an age when most Time Inc. managing editors were finishing rather than just beginning their tours of duty. A Brown University graduate, he had written popular fiction and edited pulp magazines before coming to *Time* in prewar days as a National Affairs writer. "In 1939 the world seemed to be going to hell. I couldn't go on writing love stories," he explained. A dozen years and 60 cover stories later, Norton-Taylor transferred to *Fortune*, where, in 1958, he was named executive editor. Curiously, although rockribbed Republican in his politics, Norton-Taylor was not much enamored of businessmen, whom he regarded with "a good deal more suspiciousness . . . than normal journalistic diligence would require," Donovan observed. But he considered Norton-Taylor "an excellent literary editor, with a strong dramatic sense."

Several staff changes at *Fortune* followed Norton-Taylor's appointment. Assistant managing editor William H. (Holly) Whyte Jr., out of whose perceptive *Fortune* pieces had come the popular book *The Organization Man*, resigned. Filling the vacancy was Max Ways, 55, formerly a *Time* senior editor, more recently the Time Life news bureau chief in London. John Davenport, 56, *Fortune*'s other assistant managing editor under Donovan, remained during Norton-Taylor's tenure. In June 1961 *Time* senior editor Louis Banks was brought over to be *Fortune*'s third assistant managing editor. Late the following year, the magazine acquired a new art director as well. Leo Lionni was succeeded by his deputy, Walter Allner, an alumnus of Germany's famous Bauhaus, who had come to *Fortune* in 1951 after a distinguished career in Europe as an abstract painter and designer. Allner's cover designs for *Fortune*— on one occasion employing a fanciful assemblage of mashed tin cans; on another, of items representing 116 of one year's Fortune 500 companies—were a notable feature of the magazine for more than two decades.

Together, the trio of Norton-Taylor, Ways and Davenport constituted not only the grayest but probably the most conservative editorial directorate of any Time Inc. magazine—"a bristling Adam Smith axis," Donovan referred to it jokingly. It was also the most scholarly. Norton-Taylor was quite philosophical in his bent, something of a theologian, who for years had been working on a biography of John Calvin in blank verse.* Davenport, brother of onetime *Fortune* managing editor Russell Davenport, was an expert on international monetary questions and had, from 1949 to 1954, edited *Barron's*, the financial weekly. Ways, Jesuit educated, a reporter on the Baltimore *Sun* and editorial writer for the Philadelphia *Record* before joining Time Inc. in 1945, was very close to Luce; he had been, at *Time*, the chosen interpreter of Luce's thinking, much as Jack Jessup had been at *Life*. "The intellectual head of the table,"

*The book, entitled *God's Man*, was published as a novel in 1979 by Baker Book House.

Luce once remarked, in a felicitous description of Ways. A large, rumpled man, he was something of a loner, inclined to commune directly with Luce rather than whoever happened, at the moment, to be sitting in the managing editor's chair. The difficulties this created were more than compensated for by Ways's gifts, as a writer, for sagacity on short notice.

Among the senior writing staff, who made up *Fortune*'s board of editors, viewpoints were more mixed. The board itself was a hierarchical peculiarity, duplicated at no other Time Inc. magazine; it served no editorial function except to meet periodically to dine expensively and, on occasion, to ratify the managing editor's selection of new members. Several veterans from prewar days remained. Gilbert Burck was *Fortune*'s most prolific writer by far; in 35 years with the magazine he would, eventually, set a record of producing more than 350 major articles. Charlie Murphy, the magazine's Washington-based specialist in defense and intelligence matters, was an imposing figure who had been in journalism since 1926 and had done almost everything. He had worked on the Boston *American* in the days of the prototypical *Front Page* editor, Walter Hovey; had written editorials for the New York *World* under Walter Lippmann; had gone to the South Pole with Admiral Richard E. Byrd and helped write Byrd's book about the expedition. He had also ghost-written the Duke of Windsor's memoirs, *A King's Story*.*

More recent arrivals on the board of editors included Mary Johnston, who had become chief of research in 1955 and was to hold that job for more than three decades; she turned an already admirable research staff into one as formidable as any in the Time & Life Building and perhaps in all journalism. Richard Austin Smith, a former Washington correspondent for *Time*, had become *Fortune*'s expert on corporate misdeeds and mismanagement and was sometimes accused of writing like a prosecuting attorney. Sanford Parker was a brilliant economist who, although he suffered from agoraphobia and rarely moved outside his Manhattan neighborhood, made *Fortune*'s Business Roundup the most authoritative economic forecast then being published for a general audience. Charles E. Silberman, a former economics instructor at Columbia University without previous journalistic experience, became *Fortune*'s leading writer on education and race-relations problems. T.A. (Tom) Wise, an acquisition from the *Wall Street Journal*, specialized in financial and investment matters.

*G.P. Putnam's Sons, 1951.

181

Norton-Taylor had been in the job only a few months when the editor-in-chief, hearing what he called "sounds in the engine room," began wondering aloud whether it might be time, yet again, for an editorial overhaul of *Fortune*. "A New Prospectus, even though mainly reasserting the main merits of [the] existing *Fortune*," Luce wrote, "would help to 'validate' the new managing editor. It would force the Old Guard to modernize itself . . . and it might even be useful to J. Howell [John Howell, *Fortune*'s advertising manager]."

Norton-Taylor was skeptical. His private view was that revising a magazine's formula was "like trying to revise a wrought-iron fence." He duly took time off, however, to work up some thoughts for Luce, which he presented in January 1961. The *Fortune* layout could stand some restyling, he conceded, but "no new chrome, no tail fins." *Fortune*'s "neglect of the art of story telling" could be remedied. "Stories of rascality seem to enchant our law-abiding readers," he observed. He listed several specific projects that *Fortune* was then planning, including a series on personal investing and a 12-part history of American business from prerevolutionary days to the present, for which John Chamberlain, author of many of the prewar *Fortune*'s corporate profiles, had been recruited as writer. But on the whole, Norton-Taylor declared, "my unexciting conclusion is that we shouldn't make any basic changes [in *Fortune*]. Paine and Donovan have passed along a very good thing."

Succeeding months saw a number of outstanding articles. In the April 1961 issue was a notable tale of corporate rascality: the first of a two-part series by Dick Smith on "The Incredible Electrical Conspiracy," recounting the secret codes, clandestine meetings, faked travel vouchers and other details of the collusive bidding by several major electrical manufacturing firms, which resulted in the biggest criminal prosecution ever brought under the Sherman Antitrust Act. That same issue also carried Silberman's report on "The Remaking of American Education," which was to affect profoundly Time Inc.'s thinking about its own role in education. In September the promised series on personal investing began; it was to evolve into a regular *Fortune* column.

In January and February 1962 came another blockbuster by Dick Smith that was destined to be long remembered around Time Inc. This was an examination of "How a Great Corporation Got Out of Control." The corporation in question was General Dynamics, whose $425 million loss was the "biggest product loss ever sustained by any company anywhere." Recalled Smith:

182

Obviously, this was a business story that demanded *Fortune* coverage . . . The catch was that General Dynamics' chairman was Frank Pace, then . . . a highly regarded member of Time Inc.'s board of directors . . . We had to do the story, otherwise it would look as if we'd chickened out; further, if we found Pace at fault in the $425 million loss, we couldn't do less than say so. Dunc [Norton-Taylor], quite equal to the diplomacy involved, set up an exploratory lunch with Pace and his people. And there, as my neck seemed to stretch farther and farther out along the white tablecloth, I felt constrained to put the painful question: if we find mistakes have been made, Mr. Pace, you understand that we will have to assess the responsibility for them? He understood, and he would cooperate fully in getting at the facts . . . When Pace read the first draft on Part One, he informed *Fortune* the magazine could announce his resignation as chairman in Part Two.* When editorial director Donovan took a proof of the story in to president Linen, Pace's old and good friend, he emerged an hour or so later without a mark on it.

After 1960, when *Fortune* had earned just over $2 million, pretax, on revenues of $12,646,700, the magazine's profits sagged. A decline in advertising page sales was part of the reason; the rising cost of maintaining circulation also hurt. Hank Luce, who was then serving as *Fortune*'s circulation director, was worried also by the aging of the magazine's readership; the median age was up from 44 in 1960 to 46 in 1963. A survey of readers tended to confirm the impression that *Fortune* was "unique . . . superior . . . authoritative," but was also seen as "a spokesman to and for BIG business" and published for an audience that was "higher up . . . somewhere else." Additionally, *Fortune* was too bulky a package, "physically big to hold and handle, to read and carry"—a criticism to which the publisher's office was becoming quite sensitive.

For the troubles *Fortune* was experiencing, publisher Del Paine was inclined to blame the editorial product. Given to growling his opinions rather than voicing them (a colleague once told him: "Del, if you spoke English, you'd be bilingual"), Paine was explicit enough in writing. And he complained to Luce that the magazine

---

*As a matter of fact, the second installment, in February, went to press before Pace's resignation, but *Fortune* carried the appointment of his successor in the March issue. Pace remained on the Time Inc. board of directors.

was editorially ill-defined, that early improvement was unlikely and that the editor-in-chief and his deputy should take a firmer hand. In January 1964, Paine let fly again:

> Evidence that there is something wrong with *Fortune*'s editorial performance can be quickly summarized: 1) Circulation is hard to get and too costly. 2) Advertising sales in its 1964 selling season is meeting increasing resistance to the *Fortune* proposition . . . Even our friends worry about the magazine's urgency and timeliness.

Paine went on to list his specific complaints and offer some editorial suggestions of his own—a final salvo, as it turned out, since in a general Time Inc. publishing reshuffle that followed a month later, Paine was shifted to the corporate staff as head of the company's new research and development department. Succeeding him as *Fortune* publisher was former domestic news service chief Jim Shepley, most recently assistant publisher of *Life*.

Coincidentally, in a move to strengthen *Fortune*'s editorial management, assistant managing editor Louis Banks was promoted to executive editor. Ways was named associate managing editor, to assist in forward planning and to handle the editorial page. Two younger editors, Robert Lubar and Daniel Seligman, joined Davenport as assistant managing editors, giving *Fortune* what Donovan, looking back on his own days as managing editor, described somewhat enviously as "a luxurious editing staff."

Paine's farewell blast had, nonetheless, struck an unusually responsive chord with Luce, who wrote *Fortune*'s senior editorial group saying that he had been intending to produce "a major memo" about the magazine but "now Del Paine . . . has done some of my work for me." For a while, Luce considered subjecting *Fortune* to another rethink; in a session with Banks, he indicated he was toying with the idea of making *Fortune* into "quite a different magazine." The impulse to remake *Fortune* passed shortly, Luce deciding that nothing so "portentous" as a new prospectus was needed. But he did pick up on several of Paine's specifics, notably that *Fortune* should increase the number of stories to provide more variety and topicality. And he enthusiastically endorsed Paine's proposal that *Fortune* take on the "new editorial mission" of reporting science's impact on the social order or, as Luce delineated it, "the vast subject of radical change in the conditions of human life."

While Norton-Taylor began the editorial adjustments Luce suggested, Max Ways undertook to articulate Luce's larger thoughts.

184

The resulting essay, "The Era of Radical Change," which ran in the May 1964 issue, was a virtuoso performance on Ways's part—quickly produced, pulling together strains of thought from a diverse group of authorities from Charles de Gaulle to physicist Robert Oppenheimer to define the rapidity and scope of change that was making the present era different from anything in the past. Much quoted, Ways's article established a theme that was reflected in subsequent speeches by Luce, Donovan and other Time Inc. executives. It was also adopted by *Fortune* as the keynote for a general sales campaign.

In the midst of these changes, another assignment was thrust on *Fortune,* somewhat in the nature of a salvage job. This was to take over "a major part" of the editorial franchise of *Architectural Forum,* which, it was announced, would cease publication with the September 1964 issue after 32 years under Time Inc. ownership. And, with *Forum's* demise, *House & Home,* its younger sibling serving the residential building trade, was being sold to McGraw-Hill Inc., the U.S.'s largest trade journal publisher.

Apart from *Letters,* a short-lived supplement to *Time*'s Letters section that the company had published in the mid-1930s, these were the first magazine failures in company history. Their end was not unexpected; both magazines had been living on borrowed time. *House & Home,* despite its 137,000 circulation, the largest net paid of any monthly trade journal, had only once during its 12 years been even marginally in the black. *Forum* was highly respected professionally; the New York *Times* editorially eulogized its "influential and broadly beneficial role [as] a force for better building" that went far beyond *Forum*'s 64,000 circulation, extending to government and corporation circles as well. But *Forum* had not made a profit since 1950.

The two magazines' losses were not great. In 1963 they aggregated $432,300 on revenues of $4.6 million. But the latter figure—amounting to less than 2 percent of Time Inc.'s total magazine revenues—was the measure of a basic problem. The traditionally small-budget trade journal field was not really one for Time Inc. to be in. A statement in *Forum* by Joseph C. Hazen Jr., the Princeton-trained architect who earlier had edited both magazines and was their joint publisher at the end, made that point:

Perhaps one of *Forum*'s insuperable difficulties has been that the cost structure of a small magazine within a large publishing enterprise tends to move up to the standards set by the big, broad-audience magazines, so that the usual advantages of size become disadvantages to a small publication. This has been true for us.

House & Home went to McGraw-Hill for the virtual giveaway price of $100,000 plus the value of its paper inventory and other assets. McGraw-Hill declared its intent to keep "the magazine and its staff as intact as possible," and about half the top staff did move with the magazine; Hazen and *House & Home*'s last managing editor, Gurney Breckenfeld, were among those remaining with Time Inc.

No buyer was in sight for *Forum,* however, and the announcement of its imminent closure provoked a flood of protests from architects, many asking the company to reconsider. "We are not losing just one architectural magazine but in a sense the only one," wrote Philip Johnson. Within the company also, there were attempts to save it. Del Paine, whose duties as *Fortune* publisher had, at one point, included co-publishing *Forum,* drafted a proposal that Yale—a pioneer of architecture on the university campus, as well as his and Luce's alma mater—assume publication with a small transitional subsidy from Time Inc. Luce personally took the offer to Yale president Kingman Brewster, but the university declined, with regrets. So, later, did the University of California at Berkeley.

A month after *Forum*'s last issue, a new Structure & Design department inaugurated *Fortune*'s expanded architectural coverage—four pages dealing with a range of topics from the Ford Foundation's new "greenhouse" headquarters building in Manhattan to the aesthetics of the San Francisco Bay area's proposed rapid transit system. Time Inc. continued meanwhile to search for a possible taker for *Forum.* Before year's end one was found: the American Civic and Planning Association, a nonprofit organization devoted to urban improvement. Publication of *Forum* resumed in April 1965, under its last Time Inc. managing editor, Peter Blake, with former general manager Lawrence Mester as publisher. Other changes of direction and ownership followed in subsequent years; in 1974 *Forum* finally went under.

Paine had been at the helm of *Fortune* almost a quarter century—first as managing editor, then as publisher—when he left the magazine in 1964. The departure of this familiar figure, and the appointment of Shepley to succeed him, aroused mixed emotions. "Sullen but not mutinous"—so business manager Edward Patrick Lenahan, a *Fortune* veteran himself, described the mood as Shepley arrived from *Life*. Shepley had a reputation as a rough, abrasive administrator; his taut look and manner reminded some of a Marine Corps drill sergeant. A much read newsletter of the publishing trade referred to him as Brass Knuckles Shepley, and the nickname stuck (Shepley learned to smile about it). In his off hours, Shepley, an accomplished and fanatic yachtsman, went in for ocean racing.

It was on the editorial side that Shepley had made his name and where he had come to Luce's attention. Shepley had left Dickinson College to become a reporter on the Pittsburgh *Press*, going from there to the United Press's state capital bureau in Harrisburg where, he recalled, "I was so brash and stayed up all night and forced my name on the wire so often" that the UP transferred him to Washington. In 1942 he was hired by *Time* and sent to cover the China-Burma-India theater. Subsequently commissioned in the Army and assigned to help prepare General George C. Marshall's war reports, Shepley accompanied the Army Chief of Staff to the Potsdam conference and, later, on his mission to China. Rejoining Time Inc., Shepley was named Washington news bureau chief in 1948.

"The godfather of investigative reporters . . . mean, suspicious, cynical and brilliant," as onetime Secretary of State William Rogers described him, Shepley came to figure in the news himself, in 1954, as co-author of a controversial book on the building of the hydrogen bomb*; and in 1956 as author of the *Life* article on John Foster Dulles that provoked the furor over "brinksmanship." In 1960 Shepley had taken a leave of absence to work in Nixon's presidential campaign.

The decision to send Shepley to *Fortune* as publisher was a gamble, Heiskell admitted: "He was brilliant, irascible, explosive, grating, and with fear and trembling Hedley [Donovan] and I made him publisher and waited for *Fortune* to explode in our faces. While there was quite a lot of noise, it didn't explode."

Shepley and the publishing team he brought with him—Lee Heffner, from *Life*, as *Fortune*'s new advertising sales director, and John Philip Sousa III, from *Time*, as assistant publisher—faced a difficult situation. Advertising page sales, budgeted for a decline, were falling even below budget. According to Shepley, "the competition was cultivating the impression that *Fortune* was not much read—that it was a coffee-table ornament." The year proved to be

The Hydrogen Bomb: The Men, The Menace, The Mechanism (David McKay Company, 1954). The co-author was Clay Blair Jr.

187

Fortune's worst in a decade. Time Inc.'s weekly magazines all made substantial gains, with *SI* finally going into the black. *Fortune* alone lost ground, its net income dropping to $733,500.

This was the low point, however. Shepley was a vigorous and decisive publisher who, in the words of Lou Banks, watching from the editorial side, "got *Fortune* talked about." That fall, with the help of subscriptions inherited from *Architectural Forum* when it ceased publication, *Fortune*'s advertising rate base for 1965 was pushed to 420,000. The circulation increase, coupled with a 370-page improvement in ad sales, resulted in an almost doubled pretax profit in 1965.

In August 1965, the changes in *Fortune*'s top editorial lineup begun a year earlier were completed. Banks was named to succeed Norton-Taylor who, by his own choice, returned to *Fortune*'s writing staff. In making his first managing editorial appointment after taking over from Luce, Donovan had moved slowly. Luce had a hard time restraining himself as the new editor-in-chief weighed his decision. Said Banks: "My feeling is that the appointment was a collaboration between the two of them; that Harry wanted to get on with it but Hedley's way was to sit back and watch and be skeptical about things. Harry had me to dinner at his apartment and was congratulating me but he couldn't quite tell me why . . . He said, 'Well, I think you're going to have a lot of responsibilities soon and I just want you to go ahead and put a good magazine out. But of course I can't say anything yet because Hedley hasn't decided' . . . And then ultimately Hedley did. After having audited my books like Price Waterhouse, he consented."

Donovan's deliberation paid off. In Banks he acquired not only an innovative managing editor for *Fortune* but a future editorial director for Time Inc.—the post that Donovan himself had held under Luce. Banks, who was 49 when he took over *Fortune*'s top post, was a slim, quiet man, a briskly efficient executive who had served in editing and writing positions on both *Time* and *Life*. A self-styled "Depression kid," Banks had moved with his widowed mother from Pennsylvania to southern California because the living was cheaper, and had started newspaper work while at the University of California at Los Angeles as a campus stringer for a small Beverly Hills newspaper. He went to Hearst's Los Angeles *Examiner* after graduation, saving enough money to take two long and instructive summer trips: in 1938 to Europe, in 1940 to East Asia where Japan and China were already at war. From World War II service in the Pacific as a Navy pilot, Banks returned to work for *Flying* magazine, afterward joining *Time*'s Los Angeles bureau. Sid James, then bureau chief, introduced Banks to Time Inc. work habits. "I asked about my hours," Banks said. "Sid said: 'On this job your time's your own. But you'll soon discover it all belongs to us.' Those were the most honest words ever spoken."

After a turn in the Washington bureau, Banks came to New York to write for *Time*, becoming National Affairs editor in 1956. In 1961 Luce recruited him for *Life* to produce a weekly news roundup—promptly dubbed "Banksville"—then being planned as a feature of the "new" *Life*. Recalled Banks: "Harry was always trying to put words into *Life* and pictures into *Time*." Later that year Banks moved to *Fortune*. His first full-length article, on the U.S. judicial system, entitled "The Crisis in the Courts," won an American Bar Association award for outstanding public service.

Banks's accession to the managing editorship in 1965 marked a generational revolution in *Fortune*'s top echelon. At a black-tie staff dinner that Donovan gave for Norton-Taylor, Ways and Davenport shortly thereafter at New York's St. Regis Hotel, the atmosphere fairly crackled with references to "*Fortune*'s newly constituted geriatric ward" where, Ways declared, the departing editors could be seen "in the future, waving our crutches at each other." Emotions subsided eventually, however, and all three men remained valued contributors to *Fortune*'s pages. Ways entered into one of his most productive periods, remaining on *Fortune*'s active list four years beyond the normal retirement age and continuing after that to write occasional articles for the magazine.

"*Fortune* was caught at a crossroads, not knowing which economic philosophy it believed in," Banks remarked of the split that had prevailed at *Fortune* in the years immediately preceding the change of editors. "The Keynesians were coming on . . . but on the other hand, there were the classical economic traditionalists whose influence was still strong"—too strong, in his view.

Under Banks, who described himself as a liberal Republican, *Fortune* was to undergo a marked ideological shift. In a way, it was a return to the magazine's origins, to a greater preoccupation with business activity in relation to the public interest. Not since New Deal days, perhaps, had *Fortune* been so involved in questions of public policy as during this period.

The magazine was also to become more current, to acquire what

Banks called "a news denominator . . . I'd like to say that *Fortune* became more highly topical, ahead of the news on serious questions, more perceptive about the nature of the American corporation [and] that we saw the relationship of business to the news."

An important aspect of the news of American business in the middle and late 1960s was the unprecedented demands put on it by government and by the rising forces of social protest. To both, *Fortune* responded sympathetically. In Washington, it found much to commend in the Great Society legislation that was rushed to enactment in the early days of the Johnson administration. It gave a more than tolerant reception to the "new economics" of managing money and credit supply to produce sustained growth, as expounded by the President's economic advisers. In its reaction to social disorder, and to the new questions this posed of corporate responsibility, *Fortune* took the line that it was indeed the business of U.S. business—and *Fortune*'s also—to help find solutions to the underlying problems.

"Our job in this [age of social responsibility] is twofold," Banks wrote to one of *Fortune*'s advertising executives, explaining the magazine's editorial philosophy, "[first] to raise warning signals . . . for business in anticipation of [social] changes; and [second] to report how management does, or does not deal with the questions as they arise." He went on:

> *Fortune* has always assumed business's social responsibility and the news about today is that everybody suddenly assumes it too. This confronts corporate management with pressures, demands and opportunities unlike any it has ever faced before. So we were among the first to talk about air pollution in realistic business terms, and so we have spent a lot of energy and effort in outlining the problems of decaying cities, deteriorating countrysides, rising urban [minority] populations, etc. . . . I think . . . we have tried to avoid the kind of sociological handwringing that goes with the usual reporting of mankind's unhappy condition, and tried clearly to state and define the problem, usually with some recommended course of business action.

In January 1968, when the embers of the nation's worst urban rioting were cooling, a special *Fortune* issue on "Business and the Urban Crisis" assessed the U.S. corporate capacity for helping deal with the race problems of cities already "functionally enfeebled for reasons that pertain mainly to white, not black, America." A year later, another special issue, entitled "American Youth: Its Outlook

Is Changing the World," probed the causes of generational conflict that made "this rebellion something special . . . a serious matter."

To replenish his editing staff, Banks named two new assistant managing editors: Walter Guzzardi Jr., a scholarly Princetonian who had been in charge of Luce's personal office in Rome and had afterward become the Time-Life News Service bureau chief there; and Murray Gart, a former news service bureau chief in Chicago and London. Gart's appointment was aimed specifically at strengthening *Fortune*'s reporting of the U.S. political scene, where he brought impressive credentials from his days in charge of *Time*'s Midwest coverage. As it turned out, Gart remained with *Fortune* only until 1968, when he took leave to join Nelson Rockefeller's short-lived presidential campaign effort. Not long after his return to Time Inc., Gart became news service chief.

William Bowen was added to the ranks of *Fortune*'s assistant managing editors in 1969. He had moved over from *Time* to become one of *Fortune*'s shrewder reporters and more stylish writers. He had scored a journalistic coup in April 1966, with the first thorough cost accounting of the Vietnam War, cutting through Defense Department figures to reveal that the U.S. buildup would cost billions of dollars more than had been previously estimated. During the 1960s, *Fortune* developed several young writers who were to add luster to the magazine for years. An experienced researcher, Carol Junge Loomis turned writer and helped launch the "Personal Investing" column. Her lucid analysis of complex situations won wide admiration and her corporation stories were considered among the best *Fortune* had ever published. In 1968 she became the first woman writer to be elected to the board of editors.

Richard Armstrong, a genial, unflappable Mississippian who had once worked for *Time*, came to *Fortune* as a writer and soon worked his way into the editors' ranks, as did Allan Demaree, who had been acquired upon completing a Nieman Fellowship. Edmund Faltermayer, an alumnus of the *Wall Street Journal*, had got the jump on the environmental movement with his March 1965 article on "The Half-Finished Society," questioning whether environmental disorder need be a by-product of enterprise capitalism. Another *Wall Street Journal* alumnus to join *Fortune* was William S. Rukeyser, one of a noted family of financial writers and commentators. Banks flew to Britain to lure him away from the *Journal*'s London bureau in 1967. "It was one of the best things I ever did," said Banks later. Five years later Rukeyser was to become the managing editor of the newborn *Money*.

One *Fortune* practice, a relic of the magazine's earliest days, fell by the wayside during Banks's editorship. No longer were the subjects of *Fortune* articles allowed to have prepublication looks at what the magazine proposed to say about them. The practice had originated at a time when businessmen were unaccustomed to being questioned—at least as *Fortune* proposed to question them. By furnishing them with drafts of the articles, *Fortune* aimed at allaying their skittishness. Whatever the purpose, it was a dubious journalistic practice. If there were benefits in elucidating difficult technical points, there were offsetting difficulties in dealing with the subjects themselves, and in any event *Fortune*'s journalistic independence was compromised. In August 1967, a brief directive to the staff from Banks ended the procedure.

In 1966 *Fortune* had recovered from its slump enough to celebrate its best financial year since World War II. Nevertheless, the search continued for ways to beef up its profits. One was to launch, in mid-July 1966, a 13th issue. It was built around the annual *Fortune* directory of the 500 leading American industrial corporations. A 14th issue was added in the fall of 1967, centered on the annual list of the 200 largest industrials outside the U.S. Both issues were fleshed out with relevant short articles. They also reaped a rich harvest of ads. But as the regular issues that had featured the two lists, especially the 500 issue, had always been popular with advertisers, the question arose whether the extra issues produced a net gain. In 1969 a judgment was made that they did not, and they were dropped.

Shepley's term as publisher turned out to be a lively and fruitful one for *Fortune*. It was also a brief one. In 1967 he succeeded Bernhard Auer as publisher of *Time*, and *Life*'s associate publisher, Art Keylor, 46, was appointed to take his place. A Harvard Business School graduate who had served in naval aviation during World War II, Keylor was shrewd with numbers and was considered one of Time Inc.'s best analysts of the complex mathematics of magazine publishing. He was destined to stay at *Fortune* only a year before moving upstairs to take a succession of corporate jobs.

But Keylor had time to study the magazine and send a memo to top management appraising "the realities of *Fortune*'s current situation." With high editorial quality, almost the maximum number of ad pages expectable for a monthly magazine, high advertising and circulation prices, "*Fortune* seems to have all the ingred-

ients going for it necessary for a completely successful operation
. . . What's lacking? *Too few people buy it and read it.* Or, to put
it another way, the money and effort put into it requires a larger
audience . . . than we have currently to make it work acceptably
as a business."

The question of readership had been a major concern likewise
at the extended editorial review sessions that Donovan and Luce
had held with Banks and his senior colleagues in late 1966. Shepley
had also participated. He and Donovan were in agreement that
Fortune's audience was too small. Net paid circulation was then
approaching 450,000, but *Fortune*'s "natural circulation . . . is
closer to a million," Shepley declared. Banks, for his part, saw
Fortune broadening its readership by extending its editorial franchise, aiming at an international audience as well. "The opportunity is no secret. There are new business and economic journals
springing up in nearly every industrialized country of Europe . . .
Yet as anyone who travels can tell you, *Fortune*'s reputation as the
spokesman for business is towering in all the areas where it is
known," Banks wrote in preparation for the first meeting.

On the need for *Fortune* to expand its foreign business reporting
there was no argument. It had been increasing markedly under
Banks's editorship, and in the wake of the review sessions a further step was taken. In mid-1967 *Fortune* established its first overseas editorial office. Assistant managing editor Walter Guzzardi
moved to Brussels to supervise European coverage.

There was much argument, however, about Banks's other proposal: that in preparation for assuming the editorial role of spokesman for what Banks termed "the business internationale," *Fortune*
should consider converting from monthly to biweekly publication.
Without change, Banks felt, *Fortune* faced a limited future. "*Fortune*'s editorial vitality is . . . imprisoned by its present form."

Among the editors, enthusiasm for a change in publishing frequency was restrained. Luce was cool too, preferring to maintain
Fortune in its present form, but possibly supplementing the existing
monthly with a quarterly, published separately and edited specifically for a more internationally minded business audience. Donovan
thought biweekly publication was worth "a serious probe." He felt
that "two or three able people for two or three months" should
study its editorial feasibility. The following February, Banks
appointed an exploratory committee, under Max Ways's direction,
to work out a concept for "a biweekly *Fortune* . . . which could
comfortably circulate to a million of the world's most important

English-speaking readers in the business-government-university complex."

A copy of Banks's instructions to the study group went out to Luce in Phoenix on February 15, 1967. Luce jotted a reply the next day and put Banks's memo aside on his desk; it was among the papers found there after his death two weeks later. "I was glad to have your memo on the Exploration," Luce had written Banks. "It is quite persuasive and softened me up somewhat."

CHAPTER

12

Luce's Final Years

LUCE DIED IN PHOENIX on February 28, 1967, five weeks short of his 69th birthday. In the three years since his retirement in 1964, he had begun writing a book—the first in his half-century as a journalist. It was partly a memoir of his involvement with men and events in contemporary history, partly an attempt, as he put it, "to trace in broad but hopefully accurate terms, the rise and the uses of power of the United States and . . . to assay to what degree and in what ways [it] achieved greatness and in what ways it fell short." By July 1966 he had roughed out 12 of the 15 chapters listed in the draft manuscript's table of contents. These 12 covered the period from the U.S. entry into World War II to the Kennedy presidency; a 13th chapter, on the achievements of American business enterprise in the postwar period, was written later. Two other chapters remained unwritten at the time of his death. One was on alienation in modern American life, the other on the Great Society; sketchy notes indicate that Luce may have had additional subjects in mind.

The completed chapters, transcribed from Luce's handwriting by his secretary, total 126 double-spaced pages, about 40,000 words in all, and are themselves rather bare and sketchy. Luce is speaking more than writing. His thoughts outpace his words. Though his individual observations are provocative, the work as a whole is disjointed—an outline of a book still taking shape. Luce as editor might have sent it back to writer Luce for more of the detail, color, quote and anecdote that characterized the writing in his own magazines.

Luce begins by explaining his much-criticized definition of the "American Century," as proclaimed in a February 1941 article he wrote for *Life*. It was, he says, a prophecy of what would come to pass: that the U.S. would enter World War II, that it would emerge victorious and assume "world-wide responsibilities for human freedom." In that mission, the U.S. had failed in China but succeeded in Western Europe; Korea was "proof of America's resolution but proof also of our nervous reluctance to become involved in Asia." Now, in Vietnam, Luce saw a "turning point" at which, "after 20 years of effort and experience, the United States will be able to make clear to all mankind what rules of international behavior we intend to uphold and in what ways we will preserve purposes with power."

In a three-part chapter entitled "World Order" Luce sets up the confrontation between Communism ("an eschatology") and the American Proposition (for Luce, always capitalized). He does it in metaphysical terms, contrasting Communism's "one and only dynamic, confident and demanding faith in a world of men which had lost faith in faiths" with the "American consensus that this is a moral universe and that therefore certain highly probable corollaries follow—such as the imperishable value of human freedom in general and of individual human beings; such as the quest for justice."

In his assessment of political leaders, Luce is still contemptuous of Franklin Roosevelt, but gives belated due to Truman as "one of the great American presidents" (although Luce still faults him for firing MacArthur). Kennedy is memorable more for style than substance: "Style! That is the word . . . What was important about President Kennedy was not what he did but who he was. In this period of the American Century what millions of can-do Americans needed was not so much the capacity to do as the courage to be."

Curiously, Luce is rather tepid about Eisenhower, who presided over "eight . . . great years [when] nothing turned out badly for the Republic," but who was passive toward McCarthyism and remained aloof when "the Negro revolution began. Ike did not lead it, did not identify with it . . . Some like to imagine a scene where, instead of sending the National Guard into Little Rock, he, Ike, had gone there himself and taken Negro children by the hand and led them into school. I like to imagine it myself."

John Foster Dulles is the American contemporary whom Luce most admires: "the greatest of the Cold War warriors" who was nonetheless a man of peace, of "Christian faith . . . more specifically, faith in Christ," and of "fidelity to principle," who wished for America "only that it should be true to itself—to its best self." For Luce, Dulles's dedication to the rule of law in conduct of American policy was such "that if John Foster Dulles had lived another year, something at the highest level would have been done about world law—meaning the essential leadership of the United States in that salvific cause."

The book was one of the few pieces of unfinished business left by Luce. As his associate Jack Jessup observed, "One of his most graceful achievements was the way he got offstage. He began preparing for retirement in 1959, turned his editorial responsibilities over to Hedley Donovan in 1964, left Time Inc. in excellent running order and enjoyed three years of personal peace without any suspension of intellectual activity or interests." Another friend remarked on Luce's ability to "cut off pieces of his life in slices, like bread."

Colleagues had wondered how Luce would take to retirement, and Luce himself admitted to some difficulty in keeping to his place after he ceded his post to Donovan. "I have to watch out that I don't get in Donovan's hair," he once confided to an old Time Inc. associate, adding, however, "I do reserve the human right to talk to managing editors and writers and correspondents without going through channels."

In this respect he was very active. He followed the magazines and the company's book projects, sending off memos showing his customary mixture of philosophical observations, occasional criticism and fascination with unusual snippets of information. He continued to travel in the U.S. and abroad, dropping in on the Time Inc. news bureaus wherever he went, gathering the correspondents at the luncheon or dinner table, probing them in his familiar way. He continued to give speeches, one or more a month, to professional, academic and church groups, expounding on his favorite themes of American destiny, human purpose, the rule of law, journalism's responsibilities and the interaction of Occident and Orient. He was also spending considerable time on the United Presbyterian Church's $50 Million Fund drive, and in promoting a National Presbyterian Church and Center for Washington, D.C.* In addition, he

*The project, dedicated in 1970, includes the Henry Robinson Luce Tower of Faith, a 173-foot campanile.

and Clare were planning another house, this one on the Kahala beachfront in Hawaii, near Honolulu. Upset by the architect's extravagant design, Luce one night sketched his own plans for a two-story house, including all the rooms he wanted—but omitting a stairway to the second floor.

In the fall of 1964, just before departing for Greece and the Far East, Luce delivered some comments on the outline for *Life*'s projected year-end special issue on the Bible. The "fundamental matter" absent from *Life*'s proposed treatment, Luce felt, was "Christianity . . . When we turn from the Old Testament to the New, what has to be said is that, according to Christian faith, something happened . . . A babe, not a guru, was born." He also left with *Life* a review he had written of the collected reflections and essays of Pierre Teilhard de Chardin, the French Jesuit paleontologist-philosopher to whose hopeful views of man's future Luce was particularly attracted; his review, extolling "the splendor and joy" of Teilhard's vision, ran in October.

The months following Luce's return to the U.S. were busy ones. In December he was debating China policy at the University of California in Berkeley and writing an article for the forthcoming 35th-anniversary issue of *Fortune*. In February 1965, he participated in an international convocation of statesmen, diplomats, theologians and scholars who gathered in New York, under the inspiration of Pope John XXIII's encyclical, *Pacem in Terris*, to study the requirements for establishing world peace. In March he toured U.S. Air Force bases in Ohio and Alabama as chairman of the Air University's board of visitors, and in April, took up residence at Yale as a Chubb Fellow—visiting his alma mater as a leader in public life. In September, after a month in Hawaii, Luce went to Washington for a world law conference, then addressed the annual dinner of the Magazine Publishers Association in New York. The following month, he left for Europe. He spent five days in Rome observing the Vatican Council and had an audience with Pope John XXIII's successor, Paul VI, who had just been the subject of a *Time* cover story. The magazine was on the Pope's desk, and afterward Luce demonstrated the papal reaction to the article. "He went like this," Luce said, imitating a very Italian gesture—hand thrust outward with the palm down and rocked gently to indicate mixed pleasure. From Italy, Luce went on to Britain and Germany for meetings with business, political and publishing executives. December found him in California for a speech to San Francisco's Commonwealth Club.

During the winter and spring of 1966, Luce was almost continually

198

in Phoenix working on his book. In May he went to the Iowa corn country on pleasant personal business—to be officially "adopted" by the town of Oskaloosa, population 11,053. Luce's adoption by this marvelously named farming community had its origins in a chance remark he had made years before to a Time Inc. gathering, when he observed that the one thing his birth in China deprived him of was an easy answer to that question Americans always asked one another: Where are you from? Picking a name whose quintessentially American sound obviously appealed to him, Luce had said: "I would give anything if I could say simply and casually: Oskaloosa, Iowa." That remark, quoted in Kobler's *Saturday Evening Post* profile, had provoked a response: Oskaloosa voted to award him the American birthplace he lacked. On May 30, Luce graciously thanked Oskaloosa's ruling fathers for their "inspired gift of home-township" to him.

Luce was less gracious speaking at *Life*'s Hunt Ball—managing editor George Hunt's annual dinner for the staff—a few days later in New York. Luce rarely disavowed publicly anything published in his magazines. This evening he did, attacking a recent article by one of *Life*'s talented younger writers, Barry Farrell, on the beat poet Allen Ginsberg, in which Farrell compared Ginsberg with Walt Whitman. Angered by the comparison, Luce criticized Farrell's article from the lectern and continued the argument afterward, savaging Farrell personally, quoting Whitman at length from memory and challenging Farrell to match Whitman's lines with Ginsberg's. "The greatest unpleasantness I have ever had with our editorial staff," Luce remarked later.

In October 1966 Luce made his last trip abroad, joining 26 other American corporate executives on a two-week *Time* news tour of Eastern Europe. In company with Time-Life News Service correspondents, the group flew to Vienna, motored past the barbed-wire and watchtower-guarded Iron Curtain into Hungary, and went on from Budapest to Bucharest, Warsaw, Prague and Belgrade for meetings with government chiefs and other leading figures.

Luce's strenuous schedule evoked warnings from his physician in Phoenix, Dr. Hayes Caldwell, Mrs. Luce later recalled:

I had heard Dr. Caldwell criticize him about smoking cigarettes, bounding around the world, etc., warning him that these things would shorten his life, but he said to me, "My father never drank and never smoked and died of a heart attack the night of Pearl Harbor at age 73. I am taking off six years for the abuse that I give myself, but I am adding three or four years for what modern science now knows."

Commented Mrs. Luce: "He was right the first time." Some friends felt Luce was showing the strain. One longtime acquaintance saw him walking alone in Central Park one winter afternoon and was struck by his appearance; he seemed suddenly aged.

His schedule nevertheless remained full. In November he spoke to the University of Syracuse School of Journalism on the problems of journalism in adapting to an era of radical change. Published in the January 1967 issue of *Fortune*, Luce's speech was much quoted after his death. He criticized the press for its failure to "adequately spread the news of knowledge [and] present the patterns of order" in everyday life—"what we call, in the trade, slow news." And at the beginning of February, he was again in California for the last speech of his life, a discussion of the differences between Orient and Occident, delivered to the Associated Students of the University of California at Santa Barbara.

Luce took as his text Yale philosopher F.S.C. Northrop's statement that "the most important ideological conflict confronting our world is the one rendered inescapable by the major event of our time—the meeting of East and West." Agreeing with Northrop's premise, Luce argued with Northrop's conclusion, that Eastern and Western thought were complementary. For in Luce's view, traditional Eastern cultures and civilizations were "shattered" by their 19th century contact with the West, and "do not exist for effective purposes at the moment . . . East has little to say or to propose to the West"—nor would it have for the next 50 years, Luce believed. Thus it was up to the West, which had given the Orient a taste for the modernity that was making Asian cities from Bangkok to Tokyo look increasingly alike, now to "speak to the East out of our complex experience and faith" of those higher values of the Western tradition, individual freedom with order, liberty under law.

From Santa Barbara, Luce drove back to Los Angeles with bureau chief Marshall Berges, quizzing him on the bureau's current story list and offering suggestions of his own, including one on Hawaii's ethnic mix, which Luce felt was overdue for treatment in *Time*. Had the inhabitants of America's 50th state become Americans, Luce asked, or were they still Japanese, Chinese or whatever? What did George Washington—or Lyndon Johnson—mean to them? In Phoenix, Luce wrote his last piece for publication, the introduction to a new Time-Life Books project, a series of paperbacks called *Time* Capsules, each recounting a year of recent history as reported in the pages of *Time*. The first *Time* Capsule was for 1923 and in his introduction—which he instructed senior staff editor Tom Griffith to edit as he wished or discard entirely—Luce nostalgically evoked that year of *Time*'s launching:

At last, after a year of preparations and frustrations, the first issue of *Time*, dated March 3, 1923, was going to press. Soon after midnight, with Briton Hadden in command, almost the entire editorial staff was transported in three taxis from East 40th Street to the Williams Press at 36th Street and 11th Avenue, New York.

There, until dawn, we stood around the "stones" (tables) of the composing room . . . It was daylight when I got home and went to sleep. That afternoon, I found an uncut copy of the little magazine in my room. I picked it up and began to turn through its meager 32 pages (including cover). Half an hour later, I woke up to a surprise: what I had been reading wasn't bad at all. In fact, it was quite good. Somehow it all held together—it made sense, it was interesting.

In mid-February, Luce was in New York for the monthly Time Inc. board meeting. He visited Yale on Alumni Day and posed jauntily sporting a bowler hat and a smile, for a photograph with President Kingman Brewster and the author of a new book about Yale. He also was host at a Time Inc. editors' lunch for Prince Bernhard of the Netherlands. Luce was his usual brisk, brusque self, launching into a torrent of questions before his visitor was even fed.

Later that month Luce was in California again, this time not on business of his own, but to accompany his wife, who was giving a speech at the Commonwealth Club. As always, he had arranged to leave no time unfilled. In the suite at the Fairmont Hotel, he had *Time*'s San Francisco bureau chief Judson Gooding phone managing editor Fuerbringer in New York to relay some tips Mrs. Luce had picked up on the then current Kennedy assassination controversy, which Luce thought might be useful for *Time*. He then got on the phone himself and playfully needled Fuerbringer with another fact he had just been apprised of: Did Fuerbringer know that Chicago had just had its 1,000th gangland killing?

The next day came Mrs. Luce's speech, entitled, "The U.N.—Services Unrendered," to which Luce, after reading, decided to add an upbeat ending: the U.N. symbolized the world's desire for "peace through international cooperation [and] we, as a nation, dare not unilaterally declare it to be hopeless." Luce's lines, his wife said later, stole the press play from hers.

The Luces flew back to Phoenix that evening, Friday, February 24. Saturday was another full day. Luce hacked around the golf course, wrote memos and letters, including a thank-you note (about which he was always meticulous) to Gooding in San Francisco, held a luncheon discussion with the dean of the University of Chicago Divinity School about endowing a professorship, had a General Motors executive in for cocktails and dined with Mrs. Luce and neighbors at a Phoenix hotel.

Contrary to his usual habits, Luce was not up and dressed when the cook brought breakfast of orange juice, coffee, French toast and bacon into his bedroom Sunday morning. Ten minutes later he called her to take the tray away: "It isn't that the food isn't good. I just don't feel well." He went into the bathroom and vomited. He passed a restless morning, wandering about in stocking feet, vomiting intermittently, spitting up some blood, protesting to the doctor who came shortly after noon that he was all right—he had just swallowed some blood after a nosebleed. His pulse and blood pressure tested normal, but Luce was under the covers and dozing before the doctor left. Late that afternoon he got up, spread the bedroom curtains to the sunset, padded off to the kitchen for a glass of milk, his first food of the day. He tried eating supper with his wife in her room, but after a few spoonfuls of soup he vomited again. Again the doctor came, again Luce insisted he was all right, again his pulse and blood pressure were normal. A nurse came to stay that Sunday night, however.

There was minor consternation in the kitchen Monday morning when Luce, up again, wandered in asking for cornflakes. The house was out of them. Luce ate another dry cereal but again vomited. At noon, the doctor, who earlier had reserved and then canceled a hospital room for Luce, ordered an ambulance. Protesting that he could at least stand on his own feet, Luce walked out and climbed in, carrying his shoes and an armful of books including his Bible and a paperback Perry Mason mystery. To Dr. Caldwell, checking in on him later, Luce confessed, "I seem to be unusually sleepy." That evening Mrs. Luce left the hospital. When she phoned him around 10 p.m., Luce said he was feeling better and would watch a Perry Mason rerun on TV in his room; she said she would be doing the same at home.

He slept badly that night. Several times the nurses heard him get up and pace around the room. The last time was around 3 a.m. "There was criticism that the nurses should have restrained him," Mrs. Luce said later. "But knowing Harry Luce, able to sit up in bed and watch television, I don't believe he could have been restrained." He got up to go to the bathroom, was heard to say, "Oh God"—and the nurse rushed in at once, but he was almost gone. Death, attributed to a coronary occlusion, came a few minutes later, at 3:15 a.m.

Coincidence marked his death, as it had Hadden's long before. Hadden died on February 27, 1929, six years to the day after *Time*'s first issue went to press; Luce died 44 years to the day after he had awakened in his room to pick up a printed copy of that first slim issue and leaf through its pages.

Memorial services for Luce were held in the Madison Avenue Presbyterian Church, where he had worshiped for 43 years. The congregation included Governor and Mrs. Nelson Rockefeller, the Richard Nixons, diplomats, publishers, academicians, theologians. A private hookup linked the overflow gathering in the church to two other gatherings in the Time & Life Building. In a graceful and perceptive address, Luce's pastor, the Scottish-born Reverend David H.C. Read, found consolation that in Luce's sudden passing "there was no lingering, no slow decay. He went into the world unseen with a promptness—one might almost say a punctuality—that marked his mortal life. *We* were not ready for this departure, but we can believe *he* was." Dr. Read paid tribute to Luce's personal impact as "one of the great decision-makers of our time . . . a man of unlimited imagination who reveled in hard facts . . . an intellectual who yet became the world's greatest popularizer of philosophy and art." But above all, said Dr. Read, Luce was a man of faith:

> That faith was not a vague quality of humanistic hope [but] a quite specific faith in the sovereign God and Creator through Jesus Christ his Son . . . Its theological emphases were in the very grain of his thought and life.
>
> Luce's belief that behind the chaos of men and nations there is a divine purpose accounts for his fascination with news of all kinds, and his passionate conviction that both the nation and the world have a destiny to be pursued . . . He was not ashamed, in a sophisticated environment and a nihilistic age, to see life as a pilgrimage—a pilgrimage with a purpose and a goal . . . So though his modesty might resist, I believe his feeling for

history and for the English language would approve if I conclude this tribute by quoting from Bunyan's hymn:

> *Who would true valour see,*
> *Let him come hither:*
> *One here will constant be,*
> *Come wind, come weather;*
> *There's no discouragement*
> *Shall make him once relent*
> *His first avowed intent*
>   *To be a pilgrim.*

Years before, Luce had picked his burial site. It was on the grounds of what had once been the Luce winter home, Mepkin plantation, in the pine- and live-oak-forested countryside along the Cooper River north of Charleston, South Carolina, now a Trappist monastery.*

To Mepkin, Luce's body was flown from Phoenix in a sealed coffin. The burial rites the day following the funeral were ecumenical. Led by Mrs. Luce and the abbot, the small family group and a few guests walked through the woods to the graveside where the monks, who had already sung a requiem mass for Luce in their own chapel, gathered to sing the opening hymn. The Reverend Leslie Severinghaus, husband of Luce's sister Emmavail, conducted the Presbyterian service. Luce's intellectual companion, the Jesuit theologian John Courtney Murray, spoke two aspirations; the monks sang a final hymn. Halfway around the world on that same Saturday, March 4, Luce's passing had already been marked by his friends in Nationalist China, at memorial services in the chapel of Taiwan's Tunghai University. The services there were trilingual: prayers in English; Scripture in Chinese; the anthem, Palestrina's *Adoramus Te*, in Latin. Several days later, in a Requiem Mass at the Church of St. Thomas the Apostle in Phoenix, Father Murray called Luce "an ecumenist before ecumenism."

Editorial comment was provoked worldwide by Luce's death, much of it lauding him in the same terms: Luce had been a "towering" figure, the most influential publisher of his century, whose presence inhabited his magazine and who had, almost singlehanded, "revolutionized" American journalism. Some dissents were recorded.

---

*Bought in 1936, soon after the Luces' marriage, extensively improved, rarely visited by them during World War II, the Mepkin buildings and a large portion of the land were sold to the Cistercian Order in 1949, a few years after Mrs. Luce's conversion to Catholicism.

Wrote the Manchester *Guardian's* veteran U.S. correspondent Alistair Cooke: "Like John Foster Dulles, [Luce] regarded himself, with terrifying modesty, as a soldier in the army of Christ; that is to say, as a warrior to whom the nation's wars, once they are begun, are holy wars."

There were unexpected reactions. Moscow's *Literaturnaya Gazeta* front-paged Luce's picture, awarded Time Inc. a special place in "the network of American propaganda" but went on to praise the absence of "horoscopes or screaming sensationalism" in the magazines' pages and to credit Luce with "taking into account the growing intellect of the reader." Rome's *Il Messaggero*, in an ultimate feminist tribute that Luce himself would have enjoyed, headlined its obituary: "The husband of Clare Boothe Luce has died."

A flood of personal reminiscences was loosed by his passing, testimony to the cliché that he had indeed become a legend in his own time. Former *Time* managing editor Matthews, who had parted with Luce in some bitterness, recalled him appreciatively. So did another old associate who afterward turned caustic, former Time Inc. general manager Ralph Ingersoll, author of a cruel novelistic caricature of Luce and his wife.* Now, in a bylined Washington *Post* article, Ingersoll paid tribute to Luce's "important imprint . . . the imprint of his faith in words—in words that communicate, in the legitimacy and importance of communicating, in the basic, total and inherent worthwhileness of dedicating one's life to words."

All the Time Inc. magazines carried appreciations of Luce. *Life* devoted 13 pages to his life and thought, with an editorial tribute, "The Values That Shaped His Work," by Jack Jessup. These were "liberty, reason and conscience, and they will surely bridge his era to whatever follows."

Time carried ten pages and a cover portrait; thus, "possibly the most prestigious living American who never made *Time's* cover," as Kobler's profile phrased it, made it in death—but only after considerable debate among the editors. Fuerbringer, for one, was opposed to a cover portrait, wondering how Luce himself might have felt about it. The subject had come up only a few years earlier when *Time* was celebrating its 40th birthday and there was a proposal that Luce be pictured on the cover of the anniversary issue; Fuerbringer, who had mentioned this to Luce, remembered his reaction: "There

The Great Ones: The Love Story of Two Very Important People (Harcourt Brace and Company, 1948).

was a pause that took ten seconds longer than his usual pause and he said, 'You see, I considered it. I am against it.'" This time the advocates prevailed. Luce's face, quizzical, smiling slightly, stared forth from *Time*'s cover in a line drawing by Robert Vickery. Inside the magazine were two stories recounting Luce's career and assessing his work, as well as boxed quotes from his speeches and writings; in place of the magazine's usual Letter from the Publisher, was a personal farewell to Luce entitled A Letter from the Staff. Written by associate editor Doug Auchincloss, it offered an affectionate tribute to a boss who "essentially and always . . . was a reporter and writer and editor like ourselves."

> For this we warmed to him and looked to him and trusted him. And he did us. "I am proud to be with you, and I am proud that you are with me," he once told a group of us. "And there is only this self-flattery in that statement: if a man is known by the company he keeps, then this is the company which in my life I have managed to keep, and this is the company by which I would like to be known."
> And this is the company we will try to keep.

At his death, Luce beneficially owned 1,012,575 shares, or almost 15 percent, of Time Inc.'s outstanding stock, worth slightly more than $109 million, on which his yearly dividend income was then approximately $2.4 million. To Mrs. Luce, he willed in trust 180,000 shares of stock, worth about $19 million; she also received their Fifth Avenue apartment, the house in Phoenix, the property in Hawaii. Another 143,100 shares, worth about $15 million, were placed in trust for Luce's two sons by his first wife: Henry Luce III, then Time-Life news bureau chief in London, and Peter Paul Luce, then a management consultant in New York.

Roughly half of Luce's personal stock holdings had been set aside in 1961 for the Henry Luce Foundation, Inc., created in 1936 in honor of Luce's father and engaged, at the time of Luce's death, in promoting Christian education and intellectual exchange between Far Eastern countries and the U.S.* Luce's will bequeathed another 149,465 shares to the foundation, which, with the 191,029 shares it already held, made it the largest single stockholder in Time Inc., with 880,494 shares, or 12.7 percent voting control. President of the

---

*The Luce Foundation has, since 1967, broadened its scope in various directions that include funding academic chairs in the humanities and social sciences, making grants to organizations concerned with public policy and implementing a scholarship program in American art.

foundation was Henry Luce III; other members were Luce's sister Elisabeth and her husband, Maurice T. Moore, Peter Paul Luce, Roy Larsen, Charles Stillman.

Luce left his executors and trustees a free hand in managing his estate but stipulated clearly his desire for the company. "Time Incorporated is now, and is expected to continue to be, principally a journalistic enterprise and, as such, an enterprise operated in the public interest as well as in the interest of its stockholders," he declared.

He knew what he wanted for Time Inc., just as he knew his mind about his country and his church—and himself. In *Fortune*'s April 1967 issue, Luce's longtime friend Eric Hodgins recalled "the last dinner we were ever to have." After the meal, Hodgins wrote,

> The talk turned, I don't know how, to all the flocks of books and articles then current about the identity crisis, so called. I said I was agin 'em. Harry slapped the table with his open palm. "So am I," he said. "They're preposterous. And besides, I've never had the faintest trouble knowing who I was." There came one of those famous Luce pauses that said to the experienced listener, *Don't talk; I'm thinking*.
>
> "Now my *opinion* of myself," he resumed, "is another matter; *this* has varied widely from time to time. What's more, I can tell you, if you care to know, that I think my wife's opinion of me varies someplace between my own opinion and the public's opinion. But identity crisis—no!"

The Urge to Diversify

CORPORATE MANAGEMENT had no intention of turning Time Inc. into a conglomerate. But in the supercharged economic atmosphere of the 1960s, the company was caught up in the prevailing enthusiasm for rapid growth by acquisition and diversification. In February 1962, with the Silver Burdett acquisition just about complete, and with foreign television investments and foreign-language magazine publishing ventures in train, Heiskell wrote his executive colleagues a memo which, he said, "might be entitled, 'Where is Time Inc. going?' " In it Heiskell described (with characteristic candor) what he saw as a central problem:

> From time to time a combination of instinct, excess energy, and a certain amount of logic propels us into a new venture. We do weigh the new project against existing commitments but at no point that I know of has Time Inc. sat back and attempted to outline a general plan for future activities that might serve as a framework for evaluating the new project.

Heiskell was not proposing a solution, but simply asking his readers—president Linen, editorial director Donovan and executive vice president and treasurer Brumbaugh—to ponder the problem. "At no time in our history have so many new ventures been up for consideration as in this very month," Heiskell observed. As the first

Larry Burrows in Vietnam in 1966. Burrows covered the Vietnam war for *Life* from 1962 until his death in a South Vietnamese helicopter shot down over Laos on February 10, 1971.

Thomas Griffith, assistant managing editor *Time* 1960-64, senior staff editor 1964-67, editor *Life* 1968-72.

George Hunt, managing editor *Life* 1961-69.

Life photographer Paul Schutzer in Vietnam in 1965. He was killed in June 1967 while covering the Six-Day War in the Middle East.

Photographer Ralph Morse, who joined the *Life* staff in 1942, has covered the space program for over 27 years.

...taff gathering in 1972.

...ont: John Dominis. First row: John
...engard, Lee Balterman, George Silk,
...rence Newsome, Robin Ward,
...scilla O'Neill, Bernadette
...ngford, Richard Swanson, Arthur
...atz, Farrell Grehan, Ralph Morse,
...nry Groskinsky. Second row:
...rnice Schutzer, Fern Schad, David
...ness, Richard Pollard, Robert
...emian, Ann Drayton. Third row
...ted: Nina Leen, Barbara Baker,
...n Moser, Bridgit Scheideler. Third
...v standing: Frank McCulloch, Co
...ntmeester, Harry Benson, Richard
...lley, Sean Callahan, Ralph Crane,
...chael Mauney, Margaret Sargent,
... Eppridge, Thomas Flaherty,
...nald Bailey, Edward Thompson,
...rk Kauffman. Back row: Herbert
...th, George Karas, Albert Schneider,
...udon Wainwright, Lynn Pelham,
...ilip Kunhardt, Gjon Mili, Ralph
...aves, Frank White, Carl Mydans,
...y Rowan.

Eleanor Graves, assistant managing editor of the monthly
Life 1978-80 and executive editor 1980-82, and
Ralph Graves, managing editor *Life* 1969-72, editorial
director Time Inc. 1979-83.

Louis Banks, managing editor *Fortune* 1965-70, editorial director Time Inc. 1970-72.

Richard Armstrong, executive editor *Fortune* 1977-   .

Carol Loomis, member of the *Fortune* board of editors and senior writer.

Daniel Seligman, *Fortune* executive editor 1970-77 and associate managing editor 1977-

ncan Norton-Taylor, managing
tor *Fortune* 1959-65.

Robert Lubar, managing editor *Fortune* 1970-80.

ry Johnston, member of the
tune board of editors and
ef of research 1955-   .

tney Westerfield, *Fortune*
blisher 1969-73.

Edward Patrick Lenahan, publisher *Fortune*
1973-75 and 1979-84.

Jerry Korn, managing editor Time-Life Books 1970-82.

Maitland Edey, editor Time-Life Books 1966-70.

e-Life Books: Jerome Hardy, publisher, 1960-64, (*Life* publisher 1964-69); Joan Manley, publisher 0-75, Time Inc. group vice president–books 1975-84; Norman Ross, editor, 1960-66.

Francis Keppel, chairman General Learning Corporation 1966-74.

The Time Inc. Books Group in 1977.
Left to right: Herbert Schutz, president New York Graphic Society; John McSweeney, president Time-Life Books; Edward Fitzgerald, president Book-of-the-Month Club; Arthur Thornhill Jr., chairman and president Little, Brown; Zachary Morfogen, managing director Books & Arts Associates.

Edward Thompson with astronaut John Glenn in 1962. Thompson was managing editor of *Life* 1949-61 and editor 1961-67.

step in an effort "to put on paper some logical concepts of the role that Time Inc. should play in the next decade," he offered five observations:

a) We are in the communications business in the broadest sense and in none other unless it in some way buttresses our major function.

b) The communications business is changing and will probably change at an even faster rate.

c) The satellite communications system probably has more revolutionary implications for publishing than did TV.

d) If school keeps, leisure time will increase but not as fast as added activities will be invented to fill it.

e) Timing is the key element to success. We have two negative examples on this count. We just about missed the boat on TV and we were three years late in getting into book publishing.

Before making any major moves, the company took a smaller step that was at least as important for its symbolic as for its practical meaning. In May 1964, after 33 years of being traded on the over-the-counter market, Time Inc. stock was listed on the New York Stock Exchange. The move was overdue. Then more than now, over-the-counter stocks were considered speculative, even dangerous; the market in them was occasionally tainted by scandal. Time Inc., moreover, was one of only five among the 200 largest U.S. industrial firms *not* listed on the NYSE. Going on the exchange's Big Board would open up a larger market for Time Inc. stock, attracting the institutional investors who shied away from unlisted issues. One further advantage: the stock could be more readily used in paying for acquisitions.

Throughout the 1960s and into the 1970s, Time Inc. acquired a number of enterprises, large and small, with mixed success. Opportunism played a part in selecting them; a desirable firm happened to be on the block because its management wanted to sell out. But the expansion was not indiscriminate. There was a pattern and a logic to it, which was, essentially, that the acquisitions should somehow fit into and augment Time Inc.'s own capabilities. Thus the merger with Temple Industries, which is discussed in chapter 18, was viewed as a way to reinforce Time Inc.'s own forest products subsidiary. And the numerous acquisitions in filmmaking and television (see chapters 8, 22 and 28) were seen as ways to adapt Time Inc. talents to the new technologies in the communications market.

The spectacular initial success of Time-Life Books led to its

209

becoming the nucleus of several diversification efforts. Some of these were intended to exploit the possibilities of mail-order marketing. But one venture had a loftier aim: to enlarge and strengthen Time Inc.'s foothold in what was beginning to be known as the knowledge industry.

This foray began, literally, at the 19th hole. One summer afternoon in 1964, Linen and John Lockton, treasurer of General Electric, ran into each other at the Round Hill Country Club in Greenwich, Connecticut, and ambled into a long conversation over martinis. Lockton put a question to Linen: Was Time Inc. for sale? The answer was no—but the two kept talking, finding shortly that they shared an interest in the business possibilities of education. Both men were struck by what seemed an obvious opportunity for GE, a huge and successful electric and electronics equipment manufacturer, and Time Inc., whose mission from the beginning had involved popular education, to go into business together as a powerful team. The two did not get much more specific than that in this first conversation, but within a few weeks their companies began explorations and negotiations that resulted, just over a year later, in the creation of a large new joint venture: the General Learning Corporation.

The idea of combining two disparate enterprises in a joint effort of this nature was not an inspiration from the blue. Rather, it reflected the spirit of the times. There was a perception—which had rapidly become conventional wisdom—that education was on the brink of a revolution. First had come the near panic over adequacy of the American educational system, following the Sputnik launch. Then came breakneck development of the computer, suggesting that this might make an efficient new teaching tool in the classroom. As early as 1961, a *Fortune* article by Charles Silberman had discussed "the remaking of American education," including the use of programmed instruction. Now it seemed to be happening.

But could the schools pay for this expensive new teaching technology? Passage of the Elementary and Secondary Education Act of 1965 seemed to provide the answer, authorizing large federal grants to public schools—and allowing the funding of research by profit-making, as well as nonprofit, institutions. Companies were not slow to see the potential; even before the Elementary and Secondary Education Act, major electronics firms such as Xerox and IBM had begun acquiring publishers or manufacturers of educational materials. The trend was described in *Fortune*'s August 1966 issue, in another Silberman article titled, "Technology Is Knocking at the

Schoolhouse Door":

> The past year has seen an explosion of interest in the application of electronic technology to education and training. Hardly a week or month goes by without an announcement from some electronics manufacturer or publishing firm that it is entering the "education market" via merger, acquisition, joint venture or working arrangement.

Largely through Silberman's efforts, Time Inc. management was already well briefed. In 1962 and 1963 Silberman had written several memos on education for corporate research and development that remained consistently useful. Luce had responded to one: "A vast and intricate subject. This study will undoubtedly do a lot to 'modernize' us." Meanwhile, an R & D staff set up by the book division was studying possible experimental projects in education for Time Inc. and Silver Burdett to pursue. Thus, by the time Linen and Lockton had their conversation at the Round Hill Country Club, the joint venture they talked about not only looked perfectly logical—it seemed practically foreordained.

As negotiations proceeded in secret, it became clear how different Time Inc. and GE were. GE, then 12 times bigger than Time Inc. with sales of $4.9 billion, called up platoons of financial analysts and presented elaborate business plans. Time Inc.'s approach, while historically no less successful, was certainly more seat-of-the-pants. As Andrew Heiskell later marveled, "I had never seen a business plan before. I was absolutely overwhelmed."

The negotiators worked long and hard. When the northeastern U.S. was darkened by the famous power blackout the night of November 9-10, the lawyers at work in the Time & Life Building barely missed a beat. Their source of light, a participant recalled, was "beautiful beeswax candles supplied by the *Life* photo lab." Through such efforts a complete proposition was readied for consideration by the Time Inc. board of directors on November 19, 1965. To the venture Time Inc. would contribute its textbook publisher, the Silver Burdett Company, while GE would become an equal partner by contributing $18,750,000 in cash, which had been calculated as the value of Silver Burdett. The new venture's sales were projected to reach $40 million by 1970, surpassing the forecast sales of Silver Burdett's textbook business; losses meanwhile would be from $3 million to $7 million yearly. The expected early losses were justified with a confident prediction for the years beyond 1970:

211

During the 1970-75 period we anticipate that conventional text-book sales through Silver Burdett will make only a small contri-bution to growth [but] that new educational systems sales will rise at an explosive rate. Basically this growth will be made pos-sible by the investment in research and development expenses incurred in the 1966-70 period.

On January 4, 1966, the new company formally came into being, and in April it was named the General Learning Corporation. Its presi-dent, Richard L. Shetler, came from GE. An electrical engineer, Shetler had managed the company's defense-program division; he had also supervised the company's think tank. The chairmanship of GLC went, at the start, to Roy Larsen of Time Inc., whose strong personal interest in education made him a logical choice for the post. But after a few months, Larsen found a highly qualified replacement in Francis Keppel, former dean of the Harvard Gradu-ate School of Education and at the time an Assistant Secretary of the Department of Health, Education and Welfare. Keppel had been involved with education since graduating from Harvard, and had held a number of posts with the university before President Kennedy appointed him Commissioner of Education in 1962.

Keppel took over GLC's New York headquarters, while Shetler oversaw the Washington office. With offices and officers in place, the company quickly plunged into an ambitious portfolio of proj-ects—educational games and toys for the very young, films for the older set and computer programs for elementary and high school students.

Within a very short period of actual operations, the depressing truth sank in on everyone involved: GLC was an idea whose time had not yet come. The problems were many and fundamental. As Keppel later noted, recalling his experiences in GLC's many plan-ning meetings, "The assumptions were wrong. The basic assump-tions were always in the first three charts. It took me $5 million to learn not to let them go past the third chart."

It had been ᵣssumed, for example, that GE and Time Inc. would together be admirably equipped to sell GLC's product. In fact, no one in either company was. The GE people, who were experts at persuading government administrators to make multimillion-dollar purchases, were at sea in a world where each sale could require con-vincing a local school board and perhaps individual teachers as well. The textbook salesmen from Silver Burdett knew that world but were never comfortable selling GLC's new products. The public

212

schools remained, as always, agonizingly slow to adopt new techniques and technologies, and the federal aid to public schools proved less bountiful than anticipated. A fact generally omitted from the heady early discussions of GLC's future was that less than 2 percent of education budgets was spent on materials directly related to classroom teaching; the vast bulk of the money went for salaries. Moreover, by current standards those mid-'60s computers were impossibly huge and expensive, beyond the reach of most school systems—even with federal help.

The lesson was clear: that while GLC could continue in business, it could not continue as the company it had started out to be. In February 1967, just over a year after it began, GLC shrank its Washington office by 75 employees, nearly half the total. Shetler went back to GE, and Keppel took over the presidency. From that time on, the company sold its "software" in the form of distinctly low-tech products, such as filmstrips and recordings. The really ambitious computer-related products, now viewed as unsalable, were never produced at all. This drastic redirection of GLC was Keppel's most important decision as president; Heiskell said, "It saved us millions."

General Learning did respectably well in the early 1970s, its final years, under a new president, John Backe. As a much smaller and slower-growing enterprise than originally planned, GLC needed a tough businessman at the helm, and Backe was one. A former jet pilot for the Strategic Air Command who had been in computer marketing at GE before he moved to Silver Burdett in 1966, Backe became president of the textbook firm in 1968 and took over from Keppel at the end of 1969, demonstrating in both positions an ability to tighten up and turn around operations with considerable speed. His talent was apparent to others: in 1973 Backe left Time Inc. to run the Education and Publishing Group at CBS; he was president of that corporation from 1976 to 1980.

In 1974, GLC was sold to Scott-Foresman, the textbook publisher, for some $20 million. Time Inc.'s monetary loss was $11 million, the loss in unrealized expectations not negligible either. Corporate post mortems on GLC faulted mainly its timing. It was not until a decade or more later, two decades after technology's knock at the schoolhouse door, that computers began entering the classrooms in quantity. The computers of the 1980s were more advanced than the product available to GLC—far cheaper also, sometimes even donated by manufacturers as a promotional effort in the burgeoning youth market. Nor had Time Inc. been alone in its misjudgment of

213

the opportunity; most of the similar enterprises set up at the time of GLC suffered a similar fate. "One of those mad rushes into the future that big corporations do now and then," one Time Inc. executive remarked later of GLC. Heiskell's assessment was somewhat blunter: "A fabulous failure."

Time Inc.'s diversification, as it continued, had met some resistance from Luce. His view of the General Learning venture is not recorded, but it must be assumed that had he had any objections, they were countered by Larsen's strong advocacy. However, just as GLC was coalescing, another venture came up—in motion pictures—where Luce put his foot down, quite hard.

The occasion was a proposal from United Artists in December 1965 for a possible merger. The suggestion fell on some receptive ears among Time Inc. management, where there was growing consensus that the company should be turning its talents to movie and television filming. As a potential Time Inc. partner in this field, UA was attractive: the studio was well regarded and was currently "hot," earning about $12 million that year, just over a third of Time Inc.'s net.

Linen and Baker, who was then scouting corporate development opportunities, pushed for serious consideration of a link with the movie firm. Linen, in a memo to Luce, cited profit as "a major reason for taking a hard look at United Artists . . . I see in our current activities a continued healthy growth, but it will be a less dramatic growth in profits than we have seen in the last three years. One way to improve that pattern is by acquisition . . . In my opinion . . . we should look for a large one." Exploratory talks between United Artists and Linen, Baker and other Time Inc. executives got as far as suggesting a stock exchange involving some 1.5 million shares of Time Inc. stock, then selling at $100 a share.

At this point Luce, in Phoenix for the holidays, was apprised of the thinking in New York. Larsen had doubts about pursuing the deal; Baker, reporting to Luce on the conversations in New York, noted that Larsen considered United Artists' film activities as having "little or no bridge to anything that Time Inc. now does or actively contemplates." Former chairman Tex Moore, who was also Luce's brother-in-law, was even more adamantly against it. Moore saw financial danger in assuming United Artists' large debt; moreover, paying the estimated price in Time Inc. stock, he figured, risked diluting Luce's control of the company by as much as a quarter. A handwritten letter from Moore, urging caution and pleading his concern that "this kind of a marriage . . . would . . . affect our image and our journalistic position," went out to Luce in Phoenix just as a written proposal arrived from Baker.

Luce's reply, in early January 1966, addressed to Linen, was a crushing negative. After citing the drain on management time that a United Artists tie-up could entail, as well as "conflicts . . . in the field of taste and standards," Luce let fly sarcastically:

> Ed Baker performed a nice piece of rationalization in suggesting that we should broaden our scope from mere education to leisure. This of course would entitle us to engage in practically anything, including horse and dog racing. (Is *Racing Form* for sale?) As a matter of fact, his rationalization has suggested to me several schemes which we might consider. For example, the organization of Culture Tours. But I think I would exclude the service of anaesthetizing people by T.V.
>
> Anytime you want to spend an evening discussing the future of Time Inc. in the broadest terms, just let me know. I'd be more than happy to join in.
>
> Happy New Year!

Luce's letter ended the matter. The United Artists deal was not pursued further.

A year later, after Luce's death, Time Inc. did go into motion pictures, purchasing 300,000 shares of Metro-Goldwyn-Mayer stock to obtain, as the annual report to the stockholders declared, "an investment position in the rapidly developing technology of motion pictures, television programming and the music and record industries." A $17.7 million investment, MGM was to yield little by way of return except corporate headaches (see chapter 22).

The search for acquisitions, meanwhile, had taken Time Inc. overseas again. The company's experiences here had been mixed, to say the least. By the mid-1960s, as recounted earlier, neither the foreign television investments of Time-Life Broadcast nor the magazine ventures that Time-Life International had undertaken with foreign publishing partners were working out as planned. Management had not yet given up, however. One success story to offset the disappointments elsewhere was in the books field, where the Time-Life series books—the Life World Library, the Nature and Science series—were selling briskly in translation. In fact, between 1964 and 1966, Time-Life Books' sales outside the U.S. and Canada had doubled, from 2 million to 4 million volumes. To build on this base, expanding the company's international book business through investment in foreign publishing houses, had seemed both logical and attractive.

Acquisitions began with the purchase, for $1,950,000, of a 46 percent share in Editions Robert Laffont, a French publisher, approved by the Time Inc. board of directors in late 1965. Laffont, founded in 1941, was a small, aggressive firm that had scored with several best-sellers of its own, but which also did a large business distributing French translations of American best-sellers. It was for this reason that Laffont, wanting capital, found the Time Inc. tie-up attractive. Partnership with one of the major U.S. trade book publishers, such as Doubleday or Random House, could hinder Laffont in doing business with the others; in this sense Time Inc., while a force in the books field itself, was noncompetitive.

The advantages for Time Inc. in the Laffont connection were outlined to the Time Inc. board by TLI managing director Bear, who explained that this would be the first of similar deals to follow. "This proposal reflects the conviction of TLI management that expansion of book sales overseas can best be realized through local book-publishing firms in which Time Inc. holds a substantial interest." Bear advanced several specific arguments:

Until the present, books marketed by TLI have been translations of Time-Life books created for the American market. They have succeeded overseas because of their general excellence, but we feel they would be more successful still if the content were to be adapted with competence and grace for each language or culture area . . .

A substantial interest in Laffont and similar companies elsewhere would also bring us a thorough inside knowledge of and entrée to the various local sales and distribution methods . . .

Part ownership of Laffont would keep us aware of other publishing opportunities in magazines, textbooks, and book clubs on the French scene, and make possible sale of Laffont's own line in other countries . . . The trend in book publishing is to cross national boundaries and we must be at the forefront of this trend.

Importantly, the professional competence of book-publishing associates in other major markets of the world could result in cross-stimulation among Americans, French, British, Germans and others which could perhaps produce more imaginative ideas and more efficient execution than we could produce our-

216

selves. The purchase of a series of book-publishing firms would add a new dimension to our overall publishing activities abroad.

Purchase of the Laffont shares—acquired from rather unlikely sources, the United States Steel Pension Fund and the Morgan Guaranty Trust Company, who had held them jointly through a small investment company—was completed in October 1966. Luce had not been overly enamored of the Laffont deal, remarking during a discussion of troubles that *Fortune* was experiencing about that same time that he would "rather invest capital in *Fortune* than in buying a French book publisher." But he posed no formal objection, and the company pushed ahead with other transactions already in the works.

That same October, Time Inc. purchased an 18 percent interest in Organización Editorial Novaro S.A., a leading Mexican magazine and book publisher. Meanwhile, four TLI executives—Raimund von Hofmannsthal, Peter Galliner, Zachary Morfogen and Paul Hush—had toured Germany in September and had held talks with eight publishers with a view to buying an interest in one. They eventually settled on Rowohlt Taschenbuch Verlag GmbH (Rowohlt Pocketbook Publishing Company); Time Inc. bought a one-third interest for $1,250,000 in October 1967. Two years later came the purchase of a 40 percent interest in the British publishing house, André Deutsch Ltd. That same year, 1969, Time Inc. also went into in a joint venture with Salvat Editores S.A., a Spanish publisher, to distribute books and records by direct mail.

The foreign publishers, along with the company's other book interests, constituted a group called Books & Arts Associates, which was expected to generate a productive exchange of ideas. A small Time Inc. staff in New York maintained liaison among the members. The anticipated synergism, however, did not occur, perhaps because of geographical dispersion, perhaps because of national cultural differences. Although Time Inc.'s foreign publishing investments remained sound, individually, and modestly profitable, the predicted trend toward transnational publishing never materialized in any significant way.

But the company had been able to make a small publishing acquisition at home that fitted well with the themes of diversification and education. In 1966 it bought the New York Graphic Society, the world's largest reproducer and framer of fine arts and a publisher of high-quality fine-arts books. The price was 45,000 shares of Time Inc. stock, then worth about $4,050,000. Anton Schutz, a German artist, had founded the firm in 1925, and his son Herbert was now running it. It never became especially well known or important in the company's affairs, but it was a worthwhile acquisition for its profitability and prestige in the field.

One area—an obvious one, some felt—had remained unexploited in all this diversification. This was in the publishing of so-called "trade" books, the volumes of fiction and popular nonfiction that occupy the largest space on bookstore shelves. Innovative as the Time-Life series books had been, hugely successful as they were, the company was watching the best-seller lists—based on bookstore sales of trade books—from the sidelines.

In 1966, under Baker's direction, Time Inc. began scouting around for a trade publisher with a reputation for high quality. Several fit the bill, but for a number of reasons management's attention kept returning to one in particular: the Boston house of Little, Brown and Company.

Its credentials were excellent. Since 1837, when Messrs. Little and Brown took over a Boston bookshop and decided to publish as well as to purvey books, the house had consistently published distinguished works. It brought out James Russell Lowell's first volume (*A Year's Life*) and the first legal works of U.S. Supreme Court Justice Joseph Story. When John Bartlett became a partner of the firm in 1859, he brought along the rights to his *Familiar Quotations*. By the end of the century, the house had published Fannie Farmer's *Boston Cooking-School Cook Book* and had bought the rights to works of Edward Everett Hale, Emily Dickinson and Louisa May Alcott. More years brought more major books: Remarque's *All Quiet on the Western Front*, Nordhoff and Hall's *Mutiny on the Bounty*, Hilton's *Goodbye, Mr. Chips* and works of Evelyn Waugh, Ogden Nash, John P. Marquand, J.D. Salinger, John Fowles, William Manchester.

Beyond this impressive list, the firm had a thriving business in medical and college texts. It was this aspect of Little, Brown's operations that had made the firm's two principal officers—Arthur H. Thornhill Jr., president, and his father, Arthur senior, chairman—receptive to Time Inc.'s approaches. The Thornhills wanted to expand the medical and college textbook divisions' business; looking ahead, they calculated a likely need for additional capital.

Both men had long associations with the company. Arthur senior, joining the firm in the shipping department in 1913, had become its third president in 1948; in 1962 his son had succeeded him. Now, considering the two customary options open to them for raising the needed capital—a stock sale or borrowing—the Thornhills hesitated. All of Little, Brown's stock was then in the hands of its employees, who were required to sell it back to the company when they left. If shares were in public hands and freely traded, there was a risk of outsiders accumulating a large block and dictating Little, Brown's policies. Arthur junior, chief executive and negotiator for Little, Brown's future, had the typical New England aversion to debt. That left the alternative of selling stock to another company.

First contacts between Thornhill and Time Inc. in April 1967 had the aspects of a family reunion. Handling the introductions was Robert Manning, editor of the *Atlantic Monthly,* who had headed Time Inc.'s London news bureau in the late 1950s. Representing Time Inc. was Frank White, who had been bureau chief across the channel in Paris at the same time. After a session with Thornhill at the Tavern Club in Boston, White reported happily to Baker and Time-Life Books publisher Rhett Austell: "Arthur went out of his way to underscore the high esteem that he and his father hold for Time Inc. as a company and for the several people in Time Inc.'s management whom they know either professionally or personally." He added: "Thornhill did make it clear that Little, Brown would not consider any arrangement for the future that would not guarantee the continuance of the company's name, autonomy and management."

As the next step in the courtship, White arranged for Thornhill to come to New York and meet Baker, Austell and Linen. Thornhill later recalled: "The chemistry was right . . . When Jim Linen said that 'Time Inc. wanted to help make Little, Brown the best damn book-publishing house in the world' it was good enough for me."

The chemistry worked well: within nine months, the deal was completed. There had been two potentially sticky points. One was a pending Justice Department action against 18 publishers, including Little, Brown and Company, charging collusion in setting prices to libraries for books with heavy-duty bindings. The other was Internal Revenue Service approval for a tax-free transaction between Time Inc. and Little, Brown. Both matters were settled. Little, Brown and the other publishers reached agreement with the Justice Department, without admission of guilt, before Time Inc.'s purchase; IRS approval for a tax-free transaction followed later. Negotiated between Baker and Thornhill, the purchase was announced in January 1968. The price: 170,000 shares of Time Inc. stock, worth $17 million. With the announcement, a brief literary storm blew up.

Several of Little, Brown's authors protested the sale, citing it as another gobbling of a small publisher by a much bigger one and accusing the gobbler, in this case, of conservative political bias. The Thornhills, no less concerned than their authors with maintaining the firm's independence, shrugged off the protests. The storm passed, and the partnership proved a boon to both sides. Little, Brown got the needed capital infusion, kept its independence and remained headquartered in its landmark town house at 34 Beacon Street, across from the Boston Common. Thornhill remained president.

For Time Inc., the Boston connection brought consistent profit. A year after the merger, Little, Brown's controller sent a quarterly financial statement to Bear, showing sales and earnings well above budget. Forwarding the report to Baker, Bear scribbled a note expressing a sentiment that could also have been written ten or 15 years later: "Continues to be the gem you discovered."

Less gemlike was a small acquisition that was briefly in the company portfolio during the early 1970s. This was Haverhill's Inc., a small San Francisco mail-order house that Time Inc. bought in September 1971. On the surface, the Haverhill acquisition seemed a long stretch from Time Inc.'s usual interests; actually, it represented an attempt to expand the mail-order activities that Time-Life Books had already got into, seeking to use its subscriber lists of book buyers for the marketing of related merchandise, e.g., cookware sales to cookbook purchasers. Here, Haverhill's offered both the mail-order expertise of its owner, Gerardo Joffe, and an attractive product line. Haverhill's specialty was small, somewhat exotic items made by foreign manufacturers (a windup shaver was a big seller) on which Joffe held exclusive U.S. distribution rights. Haverhill's direct competition was minimal, its markups substantial. Sales were promoted by small ads, running with great frequency in selective newspapers and magazines—every day in the *Wall Street Journal*, every week in *The New Yorker*.

As a money-maker, Haverhill's was tiny. Reported earnings were $35,000 in the nine months leading up to Time Inc.'s consideration of it; the year before it had lost $6,800 on sales of $1.4 million. However, there were good reasons why Haverhill's might do better under Time Inc. ownership. Access to Time-Life Books' mailing lists would enhance its selling power; Haverhill's could advertise in the company's magazines at little or no cost. As the purchase proposal presented to the board pointed out, "Much of the space provided by the magazines will be 'remnant' space for which presently they receive no revenue." On that basis, Ralph Gallagher of the book division and Nicholas J. Nicholas Jr., a rising figure in the corporate controller's office, estimated that Haverhill's annual profits would reach $360,000 five years after acquisition. One Time Inc. board member, Rudolph Peterson, president of Bank of America, raised objections, questioning how much Time Inc. knew about Joffe, but the transaction went ahead. On September 24, 1971, Time Inc. bought Haverhill's for 18,000 shares of stock, then worth just over $1 million.

Haverhill's then proceeded to do much worse than it had ever done independently. Joffe's entrepreneurial operating styles and Time Inc.'s did not fit and it was hard for the parent company, a continent away, to oversee Haverhill's operations. In early 1974, as the U.S. dollar weakened on the international markets, Haverhill's strategy of selling imported merchandise turned disastrous. In mid-1974 Time Inc. put Haverhill's on the block, and after failing to find a buyer, liquidated it in December 1975. During its four years under Time Inc. ownership the firm had lost $2.4 million.

Coincidentally, during this same period, Time Inc. was pulling back from another subsidiary enterprise, Printing Developments Inc. Supplying printers worldwide with technological services and products developed at Time Inc.'s Springdale, Connecticut, research laboratory, PDI had grown by 1973 to be an $18 million business, with pretax profits of $2.8 million. PDI was operating in seven European countries, Japan, Mexico and the U.S., where publications as diverse as *Playboy* and the New York *Times* Sunday Magazine were being printed from color plates produced by PDI's electronic scanners. But PDI's product development costs were mounting, and the enterprise was facing a situation familiar to many technological pioneers—of being threatened by newer, lower-cost competitors. In 1971 Robert J. Edmondson, formerly PDI's chief financial officer, succeeded John Lyons as president. That year, the Springdale laboratory was sold. In 1976, PDI's manufacturing operations in printing plates and chemicals were sold to Wheelabrator-Frye, Inc., for $12.3 million. Three years later, the sale of its color scanning business in Japan marked the end of PDI.

If Haverhill's had been a long stretch from Time Inc.'s normal lines of business, an enterprise called SAMI, which the company got into in 1965, seemed even longer. Obscurely launched and improbably named—in fact, for a dog—SAMI went on, after some initial years of discouragement, to become a tidily profitable addition to the corporate portfolio.

In its inception SAMI owed little to the large ideas then inspiring Time Inc.'s expansion plans. Rather, it was conceived originally as a local marketing statistical service for Time-Life Broadcast. The venture began in the mind of J. Clarke Mattimore, a former advertising executive who was consultant to the Time-Life Broadcast division. The company's stations, in researching their markets, were seeking ways to measure the movement of goods, brand by brand, in local stores. Mattimore's solution was brilliantly simple: since it was too hard to monitor retail merchandise movements, the measure should be made at the wholesale warehouse, where careful records were kept, often on computer tape. With shelf space at a premium, stores kept inventories lean; reorders thus were an excellent indicator of retail sales. This information could be gathered and organized. Didn't it make sense, Mattimore reasoned, that manufacturers would want to know how their products were selling city by city? And, in the case of chain outlets, the flow of items passing through their individual stores?

Astonishingly, there was then no fast and reliable supplier of this information. The A.C. Nielsen Company provided national sales data based on a survey of 1,600 stores across the country; it had no figures, however, for individual markets. Moreover, Nielsen's national survey took eight weeks to prepare. Mattimore's proposal was to collect warehouse shipment figures from several major cities, and organize them for sale to manufacturers within two weeks.

Powerful computer capacity was needed; this happened to be available at 540 North Michigan Avenue in Chicago, where Time Inc. operated sophisticated IBM machines servicing the world's biggest list of magazine subscribers. These IBM giants had never been running full time. Here was a way to use their idle hours.

Mattimore began by testing the idea in Grand Rapids, where Time Inc. owned television station WOOD. The results were heartening: grocery chains were willing to sell their warehouse data, manufacturers were eager to buy. The experiment was so successful that in November 1965, Broadcast's president, Wes Pullen, proposed setting up the service nationwide. Approved by the Time Inc. board, the company began operations in January 1966 with Mattimore as president. For the firm's name, Mattimore looked no further than his Llewellin setter, Sammy. Only later did he and others contrive the less than felicitous title of Selling Areas-Marketing, Inc. So the enterprise referred to since as SAMI was christened.

SAMI's early life was a struggle. It ventured into the world with a verbal commitment from a single client, the Jewel Tea Company. But Jewel almost immediately backed out, so unnerving Mattimore that he gave brief thought to scrapping the whole effort. Worse, Jewel quit SAMI to sign on with a recently established competitor, Speedata, offering lower prices than SAMI. For five years SAMI grew large but lost money in the battle with Speedata.

Denouement came unexpectedly in 1970. Speedata declared bankruptcy. It had been showing earnings by the accounting artistry known as capitalizing expenses; actually it was taking losses. Speedata's collapse was a turning point for SAMI. Growing from then on, SAMI by 1980 had attracted more than 450 clients and was gathering information from markets that accounted for 77 percent of national food-store sales. Earnings, surpassing $11 million, prompted this comment from Ralph Davidson, speaking as chairman of Time Inc.: "We'd love to have ten SAMIs."

The Great Newspaper Hunt

THE NEWSPAPER ITCH was an old one around Time Inc.
Hadden, in the little notebook where he jotted ideas for
future corporate expansion, had listed "Daily Newspaper"
along with various other publishing projects he had in mind, including a "Bus. Mag.," a "Spt. Mag.," and a "U.S. History Bk."

Luce was not immune either, and once had come close to buying
Los Angeles' afternoon tabloid *Daily News*—how close was
recounted later by *Sports Illustrated*'s Sid James, who was Time-Life
news bureau chief in Los Angeles when Luce and a group of Time
Inc. executives came out to look at the paper in November 1941.
According to James, Luce had considered the *Daily News*'s chances
"reasonably good" despite competition from the dominant Los
Angeles *Times* which, although fat with advertising, was then journalistically quite flabby; Luce departed Los Angeles, James remembered, "with a deal practically settled." James was to check out a
few further details and telephone Luce Sunday afternoon at his
home in Greenwich, Connecticut, preparatory to a meeting scheduled in Luce's New York office the next day. That Sunday morning,
a springlike day in Los Angeles, James and friends, including Dick
Pollard of *Life*, went out to play touch football. Recalled James:

Shortly before noon some kid who had been sitting in one of

our cars watching our antics . . . idly listening to the radio, stopped our game with news about "some Japs dropping bombs on Hawaii" . . . We rounded up the entire staff and worked flat out for 40 hours covering the bedlam of Los Angeles which, as rumor had it, would be the Japanese's next stop . . .

It was three days before we could even get a telephone line to New York. When I finally talked to Luce . . . we passed a small joke about the irony of fate and Harry closed with: "Gee, wouldn't it have been fun? But we've got our hands full now." We never talked about it again.

But even before World War II ended, newspaper projects were being resuggested. On May 7, 1945, the day of the German surrender in Europe, Stillman sent Larsen the outline of "a fairly complete plan" for a Time Inc.–owned or -franchised newspaper group delivering "an identical national and foreign news daily paper in all principal cities of the U.S."—a proposal that in a way foreshadowed *USA Today,* launched nearly 40 years later by the Gannett chain. (Stillman's idea was to have supplementary local news and advertising, varying by city.) Nothing came of it, nor of a proposal in 1949 by Larsen and Howard Black for publishing weekend newspapers compiled from left-over *Time*, *Life* and *Fortune* editorial material. "I doubt if you could get any self-respecting young editor to work at the sewer outlet of our factory," remarked John Shaw Billings, then Luce's editorial deputy, in scuttling that project.

By 1966 the proposition that Time Inc. seek out newspaper properties was current again. A corporate development department had been formally established, and newspaper publishing was one of several areas that Donovan, as editor-in-chief, chose for study; the acquisition of a daily, Donovan commented later, would not only provide another outlet for Time Inc.'s existing talent but "would be useful as a talent source. I also was attracted to the idea of having at least one paper in some non-New York city. That would be good for us, good for the editor-in-chief and good for others too, to go out and get our noses rubbed in the problems of Boston politics, for instance." Moreover, as a Time Inc. management presentation to the board of directors later declared:

Newspaper publishing, as a function of Time Inc.'s several resources—editorial, managerial and financial—could contribute in an orderly and sustained way to the company's general economic health and growth.

In command of the newspaper search, as head of corporate development, was Edgar Baker, formerly managing director of TLI. Working with him was Frank White, who had also been dealing with Little, Brown. A 1938 graduate of Stanford, where he had been lightweight boxing champion, White had broken into newspaper work with the old United Press and had served in Southeast Asia with the OSS. Joining Time Inc. in 1948, he had served as news bureau chief in Rio, Bonn and Paris before switching in 1960 to the publishing side.

From the standpoint of profitability, the outlook for newspapers was good, particularly for small-city dailies in monopoly situations, the corporate development department reported in August 1966. The report, by a young Harvard Business School graduate and recent recruit to Time Inc., Nick Nicholas, was based on close examination of three newspaper operations in Ohio, Virginia and Pennsylvania and a wider look at the industry's prospects generally. In the operations Nicholas studied, profits were running from 18 to 23 percent pretax; in the industry as a whole, the number of dailies appeared to be stable at about 1,750 and ad revenues were rising faster than U.S. gross national product. With the rapid rate of household formation in the U.S., newspaper circulations would rise even faster over the next 15 years. Meanwhile, Nicholas noted, technological improvements promised to revolutionize the industry— albeit at high investment cost.

Luce was drawn into the discussion. Four weeks before his death in February 1967, he jotted some "Notes on the Newspaper Question" (marked "Strictly Confidential") indicating that for him, editorial considerations remained uppermost in any newspaper venture. "It must, of course, pass the economic test," Luce wrote, "[but] the main attractiveness to us would be to give the paper greater general distinction and to make it an influential voice in the nation . . . a newspaper that speaks vigorously for Progressive Conservatism— 'the sound of an American.' " Then, in a characteristic touch, he added: "Besides editorial stance and serious reportage, there are other matters of vital importance to the health of a newspaper— such as Women's Pages, Food, Diet, Ann Landers, Society Page, Comics. And shall we courageously turn our backs on Astrology?"

While the scouting for newspaper acquisitions continued, turmoil in the New York newspaper situation sent the company in a new direction. In May 1967 the *World Journal Tribune*, the awkwardly named amalgam of three money-losing New York newspapers—the

World-Telegram & Sun, the *Journal-American* and the *Herald Tribune*—finally failed, leaving the city with a single afternoon paper, the tabloid New York *Post*. The New York *Times* declared its intention to explore the void that had suddenly opened up. Time Inc. decided likewise, assembling an informal task force of a dozen or so ex-newspapermen on the staff to tap sources in the industry. *Time* senior editor Marshall Loeb was assigned to prepare a formal report.

The investigators generally agreed that Time Inc. should be in daily journalism, but not in New York, either in the afternoon or morning field. "New York City offers . . . probably the lowest advertising rates and the worst union problems," Loeb reported, summing up the competitive picture. "The wrong investment in the wrong place at the wrong time."

Already, in fact, Time Inc. had what appeared to be better prospects elsewhere. In June 1967, corporate development's canvass of the newspaper field, which had ranged as far as Texas and California and had also included contacts with the *Star* in Washington, D.C., produced a seemingly solid prospect just across the Hudson in New Jersey: the Newark *Evening News*. Founded in 1883, the *Evening News* was a New Jersey institution, the state's newpaper of record, considered by some the best afternoon daily in the Northeast. With a daily circulation of 278,000 and 423,000 on Sunday, it carried double the advertising of its morning rival, the Newhouse-owned Newark *Star-Ledger*. The owners of the *Evening News* were two brothers, publisher Richard B. Scudder and president Edward W. Scudder Jr., grandsons of the paper's founder, and their uncle, Wallace M. Scudder. Both brothers had other interests as well. Rather than neglect the *Evening News* further, they said, they preferred to sell out.

In its operations, the paper offered a strange mixture of new and old. Recently, the Scudders had put $12 million into new plant and presses, yet in the accounting department, one former *Evening News* man recalled, records were still kept in "a single, dog-eared general ledger of the kind Bob Cratchit kept for Ebenezer Scrooge." Numerous other archaic touches marked the paper's operating practices.

In July 1967, only weeks after the company began talks with the *Evening News*'s owners, Newark erupted in bloody racial rioting. In the aftermath, Donovan and Frank White toured Newark. They were shaken, but the conviction remained that Newark's largest paper could contribute significantly to civic restoration. "There was a strain of piety that was very much in our newspaper concept," White commented. "We weren't only interested in acquiring papers; we wanted to find a place where there was a real need, where Time Inc.'s resources could do some good. That strain of *pro bono publico*—it appealed very much."

And with Newark calm again, the *Evening News*'s prospects appeared good. The city was the center of the U.S.'s 12th largest retail market area. Beyond the decaying downtown districts lay the newer suburbs, where much of the paper's readership was concentrated. Increases in subscription prices and advertising rates, together with faster newspaper deliveries from the new presses, were expected to lift the paper's 1968 pretax income to $2 million. Using one rule of thumb for evaluating newspaper properties—one and a half times annual revenues—Baker estimated the probable asking price at $50 million but believed Time Inc. might get the paper for $40 million in a tax-free exchange of stock.

Management's first pitch to the Time Inc. directors, that September, for approval of the *Evening News* purchase was unfortunately timed. The company was then planning a $17 million investment in MGM stock, and the Little, Brown acquisition; faced with additional outlays for Newark, the board hesitated. Was the company overreaching itself? As the discussion was reported in the dry language of the board minutes:

> The outside directors indicated a need for appraisal of the present position of the Corporation as a whole and particularly its capital requirements and resources, and the need of a well-thought-out and present plan and policy with respect to future development of the business.

It was not only the outside directors who were doubtful. Stillman was flatly opposed, on the grounds that newspapers were "a union-riddled business," and Time Inc.'s open-shop magazine production operations could become vulnerable to union pressure.

But a second management pitch to the board in October won approval. It was hedged, though, with the condition that "any further proposals for acquisitions in this field would have to await a period of operation that could prove the validity of the acquisition and of the operation of newspapers by Time Inc."

Four days before Christmas, agreement was reached with the Scudders. The sale price came to $37.5 million, to be paid partly in

325,000 shares of Time stock, and partly by Time Inc.'s assumption of $5 million of *Evening News* debt. Formal announcement was made on February 14, 1968.

The agreement did not last long. Seven weeks later, the deal began falling apart under the impact of the *Evening News*'s audited figures for 1967 and its revised projections for 1968. Nick Nicholas, who was back in the controller's department when the figures arrived, recalled: "The numbers were unexpected, just catastrophic, off something like 80 percent—enormous." Classified and display advertising linage was down; costs, including retroactive pay raises for the *Evening News* staff, were up; accounts payable and bad debt had risen. For 1967, operating income was $2,115,000 less than anticipated; by Time Inc.'s calculations the paper's 1968 profit would be a bare $150,000 instead of the $1 million previously projected.

The Time Inc. negotiators had until then accepted the figures provided by the *Evening News*, and even now they believed that the Scudders were as distressed as they were by this belated revelation of the paper's deteriorated condition. The bad news reached the Time & Life Building on Friday afternoon, April 5. Nicholas remembered Brumbaugh, a skeptic from the start, walking into his office, twirling a large cigar and "smiling like a Cheshire cat."

That Sunday morning, a handful of senior executives, including Linen, Heiskell, Donovan, Larsen, Stillman and Brumbaugh, met at Linen's home in Greenwich to go over the figures again. Frank White sat in for Baker, who was in Europe. White recalled the session: "Almost instantly a consensus developed that we just couldn't go further with this . . . We tried to draft a statement. Various people tried their hand . . . When the meeting broke up, we had to decide who should tell the Scudders. Everyone looked stonily at me: '*You're* going to tell them!' " The following morning White and Nicholas drove over to Newark. "It was pretty dramatic. They were pretty upset—there was a lot of 'you'll hear from our lawyers,' " White remembered. "We didn't stay for lunch, I can tell you that."

That was not quite the end of the affair, however. In December the *Evening News* was again offered to Time Inc., at a suggested price around half the earlier figure. The company was not interested. In February 1970, the Scudders sold their publishing and related interests to Media General Inc. of Richmond, Virginia, for stock valued at approximately $50 million. Media General brought in new management and applied drastic economies, which in turn provoked a strike. With its presses and Sunday franchise sold to the rival *Star-Ledger* and its circulation down below 140,000, the *Evening News* finally ceased publication on August 31, 1972.

Although a disappointment, the Newark episode was not a deterrent to Time Inc. in its ambition to become a newspaper publisher. Quite the opposite. In May 1968, three weeks after the purchase agreement for the *Evening News* collapsed, the change in managing editors at *Time* left Otto Fuerbringer free for a new assignment. Donovan announced that this would be to a new corporate post as "chief explorer of Time Inc.'s interests and opportunities in the newspaper field . . . The company hopes to develop a role in daily newspaper journalism, and we are asking Fuerbringer to take charge of our studies of where, when and how."

Fuerbringer had, as noted earlier, worked ten years for the St. Louis *Post-Dispatch* before he came to *Time*. His new assignment not only signaled an acceleration of the newspaper search; it also marked the beginning of a second career at Time Inc. for the 57-year-old former editor, who in the decade ahead would go on to direct the company's magazine development group and to oversee the launching of both *Money* and *People*.

Rather quickly, Time Inc.'s newspaper division, as the Fuerbringer operation was subsequently named, had a number of prospects in view. There was serious examination of the Boston *Globe*, also of the Perry Publications, a chain of 13 Florida dailies including the West Palm Beach *Post* and *Times* and the Pensacola *News* and *Journal*, 11 weeklies and two magazines. Discussions in both cases foundered on the question of price.

But in April 1969, Time Inc. got into newspaper publishing at last. Along with acquisitions, Fuerbringer had been scouting the possibility of entering metropolitan daily newspapering by the periphery—establishing a base in the suburbs, serving the commuter trade, and moving in from there. Chicago was one of the newspaper markets Fuerbringer had in mind, and when a chain of weeklies in the area came up for sale, he recommended purchase.

For $1,350,000, plus assumption of $2,125,000 of debt, Time Inc. bought the Pioneer Publishing Company of St. Charles, Illinois, owners of a commercial printing plant and 22 weekly papers with a total circulation of 118,000 in the suburban belt from beyond Oak Park in the west to the North Shore communities along Lake Michigan.

Put together mainly in the 1920s by Telfer MacArthur, the brother of playwright Charles (*The Front Page*) MacArthur, the Pio-

230

neer group had roots going back a half-century. Ernest Hemingway, as a teenager, had delivered Pioneer's Oak Park publication, *Oak Leaves*, and during his World War I service in Italy had had the paper sent to him there. On revenues of around $5 million, the papers were modestly profitable, although modernization of Pioneer's commercial printing facilities in 1968 had put the company temporarily in the red.

Fuerbringer outlined the newspaper division's strategy in a memo to Heiskell:

> The significant fact about the acquisition of Pioneer is that it gives us an opportunity to advance our theory that today's best and most economical opportunity for entering daily journalism in big urban areas is to come into the suburbs with an afternoon paper. Such a paper should be based on existing small dailies and weeklies, using their already established community acceptance and their existing printing plants. We thus avoid the necessity of buying a successful big-city daily at an astronomical price; we sidestep the high cost of starting a new paper from scratch; and we minimize the possibilities of antitrust intervention.
>
> Such a move . . . does not exclude our interest in acquisitions of middle-sized papers, especially in growth areas, or in papers in newly urban areas that are not bedeviled by a decaying core city. The two types of enterprises are not mutually exclusive.

In the Chicago area, Fuerbringer said, the newspaper division had its eye also on two other groups: Lloyd Hollister Inc., publisher of ten tabloid semiweeklies with a total circulation of 65,000 in the affluent North Shore communities from Evanston to Lake Forest; and the Pickwick and Franklin Park Publishing Companies, whose nine weeklies had a circulation of 50,000 in the suburbs westward from Skokie to Des Plaines and south to River Grove. Also in the newspaper division's sights were suburban newspaper properties in the Los Angeles and the San Francisco Bay areas.

Time Inc. bought the Hollister North Shore Chicago papers in September 1969, together with Hollister's commercial printing operations, for $4,950,000. With revenues in the same range as Pioneer's, the Hollister group was well established and highly respected. The Evanston *Review*, the chain's strongest paper, had won both national and state awards for excellence in the nondaily newspaper field. The following year, Time Inc. moved to buy the Pickwick and Franklin Park chains as well, but backed off under the threat of antitrust action by the Justice Department. It was not until 1979 that these purchases were finally completed.

Time Inc. did not, as it turned out, go further with the project of creating a Chicago area daily. No formal decision was made. In the rather unsettled corporate climate following the executive changes of August 1969 (see chapter 16), the idea was simply set aside.

Newspaper acquisitions continued to be discussed, however. In March 1970, news reports that the Times-Mirror Company of Los Angeles was talking with the owners of Long Island's thriving afternoon daily, *Newsday*, prompted suggestions within the company that Time Inc. also tender an offer. Nothing came of the proposal, and over the following two or three years the company's interest in daily newspapers faded. Whether Time Inc. should even retain ownership of the Chicago suburban weeklies was questioned.

Purchase of these weeklies had, indeed, taken the company into another province of journalism—a small world of chronicling church suppers, weddings and women's lecture meetings, of assuaging local sensitivities, of dealing with merchants and town officials who thought the proper function of the press was to promote rather than to report. For Time Inc., the transition was not easy. On the publishing side too, where commercial printing constituted half the business, it was a different operation from what the company was accustomed to.

Following the Hollister purchase in September 1969, Time Inc. merged the two newspaper groups into one wholly owned subsidiary, Pioneer Press Inc. Fuerbringer became chairman. J. Richard Munro, formerly general manager of *Sports Illustrated*, was named president, only to be recalled to New York three months later to become publisher of *Sports Illustrated*. After his departure, there was a succession of executive shifts at Pioneer; finally, in 1978, David Simonson was named president. A former New York advertising man, more recently publisher of a New York suburban newspaper, Simonson had also been a newspaper reporter, editor and syndicated cartoonist, and at Pioneer Press continued to draw a weekly editorial page cartoon for the group's papers. Simonson remained president throughout Time Inc.'s ownership of Pioneer Press.

With the merger of Hollister and Pioneer, overlapping newspapers of the two chains were combined. Commercial printing operations were consolidated, and Pioneer's money-losing St. Charles plant was sold. Under Time Inc. ownership the papers were also given an editorial overhaul. In December 1969, Don Sider, 36, was brought in from the Time-Life News Service as the Pioneer publications' editor. Born in Chicago, Sider had spent ten years with the St. Petersburg *Times* in Florida, where he was editor of news features and the Sunday magazine editor. Joining *Time* in 1966, Sider had served in the Miami and Saigon bureaus and, most recently, as bureau chief in Detroit.

An energetic man who liked to go skydiving on weekends, Sider sharpened the Pioneer papers' writing and reporting, instituting livelier photography and a generally brightened format, with redesigned picture covers. The obligatory reporting of Boy Scout and Kiwanis club activities continued, but coverage was broadened to include subjects previously considered too controversial for suburban newspaper treatment: abortion, drugs, student dissent, racial friction. One series of articles, running in all the Pioneer papers and entitled, "The Root of Suburban is Urban," related the linkage of suburban issues to those of the cities. Another bold story, "Where Shall They Sleep?", broke silence on the dilemma of parents as their college-age children brought friends of the opposite sex home for the holidays.

Suburban readers noticed the editorial changes—not always with pleasure. Complained a Glenview subscriber: "Obviously, you people at Pioneer Press have turned your newspapers over to young radicals who would be an asset to underground publications in Haight-Ashbury or Chicago's Old Town." Sider, reporting to New York headquarters, conceded that the papers were suffering from their audiences' "darkest suspicions about the invaders from the East . . . carpetbaggers—'not local, too liberal.' " Still, he felt Pioneer weeklies could be fairly described as "18 pretty good, usually interesting, easy-to-read papers that cover their communities . . . as well as any papers can, given the economic realities of community journalism . . . honest, fairly brave . . . moving out of the oldtime safety of 'news guaranteed not to offend anyone' . . . We aren't innocuous. We are speaking to things that concern, or should concern, our readers."

The first venture that Time Inc. made into newspaper publishing, Pioneer Press was to remain as the last. In 1978, as related in a subsequent chapter of this history, the company bought the Washington *Star*, only to abandon publication three years later after substantial losses. Pioneer Press, in contrast, prospered, showing healthy returns on both investment and sales, despite initial losses on the group's commercial printing operations. Between 1975 and 1977 divisional income doubled, reaching $2,169,000 on revenues of $10,674,000. In 1977 Time Inc. increased its investment in Pioneer with a $1.6 million computerized copy processing system designed to serve all the group's papers.

Operationally, however, Pioneer largely remained apart from the parent company—neglected, as the Pioneer staff saw matters. With one or two exceptions, there was no interchange of editorial staff between Pioneer Press and Time Inc. after Sider's departure in 1972, and on the publishing side the company remained rather in the position of an absentee landlord. A 1975 report to group vice president Bear, the corporate overseer of Pioneer's affairs, put the relationship in blunt terms: "It is hardly heresy to suggest that Time Inc. probably does not need this chain of weekly newspapers today . . . The purpose behind the purchase of the papers has more or less evaporated. Consequently, Pioneer is something of an appendage to the corporation, a vestigial tail that the dog wouldn't bother to wag if he could."

But even as an appendage Pioneer continued to grow, in 1978 adding three papers from the Southtown Economist newspapers at Oak Park, and in 1979 the ten weeklies of the Pickwick Papers chain. Eventually, with consolidations, Pioneer was publishing 30 weeklies in all, with a total circulation of 148,000.* In 1982 Pioneer launched a glossy quarterly, entitled *Q*, with a circulation of 30,000 spread throughout the North Shore region.

In 1981, Pioneer Press's operating income went over the $3 million level, continuing to rise thereafter. But the question of whether Pioneer, whose business was essentially local, fitted with Time Inc.'s other interests, which were national and international in their scope, was finally answered in the negative. "There is no compelling rationale for retaining one such property [as Pioneer], nor is there any strategic plan to acquire additional properties of this type," manage-

*They were: the Park Ridge *Advocate*, Niles *Spectator*, Skokie *Review*, Morton Grove *Champion*, Franklin Park *Herald-Journal*, Schiller Park *Independent*, River Grove *Messenger*, Rosemont *Progress*, Des Plaines *Highlander*, Edison Park-Norridge Park-Harwood Heights *Citizen*, Evanston *Review*, Wilmette *Life*, Winnetka *Talk*, Glenview *Announcements*, Northbrook *Star*, Glencoe *News*, Deerfield *Review*, Highland *Park News*, Lake Forest *Lake Forester*, Vernon *Review*, Oak Park *Oak Leaves*, Elmwood Park *Elm Leaves*, River Forest *Forest Leaves*, Melrose Park *Herald*, Maywood *Herald*, Libertyville *Review*, Mundelein *Review*, West Proviso *Herald*, Forest Park *News* and the *Weekend World* in Oak Park.

ment informed the Time Inc. board in late 1984, in seeking approval for sale of the papers to the Chicago-based Field Corporation, a successor company to Field Enterprises. The price was $24.6 million; the capital gain to Time Inc., $12 million.

"We Believed in the Ultimate Can-Do"

I N CONVERSATION with Hedley Donovan in the White House in March 1968, Lyndon Johnson voiced the hurt he felt when Time Inc., long a supporter of his policies in Vietnam, finally turned against him. Donovan recalled the President's words, spoken more in regret than anger. "He said he had only been doing 'what you fellows wanted me to do all along.' But now, the change in *Time*'s position had made it impossible to conduct the war." The President had added quietly, "I don't think this would have happened if Henry [Luce] were still alive."

Johnson shared a common misconception: that it was Luce, the hard-liner on China, who had dictated Time Inc.'s early hard line on Vietnam. There was a certain superficial plausibility to this belief. A militancy of tone had once invited the gibe that Vietnam was "*Time*'s house war." Strongly supportive throughout the early and middle 1960s—"the right war, in the right place, at the right time," a much-cited *Time* Essay declared in May 1965—the Time Inc. magazines began shifting position within eight months after Luce's death. Guarded language in *Time,* softening that militancy, first signaled the change; a *Life* editorial calling for a halt to the bombing of North Vietnam moved Time Inc. further away.

But in truth, Luce, even in earlier years, had taken little part in formulation of the magazines' policy on Vietnam. After he had turned the editor-in-chief's responsibility over to Donovan in 1964, Luce visited Saigon in the course of a long Asian tour but hardly mentioned Vietnam in notes he wrote after his return. "Luce . . . was not greatly preoccupied with Vietnam . . . and had become more relaxed about China than you might think," Donovan recalled. "He adopted my [positions] as his . . . stance on Vietnam, but I think he was also enjoying having someone else take the final responsibility for such positions."

The war in Vietnam tore the company emotionally and politically, as it did the rest of American society. From the start it had also posed, most acutely, that question inherent in the Time Inc. system of collective journalism: Whose views should prevail in print, the reporter's or the editor's?

As late as the spring of 1962, only about half a dozen American correspondents were resident in Saigon. Most U.S. publications, *Time* and *Life* included, were covering Vietnam out of Hong Kong. Time Inc.'s two senior men in the area, *Time* bureau chief Stanley Karnow and *Life*'s Asian regional editor Milton Orshefsky, had both been based previously in Paris, where they had reported, from a distance, on France's losing war in Indochina; neither was optimistic about the current prospects in Vietnam. "A fragile state, government in the ancient Mandarin tradition by a single man and the few people he trusts—mainly members of his family," Karnow informed New York in 1960, describing South Vietnam under its autocratic and secretive president, Ngo Dinh Diem; his brother, the chief of state security, Ngo Dinh Nhu; and Nhu's beautiful but much feared wife.

Charles Mohr succeeded Karnow in the summer of 1962. A husky, sandy-haired Nebraskan, then 32, Mohr had caught Luce's eye when, as bureau chief in New Delhi, he had escorted the editor-in-chief on a trip through India in 1961. In a speech afterward at Columbia University, Luce extolled Mohr's zestful reporting from India and the "passion to be a journalist" that had led Mohr, earlier, to combine studies at the University of Nebraska with full-time work on the Lincoln *Star*. Before going to India, Mohr had been *Time*'s White House correspondent.

By his own account, Mohr arrived in Vietnam feeling the war could be won militarily: "In May 1962, I was very gung-ho." By fall Mohr shared the doubts of his journalistic colleagues, and by the following March he was openly challenging the *Time* editors' more upbeat views. Mohr wrote chief of correspondents Dick Clurman:

"In the briefest possible summary my opinion is: the situation stinks."

In May 1963 the Diem government's troubles with its militant Buddhist opposition began, and in June came the first protest suicide, the self-immolation of a 73-year-old Buddhist monk whose kneeling figure, enveloped in flames, produced a photograph that shocked the world. In July, after the announcement that there would be a new American ambassador, Henry Cabot Lodge, *Life* warned editorially: "If Diem doesn't change his ways, the U.S. may have to consider supporting another government." *Time* likewise, in a cover story evaluating Diem's position, discussed quite matter-of-factly the likelihood of his being toppled in a coup.

The cover portrait was of Diem's sister-in-law, Mme. Ngo Dinh Nhu. Mohr interviewed her for ten hours and won from her the comment, "You know, I have told you things I have never told anybody else." His file, which he expected would result in his expulsion, began on a doomsday note: "Vietnam is a graveyard of lost hopes, destroyed vanity, glib promises and good intentions." That line was not in the published story. But the magazine's characterization of Mme. Nhu as the "fragile, exciting beauty" who was "probably more feared than any other man or woman" in South Vietnam, was severe.

Mohr's files won enthusiastic praise from the editors. Mohr himself was less enthusiastic about the thrust of the cover story. In an agitated letter to deputy chief of correspondents John Boyle, he complained that the story's "tone was terribly mild" and did "*not* convey something which I believed; that [Mme. Nhu] not only may cause the fall of the government but that she and the government *deserve* that fate." Mohr also charged the editors in New York with "a consistent pattern of contempt" for his reporting, and for taking sides in the press war against him and other correspondents in Vietnam:

> I also have to ask why the pro-Diem editors of *Time* insist on referring to the American press in Saigon as "anti-Diem" . . . or "vociferously anti-Diem." Or that . . . the press "paints it black" . . . I have come to the conclusion that an attempt is being made to discount or discredit American reporting from Vietnam. This frankly bewilders me . . . *I* am one of the "reporters in Saigon" and *Time* is shelling its own troops.

Mohr's letter, relayed to Fuerbringer, set off the predictable explosion at the receiving end. Henry Grunwald, the senior editor in

charge of the World section, was incensed. Clurman, declaring himself "quite literally flabbergasted" by Mohr's letter, assured him that
his reporting was indeed being heeded. Mohr backed off, apologiz-
ing to Clurman and Fuerbringer for the "bad taste" of his remarks
about the *Time* editors. "I used my elbows and knees a bit," Mohr
wrote, "and I am sorry about that."

Temporarily smoothed over, the dispute broke out again with two
stories in *Time* two weeks later. One was a piece in the World section, reporting a valiant South Vietnamese army stand against the
Vietcong just north of Saigon; the other a story in the Press section
sharply critical of the American correspondents in Saigon who, *Time*
charged, were biased against Diem and unwilling to report anything
good about the regime and were thus "helping to compound the
very confusion [they] should be untangling for . . . readers back
home." The article acknowledged the official deceit and hostility
that newsmen in Vietnam had to contend with:

> Such uncommon pressures unite the newsmen to an uncommon
> degree. They work hard . . . But when they meet and unwind—
> in the field, in their homes or in the cameraderie of the Hotel
> Caravelle's eighth-floor bar [a popular press rendezvous in Sai-
> gon]—they pool their convictions, information, misinformation
> and grievances . . . The balm of such companionship has not
> been conducive to independent thought . . .
>
> The Saigon-based press corps is so confident of its own con-
> victions that any other version of the Vietnam story is quickly
> dismissed . . . Many of the correspondents seem reluctant to
> give splash treatment to anything that smacks of military victory
> in the ugly war against the Communists, since this . . . weakens
> the argument that defeat is inevitable so long as Diem is in
> power.

Fuerbringer, who had ordered the Press story, considered the situation—the ongoing controversy over the reporting out of Vietnam—
eminently newsworthy. "[Columnists] Joe Alsop and Marguerite
Higgins were writing about the press corps. Kennedy was complaining," Fuerbringer said later. "To infer we ran the Press story
because of Charley Mohr is 1,000 percent wrong." Nonetheless, it
provoked strong protest from Clurman, as chief of correspondents.
He and Fuerbringer lunched together the day the Press story was
closing for print. Clurman argued in vain for changes, later cabling
Mohr that *Time* was publishing a story that he felt would be
regarded in Saigon as "most seriously compromising your position"

among the correspondents there. Clurman also informed Luce and Donovan of the dispute, characterizing the Press story as one that "takes a germ of truth and converts it into what I regard as a major piece of wrong and unproved criticism."

Fearing Mohr might resign, Clurman invited the correspondent to meet him in Paris for a talk. Mohr arrived in Paris angry not only at the Press story but the World story praising the South Vietnamese army's performance against the Vietcong, which he thought was contrary to his own reporting of the battle: "The military fiasco I reported had been turned around into a victory." He wanted to quit. During a long weekend of argument, he himself suggested a compromise: a second Press story, not flatly repudiating the first, but rather noting the continuing controversy over the war reporting from Saigon and offering Mohr's view, under his byline. Somewhat dubious, Clurman flew home to talk to Luce, telephoning Mohr shortly afterward that the editor-in-chief was, in effect, standing by his managing editor. Luce could not agree to a bylined piece by Mohr but did consider a second Press story "a terrific idea." Clurman proposed that he and Mohr do it together.

Once on the ground in Saigon, though, Clurman changed his mind, counseling against a second Press story. He cabled Luce, Donovan and Fuerbringer: "Our story was out of kilter in such deliberately irremediable ways that it's next to impossible right now to run a story in print setting matters straight." He arrived in New York to find his advice overridden; a second Press story was already in preparation. Worked over by all hands and shown to Luce before he departed for a weekend out of town, the story examined at three-column length what *Time* called "currently the biggest intramural story in U.S. journalism"—whether the Saigon correspondents' "sense of mission" had affected their judgment, whether they had thus "given their readers an unduly pessimistic view of the war . . . It is not an idle question, for Washington policymakers, receiving considerable conflicting information of their own, have relied a good deal on what they have read in the public prints."

Citing both the accusations against the Saigon press corps and the correspondents' own defense, the *Time* story edged toward a retraction—something *Time* did rarely. It also aired *Time*'s in-house dispute:

In its September 20 issue . . . *Time* found the Saigon reporters to be working hard under extremely difficult conditions, but also found them . . . severely critical of practically everything.

240

What they reported about the course of the war was seriously questioned in Washington; what they wrote about the deterioration of the Diem government (not sufficiently emphasized in the *Time* story) was correct—and confirmed all around . . . In emotion-taut Saigon, the *Time* story was resented. Charles Mohr, *Time*'s Southeast Asian bureau chief, resigned.

Less than a month later Diem was overthrown in a South Vietnamese army coup. Military government began, with no discernible improvement in either the military or the political situation. In March 1965, sustained air attacks on North Vietnam commenced. That same month two Marine battalions, the first American combat troops in Vietnam, were landed at Danang. Donovan strongly supported the U.S. actions, and a *Life* editorial in July showed it: "The reasons for U.S. involvement [in Vietnam] have been thoroughly debated and the case for our staying there . . . may be considered closed." Dissent was growing, however, most vocally in the academic community, and Johnson's dispatch of U.S. Marines to the Dominican Republic three months earlier had intensified the argument over American military intervention abroad. But here also, a *Life* editorial, reflecting Donovan's views, came down firmly on the President's side.

In November 1965, Donovan made his first trip to Vietnam. *Life* managing editor George Hunt had preceded him earlier that year and returned in agreement with American military objectives. However, as a combat veteran of island warfare against the Japanese in World War II, Hunt was incredulous at the military establishment he found in Saigon: air-conditioning everywhere, swarms of soldier-clerks ("typewriter commandos"), individual place cards at a dinner for five at General William Westmoreland's headquarters. Donovan spent ten days in Vietnam, touring a dozen of the country's 43 provinces and flying on a bombing mission along the Ho Chi Minh Trail. On his return, he wrote "Vietnam: The War Is Worth Winning," the preface to a 31-page special section in *Life*'s February 25, 1966, issue:

The war in Vietnam is not primarily a war about Vietnam, nor even entirely a war about China. It is a war about the future of Asia. It is very possibly as important as any of the previous American wars of this century.

In fact this ugly, maddening, big-little war may some day be remembered as a historic turning point . . .

241

By summer [1966] the effects of all our effort should really begin to be felt on the battlefields. A point comes in a war when momentum develops: cumulative and multiplying effects spread across a whole theater; one action goes well, and things seem to go better in half a dozen other places. The momentum was running strongly for the Vietcong in early 1965. It could be running strongly for our side in late 1966.

In Donovan's estimate, "late this year or early next" could see de-escalation of the North Vietnamese military infiltration of the south and the "end of the big-unit war," which would constitute "the first installment of 'victory.' " The second installment could come in the early 1970s as Vietcong activity was reduced to a "police problem," after which all or almost all American troops could be brought home.

The article delighted Luce. "The best thing by far written on Vietnam, ever," he wrote Donovan.

Donovan's schedule for early victory had raised a few eyebrows among Time Inc.'s Southeast Asia correspondents. But most still felt the war was ultimately winnable, provided that the U.S. was willing to commit the necessary forces. The troop buildup was in progress; the results were not in yet. To this extent, reporters and their editors in New York were not as much at odds over the war as they had been in 1963.

The atmosphere, too, had improved considerably. Much of this was due personally to the new Hong Kong bureau chief, Frank McCulloch, who arrived in January 1964. McCulloch was then 44, older than most correspondents covering the war, and had been in newspapering since his teens. A muscular, billiard-bald, wisecracking character who seemed to come straight out of Central Casting, McCulloch had worked his way through the University of Nevada as a reporter and proofreader on the Reno *Gazette*. After knocking about on various papers in the Sierra Nevada gold-mining country and serving a wartime hitch as a Marine Corps sergeant, McCulloch had joined *Time* in 1953 as a correspondent in the Los Angeles bureau. He had done the reporting for a 1960 *Time* cover story on Los Angeles *Times* publisher Norman Chandler; this had led to his appointment as day managing editor of the *Times*. The reporting urge persisted, however, and when Luce, at Clurman's suggestion, phoned him in late 1963 proposing that he rejoin *Time*, McCulloch accepted and Clurman assigned him to Hong Kong.

242

McCulloch went out to Hong Kong knowing he would catch some of the resentment still felt by resident correspondents over the *Time* Press story that had provoked Mohr's resignation. "That story shocked me when I read it," said McCulloch. Now, as he prepared to take over the bureau, "It gave me a lot of qualms. As the new boy on the block I knew I'd get jumped in a hurry."

It was a tribute to McCulloch himself that when he left four years later, he ranked among the most respected correspondents in the area. "He inspires trust from his sources, respect from his colleagues and almost fanatical loyalty from his staff," a *Time* colleague wrote. "He gets up earlier, digs harder and goes to bed later than anyone else."

Before departing from New York, McCulloch said, he was told he had the confidence of the editors; he was not sent out with instructions to change the political orientation of the reporting. Clurman, trying to repair the news service's relation with the editors, told McCulloch: "Look, there's no point in trying to lay blame [in the Mohr affair]. The system is such; you know what it is." McCulloch, for his part, was inclined to be philosophical. He was annoyed by the magazine's tendency to be excessively optimistic and to overplay American feats of arms. Years after the event, *Time*'s account of the siege of Plei Mei in October 1965, which gave credit mainly to a few U.S. special forces troops and not to the valor of South Vietnamese troops in holding off the North Vietnamese attack, still rankled with McCulloch. "When we went out there afterward, we were either laughed at or cussed. I was mad as hell," McCulloch said.

He also resented what he considered *Time*'s "vindictive . . . endless vendetta" against the Saigon press corps. However, he did appreciate the problem the editors in New York had in reconciling the divergent views they got from the Saigon and Washington bureaus. "I don't know how in non-byline group journalism you avoid that," he remarked later. "In the byline system you would have Frank McCulloch in Saigon side by side with John Steele [the *Time* bureau chief] in Washington and let the reader make up his mind . . . Naturally, we got furious about it at times. What was particularly upsetting was that we'd be there looking at it. But they in New York would say, 'There are things you in Saigon don't know.' How do you answer that?"

Several factors tended to tip the balance toward the Washington view: propinquity, political sympathy and, not the least, the access the President was giving Time Inc. Like Kennedy before him, Lyndon Johnson cultivated *Time*. According to John Steele, "He too regarded it as this tremendously powerful instrument and was determined to play it for all it was worth . . . A reporter could be summoned at 4 o'clock in the afternoon although there was no particular reason for seeing the President. Then he would deliver a two-hour monologue. I felt embarrassed taking up so much of the President's time. He would sit there with his feet up, drinking Dr Pepper and giving his rationale for events in Vietnam."

The President, through his National Security staff, was also making a good deal of classified material available. "You could say it was one-sided," Steele acknowledged. "Of course it was, but it was the best information available. It was what the President and his National Security Council were getting . . . Sitting in the White House basement [the NSC offices] we were allowed to read captured enemy documents also. Sometimes you could quote them, sometimes you couldn't, but we were able to use a great deal, and by and large we did it fairly judiciously."

Fuerbringer had a different view: "Our fault was not so much that we believed what our Washington correspondents were telling us—from Pentagon sources and from Uncle Lyndon—as that we couldn't conceive that America couldn't get its act together and win." In November 1965 he went to Vietnam, talked with Westmoreland and others, got the customary military briefings and was taken to see the huge deep-water port that American engineers were constructing at Cam Ranh Bay. The Cam Ranh installations made a powerful impression on Fuerbringer, as they did on most visitors; half-facetiously, he suggested that the post facilities be shown to enemy commanders as well, as a bit of psychological warfare. "When I saw Cam Ranh Bay with McCulloch, it was hard not to think that as soon as all this power was applied with the military skill we had shown in the past, we would win . . . Despite Korea, we believed in the ultimate American can-do."

Vietnam was the longest war in American history. Scores of correspondents and photographers served there, a mixture of combat veterans from World War II and Korea and younger men covering their first war. When McCulloch arrived, the Hong Kong bureau was responsible for a huge area—not only Vietnam but all of Southeast Asia, including Indonesia and the Philippines, plus long-distance monitoring of mainland China. Among those who then and later covered the war for *Time,* some resident in Saigon and some commuting from Hong Kong, were John Shaw, James Wilde, Don Sider, Jonathan Larsen, Donald Neff, William McWhirter, Bruce

Nelan, Marsh Clark, David DeVoss and James Willwerth. Loren Fessler, an ex-OSS man and Chinese-language scholar, handled the China watch.

Then in charge for *Life* as Asian regional editor was Robert Morse. Other *Life* correspondents over the years included John Mulliken, Don Moser, John Saar, Sam Angeloff and Michael Mok. A parade of staff and contract photographers, mostly on short assignments, provided picture coverage. Among them were John Dominis, Paul Schutzer, Terry Spencer, John Loengard, Co Rentmeester, Richard Swanson, Carl Mydans and Le Minh. Former *Life* photographer David Douglas Duncan flew in to record the anguish of the Marines under siege at Khe Sanh in 1968. Above all there was Larry Burrows, who covered the war for *Life* for nine years until his death.

By early summer 1966, the demands on Hong Kong had become so great that Saigon was designated a separate Time-Life news service bureau. McCulloch remained senior correspondent for Southeast Asia, continuing to shuttle in from Hong Kong to assist in the war coverage. Heading the Saigon bureau was Simmons Fentress, 41, a genial man, sometimes given to righteous anger, who had broken in on North Carolina newspapers and had joined *Time* in 1961 after a Nieman Fellowship at Harvard. By local standards, the Saigon bureau was rather grandly set up in a villa of its own, with a full complement of Vietnamese help. Rare among news organizations in wartime Vietnam, the bureau also had a direct telex line to New York, which Time Inc.'s communications director, John Striker, had adroitly wangled from the Vietnamese postal-telegraph authorities. McCulloch, writing to New York as Fentress arrived, described how the bureau had grown:

The first time I came to Vietnam, early in 1964, we worked from John Shaw's apartment on Cong Ly Street and my single room in the Caravelle Hotel . . . Hong Kong staffers moved in and out as the news demanded . . .

As the war grew, so did the bureau. At first, we fitted very well into Room 6, Continental Palace, 132 Tu Do Street. Then wall maps, correspondents, office help, Teletype operators, weapons, boots, helmets and all the other impediments of covering a war began to proliferate.

On more occasions than not we had up to 15 people working in one hotel room. When the air conditioning was off, as it frequently was, and the floor lamps were at full brilliance and the

Teletypes heated up and numerous correspondents were in the throes of creation, well, the room was something more than cozy . . .

The quarters to which we have just moved [are at] 7 Han Thuyen . . . Directly across the street is one of Saigon's few parks. Half a block away . . . is the city's Catholic cathedral, and just the other side of that, the cable office and post office. It is a justifiably coveted location . . .

The villa is a small one. Our office occupies the entire ground floor, and while we're still pretty well packed in, the sardine atmosphere of Room 6 is a thing of the past.

Time chose the opening of the Saigon bureau as the occasion for another critical look at the American press establishment in Vietnam. In vain, McCulloch fought to get the story postponed, cabling the editors: "I can think of nothing calculated to do Simmons Fentress more harm and to get him off to a more difficult start in this extremely difficult town than a story dissecting his colleagues . . . What a combination: Fentress arrives and immediately does a knife job on other newsmen, and McCulloch departs and on the way to the airport helps drive the knife home."

Clurman, reading the story in New York before it went to press, tried to reassure McCulloch: "The Press story, while not exactly to my liking, shouldn't make any of you jump ship." He was right. But a few months later, *Time* resumed its criticism of the Saigon correspondents with a Press story quoting extensively from a *New Leader* article by the retired Army brigadier general and military historian, S.L.A. Marshall. Comparing the Vietnam newsmen unfavorably with those he knew in World War II and Korea, Marshall accused them of neglecting combat reporting for stories "that will make people squirm and agonize. The war is being covered primarily for all bleeding hearts," not for the "simple souls who would like to know how it is being fought and how good are the chances [for a] military victory." When that issue of *Time* reached Vietnam, Fentress blew up. "*Time*'s pickup of the S.L.A. Marshall piece had the Saigon press corps on its ear," he cabled New York, complaining that for *Time* to let Marshall "lecture from our pulpit in such gross terms without even a line of comment from us . . . reflects upon every reporter here, including *Time*'s own."

Donovan too had been upset with *Time* over Vietnam. In June 1966, the U.S. had stepped up its air attacks on the north. As carrier-based Navy planes and Air Force bombers from bases in South Vietnam and Thailand swept in to bomb the oil storage depots outside Hanoi and at Haiphong, *Time* ran a cover story on Defense Secretary Robert McNamara, lauding the escalation. The story and the cover slash, "Raising the Price of Aggression," triggered a sharp exchange of memos between the editor-in-chief and *Time*'s managing editor.

Donovan wrote Fuerbringer: "Occasionally a kind of cheerleader tone turns up in [*Time*'s] treatment of the war and Washington decisions about the war. The effect is to make us sound like uncritical champions of a policy which, God knows, has its agonizing moments." Donovan thought the story contained much excellent detail on the raids—"the best report on all this I've seen in one place." But, he added:

> I am much distressed by much of the surrounding commentary . . . that the U.S. must be determined to win in Vietnam "at any price."
>
> I argued in my *Life* piece [February 25, 1966] that with sustained air pressure against the North, and eventually about 400,000 U.S. troops on the ground, we ought to be able to win the present phase . . . I still think that's not a bad guess. But if it's wrong, am I in favor of 500,000 troops? Yes. 600,000? 750,000? I would begin to wonder.
>
> I would not expect him to say so out loud, but I am sure there must be some cutoff point in L.B.J.'s mind, or at least a point where he would reexamine all those "options" he's always preserving. *Time* ought to keep some options too, or at least refrain from issuing such stupendous blank checks.

"*Time* has not been and does not intend to become an automatic Johnson cheerleader," Fuerbringer replied, adding that Donovan had "missed the forest in favor of chopping down some of the trees . . . The U.S. had taken a major and necessary decision; the Hanoi-Haiphong bombings were a military masterpiece. Thus the story had a strong and justifiably admiring tone."

Vietnam was becoming a touchy issue with Donovan. On a European tour he had lunch with the Time-Life staff in Paris, and the question of European attitudes toward the U.S. had come up. Afterward, one correspondent recalled "blurting out that the American image would not improve unless we got rid of that goddamned Vietnam war. When I said that, Donovan looked as if I'd slapped him across the face with a wet towel."

Antiwar sentiment in the U.S. was spreading as Donovan made a second visit to Vietnam, in May 1967. There had been demonstrations against the war in New York and San Francisco. Martin Luther King Jr. had publicly urged draft evasion and Senator Robert Kennedy called for a bombing halt. American troop deployment in Vietnam was already past 400,000 and edged toward the half-million mark by the end of the year. There were more casualties in 1967 than in all the previous years of the war combined. "The U.S. has gone far, far beyond the point of no return in Vietnam and there is no escape except in defeat," *Fortune* declared in the foreword to a special section on "Vietnam 1967" in the April issue, which examined not only the military situation but the managerial aspects of the war effort. One article was written by John Mecklin, who had served from 1962 to 1964 as U.S. Information Chief in Saigon (while on leave from *Time*). He saw only marginal prospects for the rural pacification program. Assistant managing editor Walter Guzzardi found "confusion . . . and frustration the order of the day" among American officialdom both in Washington and in Saigon. Only from *Fortune*'s Charles Murphy was there a hopeful message—General Westmoreland's military strategy was working "brilliantly."

Donovan was less sure. In *Life*'s June 2, 1967, issue, he backed off his earlier timetable for victory. "Some overoptimistic Americans . . . this writer included, had expected by now to see the beginnings of real momentum in Vietnam, the multiplier point where success in one theater or aspect of a war starts to breed success in many others. It certainly hasn't happened yet." However, it was success deferred, not denied, that Donovan saw. "Vietnam: Slow, Tough, But Coming Along," the article was headed, and the final paragraphs set a new timetable—perhaps another nine or ten months before "our Vietnam policy could be looking like a success," another couple of years before U.S. troop reductions could begin.

It was the last prediction of victory that Donovan risked. During the summer, his own growing doubts, added to those of other Time Inc. colleagues, took over.

In June 1967, Donovan delivered the commencement address at New York University. Publication of extensive excerpts in the publisher's letter of *Time* underscored the importance he accorded the speech. After contrasting the Vietnam war with "the popular war, even . . . romantic war" that Israel had just fought and won in the Mideast, Donovan got to his announced subject—a subject that, he said,

248

I am not sure . . . is being taught today in any major American university. I am speaking of the ability to be wrong . . . Journalists have never been notoriously eager to acknowledge their mistakes. Many, indeed, have perfected a smooth, effortless way of taking a new position without ever noting that they once held quite the opposite view.

Perhaps the students could teach all Americans how to be wrong, Donovan observed:

I know many students . . . have felt deeply, and spoken up strongly, on Vietnam . . . Some of you will turn out to have been wrong . . . How to be *right* is something of an art, too, and some of you will get a chance to show your skill at that, when the Vietnam results are finally in . . .

It's a very tough proposition. We may fail . . . But you know, we may just succeed. And if that happens I hope that the many thoughtful, dedicated Americans who opposed the policy will be glad to acknowledge that their country is sometimes capable of even more than we should have dared to dream.

Donovan said later that the succeeding couple of months were decisive for him; he was already swinging more into line with the skeptics among his Time Inc. colleagues, in particular *Life* assistant managing editor Ralph Graves, senior staff editor Tom Griffith and chief of correspondents Dick Clurman. In Donovan's recollecton, "It was about this time that Clurman . . . who had been going to Vietnam two or three times a year for several years, which gave him a very valuable perspective, concluded the war was just about hopeless. I was by no means that pessimistic but was budged a certain distance by Clurman's views." A reunion Donovan had just had in Vietnam with his son Peter, who was doing Peace Corps-type duty with the International Voluntary Services in the Mekong Delta, also made an impact. "Peter had been enthusiastic about the war, a strong believer. [But] by the spring of 1967 he was discouraged by the corruption and the situation in the delta. He thought it was insoluble."

On his return from Vietnam, Donovan said, he had been struck by the change in American opinion—"an important broadening of domestic opposition to Vietnam" shared even by "relatively conservative businessmen and politicians." The impression was confirmed during a vacation Donovan spent at home among "my mainly Republican neighbors" in Sands Point, Long Island. "I was struck

249

by how many Republican, conservative women were totally opposed
. . . It wasn't that I had to go to Sands Point to discover these sentiments, but even there one couldn't get away from them." After
what he had seen in Vietnam, Donovan also found it "morally
objectionable" that the war had entailed no civilian sacrifice on the
home front.

In small, deliberate steps, Time Inc.'s policy began to shift. In
July, Donovan, exercising the editor-in-chief's prerogative, sat in for
Time managing editor Fuerbringer. In the August 4 issue, *Time*'s
World section questioned the South Vietnamese army's fighting abilities. The writer, Jason McManus, later recalled the discussions he
had with Donovan: "It was a conscious decision to raise doubts
about the war . . . Characteristically, Hedley insisted that it be not
a lede [*Time*-ese for the lead-off story in a section] but a three-column story inside." On Fuerbringer's return in mid-August, Donovan sent him a confidential memo suggesting that stories reporting
progress in the war needed "a note of wariness." In September *Life*
interpreted South Vietnam's presidential elections as having given
the new Thieu-Ky government a "mandate to talk" peace with the
enemy. In October, in a carefully considered articulation of company policy, a *Life* editorial proposed that the U.S., on its own,
make a peace gesture.

The editorial was argued out at a Time Inc. managing editors'
lunch in New York at the end of September. Some 15 senior editorial executives from all the magazines and the news service were
present. The majority favored editorial advocacy of a more conciliatory American policy in Vietnam; afterward, Donovan remembered
three or four—others only a couple—who were still opposed. One
of the dissenters, Washington bureau chief Steele, recapitulated the
debate in a guidance message for *Life*'s editorial writer:

> The discussion, I believe, centered on three themes: The first
> was whether or not our Vietnamese enterprise is worth the
> effort in terms of U.S. men, money, national preoccupation and
> effort. The second was whether or not the United States
> should, on a unilateral basis, de-escalate the war with a bomb-
> ing pause over North Vietnam or a portion thereof. This was
> the most immediate question before the house. The third was
> . . . whether or not public disquietude, indeed opposition,
> makes our government's stance in Vietnam untenable as now
> constituted.

It was the second of those themes to which *Life* addressed itself.

250

"The Case for Bombing Pause Number 7," as the editorial was entitled, was originally planned to run in the issue dated October 13. Finished at 2 a.m. the day the magazine went to press, it showed too much of the writer's late-night sweat; Donovan, reading the proof when he came to work the next morning, ordered the editorial pulled. In a hasty makeup change, a full-page ad ran in its place.

The delay served to get the wind up at the White House. Over the weekend, while the *Life* editorial was being rewritten, a Washington *Post* story out of New York tipped its content. "An important shift of policy for the publication, generally associated with a hawkish position on the Vietnam conflict," was in preparation, the *Post* reported, adding that "there is a special irony in *Life*'s change of heart in that the Far East was Luce's lifelong interest and the place in which his hard-line anti-Communism found its greatest expression." Shortly, Lyndon Johnson was on the phone. Could the editor-in-chief come down to Washington? Donovan recalled: "I felt there was nothing new to be said." Then Secretary of State Rusk offered to come to New York. Donovan gave him the same answer.

Reworked by Donovan, the editorial appeared in the October 20 issue. Conceding the failure of the six previous U.S. bombing halts—three holiday respites, three to allow a "signal" from Hanoi that never came—the editorial presented the case for a seventh mainly in terms of recapturing political support, at home and abroad, for a cause that was increasingly being questioned. Then *Life* itself edged toward the questioners:

> *Life* believes the U.S. is in Vietnam for honorable and sensible reasons. What the U.S. has undertaken there is obviously harder, longer, more complicated than the U.S. foresaw . . . We are trying to defend not a fully born nation but a situation and a people from which an independent nation might emerge. We are also trying to maintain a highly important—but in the last analysis not absolutely imperative—strategic interest of the U.S. and the free world. This is a tough combination to ask young Americans to die for.

Two subsequent *Life* editorials in January 1968 advocating a shift to a "southern strategy" of seeking negotiated peace in South Vietnam while de-escalating the war in North Vietnam, marked a further evolution of Time Inc. policy. Two months later came Donovan's visit to the White House, where Johnson claimed that matters would have been different had Luce been alive.

The surprise Communist attacks at Tet, at the end of January 1968, broke the truce both sides had declared for this holiday marking the lunar New Year—in Vietnam, traditionally a time for gaiety and family reunions. Quite coincidentally, Tet caught Time Inc.'s Southeast Asia bureaus in transition. McCulloch had just left to become *Life* bureau chief in Washington; succeeding him in Hong Kong was Lee Griggs, 39, who as Africa correspondent had covered the fighting in the Congo and later, as Beirut bureau chief, the Six Day War in the Mideast. Fentress left Saigon, to be succeeded by William Rademaekers, who had previously covered Eastern Europe.

The Vietcong struck Saigon at 2:48 a.m., Wednesday, January 31. A little more than an hour later, Rademaekers telexed Clurman in New York:

> Attack is still going on. Terry and Cantwell [correspondents Wallace H. Terry II and John Cantwell, recent additions to the *Time* staff] report heavy mortaring few blocks away. Dick Swanson sitting on roof of *Life* villa. Ambulances moving through streets.

Hitting the major cities, 30 provincial capitals, some district towns and South Vietnamese and U.S. military installations, the Tet fighting raged into March. Nowhere was it heavier than in Hue, the fortress capital of Vietnam's warlords and center of Vietnamese religious life. From the besieged Marine outpost at Khe Sanh, *Time* correspondent Hugh D.S. (David) Greenway—"in a class by himself, way too much physical courage," McCulloch remarked of him—flew in to join Marine and South Vietnamese forces fighting to retake Hue in a three-week, house-to-house battle that was possibly the longest and fiercest single action of the war. Greenway, 32, was wounded in the assault on Hue's thick-walled Citadel, in the imperial compound at the city's heart. Back in Saigon, Greenway telexed a low-key, almost casual report:

> The Marine company I was with found itself pinned down among the ruins of the east wall of the Citadel . . . [They] were taking very heavy casualties and were moving very slowly in that part of the city—a half a block a day was considered a success.
>
> One squad was told there was a NVA [North Vietnamese army] machine-gun crew up ahead that was holding up the entire advance, and they were to try to knock it out. I decided to go along and we crawled up a few yards to a free-standing

252

wall that would give us some cover . . . The rest of the platoon, including a tank, were giving us covering fire and the din was terrific.

We all reached the wall safely when one Marine stood up to look through what was once a window. An NVA soldier dropped him with a single round through the neck from about 20 yards away. He was still alive, but sucking air through the wound, so the corpsman and I dragged him back to the company command post while the others covered our retreat . . .

The idea was for the reporters to help carry the man farther back to the rear so as not to take riflemen off the line . . .

We were all bunched up trying to carry him, when a lucky mortar round came in a few yards away and blew us into the ditch. There was a lot of yelling and screaming, as there always is in that kind of situation. Al Webb [of UPI], myself, the corpsman and the Marine were hit in the legs . . .

I found out later that the poor chap that we were trying to get out in the first place died in the battalion aid station before he could be medevaced out. An hour later we were all brought out on a helicopter—rounds slamming into the sides from a hostile countryside—but everyone was so glad to see the last of Hue for a while that nobody cared.

At the end of March, Lyndon Johnson quit the presidential race and partially halted the bombing of North Vietnam. In May the Paris peace talks began, only to stall when Hanoi insisted on a total bombing halt. The impasse continued through the November 1968 elections and into the first months of the Nixon administration.

At the end of February 1969, a *Time* news tour group of 25 leading American corporate executives visited Vietnam in the course of a 16-day swing through Asia. Donovan, Shepley, Heiskell and Linen were among the Time Inc. contingent accompanying the businessmen. For Donovan, the Vietnam visit offered some evidence that under the new U.S. commander in Vietnam, General Creighton Abrams, the military situation had improved. From Saigon the businessmen had been flown out to military posts in the countryside, under conditions of apparently greater security than Donovan had encountered on his last visit. "Three years ago when I went there, they had two gunships escorting the chopper," Donovan said, pointing to the areas on the map. But on this trip, he noted, "We were flying unescorted everywhere. That's a rough measurement of what they think is on the ground." Donovan proposed that the news tour group vote on whether they would support a continued, but modestly reduced, American military commitment to South Vietnam. All but three of the group said they would.

It remained for *Life* to illustrate, in human terms, the price of still heavy American military commitment. The occasion was the routine announcement of U.S. casualties for the week of May 28 to June 3, 1969, during which 242 men had died, as the Pentagon put it, "in connection with the conflict in Vietnam." *Life* set out to find and publish the picture of every one of those men.

The week was chosen deliberately—"a span of no special significance," *Life* said, in which the numbers of dead were "average for any seven-day period during this stage of the war." Of the 242, *Life* managed to get photos of all but 25, who either could not be located or whose families refused to furnish one. Together, the 217 whose pictures did run formed a portrait gallery covering 12 pages of *Life*, running five pictures to a row, 20 to a page, passport size, each identified by name, age, rank and hometown.

These young faces looking from the pages silently made the most powerful statement that any Time Inc. magazine—perhaps any American publication—had yet made about the war. Most of the dead were in their 20s, many in their teens. Twenty-five were black. Two were pictured in cap and gown at high school graduation, a moment of youthful promise. One, a much-creased dime-store portrait that a relative fished from a wallet, was hardly usable, but the *Life* photo lab had managed to put it in shape to print. From inscriptions on the backs, from interviews and from letters, *Life* assistant managing editor Loudon Wainwright, who had proposed the project to *Life*'s newly appointed managing editor Ralph Graves, briefly recorded the circumstances of some of the young men's lives and deaths. There was no other text. The pictures were the story.

The impact of the story was enormous, not the least on the *Life* staff who put it together. "I have never seen such intense devotion to a single story," Graves said, "It wasn't because we were all a bunch of doves—as usual there was a wide mix of feelings about the war. It was because we thought it so important to turn those weekly numbers into faces. Even after we had worked on it for several weeks, seen all the layouts and approved the text, we were astonished at how powerful it looked in the magazine. Some readers suggested we do the story every week. One reader (who obviously thought *Life* could do anything) proposed that we do an identical

254

story on the North Vietnamese dead, presumably with snapshots and hometown information."

Two weeks later, a *Life* editorial entitled "The New Arithmetic of Vietnam" measured the price—36,500 American lives and $83 billion expended over five years—against the nation's remaining interest in Vietnam, and declared that the U.S. strategic stake needed reexamination.

Antiwar sentiment in the U.S. was rising. At Time Inc., it took organized form in October 1969 with a Moratorium Day peace rally in the Time & Life Building auditorium. Similar observances— planned as deliberate interruptions in the business-as-usual routine to permit demonstrations of opposition to the war—were scheduled across the nation. A petition signed by 462 Time Inc. employees had requested use of company facilities. Somewhat hesitantly, manage- ment granted the request, "on the strict understanding that it was taking no official position on the Moratorium itself." The rally was moderately well attended. *Time* publisher Hank Luce showed up "to see what was going on." In all, 645 signatures were gathered for a telegram to President Nixon demanding a troop withdrawal. The meeting did not result in any direct challenge to management. Nonetheless, some in management were worried. One memo to Donovan's office saw Moratorium Day pointing "in the direction of increasing staff pressure on editorial and corporate positions."

That became evident in May 1970, after the shooting of four stu- dent protesters at Kent State University in Ohio. Emotions were already inflamed with the revelation of the My Lai massacre and the news that Nixon was opening a new war front in Cambodia. Several petitions were circulating at Time Inc. One asked that the company auditorium be made available for "dissenters" to be heard. Another called on the magazines to "pursue the objective" of U.S. troop withdrawal. A third asked the managing editors of *Time*, *Life* and *Fortune* to take a "strong editorial stand" against the Cambodian incursions and the resumption of bombing in North Vietnam, adding that if the managing editors would not "condemn these actions," the staff request be at least acknowledged in the magazines. There were 332 signatures on the latter petition.

Management rejected the petitions, and in a memorandum to the staff as a whole, Donovan explained the company position. It was in the pages of the magazines, not in employee "political meetings, no matter how worthy," that Time Inc. should explore "the issues

255

of the day," Donovan said:

> If it appeared that the [Time Inc.] auditorium was being used for expressions of dissent against the policies we must write about, our coverage of these policies (and of dissent itself) would be suspect.

Therefore, there would be no repeat of the Moratorium Day rally or any other use of Time Inc. facilities, Donovan declared. As for publicizing the staff petitions against U.S. policies in Southeast Asia, Donovan insisted that while the editors respected the concerns of the staff, they could not "report in their editorial columns on these petitions (though I am aware that other publications may do so)." Donovan went on:

> I must reaffirm a general principle of editorial responsibility in Time Inc. Our readers are entitled to assume that our editorial position on any topic is based on the views of the Time Inc. people professionally assigned to that topic, working under the direction of the editors identified on our mastheads. This system does not guarantee infallibility, but it does clearly locate responsibility. I think it makes for stronger journalism than if our editorial positions were based on samplings of general sentiment within the staff.

Donovan's declaration settled the policy question. "Hedley . . . this is a superb, firm restatement of editorial responsibility," Roy Larsen jotted on his copy of Donovan's memo. It did not, however, quiet the protests. Time-Life Books researcher Carol Isenberg wrote accusing Donovan of "gross insensitivity . . . You say to us . . . 'fine, but make sure it's after 6 o'clock.' " *Time*'s public affairs director Robert Sweeney, commenting on the company's reception of the staff delegation that presented the petitions, feared that "we sent them away convinced that Time Inc. management was . . . out of touch with what's going on right under its nose. Admonishing that this building was, in Harry Luce's words, 'Built for work,' we implied, in the context *we* used it, that the business of business is still business. Do any of us . . . really believe that?" From Winston (Tony) Cox of the controller's office came a complaint that Donovan seemed to be addressing himself only to editorial staff: "We nonedit employees are equally concerned."

In any case, in the wake of the October Moratorium Day demonstrations, Donovan, in a signed editorial entitled "Winding Down the War on Our Own," suggested that Nixon aim for a reduction of

U.S. troops in Vietnam, then just under the half-million mark, to no more than 150,000 by mid-1971. Donovan also derided Nixon's expressed fear of being "the first American President to lose a war. He might, however, if he and we are lucky, become the third President to settle for a tie. The others were James Madison (War of 1812) and Dwight Eisenhower (Korea), perfectly respectable company for any President to keep."

In July 1970, under the headline, "Vietnam: Time to Fix a Date," *Life* urged a faster troop pullout, calling for "all American participation in the war" to terminate "by no later than the end of 1971." By February 1971, the war had widened further with the U.S.-supported South Vietnamese invasion of Laos—a military action that *Life* considered "a precautionary action that is perfectly consonant with winding down the U.S. military role." In a signed Essay in *Time* in June 1971, Donovan conceded that a pullout by year's end was now impractical. "But a deadline of April 1, 1972, or July 1, could be met," Donovan wrote, adding that the withdrawal should be total: all combat and support forces, land, sea and air, out of Vietnam; all air operations, land- or carrier-based, over Vietnam, Laos and Cambodia ended.

By the time Donovan's April 1972 deadline arrived, Nixon's systematic withdrawal left 95,000 troops still in Vietnam. In an attempt to wring concessions from the North Vietnamese, Nixon ordered a fierce bombing attack on Hanoi and the nearby port city of Haiphong. By August, *Life* noted, the U.S. had "dropped more tons of bombs on a little Asian area than were dropped on all fronts in World War II." That month the last U.S. combat ground forces in Vietnam were deactivated. In January 1973, a cease-fire was signed in Paris, leaving South Vietnam segmented pending an eventual peace agreement. In March, 11 years of American military involvement ended; the last U.S. troops departed.

Gradually Vietnam faded in news interest and merged into the larger Southeast Asian story, much changed since the resumption of relations between Washington and Peking. In November 1972, the Hong Kong bureau was taken over by Roy Rowan, a former assistant managing editor of *Life* and an old Asia hand, who had filed eyewitness reports on the Chinese civil war in the late 1940s and on Korea in 1950-51. In Saigon, bureau chief Stanley W. Cloud gave way to Gavin Scott, a veteran of Mideast and Latin American coverage. It was a measure of the relative calm of Saigon that Scott brought his family there and put his children in school. "It was a

257

time that suited a novelist more than a journalist," Gavin Scott remarked of Saigon's last years. "There were so many signs of collapse. The only guessing game was how long it would take."

The answer came in March 1975 when, in the face of an estimated 16 North Vietnamese invading divisions, the South Vietnamese army's withdrawal from the North-South demarcation line turned into a rout. The Khmer Rouge tightened their hold on Cambodia, closing in on Phnom Penh. In mid-April *Time* correspondent David Aikman, who had flown in from Hong Kong to record the Cambodian capital's final weeks, was airlifted out to the Gulf of Siam.

Saigon's climactic moment was approaching also. The American embassy was drawing up evacuation plans for U.S. nationals, including correspondents. But for Time Inc., as for other news organizations, the question was whether their Vietnamese staffs would be included. Embassy officials were evasive; the South Vietnamese bureaucracy, controlling exit permits for its nationals, was obstructive if not worse.

In late March, chief of correspondents Murray Gart flew to Hong Kong to supervise arrangements for the company to evacuate the Vietnamese local staff on its own. One such effort had already failed. A Cathay Pacific jet chartered jointly with the New York *Times* had flown into Saigon but Time Inc.'s staff had not been allowed to board. From Hong Kong, Gart cabled a plea to President Ford for American embassy assistance, citing "what we regard to be a clear moral responsibility" to the company's Vietnamese employees whose "long and loyal service to the purpose of trying to keep the American people informed . . . surely merits special consideration." In the event of a Communist takeover, Gart later noted, "Their lives would not have been worth a nickel." Moreover, Gart said, there were *Time* staffers who owed their lives to their Vietnamese colleagues.

Amid the mounting uncertainty in Saigon, several schemes for spiriting out Time Inc.'s local employees were explored. One by one, they failed. With the help of a Chinese shipping magnate in Hong Kong, a sealift was arranged; the Vietnamese staff would sail by small craft to an offshore rendezvous with an ocean-going tug, which would then ferry them to safety in Hong Kong—risky business, since pirates were already overtaking escape boats and throwing passengers overboard. In a coded cable that referred to the local staff as photographic "film" being "transshipped to a processing center" in Hong Kong, Gart outlined the plan to Rowan in Saigon. "We will have to be absolutely sure the shippers understand . . .

that risk since insurance is impossible for undeveloped rolls of film."
In any case, the "shipment" never came off. The South Vietnamese
navy boarded the tug and sailed it out of the area.

Two airlifts were tried. The first, a West German charter devised
by Time Inc. president Shepley's son, Steven, failed when a dis-
turbed South Vietnamese jet fighter pilot bombed President Nguyen
Van Thieu's official residence and the charter pilot decided not to
land. A few days later, a twin-engine Convair hired in Singapore
reached Saigon, under cover of being on a "mercy mission" to
Phnom Penh, only to be impounded by Vietnamese authorities after
the pilot got into a shooting scrape.

With escape routes rapidly closing, Gart flew home to plead personally with Secretary of State Kissinger that the local staffs of all
American news organizations be included in the U.S. government's
Saigon evacuation plan. Gart's plea carried; at the end of a day that
Gart spent parked outside Kissinger's office, waiting for an
answer—Kissinger himself was tied up with a visiting official delegation—word emerged that the American ambassador in Saigon was
being instructed accordingly.

On April 23, a cable from Rowan in Hong Kong informed Gart:

EIGHT COLOR ROLLS BY DANG, SIX ROLLS BY LEMINH, AND
FIVE ROLLS BY MRS. AN SHIPPED THIS AFTERNOON. FILM WILL
BE PROCESSED EITHER AT CLARK OR GUAM LABORATORY.

Thus confirmation arrived in New York that the Saigon bureau's
telex operator Nguyen Thuy Dang and photographer LeMinh and
their families, together with the family of reporter Pham Xuan An,
19 persons in all, had been flown out to safe haven at U.S. military
bases in the Pacific. A second group of 18, consisting of Saigon
office manager Tran Thi Nga and telex operator Luong Xich Long
and their families, followed four days afterward. With Time Inc.'s
help, all were settled later into homes and jobs in the U.S.

At that, it had been a close call for the second group that Rowan
led to the Saigon airport. Blocked at the gates by South Vietnamese
air police who would not be budged, even for a 100,000-piastre
bribe folded in Rowan's passport, the group missed its scheduled
evacuation plane entirely. They caught another the next day only
after the CIA loaned Time its "black bus" for clandestine transport,
which Rowan bulled through the airport gate. Rowan concluded his
account of the exodus: "That's the saga of the last 'film shipment.' "
Donovan later commented, "Murray did a hell of a job getting those
people out."

To that saga there was, however, a postscript. The bureau's local reporter, Pham Xuan An, whose family had left in the first group, stayed on in Saigon himself. "I am a Vietnamese and a journalist and evacuation is only one chapter of the story," he explained. A slight, wiry man, almost dwarfed by the large cigar habitually in his mouth, An was, in the opinion of many American correspondents in Vietnam, the country's best reporter, with extraordinary contacts in the government and the military. He had spent a couple of years as a student in California on a U.S. government grant and had worked briefly on the Sacramento *Bee*. He joined *Time* as a stringer in 1966, was promoted to the regular staff and put on *Time*'s masthead in 1971.

With the departure of *Time*'s American staff, An took over the reporting from Saigon, cabling New York a few hours after Rowan and the others had left: "Here is Pham Xuan An now. All American correspondents evacuated because of the emergency. The office of *Time* is now manned by Pham Xuan An." Over the succeeding months he continued to file intermittently. The next year, An's wife and children, at his request, rejoined him in Saigon. In April 1976, An was shifted from staff correspondent to stringer status, and later he dropped out of sight of Western newsmen.

In 1980 stories began to emerge about An's double role: he had held the rank of lieutenant colonel in the National Liberation Front, the Vietcong, while working for *Time*; in 1976 he had been declared a national hero and now held high rank in Vietnam's Communist government.

In addition to everything else, Vietnam had been an exceedingly dangerous place to cover. Time Inc. journalists had met death elsewhere during this period. In June 1967, *Life* photographer Schutzer rushed from Vietnam to cover the Six Day War in the Mideast, only to be killed in the first hours of fighting during an Israeli tank thrust into the Gaza Strip. In October 1968, Priya Ramrakha, a Kenya-born photographer on assignment for *Time,* was caught in ambush by Biafran rebels in Nigeria. But in terms of total casualties, Vietnam was—for Time Inc. correspondents and photographers—the bloodiest war of any. As was characteristic of any guerrilla war, there was no distinct battlefront; death lurked everywhere. Two Time Inc. journalists were killed by enemy fire; two were taken prisoner, one to die somewhere in captivity; eight were wounded.

Time correspondent John Cantwell was the first to be killed. He was 30 when he died. A cheerful, teetotaling health-food addict and bird fancier, fluent in three Chinese dialects, Cantwell came to *Time* from the AP in Saigon in 1967, after years with daily newspapers in Australia and Hong Kong. His death, in May 1968, was murder. With four other journalists, Cantwell had driven into Cholon, the Chinese section of Saigon, to investigate recent battle damage when the group was caught by a Vietcong patrol. Though the newsmen were in civilian clothes and identified themselves—*"bao-chi, bao-chi"* (reporters)—the Vietcong opened fire on them with automatic weapons. All but one were killed; a photographer escaped by playing dead.

In 1970 *Time* photographer Sean Flynn, 28, was captured in Cambodia and is assumed to have died in captivity. Flynn, as handsome as his father Errol, with a daredevil reputation to match, had been a game warden in Kenya, a fashion photographer in Paris, a big-game hunter in Pakistan and briefly a film actor, before coming to Vietnam as a freelancer, in 1965.

On April 3, 1970, along with *Time* correspondent Burton Pines, Flynn drove into the Parrot's Beak area, a prong of Cambodian territory jutting into Vietnam west of Saigon, trying to verify the U.S. air and artillery strikes that Washington was then vigorously denying. Flynn and Pines were almost trapped between two Communist patrols that appeared from the roadside; Pines, who was driving, got their car out of range before the enemy could react. Two days later, Flynn went into the Parrot's Beak again, this time in company with CBS cameraman Dana Stone, both riding rented Honda motorcycles. The next day, Cambodian villagers told of seeing the Vietcong capture two Westerners on motorbikes and lead them away. Months afterward, a Dutch journalist reported hearing from North Vietnamese sources that Flynn might still be alive, but despite intense probing by the Saigon bureau, no confirmation ever came. When and how Flynn died was never known; at the end of the war, Flynn, Stone and 19 other newsmen, all but one of them captured in Cambodia, remained among the missing.

Four months after Flynn disappeared, *Time* correspondent Robert Sam Anson was taken by North Vietnamese soldiers outside the Cambodian capital of Phnom Penh. Anson, then 25, the newest man in the Saigon bureau and the most vehemently antiwar in his views, had been hired by *Time* out of Notre Dame University in 1967 and had come to Vietnam in late 1969. He was in Cambodia just after Prince Norodom Sihanouk was deposed. Driving alone north of Phnom Penh on August 3, 1970, Anson encountered a patrol of North Vietnamese riflemen whom he first mistook for

261

Cambodians. Dragged from his car and marched to a bunker deep in the bush, Anson expected to be shot. "So this is how it ends, I thought. In some rotten little hole, where no one will find me," he wrote later. The soldiers poked their guns in. Anson closed his eyes and waited. But his captors were only motioning him to get out and move along; there was too much enemy mortar fire to stay there, too many enemy planes overhead, they indicated. Loosely tied, Anson was marched farther into the bush, then taken from place to place under North Vietnamese and Khmer guard, while Time Inc. made diplomatic approaches worldwide—to the United Nations, to the North Vietnamese delegation in Paris, to Prince Sihanouk in exile in Peking—trying to secure his release. Contacted by Gart, the Reverend Theodore Hesburgh, president of the University of Notre Dame, approached the Pope. (According to Gart, "Hesburgh said, 'We've still got someone in Hanoi. Let me call the Holy Father and see what he can do.' ") Finally a message came from Sihanouk that Anson was being released. On a Sunday three weeks after he was captured, the rented Ford Cortina was returned to him, along with his reporter's notebooks; unharmed but considerably thinner, Anson drove back to Phnom Penh.

The last Time Inc. casualty was Larry Burrows, the English-born photographer who was undoubtedly *Life*'s preeminent photojournalist of the war. Burrows first worked for *Life* in 1942, at 16, as a darkroom helper in the London bureau's photo laboratory, and came to Vietnam as a staff photographer in 1962. Tall and gaunt, wearing thick spectacles, Burrows loped rather than walked into battle—"either the bravest man I ever knew, or the most near-sighted," a colleague said of him. In 1966 Burrows became the only two-time winner of the Robert Capa* award "for superlative photography requiring exceptional courage and enterprise."

Burrows's photography made up no less than 22 *Life* covers during his nine years in Vietnam. His photojournalism ranged from grim combat reportage, for which he sometimes supplied his own text, to poignant picture essays on the child victims of the war. His last published work pictured the accidental bombing of South Vietnamese troops by American aircraft. Burrows and *Life* correspondent John Saar themselves barely escaped the carnage. The story, "A Frantic Night at the Edge of Laos," was just going to press in *Life's* February 19, 1971 issue when word was received of Burrows's death. A South Vietnamese helicopter, carrying him and four

*Capa, a *Life* photographer during World War II, was himself killed in Indochina, on Time Inc. assignment, in 1954.

other newsmen on a mission over Laos, went down under heavy antiaircraft fire and burned; no one aboard escaped. Afterward, *Life* bureau chief Don Moser wrote this tribute to Burrows:

> Correspondents and photographers came to Vietnam and went; he . . . intended to stay till the end . . . A war photographer is by definition a recorder of the suffering of others, and Larry used to worry about that. He said, "It's not easy to take a shot of a man crying, as though you have no thoughts, no feelings . . ." He took such pictures again and again because to him they were the ones that showed the truth of the war. Yet there were occasions when he would turn away from a scene of human grief out of concern that his presence would aggravate the feelings of those involved . . . He was an old pro who had not, along the way, grown cynical . . .
>
> The courage he had was cool, intellectually and emotionally under control . . . If he stood up in a firefight it was because he had to get the picture. If he did not wear a helmet or a flak vest it was not from bravura but because the armor impeded him.
>
> Because he had come through so much unscathed, people began to think he was invulnerable . . . But Larry knew perfectly well that he was not . . . He said once, "I will do what is required to show what is happening. I have a sense of the ultimate—death. And sometimes I must say, 'To hell with that.' "

CHAPTER
16

The End of
"Family-Style" Management

ROM A "SMALL BIG BUSINESS," as Luce had once described Time Inc., the company had gone to indubitable status as quite a big Big Business, and in 1969 began facing up managerially to the consequences of its size. With annual revenues exceeding $600 million and coming from many sources, the company could no longer operate as if it were simply the publisher of four magazines. The changes begun that year were completed by the end of 1972. Time Inc. found itself with new top managers, a new management structure and an important rearrangement of the business it was in and wanted to be in—in all, a new character that would see it through the 1970s.

No single event prompted the changes. The most immediate spur to action, though, was the depressing profit picture. Since 1961, Time Inc.'s earnings had marched steadily upward; while revenues doubled, profit quadrupled, reaching an after-tax net of $37,253,000 in 1966. This turned out to be a peak that was not surpassed for another seven years.

For 1969, the net was down to $23,916,000 and in April of that year, at the annual meeting of Time Inc. stockholders, management had had to report an actual loss of $300,000 for 1969's first quarter. The declared loss came only two days after another blow to the corporate image. This was a front-page article in the *Wall Street Journal* that had hit with devastating impact within the Time & Life Building, and knocked Time Inc. share prices on the New York Stock Exchange down seven points in a single day. "Hard times have come to Time Inc.," the *Journal* article announced, going on to list various troubles facing the company: the competition *Time* was encountering from *Newsweek*, *Life*'s advertising sales decline, the losses on such nonpublishing ventures as General Learning, SAMI and Latin American television.

Heiskell and Linen were subjected to sharp questioning about the *Journal* article at the stockholders' meeting. The downward slide in Time Inc. stock continued. Trading for around $100 until the end of 1968, the stock fell to about a third of that by mid-1969. In the opinion of investors, nearly half a billion dollars had been wiped off the market value of the company.

That in itself was enough to give pause, but there were other good reasons for a managerial reappraisal. The company had, of course, been the realm of a single man for most of its existence, and that in turn had shaped the way it was run. No one had ever been designated chief executive officer. As long as Harry Luce was alive, this was neither necessary nor possible; even after Heiskell was named chairman and Linen president in 1960, there was no doubt about where the final authority still lay.

After Luce's death in 1967, the lack of a formally designated c.e.o. had not caused any important problems internally. The managerial triumvirate—chairman Heiskell, president Linen and editor-in-chief Donovan—continued to work well together, as they had before. But the arrangement was unusual among companies of Time Inc.'s size, and it had about it the feeling of an unresolved situation. When it came right down to it, who, after all, was really running the show? As Heiskell recalled, "People were already confused by the division of power between church and state, and then to have state also split in two—it struck them as being a little silly. I didn't think it was." But among some of the company's outside directors, doubts persisted. Gaylord Freeman expressed the feeling well in a letter to Heiskell:

> I have not felt that a triumvirate, nor even a partnership, is the right way to run an important and difficult business. Unless one man feels the responsibility, difficult judgments will be avoided and unwise choices will be made because no one wants to say no.

There was perhaps a more serious anomaly in the structure of Time

Inc.'s top management: it had not altered to accommodate the enormous enlargement of the corporate portfolio. Heiskell had taken steps to enlarge the Time Inc. board, enlisting more outside counsel. Freeman became a director in 1962. In 1967 Rawleigh Warner Jr., Mobil Oil Corporation's president, was elected. The following year John Gardner, former Secretary of Health, Education and Welfare and then chairman of Common Cause, and Alexander Heard, chancellor of Vanderbilt University, were chosen, and for the first time outsiders outnumbered insiders, by eight to seven. In the direction of the company's day-to-day business, however, the arrangements were as always, with the managers of each magazine reporting directly to the top. As the company added new enterprises this approach had been simply extended, with the managers of the new units also reporting directly to the top.

That was workable for a while, but less so as the load on Heiskell and Linen increased. They found themselves asked to oversee the management of General Learning; SAMI; Little, Brown and Company; the New York Graphic Society; Printing Developments, Inc.; Eastex; Time-Life Broadcast; and of course the business sides of four magazines and Time-Life Books. By 1969 the organization chart showed that chairman and president had under them a total of 43 vice presidents, plus a clutch of financial officers. In June an assistant to Heiskell sent him a memo suggesting a restructuring of management (one of several such proposals in the air around that time). His central, accurate point was that Heiskell and Linen were "required to make too many decisions on far more subjects than you can begin adequately to understand."

These problems combined in a powerful buildup of pressures that had its effect in August 1969 with rearrangement of the organization chart and changes in many of the names in the boxes.

The most important changes were at the very top. Heiskell, remaining chairman of the board, was given the additional title of chief executive officer. At last, one person was unambiguously in charge. Heiskell disdained the new title—"pretentious," he called it—and used it as seldom as possible; but the meaning, not the words, was what counted.

Linen, who had been president for nine years, became the board's executive committee chairman, a job held up to then by Roy Larsen, who became vice chairman of the board. Linen had been a busy and peripatetic president, jetting tens of thousands of miles each year to give Time Inc. a presence around the world. But as the company's earnings and stock price sagged, management saw a need to shift gears. Like a baseball team manager who is replaced after a losing season (even if the season was not entirely his fault), Linen was moved out of the presidency. It was a difficult action to take; Linen, a warm and outgoing man, eased the situation considerably by his own graciousness. There were several reasons for the corporate move. Inescapably, Linen was identified with some of Time Inc.'s more troubled ventures, notably General Learning. His travels too, on behalf of the company and his own interests, had kept him away from the office almost as much as he was in it. The strain affected his health; a few months earlier, he had suffered a stroke; later came another. Linen admitted afterward, "I didn't take the rest I should have." Presiding over Time Inc. was a stressful job for the healthiest of men, and there were doubts that Linen was any longer up to it.

Replacing Linen as president, with the added title of chief operating officer, was *Time* publisher Jim Shepley. His background as a successful journalist who had leaped over the partition to the publishing side and succeeded there, outstandingly, made him a logical candidate. His ability at cutting through flummery to get to the nub of a problem, his willingness to be tough as nails in dealing with it, were recognized and appreciated. With his appointment the team was in place—Heiskell, the tall, expansive, cosmopolitan chairman, and Shepley, the wiry, aggressive, intense president—that would guide the company through the 1970s.

The change in the corporate presidency was followed by the creation of three executive vice presidencies. One such position already existed, held by David Brumbaugh, originally as corporate treasurer and now as chairman of the finance committee. In December 1968 Brumbaugh had succeeded Stillman in that post, succeeded in his own by assistant treasurer Dick McKeough. The three positions added were new jobs, a new layer of management interposed to sort out the lines of authority under Heiskell and Shepley and give each of three large groups of corporate operations a single overseer. Bernie Auer, a former publisher of *Time*, took overall charge of the magazines; Rhett Austell now supervised all book operations plus broadcasting, films and records; and Art Keylor, who had been named the company's first group vice president in 1968, got expanded responsibility for production of all publications, subscription services and management of the company's real estate.

The three new executive vice presidents, plus chief financial officer Brumbaugh, reported to Shepley. Shepley alone reported to

Heiskell. "The one smart thing I did," Heiskell commented later. It didn't mean, though, that Heiskell was isolated. "I certainly felt entitled," he said, "to talk to any of the managers, to keep informed. About that time I started an every Wednesday lunch, and that was part of informing myself and a forum for exchanging information. It was Shepley, the group vice presidents, the editor-in-chief, a few others. We would start at noon and usually continue for three hours. It became a very effective instrument of management."

Shepley's elevation to the presidency triggered other executive changes. Succeeding him as publisher of *Time* was the former publisher of *Fortune*, Hank Luce. Luce had been in London as the news service bureau chief at the time of his father's death and remained abroad for several months thereafter. He enjoyed the job and had been quite a figure on the local scene. But as a Time Inc. director, and as a trustee of the Luce Foundation voting its shares, he had been commuting frequently to New York; in the spring of 1968, he had moved back permanently to the *Fortune* post. (A *Life* special report Luce had written on his departure from London, examining England's current economic, social and educational woes, stirred up Fleet Street as had few pieces in Time Inc. publications in recent years.)

Now, with Hank Luce's departure for *Time*, *Life* assistant publisher Putney Westerfield took over at *Fortune*. At Time-Life Books, the vacancy created by Austell's move to an executive vice presidency was filled by the appointment of Walter Rohrer as publisher. Formerly TLI's man in Paris, Rohrer had been serving as associate publisher under Austell. At Time-Life Broadcast also, there was a shift. Vice president Wes Pullen left to become an assistant to Heiskell. Succeeding him was Barry Zorthian, a recent arrival at Time Inc. after 20 years in government information service. Another of the company's ex-Marines, Zorthian had once been a newspaperman and broadcasting newswriter; from 1964 to 1968 he had been chief public affairs officer at the American embassy in Saigon.

Amid the reshuffling Shepley had the inspiration to make TLI managing director Charley Bear his assistant. By now it was becoming evident that Bear played a unique role in corporate management. A short, energetic, cheerful man who had spent most of his career dealing, from his New York base, with Time Inc.'s worldwide operations, Bear had acquired a knowledge of the company and its people that had rarely been matched. Because of his knowledge,

268

because of his engaging and accessible manner, Bear had become sought after as confessor and adviser—"the corporate rabbi," as a later Time Inc. c.e.o. was to describe him. Bear was, in addition, a prodigious worker. He kept two secretaries busy full time. It was said that if someone gave Bear 14 problems in one day, he would do something, and just what it deserved, about each one before he went home. His observations on all parts of the company's business, pointed and often dryly clever, were highly valued.

Completed by the end of 1969, Time Inc.'s conversion from its former "family-style" managerial structure (as Bear called it) put the company in better shape to deal with the problems it faced. One went beyond Time Inc. This was the changed social and political atmosphere in which all corporations were now operating—radically different from 1960 or even from a more recent period, the latter years of Luce's life. Managerial performance also was being scrutinized more carefully, not only from outside the company but from within, among employees. The *Wall Street Journal* story, one of several appearing in the business press about that time, had an unsettling effect on the morale of Time Inc.'s own staff. Additionally, there were grievances building up among the company's large and articulate female contingent, which would shortly lead to their filing formal charges of discrimination against Time Inc., and discontent among the magazines' editorial staffs that would lead to the first strike in Time Inc.'s history (see chapter 26). Already there had been the challenges to the Time Inc. magazines' editorial position on Vietnam, implicit in the October, 1969, Moratorium Day gathering in the Time & Life Building auditorium.

Not long after, in February 1970, Heiskell took a moment during a European tour to muse on these matters. That month marked the third anniversary of Luce's death, and on stationery of the Hotel Ritz in Paris, Heiskell jotted down some thoughts:

Henry R. Luce died on the right day. For that day, month and year marked a major turning point for the United States. It was at that point that the principles that had guided us for decades had eroded so much as to be meaningless. Not for all America but a sufficient percentage to prove that this was indeed a new watershed.

What went by the boards? Well, among others:

The belief in the perfectibility of man.

The belief in "just" wars.

The near automatic acceptance of existing institutions.

The belief on the part of the young that the experience of their elders had validity.

The hope that somehow technology could sooner or later solve any and all problems.

Time Inc. - H.R.L. was one of the establishments. And that's how he wanted it. Ideologically directed within a nation which by and large had a clear-cut notion of what was right and what was wrong.

In today's world he would have been miserable. But perhaps we need to face up more explicitly than we have that running Time Inc. or other national communications organs is and will continue to be far more difficult than it was. If the editor speaks with great authority, his staff will look on him with amazement and the bright young men will not come aboard. Whereas you tended to have two opposing audiences—one with you and one against—you now have many different reactions to what you print.

I guess that the problem of leadership is bothering quite a few people within the company. In some cases because of failure on our part, but mostly because leadership is more difficult to exercise in today's world. Do our people understand that and if not, what can we do? Should we speak more clearly as we do not have the cumulative institutional impact of H.R.L.? And of course the situation is aggravated by the drop in profits which some connect with the demise of H.R.L.

Closer to home were the worries concerning the publishing industry's future. These had nagged at Time Inc. for years, increasingly so with television's apparently unstoppable growth. While publishers in the early 1960s had fretted over the possibility that magazines were a "mature" product, the concern as the decade ended was far more serious: that magazines—and the printed word in general—might have reached the end of the trail. In publishing circles, Marshall McLuhan, the Toronto professor who insisted that "the medium is the message," was quoted ominously to the effect that movable type was a quaint and obsolete technology being rapidly superseded by the electronic media. Scary stuff for print men.

Yet it appeared to some as if this might just be true. At Time Inc., the trends looked potentially devastating. "It was the terrible numbers game—the loss of ads to TV—that influenced everybody's thinking," Bear said. "We were getting such a skunking."

To grapple with the problem, top management began meeting on

270

weekends at Heiskell's home in Darien, Connecticut. Presumably Time Inc. would have to take advantage of the new technologies in ways that would capitalize on its established strengths. But how? In one of many attacks on the problem, Heiskell had circulated some memos on "technology and its probable impact on Time Inc." to Brumbaugh, Donovan and Linen in early 1969. Brumbaugh replied at length, puzzling over coming changes in the media, their likely speed and how Time Inc. could prosper in the new world. His conclusion:

> Aren't we back to gathering, editing and disseminating news and information by words and pictures in some form as our important function? What is that form to be? Here is where clarification is needed it seems to me.

Seeking such "clarification" became one of management's main occupations in the following years.

Corporate planning was not being well handled; that was recognized. Not a conglomerate, Time Inc. was tending to act like one. Individual divisions were pursuing a variety of individual projects, both publishing and nonpublishing; some systematic way was needed of deciding what Time Inc. should try and what it should leave alone. In 1969 Dick Clurman, now vice president in charge of editorial development, was asked to devote himself to the question. After ten months of inquiry, he reported in a confidential letter to Heiskell, Shepley and Donovan: "Any reasonable management consultant looking over Time Inc. would certainly conclude we should right now make a clear decision about our development activities." Clurman was unsparing:

> The 20 or so projects being worked on around this building are undertaken with no sense of urgency, deadline or even hard work. They seldom invoke our best resources. Many of them, suffering from dispiritedness and lack of objective, simply fade away, with the possibility that we are souring by sloppy exploration potentially valid enterprises . . . the field of development for Time Inc. is surrounded by amateurism, and hipshot suggestions from all sides, almost none of which are useful but send us off in all directions, including especially directions that we've already gone over, or in which we already have established expertise.

Clurman's proposed solution was "a development unit with someone designated to run it—really run it . . . Without such a change, only luck or accident will get us into consequential new ventures."

What large principles would guide a development department? Bear, for one, thought the company's larger goals should be formally stated, and at Shepley's request put his thoughts on paper. His reasoning: "Surely more could be accomplished divisionally if we were to have a better idea of where we want to get corporately." He proposed "a broad corporate plan, simply and generally stated, which establishes for working purposes the objectives of the company and an order of priority for addressing them." Shepley sent the memo on to Heiskell, with a penciled note in the margin:

> I asked Charley to write down his thoughts on planning which he has been communicating orally. I told him there was more planning than met the eye, but that it now is filed in the seat of the chairman's (and/or the president's) pants.
>
> Many of his arguments are well reasoned, but I remain worried about "planning" in the context that we might actually *adhere* to a plan. There is of course one point on which Napoleon and Von Clausewitz found themselves in full agreement: planning is valuable but no battle goes according to plan.

A few months later, Heiskell asked three of the outside board members—Gardner, Heard and Sol M. Linowitz, diplomat and senior partner in the international law firm of Coudert Brothers—to look at Time Inc.'s long-range planning and report back to him. They recommended that Time Inc. eschew the conglomerate form it was taking on and instead "be a company with a coherent mission," presumably in the communications field. As far as new ventures within the mission were concerned, the committee saw much room for improvement. "We came to believe, rightly or not, that the company had gotten involved in a variety of activities without due consideration," they reported. As a remedy, they favored a proposal much like Clurman's: a "business analysis unit" attached to the chairman's office.

None of these proposals was adopted. Formal planning remained located where Shepley indicated. But nonetheless, facing the exigencies in Time Inc.'s three main areas of business, management did take a series of decisions that, over the next couple of years, set the corporate course for the 1970s. These were: to get out of radio and television broadcasting and into programming and ownership of cable systems; to move into forest products in a larger way; and finally, to bet on the future of magazines and create new ones. Time Inc.'s moves in forest products and magazine publishing are discussed in later chapters; the turnabout in television, starting with the sale of the broadcast properties, was already under way.

The company, as recounted earlier, was by then cutting its losses in Latin American television. In the case of the domestic stations, which were solidly profitable, earning over $6 million before taxes in 1970, the decision to sell was part of a larger aim, which executive vice president Austell outlined in a highly confidential memo to Heiskell and Shepley:

> In the briefest outline we are working to:
> 1) disengage from all of our investments in Latin America;
> 2) sell all of our U.S. stations;
> 3) substantially increase our stake in CATV;
> 4) develop marketing capability in the field of in-home cartridge television; and
> 5) become a leading force in programming for all forms of film and electronic media.
>
> Patently such a strategy cannot be publicly disclosed . . . Unless the way is carefully prepared, it may appear to the uninformed—outsiders as well as insiders—that Time Inc. is making a desperate withdrawal from the field of electronic communications for whatever reason. Thus, until we're much further along, we will speak publicly only about individual parts of the program and then only as each of them matures.

Moreover, broadcast properties were judged to have peaked. "We consider them overvalued at current market prices," Austell wrote. "The rate of increase in broadcast earnings has topped out and shows no signs of long-range recovery." In contrast, he believed, cable could develop into "a truly revolutionary system of communication and . . . Time Inc. should be in on the ground floor in a big way."

The stations went on the market in the summer of 1970 with a value estimated by the company at $80 million. A few offers came in, the most serious from the Combined Communications Corporation of Phoenix. That went by the boards when it became apparent that Combined Communications was too highly leveraged to be able to obtain sufficient bank guarantees. McGraw-Hill had been watching the negotiations from the sidelines and quickly stepped in. Within two weeks a price of $80 million was agreed to in principle, and the deal was announced on October 30, 1970.

A year and a half of legal wrangling followed. An FCC regulation prevented a company from owning television and radio properties in the same market. Both companies knew about the rule (Time Inc. had been exempted by a "grandfather" provision), but had thought that McGraw-Hill could sell off the radio operations after buying the whole package. No deal. Time Inc. had to sell the radio stations, which it did, to various buyers, for a total of $11 million. A coalition of black and Chicano groups pointed out another FCC rule that required that it be "in the public interest" for any purchaser to buy more than two TV stations in the top 50 markets. The Time Inc. package contained three such stations—Denver, Indianapolis and Grand Rapids—so Grand Rapids was taken out of the group and the aggregate price cut to $57,180,000. The deal for the remaining four stations was finally closed on June 1, 1972. (Time Inc. would sell the Grand Rapids station ten years later for $32 million.)

In 1970, Time Inc.'s fortunes hit bottom. After-tax profit sank to $20,627,000, down 45 percent from 1966's peak. "The pits," Heiskell later called that period. In the course of it, a company-wide economy drive was decreed. It hit everywhere, most painfully in staff reductions. Through attrition, early retirements and outright dismissals, the overall head count in publishing operations was brought down some 15 percent during the next couple of years.

Corporate finances also underwent reorganization. As a measure of fiscal discipline on the managers of the individual corporate divisions, the company introduced the elementary practice of charging them for the corporate capital they used, on the same basis as if the funds were borrowed from a bank. The capital charge became a tool for more accurately measuring each division's corporate contribution. Likewise, for the company itself, an overall financial goal was established: a 10 percent minimum return, after taxes, on invested capital. Time Inc.'s 10 percent goal was not ambitious for its day, but the company was still far from reaching it; the 1972 return, for instance, was 6.4 percent.

Life remained the great unsolved problem, its huge and growing losses the principal burden on the corporate P & L statement. The elimination of *Life*'s two overseas editions lightened the burden somewhat. *Life en Español* was terminated with the December 1969 issue, *Life International* a year later.

In 1970 also, Heiskell moved to extricate the company from another relic of *Life*'s more prosperous past: the costly papermaking venture at St. Francisville, Louisiana, that the company had undertaken in 1956 with Crown Zellerbach to supply *Life* with lightweight coated magazine paper at below-market prices. The sole exception to a Time Inc. policy of not being its own supplier, the St. Francisville project proved the rule's prudence. Mechanical troubles plagued the mill from the start. *Life*, committed to buy half of St. Francisville's output, calculated it had paid more than $2 million over the market price for its paper; Time Inc.'s investment in the project, meanwhile, mounted to $15 million. Negotiations for sale of Time Inc.'s interest to Crown Zellerbach—eventually concluded with nearly a $10 million loss to Time Inc.—were still in progress at the end of 1972, as the company approached a decision on the future of *Life* itself.

Reflecting on the weekly magazine's death, which came in December, Heiskell remarked, "For my first ten years [as chairman] we really didn't do much. It was *Life*. We spent all our time worrying about *Life*, leaning over backward to solve its problems. When the moment finally came that we saw that in fact we couldn't save *Life*, then we got moving."

Ahead, in fact, was the company's most active, expansive, prosperous decade.

Requiem for Life

LIFE'S ILLNESS WAS TERMINAL. For a while it had looked otherwise; in 1966, the magazine had an operating profit of $10,325,000 on revenues of $164,895,000—the best showing since the booming 1950s. But recovery turned out to be only remission. The following year, profits fell by half and in 1968 *Life* was only marginally in the black. Between 1969 and 1971, the cumulative losses were more than $47 million. Thus was posed the decision that the company, partly out of pride and sentiment, had long been dodging. The idea of Time-Life without *Life* was not easy to face up to.

For all three of the mass-circulation magazines—the weekly *Life*, the fortnightly *Look* and *Saturday Evening Post*—the years from 1966 onward had been very hard. As television's share of advertising revenues rose, that of general magazines leveled off, while the shares taken by *Life*, *Look* and the *Post* all declined. Meanwhile, circulation became ever more costly to get, and hold. At one point, the president of the *Post*'s parent Curtis Publishing Company described the ruinous competition among the three magazines as "a race to the poorhouse." That race was won by the *Post*, which ceased publication in February 1969. *Look* lasted two years longer, folding finally in October 1971.

The departure of its chief competitor did not solve *Life*'s two basic publishing problems. One was the inability to earn a healthy profit on its circulation revenue. This was a chronic problem, the inevitable result of the cut-rate subscription pricing that *Life* and its competitors had engaged in during their long battles for readership. *Life* publisher Jerry Hardy noted in 1965 that the magazine, then selling for 35 cents on the newsstand but discounted to less than 10 cents in some subscription offers, was costing the company 16 cents more per copy to produce and deliver than readers paid. For each additional cent that could be obtained from the reader, *Life*'s overall profit could be improved by $3.5 million annually, Hardy pointed out in a memo to top management; it was here, rather than on the advertising side, where lay "the best chance to change the basic economic structure of *Life*."

Life's other problem, faced by a succession of advertising directors—James Dunn, who succeeded Clay Buckhout in 1961; John Crandell, who followed in 1966 and Lee Heffner, who came in 1969—was that, because of the circulation race, advertising page rates had been pushed too high, particularly for the mass-selling merchandisers of soaps, foods, cosmetics. Looking back on this period, the advertising trade magazine *Media Decisions* observed in 1971 that "by 1966 page rates had passed some significant levels. A color page . . . was now over $50,000. It was also more costly than a minute on prime-time television . . . As circulations, costs and rates rose . . . the same [advertising] dollars bought fewer pages. 'They were just about pricing themselves out of the market,' is the way so many media directors put it that we don't know which one to quote."

In early 1968, Martin Ackerman, 36, then a barely known New York lawyer specializing in corporate acquisitions, bought control of Curtis. In his first move to save the *Post*, Ackerman proposed halving its circulation and selling off 3 million names on the *Post*'s subscriber list (fewer after eliminating duplications). In so doing, Ackerman introduced a new element of uncertainty into the *Life-Look* battle. For still fresh in Time Inc. memory was the disposition of the *Collier's* subscription list when that magazine died in 1956. The *Collier's* names had gone to *Look*, which was thus able to match and then draw slightly ahead of *Life*. "It became an article of faith that this would not happen again," one *Life* advertising executive remarked.

Now, in 1968, the stakes seemed equally high. "*Life* could lose . . . at least 240 advertising pages should *Look* jump to a command-

277

ing edge in circulation," Hardy predicted in a memo to the Time Inc. board of directors. "Far more important, we believe, is that *Look* magazine at 8.5 million circulation, and a lower cost per thousand than *Life* . . . could start an advertising trend away from *Life* that would be very difficult to stop."

Decision on the *Post* subscribers came at a meeting of some 15 senior Time Inc. executives, among them Linen, Heiskell, Brumbaugh, Keylor, Auer and Hardy, at Heiskell's home in Darien, Connecticut, one Saturday morning in May 1968. There were questions about the ruinous numbers game that *Life* was caught in, but not many, according to one participant's account. The trickier question involved negotiating tactics: how to forestall a possible private deal between *Look*'s owner, Gardner Cowles, and Ackerman of the *Post*. Time Inc. under SEC rules had to notify Ackerman of the company's intent, yet it could only guess at Cowles's interest. Recalled Charles Linton, then serving as Time Inc.'s legal counsel: "The rest of the day was spent in figuring out how we could make our pitch in a meaningful way—how we could outbid Cowles without knowing what his bid was. It was like shooting craps in a hat. We didn't know to what extent we were being made a patsy. From Ackerman's standpoint, he had the greatest hole card in the world: two people interested in what he had without either knowing what the other was willing to pay."

Cowles did not contest Time Inc.'s bid. On May 17, *Life*'s publishing staff was assembled to hear announcement of the deal. "To permit continued publication of the *Saturday Evening Post* on a healthy financial basis," a statement issued jointly in Linen's and Ackerman's names declared, Time Inc. was lending Curtis $5 million as prepayment for printing *Life* on Curtis presses as well as *Life*'s use of the Curtis newsstand distribution system and its subscription sales subsidiary. In return, an unspecified number of *Post* subscribers were to be transferred to the *Life* list.

Later, the purchase of the *Post* circulation came to be seen as a mistake—a fatal turning onto a course of accelerated growth from which *Life* eventually, and much too late, had to retreat. But it was not so viewed in 1968. Looking back years later, John Watters, *Life*'s general manager at that time, reflected:

In hindsight—hindsight—getting that *Post* circulation was the colossally wrong thing to do. But I remember the day in May when Hardy went before the board of directors to explain it to them. It was like watching the returning conqueror of Gaul before the Roman senate. It may have been a wrong deal but there wasn't the slightest hint that anybody up there thought so that day. Hardy was a hero.

On the *Saturday Evening Post* side, there were some who regarded the deal with suspicion. Managing editor Otto Friedrich (who later became a senior editor on *Time*) felt that *Life* had taken the *Post*'s best names: "By any estimate, *Life*, far from doing us a favor, drove a very hard bargain, but its talent for negotiation was equaled by its talent for public relations. Somehow, the deal was made to sound as though Time Inc. had acted out of charity."* In any event, the *Post* was not much helped. Nine months later the magazine went under, having drawn only half of Time Inc.'s $5 million advance. Nor did *Life* benefit greatly, except in numbers; transplanted to *Life*'s lists, the *Post* subscribers showed a poor renewal rate.

In October, with the first increment of *Post* names, *Life*'s circulation rate base was raised to 8 million and another boost, to 8.5 million, was announced for January 1969. Reflecting the increases, *Life*'s advertising page rates went to $42,500 for a black-and-white page, $64,200 for four-color vs. *Look*'s $37,000 and $55,500 respectively. Including pass-along readership, *Life*'s total audience was now estimated at 48 million—"larger than any other single communications medium in the world," *Life* promotion copy boasted.

Now that the war of the mass magazines had been reduced, effectively, to two combatants, the editorial pressure on *Life* was heightened, Donovan felt. "I think we are coming into a quite critical six to 18 months for *Life*," he wrote managing editor Hunt, going on to declare:

> With the disappearance of the *Saturday Evening Post* as a big magazine, and our own circulation acquisitions, a lot of people are going to be forming first, or fresh, impressions of *Life*. So it is a period of tremendous editorial opportunity. As we know too well, it is also a period of precarious P & L. I can't help feeling that the next 50 or so issues could determine the health of *Life*—and to a considerable degree the health of Time Inc.— for some years to come.
>
> We must figure out how the many separate strengths of *Life* can be made to coalesce into a clear personality or character for the magazine as a whole . . . *Time* has benefitted enormously

Decline and Fall (Harper & Row, 1970), p. 353.

from its sharply defined (and not universally admired) personality . . . *Reader's Digest, New Yorker, Playboy*—all huge successes and easy for readers (or detractors) to characterize in a word or two. I don't think of *Look* as having a clear-cut personality; I would be nervous if they developed one.

With this, Donovan asked Hunt for "a fresh try at defining the magazine—just for ourselves, for the time being." It was a familiar exercise, undertaken repeatedly in Luce's day and continued, no less exasperatingly for the *Life* staff, under Donovan. "We were just plagued with all those attempts to redefine *Life*," commented former assistant managing editor Robert Ajemian. Hunt's habit was to take his colleagues out sailing on his sport-fishing boat and talk about *Life*. Ajemian recalled one summer day's cruise where "George announced at the start that we were going to spend our time getting a definition of *Life* on paper for Hedley. The more we all talked, the more we realized you couldn't define *Life* like that." Donovan admitted as much in writing Hunt: "Vexed editors, managing and otherwise, have sometimes said to me: pick up this week's magazine—that's what *Life* is! Or (a better answer): pick up a month of *Life*—that's what we are." As Hunt put it later, *Life* was "taking the world and putting it into the lap of the reader every week—dammit, that's what we were doing. The best definition of *Life* was *Life*."

In May 1969 Hunt completed his eighth year in the job—the term of office he had set for himself, Donovan noted in announcing the appointment of Ralph Graves as *Life*'s new managing editor. After a transatlantic cruise on his yacht, *Baraka*, Hunt returned in 1970 to develop television projects for the company.

Life's new managing editor—"an intense, athletically built man of 44," as the New York *Times* described him—had spent virtually his entire professional career on the magazine. Born in Washington, son of a *National Geographic* editor who died in 1932, Graves passed part of his boyhood in Manila with his stepfather, Francis Sayre, U.S. High Commissioner to the Philippines. Following six months on a Texas cattle ranch (his stepfather believed that "every kid should be in touch with the land," Graves explained) and a year at Williams College, he served in the Pacific as an Army Air Corps cryptographer, returning after the war to earn his bachelor's degree from Harvard. He joined *Life* in 1948 as a researcher, went on to become a writer, Chicago news bureau chief, articles editor and then assistant managing editor. On the side, he also turned out two novels. In 1968 he went upstairs to succeed Tom Griffith as senior staff editor assisting Donovan.

Graves came back to a magazine that was undergoing a painful squeeze—"pinchy times," as one editor put it. *Life*'s spending habits were always under fire from management, although its editorial costs remained lower than those of any other Time Inc. magazine in relation to total costs, and little more than half, in percentage terms, of *Time*'s. But *Life*'s conspicuous consumption made it a target. The year before, Hunt had informed Donovan's office that "the party-giving rights of bureau chiefs have been rescinded." Several of New York's costlier expense-account eateries were also placed off limits.

Staff cuts had begun, and with Graves's arrival, the Time Inc. unit of the New York Newspaper Guild questioned management about rumors that further, more drastic cuts were planned. The rumors were shortly confirmed. Over the following year, some 50 of *Life*'s nearly 300 editorial staffers were let go. It was unpleasant business, but Graves took on much of it himself, and in his colleagues' view handled it compassionately. Places were found for a number of people at Time-Life Books.

In June the new managing editor addressed the entire editorial staff. The midmorning assembly, without benefit of the usual refreshments—"no coffee, no Danish," as one staffer recalled—was in keeping with *Life*'s new, austere style. Graves, by his own admission "not the inspirational type," declared that he planned a "rather blunt" speech:

> These are obviously hard times for general magazines . . . and obviously and specifically hard times for *Life*. We have television on one side of us and more and more specialized magazines on the other. Our job is to make readers care about this magazine. Not because it is an institution—never let us forget that the *Saturday Evening Post* was an institution long before *Life* was invented.

Great news events, Graves said, made people care. "An assassination, that first trip around the moon, Jackie's wedding, the Columbia University riots—everybody cares." But he had looked back over three years of *Life* issues and by his count there were only about ten great events per year. "We are never going to make a living for 50 issues a year [on] our coverage of ten super news events." Rather, *Life* had to search out stories that would involve *Life*'s readers and "touch their daily lives."

281

The trouble with us is that we can do *Life* stories on almost any subject. We are the most can-do magazine ever invented. We have the manpower, the talent, the know-how, the technique, the tradition of sparing no horses and no dollars . . . to produce a publishable story on almost any subject . . .

Well, I am not interested in stories that are merely publishable . . . Our stories have to *count*. They have to *matter*.

Graves wanted more controversy, more attention to America. "Maybe it is not the best country or the happiest, but it is where the action is . . . the youth revolt, the Vietnam crisis, the Pentagon, the leisure age, the black militants, the good life and the bad life . . . It is therefore *Life*'s most interesting subject."

And finally, a reminder of *Life*'s primary journalistic aim: those staffers who were not picture-minded should depart. Said Graves:

We need to put more emphasis on pictures and less emphasis on text. *Life* is still a picture magazine. I seriously recommend that all reporters and young writers who are interested in their own bylines but don't really care about pictures should go look for a job somewhere else . . . they have no real future on this magazine.

The power of the picture was demonstrated, unforgettably, in one of the first issues after Graves took over: the June 27, 1969, *Life* featured a gallery of one week's war dead in Vietnam (see chapter 15). The issue marked an auspicious beginning for the new managing editor. The August 29 issue was also much talked about, with ten pages on the Woodstock rock festival (from which photographic coverage *Life* later assembled a special issue) and the first 26,000-word installment of Norman Mailer's three-part treatise on the Apollo lunar voyages titled "A Fire on the Moon."* Then, in the December 5 issue, came *Life*'s grisly record of the My Lai massacre in Vietnam, with six almost unbearable pages of color from an Army photographer present at the scene, supplemented by a reconstruction of the event by a *Life* reportorial team, based on interviews with U.S. Army witnesses and some Vietnamese survivors.

In the shift of managing editors, Griffith had remained editor of *Life*. This peculiar tandem, which Luce had devised—of a managing editor responsible for hiring, firing and week-to-week editorial direction, with a co-equal editor responsible for "tone, emphasis,

---

*The sections appearing in *Life* were part of Mailer's book *Of a Fire on the Moon* (Little, Brown and Company, 1970).

policy" and long-range planning—had not really worked before. It did with Griffith and Graves. They meshed well. In his earlier days on *Time*, Griffith had been both National Affairs and Foreign News editor; on *Life*, he provided a politically savvy approach to controversial issues and, in the editorial page that he edited and later wrote, a sophistication that in Graves's opinion had not been evident for some years.

There were other staff changes. *Life*'s art director, Bernard Quint, was succeeded by Irwin Glusker, formerly senior art director at American Heritage. Assistant managing editor Roy Rowan, who had been a contender for the managing editorship, left to take on a corporate assignment. Bob Ajemian and Phil Kunhardt stayed on as assistant managing editors; later they were joined by Don Moser, formerly *Life*'s Far Eastern editor; Dick Stolley, who had been in charge of the magazine's European, African and Mideast coverage; and Dave Maness, formerly *Life* articles editor, who became Graves's deputy for administration. *Life* columnist Loudon Wainwright also joined the editing team briefly, then went back to his first love, writing.

In March 1970, Graves sketched for the board of directors the principal changes under his editorship. Five news bureaus had been shut down: Miami, Beirut, Vienna, Moscow and Rome. Five of *Life*'s old departments—editorial fiefdoms—had been eliminated, most notably Miscellany, Sports and Fashion, where the redoubtable Sally Kirkland had long held sway. "The purpose was not to eliminate those subjects from the magazine, but to get the staff thinking in broader terms," Graves explained. *Life*'s photographic content had been increased with a Gallery section of pictures for pictures' sake near the front of the book and, to close the magazine "with some irreverence and unexpectedness and humor," four pages of photos entitled Parting Shots. *Life*'s wordage—that Norman Mailer blockbuster notwithstanding—had been trimmed and *Life*'s lengthy historical series "pretty much [done] away with . . . We were running out of ancient empires, besides."

These were the easiest changes to label, Graves told the directors. More important, he felt, was *Life*'s changed approach to the news: "Instead of depending on pure news events, the kind that make daily headlines and appear on the Huntley-Brinkley show, we now concentrate on what Tom Griffith calls 'news that's in the air.' "

Graves felt confident about *Life*'s future. He got an appreciative laugh from the Time Inc. directors when he described how *Life* investigative reporter Bill Lambert, after being romanced with an attractive New York *Times* job offer, had turned around "and investigated *Life* . . . He came back to me this last week and said, 'Listen, *Life*'s all right. I'm going to stay here.' "

In the wake of the mid-1969 changes in corporate managment that took Shepley from the publisher's job on *Time* to the presidency and established three new executive vice presidencies, there was an unexpected change at *Life*. Publisher Jerry Hardy quit Time Inc. to become the executive vice president of the Dreyfus Corporation. Replacing him at *Life* was Garry Valk, 49, who had been publisher of *SI* for the previous four years.

During Valk's tenure at *SI*, the magazine had flourished, and he made the move to *Life* reluctantly. His view was reflected in a story he told (claiming, however, that it was "apocryphal") about his conversation with Heiskell. Valk: "But Andrew, there are a dozen people in the Time & Life Building just as qualified to be publisher of *Life*." Heiskell: "Yeah, but the other 11 have already turned it down."

It was recognized, in projections made before Valk took over, that *Life* would suffer a large initial loss in taking on the *Saturday Evening Post* circulation, most of it reflecting the costs of producing and delivering the extra copies of *Life* being provided free to former *Post* subscribers. But this would be a onetime outlay, which would be more than covered by increased circulation and advertising revenues in the succeeding three years.

Other projects to improve *Life*'s income were also under study as the new circulation increases took effect. One was the old idea of *Life* supplements to be offered subscribers according to their particular interests in food, travel, television, cinema, etc. Now working on a similar proposal was a group headed on the editorial side by assistant managing editor Kunhardt and on the publishing side by assistant publisher Putney Westerfield, who had been brought over from *Time* in 1968 to supervise *Life*'s long-range planning. In January, testing began on the first two supplements, one on food, the other on movies. Though readers were interested, they proved unwilling to pay what would have been an economic price for the supplements, which meant that advertisers would have to be asked to make up the difference. The project was abandoned.

By early 1970 it was apparent that the projections made when *Life* acquired the *Post* circulation had been overly optimistic. On circulation income, *Life* was doing fairly well. In January the cover price had been upped a dime to 50 cents and subscription prices had been raised to $10 a year; renewals were strong. But in advertising, *Life* in 1969 had fallen nearly 60 pages short of the 2,450 pages projected earlier, and would likely be 350 short in 1970, Heiskell informed the board in March. Actually, the shortfall was 450, and advertising went under 2,000 pages for the first time. The only consolation was that *Life* was "suffering neither more nor less than other print media," Heiskell said, noting that *Look* was also in trouble.

With this he broached—for the first time to the Time Inc. board— a shift to biweekly publication: "*Life* as a biweekly . . . might well be acceptable to the advertising fraternity. However, after *Collier's*, the *Post* and now *Look*'s questionable position, we would spend two years arguing that this was not a prelude to demise . . . It looks like a poor bet."

Heiskell saw grounds for hope in *Life*'s present course. First, "a very positive attitude toward our editorial product. This wasn't the case two years ago." Competitively, too, *Life*'s position was improving. Two marketing studies, one by *Life* itself, another by General Foods (with financing also from *Life*, *Look* and *Reader's Digest*) documented the impact of mass-magazine advertising and put *Life* "back in contention in terms of package goods." Meanwhile, Heiskell said, the proliferation of commercials had diminished the cost effectiveness of TV advertising.

But it was "*Life*'s importance to the overall welfare of the corporation" that Heiskell stressed. Even with 1970's projected loss of $10 million, *Life* could be considered a breakeven proposition. It accounted for nearly $55 million of Time Inc.'s deferred income— prepaid subscription revenue. It carried $7 million of corporate overhead. Its purchasing leverage, mainly for paper, was considerable. *Life*'s name and subscriber lists for Time-Life Books and record sales were worth more than $5 million now, and would be worth more in the future "in view of a rapidly increasing Time Inc. interest in going into other businesses such as a travel club, home films, sale of carefully selected merchandise, book and art clubs, etc. The prime reason we believe such new ventures . . . would be possible is our ability to advertise them on a cost basis in *Life* and send direct mail to *Life* subscribers." Heiskell felt the company had no choice except to keep going and try to position *Life* again "as a really essential advertising medium . . . This last year has been clear proof of how *Life* can be nearly poor-mouthed out of existence."

The competitive picture was already changing rapidly. The following month, *Look* announced it was cutting back its circulation rate base from 7,750,000 to 6.5 million effective in October; shortly after, *McCall's*, *Holiday* and the men's magazine *True* also announced circulation reductions. In August Congress had passed the Postal Reorganization bill, which presaged large postage increases. In September a strike hit General Motors just as production of the next year's models was to start. The ensuing cancellation of some automotive advertising contributed further to the already perceptible sag in *Life*'s ad page sales.

In a reappraisal of *Life*'s situation, undertaken during August and September, biweekly publication was considered again. The choice was between a biweekly with the present 8.5 million circulation and one with 7 million. For both, advertising projections indicated page sales well below 1,700 for the next two years, which with a reduced publishing frequency would result in sharply reduced revenues without a commensurate cut in costs. On October 1, a compromise decision was announced. *Life* would remain a weekly, but with its circulation cut to 7 million effective in January 1971. Advertising rates would be lowered proportionately—in the case of color pages, from $64,200 to $54,000. Declared Valk: "This course of action will enable *Life* to continue to offer advertisers a high-quality weekly audience at a significantly lower dollar figure."

With the circulation cutbacks came Valk's announcement that the magazine's last two surviving international editions were being folded. Following *Life*'s South Pacific editions, which had died in September 1968, and *Life en Español*, which perished in December 1969, *Life International* and *Life Asia* would cease publication with the last issues of December 1970.

The moves to save *Life* inevitably drew an unfavorable press reaction. The *Wall Street Journal* recalled that "magazine industry experts . . . had privately criticized [*Life*'s] 1968 circulation jump as risky." Commented *Time*'s rival, *Newsweek*: "After having seemingly won a long, bitter, three-way circulation war with *Look* and the late *Saturday Evening Post*, *Life* magazine revealed last week that its victory turned out to be more Pyrrhic than profitable." However, *Newsweek* discounted the speculation that Time Inc. might fold *Life* altogether: "Paradoxically, it might be cheaper for the company to carry *Life* than to kill it. 'Any magazine that is thinking of folding now has got a bear by the tail,' says one New York publisher. 'It has to pay off all those subscribers because there's nobody you can lay them off to these days.' "

At that somber moment came the welcome intrusion of an extraordinary journalistic coup. The cover of *Life*'s November 27,

1970, issue—picturing the deposed Soviet leader Nikita Khrushchev in full oratorical flight, his finger stabbing the air—announced the beginning of a series of articles entitled "Khrushchev Remembers," which *Life* had been preparing since 1969. In a prefatory Editors' Note, Graves explained:

> For more than a year a very small group of people at *Life* has been sitting on a very large secret: the reminiscences of Nikita Khrushchev. We could make no public reference to the subject, and we could not even talk about it around the office. . . We were certain that the Soviet government would raise the question of authenticity or even denounce the work as a fake. Indeed, just last week the Soviet news agency Tass published a statement from Khrushchev . . . that he had not "passed on memoirs or materials of this nature" and that the project was therefore "a fabrication." Knowing a year ago that such comments would be forthcoming, we had to be sure that what we had was *not* a fabrication.

The details of how Khrushchev's testament became available to *Life* are known by only a handful of Time Inc. executives. The names of some of the Soviet intermediaries and some facets of the deal still remain locked in a safe to which the authors of this volume have not had access. Full details may not yet be known within the U.S.S.R. In the view of Strobe Talbott, Time Inc.'s translator of the Khrushchev material, "There are officials who know bits and pieces but not, I think, the whole story . . . The Soviet Union is less monolithic than conventional wisdom would have us believe. Sparrows do fall."

Since his fall from power, Khrushchev had been confined to a seven-acre country estate outside Moscow. Under constant surveillance by security guards, the old man had few freedoms left except to talk with nearby villagers and occasional visitors. But it was rumored in Moscow that he was also putting his thoughts on tape. In 1967 the NBC network obtained enough taped Khrushchev quotes and movie footage for a two-part news special called "Khrushchev in Exile." Doubtless there was more material—his personal story. The question among Western correspondents in Moscow was who would lay hands on it first. Time Inc.'s advantage, as the subsequent negotiations were to indicate, was that it could offer simultaneous book and magazine publication, the latter through Time Inc.'s trade book subsidiary, Little, Brown and Company, as well as television exposure through Time-Life Films.

First indications that Time Inc. might get Khrushchev's reminiscences came from *Time* correspondent Jerrold Schecter, in the spring of 1969, a few months after Schecter arrived to reopen the magazine's Moscow bureau. Time Inc. had been in a somewhat curious situation in Moscow. In 1964 a *Time* cover story on Lenin, mentioning the fact that the Soviet saint had a mistress, had resulted in the expulsion of correspondent Israel Shenker, and since then the magazine had been excluded completely except for occasional visits by transient correspondents who came in on tourist visas. *Life*, on the other hand, had been allowed to maintain its Moscow bureau, and also had one local staffer, Felix Rosenthal, a Soviet citizen who had served as Benny Goodman's interpreter during the bandleader's 1962 Russian tour and was subsequently hired by *Life*. In January 1968, Donovan had come to Moscow with *Life* managing editor George Hunt for an interview with Soviet Premier Alexei Kosygin, and in the rather cordial aftermath of that encounter, Donovan had pushed through the reinstatement of a Moscow bureau for *Time*, with Schecter as the designated correspondent. Now, though, in the budget pinch of late 1969, *Life* was closing down its Moscow bureau; Schecter remained Time Inc.'s sole representative.

Schecter combined reportorial experience with an entrepreneurial flair that served the company well in the Khrushchev negotiations. Then 36, he had begun stringing for *Time* in Japan during his off-duty hours as a U.S. Navy officer. After a year on the *Wall Street Journal* he came back to *Time* as a writer in the Business section, then went to the Far East as a correspondent, eventually becoming *Time*'s Washington-based diplomatic editor.

Initial reaction at Time Inc. to the proffered material was extreme suspicion. On the instruction of chief of correspondents Murray Gart, Schecter flew home to brief Donovan. In early November, Gart went to Moscow to check further, personally. There—incongruously enough, during the anniversary celebrations of the Bolshevik Revolution—Gart spent a whole day talking with the Soviet intermediaries and listening to a tape, while Schecter provided a running translation. On his assessment of "the flavor of the thing," Gart recommended that Time Inc. proceed to the next stage. Thereupon the "Jones project," as it was code-named around the Time & Life Building, got under way with Gart serving as the project's editorial executive working with Little, Brown's Larned G. (Ned) Bradford. ("How's Jones?" became a question at *Life* when Khrushchev had a heart attack in October 1970, at a critical stage in the publishing preparations.)

In all, 180 hours of tapes, both reel and cassette, and 820 pages

288

of Russian transcripts were delivered to Time Inc. for the two volumes that Little, Brown published, the four installments that *Life* excerpted from the first volume, and the two installments from the second volume that appeared in *Time* following *Life*'s demise.* The material arrived in the U.S. by several routes—"in the usual way that underground stuff gets out of the Soviet Union," was as much as Schecter felt free to say. One parcel landed in Cleveland, Ohio.

Spectrographic analysis was made by the Voiceprint Laboratories of Somerville, New Jersey, using for comparison a United Nations recording of Khrushchev during his appearance at the 1959 U.N. General Assembly. The analysis established conclusively that it was indeed the Soviet leader speaking on the smuggled tapes. There were pages missing in the transcripts and gaps in the tapes, but no evidence of tampering. Voiceprint Laboratories reported that 175 hours of tapes were unmistakably Khrushchev. On the other four and a half hours the voice was less certain; Khrushchev had had trouble at first with the primitive equipment, and sometimes put the microphone on top of the recorder. The subject matter of these portions (some incidents of World War II, Khrushchev's visit to Britain in 1956) did not suggest that there had been any doctoring, however. Indeed, the background noises of dogs barking, dishes rattling in the kitchen, birds singing and children playing while he was outside in the garden, all recorded sharply on the German machine that Khrushchev later used, further supported the tapes' authenticity.

But the material, as first transcribed, was unpublishable—"an unholy mess," in Talbott's view. Then a 23-year-old graduate student of Russian literature at Oxford, Talbott had gone to Yale and worked briefly as an editorial writer on the Cleveland *Press.* Spotted by Time Inc. as a likely prospect when he went to Oxford as a Rhodes scholar, Talbott had interned in *Time*'s London and Moscow bureaus in the summers of 1968 and 1969, and was back at Oxford when he was told "to get my best Russian dictionary and come up to London." Working initially from the Russian transcripts, which he later compared with the tapes, Talbott found Khrushchev's recollections confused but completely absorbing, containing "an incredible wealth of historical material."

Edward Crankshaw, the British expert on Soviet affairs and biographer of Khrushchev, whom Bradford enlisted to provide historical guidance for the project, was similarly convinced. Crankshaw admitted in his introduction to the first volume that he, too, was not told

Life November 27, December 4, 11 and 18, 1970. *Time* May 6 and 13, 1974.

how the material was obtained. However, he was certain that it was Khrushchev speaking, and to Crankshaw, Khrushchev's motivation, apart from self-justification, seemed evident:

> Nobody now active and in office is attacked directly. The main target of criticism is Stalin . . . I think it may be assumed that the chief concern of the person, or persons, responsible for releasing these reminiscences to the West—it certainly appears to be one of Khrushchev's chief concerns—was to counter the current attempts [in the U.S.S.R.] to rehabilitate Stalin.

In February 1970, the contract was signed for the Khrushchev material, providing for payment of $750,000 through a Swiss bank. All rights—"even ballet," one editor noted, playfully—went to Time Inc. Final discussions that summer set the publication protocol, which Schecter summarized in a message to New York: the material was not to be presented as a "memoir" but only as "reminiscences." Confidentiality should be maintained until the last moment. "If the first leaks suggest a sensation, we can expect a sensational and potentially devastating response," Schecter wrote. "It is imperative that although we speak of a Russian manuscript we do not directly mention its author. Rather, the formula is that the manuscript contains material that was collected and put on paper by persons with permanent access to the subject over a long period of time [avoiding] any indication of the subject's role in the project."

With these conditions in mind, *Life* senior editor Gene Farmer began preparing four excerpts totaling 35,000 words for publication in the magazine. Shortly afterward, *Life* opened the bidding for foreign newspaper and magazine syndication. It was a blind auction. Gedeon de Margitay, *Life*'s Paris-based syndication chief, made the rounds with a kit containing Talbott's characterization of the work and Crankshaw's introduction, but no actual Khrushchev excerpts nor any information about the source. Buyers were told by De Margitay that "we were taking a gamble and I was asking them if they'd like to gamble along with us." Explicitly, the buyers were forbidden by contract to speculate in print on the origin of the Khrushchev material beyond what Time Inc. had told them. Even under these conditions, sales were brisk. In all, European, Latin American, Mideast and Asian publishers paid a total of $880,000 for publication rights, more than covering Time Inc.'s outlay. No syndication was offered in the U.S.; *Life* intended capitalizing fully on exclusivity on its home ground.

Khrushchev in print was a worldwide sensation. *Life*'s coup set off a speculative flurry in which, inevitably, publishing rivalries played a part. In Europe especially, newspapers and magazines that had not got rights to the Khrushchev reminiscences challenged their authenticity. Among publications accepting the Khrushchev memoirs as genuine, also, there was questioning of motive and source—the why and how of Khrushchev's unburdening himself to an American publisher.

Press attention focused on the possible role of an enigmatic figure who called himself Victor Louis. He had been imprisoned under Stalin; now liberated, he served as Moscow correspondent of the London *Evening Standard* and lived in capitalist affluence, with an English wife, a seven-room Moscow apartment, a suburban dacha with sauna and tennis court, a Porsche and a Mercedes in the garage. The New York *Times* described the multilingual, 42-year-old Louis as a man "who doubles or triples as a newsman, literary hot-goods salesman and, it is suggested, secret police agent." It was reported that in 1967 Louis had attempted to discredit the autobiography of Stalin's daughter Svetlana, titled *Twenty Letters to a Friend*, which was then being sold to Western publishers (*Life* bought the first U.S. serial rights and published excerpts in its issues of September 15 and 22, 1967). Earlier, he had attempted to produce a pirated version of *My Fair Lady* for Soviet audiences. There were numerous suggestions that Louis had been the agent in the Khrushchev transaction. According to a Danish paper, he had been registered at the Hotel d'Angleterre in Copenhagen in August 1970, at the same time Gart was in town for a regional conference of Time-Life European correspondents. (The report was correct.)

Time, not privy to *Life*'s secrets—and uncertain, as one *Time* editor remarked, "whether *Life* had been given a piece of Soviet disinformation"—was unable to confirm or deny the speculation. *Time* did, however, do some speculating on its own about the persons around Khrushchev who could have taped or transcribed material and passed it along: Khrushchev's son-in-law Alexei Adzhubei, exeditor of *Izvestia*; Khrushchev's granddaughter Yulia, a onetime journalist; and her late husband Lev, formerly editor of an English-language Soviet magazine. "The family abounds with possible Boswells," *Time* observed.

Prudently, the news service had transferred Schecter before the Khrushchev reminiscences appeared. The Soviet reaction was as *Life* had anticipated, even to the extent of a denial from Khrushchev's wife. "Impossible . . . a joke," she was quoted as saying. Khrushchev's own denial, however, was seen as less than categorical; he disavowed delivering "material of a memoir nature" to any publisher, but not the fact of this material's existence. Although some Soviet specialists continued to profess doubts, the weight of expert opinion swung to Time Inc.'s side. In 1972, after Khrushchev's death, the original tapes were retrieved from a Swiss bank vault and brought back to the U.S. for presentation to the Oral History Collection at Columbia University. De Margitay was the courier. In a scenario "right out of an Eric Ambler novel," as he described it, De Margitay flew to Switzerland where, following his instructions, he went to the steps of a church in Lucerne that was high on a hill, visible from all sides. The contact man appeared, exchanged a few words with De Margitay in accented French, handed him a plastic shopping bag containing the tapes and departed. That afternoon De Margitay flew back to New York. The tapes passed through U.S. Customs without so much as a glance.

Khrushchev died of heart disease in September 1971, ten months after the first volume of his reminiscences appeared. A copy of the book had been delivered to him several months before that. He was pleased with the presentation, according to Time Inc.'s information, and encouraged to continue taping. A second volume was published posthumously. It contains the touching valedictory: "After being sick . . . I'm tired, almost too tired to go on. But nonetheless I'm determined to leave my memoirs for future historians so that they may know my viewpoint, my judgments and the reasons for my judgments." Khrushchev's kin reiterated his sentiments posthumously; more than a decade after his death a close family member personally conveyed satisfaction to Time Inc. with the way the project had been handled.

The success of the Khrushchev reminiscences was a morale booster for the *Life* staff. Donovan, at a pre-Christmas party in December 1970, hailed the project as "surely a tremendous asset for other ventures in *Life*'s future," and went on to scotch the published rumors—he cited *Newsweek*'s in particular—that *Life* was folding:

> I hope I don't shock anyone in this room if I say we *could* stop publishing *Life*, and we *would* stop publishing *Life* if we thought it was not going anywhere. The point is that we *choose* to publish *Life* . . . not . . . because we are stupid at arithmetic [or] out of stubbornness or sentiment. Though we have a bit of both—and it does help at times . . .
>
> We are publishing *Life* because we believe *Life* has important

work to do, now, and as far as we can see ahead . . . And from all previous Time Inc. experience—here I will be a little commercial—we continue to believe that a magazine doing an outstanding editorial job will also succeed in the marketplace.

Time Inc. was also putting a bit more money into the magazine, Graves informed the staff. "After two years of massive cuts in head count, production costs and general edit," he noted, a half million dollar increase in the editorial budget had been negotiated for 1971, permitting *Life* now to "feel freer to go up four pages when we need to, to run a couple of extra spreads of color . . . even to take some gambles that don't come off."

The money seemed well spent; 1971 was a good year editorially. A March issue scored a near sellout on the newsstands with a cover photo by photography buff Frank Sinatra and 8,000 words of text inside by Norman Mailer on the Muhammad Ali-Joe Frazier heavyweight title fight. In April came 21 pages of color on China, until then virtually forbidden territory to American visitors. The accompanying text by Communist China expert Edgar Snow recounted his conversations with Mao Tse-tung, in which Mao dropped the hint that led the following year to President Nixon's historic visit to Peking. In June, *Life* had another near sellout on the newsstands with ten pages on the White House wedding of Tricia Nixon and Edward Finch Cox. In July, *Life* published the results of its amateur photography contest, which had attracted more than 1 million entries from 100,000 participants. In October began a new five-part series of pioneering medical photographs by Lennart Nilsson, showing in microscopic closeup the workings of the human brain.

On the publishing side likewise, the year had begun encouragingly. While advertising revenues were expected to drop by $13 million as a result of lower page rates, circulation income was budgeted to improve by $8 million, thanks to higher subscription prices, the reduced volume of new subscribers needed to replace nonrenewers and the elimination of all paid-during-service (PDS) subscriptions. These last were peddled by door-to-door or telephone solicitation and paid for on the installment plan. They were a quick way to increase circulation but had few other merits. Sold at a discount, usually in combination with other magazines, PDS subscriptions had a poor renewal record, and were regarded unfavorably by advertisers.

The decision to end PDS subscriptions gave Time Inc. the chance to rid itself of a growing corporate embarrassment. This was its own

PDS subsidiary, Family Publications Service, Inc., jointly owned with *Parents* magazine until 1966, when Time Inc. acquired it entirely. FPS had been a flourishing business in *Life*'s halcyon years; its president reputedly earned more than Luce. ("But you wouldn't like the work, Harry," Roy Larsen pointed out, when Luce complained.) Like other subscription solicitation firms, however, Family Publications Service was coming under increasing federal and local government scrutiny for high-pressure sales tactics. In an attempt to clean up suspected irregularities at certain of FPS's 32 field sales offices, *Life* general manager John Watters was reassigned in December 1970 to supervise the operations of FPS and a related business, the Life Circulation Company.

In January 1972, Time Inc. shut FPS down completely. To prevent branch managers from destroying records, the closure was conducted like a military assault, with three-man teams—a lawyer, an accountant and a uniformed but unarmed Pinkerton guard—marching into all the FPS offices across the country simultaneously, at 12 noon Eastern Daylight Time. Scenes of high tension and occasionally low comedy ensued. Loyal secretaries tried to flush papers down the toilet. An FPS employee pulled a pistol from a bottom drawer as he cleaned out his desk. Recalled Watters: "He was a gun collector but our team didn't know that, and I guess it *was* a sight watching them falling over each other as they scrambled for the door." Not until 1974 was FPS finally dissolved, at a cost of nearly $1 million in legal fees. The Life Circulation Company, renamed Dialogue Marketing, was sold in 1972.

All projections for *Life*'s future were, however, upset by the news from Washington. Among the various economies planned for 1971 was a fractional reduction in *Life*'s page size, to save paper weight and cut the magazine's enormous postage bill; together with an earlier switch to a lighter paper stock, this could save nearly $2 million. But in February 1971 came the announcement of vastly increased second-class (periodical) postage rates proposed by the U.S. Postal Service. Although the magazine industry had expected some second-class rate hikes as the result of Congress's creation of this new agency to replace the old Post Office Department, the increases actually proposed came as a shock: 142 percent over the five years 1972 through 1976. In Time Inc.'s case they were estimated to run much higher, around 176 percent, because of the magazines' paper weights, their publication frequency and national distribution patterns. *Life*'s postage bill would rise $2 million in 1972 and more later.

Going public with its protest in a *Life* editorial, Time Inc. charged that the Postal Service's "astounding" proposal "quite literally threatens the survival of much of the publishing industry."

Last year the pretax earnings of all magazines were probably about $50 million . . . If the proposed increase were adopted, magazines would have to find an additional $130 million to pay for mail service by 1976—more than twice their 1970 profits! For Time Inc., it's possible to be quite specific. Our four magazines earned $11 million before taxes last year; over the next five years the bill for mailing these magazines to subscribers would rise by about $27 million.

One magazine publisher who decided not to take the risk of finding that extra income was Gardner Cowles Jr., owner of *Look*. On September 16, Cowles Communications Inc. announced that *Look* would fold with the October 19 issue. Time Inc. took the occasion to attack the Postal Service again, in a corporate statement:

It is always bad news for this country when a responsible journal is forced to close down. It is particularly bad news when that development is, in part, engendered by an arm of the government.

Nor was *Look*'s demise unmitigated good news for *Life*, despite the elimination of its last competitor in pictorial journalism. From Cowles, Time Inc. picked up some bits and pieces, including $2,850,000 worth of Des Moines real estate that formerly housed *Look*'s subscription service operations, and an agreement to transfer part of *Look*'s subscriber list to the *Life* lists as needed (at $3 a name) to maintain *Life*'s circulation rate base. But *Life* was left isolated in its field. For all the brave Time Inc. declarations that *Life*'s situation was comparable to that of the victors of the metropolitan newspaper wars where "in many cities, one strong newspaper has survived . . . and has prospered," gossip in the magazine trade said exactly the opposite. There was immediate renewed speculation that *Life* could not make it for long, either.

Within Time Inc., a corporate reappraisal completed in November 1971 concluded, "The departure of *Look* from the market does give us a flexibility in planning changes [in rate base, etc.] for 1972 which we did not have before." Beyond that, there was not much reason for optimism. Advertising for the first three quarters of 1971 was down, with particularly heavy losses in food advertising. (The General Foods account was an exception; that company tripled its

295

schedule in *Life* during the year.) The greater problem, however, was circulation. For 1971's second half, it appeared that *Life* might fail to make its guarantee, falling some 16,000 below rate base; this raised the unpleasant prospect of refunds to advertisers.

Life was, in fact, back to the same choice it had faced 18 months earlier—between continuing as a weekly and going biweekly—but in either case, circulation would have to be cut. Up against an advertising ceiling and having reached the floor in reducing physical costs, *Life* could survive only by improving circulation profitability. As the publisher's office put it, "We must *reduce circulation* through a contraction in rate base or a change in publishing frequency, again with a rate base cut. A reduction has a dual impact: it allows us to increase the price we charge subscribers, and it reduces the cost both in total and on average to acquire subscriptions."

On November 23 a special board of directors meeting ratified management's choice. *Life* would remain weekly but its total circulation would be cut again, this time to 5.5 million, while at the same time the subscription price would be raised by slightly over 20 percent. There would be a corresponding 18 percent reduction in advertising page rates.

At this point in the dismal numbers game, *Life* made a pre-Christmas announcement: in March 1972 it would begin publishing the autobiography of the billionaire recluse, Howard Hughes. The news was stunning, "perhaps the most momentous editorial announcement in years," *Life*'s senior circulation executive, Robert Cowin, termed it. Offering a mixture of Hollywood sex, corporate intrigue and aviation adventure, the Hughes story surely would have been a journalistic sensation—had it been authentic.

Hughes had been totally unreachable, virtually invisible, for over a decade. Inheritor of a Texas oilfield equipment fortune, he was reputedly worth more than $3 billion. He had been a record-breaking aviator, aircraft designer and builder, Hollywood producer, creator of stars and collector of starlets, airline entrepreneur, real estate operator and Nevada hotel and gambling-casino owner. Then suddenly, he had retreated into hermetically sealed isolation in a series of tropical or desert hideaways behind phalanxes of bodyguards. Living on a bizarre diet, shunning germs and all outside contact, Hughes had been heard from only in scrawled messages and late-night calls on scrambler telephones; he had not even come out to defend himself in a $50 million lawsuit brought by a longtime associate. The last journalist to interview him face to face was Time-Life correspondent

Frank McCulloch, who in 1971 was the news service's bureau chief in New York. As Los Angeles bureau chief in the late 1950s, during Hughes's fight to maintain control of Trans World Airlines, McCulloch had often been routed from bed to listen to Hughes's telephone monologues. When McCulloch went to Southeast Asia in late 1963 the calls from Hughes followed him there.

Thus there was a certain crazy plausibility to the tale about Hughes that an expatriate American novelist named Clifford Irving had brought to the McGraw-Hill Book Company and McGraw-Hill, in turn, had brought to *Life*. Irving, something of a drifter, four times married, was then living on the island of Ibiza off the Spanish Mediterranean coast. There he had met Elmyr de Hory, a picaresque, Hungarian-born art forger whose fake Picassos, Matisses and Dufys had fooled experts all over the world. Irving claimed that his sympathetic biography of De Hory, published in 1969 by McGraw-Hill, caught Hughes's fancy, and that in subsequent correspondence with the billionaire recluse he had been authorized to write Hughes's biography as well. "It would not suit me to die . . . without having stated the truth," Hughes had supposedly written Irving.* Hughes was at that time immured in a suite atop a Bahamas hotel that bristled with James Bondish electronic protective devices. But, according to Irving, Hughes had emerged to rendezvous with him at various exotic locales, to which Irving was directed by mysterious Hughes intermediaries.

Irving brought his tale to McGraw-Hill in February 1971, supporting his account with purported correspondence in Hughes's handwriting on lined yellow legal paper. Irving relayed Hughes's price: $500,000, to be deposited to his account in a Swiss bank. An additional $100,000 was to go to Irving. Secrecy was to be total; otherwise Hughes would back out. In fact, Irving said, he himself could not reach Hughes but rather had to wait for Hughes's calls to him, and if Hughes got wind of any others being involved in the project he would cancel everything. Similar secrecy was written into the $250,000 contract *Life* signed with McGraw-Hill for magazine rights. As with Khrushchev, Hughes's identity was to be screened under a code name, in this case "Octavio," and knowledge of Project Octavio was to be limited to "an absolute minimum of responsible officers of *Life*." In the contract was an important escape clause: if Hughes failed to authorize the book before publication, all money paid by *Life* would be refunded.

*Clifford Irving: *The Hoax* (The Permanent Press, 1981), p. 44.

The proposition seemed irresistible, as Donovan told the Time Inc. board of directors afterward:

> We were not in the beginning asked to risk anything, in money or time . . . What we were getting, on the other hand, was a hold on all magazine rights worldwide to what might develop into a fabulous journalistic property.
>
> Putting it another way, I would have hated to wake up some day last summer and read that *Look* magazine, which you will recall still existed then, was about to publish the autobiography or authorized biography of Howard Hughes. I would have hated for that matter to read that the New York *Times* was about to come out with Howard Hughes in 18 daily installments.

Irving was introduced to Graves at a lunch arranged by Beverly Loo, the executive editor at McGraw-Hill. With him Irving brought the "letters" from Hughes. They were more than passable forgeries, as events would demonstrate—Irving had used as a model an actual letter of Hughes's that *Life*, most providentially for Irving, had reproduced the preceding January as part of a story on Hughes's continuing legal troubles. Graves read the letters carefully, and was particularly struck by something he saw in one of them: "The way he writes the letter *I*. You see here. The way he's gone over it twice . . . That's a habit of his. I've seen it before in other letters, the ones in our file."* That was only the beginning of a number of breaks that fell Irving's way.

With his researcher, Richard Suskind, an American living on Majorca, Irving set off around the U.S. to gather background material on Hughes to flesh out the personal "interviews." At the Pentagon, Irving ran into a cooperative official who supplied information on the operations of Hughes Aircraft Co. and Hughes Tool Co., including military projects. At the Library of Congress, Irving survived frisking by a suspicious guard as he duck-walked out cradling in the seat of his pants a thick volume of Hughes's testimony at 1947 Senate hearings. Then Irving gained access to Time Inc.'s own files on Hughes, dating back to pre–World War II days.

Normally closed to outsiders, Time Inc. files had on occasion been made available to writers working on projects for the company, and Graves gave instructions accordingly. Because of the secrecy imposed on the project, however, very few in the company knew this. Those few did not include Time Inc.'s in-house authority,

The Hoax, p. 69.

Frank McCulloch, who, as a matter of fact, had once signed a contract to write a Hughes biography himself. (After a couple of days' reflection, McCulloch had thought better of it and returned the publisher's advance.)

For his day in the Time-Life library, Irving arrived with camera and magnifying lens, but no other special equipment. Ushered to a locked room by *Life* assistant managing editor Dave Maness, Irving was provided with an almost complete dossier—the handwritten notes of a *Time* correspondent who interviewed Hughes after his 1938 round-the-world flight; accounts by former Hughes aides of his business contacts and amorous assignations; a report from McCulloch on Hughes's controversial 1956 loan to Richard Nixon's brother Donald; clippings from *Time, Life, Fortune*, the newspapers. Irving found it "a treasure trove." Spreading the pages on a windowsill, he photographed for seven hours without a break.

Subsequently, Irving got another piece of serendipitous help from a pirated photocopy of the unpublished memoirs of a former Hughes lieutenant. Appended to it was a ten-page, single-spaced memo dated October 30, 1958, from McCulloch in Los Angeles to Jim Shepley, then chief of Time Inc.'s domestic news service in New York. It was a verbatim record of a telephone call from Hughes, asking McCulloch's assistance in heading off a projected *Fortune* article on the troubles at TWA, which Hughes then controlled. The memo had probably been copied by someone with access to the Los Angeles files, and it fell into Irving's hands in the course of his "research." He said, "[It] gave us Hughes's conversational patterns, his expletives, his spoken syntax, manner of response, love of clichés and mangled metaphors."* With this and their other research in hand, Irving and Suskind sat down in Ibiza with a tape recorder and, taking turns at impersonating Hughes, began re-creating Irving's "interviews" with him at their various secret meetings. So persuasive were the results that when Irving flew to New York with nearly a thousand pages of transcripts, all doubts on *Life*'s part vanished. Later, in *Life*, Graves described the first reading of Irving's material:

> At 9 o'clock on the morning of September 13 three McGraw-Hill editors and two *Life* editors met in Cliff Irving's two-room suite in New York's Elysée Hotel . . . We spent two days going

*The Hoax, p. 129.

through the boxes of paper, passing batches of pages down the line from one reader to another.

It was marvelous stuff. Outspoken, full of rich and outrageous anecdotes. . . . his private life, his opinions, his crotchets. . . We finished with the conviction that these 1,000 pages of talk were authentic.

And highly marketable. On the basis of the transcripts alone, Dell paid $400,000 for paperback book rights. The Book-of-the-Month Club (not yet owned by Time Inc.) paid an exceptionally high $350,000. *Life*, preparing for its own publication, commissioned David Walsh, an artist friend of Irving's, to paint scenes re-creating his meetings with Hughes, as a substitute for the photographs that "Hughes" refused to pose for.

Meanwhile, on a trip to Switzerland, Irving's German-born wife Edith had established a banking channel for the deposit of McGraw-Hill's checks made out, at Irving's request, to "H.R. Hughes." For anonymity's sake, Irving explained, Howard R. Hughes preferred using only his initials in this project. The same preference for initials was expressed by Edith Irving when, using an altered Swiss passport in the name of Helga R. Hughes, she opened an account with the Swiss Credit Bank in Zurich, explaining that as a businesswoman with offices in Paris and New York, she was known simply as H.R. Hughes.

So endorsed, McGraw-Hill's first check, for $275,000, drawn on the Chase Manhattan Bank in New York, cleared without difficulty. The Swiss Credit Bank attested the H.R. Hughes signature as corresponding to that of the H.R. Hughes holding the account. Chase Manhattan, stamping the check in the usual way, "Prior Endorsements Guaranteed," paid Zurich and notified McGraw-Hill accordingly. A McGraw-Hill editor in turn notified Time Inc. that it had "a check signature guaranteed by Chase Manhattan Bank," evidence that Howard Hughes had received payment.

Capping everything was a letter that arrived in November, supposedly handwritten by Howard Hughes and addressed to McGraw-Hill's Harold McGraw, authorizing the firm to announce the Irving-Hughes book.

With that announcement, on December 7, the pyrotechnics began. Instantly, executives of the Hughes Tool Company, parent firm of the Hughes interests, challenged the book as "a fake and a fraud," threatening legal action to stop publication. Chester Davis, counsel to Hughes Tool, insisted that the rights to any Hughes biography were owned solely by Rosemont Enterprises, a Hughes-owned company. Time Inc. and McGraw-Hill stood their ground.

Time Inc. had reason to feel confident. In addition to the "guaranteed" signature on McGraw-Hill's check, there was "the real clincher," as Donovan called the nine-page letter to Harold McGraw. Correctly postmarked (Suskind had flown to Nassau in the Bahamas to mail it), the letter had been submitted for handwriting analysis to the same expert who analyzed the genuine Hughes letter that *Life* had published in January 1971. His opinion: both letters were by the same hand, the chances of forgery "less than one in a million."

"As we learned later," Donovan commented, "that one number in a million came up." The probability began looming, unpleasantly, a week following the announcement. *Life* had still not brought Frank McCulloch into the picture; he only learned of the Hughes project, he said, in the newspaper he read on the train to work. On the afternoon of December 14, McCulloch got a telephone call that he was to remember vividly. "Stand by for a call from Mr. Hughes," a male voice declared. Then Hughes came on. "All those wearying hours I'd listened to that nasal, whining voice—there was no mistaking it," McCulloch said. "Hughes wanted to know what the [obscenity] us guys were doing. Had we gone crazy? He had never heard of Clifford Irving."

As McCulloch stalled for time, Hughes said he would talk again at 7 p.m. Present with McCulloch that evening were vice president for corporate and public affairs Donald M. Wilson and Time Inc.'s chief editorial counsel, John F. (Jack) Dowd, as well as Chester Davis on behalf of the Hughes Tool Company. After dialing by credit card and concealing the number, Davis handed the phone to McCulloch. When McCulloch asked to tape the conversation, the man on the line turned down the request and launched into a repetition of the afternoon's tirade.

Belatedly, all inhibitions on a thorough investigation of Irving's veracity were removed. *Life*'s former investigative reporter Bill Lambert, now with *Time*, began to use sources in federal and international law enforcement agencies. Time Inc. lawyers flew to Nevada to gather authenticated Hughes documents, including his pilot's log and fingerprints from wartime military files, for further handwriting comparisons.

Incredibly, Irving's story stood up. By an inexplicable oversight on *Life*'s part, McCulloch was still not informed that Irving had been allowed to see the Time Inc. files on Hughes; after reading

Irving's manuscript and spending two hours alone with him, McCulloch came away impressed by Irving's evident familiarity with the man. Preliminary checking for accuracy of the three 10,000-word excerpts (from the 230,000-word book) that *Life* planned to publish revealed no serious factual discrepancies. If anything, *Life* researchers told the editors, the material checked a little too easily, coinciding closely with the facts of Hughes's life as reported by Time Inc. correspondents over the years. More astonishing was a second, independent comparison of forged and authentic Hughes handwriting samples, by a firm of leading courtroom authorities. Reported Osborn Associates of New York: "The evidence that all of the writing was done by one individual is, in our opinion, irresistible, unanswerable and overwhelming." At the McGraw-Hill offices, Irving underwent a lie-detector test, but again his luck held: the test results were inconclusive.

On January 7, 1972, came another denial from Hughes. The setting was a freakish press conference in a Los Angeles hotel, where seven journalists who had once known Hughes well sat confronting a telephone amplifier, from which emerged a disembodied voice claiming to be Hughes, speaking from his Bahamas hotel. "I don't remember any script as wild or stretching the imagination as this yarn . . . I don't know Irving, never saw him." The quavering Texas drawl, the rambling descriptions of aviation minutiae convinced his listeners that it was indeed Hughes. Irving, however, pointed to "discrepancies" in Hughes's answers.

Caught uneasily in the middle, McGraw-Hill and Time Inc. continued to profess faith in Irving's book. *Life*, advancing the publication date, announced that excerpts would start running in the magazine's February 11 issue, four weeks away. McGraw-Hill set its book publication date for March 6. Chester Davis went to the New York State Supreme Court for an injunction to block both publishers.

"The Hughes Mystery," as *Time* labeled the cover story in its January 24, 1972, issue, was now practically the biggest news story anywhere. Reporters swarmed to Ibiza looking for more on Irving, and into the Bahamas for more on Hughes.

One matter that remained to be resolved was the McGraw-Hill checks to H.R. Hughes, now totaling $750,000, that had cleared through the Swiss Credit Bank in Zurich. In mid-January, at a discreet breakfast meeting in the Zurich airport, Time Inc.'s Geneva stringer Robert Kroon put two questions to an old news source of his, a vice president of the Swiss Credit Bank: Could he say whether Howard Hughes had an account at the bank? And if so, was the account number the same as the one shown on McGraw-Hill's checks? The bank official shook his head: *"Das ist unmöglich!"*—impossible. Kroon, a multilingual Dutch newspaperman and television correspondent who had reported for *Time* for two decades, prodded gently. A possible crime was involved; this was a major news story; the bank risked embarrassment. Finally, Swiss bank secrecy—"sanct but not sacrosanct," as Kroon wisecracked in a cable to New York—lifted just slightly. It lifted more when Brussels bureau chief Roger Beardwood arrived to press further, informing New York that if bank officials could talk directly with the Time Inc. and McGraw-Hill principals in the case, "they might have something interesting to report."

But it was a guessing game that ensued when Time Inc. vice president Charley Bear and McGraw-Hill representatives flew into Zurich two days later. "It was like charades," Bear said. The bank would volunteer no more than that it was "definitely not the signature of the famous Howard Hughes . . . But we were allowed to guess. I asked: 'Was it a black?' No. Then: 'Was it a woman?' Big smiles on their faces. Then, and you won't believe this," Bear continued, recounting the bank's description of the bewigged female who had opened the H.R. Hughes account, "we got so fascinated with that business about a black wig that we thought it was [art forger] Elmyr de Hory—in drag."

Time Inc. got the word from Zurich just after its lawyers had come back from a morning in court defending Irving's veracity and arguing to quash Davis's request for an injunction to stop publication. They returned to court in the afternoon to report that publication was being delayed voluntarily until "questions concerning the Swiss bank account [are] fully resolved."

Life now prepared a cover story of its own on the Hughes-Irving controversy, with a cover portrait of "Hughes" drawn by Irving's painter friend David Walsh and a text piece inside by Graves tracing the intricacies of the Irving saga to date but not yet suggesting fraud on Irving's part. Together with the cover portrait, the Graves text piece appeared in *Life*'s February 4 issue—although not in its original form. Seventeen hours after *Life*'s press run started, but in time to stop distribution of the copies already printed, the truth was wormed from Irving by Frank McCulloch and John Goldman, a Los Angeles *Times* reporter.

Returning from Ibiza two days earlier, Irving had found his edifice of lies collapsing. U.S. postal inspectors, federal and New York State grand juries were waiting to question him. Swiss authorities were also closing in; in Zurich the bank had revealed publicly what it told Time Inc. and McGraw-Hill privately about the black-wigged woman. Denying his wife's involvement, Irving fled to the New York home of his lawyer,* where McCulloch and Goldman found him. There, at 1 a.m. on January 28, Irving, exhausted and croaking with laryngitis, admitted finally that "Helga R. Hughes" was indeed his wife. McCulloch recalled bursting from the session with Irving and looking for someone around the Time & Life Building at that dead hour of night who could order the presses stopped. "Only time in my life I ever said, 'Stop the presses!' " McCulloch said. Someone on the production side was found, and in Chicago the press run was halted and the pages replated to report Edith Irving's complicity in the fraud that closed the circle of deceit.

In his rueful postmortem to the Time Inc. board of directors, Donovan noted that the contractual arrangements with McGraw-Hill had prevented *Life* from running its own investigation of Irving before the book was announced. "The linchpin of the swindle," as Donovan called it, was the secrecy that Hughes had supposedly demanded. "This ruled out a lot of things, including 'bringing in' McCulloch," Donovan said, answering criticism that the company's in-house authority on Howard Hughes had not been consulted earlier. As it was, Donovan felt the damage was limited. He conceded that in this affair, the corporate succor given *Life*'s editorial side "did a lot to help reduce or contain possible embarrassments for Time Inc. . . . I have never been completely certain, in the church-state analogy, which part of Time Inc. is which, but assuming the editorial departments are the church, I have to say that church got us into this and state has been very active in helping to get us out."

Donovan assessed the costs—investigative and legal expenses, wasted executive time, *Life*'s replate, and a "fair bit of kidding . . . some quite friendly, some on the rough side" that Time Inc. had been taking in the publishing trade. But publisher Valk "detected no damage to *Life* among our advertisers," Donovan reported. As for *Life*'s standing with its readers:

> I think we have to assume there is going to be some harm done, at least temporarily, to our reputation . . . a certain credibility gap to overcome. If our next sensational story is okay, and then we come along with another one a bit later that also checks out, I think then we would have successfully put this affair behind

---

*Who turned out to be Martin Ackerman, former owner of the *Saturday Evening Post*, from whom *Life* had bought the *Post*'s subscriber list.

us. Some nice people come up to me and say you have had millions of dollars of free publicity, or what wonderful innocent fun you've given all of us, etc., etc. No doubt these are offsets to the embarrassment of being fooled, but not quite total, I think.

Three weeks after Donovan spoke, Irving was indicted for conspiracy to defraud, forgery, perjury and other charges, for which he eventually served 17 months in federal prisons. Suskind, sentenced under New York State law, served five months. Edith Irving served two months of a two-year federal sentence and then returned to Switzerland where, sentenced again, she served 14 more months.

In the retrospective view of most of the people on the magazine, the Irving hoax did not hasten *Life*'s demise. But the struggle for survival grew harder. "Like pushing a safe through sand," publisher Valk described it. With the November 1971 decision to cut circulation back to 5.5 million went another staff reduction, this time involving about 90 persons out of 450, divided equally between the editorial and publishing sides. Among the editorial casualties were the *Life* investigative team and a number of valued veteran writers and photographers. Further economies continued through the year, touching every aspect of the magazine's operations. When *Life*'s London bureau chief, Jordan Bonfante, was left without secretarial help and asked approval for $25 weekly for the part-time services of a *Time* secretary, he was turned down.

Adding to the strain was the renewed agonizing over *Life*'s editorial approach: Should it be radically revised, in an attempt to regain readership? Donovan's deputy, editorial director Lou Banks, felt that *Life* should "lower its sights . . . become the magazine of the blue collar—reflecting the best sensibilities of the blue collar." Tom Griffith took a different tack in a note to the other top editors of *Life*:

> Is it possible at this late date to think about a totally different *Life*? Common sense says that tradition, Time Inc. habits of thought, and reader expectancy keep us from straying too far. More sensational? We could promise more boldly, but . . . to the degree the exercise was seen to be souped up [it] would be taken as desperation tactics. Sexier? In the world of *Playboy*, etc., you have to go too far to be even noticed. More pop? . . . I don't think this the route to be taken to be considered more *essential*. Heavier, then? Too many magazines already there.

305

Of all the ways to change *Life* dramatically I can think of only one which would be consonant with our past and present, while giving us a chance to make a new start. It would be simply to declare that henceforth *Life* intends itself to be a magazine for those under 35 . . . an audience that is in fact a lot more to our way of thinking than the middle American we comprehend so little . . . We wouldn't in general have to change our contents or range of interests much at all (reviews, news coverage, text pieces, essays), but our outlook greatly.

Neither proposal was seriously examined. Several new features were, however, added to the *Life* formula. Among them were the *Life* questionnaires, which asked readers to "make their voices heard" on major social issues treated in *Life* stories. A *Life* questionnaire on crime provoked 45,000 reader responses; one on marriage 60,000. While the magazine remained painfully thin, it could still carry great editorial impact; one of *Life*'s most powerful text pieces in years was Tommy Thompson's May 1972 account of an anguished father who shot his drug-addicted son.

Seeking also to gain more picture space, Graves, with Griffith's backing, proposed dropping *Life*'s regular editorial page. Donovan rejected the idea. The *Life* editorial had always been the voice of Time Inc. where company policy was enunciated. Said Donovan:

You—and others, me included—and Time Inc. have been devoting tremendous effort to keeping this magazine going. One reason . . . is the belief that *Life* is an important place to say important things to a particular audience . . . to express what Time Inc. "stands for." Not just for the sake of being "on the record"—somewhere—with our views but actually in the hope of influencing people.

It was a theme Donovan returned to as pressures from outside directors on the Time Inc. board mounted for management to make up its mind about *Life*. Gaylord Freeman and Rawleigh Warner were particular gadflies among the directors. Freeman questioned whether the church-state division of editorial and publishing responsibilities at Time Inc. was not obscuring management's primary obligation to its stockholders: to maximize profit. Donovan replied in a memo to Heiskell, conceding that "perhaps we would have come to earlier or better decisions about *Life* if the final responsibility devolved on one man instead of three, or two." However, he

306

added, "I would argue that the magazine is capable of such a significant contribution to the quality of American life that Time Inc. would be justified in publishing it at a very modest rate of profit—lower than we would accept for the company as a whole." But Donovan "would not argue that *Life* should be published at a loss over any great length of time—that would imperil too many other things we do."

The approach of fall, when *Life* had to budget for the next spring's subscription mailings, increased the pressure for decision. Circulation was not holding up well. The barometer of newsstand sales, a small but sensitive indicator, showed that 1972's sales to date were lower than 1971's for all but a few issues. More important, subscription renewals were proving disproportionately costly to get. Returns were "some 20 to 40 percent *below* what is necessary to make any sense out of selling by direct mail," a report to publisher Valk warned.

Advertising was not holding up either. For 1972's first three quarters, ad page sales continued slightly better than the corresponding periods a year earlier. This was partly the result of Valk's missionary work along Madison Avenue where he had discussed *Life*'s situation with "unheard of . . . honesty," as the New York *Times* advertising columnist reported. But fourth-quarter orders were off again. As Valk was to put it later to the Time Inc. board, *Life* was finding itself "in a booming economy with a fading advertising picture. *TV Guide*, *Reader's Digest* and the three women's service-store books are announcing record revenue increases, so there's money being spent that we're not getting . . . Whereas a year ago we were positioning ourselves for new or additional space from *Look* users—i.e., Bulova, Hiram Walker, Heublein—as well as additional space from the tobacco sector . . . there are now no such increases on the horizon."

Once more the choice was before management: to reduce *Life* circulation to some undefined lower level—for working purposes, 4.5 million was picked—and sell this new, smaller audience to advertisers; or simply to pull the plug at last. Climaxing the discussions was a small session in a company suite at New York's Hotel Dorset, attended by Heiskell, Shepley, Valk, magazine group vice president Art Keylor, chief financial officer Dick McKeough and corporate circulation director Kelso F. Sutton. Recalled McKeough:

We had kept watching the numbers very carefully. By August it was clear we couldn't make it . . . It wasn't just that we were

307

losing money. It was the projections. They were very, very grim
. . . Finally, after a long discussion Andrew got up and said,
"Yes, I'll talk to Hedley." A consensus was reached—a feel of
what we were going to do—by late in September. It was kept
secret till December.

In the interim, much had to be got ready: an analysis for the board
on the corporate implications of amputating this huge arm of Time
Inc.'s publishing operations; arrangements to cut off paper supplies
and printing contracts; a plan to deal with *Life*'s deferred income
liability—"the overwhelming balance sheet item confronting us in
any consideration of termination," said Keylor.

This liability, *Life*'s unfulfilled obligation to subscribers to deliver
magazines, for which they had already paid and for which they
could legally demand cash refunds, had been reduced somewhat by
the earlier circulation cutbacks. But the deferred income liability
("DI" in corporate accounting shorthand) still amounted to $41.4
million. The whole question was a touchy one; corporate procedure
in such instances was subject to scrutiny by the Federal Trade Commission. "It was scary, they could make you or break you," a Time
Inc. lawyer remarked after a scouting trip to Washington to test the
FTC's current mood. No firm guidance was forthcoming. In the end,
the company decided to take its chances, offering subscribers a mixture of cash refunds, subscriptions to other Time Inc. magazines,
books and other products.

Because of the SEC requirements on disclosure of information
affecting stock prices, the tightest security prevailed as the preparations for shutdown proceeded. Griffith was away on sabbatical
leave, writing a book; Graves, the only one on *Life*'s editorial side
to be given advance warning from management, was not told until
two weeks before the board meeting. He dined with Donovan in a
private room at New York's Century Club, the conversation stop-
ping every time the door creaked and a waiter came in. Donovan
was so guarded in his conversation that Graves at first missed the
point. He took Graves "carefully through the numbers, through all
the projections and the losses . . . how terribly serious things were,"
Graves recalled. "But somehow I missed a crucial fact—that they
were predicting a $17 million loss for the next year [1973]. The next
morning we talked again and this time I heard that $17 million
figure. I said, 'That's impossible' . . . Hedley said, 'Yes, and that's
why we have to stop publication.' "

Administrative necessity forced Graves to take one other editorial colleague into his confidence; otherwise, the charade continued to be played through. Preparations continued for the installation of *Life*'s first woman bureau chief in Washington: Bonnie Angelo, who had been appointed just a few hours before Graves learned from Donovan there would be no *Life* bureau for her to command. (Five years later, Angelo became the first woman to head Time Inc.'s London bureau.) *Life*'s advance scheduling continued for the coming year, including a story due for the first issue in January on the response to a children's questionnaire the magazine had published the preceding October. Some 250,000 boys and girls aged six to 12 had replied; 5,000 of them had enclosed letters further expressing their hopes and fears. "When I knew there wasn't going to be a first issue in January, I couldn't stand the thought of all those 250,000 kids who had answered," Graves said. By pushing the writer assigned to the story, he squeezed it into *Life*'s final issue. "I said I had to have it early for layout reasons, for space planning."

For the special board meeting that ratified management's decisions to suspend *Life*, secrecy dictated the choice of a hotel not often used by Time Inc., the Hampshire House on Central Park South. All the directors were present except two, who had been informed; a third, Rudolph Peterson, was traveling in Cyprus and could not be reached. As senior executive in charge of the magazine division, Keylor reviewed the options. The alternative of a *Life* at 4.5 million circulation was not viable, even, Keylor said, "ignoring the competitive situation it posed for our sister publication—*Time*." *Life*'s losses at this lower circulation level would still come to $10.8 million in 1973 and $12.4 million in 1974, although for bookkeeping purposes this could be trimmed by $4 million each year to take into account *Life*'s share of corporate overhead and its contribution to other company enterprises.

Elimination of *Life*'s losses from the corporate balance sheet would improve Time Inc.'s after-tax earnings by $6.6 million in 1973 and $5 million in 1974, McKeough told the board. But then there were the expenses of termination, including severance pay for 600 to 700 employees, about half of them on *Life*'s staff, the others in various service departments; the obligation to compensate subscribers; disposal of *Life*'s paper inventory; and the write-off of other fixed assets, including printing equipment used only by *Life*. These expenses would of course be partially offset by tax recovery resulting from the shutdown.

The net cost of suspension, after all offsets, was estimated at $7.3 million. "The company can afford this additional cash outlay over the next two years without, in my estimation, impairing its rather strong financial position," McKeough said. Though the final one-time loss, as noted in the company's annual report the following April, came out somewhat higher at $8.3 million, the New York Stock Exchange read the news of *Life*'s suspension as bullish: within two trading days of the announcement on December 8, Time Inc. stock rose by ten points to $59.

To wrap up the remaining technical details, and also to delay the requisite SEC notification until preparations for notifying the *Life* staff were complete, the board of directors delegated final authority to suspend publication to its executive committee. A ten-minute meeting in Heiskell's office the afternoon of December 7 satisfied that formality, determining that *Life*'s December 29 issue would be its last.

Life's entire crew, on both editorial and publishing sides, was summoned to a meeting at 10 o'clock the next morning when the news would be revealed, simultaneously with the public announcement and with suspension of trading in Time Inc. shares on the New York Stock Exchange.

Graves and his senior colleagues divided up the names on the editorial staff list and spent a good deal of the night telephoning, while Valk and his associates did likewise on the publishing side. "You really would have thought that evening that none of us had lost our jobs," Graves remarked later. "It was as if we were covering a story again, getting organized, feeling the excitement of a project we were doing together." One who was informed was Clare Boothe Luce—a courtesy to her as Luce's widow, and as one who had brought her own journalistic talents to bear on *Life* when Luce was working to create it. Reached at her home in Hawaii, she was not surprised by the news. "I was wondering," she told Charley Bear, "when you fellows would get around to it."

As the New York staff gathered the next morning, messages began going out to *Life* offices overseas, and to correspondents and photographers on distant assignments. Photographer George Silk, roaming the Himalayas for a picture essay on Nepalese game preserves, was reached by cable in Katmandu. Others, closer at hand, registered their dismay and disbelief when *Life*'s director of photography, Ronald Bailey, broke the news to them by phone. *Time* correspondent Marsh Clark covered the scene in the *Life* offices:

To John Loengard, on assignment in New Orleans for an essay on jazz, Bailey said, "Go ahead and finish the assignment tonight." To Alfred Eisenstaedt, one of those who helped make *Life* the great magazine it was, Bailey said softly, "Yes, Eisie, they decided to shut it. Yes, Eisie, I know it's unbelievable." Ralph Morse, who has been with the space program since its inception, called in from Cape Kennedy. "Sure, Ralph, why don't you go ahead and take that vacation," Bailey told him . . . "Yes, it's dead," Bailey said mournfully to Bill Eppridge, calling from Los Angeles. "Come on in and we'll have a drink," he told John Zimmerman.

The staff meeting was emotional, at times tearful. Heiskell's eyes glistened as he recalled his own days on *Life*, and the magazine's achievements. Graves was unable to get through the final words of his written speech, and even Valk, a publisher not known for sentimentality, was so choked up he could barely say his lines. The following week, more businesslike considerations prevailed; *Life*'s final issue had yet to be put together, and the job search for *Life* staffers—the 320 survivors out of a group that once numbered double that—had to be organized. In the end, and with the help of a hiring freeze imposed on other divisions of the company, many were accommodated, more or less satisfactorily.

Dated December 29, 1972, appearing on the newsstand just before Christmas, *Life*'s final issue—the last of 1,864 published since the magazine's founding in November 1936—was devoted to a review of the year in pictures. The cover was a montage; tucked in the lower right-hand corner, inserted by the layout staff, was the word Goodbye. At the front and back of the magazine were farewell messages from Donovan and Graves, noting the large and generous outpouring of letters from readers regretting its closing. "People took *Life*'s closing very personally; some are already saying they will always remember just where they were when they heard the news," Donovan wrote, adding a reminder that this was not necessarily the last they would hear of *Life*. "We still own the name *Life*, of course, and it is not impossible that the familiar red-and-white logotype will reappear someday on a new kind of Time Inc. magazine."

A Marriage in Texas

NOT ONLY IN THE PUBLISHING TRADE, the announcement on February 15, 1973, came as a jolt: Time Inc., the Manhattan-based publisher of *Time*, *Fortune*, *Sports Illustrated*, the recently suspended *Life* and the newly launched *Money* magazine, publisher also of Time-Life Books, was merging with Temple Industries, producers of lumber, plywood and other building materials, headquartered in Diboll, Texas. Within hours of the announcement, an executive of the Madison Fund, which held almost $5 million in Time Inc. stock, telegraphed Heiskell:

> URGENTLY REQUEST THAT YOU RECONSIDER THE TEMPLE
> MERGER . . . YOU ARE NOT A BUILDING MATERIALS COMPANY.
> HISTORY STRONGLY INDICATES THAT MANAGEMENTS ARE
> UNSUCCESSFUL IN FIELDS FOREIGN TO THEIR NORMAL
> BUSINESS . . . AS AN OWNER OF 90,000 SHARES OF TIME INC. I
> HAVE BEEN VERY PLEASED WITH AND AN ARDENT SUPPORTER
> OF THE CORPORATION'S MANAGEMENT. THIS MOST RECENT
> MOVE LEAVES ME DISILLUSIONED. PLEASE RECONSIDER OR I
> MAY HAVE TO.

The investment firm of Loeb, Rhoades rendered a similar verdict in an internal memorandum:

The timing of the acquisition of Temple Industries by Time Inc. is wrong and should lead to a dilution of Time Inc.'s earnings, which are now in a good uptrend following the suspension of *Life* magazine. We view the merger, therefore, as untimely.

Around the Time & Life Building also, as Heiskell acknowledged, "there was much upset. This was viewed as nearly treason to the cause." *Life*'s disappearance had hit Time Incers hard, raising questions about the company's future; the Temple merger raised more. *Fortune* staffers at least saw humor in the news. They plastered their office doors with fanciful new titles in what they imagined might be the new Time Inc.: "Vice President for Leaves, Twigs and Bark," "Branch Manager."

Ultimately, those who questioned the Temple merger were proved partly right. But not because Temple was alien to Time Inc.'s present interests. The problem was, rather, that soon after the merger the building materials industry fell into a decline that persisted through the 1970s. Temple, strong and excellently managed, suffered less than many of its competitors, but it could not avoid suffering—and neither could Time Inc. As the lean years continued, an unhappy fact about the nature of the forest-products business came home to Time Inc. Timber and wood pulp were commodities, basically indistinct from similar products made by others, the price determined by factors beyond the company's control.

The widespread surprise that greeted the Temple merger when it was first broached suggested that many people, in and out of the company, were only vaguely aware that for years Time Inc. had been making products from the trees of east Texas and that these operations had given a considerable lift to corporate profits. Even the Wall Street analysts who followed Time Inc. paid scant attention.

It had all begun decades earlier, in the 1930s, when treasurer Charlie Stillman was roaming the country seeking paper supplies for *Life*. Stillman found great potential in the eastern Texas holdings of the Houston Oil Company and in 1941, Time Inc. began buying Houston Oil stock. Eleven years later, the two companies formed a joint venture, the East Texas Pulp and Paper Company—Eastex, as it was universally known. By 1956, Time Inc. had become the sole owner of this company, which operated a fast-expanding mill at Evadale, and possessed 660,000 acres of nearby timberland. Eastex's profit performance was chiefly owing to the skillful guidance of

R.M. (Mike) Buckley, who had been hired away from a Washington paper firm to run Eastex a few months after its formation; he ran it until he retired in 1975. A sharp-eyed, sharp-featured man, Buckley was, in Heiskell's recollection, "a star dictator." He wanted minimum interference from Time Inc.'s faraway headquarters, and he reported back only the minimum necessary information. Given Buckley's success, the arrangement satisfied all parties. Producing a wide variety of pulp and paper—virtually none of it for the Time Inc. magazines, other grades being more profitable—Eastex, during its first 15 years of operation, tripled production and raised pretax income by $15 million to more than $17 million. In 1971, a poor year in the magazine business, Eastex was the source of 34 percent of Time Inc.'s pretax profits. The following year, the last one before the Temple merger and a much better year for magazines, the figure was 31 percent.

Eastex and Temple were neighbors. Temple owned almost as much land as Eastex, about 475,000 acres. In 1970 Eastex sold 25,500 acres of its holdings as part of Rayburn Country, a land development subsidiary, to Temple Industries; this and other land sales since 1960 reduced Eastex's acreage to 585,000 by 1972. The two companies' holdings, mainly along the Neches River, were intermingled.

Temple was by far the older enterprise. It had been founded by Thomas Lewis Latané Temple, 34, an Episcopal minister's son who in 1893 had bought 7,000 acres of pinewoods from a man named J.C. Diboll. The land was cheap; the area had been settled mainly by farmers, who considered uncleared land next to worthless. Temple built a sawmill and, because of the remoteness of the site, which is about a hundred miles north of Houston, also built a settlement for the workers, which he named Diboll.

Temple's firm, the Southern Pine Lumber Company, was one of several timber empires built in the area around that time. Temple outlasted most of them, one reason being that he was determined from the beginning not to run out of trees. Consistently buying more land than he cleared, Temple cut only selectively, leaving some timber standing. By the time he died in 1935, Southern Pine owned more than 200,000 acres of land.

In the following years the company flourished, remaining always in family hands. By 1972 it was being run, still from Diboll, by Arthur Temple, 52, grandson of the founder. Standing just over six feet tall and built as solidly as a bear, Arthur had the confidence and daunting manner of a man with nearly total control over a large business and a small Texas town (population 3,557). At the same time, he could turn on an irresistible, softly drawling Texas charm. For relaxation he loved to go hunting or fishing deep in the woods. But he resented being thought of as some sort of back-country yahoo. He pointed out that his father and uncle had both attended Williams College, and he had been exposed to New York and the eastern seaboard by summers spent at his maternal grandparents' home in Quogue, on Long Island. Temple considered himself a progressive on matters of race relations and minority hiring. "We were among the first to integrate down here," he said, recounting the example of a local café:

> One day the lady who ran a little restaurant down here for us called me up all hysterical. Now we had blacks in the mills by this point and our school was integrated too. But the restaurant had been quiet. She called hysterical telling me that "We've had word that some of those civil rights people are on their way over here to eat. What'll I do?" "Well," I told her, "that's easy. Serve 'em." "Well," she said, "what if my waitresses won't serve them?" That was possible in those days. So I told her, "Well, if the waitresses refuse to serve them, you give 'em menus and call me up. Lottie [his wife] and I will come down there and serve them ourselves. But before you call, make sure you tell those waitresses that we're coming."

The restaurant was integrated from then on.

At work, Temple indulged a boss's quirks. From his desk a small sign shouted: Do It RIGHT, But Do It RIGHT NOW. He constantly chewed on a cigar but only occasionally lit it. He was almost completely bald and wore a hat most of the time. Business suits were not his idea of comfortable clothing, and on the average day in Diboll there was no need to wear one.

Temple had known from youth what he wanted to do with his life, and college had not held much allure for him. He had attended the University of Texas at Austin for a year and the following fall had enrolled at Williams, but he left after a week. "Truth was, I wanted to get married, and in my family if that's what you want, they just say, 'OK, that's your decision. But if you do it, you should get a job and be prepared for it.' I just wanted to get to work and start earning some money. I don't want to sound like a know-it-all or anything, but I really wasn't learning anything." Temple felt differently, however, about his World War II service as an enlisted man in the

Navy: "The best thing that ever happened to me. It taught me humility in spades."

Joining the family firm as a common laborer, Temple became a bookkeeper, then manager of a lumberyard. He also formed a little construction company and a concrete company of his own, and in 1948 took leave of absence from Southern Pine to give them full-time attention. "I was only gone a couple of months when my cousin, Henry Temple, died. Now he had been running the mill at Diboll. The family got together and they asked me to come back and run the mill. I was only 28 years old when that happened. But I did it. Eventually I folded my own companies into Southern Pine."

It soon became apparent that Temple was a superb manager. As *Fortune* pointed out in an admiring item in 1960, he re-engineered the sawmill at Diboll so that 1,000 feet of lumber could be produced in 12 man-hours instead of 40. He renovated his company's old railroad line between Diboll and Lufkin, then arranged for its use by an industrial subdivision in Lufkin that he had sponsored. He moved the company's headquarters from Texarkana, where his grandfather had set up the company, to Diboll. He began selling to workers the company-owned housing they had been forced to rent for years, and helped them set up a credit union so they could borrow from themselves instead of the company. And while sales had been stagnant for several years when he took over, he quadrupled them within a decade. Temple diversified his company into mortgage banking, real estate and the manufacture of mobile homes, furniture and building materials such as wall paneling and fiberboard. He also renamed it. By 1972 Temple Industries had 3,800 employees in plants and offices, principally in the South, and earned profits of $9.6 million on sales of $99.6 million. Time Inc., in comparison, that year had 10,000 employees, netted $22.4 million on sales of $511 million.

Being in similar businesses in the same region, Temple and Time Inc. were involved with each other in many ways for many years. Arthur Temple's first encounter with a Time Incer was not only pleasant, it was profitable. In the early 1950s Stillman, the architect of Eastex, was a guest at a Temple hunting lodge called Scrappin' Valley. Eastex was then still jointly owned by Time Inc. and Houston Oil, and during an early morning walk around the Scrappin' Valley lake Stillman explained to Temple how he hoped that someday Houston Oil would break up, with Time Inc. taking over Eastex. Temple liked the sound of that scenario and soon bought Houston Oil stock, at around $17 a share. When the breakup was announced a few years later, the shares were going for $155 each.

Others at Time Inc., including Andrew Heiskell, became acquainted with, and impressed by, Temple at the annual conferences on housing sponsored by *House & Home* in the 1950s.

In addition to the personal acquaintanceships, there was a substantial business link between Eastex and Temple arising out of their differing needs for wood. Temple used mostly saw timber—large pines and hardwood suitable for cutting up into lumber or for use in plywood. Eastex mainly needed pulpwood—smaller trees that can be hacked into chips and sawdust and eventually turned into paper. Each company thus had some of what the other needed; Temple was the principal buyer of Eastex saw logs, and the second largest supplier to Eastex of pine chips and sawdust.

In the early 1970s, each company saw powerful reasons for merging. Turning trees into lumber produces quantities of chips and sawdust, which Temple Industries wasn't using to make paper, though it did sell some to papermakers, such as Eastex. But Temple thought that his company should be making every important product that comes from trees. "In the forest-products business, we like to use every single scrap of that wood," he pointed out, "and I needed a paper mill." But to build a mill would be staggeringly expensive.

Another factor that sharpened Temple's interest in a merger was that his son, Arthur III (known as Buddy), was mapping out a career in politics, not lumber. When asked, he told his father frankly that he was not interested in running the family firm. Accordingly, Temple began looking for a large papermaker with which to merge. In 1971 he negotiated seriously with the Champion Paper Company, but at a late stage that deal fell through because an agreement on price could not be reached; a prime concern of Temple's was the size of Champion's West Coast timber reserves.

Time Inc., meanwhile, had concerns of its own. Mike Buckley would turn 65 in 1974, and there was no one in Eastex's ranks who looked like a promising successor. In addition, a Temple merger with a major paper company like Champion could deprive Eastex of an important source of sawdust and chips. By merging with Temple, Eastex would not only protect that source, it would also gain access to hardwood and pine pulpwood Temple had in good supply.

It is impossible to say who first conceived of the merger. Considering the logic from both companies' points of view, it seems most likely that it occurred to several people independently. In Heiskell's memory, "I said to Mike [Buckley], 'Why don't we buy Temple?'

317

Mike said, 'Jesus, I thought that you guys felt you had enough with Eastex.' I said, 'Not necessarily; I am beginning to like trees.' " Arthur Temple recalled taking a fishing trip with Mike Buckley in the summer of 1972, during which they talked about a merger. "I told Mike that I'd like to merge with somebody and that I'd like for him to talk to somebody up in New York about it." Buckley remembered first talking to Temple about the idea sometime around 1970; then on and off, as Temple considered Champion and other prospects. A turning point came in the autumn of 1972 when Buckley told Temple that Time Inc. management felt the time was ripe for such a move. As Buckley put it, "We might as well get married. We've been sleeping together for years."

More important than who thought up the deal was that these three men were soon pushing it. Heiskell had asked the investment firm of White, Weld to prepare a confidential analysis of Temple Industries. The resulting study confirmed three advantages of merging: Temple's strong management would balance Eastex's weakness in that area; the merged company would gain economies from joining their contiguous timberlands; and Eastex could expand more cheaply by merging with Temple than by doing it from scratch.

Buckley, after conferring with New York, proposed to Temple that his company merge with Eastex. Temple didn't think that was even worth considering: "I told him that I wanted to merge with Time itself, not with any subsidiary."

Time Inc. accepted that condition, and the negotiations continued into 1973. Leading Time Inc.'s team was chief financial officer Dick McKeough; his counterpart from Temple Industries was Clifford Grum, who had left a Dallas bank four years earlier to become Temple's financial vice president. White, Weld produced another report on Temple in January and again came to a favorable conclusion: "Despite the company's exposure to residential and nonresidential construction activities, with the former expected to be generally flat through the balance of this decade, we feel that Temple is in an excellent position to continue its fine rate of growth." The reasons, in White, Weld's opinion, were that Temple was integrated forward into products like wall paneling and backward into raw materials; that the company was technologically innovative in the production of plywood and particleboard; and that its management, led by chief operating officer Joe C. Denman Jr., a veteran of 22 years with Temple, was excellent. Heiskell and Shepley were well aware of Temple's vulnerability to cyclical trends in construction,

318

but they believed that federal housing subsidies would even out those ups and downs in the future.

In February the two companies signed letters of intent to merge by exchanging shares. All of Temple's stock—about 6.2 million shares, then valued at $129 million—would go to Time Inc. In return, Temple stockholders would receive half a share of Time Inc. for each Temple share. During the spring of 1973 Time Inc. and Temple Industries studied each other's operations, timber inventories and financial outlooks. Visits were exchanged, discussions held, necessary documents filed. Directors of both companies approved the exchange in August. There quickly followed a special meeting of Time Inc. stockholders and, in Diboll, of Temple stockholders. The deal was complete.

There were several immediate consequences. Arthur Temple and his first cousin, W. Temple Webber, chairman of Temple Industries' executive committee, were elected to the board of Time Inc. Arthur Temple and Mike Buckley split operating responsibility for the new company, which was to be called Temple-Eastex; Buckley felt that while Eastex was the bigger company, Temple's "old Texas" name should come first. Perhaps most important, the former shareholders of Temple Industries now owned about 30 percent of Time Inc. Since members of the family had owned more than half of Temple Industries, they now held at least 15 percent of Time Inc. The largest single holding, about 4 percent, belonged to Temple's aunt, Mrs. Georgie Temple Munz, then 82. Even the Luce Foundation, which had received the greatest portion of Henry Luce's stock when he died, now held only 10.9 percent.

The Temples' apparent new power over Time Inc. caused concern that this small group of Texans might now take to meddling in the magazine business. But those fears ignored some important facts. Relatives and former associates of Luce plus Time Inc.'s top management and the Luce Foundation collectively owned from 18 to 20 percent of the company—a safe margin. In any event Arthur Temple had no wish to become a publisher. He and Heiskell had already discussed the point.

Recalled Heiskell: "I said, 'What do you want to be?' Temple replied that he wanted to run his company for two or three years and then turn it over to Joe Denman. By that time Buckley would be 67 or 68 and Denman would get to run Temple-Eastex. I said, 'And what do you want to be at Time Inc.?' and he said, 'I would like to be like what Roy Larsen is now.' I said, 'You mean vice chairman in an avuncular fashion?' and he said, 'That's exactly what I want.' And that is exactly what happened." Jim Shepley—who was, according to Temple, "the key guy in making the Temple-Time tie-up work so well" during the middle and late '70s—described Temple as "a businessman who understands church-state," and "who never attempted to interfere with the magazines' role." Temple's considerable management talent was, indeed, to prove one of the most valuable assets Time Inc. received in the merger.

The merger had little effect at the operational level. Temple would continue to run itself just as it had. But it made sense for each company to have some representation in the other's camp. From New York to Diboll, therefore, went Time Inc. controller David Dolben, who became Temple-Eastex's financial vice president. Adjusting to life in east Texas turned out to be more pleasure than pain for Dolben and his family. "We just plunged right in. We didn't have any trouble. There was a delightful scarcity of Yankees in that area, so everyone welcomed us." Dolben and his wife returned to New York in 1979, when he became Time Inc.'s financial vice president. But their two daughters, who became adults during the family's time in Texas, liked it so much that they stayed.

Dolben was able to become financial vice president of Temple-Eastex because the previous holder of the job at Temple, Clifford Grum, came to New York as Time Inc.'s new treasurer. (Dolben ended up buying Grum's house in nearby Lufkin, Texas: "There weren't a lot of other places on the market," he explained.) Time Inc. management had got to know Grum during the merger negotiations, and they were impressed. "I had trouble understanding him because of his accent," recalled Heiskell, "but he struck me as being terribly savvy." When the merger went through, Heiskell told Temple, "This guy's got a real future. I'll steal him away from you." Temple's response: "Over my dead body." After Temple came around and Grum moved to New York, he earned a reputation as a brilliant dealmaker, adept at discerning what the other side wanted and reconciling it with Time Inc.'s wishes.

Temple-Eastex began life with promise. It turned out that 1974, the first full year in which Temple and Eastex were a combined unit, was a record year in the paper and paperboard industry. The division produced pretax profits of $52.8 million, a good deal more than the $44.3 million contributed by publishing, and 59 percent of Time Inc.'s pretax earnings. Furthermore, those forest-products profits proved to be the fastest growing in the company. If Temple and

Eastex had been a combined unit in 1973, their pretax profits would have been a healthy $39.8 million. The 1974 figure represented a 33 percent increase.

Temple Industries brought Time Inc. something that many, especially on Wall Street, thought it badly needed: greater tangible assets. Though on balance disapproving of the Temple merger, Wall Street at least saw one virtue in it. A typical publishing company owns practically nothing in the way of factories and machines; its most valuable assets, as the old saw has it, go down in the elevator every night. Already financially stronger than most publishers, Time Inc. had additional and hugely valuable physical assets in Eastex; now the Temple acquisition had nearly doubled those assets.

Indeed, Time Inc. presented just this argument to the two principal bond rating agencies, Standard & Poor's and Moody's, in the summer of 1975. The company was contemplating a bond issue and sought a high investment-grade rating so it could keep interest costs down. Time Inc.'s 60-page presentation to the rating agencies made a powerful case: even after this bond offering, and even counting no other assets but its land, the company's total long-term debt would represent less than $150 per acre. In fact the land, by conservative valuation, was worth $500 an acre. Impressed, the agencies gave Time Inc. a double-A rating, raising the company to a new level of respect in the financial community. The importance of the new assets was unquestionable: Thomas J. Watson Jr., chairman of the executive committee of IBM and a member of Time Inc.'s board, was only half joking when he proclaimed that he was delighted with Time Inc. stock "because there are three trees behind every share."

Together, the Temple and Eastex landholdings comprised 1.1 million acres of forest land, an area greater than the entire state of Rhode Island. After the merger, a further 27,000 acres were set aside for the federal government to acquire for the Big Thicket Natural Preserve, 85,000 acres of virgin bottomland forest along and west of the Neches River, authorized by Congress in 1974.

Congressional action had been contemplated for nearly a decade, and while the legislation was pending, Eastex and others had joined Temple in a voluntary moratorium on cutting in the Big Thicket area—"at considerable financial sacrifice in Temple Industries' case," Temple told a House subcommittee in 1973. The question, nonetheless, was a touchy one; Time Inc.'s dual role as publisher and forest landowner had already led to some uncomfortable intracorporate schisms.

In July 1970, in an article entitled "Moving in for a Land Grab," *Sports Illustrated* declared: "Lumber-industry attacks on public lands have long been notorious. Lumbermen's politicians fought creation of national forests, and today in those forests the industry gouges muddy labyrinths of roads, scalps whole sections and leaves impenetrable deserts of stumps and slash." Reading this, Eastex's Mike Buckley angrily protested to New York; the National Forest Products Association, of which Eastex was a member, sent a stream of letters and telegrams. Eventually, Heiskell, Donovan and Shepley were drawn in to defend *SI*'s position. Two years later, in April 1972, a *Life* article on the ivory-billed woodpecker—a rare, if not extinct, species that recently had been sighted in the Big Thicket area—noted the presence of loggers in that region, with a footnote mention, also, of Eastex's active reforestation work. (In a separate note to *Life* editors, writer Don Moser reported that the company with the best reputation among conservationists was Temple Industries.) Again Eastex complained; again it was necessary to reaffirm the Time Inc. magazines' editorial independence.

For all the corporate assets that Temple-Eastex's landholdings represented, the division's contribution to corporate profits was largely dependent on the performance of the building industry, which, unfortunately, was then coming in for a series of hard knocks: the energy crisis beginning in late 1973 (and another one in 1979), the severe recession of 1974–1975, the beginning of double-digit inflation. With mortgage rates soaring, housing construction in the U.S. sagged.

In 1972, when Time Inc. and Temple began merger talks, new housing starts had totaled 2,379,000, the highest number recorded to date. It would also be the highest number for at least the next ten years. By 1975, housing starts had fallen to a little more than a million. Time Inc.'s 1975 presentation to Moody's and Standard & Poor's noted the decline and predicted that housing starts would recover to 2 million by late 1977. This forecast was right on target, but it failed to predict that this level too would be a peak. After remaining virtually unchanged in 1978, building starts plunged again in 1979, then fell further in 1980 and further still in 1981. The housing cycles that Heiskell and Shepley had hoped were a thing of the past proved instead to be worse than ever.

The effect on Temple-Eastex was predictable. Its building materials division lost money in 1974 and again in 1975, improved in 1976 and managed to earn a record pretax profit of $30 million in 1977, the year housing starts hit 2 million. The following year was the division's best ever: its pretax profit was $43.1 million. Then, however, came the inevitable decline, with pretax profits of only $15.2 million in 1979 and a pretax loss of $3.8 million in 1980.

While earnings were falling short of expectation, the need for capital investment far exceeded what had been anticipated at the time of the merger. This was partly an effect of higher-than-expected inflation, but there were operational reasons as well. In 1973 Eastex undertook a three-year, $65-million program to enlarge its Evadale mill; productive capacity was increased 15 percent. Regular maintenance of the plant suffered during expansion, however. By 1977 it was clear that large-scale renovation was necessary; a $100-million project, begun the following year, was completed in 1980. Temple bought a new particleboard plant for $9.5 million in 1978 and completed a new headquarters building in Diboll in 1979, in addition to modernizing many of its other plants for greater efficiency as the building materials market shrank. Chiefly because of the demands of the capital-intensive forest-products operations, Time Inc.'s capital needs, which in 1975 had been projected at $258 million over the next four years, actually came to $448 million.

In September 1975, Mike Buckley, who had turned 66, began the transition into retirement by assuming the new position of vice chairman of Temple-Eastex. Arthur Temple, who had been president and chief of operations, replaced Buckley as chief executive of Temple-Eastex and group vice president, for forest products, of Time Inc.

A few months later Temple unwittingly gave a celebrated and much regretted interview to *The Village Voice*, the New York weekly. It happened when an old acquaintance, William D. Broyles Jr., then editor of *Texas Monthly* (later, briefly, editor of *Newsweek*), telephoned to ask if he could come by Temple's Diboll office and chat. Broyles arrived with another man—"a scruffy-looking guy; I thought he was Bill's driver or something," Temple recalled. Broyles's guest sat in on the chat, during which "Bill asked me if I was going to move Time Inc. down to Texas. It was kind of a joke. I explained to him that there were parts of that operation that just couldn't be anywhere else but New York. Then I said that, of course, there were pieces of it that it probably wouldn't make any difference if they were in Oshkosh or Atlanta. We rambled some more but it was just hypothetical speculation. I understood that this whole thing was off the record and really just a chat with Bill. Wham!"

The "scruffy-looking guy" turned out to be Alexander Cockburn, a left-wing columnist for the *Voice*, and he wrote a dead-serious article about the chat. He detailed the Temple family's extensive ownership of Time Inc. stock, then quoted Temple as saying "I don't see why Time Inc. should be in New York" and wondering why *Fortune* couldn't be in Boston or Atlanta, *People* in Los Angeles, *Sports Illustrated* in St. Louis and *Money* in Austin. The article, appearing just a few weeks after the employees of Time-Life Books had been told they would be moving out of New York City to a lower cost location (see chapter 23), created an uproar in the Time & Life Building. Firm assurances that no such moves were planned quelled the panic, but Arthur Temple protested that "I just never said what they said I said, and even the few parts they got right, they twisted."

In accordance with his understanding with Andrew Heiskell about his role at Time Inc., Temple remained chief executive of Temple-Eastex for only a short time. In December 1977, at age 57, he turned that post over to Joe Denman, as planned, while remaining chairman of the Temple-Eastex board. In 1978 he joined Roy Larsen as an "avuncular" vice chairman of Time Inc. Avuncular may never have been the right adjective for the forceful Temple— "I'm avuncular with teeth" he once explained—but Time Inc.'s managers were glad to have him stay on the board. "He comes up once a month if the weather is all right," said Heiskell. "It works well, and we have an invaluable adviser." He was cherished, among other things, for his earthy metaphors. During a board discussion of a minor but bothersome problem, he remarked: "We'd better pull that snake out on the road and see how long it is before we try to kill it."

It was while serving as Temple-Eastex's chairman that Arthur Temple engineered the biggest acquisition in Time Inc.'s history up to then, larger even than the Temple acquisition itself. This was the Inland Container Corporation of Indianapolis, whose business was making corrugated boxes and containerboard. The impetus for the purchase came from a research report Temple-Eastex had commissioned in 1976, from the Stanford Research Institute, a leading consulting firm. Asked to identify the paper industry's areas of greatest promise, SRI recommended kraft linerboard, used in the manufacture of corrugated boxes. Demand was rising and would probably continue strongly upward for the next 20 years. Eastex might want to expand its operations in this area—it already had a packaging division—but a better idea, the report suggested, would be to buy an established, integrated producer.

There were several such companies, but Arthur Temple especially liked the looks of Inland. It was fourth largest in its industry, big enough to be strong but small enough to buy. It was highly integrated: with Mead Paper it jointly owned Georgia Kraft Co., which had 950,000 acres of trees. It owned 28 box manufacturing plants, and it owned companies that produced the ink and tape used in box-making. It was also well managed. Henry C. Goodrich and Clinton G. (Jack) Ames Jr., Inland's chairman and president respectively, had achieved one of the better records in the industry.

First conversations between Time Inc. and Inland in early 1977 were inconclusive, but by fall both sides were ready again. Negotiations continued through the winter, and by May 1978 a complicated deal had been struck. Time Inc. would exchange a fraction of a common share and a fraction of a newly issued preferred share for each Inland share, up to two-thirds of the total; for the rest of Inland's shares it would pay $35 each. The total price came to about $272 million. In urging Time Inc.'s board to approve these items, Arthur Temple pointed out that Inland's timber holdings alone were probably worth more than the cash and stock that Time Inc. was offering for the whole company. Approved by the board, the acquisition was completed on November 14, 1978.

The following year, Henry Goodrich resigned to become president of Southern Natural Resources, Inc. He remained on the Time Inc. board, to which he had been elected, as an outside director. Succeeding him at Inland was Jack Ames, 57, who was to run the company as long as Time owned it.

Wall Street's first reaction to news of the acquisition, the preceding May, had been suspicion. Time Inc. stock had immediately fallen a few points, with one stock analyst remarking that "Time's acquisition of Inland raises questions in people's minds as to what kind of equity they own. How much in the direction of a conglomerate does this company want to go?" Another thought that it was not a bad move, just not "as sexy, glamorous, or exciting" as the company's other recently planned or completed acquisitions closer to Time Inc.'s main interests, in publishing. But the stock recovered from that tumble, and over the next few years Inland performed better than expected. In 1979, its first full year as part of Time Inc., it turned in pretax profits of $43 million, nearly matching Temple-

Eastex's contribution. The next year, Inland's pretax profit jumped to $53.1 million.

The Inland acquisition completed Time Inc.'s portfolio of forest-products enterprises. By any standard they formed an impressive segment of the business, with sales in 1980 totaling $1.04 billion and pretax profits, though down from the year before, at $87.3 million—not much less than the $96.8 million Time Inc. earned in publishing. However, the capital needs of the forest-products operations were posing a problem for corporate finances. Even as the Inland Container acquisition was in train, Heiskell and Temple were already talking of the possibility of spinning off all these ventures into a separate corporate entity.

Changing Time

T HE YEAR 1968 had been one of extraordinary turbulence. In January the Tet offensive erupted in Vietnam. In April, Martin Luther King Jr. was assassinated; in June, Robert F. Kennedy. In May began the French student riots that nearly drove Charles de Gaulle from power. In August, Soviet tanks rumbled into Prague. That same month in Chicago, on the streets outside the Democratic National Convention, antiwar protesters fought televised battles with Mayor Richard Daley's police.

In the spring of that stormy year, Henry Grunwald succeeded Otto Fuerbringer as managing editor of *Time*. The impact of great events and the editorial challenge in covering them were very much on Grunwald's mind as he took over. At a staff dinner honoring his predecessor, he remarked: "I sometimes have an almost palpable sense of the world refusing to fit into our departments and sections, . . . of events trying to burst out of our neat organization, to burst out of the orderly measure of our columns. What is to be done about that? My notion is to let it happen . . . Let people and events and ideas struggle and push into new forms and new shapes in our pages, both physically and intellectually."

Happen it did. During Grunwald's editorship the *Time* formula was, in his word, "bent" into more new shapes than ever before. *Time*'s group journalism was modified with the appearance of signed pieces, some by outside contributors. *Time*'s focus shifted more toward issues and away from personalities. On occasion, virtually the entire magazine was devoted to a single subject. Noticeably, *Time* became more nuanced in its political judgments, less assertive in stating them. Major stories grew longer, more expository, moving *Time* further away from the charter that Luce and Hadden had drawn up for their magazine: to provide a quick, comprehensive news review. Looking back, on the occasion of *Time*'s 50th birthday in 1973, Grunwald declared: "We have had to revise the definition of what makes a newsmagazine."

Immediately spurring that revision was the competition of television, which he felt had now usurped *Time*'s original function. Speaking to a gathering of *Time* writers in Bermuda shortly after he took over as managing editor, Grunwald observed:

> *Time* began with a very brilliant, seemingly simple idea of being a weekly summary of the news. Well organized, reasonably clear, reasonably brief, for the famous "busy man" who was mentioned in the prospectus of the founding fathers.
>
> But actually . . . the job of *Time* was never quite that simple. There was always a tremendous amount of selection involved; a tremendous amount of comment through the selection; a tremendous amount of additional judgments and values given by the writing and, more recently, by the reporting. So that . . . we are really more than a newsmagazine, and have been for quite a while.
>
> But . . . TV has completely changed the conditions in which you sit down at a typewriter. There used to be a notion that people didn't really know about an event until they read about it in *Time*. I'm not sure that this was ever right, ever justified, but it certainly isn't now . . . .The kind of *Time* item that says little more than a radio or TV news bulletin . . . that merely pieces together a mosaic, no matter how orderly or attractive, of already reasonably familiar facts is no longer justified . . . Where we must truly succeed is in what we *add* to the familiar event.

Other factors besides television were, in Grunwald's view, impelling changes in *Time*: the competition of specialized publications catering to the particular interests of segments of *Time*'s audience; the fresh appeal of the so-called "new journalism," which was creating a reader taste for more personalized reporting; the challenge of better educated *Time* readers, "a great deal more sophisticated than they used to be and than we sometimes assume." Younger readers especially, Grunwald suggested, resisted *Time*'s pontifical tendencies; they evinced "a certain impatience with all oracles and voices of authority that are put forth perhaps too smartly and too blatantly." Vietnam was a case in point. Grunwald acknowledged that *Time*'s previously hawkish line—then in the process of change—had "alienated a lot of the younger readers." Although *Time*'s earlier position was "a defensible line at the time," he now felt it was "wrong . . . I say this in hindsight, honestly."

In December 1968, two months after his Bermuda talk, Grunwald met with *Time*'s overseas correspondents in Paris. And early in 1969, the Washington bureau correspondents convened at Airlie House in Virginia to discuss national coverage. These meetings, together with a conference that Fuerbringer had held with his senior and assistant managing editors in November 1967, at Easthampton, on Long Island, with Donovan in attendance, constituted an extended editorial review of *Time*, probably the most thorough self-examination the magazine had undergone in more than a decade.

Candor prevailed. The discussions were uninhibited. At Easthampton Donovan criticized the quality of *Time* writing. In Bermuda the writers in turn complained about the pressures, both personal and professional, imposed on them by the *Time* editing system; one unforeseen consequence of the Bermuda session was that it planted the seeds of a writers' rebellion that culminated, eight years later, in their joining the first editorial strike in Time Inc.'s history (see chapter 26).

Most clearly in evidence at the meetings was the extent of the ferment on *Time*, the widespread urge for experimentation, shared by editors, writers and correspondents. "Change is what seems to be on all our minds," Grunwald observed at Bermuda. "I don't think I was appointed managing editor of *Time* to preside over the status quo." Grunwald stated his own proposals for changes at *Time*—essentially, in its editorial approach:

> We must not break the formula, but bend the formula . . . The magazine must become more intelligent and, although I hate to use the word, more intellectual. By that I simply mean that we can make greater demands on the reader . . . greater demands on ourselves. [We] must really avoid oversimplifying complicated situations. We should never shy away from history, philosophy, or theory; at present we do shy away from these things quite a bit . . .

And above all, we must do much more to develop expertise

in many fields . . . This is . . . particularly true and urgent in the front-of-the-book sections, which I think are often quite shallow . . .

In addition to making *Time* more intelligent, I think we must make *Time* freer . . . Our journalism must become more personal—this goes for correspondents and writers . . .

I think we must render our judgments . . . in a different spirit. I think we must render them less arbitrarily, much more coolly and perhaps occasionally with a becoming sense of fallibility—which is not at all the same as being wishy-washy or qualifying everything. I also feel that we ought to counterpoint our own opinions, our own judgments, with quite a bit of opinion from the outside.

But this freer, more personal journalism, less arbitrary in its judgments, implied no abdication of the managing editor's authority; in this respect Grunwald was no different from any of his predecessors:

The editor of *Time* must substantially believe in the stories we print. He must be personally committed to them because otherwise he is . . . abdicating responsibility . . .

I can and must make certain decisions at *Time* . . . If there's a *Time* writer who feels that we are constantly and plainly wrong about an issue, he has the duty to come and argue with me . . . And if a *Time* writer finds that his deepest convictions are constantly violated by what *Time* prints, he should not work for us. I don't want mercenaries—we don't necessarily pay well enough to get mercenaries anyway.

Grunwald, who was 45 when he became managing editor, was a roundish man, slightly less than middle height, with crinkled gray hair, heavy-rimmed glasses and a deep, resonant voice in which only a trace of his native Vienna remained. Urbane, multilingual, fond of food, good wine and cigars, opera and the theater, a well-read man, intellectually self-assured, he commanded both respect and some fear from the staff.

Grunwald's career on *Time*, where he had spent his entire working life, was remarkable. His family background was theatrical, literary. His father, Alfred, was a prominent Viennese operetta librettist (*Countess Maritza*) and playwright; Henry had tried writing plays himself ("now mercifully lost"). When Nazi Germany annexed Austria in March 1938, Grunwald was forced, with other Jewish children, into classrooms in the old Vienna ghetto; his father was briefly jailed. That fall the Grunwalds fled to Paris. One lunchtime in June 1940, news came of the German army's breakthrough into northern France. Leaving the lunch dishes on the table, the Grunwalds got up and left, not even locking the apartment door behind them. They went to Biarritz and then by sea to Casablanca, bought their way back to Lisbon and thence aboard a refugee-crowded liner to America. The family finally arrived in New York in September 1940.

Assiduous afternoons at the movies improved Grunwald's English immensely, and in 1944 he graduated Phi Beta Kappa from New York University, having edited the college paper and, on weekends, put in two ten-hour days as a copyboy at *Time*. Grunwald's first boss, *Time* research chief Content Peckham, remembered him as "driven, willing to work terribly hard" but also "terribly underfed"—a condition which, once cured, proved nonrecurring. Grunwald left for a few months to report for a New York trade-union paper, but returned to *Time*.

With his youth went little apparent modesty. At *Time* he was given to looking over the writers' copy and offering advice for improvement, which was not always well received. But Whittaker Chambers, then Foreign News editor, took a shine to Grunwald, encouraging him to test his hand at short items for print. The October 9, 1944, issue carried Grunwald's first published *Time* piece: 12 lines on the Soviets seeking artificial legs and arms from America for their maimed war veterans. The following year managing editor Tom Matthews gave him a formal tryout and in November 1945, still not 23, he appeared on the masthead as a contributing editor, then *Time*'s designation for its journeymen writers. That same month came his first cover story ("a nightmare"), a rush job on the opening of the Nuremberg trials—the first of more than 30 cover stories that Grunwald wrote, on subjects ranging from Pope Pius XII and T.S. Eliot to Ava Gardner and America's sexual revolution.

Fascinated but unacquainted with the American Midwest beyond having read about it, Grunwald took his first trip outside New York in 1947. A bylined piece in *Life* from Sinclair Lewis country, entitled "Main Street 1947," was the result. Very early also, he began forming some critical ideas about *Time*. A request from the managing editor for staff comments on the magazine loosed a 28-page reply from Grunwald, listing the "things that disturb me about *Time*," notably its "weekly sameness . . . signs of threatening shallowness"—an agenda of matters that Grunwald returned to during his own managing editorship, 20 years later.

In January 1951, barely 28, Grunwald became *Time*'s youngest senior editor. He was not yet entirely rid of his playwriting ambitions. Taking a leave of absence, he retreated to rural Connecticut for one last try. After six months he was back, his career uncertainties gone: "I discovered that journalism was something I was pretty good at and playwriting was something I wasn't." He was already catching the editor-in-chief's eye; scribbles in Luce's hand in the company archives indicate he was watching Grunwald.

Luce made his feelings known more directly when, in the early 1960s, he summoned Grunwald to dinner alone at his apartment. Through a secretarial mix-up, Grunwald arrived a half hour late, to find Luce highly irritated. Luce soon calmed down. "Anyway," Grunwald recalled, "he said to me, 'A little bird tells me you're restless.' I told him, 'I *am* restless. I've been here a long time now and I've seen people who've spent years here and then find themselves wandering along the corridors of power and suddenly realize that they haven't made it.' " Luce reassured him: "I think you should know that you *have* made it—at least in my mind." Grunwald suggested others who might stand ahead of him at *Time*; Luce cut him off curtly: "Not necessarily so." "He also asked me if I'd like to go to *Fortune* and become managing editor there, in due course. I said no, I didn't have that in mind . . . .We started to talk about China and various other things." The conversation was not relayed to Donovan.

As a writer Grunwald was graceful, versatile and fast; in an emergency he could be counted on to deliver, for almost any department of the magazine. As senior editor he could, and often did, dictate entire stories—an unnerving experience for associates who listened outside his office as he strolled around the room, rumbling forth the paragraphs that for most writers and editors usually came only after agonizing hours at a typewriter. On one famous occasion, when a cover story on anxiety in *Time*'s Medicine section failed to come off, Grunwald was summoned for a salvage job; overnight and largely out of his own head, he dictated 6,000 words of a new version.

In 1966, Grunwald was named an assistant managing editor. His appointment as managing editor two years later was pretty much in the cards. As Otto Fuerbringer had edited the *Time* that Luce wanted, Grunwald was the editor to effect the changes Donovan aimed at. In their discussions, Grunwald recalled, Donovan had spoken of a "less centralized" *Time*, less reflecting one man's views. Donovan said later: "I wanted more openness—more openness to the staff members who had a different point of view from what had

332

been expressed in *Time*. I wanted more openness internally, and in print." He conceded that in managerial style, the change proved not very great. "Managing editors put a powerful stamp on the magazine. Henry's managing editorship was different from Otto's but within a year people who were anti-Otto found that the new managing editor also had strong ideas and they found that they didn't like that either."

In other respects, Grunwald's accession signaled a different approach for *Time*. The preoccupations of the New York intellectual, literary, theatrical scene were Grunwald's also—"Henry was *urban*," one *Time* senior editor characterized him. There was a strong philosophical bent to his editing; coming to the United States from abroad, he was particularly fascinated by what Luce had called "the American Proposition"—those tenets of government, the product of the American historical experience, which Luce felt had given the U.S. a special global role to play. This conviction was to be repeatedly examined during Grunwald's editorship. In his politics, Grunwald was fairly conservative, positioning himself "a little right of center," and the magazine reflected this viewpoint, which had been Luce's and *Time*'s under its preceding managing editors. But the tone of voice changed under Grunwald.

"*Time* can still be very, very opinionated, God knows," Grunwald remarked later. "One didn't necessarily disagree with the substance [of *Time*'s policy]. But that tone was so polemical, so heavy, that it undercut *Time*'s credibility . . . I think this undermined, paradoxically, the very message that *Time* was trying to deliver. *Time* changed, of course, primarily under Donovan's prodding . . . It became more evenhanded and, I like to think, much fairer. I think I had something to do with it too."

With Grunwald's accession, James Keogh moved up from assistant managing editor to executive editor. Three months later he took leave to work in the Nixon campaign. The following January he joined Nixon's White House staff as research chief, a post he kept until Nixon named him head of the United States Information Agency in late 1972.

After Keogh's departure, senior editor Edward L. Jamieson, 39, took over as Grunwald's deputy. In addition to relying on him for many administrative chores, Grunwald considered Jamieson "crucial to the magazine." Something of a father-confessor to the staff, even at his young age, the Boston-born Jamieson had a keen if understated sense of humor but a stiffly formal manner. He was conspicuous around the *Time* offices for never removing his jacket at work; friends wondered if he wore it to bathe. In April 1969 Jamieson was named assistant managing editor and in 1976, executive editor.

In November 1969, senior editor Richard M. Seamon, 50, became the other assistant managing editor. A Marine Corps pilot in the Pacific during the war, Seamon was a frustrated novelist (three unpublished efforts) and former editor at the Rand Corporation. He had also worked briefly for *The New Yorker*. At *Time* he was known as an expert in science and sport and established a reputation as an expeditious if somewhat explosive administrator; in 1975 he was named head of Time Inc.'s editorial services.

Changes in the *Time* format began immediately under Grunwald's editorship. Within the first month, there was poetry. To go with the reopening of Belmont Park, Rolfe Humphries, the classicist and racing buff, contributed two columns of verse evoking the sights, sounds and mood of the historic racetrack:

> *"Riders up!" The bugle sounds First Call*
> *All eastward streams the rank processional . . .*
> *Let our eyes close, our memories watch again*
> *Fields of our favorites, from Amblecane*
> *To Zev, parading to the post, the bright*
> *Silk stable colors shining in the light . . .*

Early the following year *Time* ran its first fiction: a tale of religious harassment in the Soviet Union entitled "The Easter Procession" by Alexander Solzhenitsyn, to accompany a report in the World section on the first appearance in the West of the Russian writer's now famous novel, *The Gulag Archipelago*.

Signed opinion by outside contributors commenced with excerpts from a lecture given by Urban Coalition chairman John W. Gardner—a declaration for reforming government and society entitled "Toward a Self-Renewing Society"—which *Time* carried in April 1969 as a two-page Essay under Gardner's name. Intermittently over the following years, other signed Essays by outside contributors were to appear in *Time*'s pages, as were verbatim, question-and-answer interviews with newsworthy figures, a form of reporting that *Time*, with its preference for pithy summary, had previously shied away from.

With the introduction of a new section, Behavior, in January 1969, *Time*'s back of the book was expanded further. The new section, devoted to the burgeoning field of the behavioral sciences—of

which the growing popular interest in psychology was one facet—
was one of six sections added to *Time*'s list of contents during Grunwald's editorship. Dance was introduced in April 1969 and ran intermittently as the occasion warranted; Environment began in August
1969; Economy, an offshoot of the Business section to report on
broad questions of economic policy, in September 1971; Sexes, to
cover what *Time* described as "the oldest topic in the world and in
some respects the newest," in January 1973. The following November, with the onset of the Mideast oil crisis, an Energy section was
created. One old section, Show Business, first created in 1958 as a
catch-all for television and other forms of popular entertainment,
was revived in November 1969. (It was in Show Business that *Time*,
in January 1973, ran the cover story that provoked the greatest
reader response—most of it outrage—in the magazine's history. A
five-page description, with appropriate nude photography, of Mar-
lon Brando's sexually explicit movie, *Last Tango in Paris*, the story
elicited 12,211 letters to the editor, including 6,725 cancellations and
nonrenewals of subscriptions.)

One innovation failed—an attempt in August 1974 to reshape the
Letters section, and make it into a sort of miniature op-ed page, carrying brief commentary of current interest by authoritative or well-
known figures. Retitled Forum, it was moved from its old position
up front amid the advertisements to a new center position following
the main news sections. Forum proved difficult to sustain. Not
enough usable commentary came in voluntarily; contributions had
to be solicited; after a few months, the section moved back to its old
spot, and later to its old title.

Other innovations were more successful. By long custom, the
Nation section had led off the magazine with the major national,
usually Washington, story of the week. Starting in October 1969, a
page of American Notes—short pointed news items, frequently serving as the basis for brief political or social commentary—became the
Nation section's regular lead. That same year saw the first use in
Time of public opinion polls, conducted by an outside polling firm,
to accompany stories on a variety of subjects: Vietnam, the nation's
changing morality, Chappaquiddick, public confidence in the press.

More interesting journalistically was the creation, also in 1969, of
the *Time* Board of Economists. The idea came out of Business editor Marshall Loeb's service (on leave from Time Inc.) with the
Hubert Humphrey campaign. He observed how academic experts
assisted the candidate in drafting economic policy positions. He
thought a similar group could serve to fill *Time*'s "policy

gap . . . We journalists didn't know in advance about new policies. We needed to learn about these proposals when they were in the process of gestation . . . when they were being debated."

Recruited by Loeb to reflect the spectrum of economic thought, members of the board gathered first in October 1969, for a day of roundtable discussions with *Time* editors. Their dialogue, on two topics that were to remain uppermost in American minds over the years to come—inflation and unemployment—was excerpted for a story in the Business section. The panel, meeting four times yearly, became a continuing source of economic intelligence, pointing the way to sometimes quite prescient *Time* stories. From the start, the board attracted distinguished participants, who were to include seven past or future chairmen of the President's Council of Economic Advisers.* Similar boards were recruited later for *Time*'s Canadian, European and Asian editions.

Nixon's inauguration in January 1969 brought about a radical bending of *Time*'s customary format: a special section dealing with a single subject in greater depth and at greater than cover-story length. Entitled "To Heal a Nation," the special section was a 20-page exploration of the problems dividing the American people as the Nixon administration took office, with suggested paths to their solution. Forty reporters contributed, and the Washington bureau file alone was three inches thick. One unkind critic suggested *Time* had not so much set the task before the country as a task before the reader. In July came another special section, "To the Moon," 14 pages on the historic lunar landings. In December seven pages entitled "From the '60s to the '70s: Dissent and Discovery," appraised the character of the decade just ending ("a romantic era . . . in mystical search for a shortcut to Utopia") and probed the likely nature of the next ("a search for goals").

The following April, *Time* went a step further and devoted virtually an entire issue to a single subject: "Black America, 1970." The problem of race relations "has become so crucial to American survival that it demands unusual efforts of analysis and understanding," the Publisher's Letter declared. That unusual effort consisted of an examination, section by section throughout the magazine, of the status, accomplishments and problems of American blacks. As an

---

*The seven: Walter Heller, Arthur Okun, Alan Greenspan, Murray J. Weidenbaum, Charles Schultze, Martin Feldstein and Beryl Sprinkel. Others who served on the *Time* Board of Economists between 1969 and 1980 were Otto Eckstein, David Grove, Robert Nathan, Joseph Pechman, Lester Thurow and Robert Triffin.

336

Richard Clurman, chief of correspondents 1960-69.

Murray Gart, editor of the Washington *Star* 1978-81. He was chief of correspondents and head of the Time-Life News Service 1969-78, with the title of assistant managing editor.

Otto Fuerbringer, *Time* managing editor 1960-68, inspects a sculpture created for the magazine's cover. To the left is James Keogh, *Time* assistant managing editor 1961-68. The sculptor is Robert Berks.

Time **correspondents during Watergate hearings, 1973.** Back row: Simmons Fentress, Stanley Cloud, Dean Fischer, David Beckwith. Front row: Neil MacNeil, Hays Gorey.

onald Kriss, *Time* assistant
anaging editor 1979-83,
ecutive editor 1983- .

chard Duncan, chief of corre-
ondents and assistant
anaging editor *Time* 1978- .

Time senior editor Edward Jamieson in Saigon in 1968.
Jamieson became an assistant managing editor in 1969 and
executive editor in 1976.

chard Seamon, assistant
anaging editor *Time* 1969-75.

Hugh Sidey, Washington bureau chief 1969-77 and Washington
contributing editor 1977- . His column, "The Presidency,"
appeared in *Life* 1966-72 and from then on in *Time*.

Selecting pictures at *Time*.
Ray Cave (pointing), managing
editor 1977-   . Left to right:
Rudolf Hoglund, art director; Irene
Ramp, deputy art director; Jason
McManus, assistant managing editor
1975-78, executive editor 1978-83.

James Bell, correspondent 1942-80;
John Steele (foreground), chief of the
Washington bureau 1958-69.

Henry Grunwald (foreground), managing editor 1968-77. Left to right: John Elson, assistant managing editor 1982- ; Charles Jackson (hidden), makeup chief; Arnold Drapkin, picture editor.

Ed Magnuson, a *Time* senior writer since 1974, has written over 100 cover stories, including 20 on Watergate.

Sports Illustrated editors, July 1979.
Front row: Bob Ottum, Jeremiah Tax, Roy
Terrell (managing editor 1974-79),
Gilbert Rogin (managing editor 1979-84),
Kenneth Rudeen. Second row: Bob Brown,
Peter Carry, Scot Leavitt, Robert Creamer,
Sandy Padwe, Mark Mulvoy (managing
editor 1984-   ), Arthur Brawley.

Philip Howlett, *Sports Illustrated*
advertising sales director 1976-80,
and publisher 1980-83, Time Inc.
executive vice president 1983-   .

Andre Laguerre, managing editor *Sports Illustrated* 1960-74.

...rry Valk, publisher of *Sports Illustrated* 1965-69, of *Life* ...9-72, and of the magazine ...velopment group 1973-78.

Frank Deford, *Sports Illustrated* distinguished senior writer.

Neil Leifer, innovative photographer, *Sports Illustrated* 1972-78, *Time* since 1978.

Famous Faces of Forty Years

Towering Socialist Norman Thomas and Italian Actress Gina Lollobrigida reveal the refreshing diversity of TIME magazine cover subjects who gathered for TIME's 40th anniversary celebrations.

The party was at the Waldorf on May 6, 1963.

Celebrating *Time*'s 60th: Ralph Davidson, publisher 1972-78, and John Meyers, publisher 1978-

approach to a sensitive subject, the special issue was judged excellent by Heiskell, who was deeply involved with New York City's racial problems as co-chairman of the National Urban Coalition. Donovan had reservations. Grunwald thought single-subject issues of *Time* were something to be tried sparingly. It was two years before another one appeared; women were the subject.

Addressing the Time Inc. board, Donovan described the changes in *Time* as "perhaps not radical or startling in terms of what other publications have done, but quite sharp innovations for *Time*." A particularly sharp departure from *Time* tradition was the introduction in July 1970 of writers' bylines. Instituting bylines for *Time* writers—establishing their individual identity within the magazine's system of largely anonymous group journalism—was an emotional issue, long debated at *Time*. Correspondents already had long enjoyed occasional identification in print, and suffered fewer ego deprivations in any event; as Donovan once observed on a tour of the overseas bureaus: "You fellows are local celebrities." But for the writers cloistered in the New York office it was different. The Bermuda meeting had revealed much irritation over the lack of personal recognition. Senior editors were divided on the question: Would *Time* speak less authoritatively over the signature of a named individual?

Grunwald's proposal was that *Time*'s front-of-the-book news sections remain as they were—unsigned. For the back-of-the-book critical sections and the *Time* Essay, however, he felt there was a strong case for going ahead. Not because signed stories carried greater credibility with readers: "To the general reader . . . trust . . . is not in the men but in the institution." He found more persuasive the idea that younger readers especially liked "having a name attached . . . because it suggests a human voice, a human presence, and reduces the feeling of faceless anonymity that is supposedly so widely resented in our society." But the main reason for introducing bylines, Grunwald felt, "has to do with the ego and self-respect of the writers."

> The assumption is that they will be happier, more responsible and inspired to do better things. Putting it somewhat differently; it is felt that in these days of "participation," etc., it is simply untenable to preserve our tradition of anonymity. I consider this the most compelling argument of all . . .
>
> I am fully aware of the pitfalls. They include the possible dilution of the authority of *Time*, the conflict of responsibility between editors and writers . . .

The introduction of bylines in any section of the magazine obviously raises questions of responsibility. I think it must be made quite clear that responsibility remains with "the editors of *Time*."

Late in the following year, *Time* underwent a complete typographical redesign. The new look, unveiled with the January 3, 1972, issue, was created by art director Louis Glessmann, who had been recruited by Grunwald from *Parents* magazine. Changes began with *Time*'s name on the cover; in place of the classically elegant, rather understated lettering, a more assertive logotype, in the same type family but bolder and stronger, was substituted (the identifying subtitle, "The Weekly Newsmagazine," a fixture since 1923, had disappeared from the cover in 1968). The distinctive red border was trimmed slightly to enhance the cover illustration. Reflecting the now longer stories and larger pictures inside, *Time*'s headline type, unchanged since 1938, was also made bolder. Space opened up with wider margins between columns. Horizontal slashes of color, with drop-out white letters, set off the various departments. In a talk to the staff, Grunwald acknowledged the competitive necessity for the redesign: for an audience used to watching television, *Time* needed "more dramatic, more emphatic" presentation.

The total impact of these innovations was difficult to gauge. The publisher's circulation analysis indicated that readers favored *Time*'s increasing emphasis on issues over personalities. On the newsstand at least, subject covers sold slightly better than personality covers. *Time*'s less partisan political approach was noted by media critics (*Time*-watching remained a popular sport) and drew favorable comment. The staff generally welcomed *Time*'s new inclination toward qualified judgments but worried that there was a price to be paid—for one thing, in loss of the magazine's old flip brevity.

Early in Grunwald's editorship, Donovan had solicited a critique of the "new" *Time* from former assistant managing editor Tom Griffith, now editor of *Life*. In responding, Griffith balanced substantive pluses against what he considered stylistic minuses. "*Time* is now entitled to trust," Griffith wrote. "But this great gain has been achieved at some expense . . . a heavier magazine . . . If there is now a prevailing *Time* style, it is perhaps two parts *Fortune* (lucid, sensible, all encompassing, even-gaited, passion free) and one part jocular contemporary . . . This is certainly not the bad old *Time*, but even that which is now lighter and jocular in style often lacks what was good about the bad old *Time*: its unexpectedness, its freshness, its pertness." In notes on Griffith's memo, Grunwald dissented strongly.

A more irritating criticism was the suggestion, by some outside commentators, that *Time*'s editorial changes were a reaction to the competition from *Newsweek*. This touched a sensitive point. For *Newsweek*, long in the shadow of *Time*, had emerged as a formidable challenger for both audience and advertising. *Newsweek* had once been the alternative magazine for readers who "hated *Time*," and the alternative buy for advertisers looking for cheaper page rates than *Time*'s. Now, editorially invigorated, *Newsweek* had acquired an identity of its own; it was regarded by Madison Avenue space buyers as the "hot book," while *Time* found itself somewhat on the defensive.

Newsweek's revival owed a lot to Washington *Post* president Philip Graham, who bought the magazine from the Astor estate in 1961, and to Graham's widow Katharine, who took over the company following Graham's suicide in 1963. The new proprietors invested substantially in the property, raising salaries and hiring new editorial and publishing staff, some from Time Inc.

Editorially, *Newsweek* remained a smaller operation than *Time*. In 1968 it was estimated that *Newsweek* was still spending only half *Time*'s outlay on its news service. *Newsweek* compensated by improvisation; Osborn Elliott, the former *Time* Business writer who became *Newsweek*'s managing editor in 1959, wrote that he and his two executive editors were known among the staff as the Flying Wallendas (after a team of trapeze artists) for the editorial acrobatics they had to perform in getting the magazine out each week.* To attract attention, *Newsweek* began using billboard covers, with splashier layouts and bigger headlines over the stories inside. *Newsweek* also began hiring columnists outside its own staff, picking up Walter Lippmann from the dying New York *Herald-Tribune*, and adding more well-known names later. In 1966, it introduced bylines in its back-of-the-book sections, claiming in an aggressive promotional campaign that *Newsweek* was—in implied contrast to *Time*— "the newsweekly that separates fact from opinion." *Newsweek* also declared itself "the most quoted newsweekly."

At *Time*, the inclination on the editorial side was to treat *Newsweek* with disdain. Its "most quoted" claim drew from Fuerbringer the comment that it was "like the Chicago *Tribune* calling itself the world's greatest newspaper"; as for *Newsweek* separating fact from

The World of Oz (Viking Press, 1980).

opinion, "if they did, they would be unreadable." Grunwald was less harsh, but still dismissive. Reacting to newspaper suggestions that the format changes he was then instituting in the magazine reflected the *Newsweek* influence, Grunwald told the assembled *Time* correspondents in Paris:

> Most of you know that I have never believed in underrating *Newsweek*, and I have always thought it rather silly to automatically assume that anything they do is poor, and second best to us. I think they have been very enterprising and very good in some areas. But whatever changes I have in mind [for *Time*] have very little to do with *Newsweek*.

One advantage *Newsweek* claimed over *Time* was in greater readership per copy—more audience per advertising dollar. Traditionally, the print media measured readership by paid circulation, as attested to by the nonprofit Audit Bureau of Circulations, and it was on ABC figures that advertising rates were based. Television's advent had helped establish another measure: the size of the "total audience" exposed to the advertising message, which in the case of magazines meant counting not only readers who bought copies but also those "pass-along" or secondary readers who leafed through magazines in public libraries, doctors' offices, airplanes. *Life* in its infant days had exploited the total audience concept effectively against such older mass-circulation magazines as *Saturday Evening Post*, *Collier's* and *Liberty*; now *Newsweek* was using it to offset *Time*'s lead in paid circulation.

The first comprehensive survey of magazine audiences by W.R. Simmons & Associates in the early 1960s that had so helped *Sports Illustrated* (see chapter 9) had hurt *Time*. According to Simmons, *Newsweek*, with less than three-fifths of *Time*'s circulation, had nearly three-quarters of *Time*'s audience; this, when *Time*'s higher page rates were taken into account, pushed *Time*'s advertising cost in audience terms 24 percent above *Newsweek*'s. Subsequent surveys narrowed the differential somewhat. By 1968, *Time*'s price disadvantage was down to 15 percent.

Still, *Time*'s ad sales suffered. In 1968 *Time* fell behind in pages sold, dropping by some 300 pages to 2,913, while *Newsweek* rose nearly 100 pages to 3,008. Advertising rate and circulation increases confined the drop in profits. But the problem of total audience, as it affected advertising sales, was far from solved.

In August 1969, *Fortune* publisher Hank Luce came over to take

Shepley's place at *Time*. Remaining as assistant publisher was Ralph Davidson, who had assumed that post in March 1968, after *Time* International, of which he had been publisher, was put under the domestic division. A few months later that year, *Time* advertising director Bob Gordon went upstairs to be a corporate vice president; succeeding him at *Time* was John A. (Jack) Meyers, who had been ad sales manager in New York. In September 1968, the magazine's longtime general manager, James A. (Gus) Thomason, retired. His breezy young deputy, business manager Kelso Sutton, became general manager.

Time's new publisher, in his first statement to the Time Inc. board in December 1969, described the "perplexing" situation the magazine found itself in. Reader interest was at a peak; 1969's mail had already brought 65,000 letters to the editor, more even than in 1964, when readers' passions had been stirred up by the Johnson-Goldwater presidential race. The descent of domestic advertising sales had temporarily leveled out. But overall, *Time*'s costs were rising faster than its revenues. Accordingly, Hank Luce said, *Time* was advancing to early 1970 a planned subscription price increase, from $12 to $15, which would help boost circulation revenues from their previous level of about 25 percent of *Time*'s gross.

Also in train for 1970 was the launching of a new "demographic" advertising edition of *Time*, to be called *Time* B. Different from the regional editions, which offered advertisers a geographical segment of *Time*'s total circulation, the demographics offered a segment selected by occupation or income. (In all editions, editorial content was the same; only the advertising varied.) Earlier *Time* demographic editions had offered doctors, identified as such by title, and college students, identified by the special subscription rate they enjoyed. *Time* B was to offer subscribers identified by questionnaire as being upper-income business executives. The edition was to prove highly successful, bringing in $5 million in advertising in its first year, much of it new business. ZIP Marketing, another advertising sales device being worked on at that time— using ZIP code breakdowns of *Time*'s circulation lists to demonstrate precisely the magazine's penetration of the prospective advertisers' market areas—was likewise to prove highly effective.

Nevertheless, the pressure to cut costs remained. *Time*'s editorial outlays were coming under renewed scrutiny. *Time* was indeed an expensive magazine to produce, and some of the lavishness in its editorial operations was traditional and hard to eradicate. In 1968, Ralph Graves, then senior staff editor, gibed at the complaints he

341

anticipated from "this richly staffed, richly caparisoned organization" as an economy drive got under way. "Tears and cries of treason: What? Not have 18 *Time* copy boys?" Yet the nature of the news business made editorial outlays difficult to control; coverage of the Vietnam war alone was costing *Time* around half a million yearly. Nor was Time Inc. in the habit of choosing editors "on the basis of their budgetary ruthlessness and skill," as Donovan once explained to the Time Inc. directors. Rather, he noted, "it comes somewhat in the nature of a bonus or pleasant surprise when somebody is an extremely good editor and also reasonably good at . . . financial control."

That bonus was slow in coming under Grunwald's editorship. During 1968, late editorial closings, late cover changes and extra news color pages were estimated to have added about a million dollars to editorial costs. Subsequently, late closings were to become even more of a problem. The *Time* system itself created much of the trouble. Masses of copy, the product of a couple of hundred people, had to be funneled through one pair of hands, under one pair of eyes before the magazine was closed and ready to print. That was why one of the qualifications of *Time* managing editors was sheer physical stamina. To this, Grunwald added extreme meticulousness. He was given to ordering up numerous new versions of stories, fiddling with language and meaning. He could not let go of copy easily. At one point the situation got comic. Wrote Grunwald in a staff memo:

> I understand some of you were amused because I requested a new ending on a story that I myself had written (or more precisely, excerpted from a correspondent's file). The lesson seems obvious: almost anybody's copy, certainly including the managing editor's, needs editing.

The publishing staff, dealing with the resultant production delays, was less amused. While he was publisher, Jim Shepley had fumed constantly. On average, *Time* was eight hours late in closing, he claimed, and as a consequence, deliveries of the magazine to subscribers were back to the standards of the early 1960s, before the widespread diversification of *Time* printing operations began. It was worse for *Time*'s international editions. A missed plane connection out of Chicago, where the pages were typeset and then photographed for offset printing at plants overseas, could delay arrival a day or more at the other end. In June 1969, *Time*'s editorial deadlines were again advanced. This did not entirely cure the trouble, and publisher Luce took up the complaints where Shepley had left off.

Among the more important changes wrought during the Grunwald years at *Time* were those that involved the Time-Life News Service, its relationship with the magazine it principally served, and the role of the correspondents in the editorial process. These had been points of contention for years (see chapter 6). Grunwald was only the latest managing editor to take office resolved to end the news service's autonomy and bring it under his wing. But first he moved to settle a long-standing grievance of the correspondents—that they had no chance to check the final product of their reporting for accuracy in fact, tone or emphasis after it had been worked over by the writers, researchers and editors in New York.

The obvious solution would be to "play back" finished stories to the bureaus. The *Time* editors, however, had not been inclined to let the correspondents have such power of review, for fear that it would erode their own authority over what went into print. What could not be accomplished openly began to be done by clandestine means. The news service desk—the liaison between the bureaus and the various sections of the magazine—took to telephoning drafts of some stories to the correspondents for their comments. On rare occasions, a particularly sensitive story was put on the wire; in Detroit, where a mistake in wheelbase dimensions or horsepower in a story on new car models could be disastrous, the *Time* bureau began getting such wire replays regularly. Technological limits on communications capacity hindered the spread of this playback system; if thousands of words of edited *Time* articles had been punched laboriously into the telex every week for relay to bureaus, the result would have been prohibitive costs as well as massive traffic jams just as the magazine was about to close.

Improvements in cable facilities beginning in June 1963, guided by corporate communications chief John Striker, vastly speeded the flow of copy. From the news service's main communications centers, correspondents' files that formerly had moved on teleprinters chattering out 60 words per minute were now sped to their destination at rates of up to 1,000 words per minute. Under the direction of *Time*'s editorial production chief, Robert Boyd, a computer was introduced in 1967 to replace the old teletypesetting machines. It produced a paper tape that could easily be used to transmit stories back to the news bureaus; thus playbacks could become routine.

When he took over as managing editor, Grunwald was in no mood to continue the conflict waged between his precedessor and the redoubtable chief of the news service, Dick Clurman. He was well aware of the discontents of the correspondents and inclined to sympathize with them. Not only did he set in motion plans to institute playbacks; he went much further and, in effect, redefined the role of the *Time* correspondent. At the Paris conclave of overseas staffers in December 1968, he declared he was instructing his editors "that, other things being equal, the word of the *Time* correspondent should be taken over that of anybody else."

What was more, he announced that he would encourage correspondents to write directly for publication, to minimize the rewriting process under which they all chafed. Grunwald then issued a challenge to the assembled correspondents: the rewriting, "while galling in some ways, has served also as a kind of protection. You have been working behind a screen . . . I want you to come out from behind that screen and be there for the public to read and judge you."

In early 1969, with the presidential election and Nixon's inaugural over, Donovan made the expected change in the news service leadership. Chief of correspondents Dick Clurman left to become a corporate vice president, in charge of exploring new projects. Succeeding him was Murray Gart, 44. Gart had come to *Time*'s attention as news editor of the Wichita *Eagle* where, as a stringer for the magazine, he had covered a particularly disastrous tornado. Joining the news service in 1955, he had served in turn as bureau chief in Toronto, Boston, Chicago and London, returning in 1966 to New York to become an assistant managing editor of *Fortune*. In 1968, he had taken a short leave of absence to work in Nelson Rockefeller's campaign for the Republican presidential nomination.

The transition from Clurman to Gart was the occasion for a new look at the news service's organizational independence. Working almost entirely for *Time*, the news service comprised 31 bureaus, with 106 correspondents and 148 support and headquarters staff. It was costing almost $93,000 to keep one correspondent abroad for a year and more than $50,000 to maintain the average domestic correspondent. (By 1980, costs would rise to an average, for the news service as a whole, of $200,000 per correspondent.) From the corporate viewpoint, the question was how large a news-gathering apparatus *Time* could afford. Donovan himself had long wondered; in a memo to Luce in August 1965 he had described the news service as "either vastly overstaffed or underused"—an impression that persisted into the 1970s. Grunwald analyzed the situation in a memo to Donovan in December 1971:

> *Time* probably has the highest editorial cost per page of any publication in the world. This is partly caused by the fact that every word is produced by two editors, one writer, one or more correspondents, a researcher, not to mention various support troops . . . Our system gives us a quality generally unmatched in journalism. Nevertheless, the time seems to have come where we can no longer afford that quality, at least not to the present degree.

There should be fewer correspondents, used more selectively, Grunwald argued; writers and researchers should help with the reporting:

> To make all this work, it is obviously necessary for the news service to become part of *Time* . . . What matters is not the label, but the administrative and economic reality of running one organization rather than two.

Gart defended his autonomy no less fiercely than his predecessors. But early in 1972, a corporate review of *Time*'s editorial and publishing plans for the next five years finally forced a resolution of the debate. In April Donovan announced that, following the November presidential election, *Time* would take over the news service. The merger, he declared, "does not primarily interest me for budgetary reasons . . . It does concern me very deeply as a question of journalistic effectiveness." Donovan's conclusion was that integration would lead to "enrichment of the magazine" by more interchange between New York and the field, more writing for print by the correspondents, more "first-hand inquiry . . . outside New York" by the writers and, in the end, "a less New York–centered *Time*." Gart fought the decision to the end, reiterating in a note to Donovan— "in case it should matter to some future Time Inc. historian"—that he remained opposed. Donovan, closing off what he considered a wearisome debate, issued a plea. "Now," he wrote, "let us all get back to work."

In December, Gart became an assistant managing editor of *Time*, retaining also the title of chief of correspondents. (Gart and his successor, Richard Duncan, have been the only persons to have dual billing on the *Time* masthead.) The Time-Life News Service retained its masthead identity likewise, and, by Donovan's direction, continued to serve other divisions of the company as needed. In actual practice, relatively few things were different under the new arrangement. *Time*'s researchers, redesignated researcher-reporters in deference to the growing women's protest movement at Time Inc. (see chapter 26), came for a time under the jurisdiction of the chief of the news service. This shift drew sharp, but futile, protest from research chief Marylois Purdy Vega. There was more interchange between the bureaus and the New York staff; correspondents had previously done brief writing stints in New York, but now bureau chiefs began coming in for turns at editing.

Ironically, there was no apparent cost saving. In 1973, the first year of merger, rising travel and entertainment expense offset reductions in the domestic bureau and headquarters staff that brought the total news service head count down to 180, of whom 85 were correspondents.

In February 1972, publisher Hank Luce took a sabbatical leave. Associate publisher Ralph Davidson sat in for him, then took over permanently in June when it was announced that Luce was becoming vice president for corporate planning. There were other changes in *Time*'s business staff. Kelso Sutton departed to head a new corporate circulation department, with vice presidential rank. Succeeding him as *Time* general manager was Donald Barr, a production expert formerly stationed in Paris. The magazine's public affairs and promotion efforts were combined under assistant publisher Lane Fortinberry, a jovial extrovert of great panache. Shepley once called him "Mr. 42,"—"the only man in Time Inc. who eats twice a day at '21' " (New York's celebrity restaurant).

Davidson, 44 when he became publisher, was a blondish, muscular, outgoing man, with a talent for putting people at ease. His long service overseas, in close promixity to the news service bureaus, had made him adept in dealing with the editorial side. He and Grunwald got on well together. "Somebody forgot to tell me that publishers are supposed to be frightened of managing editors," Davidson explained.

From high school days in Los Angeles, Davidson had had ambitions to be in international business, and after finishing Stanford with a degree in international relations, he used a graduation gift from his mother to finance a long Jeep trip through North Africa. The journey resulted in his being hired later by the CIA for a two-year tour of duty in the Mediterranean region. While back in California, waiting for his CIA appointment to clear, Davidson spent several months at the sidewalk level of sales training, as a Fuller

346

Brush man. His entry into publishing with Time Inc. in 1954 was at a similar basic level, as a retail representative for *Life*, promoting food-store displays of packaged goods advertised in the magazine. He finally got his opportunity to go abroad in 1957, when he was assigned to *Time* International's ad sales office in Zurich. From there he moved to London as *Time*'s European advertising director, becoming publisher of *Time* International in 1967, and assistant publisher of the U.S. edition the following year.

Time had passed one milestone shortly before Davidson's accession. Domestic advertising revenues had gone over the hundred-million mark for the first time ever, to $101,644,000. Worldwide ad revenues of $131 million made *Time* "in these terms, the largest magazine in the world," boasted Time Inc.'s 1971 annual report. Meanwhile, the competitive situation between *Time* and *Newsweek* had stabilized; *Newsweek*'s great spurt in 1968 had proved a onetime event. Only the Simmons figures, still showing *Newsweek* with higher readership per copy, continued to nag.

A basic decision had been made in *Time*'s circulation policy: to hold at the 4,250,000 level reached in 1970. Since 1952, *Time*'s rate base had gone up every year, by no less than 100,000, and its advertising page rates had tripled over that period. *Time* was, in fact, nearing the situation that *Life* had faced: of pricing itself out of the market against television, which could, for the same dollars-and-cents outlay, deliver larger total audiences. A study done for the publisher's office warned that the cost of a 4-color bleed page in *Time*'s national edition was approaching television network rates. The study also predicted that rising paper and printing costs as well as postal rate increases would make "even modest growth prohibitively costly." *Time* would be "unable to pass along these increases to our readers and advertisers at rates that will improve or maintain our income as a percentage of revenue," said Davidson: "The advertising community was saying very clearly: 'Your rates are very high, we don't want more circulation.' "

Time's decision left an obvious opportunity for *Newsweek*, which was then at 2,725,000, to narrow *Time*'s circulation lead. To Davidson's surprise, *Newsweek* did not jump. "If I'd been *Newsweek* I would have been pushing up and up," Davidson said. "We kept waiting, but except for a year or two, they never did," *Time* kept its rate base at 4,250,000 throughout the rest of the decade.

In March 1973, *Time* reached the half-century mark. A 50th birthday celebration was in order but it was pitched quite differently

347

from the gaudy show that had marked the 40th. That huge party for *Time*'s cover subjects could not have been matched in any event. Nor would a gala have been quite fitting at that point, only three months after Time Inc. had gone through the corporate ordeal of suspending publication of *Life*. "The mood has changed," Heiskell explained. "That kind of event was right for 1963, but not for today."

A more sober schedule of events had been laid on. There was an affectionate staff party for Roy Larsen, the last survivor among the three men who had launched *Time*. Then a series of regional conferences assembled members of Congress, political scientists and Time Inc. editors to discuss ways of restoring the constitutional balance between Congress and an increasingly powerful presidency. The company also sponsored various cultural events including a tour of the U.S. by Britain's Royal Philharmonic Orchestra. And in May 1973 came the opening of the Henry R. Luce Hall of News Reporting at the National Museum of History and Technology in Washington, displaying pamphlets, newspapers, magazines and other journalistic memorabilia from pre-Revolutionary days to the present, as a permanent record of the news media's impact on the development of the country.

It was appropriate, even if coincidental, that the anniversary dinner for the staff in October, with Grunwald and Davidson as hosts, came just as *Time* was finishing the best year in its history. Pretax net income was up nearly 40 percent from 1972. Advertising sales increased by 300 pages, and advertisers were getting a bonus of an extra half million delivered circulation over the rate base.

Part of the reason for the rise in circulation was Watergate. As the crisis heated up, people were using the trial subscription forms inserted in the newsstand copies of *Time* to order at an unprecedented rate. "It would be inadequate to say merely that *Time* rose to the challenge of this big story," Donovan told the anniversary dinner audience. Rather, he went on, "*Time* has had something to do with the fact that we all perceive Watergate to be as big a story as it is"—in his view the biggest domestic story in *Time*'s history apart from the Great Depression of the 1930's. "*Time*'s 51st year truly has been a year of extraordinary fascination and importance," Donovan said. "And *Time* in its 51st year is the best magazine it ever has been."

Uncovering Watergate

L IKE NO PRECEDING PEACETIME EVENT, Watergate showed
newsweekly journalism's distinctive strength. Even if the
whole complex of events—the intelligence operation set up
by Nixon's Committee to Re-Elect the President, the actual Watergate burglary attempt, the tangled cover-up—had become fully
known all at once, it would have been overwhelmingly difficult to
sort out and fully understand. To follow the story daily, through
newspaper and television accounts, was a task requiring hours—and
it would have helped to be a lawyer. The lengthening cast of characters and their misdeeds, alleged or proved, threatened to become
a hopeless jumble: Nixon, Haldeman, Ehrlichman, Dean, Mitchell,
Mardian—now what was his job? And he told whom to do what?
Did Nixon know? And if so, was that a crime?

The newsmagazines' contribution was coherent narrative. Additionally, they contributed no small amount of original reporting. A
story demanding teamwork, Watergate displayed *Time*'s group journalism at its best. The magazine's performance also erased whatever
remained of the old accusations of Republican party bias. (Time
Inc.'s endorsement of Johnson in 1964 in a *Life* editorial undercut
that allegation earlier.) *Time*'s acceptance on campus reached a new
high; *Time* regained lost ground elsewhere. Even such an acerbic

critic as David Halberstam called *Time*'s coverage of Watergate "truly distinguished."*

In the 1968 presidential race, Donovan had not been enthusiastic about either Nixon or the Democratic candidate, Hubert Humphrey. "The charge of a grave flaw in character" haunts both men, Donovan wrote in a memo to his managing editors. "Against Nixon it is the old question of whether or not he is a principled man; against Humphrey, whether this man is in full control of himself." He also noted that "both candidates seem to have rather grubby friends." Finally, however, because the Republicans offered "political competence," *Life* declared Time Inc.'s "preference for Nixon."

That rather tepid tone did not warm during the first years of his presidency; for one thing, Donovan was growing critical of Nixon's Vietnam policy. Also, he was shocked to learn at a dinner with a fellow Minnesotan, Congressman Clark MacGregor, that even this longtime Nixon supporter was "increasingly baffled" by the President. In July 1970, at Donovan's request, Jason McManus, senior editor of *Time*'s Nation section, prepared an assessment of Nixon in the form of a report card (a favorite device of Donovan's). McManus gave Nixon a C+ on his conduct of the Vietnam War, a B+ on the economy and an F on race relations. He also complained:

> There is much talk of the President's mastery of the image arts; his image remains blurred or, better, snaps suddenly into focus and then blips out. No matter that it annoys and even infuriates the press and the opposition. Does it serve the President's and the country's interests well? We know too little about Nixon.

That measured view of the Nixon administration was reflected in the Time Inc. magazines as the 1972 presidential campaign began. A Nixon victory over the Democratic candidate, Senator George McGovern, was hardly in doubt. Less certain was whether Nixon would again choose Spiro Agnew as his Vice President, and in July a *Life* editorial suggested that Nixon could do better. *Time* was no less critical. The result was an extraordinary lunch in the vice presidential suite in the Executive Office Building on August 12. Agnew was the host; his guests were Donovan, *Time* managing editor Grunwald, McManus, Washington bureau chief Hugh Sidey and several correspondents. At the outset, Agnew announced that he had not attended the lunch in order to be interviewed, but rather to tell *Time* how displeased he was with its coverage of him. He cited sto-

---

*The Powers That Be (Knopf, 1979), p. 552.

ries and read from a list of offending quotes, objecting particularly
to *Time*'s suggestion that he was not intellectually qualified to be
President. His I.Q. was 130, Agnew asserted. And in any case, was
it for *Time* to decide who was qualified to be President? Donovan,
ordinarily a man of what Grunwald described as "massive calm,"
was quietly outraged. Sitting directly across from Agnew, looking
him in the eye, Donovan replied, as one participant recollected:

> First of all, Mr. Vice President, you work for us. The reason
> we say these things about you is that we believe they are true.
> You are not qualified to be President, and we have a responsi-
> bility to tell our readers.

No one from Time Inc. could remember having seen the imperturb-
able Donovan more indignant. Agnew changed the subject, talking
about the tapestries on the wall, and eventually the luncheon ended.
"An awkward meal," Donovan commented later.

The Watergate burglary attempt that had occurred on June 17, just
two months before the Agnew lunch, at first seemed only an embarrassment. Like most of the news media, *Time* began by calling it a
"caper." By August that view was hardening; Watergate, *Time*
declared, "promises to be the scandal of the year." On August 7,
Donovan wrote Grunwald:

> Your story this week on the Watergate 5 [the five arrested bur-
> glars: James McCord, Frank Sturgis, Bernard Barker, Virgilio
> Gonzalez, Eugenio Martinez] is excellent—I am told (by a not
> entirely disinterested source) there is plenty here to follow up
> on, which would warrant a major "investigative team" effort.

Further unsavory facts about the Nixon campaign's intelligence
operation and the way it was financed turned up in September and
October. But the details, which did not point to the President's
office, seemed to many almost niggling in comparison with the main
election issues: Vietnam, the economy, domestic unrest.

In October *Life* endorsed Nixon for President. Donovan and
managing editor Ralph Graves made the decision. *Life*'s staff
emphatically did not approve. Shortly before publication of the editorial, Graves was presented with a petition that said simply: "The
following members of the editorial staff wish to express their support and endorsement of Senator George McGovern." Of 145 staffers asked to sign the petition 100 had signed, including two of the
magazine's four assistant managing editors, all eight senior editors,

three of five staff writers, nine of 11 associate editors, ten of 13 assistant editors.

The magazine's endorsement of Nixon was lukewarm, but was not affected by the petition. Addressing itself mainly to an agenda for Nixon's second term, *Life* took a mild swipe at the Vice President ("While welcoming the recent hints of a 'new Agnew,' we shall continue to pray for the health of the President . . ."), and mentioned Watergate only in passing. There was no mention whatever of Watergate in an early draft of the editorial circulated to key Time Inc. editors, an omission that Grunwald thought unjustified. In a prepublication memo to Donovan he stated his reaction to the editorial: "Overall, I feel that the negatives of the Nixon administration should be stressed more." Grunwald cited Nixon's handling of race relations, "the air of quasi-corruption around the White House," his "frequently poor appointments." Grunwald's bottom line: "In sum, a reasonable case can be made that he deserves another term, but the price may be quite high."

A few weeks later, voters reelected Nixon by one of the largest majorities in American history. For the next two months, with Congress in recess and Nixon making news by reshuffling his Cabinet, the Watergate story receded from the news. Then, on January 8, 1973, the trial of seven men accused in connection with the break-in—the five burglars plus E. Howard Hunt and G. Gordon Liddy—began in Judge John Sirica's courtroom. Watergate quickly became the intensely hot story that it would remain for the next 18 months. Beginning in the summer of 1972 when the break-in occurred, the Washington *Post*'s Carl Bernstein and Bob Woodward had been diligently tracking the story and establishing themselves as the premier reporters of Watergate. They earned their paper a Pulitzer prize. Now other newspapers, newsmagazines and the networks raced to put their considerable resources and energies into pursuit of this twisted, elusive story.

For *Time*, the center of coverage was, of course, the Washington bureau. Many hands were involved. Bureau chief Hugh Sidey made the reportorial assignments, all the while continuing to write his column, "The Presidency." John Stacks was the bureau's news editor; Dean Fischer covered the White House; Neil MacNeil continued to cover Congress, as he had for 15 years. Others who reported on the evolving scandal included David Beckwith, Stan Cloud, Hays Gorey and Simmons Fentress. Each of these men would eventually ferret out important new details in the Watergate story.

But no *Time* reporter produced more Watergate scoops and

received less public credit for them than Sandy Smith—he wanted it that way. It was impossible to be specific about Smith's beat. He simply used his own sources, many never identified, many in the FBI. Before *Life* hired him in 1967 Smith had spent years with Chicago newspapers reporting on the Mob—which was, he insisted, "as safe as covering a Sunday-school picnic." A large, rumpled man with an easy manner, Smith had, in fact, once crashed a Mob picnic; another time he dropped in uninvited at the wedding reception given by Sam "Moe" Giancana for his daughter, pocketed the guest list and interviewed Giancana at length. (Giancana's daughter Antoinette recalled that in her book *Mafia Princess*.)* Soon after Watergate broke Smith was on top of it, tracing the money found on the burglars, discovering where signals sent by the bugging devices were picked up, unearthing dozens of other significant details. But publicity could have ruined Smith's information network. Rarely was he mentioned in print; one notable exception was when *Time* disclosed that Smith had been the source of a March 1973 story revealing that as Attorney General, John Mitchell had authorized FBI wiretaps even on White House staffers. But most weeks, Smith's explicit instruction to New York was: "First and foremost—pls delete the byline. Thanks, but no thanks, on this one." John Stacks summed up Smith as "the best pure reporter I've ever seen."

In mid-January 1973, *Time* landed the first interview with E. Howard Hunt, the mysterious former CIA operative who had helped plan the Watergate break-in. Hunt would not say anything substantive to David Beckwith, *Time*'s correspondent at the Watergate trial, or to any of the other reporters. When Hunt pleaded guilty, Beckwith passed him a business card and a quickly jotted note asking, "Well, now would you like to tell your story?" Hunt, who said that he had always felt an affinity with Time Inc. because he had briefly worked for *Life* in 1943 and had written some *March of Time* scripts, called Beckwith the next day to say that he would. Parts of the interview ran in the next two issues of *Time*.

On the last day of January, Liddy and McCord, the two Watergate defendants who had not pleaded guilty to burglary charges, were found guilty by Judge Sirica. In February the Senate created the special committee, chaired by Senator Sam Ervin, that became known as the Senate Watergate Committee; it would begin public hearings in May. In March, during Senate confirmation hearings on

*William Morrow, 1984.

L. Patrick Gray III, Nixon's nominee to head the FBI, a document became public revealing that officials of Nixon's reelection committee had tried to impede the FBI's investigation of the Watergate break-in.

A *Time* cover story on Gray followed, in the March 26 issue—the first of some 30 covers relating to Watergate. The writer was Edward Magnuson, who had come to *Time* from the Minneapolis *Tribune* in 1960 as a correspondent and was, by 1973, well on his way to becoming the magazine's all-time champion cover story writer, eventually with more than 100 to his credit. In 18 months he wrote 20 cover stories, four of them in consecutive weeks in May 1973. Magnuson's Watergate performance was virtuoso. Immersing himself in files from the Washington bureau, transcripts, newspapers and anything else relevant, Magnuson would somehow cull and order the information in his mind, then set the story down on paper lucidly and faster than one would have thought possible. The Washington bureau's John Stacks recalled: "Magnuson's incredible ability to synthesize made *Time*'s coverage superior. He was so good that we in the bureau who knew what was in all the files would still learn something from Magnuson's stories."

The break point on Watergate came on March 23, when Judge Sirica sentenced the burglary defendants—except for McCord, who had sent Sirica a remarkable letter, saying in part:

> There was political pressure applied to the defendants to plead guilty and remain silent. Perjury occurred during the trial in matters highly material to the very structure, orientation and impact of the government's case and to the motivation and intent of the defendants. Others involved in the Watergate operation were not identified during the trial when they could have been.

McCord's letter was an important confirmation of the news reports. To an unprecedented degree, *Time*'s New York editors had been asked to accept on faith a great deal of sensitive and sometimes damaging information from the bureau. They had done so—and had felt considerable heat from the administration as a result. McCord's letter, undermining many administration contentions, was welcome vindication. On April 17, President Nixon announced a new policy. Henceforth, any member of the White House staff called to testify before the Ervin committee would do so. *Time*'s cover announced: "Watergate Breaks Wide Open."

354

Soon thereafter Grunwald received a cable from senior editor McManus, temporarily on duty in Paris helping organize a European edition of *Time*. His message:

Some painful home thoughts from abroad about Watergate, based only on what I read in the [*International*] *Herald Tribune* this morning, and offered not in malice or anger, but distress and a frisson of foreboding:

If [Nixon campaign manager] Mitchell really planned Watergate from the outset, if Mitchell and [White House counsel John] Dean bribed those caught into silence, if [Nixon-fund raiser and confidant Herbert] Kalmbach was in on the espionage, is it really credible that Nixon was not involved? This is thinking about the unthinkable, a conclusion that certainly you and I, in talking about this in the past, were always unwilling to entertain. No responsible citizen wants the President of the U.S. to be guilty of a crime, because the consequences (one shies from using the word impeachment but that is what we are talking about at worst) are so calamitous and dangerous for the country. But when I think of what we know about Nixon's intimate relationship with Mitchell, how Nixon runs his ship and his psychology of gut-personal combat against his adversaries, I worry. I worry for Nixon and the country in the revelations to come, and I worry about *Time* and the role of the U.S. press more generally in the weeks to come . . . I am puzzled and dismayed at how forgiving and grateful [James] Reston and today's Washington *Post* editorial are of Nixon, full of praise that somehow the good old American system has triumphed and at last truth will out, no matter the obfuscations of the past year. The fact of the matter is that on occasion, the President of the U.S. purposefully and publicly lied to Americans . . . Have I been away too long? Is the currency of the presidency so debased, the cynicism of Americans so weary and deep now, that we are all going to give praise and thanksgiving to Nixon for deciding to tell the truth? [Or] even less than that, let the truth, or some more of it anyway, come out?

On April 10 Nixon forced H. R. Haldeman and John Ehrlichman to resign; John Dean was fired. The *Time* issue reporting these developments also contained an Essay signed by Donovan on "The Good Uses of the Watergate Affair." As Donovan saw it, Watergate had destroyed an overprotective palace guard surrounding

Nixon; it could lead to a clearer understanding of "the role of a free press in a free society"; and it "could be a historic check upon the long and dangerous aggrandizement of the presidency." But the *Time* Essay carried a feeling of a denouement, as if the crisis might have passed. Not so. The public hearings of the Ervin committee, beginning ten days after the Essay appeared, made clear that the crisis, whatever it might be, was still to come.

On May 21, four days after the hearings began, Grunwald composed a document as an aid to his own thinking, which he headed "Notes on Watergate." In it he thrashed out and settled in his own mind the question, then very much open, of whether Watergate should be allowed to overshadow Nixon's accomplishments in foreign affairs—getting out of Vietnam, nurturing détente with Russia, opening relations with China. Grunwald's conclusion: "It is very probable that in history Watergate may be more important than Peking and Moscow." For a dozen pages he followed this line of argument, becoming more convinced with each page. Regarding Nixon's still shadowy responsibility for Watergate, Grunwald asserted:

> Whether he was directly involved or not, whether he knew or not, the President obviously gave his highest trust to his aides, which is what enabled them to do what they did. He obviously established and set the rules by which these men operated. Without any further and more damaging evidence to emerge, Nixon cannot escape culpability.

By his final page, Grunwald was thundering:

> The ultimate and unspeakable corruption of Watergate would be if the American people were to decide that it does not matter. The ultimate and unspeakable act of corruption by the President, no matter what else he did or did not do, would be to confirm the American people in that corruption. The President himself has often eloquently declared that the erosion of moral fiber has been known to bring down the greatest nations. The more or less placid acceptance of Watergate would suggest a degree of moral decay in America compared to which the greatest diplomatic triumphs in Peking or Moscow—or in Brussels or in Cairo, or in Havana—would be minor diversions.

As that unforgettable spring and summer of 1973 rolled on, a fascinated public watched the televised Ervin committee hearings. These became the ultimate serial drama, promising something new in virtually every installment. Among the most stunning pieces of testimony was former White House administrator Alexander Butterfield's revelation of the Nixon tapes.

That summer also, senior editor McManus returned from Paris and resumed editing the Nation section, handling *Time*'s Watergate stories. A deft writer and an editor of considerable managerial skill, McManus had first come to Time Inc. as a summer trainee in 1957. A Rhodes scholar, he had been the Oxford stringer for *Time*'s London bureau, and in 1962 returned to Europe to be *Time*'s Common Market correspondent, based in Paris. In 1968 he was appointed senior editor in charge of the World section, moving over to Nation a year later. McManus placed a good deal of confidence in his staff and, by doing so, earned their best efforts week after week.

One of *Time*'s most important coups was correspondent Hays Gorey's early interview and continued contact with John Dean. As of May 1973, when Dean was testifying secretly to Watergate committee staffers, no reporter had spoken with him at length, and his public testimony was not to come until late June. What did Dean know? What was he saying? Gorey's repeated calls to Dean's lawyer, Robert McCandless, were not returned. Finally Gorey asked a friend, Senator Fred Harris, an Oklahoman like McCandless, to intercede. The result was that McCandless met with Gorey—and politely explained that there would be no interview. Gorey kept hounding him. Then one day McCandless took Gorey for an automobile ride, destination unannounced. They ended up at Dean's town house in Alexandria. As Dean later explained in his book *Blind Ambition*,* McCandless had decided that a talk with a reporter would help Dean's image, and McCandless had chosen Gorey because, he told Dean, "He is a good man; he hasn't made any judgments about you, one way or the other. I think he'll give you a fair piece."

Dean granted a brief interview, published in *Time*'s June 4 issue, in which he asserted that parts of Nixon's just-released account of Watergate were "not accurate at all." Not many days afterward Gorey, bearing flowers and a bottle of wine, returned to the Dean house for a second, longer interview. Said Gorey:

> I was always comfortable with John Dean, right from the beginning. I think he learned to trust me, but it took time. I think he felt reassured that he could say things to me for background

*Simon & Schuster, 1976.

357

and that we would be very fair with the information. I think we were.

Early in the fall there were major developments practically every week. Judge Sirica ordered Nixon to turn over certain tapes to special Watergate prosecutor Archibald Cox; Nixon appealed the ruling. Coincidentally, Spiro Agnew resigned as Vice President. A Court of Appeals rejected Nixon's appeal on the tapes; Nixon then announced a "compromise" plan to turn over summaries, which would be verified by Senator John Stennis; Cox rejected the compromise. On October 20 came the Saturday Night Massacre. Nixon ordered Attorney General Elliot Richardson to fire Cox; Richardson resigned instead. His second-in-command, William Ruckelshaus, balked too, so Nixon fired him. He then appointed Solicitor General Robert Bork acting Attorney General, directing him to fire Cox and close the office of special prosecutor.

It was 8:22 p.m. in Washington when presidential press secretary Ziegler announced the firings. In New York, Ed Magnuson had just handed Jason McManus a cover story on the week's Watergate developments. It now required a complete rewrite. As Magnuson remembered:

> Jason tossed it all off with the opening, if I recall correctly, "Well, I guess we'll have to start all over." That "we" sounded too easy. I was sure he meant that "I" would have to start all over. Perhaps he sensed, for the first time, a flicker of panic on my face. At any rate, he proceeded to do what very few senior editors do as well as he: verbally outline the elements of the entirely new story in a clear and persuasively logical sequence. We closed it Sunday morning. Some said the haste did not show. If so, a superb editor had patched the seams.

The Saturday Night Massacre inflamed public opinion against Nixon as nothing else had. Within an hour of Ziegler's announcement, protesters outside the White House held up signs for passing motorists: "Honk for Impeachment." And there was plenty of honking. Western Union reported processing the most concentrated volume of telegrams in its history.

In this atmosphere, some readers of *Time* inevitably blamed the messenger for the bad news. A man named Owens wrote Hedley Donovan:

Dear Mr. Donovan:
   The transfer of *Time* Magazine from an independent well run

magazine under Henry R. Luce to an oracle of the Democratic party is one of the most disgusting things in modern day journalism. You have consistently glorified the Kennedys, which well informed people know are one of the most common families ever to hit our American colonies, and have shown your hate-Nixon-get-him-at-any-price attitude.

Unless you change your attitude and become a little more non-biased I shall be forced [into] buying substantial portions of the stock and throwing you, unqualified as you are, out of office.

To which Donovan replied:

Far from having a "hate-Nixon-get-him-at-any-price attitude," the Time Inc. publications supported him three times for President. We also deplore many of the activities now shown to have been carried out by some of his most intimate advisers and appointees. These inevitably reflect on his own capacity as an executive and his own sense of propriety.

On the basis of new information, in other words, we are revising our previous opinion. The willingness to go through that painful business is known as open-mindedness.

Please feel free to buy as much Time Inc. stock as you wish.

Much happened in the following several days. The AFL-CIO called on Nixon to resign and on the House of Representatives to impeach him if he did not. Eight impeachment resolutions were introduced in the House. Nixon abandoned his "compromise" plan and agreed to turn over tapes to Sirica's court—except for some that turned out to be missing. On Sunday, November 4, Senator Edward Brooke of Massachusetts became the first Republican Senator to call for Nixon's resignation. That same day, the New York *Times*, the Detroit *News* and the Denver *Post* advised the same thing. The next day, *Time*'s issue dated November 12 appeared on the newsstands, also carrying an editorial calling on Nixon to resign.

The decision to publish the editorial had been surrounded by secrecy and uncertainty. In all its 50 years *Time* had never run an editorial. This was an explicit policy, as the magazine's 1922 prospectus had stated:

There will be no editorial page in *Time* . . . But the editors recognize that complete neutrality on public questions and important news is probably as undesirable as it is impossible.

Over the years *Time*'s position had been that it was misleading to attempt a separation of news from opinion and analysis; the distinction was usually false or impractical, *Time* maintained.

Time editors had, on occasion, considered making exceptions to the policy; Luce, too, had given thought to an editorial page. The subject had come up again as recently as ten months earlier—and Grunwald, writing Donovan, had argued emphatically against it:

> No matter what we did or said, the introduction of an editorial page would lead people to assume that we have decided after so many decades to separate and earmark editorial opinion from its reporting of the news. I tend to believe that there is virtue in the ambiguity of the way in which *Time* now expresses its views. It often gets people mad and it sometimes confuses them; a certain amount of effort had to go into figuring out whether we were for or against Nixon [in the election], for example. My hunch is that this is part of *Time*'s appeal.

But the Watergate situation was too exceptional to be governed by precedent. As the Ervin committee hearings ended, Donovan concluded privately that Nixon would have to go. He and Grunwald discussed an editorial but the timing was problematic. "It was impossible for me to advocate Nixon's resignation while Agnew was still Vice President," Donovan explained. "After Agnew left, Carl Albert was next in line. For him to succeed would have been overthrowing the 1972 election results. By late October, it was clear that Ford would be confirmed as vice president, and Albert had even said if he should succeed in the interval, he would resign as President as soon as Ford was confirmed. At that point we were ready to publish."

Because of the unusual nature of the editorial, Heiskell, Shepley and *Time* publisher Ralph Davidson, who would normally have no voice in an editorial matter, were kept informed. Eventually McManus, Sidey, news service chief Gart and assistant managing editors Ed Jamieson and Richard Seamon were consulted as well.

Grunwald wrote a draft of the editorial and sent it to Donovan and McManus for comment and suggestions. Donovan edited it. Absolute secrecy was maintained. Two pages of the magazine were held open, and Grunwald was said to be working on a *Time* Essay. Heiskell made it a point not to mention the editorial even to his wife, Marian Sulzberger, whose brother was publisher of the New York *Times*. At the last minute a researcher checked the piece for accuracy, and the necessary layout and production people were brought in. Even at that late moment, the idea of tampering with

Time's long-standing policy caused jitters. As the piece was closing, around 9:30 p.m. on Saturday, Donovan walked into McManus's office, shut the door and mused, "Should we really do this?" Before the night was out, the editorial was closed and ready to be printed. Copies went out to the wire services the next day, Sunday. The network news broadcasts carried word of it that night. The editorial began:

> Richard Nixon and the nation have passed a tragic point of no return. It now seems likely that the President will have to give up his office: he has irredeemably lost his moral authority, the confidence of most of the country, and therefore his ability to govern effectively.
>
> The most important decision of Richard Nixon's remarkable career is before him: whether he will give up the presidency rather than do further damage to his country. If he decides to fight to the end, he faces impeachment by the House, for he has indeed failed his obligation under the Constitution to uphold the law. Whether two-thirds of the Senate would vote to convict him cannot be certain. But even if he were to be acquitted, the process would leave him and the country devastated. Events have achieved an alarming momentum; additional facts that would be brought out under subpoena power at an impeachment trial could strike in many unforeseen and dangerous directions.
>
> Moreover, a trial would take at least several months, during which the country would be virtually leaderless. The White House would be paralyzed while the U.S. and the world awaited the outcome. The Republic would doubtless survive. But the wise and patriotic course is for Richard Nixon to resign, sparing the country and himself the agony.

The editorial went on to cite Time Inc.'s past support of Nixon, explain the uniqueness of Watergate, catalogue Nixon's sins and dispose of his excuses. It then concluded:

> The nightmare of uncertainty must be ended. A fresh start must be made. Some at home and abroad might see in the President's resignation a sign of American weakness and failure. It would be a sign of the very opposite. It would show strength and health. It would show the ability of a badly infected political system to cleanse itself. It would show the true power of popular government under law in America.

361

The editorial provoked 1,866 letters in the first week after publication. By year's end there were about 5,000—with 4,500 objecting, sometimes violently, to *Time*'s position; many readers canceled their subscriptions.

Within Time Inc.'s own board of directors there was commotion too. Donovan later described the incident:

> A Time Inc. director, catching up with our editorial in Hong Kong, fired off a blistering cable to board chairman Heiskell, saying that he refused to take any responsibility for the editorial. Heiskell replied pleasantly that that was just right; the editors were responsible for the magazine's views.*

One angry letter demanded special attention. It was from Clare Boothe Luce. She condemned the editorial, accusing *Time* of "deliberately trying to bypass the Constitution," and its requirement of impeachment and trial as the means of removing a President. Grunwald, replying by cable, pointed out that in the just-published issue there was a roundup of opinion that included a statement by Mrs. Luce making the same general argument and that "publishing your letter will unquestionably lead to widely and gleefully publicized stories about a feud between you and the editors of *Time*. It will be exploited by people not necessarily in sympathy with the President, you or *Time*. You may feel that this cannot be helped, but I am hoping that you will consider carefully whether you really want that." Mrs. Luce cooled off, and that letter did not run.

The rush of developments did not abate. A few days before *Time*'s editorial, Leon Jaworski had been named Cox's successor as special Watergate prosecutor. A tough Texas attorney, Jaworski had been offered the job months earlier, before Cox, and had turned it down; now, assured that he could, if necessary, take the President to court, Jaworski accepted the prosecutor's post.

In mid-November Nixon made the memorable announcement to a group of newspaper executives at Disney World that he was not a crook. Four days later, the celebrated 18-minute gap was discovered in the tape of Nixon's conversation with Haldeman three days after the Watergate break-in. The year ended with Jaworski predicting that several indictments would be handed down in January and February. Shortly, a panel of technical experts announced that the gap was the result of at least five separate erasures, and in early Febru-

---

***Roosevelt to Reagan* (Harper & Row, 1985), p. 126.

ary 1974, the House voted 410 to 4 to let the Judiciary Committee continue its impeachment investigation.

It was against this background that Jaworski, in essence, invited *Time* to invite him to dinner. A date was set, February 12; place, the conference room of *Time*'s Washington bureau; agenda, open. Attending from the bureau were Smith, Sidey, Gorey, Stacks, Beckwith, Fischer and Cloud; from New York came Grunwald, senior editors Loeb and McManus, writer Magnuson and Gart. Jaworski was accompanied by an aide, James Doyle.

Dinner began with a discussion of how Jaworski's remarks might be handled by *Time*. This was a crucial moment: Did Jaworski intend that his remarks, however disguised, see print? Gart spoke: "We're all gentlemen here." Translation: the dinner would be off the record. Jaworski then revealed his message, speaking very carefully about an extremely grave subject. "Suppose," he said, "I had heard some tape that makes it very clear that the President is guilty of criminal conduct. Suppose the President knows I've seen this incriminating material. What would the President do?"

Ed Magnuson later recalled, "Without thinking much I responded, 'Resign.' Everybody around the table laughed. Jaworski didn't."

It soon became clear that Jaworski was convinced that Nixon was guilty of an offense substantial enough to force his resignation. Although he did not say so, Jaworski had heard the tape of Nixon's March 21, 1973, conversation with Dean and Haldeman in which the three men talked about past and future payoffs to buy silence from the Watergate defendants. It indicated that Nixon was, at the least, guilty of misprision of a felony.

But why had Jaworski chosen to reveal this electrifying information? McManus's judgment was that "Jaworski was concerned about the fate of the Republic. He was concerned that the American system of government would expire, and he wanted to get out what he had to say." A slightly different interpretation came from correspondent John Stacks: "I believe it was always his intention to get Nixon to resign rather than go through the impeachment procedure. I felt that he was trying to send a message to the press and squeeze Nixon out of office."

In other words, Stacks—and most of the Washington contingent at the dinner—felt that Jaworski was providing information for publication and that *Time* should go with a story, based on his remarks, without mentioning the source. The New York contingent felt otherwise; in their view, the dinner was completely off the record and *Time* was honor-bound not to print anything about it. In a confidential file to Gart, the Washington bureau summarized the evening's discussions. But a worried phone call afterward, from Doyle, underscored the extreme sensitivity of the whole subject, and *Time* did not publish (although within two weeks the New York *Times* appeared with an account apparently based on a similar conversation with Jaworski). McManus concluded, "The importance of the Jaworski dinner was in providing the context of our future Watergate stories." Magnuson added: "Any doubts anybody was harboring were brushed away."

From the Jaworski dinner onward, covering Watergate became a chronicling of Nixon's deteriorating defenses. Donovan cautioned vigilance in the tone of the stories as evidence against the President accumulated: "God knows the unvarnished facts and inescapable inferences are bad enough." Watergate now dominated nearly every issue of the magazine, taking more pages; by the spring of 1974 *Time* was running over its editorial page budget. Some of the *Time* staff complained that the magazine was giving Watergate too much play. In fact, the back of the book—the collection of departments not tied to the hard news of the day, such as Art, Cinema, Science, Theater—was getting a smaller proportion of *Time*'s space than usual. The editors took no immediate action to solve the problem although both Donovan and Grunwald were worried about it. A natural resolution was only a few months away.

On April 18, Judge Sirica issued a subpoena, drawn up by Jaworski, for documents and tapes covering 64 presidential conversations. On April 30 Nixon released transcripts of tapes subpoenaed earlier by the House Judiciary Committee. Now the nation could read most of the conversations Jaworski had known about when he came to dinner at the Washington bureau. "Nixon's Shattered Presidency" said *Time*'s cover. A canvas of Senators and Congressmen found even conservative Republicans demanding resignation. Still Nixon held on, traveling to the Middle East and to Moscow.

Finally, on July 24, the Supreme Court ruled unanimously that Nixon must turn over the 64 tapes subpoenaed by Jaworski in April. One recorded the conversation between Nixon and Haldeman on June 23, 1972—the so-called "smoking gun"—in which Nixon explicitly directed Haldeman to impede the FBI's investigation of the break-in. It was now clear even to Nixon's defense counsel that the President could be charged with obstruction of justice, a felony. Resignation or impeachment became inevitable.

Nixon announced his resignation on Wednesday evening, August 8, and officially tendered it the next day. The issue of *Time* appearing the following Monday, dated August 19, was a special issue devoted almost entirely to the resignation, Watergate, Nixon and the accession of Gerald Ford. A tight close-up of Ford's face looked out from the cover, above the words, "The Healing Begins."

Grunwald had scrapped the originally scheduled story list by Wednesday afternoon, when it became certain that Nixon would announce his resignation that night. More than 40 *Time* staffers crowded into Grunwald's office as he began making assignments for the special issue. Some preparations had already been made. Months earlier, the Nation section had assembled an emergency duty roster of writers, reporters and researchers. Senior editor Ronald P. Kriss had drafted a review of Nixon's life and career the previous October. A biography of Ford was on the shelf, though it now had to be largely rewritten.

The issue's central article, detailing Nixon's final week, was written, fittingly, by Ed Magnuson. It was a typical job—long, detailed, clear, compelling.

Early Friday evening, Grunwald, art director David Merrill and production chief Eugene Coyle began laying out the issue. The Nation section is normally 12 to 14 pages long, but this time it ran for 47 pages. Through Saturday and Saturday night the researching, writing and editing continued. The last piece of copy closed just before noon on Sunday. Yet everyone involved recalled not confusion but rather extraordinary smoothness. According to McManus:

> It was a smoother and better closing than some other "ordinary" weeks of the previous Watergate year. It was not just the careful planning; one had a sensation that this is what it must be like playing on the New York Knicks on a good night. For everyone it was an enormously satisfying and proud week to be a journalist at *Time*.

The resignation issue of *Time* sold 527,000 copies on the newsstand—slightly more than the issue reporting the end of World War II, and more copies than *Time*, or any other newsmagazine, had ever sold before. But it was not quite the end of the Watergate story: there was one more scene to be played. In September, Gerald Ford announced "a full, free and absolute pardon unto Richard Nixon for all offenses against the United States which he, Richard Nixon, has committed or may have committed or taken part in."

Like the first episode in the Watergate story, this last became known on a Sunday morning. But unlike that clumsy burglary, the pardon demanded an overhaul of the *Time* issue that had closed only a few hours earlier. Crash reporting began; in New York, some 45 researchers, reporters, copyreaders, production and layout specialists, photographers and editors returned to work. The cover figure that week was to have been a winsome baby for a piece on the declining birthrate that did run inside. Millions of already printed covers were discarded and replaced by a new one featuring a Nixon portrait.* The new cover story, assembled and edited by senior editor Loeb, closed at 4:30 a.m. Monday, and the revised issue appeared only a day late.

Except for loose ends, the Watergate story was over. Certainly the press had been a major figure in Watergate, although its role was, in retrospect, sometimes misperceived. Sandy Smith felt strongly about the subject:

> There's a myth that the press did all this, uncovered all the crimes . . . It's bunk. The press didn't do it. People forget that the government was investigating all the time. In my material there was less than 2 percent that was truly original investigation. There was an investigation being carried out here. It may have been blocked, bent, botched, or whatever, but it was proceeding. The government investigators found the stuff and gave us something to expose.

In which exposure *Time* could, however, take some of the credit. "This company can take great pride in *Time*'s coverage over the past two years of the whole Watergate story," Donovan declared in a congratulatory message to the *Time* staff. "It has been an enormously demanding assignment, and *Time* has brought to it not only the highest technical skills but genuine insight and a steady sense of the public interest. I think *Time*'s work has made a difference."

Grunwald sent a similar memo of thanks and congratulations. He concluded with a journalistic look ahead:

> Now we will probably move into a more normal news era—not that one can ever be sure. If so, our job will in some respects be harder. The consistent drama and suspense will be missing, and we will have to find other ways of holding the readers' attention. We will have to concentrate on a great many different problems, some old, some new, find fresh stories and fresh ways of telling them.

---

*Nixon has appeared on *Time*'s cover 52 times (24 of them alone) since 1952, more than any other person.

366

One consequence of Watergate was less salutary. This was the tendency in American journalism to believe that the best formula for "holding the readers' attention" lay in adopting an adversarial role toward established institutions, notably including government, and applying the methods of criminal investigation in gathering news. Ron Kriss, later an executive editor of *Time*, thought the press emerged from the Watergate story with the belief that many other Watergates remained to be uncovered. In the single-minded hunt for scandal and iniquity, other legitimate news got short shrift. "Partly," said Kriss, "this post-Watergate fervor left the feeling that the only government reporting worth doing was government screwups and venality. This meant that the normal functions of government were neglected."

At the height of Watergate, in July 1974, a cover story in *Time*, "The Press: Fair or Foul," raised just that question. Declared *Time*:

> Many journalists fear that Watergate has created a backlash against a press perceived as having grown too powerful . . . [Even] moderate or liberal editors and publishers . . . wonder whether the press has gone too far and assumed a role greater than the public is willing to tolerate.

The "Screwballs"

I N JUNE 1972, *Time*'s international advertising sales force gathered in New York City for a five-day conference. Among those addressing the group was managing editor Henry Grunwald. He began his talk with a discussion of editorial jargon:

> Until recently, we used one term that may interest you especially. The term was "the screwballs." Somebody would say, "Who is making up the screwballs this week?" or, "I am afraid the screwballs are going to be late again."
>
> I hate to tell you this, but the screwballs were the foreign editions of *Time*.
>
> Now some of our older citizens may still occasionally use this word in a spirit of nostalgia. But, in fact, it has disappeared from our *Time* vocabulary . . . One simply cannot think of one fourth of one's circulation and revenues as the "screwballs."

On the basis of reported income, the screwballs were doing even better than Grunwald indicated, reaping profits that were consistently higher, as a percentage of revenue, than the domestic edition's. True, the international editions carried an artificially minute share of *Time*'s very substantial editorial cost, an accounting arrangement justified by the fact that except for *Time Canada*, none of them were then generating their own news: the stories reported, written and edited for *Time* U.S. were transferred intact to the internationals. Still, the figures appearing in the *Time* division's P & L statements made very good reading. In 1971, not a good year for *Time* U.S., the five international editions earned $6,851,000, vs. $13,319,000 for the domestic edition. In 1972 they were heading for $8,019,000 vs. domestic's $22,339,000.

It was a matter of concern, therefore, that the two of the five internationals that brought in the bulk of the profits—Canadian and Atlantic—were both having problems. In Canada, the nationalist political threat to *Time* had not abated; in 1970 a new government inquiry had raised new questions about *Time Canada*'s long-term future. In Europe, the difficulties inherent in editing and publishing an American magazine for a largely non-American audience were raising similar questions about *Time Atlantic*.

Time Canada's status had been left uncertain following the defeat of the Diefenbaker government in 1963; the O'Leary commission's proposals for taxing *Time*'s Canadian-originated advertising had not led to any legislation by then, or for some time after. Then, in 1965, the Liberal government of Prime Minister Lester Pearson made a move, reacting to the possibility of foreign takeover of two leading Canadian newspapers—Toronto's *Globe and Mail* by an American newspaper chain and Montreal's *La Presse*, the country's biggest French-language daily, by Gaullist interests. The government proposal, passed as part of the 1965 Income Tax Act, disallowed the tax deductibility of advertising in foreign-owned publications, but gave specific exemptions to *Time* and the *Reader's Digest*. As magazines "edited in whole or in part . . . and printed or published in Canada," both were deemed to be, in the law's convoluted legalese, "not non-Canadian." Although the law defined a Canadian periodical as one whose contents were not "substantially the same as the contents of" any foreign-owned parent, *Time Canada* appeared safe.

The exemption granted *Time* and the *Digest* touched off renewed Canadian nationalist attacks, however; Time Inc. was accused of bringing pressure on the Canadian government through Washington. Peter Newman, the Toronto *Star*'s syndicated political columnist (later to become editor of *Maclean's*, the Canadian monthly), quoted an unnamed "senior Canadian civil servant" as saying, "I had the impression that if we dared touch the Canadian operations of *Time* and *Digest*, the State Department would view it as far more serious than if, for instance, we sold armed tanks to Fidel Castro."*

The Distemper of Our Times (McClelland and Stewart Ltd., 1968), p. 225.

Pearson, in his memoirs, flatly denied the allegations.

In any event, *Time Canada* had won a reprieve. The company's relations with the Canadian publishing industry improved, in part owing to the efforts of *Time Canada*'s new managing director, Stephen S. LaRue, in helping organize a Canadian publishers' association to promote magazine advertising generally.

Transplanting editorial operations to Montreal had also paid off. Under the resident editor, John Scott, there was a recognizably more Canadian feel to the section of Canadian news that led off the edition each week. This extended even to taking political positions independent of the parent *Time*, as in 1965 when *Time Canada* gave sympathetic handling to Pearson's differences with U.S. policy in Vietnam. And *Time Canada* was producing more of its own cover stories. Hierarchically, *Time Canada* remained under the wing of an assistant managing editor in New York, and every Canadian story was wired to him for prepublication approval. But as the Montreal staff settled in, top-editing from New York got lighter and lighter until it was limited mainly to stylistic fixes. The leeway was broad: it was in *Time Canada*, in 1971, that an "unprintable" word, never seen in any Time Inc. publication, appeared. It was used by none other than Prime Minister Trudeau in the midst of a parliamentary debate. Irate at opposition heckling, he "silently but emphatically mouthed the blunt expletive: 'Fuck off,' " *Time Canada* reported. New York let the quote go through.

The "not non-Canadian" status, for tax purposes, that had been bestowed on *Time* in 1965 came up for reexamination in February 1970. Heading the renewed inquiry, this time by a parliamentary committee, was Senator Keith Davey, a Toronto public relations executive, formerly a national organizer for Trudeau's Liberal party. The Davey committee promised a repeat performance of the O'Leary commission inquiry of a decade earlier, but with a new twist: Grattan O'Leary himself, now of a conspicuously different mind, was on *Time*'s side. "I am not so sure that *Time* magazine today is not the best Canadian magazine we have," O'Leary told the Davey investigation.

Time Inc. management felt fairly confident as the hearings opened. *Time Canada* was reporting a more varied menu of news stories, the editorial staff had been enlarged, more Canadians were employed and the edition was about to be printed in Vancouver as well as Montreal. Since the locally based editorial operation had begun in 1962, circulation had nearly doubled, to 460,000, and was still growing. The same was true of advertising revenues. *Time Canada* publisher LaRue and editor Scott were grilled by the Davey committee for a full morning. Scott ably stated *Time*'s case: "We are the only magazine in Canada dealing with the news at the frequency of once a week. As for my own responsibility to Canada, I meet it simply by doing the best job I can."

Pressure on the government mounted while the Davey committee prepared its report. A close Trudeau aide confided to Ottawa bureau chief Richard Duncan that "if we don't do something, every bankrupt journal in the country will keep on blaming *Time*." In November 1970, a Liberal party conference recommended ending the tax concessions to *Time* and the *Reader's Digest* entirely. The Davey report, issued in December, suggested the same, and more.

Though it conceded that *Time* lent dimension to the entire Canadian publishing industry, the committee recommended that "the exemptions now granted *Time* and the *Reader's Digest* under . . . the Income Tax Act be repealed, and the sooner the better." Rejecting the idea of "sending the two magazines home," the committee proposed instead that the government should "make them settle here" by requiring that they "sell 75 percent of the stock in their Canadian subsidiaries to Canadian residents." This solution had "the virtue of fairness," the committee felt, and would result in "two healthy magazines, heavily Canadian in editorial content, overwhelmingly Canadian in ownership." The report added, parenthetically, "We are presuming here that a condition of the sale would be an undertaking that the names and essential character of the magazines would remain unchanged."

It remained for the Trudeau government to translate the Davey recommendations into action. The action was not forthcoming, and in the hiatus, which lasted nearly four years, Time Inc. rethought its position. LaRue began investigating ways to "Canadianize" the local publishing operation further. A public issue of stock in Time Canada Ltd. was considered, but decided against. *Time Canada*'s board of directors was, however, broadened to include several distinguished Canadians.*

Coincidentally in 1973, *Time Canada* got a new editor. John Scott

*They were: Murray G. Ross, founding president of Toronto's York University; J. Richard Murray, former managing director of Winnipeg's Hudson's Bay Company and a member of the International Trilateral Commission; Senator John L. Nichol of Vancouver, a longtime Liberal party activist who had served in Lester Pearson's cabinet; Marcel Bélanger of Montreal, a tax expert and chartered accountant. In 1974, William I.M. Turner, president of Consolidated-Bathurst, Ltd., of Montreal, replaced Murray.

left Montreal to become chief of *Time*'s London bureau. From New York, associate editor Clell Bryant arrived to take his place. Bryant, like Scott, was born in Canada and had worked for newspapers in Winnipeg and Montreal before being hired in 1962 to write for *Time Canada*. Transferred to the New York writing staff in 1968, he had on occasion flown back to Montreal to fill in when Scott was vacationing.

Soon after the change in Montreal, *Time*'s Ottawa bureau got a new chief as well. Traditionally, the post had been held by an American experienced in U.S. and foreign news reporting. Canadian critics cited this as an example of *Time*'s cultural imperialism, and when the Ottawa job became vacant in 1973, with the departure of bureau chief Lansing Lamont, *Time Canada* staffers themselves strongly urged that a Canadian be appointed to succeed him. New York rejected that idea, but did take special care in picking the new chief. Hungarian-born B. William Mader, who was then serving his second tour of duty as *Time*'s State Department correspondent, was the choice. As talented a diplomat as he was a reporter of diplomatic news, Mader found himself employing both those skills over the next two years.

In 1974 Canada held national elections. Prime Minister Trudeau enlisted Keith Davey to run his campaign. The government was reelected with a comfortable majority owing in large part to the vigorous support of Liberals in Ontario, where Davey was most influential. This was a turning point for *Time*'s Canadian edition. Recalled LaRue: "Davey began to feel his oats. He was determined to make a name for himself, and we were a part of that . . . There had always been a sort of stabbing, jabbing in the press reference to *Time Canada*'s 'privileged position' . . . We could see that we were in for trouble."

Later in 1974, as the nationalists pressed for legislation to revoke *Time*'s tax exemption, Mader warned New York:

> Within the Cabinet and the Parliament the overwhelming majority is stridently against us . . . It seems to me that if *Time* is to stay, it will have to make very substantial concessions. This would concern not only ownership but very likely content and format as well . . . Both the short- and the long-term outlook remain bleak.

LaRue was similarly briefing the *Time* business offices.

372

On November 14, 1974, magazine group vice president Keylor took the matter to the Time Inc. board. "Canadian nationalism is no longer a noisy, vaguely irritating threat to *Time Canada*. It is now a widely held and strongly expressed view—culturally, economically and politically," Keylor said, asking approval for sale of 75 percent of *Time Canada*'s equity ownership to Canadians. A sale had already been discussed with the Power Corporation of Canada for $7.5 million; other firms, including John Bassett's Baton Broadcasting Inc. and the Thomson newspaper group, were also interested. After such a sale, Keylor said, Time Inc. would continue to provide editorial material and operate the day-to-day publishing business under specific contractual arrangements.

The demand that the magazine be "heavily Canadian" in content was harder to deal with. To *Time*'s request for a definition of what was legally required, the Canadian government had not yet given a satisfactory answer. Sale of the equity would hinge on that answer, Keylor told the board.

Time Inc. also renewed its lobbying efforts. An impending meeting of President Ford with Prime Minister Trudeau in December 1974 gave Hedley Donovan the opportunity to write Secretary of State Henry Kissinger: "I take the liberty of calling to your attention a serious threat to the position of *Time* magazine in Canada, arising out of the nationalist currents that seem to be running so strongly in Canadian politics." Donovan did not ask for any specific intercession but merely briefed Kissinger on *Time*'s position. Weeks later Donovan was told by Kissinger that the whole question of *Time*'s role in Canada just "did not come up."

For the *Time Canada* staff, it was a harrowing period. Although the number of cover stories appearing exclusively in the Canadian edition and the regular Canadian news pages running each week were both increasing, the edition's Canadian critics were not mollified. "The staff of *Time Canada*," as Bryant described the experience, "was enduring a psychological siege of an intensity and duration that no one should be subjected to outside of a combat zone. For more than a year, they lived with that most stressful of all conditions, uncertainty."

Early in 1975, *Time* made a final editorial attempt to comply with Canadian demands. Founding father Scott, who had returned to Montreal as a senior correspondent, designed the battle plan. The section of Canadian news that had for so long led off *Time Canada*—"the Canada ghetto," Scott called it—would be broken up and distributed in appropriate sections throughout the magazine. "Psychologically," said Scott, "this would . . . give the whole magazine the flavor that it has been addressed to the Canadian reader." By this formula the Montreal editor, selecting stories from domestic *Time*, would look for ways to revise or amplify them, where possible, for Canadian readership. Shortly, New York dispatched Donald Morrison, a rising *Time* writer, and Irene Ramp, a skilled designer, to Montreal to help produce a dummy.

The dummy issue was presented to the Canadian government in May, with a formal request for a ruling: Would *Time Canada*, in this form, qualify as a Canadian publication under the Income Tax Act of 1965? The government still deferred its reply. Increasingly, it was becoming evident that the real intention, far from seeking the "Canadianization" of *Time Canada*, was in fact to prevent it, in order to clear the field—as officials later privately acknowledged— for Toronto's *Maclean's* magazine to transform itself from a monthly into a newsweekly. That supposition was confirmed when finally, on October 23, 1975, Canada's Revenue Minister issued a ruling on the government's requirements for editorial content: for a magazine to be considered Canadian, a minimum of 80 percent of its text had to be "substantially" different from that of its parent edition.

In the face of this impossible condition, *Time* abandoned the effort to preserve *Time Canada*'s distinctive editorial identity. It did not, however, abandon the effort to stay in Canada; rather, in a completely different plan of action, the *Time* division now proposed to offer the regular U.S. edition to Canadian subscribers at a premium price of $30 a year (Canadians had been paying just over $18; the U.S. price was then $22). The likely Canadian circulation of *Time* U.S. at this price was estimated at about 200,000—down from *Time Canada*'s 510,000. Shepley outlined the plan to Heiskell:

> At the moment we are keeping the cards close to the vest on this thinking, both because of Canadian politics and the Canadian staff, but obviously some announcement must be forthcoming fairly soon . . . It's a calculated risk . . . The Canadians can respond with punitive postal rates and other new sanctions against us. But each new step makes them look more like a banana republic and a banana republic lowering an Iron Curtain against the U.S. to boot.

On February 25, 1976, the Canadian House of Commons voted 134 to 96 to remove the tax deduction for advertisers in magazines not qualifying as Canadian. The Liberals and their allies burst out in

374

cheering and desk thumping as the vote was announced.

Publisher LaRue was ready with a statement: "The government's intention . . . is to put *Time Canada* out . . . and to prevent us from taking the necessary steps to qualify under the law as a Canadian magazine." *Time Canada* had "clearly and repeatedly stated its willingness to meet the letter and spirit of the law," but could not comply with the government's "exceptional and selective interpretation" of it. So, said LaRue, "with great regret we must announce the suspension of *Time Canada* and the Canada editorial section, and give notice to our staff." *Time Canada* published its final issue on March 1, 1976.

The business plan outlined the preceding fall was put into effect. *Time*'s U.S. edition was offered to Canadian readers. The *Time Canada* operation was dismantled. Later, editor Bryant praised the staff's professionalism and loyalty, quoting chairman Heiskell: "I have never seen a group of people hold together as these people have done." Bryant went on to say: "Perhaps the most remarkable aspect of the whole affair was not the eventual death of *Time Canada* but that it had survived for so long against so many nationalist slings and arrows." *Time Canada* director John Nichol summed up the views of some of his countrymen in a letter to *Time* publisher Ralph Davidson: "As a Canadian, I found the whole exercise childish, repugnant and stupid."

Ironically, *Time Canada*'s demise was of little, if any, benefit to Canadian magazines. The monthly *Maclean's*, founded in 1905 as "Canada's national magazine," went fortnightly as "Canada's newsmagazine" in 1975 and weekly in 1978—but lost about 15 percent of its circulation in the process.

Time, for its part, suffered no financial damage. By 1980, some 286,000 Canadians were paying $39 yearly to subscribe to the U.S. edition of *Time*, and 45,000 more bought it at newsstands. *Time* in 1980 earned a pretax profit of over $5 million in Canada—more than three times the net in 1975, the last year before *Time Canada* was forced to fold.

The editorial success of *Time Canada* had been very much in the company's mind as attention focused, in the early 1970s, on the question of *Time Atlantic*'s future. The idea of adapting *Time* editorially for European readership was not a new one. In 1953 a British *Time* was seriously studied. There had been experiments over the years at translating *Time* into French or German, most recently in 1967, when samples of each were dummied and circulated to Time-

Life International's European staff for comment—with rather discouraging results. (The translated stories, moreover, did not space to the same lengths as the originals in English, suggesting the makeup difficulties that any directly translated version of *Time* would have encountered.)

In June 1972, with the appointment of a joint editorial and publishing team to study *Time Atlantic*'s situation, the company turned to the *Time Canada* formula, a model for a *Time Europe* with stronger advertising and audience appeal. Publisher Ralph Davidson, who had spent a decade in international advertising sales for TLI, was behind the project. Composing the task force were two experienced correspondents, *Time*'s deputy news service chief Ed Jackson, formerly chief of the Rome bureau (and before that with United Press overseas), and Robert Ball, European editor of *Fortune*, previously *Time*'s European economic correspondent. On the publishing side was David Borie, a marketing specialist in the *Time* publisher's office. Additionally, the study group was asked to look into *Fortune*'s position in Europe.

Their study, completed in October, confirmed that *Time* faced a new situation in Europe—one which also offered journalistic opportunity:

> Europe has left the postwar nest. The power of the U.S. to control European events is steadily diminishing. Once we could virtually call the shots. Now . . . American influence in Europe will increasingly depend on persuasion, and persuasion depends on effective and accurate communication, plus the sense of underlying common interest . . . Americans need to know more, not less, about Europe. By the same token Europeans need to know more, not less, about the U.S . . . .It would seem the natural pride of Time Inc. to want to share importantly in this effort.

Competitively, *Time* was still ahead. It could not, in English, reach the audience the local magazines could, but its European circulation was more than double *Newsweek*'s and quadruple that of the *Economist*. *Time* took in half of all the money spent in Europe on international advertising.

Yet *Time Atlantic* rested on a fragile publishing base. International advertising was a thin field, especially vulnerable to changes in business conditions—"always the first to go in tight times," the report noted. Overall, the international advertising pot was shrinking. *Time Atlantic*'s circulation seemed stalled; 250,000 new subscriptions would be needed in 1973 to maintain the 430,000 rate base. Since 1969 ad page sales had declined; increased page rates kept revenues up. The task force reported that "1973 will be the third consecutive year in which we will offer advertisers the same circulation at higher prices."

Time had to change editorially, the study group insisted. Its prestige was still high, its American viewpoint an asset rather than a liability: "One of the most admired aspects of *Time*'s international coverage is its balance . . . the feeling that if it has an axe to grind, at least it is not a narrowly German or French political axe." But, the report warned, "we are partly living on our past reputation. We are standing on a plateau in Europe. In a few years, we could head downhill unless we do something now." Pointedly, the task force noted the international moves being made by *Time*'s competitor. With a growing New York-based international editorial staff, *Newsweek* had begun putting special regional covers on its overseas editions and running features such as business briefs, a markets column and interviews aimed at an international audience.

Unanimously, the task force recommended that *Time* "think Europe"—that is, use its worldwide news-gathering apparatus, the access the magazine enjoyed, to produce extra pages of news oriented to European interests, supplementing *Time*'s regular front- and back-of-the-book coverage. Paris was recommended as the editorial base; *Time*'s European news coverage was already centered there. In the spring of 1972, Gart had established a new European bureau under former Paris bureau chief Bill Rademaekers, through which other bureaus on the Continent as well as London now reported. *Time*'s European pages also would be written in Paris, on-scene, as in Canada.

In the end, it was *Newsweek* that forced *Time*'s hand—not in the decision, but in its timing. Davidson was ready to go ahead; Heiskell, during a visit to Paris, had heard the argument in favor from *Time*'s European advertising director, Christian Bardin. Time Inc. management was favorably inclined but not yet committed. In mid-December a *Time* correspondent, who must necessarily remain nameless, chanced on a friend, a *Newsweek* correspondent, necessarily ditto, in Spain. They chatted. *Newsweek*'s plans—to announce their European edition very shortly—slipped out. A cable from the *Time* correspondent to Gart and some hurried meetings in New York did the rest.

On December 19, less than 24 hours after the cable arrived, there were two announcements. One, a statement from Davidson's office, declared that *Time* would launch a European edition in the coming year, with a Paris-based staff to begin preliminary work in February. A half-hour later came *Newsweek's* plans for "major expansion" internationally: a new European edition and one for Asia too. The dual announcements, *Time's* and *Newsweek's*, made a single story in most newspapers. Later, Davidson savored the small triumph:

> When we overheard that *Newsweek* was going, we just jammed through our decision . . . I nearly got fired over that. I did not clear it with [Time Inc.'s magazine group]. I knew that if I had to clear it with them, it'd take a month. So I just did it . . . [They] chewed on me . . . chewed, and chewed . . . Finally Heiskell called me up to his office. He said: "In the future, don't you think you could pick up the telephone?"

It was a fast run from there to press time for *Time Europe*, a little over ten weeks later. A staff was set up in Paris under European editor Jesse Birnbaum, a relative novice in Europe but an experienced *Time* senior editor with a bright, light touch. Curt Prendergast, formerly news bureau chief in Paris and London, came aboard for the start-up. Joining the group a few months later, and bringing nearly 20 years of reporting experience in Europe, Africa and the Far East as a correspondent for the United Press and *U.S. News & World Report*, was Frederick Painton, who was to become the edition's leading writer and its sophisticated guide to European politics.

Ed Jackson, fresh from the task-force exercise that had got *Time Europe* started, was established in New York as international editor, a new post on *Time*. He was to handle the myriad details of layout and pictures, and coordinate European stories with those from the domestic edition. It promised to be a complicated and expensive procedure. Some stories, running only in Europe, would be written and edited in Paris, then fitted into the page layouts in New York before relay to the printer in Chicago, where the pages would be filmed for air shipment back to Paris for printing. To supervise the start-up, senior editor Jason McManus went to Paris; in New York, Grunwald kept a sharp eye on the proceedings, reading the story lists carefully, offering suggestions of his own for coverage.

Dated March 12, 1973, the first issue of *Time Europe* appeared in print 50 years to the month from the first appearance of *Time* in America. In the publisher's letter *Time* hailed the new edition as "the first step in our second half-century." Six additional pages on Europe led off that first issue, beginning with the first-round results of France's parliamentary elections. The *Time Europe* staff stayed up Sunday night for the election returns, went to the Paris printing plant the next day to insert the latest vote tabulations into the story that had arrived that morning from Chicago. *Time*'s European edition came out Tuesday with later figures than any of the local competitors could manage.

With *Time Europe* established and running, and showing a slight improvement in advertising sales, the publisher's attention turned a few months later toward Asia. Jackson was assigned to do a parallel study of the feasibility of "a natural sequel to *Time Canada* and *Time Europe*."

The Pacific, Jackson reported in October 1973, was an area of "difficult publishing problems . . . bannings, tariffs, vast distances." But it was an area with enormous economic potential, and here too, *Newsweek* was intensifying efforts. For Asian readers, *Newsweek* was adapting its international edition to lead off with several pages of Asian news, followed by a section on Europe (in the European edition, the order was reversed but the material remained the same). Though its total Asian and Pacific circulation was only about half *Time*'s total, *Newsweek* was pressing closer in some countries, notably Japan. The *Wall Street Journal* likewise was eyeing the Asian market. For journalistic and competitive business reasons, Jackson urged, *Time* should make a move in the Pacific. He recommended stationing an editorial staff in Asia, preferably Hong Kong, following the models of *Time Canada* and *Time Europe*.

Attractive as a locally-based Asian editorial operation appeared to be, the costs were judged too high. Instead Jackson, from his base in New York, took on the additional duty of overseeing the production of special editorial material, including cover stories, for the Asian and South Pacific editions of *Time*. In early 1976, budgetary considerations forced *Time* to bring its European staff home. With this move, amalgamating all international operations under a single editor seemed logical; Birnbaum returned from Paris to take that post.

Remaining under the *Time* publisher's office for publishing direction, the international editions became increasingly more autonomous editorially. With a growing staff, *Time Europe* and *Time Asia* were generating more of their own regional news and cover stories—at the same time, however, maintaining the predominantly American "feel" that the task force had judged to be *Time*'s basic editorial strength. In this, *Time*'s approach to magazine publishing for an international audience remained distinctly different from

379

Newsweek's. In 1980 editorial direction of the international editions changed hands. Birnbaum left for Time Inc.'s new magazine *Discover*; succeeding him was *Time* senior editor Karsten Prager, 43. Prager, German-born, had been a Southeast Asian correspondent for the AP before joining *Time* in 1965 in Vietnam; he had served for three years as *Time*'s Beirut bureau chief.

Not all the problems of *Time*'s erstwhile "screwballs" had been solved as the 1980s began. Circulation growth was slow; however, that circulation was solid and becoming steadily more profitable. Advertising revenues were fairly soaring. Of the international editions' combined pretax income of nearly $30 million in 1980, half was coming from *Time Europe*.

CHAPTER
22

A Trip to the Movies

"IT IS HARD TO VISUALIZE Time Inc. enlarging its leadership position in the information industry unless it develops expertise in informing the public through the medium of pictures that move." That conclusion of a recent corporate research study was cited as the company prepared, in mid-1967, to take its first major stake in films—a 5 percent ownership of Metro-Goldwyn-Mayer.

Time Inc. had been frustrated in most of its efforts to get into filmmaking. *The March of Time,* for all its journalistic excellence, had been a marginal enterprise financially; Time-Life Broadcast's various attempts to program for network television had failed. The MGM involvement offered what management considered a more direct route into motion picture production and marketing, for both theaters and television.

Different from the United Artists proposal, which Luce had so abruptly stopped a year before his death (see chapter 13), the MGM investment would be neither acquisition nor merger, Ed Baker, who then headed corporate development, pointed out. Rather it would give Time Inc. "a front-row observation post" in films, in a studio that "has long enjoyed the reputation of the Rolls-Royce of its industry, both in terms of product quality as well as operating results." MGM was also the second largest producer of prime-time

381

TV films and one of the U.S.'s top five record companies. "From conversations with MGM management, we know that with a holding of this size they would be happy to have us represented on the board, and it probably would be possible to place several of the younger Time Inc. executives in middle-management positions in the company," Baker declared.

The MGM investment opportunity arose through Time Inc.'s association with Edgar Bronfman, head of the U.S. operations of Seagram's, whose liquor advertising was among the Time Inc. magazines' largest accounts. Bronfman was a regular on the *Time* news tours and also a close friend of Linen, whom Bronfman had first met as a Williams College undergraduate when Linen was a Williams trustee.

Bronfman, through an investment management company called Cemp Investment, Ltd. (named for Charles, Edgar, Minda and Phyllis Bronfman, the four children of Samuel Bronfman, progenitor of the Seagram fortune), had been buying MGM stock during a proxy battle for control of the movie firm. The loser in the proxy battle was Philip J. Levin, a wealthy New Jersey real estate developer whose 560,000 shares of MGM afterward came onto the market. Bronfman, already holding 400,000 shares, invited Time Inc. to join him in a bid. Encouragement came from all sides, including from MGM management, which welcomed the proposed new shareholders' "assurance of support." The deal was consummated on September 1: Time Inc. bought 300,000 of Levin's shares and the Bronfmans the rest, at $59—a $17.7 million investment for Time Inc. Additionally, the Bronfmans bought 160,000 shares from associates of Levin, thus becoming MGM's largest shareholders, with about 16 percent of the stock.

Baker and Bronfman joined the MGM board of directors, as did Leo Kolber, Cemp's managing director. Several months later Bernhard Auer, now a senior vice president of Time Inc., and Bronfman's brother-in-law John Loeb, senior partner in the investment banking firm of Loeb Rhoades & Co., also joined the board. Wall Street speculated that a merger was in the works. None came off, of course, but within a year MGM was in the news on another score.

Dissatisfied with MGM management, Bronfman brought in a new president, Louis F. (Bo) Polk, 38, a business prodigy who had been chief financial officer of General Mills at the age of 31. Shortly afterward, in May 1969, Bronfman had himself named chairman of the MGM board. But Polk was a Hollywood novice, and during 1969 the studio's fortunes sagged. MGM stock dropped to a low of $25 in July; not long after, Kirk Kerkorian, the Las Vegas hotel owner and financier, began buying heavily. By October, Kerkorian owned more stock then either Time Inc. or the Bronfmans, and began exercising his newly purchased control. Polk was sacked, to be replaced by James T. Aubrey Jr. (known as the Smiling Cobra), who had kept CBS television on top of the network ratings in the early 1960s. Bronfman and Loeb resigned from the board, as did Time Inc.'s Auer. Edgar Baker had died earlier in the year.

By early 1970, Time Inc.'s relationship with MGM bore almost no resemblance to the one it had entered into two and a half years earlier. Control and management of the company were in unfamiliar and unanticipated hands. No Time Inc. delegates had voices on the board. Jim Linen, who had most vigorously championed the association, was no longer Time Inc.'s president. While the two companies negotiated some minor deals—MGM got the rights to make films out of Time-Life books, for example—it was clear that the close association once envisaged was not possible. From its "front-row observation post" on films Time Inc. had witnessed mainly MGM's managerial troubles. In 1972 the company took a $10.5 million write-down on its MGM investment, retaining the stock, however, as part of its portfolio, selling it off gradually until it was all gone in January 1979.

While Time Inc. was working at the corporate level to establish a position in films, individual divisions were continuing their own production efforts—not, as it became apparent, with much coordination or overall direction.

Life had dipped into moviemaking several times, partly in an attempt to get an extra payoff from its regular photojournalism. Early in the 1960s, Dick Pollard, *Life*'s director of photography, had bought a pair of 16-mm. movie cameras, burying the cost in his budget, and asked photographers to take them along on field assignments. In Pollard's view, it was "pretty damned silly to send a photographer to Outer Mongolia, Antarctica, Easter Island or on any long, expensive assignment just to do still pictures."

Little had come of these particular experiments; motion-picture and still photography proved hard to combine. But by 1968 *Life*'s film production was put on an organized basis with the establishment of a film department headed by Richard O'Shea, a former business manager for editorial operations. O'Shea developed an ambitious plan to make one-hour documentaries for commercial television, and began looking for sponsorship. Under the plan, *Life*

383

would retain editorial control but the sponsor would get a four-color advertisement in *Life* as well as an article on the subject of the program shortly before it was broadcast. Alcoa bought the arrangement, signing up for four programs at $200,000 each (it later signed up for four more). Aired by a group of independent stations tied together as the Hughes Television Network, the programs got a respectable national audience, but not the network showing originally hoped for.

At the same time, the book division was collaborating with MGM on an NBC series sponsored by General Electric. By mid-1969 Time-Life Broadcast, for its part, had produced a dozen episodes for an educational TV series called *The World We Live In*, based on books in the Life Nature Library and the Life Science Library; 14 more programs were in the works. *Sports Illustrated* also, in partnership with a Philadelphia firm, was turning out short films, running three minutes 40 seconds each—vignettes and interviews highlighting offbeat facts and odd information about a variety of sports or sport figures—for TV sponsorship by the Shell Oil Company. With a different partner *SI* was co-producing for the retail market 400 how-to-play-it 8-mm loops, and it also had a half-interest in a film about a mountain-climbing expedition in Afghanistan.

This profusion of uncoordinated efforts in the film field bothered *Life* publisher Jerry Hardy. He put his complaint in a memo to management in April 1969:

> The problem seems to be that several divisions of the company, including *Life*, are making proposals to produce films, basically for television, that cover much of the same subject matter and even solicit sponsorship from some of the same advertisers . . .
>
> A TV program on, say, wolves, produced under the auspices of Time-Life Books is not going to look very different from a film on wolves produced by *Life* magazine films or Time-Life Broadcast. I understand two films on wolves are contemplated by two Time Inc. divisions. Therefore this is not an academic question.
>
> [There is a] serious risk of alienating advertisers . . . When GE, for example, lays out something like $300,000 for a Time-Life book division film, it is likely to be upset by discovering that *Life* films or *SI* films is selling one that is different principally in being "by the editors of *Life*" rather than by "the editors of Time-Life Books."

Moreover, these small film enterprises were not being managed

384

efficiently. In July 1969 a corporate development study done for Heiskell and Linen set forth the problems:

> In the big majority, the films were of good quality, but they lost a lot of money. Another common failure . . . has been the near total lack of consistency in retention of rights for ancillary markets (education, television, syndication, etc.) . . . Nor has there been any established authority in the company to supervise production, budgets or control quality.

Hardy and the corporate development team came to identical conclusions: Time Inc. should establish a corporate division to manage its disparate film efforts. But simply combining a group of losing or marginal enterprises was not likely to produce a winner; Time Inc. was still deficient in filmmaking and marketing expertise. The development group therefore advocated acquiring a small, established film distribution firm—specifically, Peter M. Robeck & Co.

Robeck, then 52, was a Californian who had been in the film and TV business, mainly as a salesman, since leaving UCLA. He had worked for CBS, for a Los Angeles TV station owned jointly by CBS and the Los Angeles *Times*, and for RKO General before founding his own company in 1958. It produced no programs of its own, but rather syndicated programs made by others to individual TV stations around the country, also selling and renting to government and educational institutions. The company's most valuable asset by far was its contract with the British Broadcasting Corporation, for nearly exclusive rights to U.S. distribution of BBC programs to the television and educational market.

The BBC association that Robeck offered was attractive for two reasons. The BBC was a bountiful source of films, producing more than 5,000 hours of original programming annually, of which about 100 hours (both 30- and 60-minute programs) were judged suitable for American audiences. The BBC was substantial and prestigious, a desirable partner. In fact, Time Inc. was already negotiating with the BBC to co-produce a historical series called *The British Empire*, for which Time-Life Books in London would publish an accompanying series of softcover booklets.

The Robeck acquisition was approved by the board of directors on August 21, 1969—the same day as the management shuffle that included the appointment of Rhett Austell as executive vice president in charge of books, records, education and films. Robeck got 13,500 shares of Time Inc. stock, then worth $675,000; his company in turn became the umbrella under which all of Time Inc.'s film operations were combined to form a new division named Time-Life Films, with Robeck in charge. Sometime later he said of the film division, "Its mother was a mature publishing company, its father a traveling salesman."

Formation of Time-Life Films did not inhibit a proliferation of other company activities falling into the video category. Clurman, on joining corporate development, had taken video technology as his province, and in May 1970 was assigned by Austell to investigate "the editorial potential of cartridge television." A staff under Clurman experimented with cassettes of Leonard Bernstein conducting Beethoven's *Fidelio* and a sex-education program with Masters and Johnson, among others. Eventually, from Clurman's group, Time-Life Video evolved.

Meanwhile, former *Life* managing editor George Hunt had gathered a staff to develop scripts for a television pilot to be called the *Magazine of the Air*. This was described by Austell as "halfway between the 'now' television of the Cronkites . . . and documentary television." Working with Hunt was Eleanor Graves, one of Time Inc.'s more talented and versatile editorial hands. Eleanor Mackenzie (as she was then) had come to the company fresh out of Barnard College, started as a researcher-trainee on *Time*, switched to *Life* and worked as a reporter, writer and editor in just about every department of that magazine. In 1958 she married Ralph Graves, then *Life*'s articles editor. When he became managing editor in 1969 she left the staff because Donovan had "told me graciously that Ralph would have to cut the staff and it would be unpleasant and inappropriate while others were being let go that I, a wife, would remain." She then joined Hunt's unit.

Life's experience with the *Magazine of the Air* was reminiscent of Time-Life Broadcast's earlier attempts at network programming. Mrs. Graves explained: "We were naive and didn't realize that we couldn't sell it to the networks via the news departments. There was no outlet for the film." Moving on to Time-Life Video, she supervised production of a successful cassette on speed reading, with Dick Cavett as narrator, which earned more than $2 million in the ten years following its issue. In 1974, Time-Life Video was merged into the film division, and Eleanor Graves became vice president of programming and executive producer.

By then, Time-Life Films was no longer the enterprise Peter Robeck had launched with such exuberance, and Robeck himself was gone. His brief reign had started auspiciously; 1969 was a particularly good time to be distributing BBC films. The magnificent series *Civilisation* was just being released to reverent notices; much of the credit was due its distinguished author and narrator, art historian Kenneth Clark (of whom *Time* art critic Robert Hughes once remarked, "He spoke of the Renaissance as though he had commissioned it"). That series brought in U.S. revenues of more than $1 million in 1970, an enormous amount for a BBC program in America, and got Time-Life Films off to an encouraging start.

But there were problems in the relationship with the BBC. The most important concerned co-production, where distribution rights were closely linked with financing, and Time-Life Films, in order to remain the sole U.S. distributor, found itself financing far more than was wise. In just two years Time-Life Films accumulated an inventory of 39 unsalable programs. Peter Hansen, the division's manager of television program administration, described them in a memo, parts of which are grimly amusing:

MARCEL MARCEAU - An interview with Marcel Marceau [the mime], who ought to keep his mouth shut. Even the culture vultures nod off. No interest even at PBS.

MAX REMEMBERS - A whimsical dramatization of the latter part of Max Beerbohm's life. There is precious little to dramatize, and what little there is is precious, and unfortunately, we have no convenient package to absorb it, even for PBS.

PARASITE OF PARADISE - A minute examination of malaria. Not an automatic turn-on. No client, network, or station interest.

Several other co-productions seemed to be vying for the distinction of being the most anticlimactic. There was the saga of a group of mountain climbers who tried to scale Mount Everest but didn't make it. Another told the story of the woman whose husband had died without fulfilling his lifelong wish of catching a world-record marlin; she set out to catch it for him, BBC cameras following all the way, but never got a nibble. And then there was the film that followed the favored yacht in a transatlantic race. The boat didn't even place.

To be sure, there were some outstanding successes in the pile. The most notable were two famous series, both first shown on NBC: *America* (sponsored by Xerox) a 13-part series in the *Civilisation* style with Alistair Cooke as author and narrator, and *The Search for the Nile*, the story of Sir Richard Burton's punishing expedition to the source of the Nile in 1857–58. But most of the Time-Life Films and BBC collaborations remained unsold; of the $5 million TLF invested in its first three years, $3 million had to be written off.

Time-Life Films was also producing programs on its own, with mixed success. Two films made on speculation, *Khrushchev Remembers* and *The Making of the Presidency* with Theodore White as narrator, proved impossible to sell as individual programs and were never widely seen. Most successful were the documentary series *Other People, Other Places* and *The Wild, Wild World of Animals,* which were syndicated both in the U.S. and abroad.

In 1972, Time-Life Films lost nearly $2.5 million. That year, Robeck left. In his place came Lee Heffner, former advertising director at *Fortune* and national advertising manager at *Life.* Despite Heffner's Madison Avenue contacts, Time-Life Films was no more successful in placing programs on commercial television, and after a year in which Time-Life Films lost $5.2 million, Heffner moved over to chairman. He was succeeded as president by Bruce Paisner.

Paisner, then only 31, had started at Time Inc. in 1968, just out of Harvard Law School, as an assistant to Andrew Heiskell. While an undergraduate at Harvard, Paisner had been managing editor of the *Crimson*; later he worked as a reporter for *Life.* In 1970 he left Heiskell's office to become general manager of Time-Life Video, moving afterward to the film division where in October 1973 he was named the division's president. Under Paisner, Time-Life Films cut back sharply on co-productions, planning to rely less on the BBC in general. Paisner explained his thinking to the directors of Time Inc. at a dinner in November 1974:

> One of the things that most worried the new management [of Time-Life Films] was our near-total dependence on the BBC. A major part of our programming strategy has been and will continue to be to reduce this dependence, and it is gratifying to be able to report that when we chose our most successful programs (both financially and creatively) to show you tonight, three of the four turned out to be our own productions.

The three house-produced programs were the speed-reading course, an episode about Kodiak Island bears from *The Wild, Wild World of Animals,* and the first completely internal production the division ever sold to a network, the *Harold Lloyd Special.* The Lloyd program, a takeout on the comedian with a sampling of scenes from his silent films, appeared on ABC with an introduction by Dick Van Dyke. The fourth program shown the directors was one co-produced with the BBC years earlier, *The Ascent of Man,* with British scientist Jacob Bronowski as author and narrator. Not seen on American television until the following year because Time-Life Films was holding out for $3.9 million (more than twice what *Civilisation* and *America* had brought from sales to commercial sponsors), *The Ascent of Man* had the extraordinary scope and learning of its predecessors, but not the same popular appeal; Time-Life Films eventually settled for $750,000 on a sale to the Public Broadcasting Service.

Paisner by no means intended to cut all ties to the BBC, and indeed the transatlantic collaboration continued. One notably successful product was a Shakespearean play cycle, aired on PBS at the end of the 1970s.

Time-Life Films did, however, shift its emphasis toward more homegrown productions. Coinciding with the launching of *People* magazine in 1974, this policy offered the opportunity that had been envisaged when the film division was first set up. The new magazine's province seemed a natural for television; plans for a *People* program began to take shape almost immediately. By early 1976 a half-hour pilot program about actress Ann-Margret, called *People Cover Story*, was ready. The show, broadcast on ABC's New York station, was greeted with a sneering New York *Times* review, calling it "breathless digging beneath a glamorous veneer to discover still another glamorous veneer." Another *People* program, a variety show on NBC with Lily Tomlin as host, fared somewhat better—but not in the Time Inc. publications. *Newsweek* ran a neutral story; *Time* ignored it completely, leading Paisner to write a peevish note to Heiskell:

> *Time*'s failure to mention at all a Time Inc. project which *Newsweek* found newsworthy supports your feeling that we have a long way to go to coordinate our activities most effectively. In this particular instance, a story in a newsmagazine the week before the program can create public interest and raise the number of viewers, thus: 1) encouraging NBC to order more shows, and 2) increasing the circulation of *People* magazine.

The issue, a sensitive one, was to arise again later, when Time Inc. became a major force in television programming, through its Home Box Office cable network (see chapter 28), and *Time* began reviewing HBO's film offerings.

Yet despite reverses, Time-Life Films was becoming a healthy business. By 1975 it had turned a small profit. Growth was clearly dependent on expanding production, however. The expansion route chosen was a major acquisition: David Susskind's Talent Associates Ltd., purchased in August 1977 for $1,001,000 of Time Inc. stock plus an arrangement for dividing profits over the next five years. The deal was mutually beneficial. Time Inc. acquired the talents of Susskind himself and his quarter-century of experience in the tough, risky world of network production. His organization had produced everything from classy dramas (*Death of a Salesman*, *The Crucible*) to sitcoms, in addition to Susskind's own weekly TV talk show, which made him something of a celebrity. For its part, Talent Associates gained access to the financial strength of Time Inc. and a connection with a large, established distributor. As Susskind explained to the New York *Times*, "In most cases, if you produce a product and then turn it over to a syndicator, they don't give you a fair shake. Now we are blood-related, so they [Time-Life Films] will distribute all the products that we produce."

There was one early stumble as Susskind's outfit began production under Time-Life Films' aegis. This was a new effort at transferring the *People* format to TV film, which CBS scheduled for the 1978 fall season. Producer of the show was Charlotte Schiff Jones, formerly vice president of Manhattan Cable and more recently assistant publisher of *People*. A pilot program underwritten by CBS was broadcast in June. With Phyllis George, a onetime Miss America, as host, the show offered brief looks at such celebrity staples as the New York disco Studio 54, model Cheryl Tiegs, singer Pat Boone and actress Greta Garbo, all edited to move at a breakneck pace to the accompaniment of throbbing music. The reviews were vituperative. The Chicago *Tribune* found it "so lacking in taste and common decency that it would be a pleasure to see the show fold quickly." The San Francisco *Chronicle* called it "laughable." The show went bravely forward, going on the air as scheduled, only to fall an early victim of poor audience ratings.

The Susskind association nonetheless boosted Time-Life Films from a minor to a major position in its field. Owing entirely to Talent Associates' activity, TLF suddenly became the third largest supplier of made-for-television movies to the networks, after Universal and Warner. The next step was obvious and irresistible: to become a producer of theatrical films.

As a business proposition, this was riskier than making television programs. But the stakes were higher. Time-Life Films took the plunge in 1979, producing through Talent Associates a comedy

390

called *Loving Couples*, with Shirley MacLaine and James Coburn. The film failed despite its stars, but two others were already in the works. *Fort Apache, the Bronx*, a picture of life in the roughest police precinct in New York City, starring Paul Newman; and *They All Laughed*, a comedy conceived and directed by Peter Bogdanovich. When the dice were rolled, *Fort Apache* scored a hit, but *They All Laughed* had a very short run. (Bogdanovich later bought the movie from Time-Life Films.)

One success in three tries was not a bad batting average; on the strength of it, Time-Life Films increased its commitment to movie-making. Other ideas for exploiting new technologies and TLF's own resources were under consideration. One venture, launched in 1979, was the Time-Life Video Club, which, operating like a book or record club, offered members a monthly selection of video cassettes playable on home video recorders. The club correctly anticipated the growing popularity of home video. The trouble was buyer reluctance to pay $40 to $80 for a cassette that probably would be viewed only a couple of times. The market for video cassettes, as it developed, became predominantly rental; Time Inc.'s direct-mail experience did not extend to the rental business. The video club expired.

A space-age failure doomed another Time-Life Films project, a plan for distributing BBC programs and TLF's own product via satellite to operators of cable TV systems, who would pay a small monthly fee per subscriber for the service. Preparations, including leasing of a transponder on RCA's then unlaunched Satcom III satellite, were complete when Satcom, shortly after launch, bafflingly disappeared. The loss caused a scarcity of transponders and gave Time Inc. management an excuse to scrap a scheme for which there was anyway no great enthusiasm.

In late 1972, with Time Inc.'s stake in video growing—not only in films but in cable television—management in this area had been strengthened. Dick Munro, a former general manager of SI and most recently its publisher, was assigned as deputy to group vice president Rhett Austell, the overseer of Time Inc.'s video interests. Munro, then 41, was to rise fast in the corporate ranks, taking over the direction of video a couple years later and then, in 1980, succeeding Heiskell as Time Inc.'s chief executive officer. En route to the top, Munro was named executive vice president in September 1979; succeeding him as head of the video group was Gerald M. Levin, who had managed Home Box Office from its shaky beginnings to the stunning success it subsequently enjoyed. In his new job, Levin reshuffled the leadership at Time-Life Films. Paisner, with whom Levin had "profound differences," left the company and later became president of King Features Entertainment Inc. As the new head of Time-Life Films, Levin chose Austin Furst, who had been in charge of buying films for HBO, where he had established a reputation as a tough and rough negotiator.

Furst faced an immediate decision on Susskind's contract, which had been negotiated under Paisner and was now about to expire. Appreciative of Susskind's abilities as a producer, Furst considered him a poor manager and shared the general corporate unhappiness with Susskind's expensive operating style and huge budget overruns. Accordingly, Furst told Susskind that he would not "exercise" renewal rights on his contract, though he was not firing him either. Susskind thereupon began negotiating with other companies; then Furst, having second thoughts, asked Susskind to return as an independent producer. But it was too late. Susskind had already made a deal with MGM.

Even before Susskind left, Furst set out to fulfill the charter that Levin had given him "to figure out how to become a motion-picture distributor and producer." He continued to build the empire Paisner had begun on the West Coast, signing a long-term lease for a headquarters building and hiring expensive staff; almost at the same time came a wholesale firing of New York employees. Adding to the turmoil, in late 1980, was BBC's decision to end its special relationship with Time-Life Films.

Furst's expansion plans involving expenditures of $310 million over five years, never got beyond its foundations. While it was germinating, Munro, Levin and Nicholas were deliberating whether Time Inc. should remain in the risky, capital-intensive movie business at all. As Munro observed, "You can't dabble—produce four or five films a year—you have to be in the 15 movies a year range." Yet even a commitment of this kind would be fraught with danger since, as Munro put it, "distribution is the key to the movie business, and we learned the hard way. The big boys wouldn't let us in."

This was one squeeze on Time-Life Films; the other, hurting the division's expansion plans even more, was the hunger for capital being displayed by Time Inc.'s cable TV activities, whose growth was requiring millions for new financing. Against this competition, even Furst had to concede that "sensible investment strategy required us to get out [of the movie business]."

That seemed to be exactly what Time Inc. was doing when it announced in February 1981 that "an agreement in principle" had been reached with 20th Century-Fox for that company to "acquire and assume control of most of the assets" of Time-Life Films. Coming just at the time when the division, under Furst, was gearing up for a new mission, the announcement surprised both the employees and the industry. The division began to close down although no agreement was reached with Fox. Shortly, the Fox deal fell apart, to be replaced in August by one with Columbia Pictures under which that studio took over Films' production commitments, receiving syndication rights to some 200 of its properties.

Time-Life Films transformed itself into a film licensing operation. Furst departed Time Inc., buying the Time-Life Video Club and forming a new company, Vestron, to exploit its video-cassette rights. Time Inc. kept nontheatrical rights, enabling it to distribute the film properties to businesses, schools and government through Time-Life Video, the one part of Time-Life Films that was kept active.

Time Inc. would continue to participate in film production through HBO, which would help finance major films, invest in a movie distribution company and take part with Columbia Pictures and CBS in a joint venture to found a major studio. Phasing out Time-Life Films was therefore hardly the end of an era. With even more ambition and money, cable television would carry on Time Inc.'s long-standing love affair with the moving image.

Bookmakers in Alexandria

OR A DECADE, Time-Life Books continued its astonishing upward climb. The "gusher that suddenly burst from the ground," as one editor earlier described the enterprise, Books had become a far larger business in its first full year, 1961, than the 31-year-old *Fortune*. By its tenth year, 1970, Books ranked as company's second most profitable publishing operation, exceeded only by the 47-year-old *Time*.

The book division's success at selling by mail had tempted it to offer other products and acquire related companies (see chapter 13), thereby broadening and diversifying its business. Chief overseer of this expansion was Rhett Austell, who in 1964 succeeded Jerry Hardy as book division publisher. Like a number of other Time Inc. executives on the business side, Austell was an alumnus of Williams College (Phi Beta Kappa, class of 1948). After getting his MBA from Harvard, he had joined the *Life* business staff in 1950 and had begun his ascent through the company, mainly in the circulation department of *Time*. As the book division branched out into new fields, Austell's managerial responsibilities multiplied.* The 1969 corporate changes moved Austell up to a group vice presidency and

*Shortly after Austell took over, the original book operation was designated Time-Life Books and the term book division remained an internal company description of the group that included the new businesses.

his deputy Walt Rohrer took his place as publisher (see chapter 16).

One early diversification, phonograph records, was born in the corporate research and development department at just about the same time that the book division got under way. The development of stereophonic playback equipment that ordinary consumers could afford had sparked a record boom in the late 1950s and early 1960s, and Time Inc. was eager to participate. Vice president Allen Grover, Luce's longtime aide, was assigned to meet with record company executives and explore possibilities. Interest was whetted by the success of an album of classical music brought out by *Reader's Digest*, produced by RCA Victor. There followed a good deal of brainstorming about where Time Inc. could find a niche in the market. One proposal was that *Life* should put out a sort of yearbook accompanied by a record reviewing the speeches, the songs, the other sounds of that year. A deal with Columbia Records similar to the *Reader's Digest*–RCA Victor arrangement was suggested; also the possibility of financing a new invention—an 8-rpm disc—by Peter Goldmark, inventor of the long-playing record. These ideas came to nothing, but in 1962 *Life* issued a five-record set of popular songs called *The Music of Life*, produced with RCA. It sold 93,000 copies at $14.95 each, a result successful enough to merit a follow-up.

In 1964, *Life* executive editor Phil Wootton, who had proposed *The Music of Life*, moved to the research and development department, spending much time over the next couple of years designing a record series that could be sold as Time-Life book series were sold. After experimenting with a number of different ideas, titles, package designs and test mailings, Wootton's pilot project, developed from a prospectus written by *Time*'s former music critic Carter Harman, came up with the The Story of Great Music, conceived as a series of boxed albums of four records each, tracing Western classical music from the baroque era to the present. Recordings came from the Angel catalogue of Capitol Records. Each set was to include a booklet produced to Time Inc. standards, discussing that musical period; with the first album a customer ordered there would be three dividend items relating to the records (one of which, an essay on music's place in Western civilization, represented an interesting bit of moonlighting by *Time* senior editor Henry Grunwald). Research showed that the booklets were an important element in consumers' decisions to buy. William Jay Gold, text director of Time-Life Books and a onetime dance-band musician (his group was called Bill Gold and His Pieces of Eight), was named editor of Time-Life Records, newly formed under the aegis of corporate R & D. In 1966 it became a semiautonomous part of Time-Life Books.

The Story of Great Music was favorably reviewed and eventually became such a hit that the six volumes originally planned were expanded to 11; later supplements eventually brought the total to 22. Time-Life Records continued to apply the methods of Books, developing new series to bring music to a large audience by mail— The Swing Era, Great Men of Music, Giants of Jazz, among others. Although records never approached the book business in size, they did become modestly profitable.

Meanwhile, the book division was exploring ways of using its direct-mail experience to sell other products. Gourmet cookware offered in connection with the Foods of the World series did respectably well; attempts to sell the likes of typewriters and binoculars, less well. An experimental Time-Life Travel Club managed to assemble a thousand members, but it was a business for which the company had no great passion or talent, and was never cranked up to full-scale operation.

In 1970, Books adopted an idea developed by *Fortune* and launched The Executive Voice, a series of cassettes featuring business executives relating what they had been up to lately and why. After a two-year trial, editorial director Lou Banks (formerly *Fortune*'s managing editor) reported to Donovan that the venture was facing "losses into eternity" because its market was too small. The Executive Voice was silenced.

In 1966, Norm Ross, Time-Life Books' founding editor, went to the General Learning Corporation, and executive editor Maitland Edey succeeded Ross. Then 56, Edey was a Princeton graduate who had come to Time Inc. in January 1942 as a *Life* writer, leaving a few months later to join the U.S. Army Air Force, where he worked on an air intelligence magazine. He rejoined *Life* in 1946, rising to assistant managing editor four years later. Edey resigned in 1955 to write on his own and pursue his love of sailing. (In 1957 he crossed the Atlantic as a working crew member on the *Mayflower II*, a replica of the original.) In 1960 the nascent book division had brought him back as editor of the Life Nature Library.

By the time of Edey's accession to the editorship, the Time-Life Books operation had passed its early hectic period when, in Edey's description, "Books was held together by string and wire." Edey, as

396

executive editor, had once sat up all night personally rewriting a book by another author for the science series, in order to meet the production schedule. That production schedule had hardly slackened; during Edey's four years as editorial chief, Time-Life Books turned out 161 titles—one almost every two weeks. Sales totaled more than 30 million volumes.

Titles included the Time-Life Library of Art, a notably handsome series that Edey had developed as executive editor; a cookbook series, Foods of the World; a U. S. regional series, the Time-Life Library of America; and a newsy review and social history of the years since 1870, decade by decade, entitled This Fabulous Century (an idea that had come from Jack Dowd, Time Inc.'s legal counsel for editorial matters from 1944 to 1973). Production of single volumes also continued. For one, *The Cats of Africa*, Edey himself wrote the text; color illustrations were by *Life* photographer John Dominis, who had done a memorable picture series on the subject for the magazine.

By 1970, having turned 60, Edey was eager to get back to his personal writing projects. His successor was his deputy, Gerald E. Korn, known universally as Jerry. A journalism major at Boston University, Korn had dropped out to get some practical experience, returning to journalism after wartime service in Europe with the Eighth Air Force co-piloting B-24 bombers. From the Associated Press in Washington, Korn went to *Collier's* magazine as a text and articles editor, moving to *Life* after *Collier's* demise in 1957. After editing text for *Life*, moonlighting also for the new *Life* book department, where he edited *The Wonders of Life on Earth*, Korn joined the book division fulltime in 1962.

Korn was wiry, almost totally bald, somewhat birdlike in appearance. In private life he pursued wide interests, including jazz, classical music and American history. In the office he was all business, amiable and pleasant but also reserved, serious, intense. He read every word, approved every layout of every book and consequently worked killing hours. But when assistants urged him to delegate some of these chores, he would say, "This is where the fun is for me."

Korn's appointment as editor surprised no one. And only because the choice was a woman was anyone surprised about the appointment of Korn's counterpart on the publishing side, who took over shortly after. Joan Manley, then 38, was the first woman ever to become a publisher at Time Inc. She was the obvious choice for the job. As Hardy's assistant in the book division's early days, she had been assigned to make herself an expert on mailing lists. She recalled that the assignment began "one hour after I came to work. I came to a full desk, and my job was to find outside lists to sell the Churchill books," the British wartime leader's memoirs that *Life* was then publishing.

Manley became a self-taught expert on mailing lists. For the Churchill books, for example, "we rented the American Heritage mailing list because that indicated to us that the names on that list were interested in buying history books." Logical enough, but the logic didn't always hold. Manley once bought a list of sleeping-bag buyers, thinking that they'd be interested in a nature series; they weren't.

In 1963 she became circulation manager. Three years later, general manager John Watters listed her among eight "publisher-office 'stars' of Time-Life Books" in a confidential memo. "She can take on any assignment and do it well," Watters wrote. Manley rose to sales director before being named publisher.

Her rise did not stop there. In 1971 she became a Time Inc. vice president, in 1975 a group vice president and in 1978 a member of the board of directors. She always modestly attributed much of her success to luck, maintaining that if she had been ten years older she would have been blocked by discrimination against women, and if she had been ten years younger she would have encountered much more competition from other women.

While Time-Life Books was ready for a woman in high places, there was some fear that the subscribers might not be. Several forms of Manley's signature were given trial runs for promotion letters: Joan Manley, Mrs. Joan Manley, J. Daniels Manley (Daniels was her maiden name). Tests showed no difference how the mailings were signed; Joan Manley she was henceforth.

Korn and Manley took over a maturing business. It was growing and still thriving, but the early, great series—Life's World Library, Science Library, Nature Library—had run their course. New series such as Gardening, the Time-Life Library of Photography, the American Wilderness and the Emergence of Man, were in the pipeline or already in production. Not many, though, could match the popularity of the series they were replacing.

As it searched for new blockbuster ideas, the division was bolstered for a while by the remarkable success of Time-Life Books overseas. In 1968, the year that the TLI book business was integrated into the domestic Books operation, international sales amounted to 24 percent of the total. When Korn and Manley assumed command in 1970, the share had dipped to 20 percent, but it rose steadily through the ensuing decade, reaching 51 percent in 1980.

Success abroad attested to the familiarity of the Time-Life label around the world. It was not from a stranger that a Peruvian, for example, received a mail solicitation from *Libros de Time-Life Internacional*. Furthermore, the topics were usually universal in appeal: science, nature and history engaged minds everywhere. The books were published in eight languages, including Chinese and Japanese, through the company's own editorial offices in London, Tokyo and Mexico City; additionally, foreign publishers were licensed to translate the books into 21 other languages, from Afrikaans to Thai. (A lesser known venture abroad involved Time Inc. as a contractor in helping to set up an educational publishing company in Iran. The project grew out of president Jim Linen's long acquaintance with the Shah. The contract was fulfilled in the years 1976–79 and Time Inc. earned more than $2 million before the Iranian revolution erupted.)

Sales abroad, moreover, showed a high rate of profit. There were two reasons. During most of the 1970s, foreign currencies were relatively strong against the dollar and the cost of producing the books, except for translation and printing, was borne by the domestic division. For years the same color plates were used to produce the foreign-language books as in the English version; the format of the foreign books matched the English. It was only when translations into Chinese and Japanese came along that completely new plates had to be made. Later, some books were shaped more precisely to the market or even created specifically for one country, as for example *English Now*, a cassette-and-booklet language course for Japanese businessmen.

On one memorable occasion, though, the translation effort backfired. Before offering the Foods of the World volume on French provincial cooking to French subscribers, Books solicited the opinion of Robert Courtine, a French authority on cuisine—one of whose pen names was Le Grincheaux, "the Surly One." Many of M. Courtine's comments were unkind, some brutally so. As one example among many, he called a recipe for *crêpes gratinées*, stuffed with mushrooms and diced chicken, "fake grand cuisine and as ungastronomic as can be." Through some weird misunderstanding, these comments, meant for edification of the editors, found their way into print as footnotes. Horrified, Time-Life Books put the best face possible on what the New York *Times* dubbed the "self-roasting" cookbook. Each copy came with a *"cher lecteur"* letter to the reader from *rédacteur en chef* Edey explaining gamely, "We believe that the piquancy provided by this double view of French provincial cooking can only add to the ultimate enjoyment of the volume." The acerbic comments were dropped in later editions, and the first became a collector's item.

Almost from the beginning, Time-Life Books had been bedeviled by high production and editorial costs, and in the inflationary 1970s the problem got worse. In 1968 Edey had written a memo to Donovan explaining that costs were so high because the books were produced to meet the same editorial standards as the Time Inc. magazines, with their lavish use of pictures and their strenuous research, checking and editing. Edey reported that he was engineering "a radical change in our editorial procedures" by consolidating jobs and assigning smaller teams to each series. "If it works," he noted, "we will, within the next two years, have largely abandoned our magazine-type edit procedures in favor of new ones more suited to the narrower economic limits of conventional publishing." Unfortunately, he confessed, this would not necessarily keep profits at their former dazzling level, since the huge popularity of some of the early series could not be matched. Edey went on:

> I sometimes have an uneasy feeling in my brief encounters with top management that there is an assumption that we will have another Nature Library or World Library on our hands at any moment. We are trying to find such projects, and we hope we will . . . But to *expect* them is, in my opinion, unrealistic.

By 1972, Books' profits were lower than they had been at the time of Edey's memo. Korn felt no less bedeviled by cost pressures. He sent general manager Jack McSweeney a note that echoed Edey's:

> The high editorial costs of Time-Life Books result almost entirely from magazine-type operations, most particularly our heavy use of pictures, the necessity of maintaining rigid schedules, and the quality standards imposed on us by mail-order marketing.

Though Korn was experimenting with ways to trim his budgets a bit, he did not think operations could be fundamentally changed. "We are, after all, periodical publishers," he concluded. With costs continuing high and unlikely to fall, any lull in the demand for new series could spell serious trouble. Precisely this happened in 1975.

400

In a somber confidential memo to Donovan in June of that year, Korn summarized the situation:

> We are currently preparing two new series whose profitability is so marginal that they may never be launched. We are testing another series for which we have high hopes, but our hopes have been dashed so often in the past that we don't place much faith in them any longer. With one exception, no series has been tested successfully since 1973; the exception was Boating, and it had a most disappointing launch.
>
> Six series are now under way (including Records' Great Men of Music, but not counting two book series being done in London); by the beginning of 1976 the six will be reduced to four, and by mid-1977 they will all be finished.
>
> At that point, if all our worst fears are realized, Books edit could be very close to going out of business.
>
> I don't think that's going to happen—we are taking drastic measures to cut edit costs and thus improve the profitability of the two doubtful series (and all that follow), and there may be other, better tests over the horizon—but I think there is cause for concern.

Despite the "drastic measures to cut edit costs" mentioned by Korn, the situation was so grave that it required still more radical changes. As the weeks passed, Joan Manley and others in top management gave increasingly serious attention to an idea that had been in their minds for many months: moving the book division out of New York City.

It was an idea that had been many times considered by other divisions within the company. *Fortune* and *Architectural Forum* had both toyed with it; Arthur Temple had raised a furor by his offhand remark that *Sports Illustrated* could go to St. Louis, some of the other magazines elsewhere (see chapter 18). *Time* itself had once actually moved. In 1925, Luce, over Hadden's strenuous objections, had transplanted virtually the entire editorial and publishing operations to Cleveland, only to return to New York two years later. The reasons dictating the return then were still applicable to magazine publishing now: New York was not only a hugely important news center, the home of a great many advertisers and virtually all the major advertising agencies, but also a vital if maddening city offering the intellectual stimulation that few other cities could match.

New York's advantages were less important for the makers of Time-Life Books, who were not selling advertising nor reporting the news. For them the controlling considerations were financial: the costs of operating in New York City. Two were especially painful. One was the tax burden; the book division was responsible for its corporate share of New York state and local taxes, which were among the highest in the country. The other was the tab for doing business amid the luxuries of the Time & Life Building. Like the magazines, Books had to contribute also to the upkeep of Time Inc.'s library, its picture collection and photo lab, the Time-Life News Service, and other services. In 1975 its share of all this came to $4.2 million.

As the squeeze tightened, Books began reducing staff. In October 1975, it let go 24 editorial employees, roughly a tenth of the total. Without any major new series in prospect—and with the country in a full-force recession—they simply weren't needed.

A month later Joan Manley wrote management that "preliminary inquiries" into relocating had begun. Those inquiries presumed that Books would be freed of the allocated costs of the facilities in the Time & Life Building but would replace some of those services on its own, and that it would be subject to the state and local taxes in its new home. After a host of other assumptions were made about the costs of operating in other locations, it appeared as if the annual savings from a move could be about $2.9 million, less the onetime cost of moving, which figured to be in the $2 million to $5 million range, depending on location. In short, the economic case looked compelling.

Not that leaving New York struck everyone as an entirely happy idea. Korn, in a blunt memo to Donovan, made it clear that he considered it the lesser evil:

> To put the situation simply, the proposed relocation of the book division offers Books edit no operating benefits whatever. No matter where we go, our lives will be made more difficult, our books will be harder to produce, quality will be harder to maintain. But the move provides one benefit that so outweighs all else that the drawbacks become insignificant: it keeps us alive . . .
>
> I hope nobody has received the impression that if Books moves, the edit side will be dragged along kicking and screaming. Relocating was Edit's idea, and although we hate the prospect of moving from New York into the boondocks, we have never changed our fundamental position that we must do it if the alternative is to go out of business.

402

By December the decision was virtually made. To quiet the speculation among employees and in the trade, Manley and Korn announced forthrightly that relocation had "grown in recent weeks from a remote possibility to a distinct probability." They also explained the move personally at a staff meeting. The only remaining question was site, and management was already investigating several. Chicago, San Francisco, Boston and the nearby New Hampshire area, Connecticut and the Washington, D.C. area were the main contenders, each being judged on its nearness to libraries and research facilities, the availability of services and labor, living conditions, and the presumed willingness of employees to relocate there. In March 1976, Manley and Korn declared Washington the winner.

The spot eventually chosen was not in the District of Columbia but across the Potomac in the Old Town section of Alexandria, Virginia, an area being restored in the red-brick Georgian style of colonial times. One attraction was that it was less than a half-hour drive from the Library of Congress. Leasing most of an uncompleted building called the Atrium, where operations would begin in October, the division began a strenuous persuasion campaign.

The list of inducements offered was long and varied, and the fact that more Books staff, in the end, decided against the move was testimony to the complexity of employee relations in American corporate society. To acquaint New York employees with the new territory, everyone was offered a free two-day trip, a helicopter tour of greater Washington, dinner in Georgetown, a morning with a real estate agent. That was just the top of the menu. Employees deciding to move would receive five all-expense-paid days with rental car or taxi for spouse and self to go house hunting; the services of real estate agents; reimbursement of lease-termination penalties in New York; free driving lessons and the cost of Virginia driver's licenses and tags; a parking subsidy for the first year (many erstwhile New York subway commuters would have to drive to work in Virginia); reimbursement of prepaid tuition for children's schooling in New York; the services of an educational consultant; weekly round-trip travel expenses between Washington and New York for those willing to move that summer. Plus moving expenses back to New York for any employee who, after a year in Washington, didn't like it.

For all the wooing, most employees weren't sold. There was, indeed, a good deal of bitterness among the staff, who faced a choice: New York or a job. That bitterness undoubtedly helped explain why so many Books employees joined the New York Newspaper Guild strike against Time Inc. (see chapter 26) that got under way in the midst of the wooing. Moving to Alexandria meant higher costs for those whose New York apartments were rent-controlled or rent-stabilized. Many of Time-Life Books' artists, writers and editors were dyed-in-the-wool New Yorkers who could hardly conceive of working anywhere else. Some had working spouses or lovers, or children in school, who could not or would not be moved easily. Management had guessed that two-thirds of the staff would opt for the move; in fact only about one third did.

But the move seemed to serve its purpose: Books began saving money immediately. For tax purposes, Time-Life Books became a Delaware corporation, a wholly owned subsidiary of Time Inc., with Jack McSweeney as president and Manley as chairman of the board; she remained a Time Inc. group vice president. In 1977, the first full year of operations in Alexandria, total savings were calculated to be as high as $5.1 million—far more than anticipated, largely because so few New York employees moved; new workers could be hired at lower salaries and weren't immediately eligible for as many benefits as the veterans. There had been some thought of further savings through a separate union contract for the Alexandria staff that would be more in line with the needs of book rather than magazine publishing. But by the time Manley proposed the move, legal counsel had advised that regardless of relocation, editorial employees would remain covered by the Guild contract in force. Although Guild membership within Books fell by about half after the move, this had no effect on costs.

There were other substantial savings in Alexandria. Occupancy costs were 17 percent less; one practical result was that the production cost of each volume in the Gardening series was brought down from $195,000 in New York to $135,000 in Alexandria. There was some concern that the new staff, being younger and less experienced, might not be up to the quality of the old one. In fact it proved remarkably competent, and there was no loss of quality in the books.

The Alexandria-based wholly owned subsidiary, Time-Life Books Inc., was hardly a shrinking business. Its sales continued to bound upward, reaching $215 million in 1977. The following year, sales of the Time Inc. book group as a whole made an unprecedented jump—more than $100 million—thanks largely to an attractive and prestigious acquisition: the Book-of-the-Month Club.

The oldest of the book clubs, BOMC had achieved the status of an institution rather quickly after its start in 1926. The founders were Harry Scherman, formerly a copywriter with J. Walter Thompson; Maxwell Sackheim, a colleague at the advertising agency; and Robert Haas of Smith & Haas, publishers that had merged with Random House in 1936. The club was founded on the premise that people would "subscribe" to a regular monthly book just as they subscribe to a magazine. It was an original approach to book selling, much imitated by others afterward. Time-Life Books itself was a derivative, although adding another ingredient to the subscription sales formula that set its operations apart: the creation of books to fill the subscription orders. (The Book-of-the-Month Club sold only other publishers' products.) Selection of the monthly book, the club's early ads took pains to point out, was to be left to an independent board of big-name literati.

For decades BOMC was a family affair, with most of the stock held by members of the Scherman family. In 1950 Scherman's son-in-law, Axel Rosin, took over as president and eventually, chairman. In 1977 Rosin decided to retire. With no family members ready and willing to take over, he was compelled to sell. Two lucrative offers came in from large corporations, but Rosin and his president, Edward Fitzgerald, were hesitant; neither potential buyer was mainly in the publishing business. Fitzgerald, who had known Joan Manley years earlier when they both worked at Doubleday, then suggested talking to Time Inc.

The companies were not strangers. In 1974 Book-of-the-Month Club had taken over the Sports Illustrated and Fortune Book Clubs, which had been failures under Time Inc.'s management. (Even expert care could not save the Sports Illustrated club; part of its problem was that many of its members were children.) BOMC management liked Time Inc., and Time Inc. management thought BOMC had great potential. Manley, in a memo strongly advocating purchase, explained the possible synergy in such areas as mailing lists, book purchasing and fulfillment of mail orders. She concluded: "I am tempted to rhapsodize at length, but I have really said it all. I cannot imagine a better opportunity for the books group occurring within my working lifetime."

That was good enough for Heiskell and Shepley, who gave the go-ahead for negotiations. To the table came two of the most formidable names in investment banking, Peter Peterson of Lehman Brothers for Time Inc. and Felix G. Rohatyn of Lazard Frères for BOMC. They soon concluded a deal—or thought they had—and a celebratory dinner was held in the Library Suite of the St. Regis

Hotel with Heiskell, Shepley, Donovan, Manley and Arthur Temple from Time Inc., and Rosin, Fitzgerald and F. Harry Brown, executive vice president and company treasurer, from BOMC. By all accounts the highlight of the evening came when Joan Manley threw her arms around Axel Rosin and said, "Will you marry me?"

The next morning an unfortunate nuptial impediment surfaced. The negotiators hadn't actually nailed down a price. Furthermore, BOMC said it wouldn't take less than $30 a share, and Time Inc. said it wouldn't offer more than $28. The standoff lasted three months. Eventually Manley agreed and persuaded Heiskell to meet the $30 price, equivalent to $63 million total. The deal was announced in July, but not closed until December pending clearance from the Federal Trade Commission.

The Book-of-the-Month Club contributed significantly to the profits of the books group from the day it was acquired. Its profits remained steady, its franchise with the public as solid as ever. Time Inc., as new owner, saw no reason to interfere. Edward Fitzgerald continued to manage the firm, once remarking that "Time [Inc.] has been a good home. They offer us almost no advice. I manage the business, and as long as we do all right, they support us." He added, perhaps immodestly but accurately, "We are a small jewel of a company." (In 1981 Fitzgerald would move up to become chairman and chief executive officer and would retire in 1984. Executive vice president Al Silverman would succeed him as president in 1981 and later as chief executive officer, and Time Inc.'s group vice president of books, Lawrence W. Crutcher, would be appointed president.)

Although revenues of Time-Life Books continued to grow, its profits, after the first year's surge in Alexandria, did not, falling as much as 30 percent in 1981. Editorial costs and staff size climbed above New York levels. The relocation had just bought time. The declining profits partly were due to the recessions of 1980 and 1982, combined with high inflation. At the same time, there was fiercer competition for the consumer's entertainment budget; it was easy to imagine families forgoing their Time-Life Books subscription and putting the money instead into Home Box Office. The net was that Books could not pass on its rapidly climbing costs without the risk of pricing itself out of the market.

One attempt to beat the cost problem was Stonehenge Press, set up in 1979 to design and sell books produced by outside book packagers, not bearing the Time-Life Books imprint. Stonehenge failed in its purpose and was dissolved in 1983, but Books took over its two most promising series, Great Meals in Minutes and the Kodak Library of Creative Photography.

Economic environment did not explain all of Books' troubles. What continued to be most disturbing was the drying up of ideas for new blockbuster series. The most profitable series of the last half of the 1970s were three developed in the first half: the Old West, World War II and Home Repair. The new series did not do as well. There were fears the Alexandria company had lost touch with its market. There was some speculation that the problem was exacerbated by the phenomenon known as list fatigue. It appeared also that there were disadvantages to operating in Alexandria. The cross-fertilization of ideas that occurred in the Time & Life Building in New York was missed after all. It had been difficult to persuade some of Books' best promotion and marketing people to move from New York, the world center of their business. These intangibles at least partially offset the savings Alexandria delivered.

Meanwhile, the strong dollar dealt a double blow to overseas earnings. It caused U.S.-produced books to be more expensive in the local currencies of foreign countries and the profits of overseas operations to shrink when translated into dollars. The devaluation of the Mexican peso in 1982 cut the Mexican earnings by $20 million at a single stroke. In another major overseas market, Japan, currency problems were compounded by bad management and bad luck. In one unlikely deal with the People's Republic of China, Books agreed to publish 50,000 sets of a ten-volume children's encyclopedia and some volumes in the Nature and Science series. Lacking foreign exchange, the Chinese paid partially with scrolls that the sales staff believed would sell. Only later was it discovered that the Japanese public didn't care for them and the company was left with 7,300 unsold scrolls on its hands.

In short, as the 1980s began, rising costs, a tougher mail-order market and a dearth of big new ideas had called into question the whole concept of Time-Life Books. Executive changes were inevitable. In December 1980 Carl Jaeger, who had been executive vice president, took over from McSweeney as president of Time-Life Books, Inc. Jerry Korn retired as managing editor in 1982 to be succeeded by his deputy, George Constable, formerly in charge of European editorial operations in London. Also in 1982, Jaeger exchanged jobs with Reginald K. Brack Jr., the first publisher of *Discover* magazine. Brack was a feisty former ad sales director for *Time* who had a reputation for speaking his mind and acting quickly, sometimes roughly.

407

Joan Manley remained group vice president and chairman of the board of Time-Life Books, Inc., until 1984, when Brack took her place.

Time-Life Books' new management instituted several changes. To reduce dependence on mail-order selling, some books began being marketed through established trade book publishers, such as Random House, and through retail bookstores. The use of outside packagers who could produce finished manuscripts for less than it cost the editorial staff in Alexandria also increased.

Perhaps the most profound change in the Books operation would be the end of the traditional separation of church and state—editorial and publishing. This had begun to be a subject for argument between Jerry Korn and Manley. The publishing side maintained that, while an arm's length relationship was essential to protecting the magazines' editorial independence, it was not relevant to books, which were not carrying advertising and which required closer collaboration between editors and marketers. Korn commented:

> The relationship was always contentious. This may have been inevitable; both groups were able and earnest, but their goals were a little bit different. The people on edit used to complain that those in mail promotion disregarded the series prospectuses prepared by edit; the promotion people used to object that the edit side disregarded the promotion.

Backed by editor-in-chief Donovan, who felt the issue was as important to books as to magazines, Korn fought hard to maintain editorial independence. But in 1982, with Books' marketing difficulties persisting, Korn's and Donovan's successors were more amenable to compromise, and a new relationship developed: the managing editor reported to the publisher, retaining a link to the editor-in-chief, and market considerations became more dominant in shaping the editorial product. By 1984, Time-Life Books seemed well on the way to restored profitability.

...and the Girls
on the Beach

"IN AN ERA when some of the old giants of magazine publishing were failing (*Collier's*, the old *Saturday Evening Post*, *Look*, *Life*), *Sports Illustrated* grew mightily . . . in the face of television's supposedly invincible challenge to any form of pictorial journalism." Thus, the Letter from the Publisher that led off the February 11, 1974, issue of *SI* saluted the long, successful editorship of Andre Laguerre, who was stepping down after nearly 14 years—a record for Time Inc. managing editors.

Mighty was a fitting word for *SI*'s growth during this time. It had emerged from its decade in the red to become a solid money-maker. By 1970 it had achieved the second million in circulation that Luce had foreseen, and become Time Inc.'s second most profitable publication. It was the third largest of the newsmagazines, behind only *Time* and *Newsweek*, and in 1974 it had moved into fourth place among all general magazines in advertising revenue. More important, *SI* had preempted its field and, apparently, left no room for print rivals.

Nonetheless, prosperity had not come automatically to *SI*, even after it had turned the corner in 1964. It was not until 1966 that *SI* came close to reaching the 2,500-page advertising target set during Operation Breakthrough; even then sales and profits fell off again. In July 1965, publisher Sid James moved to the corporate staff and was succeeded by associate publisher Garry Valk. During the ensuing years when, in Valk's words, "we chewed up a lot of people," *SI*'s sales strategy was further refined. That strategy, Valk said, had originally been based "on the image we had projected of ourselves as a family magazine. Research proved that in reality we were a male-oriented product." In fact, the Simmons study showed that more than 80 percent of the magazine's readers were men. "As a result," said Valk, "we began to change our advertising and circulation approach . . . We changed to promoting ourselves as what we *were* rather than what we *thought* we were." *SI*'s ad staff established another important sales point: that sport played a vital role in successful business and professional men's lives, and that *SI* reached them with great efficiency.

Valk left at the end of 1969, after four years, persuaded to become publisher of the faltering *Life*. His successor at *SI* was the magazine's former general manager, Dick Munro, 37, who was brought back from Pioneer Press (see chapter 14) on Valk's urging. Munro was then an up-and-coming young executive and this brought him to top management's notice. His tenure lasted till September 1972 when he was tapped by Heiskell for a much tougher job, deputy to the group vice president in charge of book publishing, films and the troubled cable television operation. But he stayed at *SI* long enough to have the pleasure of going upstairs, in company with associate publisher Harry S. (Sandy) Steinbreder Jr., to inform Larsen that with more than $10 million in profit anticipated for 1972, *SI* would finally have paid back all of the $34 million it had cost Time Inc. to meet the magazine's losses during the bad years.

SI's next publisher was Jack Meyers, 43, an affable extrovert who came over from *Time* where he had been associate publisher. A Marine Corps combat veteran of the Korean War, Meyers had studied journalism at Michigan State and pondered a career in it, but finally got into publishing as an ad salesman. His cheery personality and fondness for sports made him a good one. He once kept a small stable of show horses. Meyers departed in 1978 to become publisher of *Time*.

Succeeding Meyers was one of Time Inc.'s most upwardly mobile young men, Kelso Sutton, then the 39-year-old deputy to the group vice president, magazines. Shortish and rather bumptious, looking as if he had just got off a college campus, Sutton had a sharp mind and breezy approach that had propelled him through a variety of company posts since his arrival 17 years earlier just out of Harvard.

410

Sutton was brought to the company by what seemed like bad luck. While he was on a ski vacation, his senior thesis (on Washington Irving) was stolen. The task of rewriting seemed so overwhelming that he delayed his plan to enter graduate school and took a stopgap job as a corporate trainee at Time Inc. instead. Within a year he was made assistant business manager of *Time*, rising thereafter to business manager, then general manager. At age 32, he headed a new corporate circulation department, and became the youngest vice president in company history since 28-year-old Roy Larsen in 1927. In 1976 Sutton gained some experience in unfamiliar territory by serving briefly as editor of the magazine development group. His stay at *SI* was also destined to be short; after less than two years he resumed his upward corporate climb, eventually to executive vice president in charge of all Time Inc.'s magazine activities. Advertising director Philip Howlett, with 22 years of Time Inc. experience in advertising sales, took Sutton's place.

SI's publishers, a capable crew under whose direction the magazine's income more than quadrupled, had an enormous asset working for them: *SI*'s proven editorial formula. "There is no question that *Sports Illustrated* is a Laguerrean concept," said senior editor Walter Bingham, an *SI* veteran on staff since 1955. "Even today, years after he departed the magazine, it still runs according to his formula." Such was Laguerre's own identification with the magazine that his replacement as managing editor, although inevitable after his many years in the job, caused considerable shock.

Donovan announced the change in October 1973, declaring that Laguerre would be leaving in February and that executive editor Roy Terrell would be taking over. "As distinguished an editorship as this company has seen," Donovan called Laguerre's long reign at *SI*, adding that Laguerre would go on sabbatical leave for a year. "A new Time Inc. assignment has been proposed to him, but he may decide to pursue career interests outside Time Inc. In whatever he does, he will carry with him the immense respect of the *SI* staff and fellow editors throughout the company."

So came the most painful change of managing editors in the two decades covered by this volume of the Time Inc. history. It highlighted a problem that the company had never quite solved: what to do with former managing editors. The managing editorship was "a very demanding experience," Donovan observed; thus it was "very good corporate policy to appoint them at an age when they would be in their most creative years." Yet this left managing editors often, at the end of their tenure, too young to retire but with no further post available to them befitting their standing or experience. On occasion, at both *Time* and *Life*, the situation had been handled by reviving the emeritus title of editor. *Fortune* had a board of editors to which ex–managing editors could return as senior writers. In other cases, corporate make-work projects had also been devised, but these were imperfect solutions.

Laguerre was aware that a change was coming at *SI*. The dilemma remained. In fact, he and Donovan had begun talking it out as early as 1972, but at the end Laguerre felt, as he told Terrell afterwards, "I've been fired." He was then 57 and had wanted to stay on at Time Inc.; the only assignment Donovan offered was to investigate the feasibility of a European version of *SI*. Laguerre was "aggrieved . . . disappointed that I had not come up something more substantial," Donovan recalled afterward. Laguerre questioned whether the European *SI* proposal was serious; Donovan assured him it was. The proposal was still pending when a *Newsweek* story by a former *SI* writer, describing Laguerre as having been "unceremoniously forced out of his job," took Laguerre's bitterness public.

That bitterness persisted. Outwardly, however, relations were somewhat improved by the time Laguerre left. Accepting the European assignment after all, Laguerre threw himself into it with considerable enthusiasm, spending four months surveying *SI*'s editorial possibilities in Britain and the Continent, while a task force under assistant publisher Peter Hanson carried on a parallel investigation of business prospects. On the Continent, multiple difficulties were foreseen but in Britain, Laguerre believed there was real opportunity. Interest in sports was "higher even than in the U.S." and with "television . . . broadening that interest, the situation recalls *SI*'s in the early 60s," he reported. Although "a gamble," a British *SI* "executed with boldness and finesse . . . could bring the company substantial profit and international prestige." Weekly lists, which Laguerre sent back from London synopsizing stories that the magazine might do, bolstered his case.

Donovan declined the gamble. He was worried about Britain's economic and political drift, and decided against the project. The following spring Laguerre went into a new magazine venture as editor and publisher of a bimonthly, *Classic*, then being planned for the elite market of thoroughbred owners and breeders. (Laguerre himself had kept a racing stable in France during his editorship of *SI*.) Several *SI* alumni, including former senior editor Andrew Crichton

412

and racing writer Whitney Tower, joined Laguerre at *Classic*, but the magazine, launched with the issue dated December 1975, lasted only until November 1979. Laguerre, already ill, had resigned in December 1978. He died a month later.

Terrell had been Laguerre's deputy and acknowledged successor at *SI* and on taking over in 1974 he made it plain that he intended keeping the magazine much as it was. He wrote the staff:

> There will be changes, of course—in our approach . . . handling . . . altered emphasis . . . and areas of responsibility—in short, just about what one would expect with any change of editorship. But *Sports Illustrated* as it now exists represents the collected thinking of a number of people, many of whom are still here. None of us is interested in abandoning, simply for the sake of change, something we have all worked so hard to perfect.

Terrell, who was then just 50, had played no small role in shaping *SI*'s development during his 19 years with the magazine. Born in Kingsville, Texas, he had been a Marine Corps pilot during World War II and worked briefly as an oilfield roustabout before returning to the Texas College of Arts and Industries for a degree in English, after which he had begun newspaper work on the Corpus Christi *Caller*. It was there that he saw a prepublication dummy of *SI*, sent around to newspaper sports editors for their comments. Terrell had his doubts about the editorial execution, but the concept of the magazine, he said, was "sensational. I thought it was the greatest idea in the world."

He immediately applied for a job and got one eight months later. His productivity and speed at the typewriter were much appreciated. As Donovan observed later, "He rapidly established himself as a knowledgeable, lively and remarkably versatile writer covering baseball, football, basketball and almost every other known sport except curling. (He plays a good many of them too.)" In 1960 Terrell was named a senior editor; in 1963, assistant managing editor; and in 1970, following Dick Johnston's retirement, executive editor. Now, with Terrell's move upward, assistant managing editor Ray Cave took over the executive editor's post.

SI's approach shifted under Terrell's editorship, as he had predicted, with more coverage of college and amateur sport, more attention to the Olympics. An outdoorsman, Terrell was more active than Laguerre, who personally shunned most sports except

413

racing and baseball. He took frequent deep-sea fishing holidays. He was also more ordered than his predecessor, and some considered him tougher on writers' copy. *SI*'s smooth functioning under his direction was reflected in a guidance memo he prepared for Ralph Graves, who as corporate editor was sitting in at *SI* while Terrell vacationed. Wrote Terrell, taking Graves through *SI*'s Thursday–Monday editorial week:

My normal routine—and train schedules—put me in the office at 9:45 on Thursdays and Fridays and at 9:30 on Saturdays and Sundays . . . I spend Sunday nights in the city and get to the office on Monday mornings between 8:30 and 10, depending on the number of post-closing celebratory martinis, etc. . . . On Sunday nights I stay until I have read and edited the last piece of current copy, including heads and captions but excluding For the Record items and the roundup section of Baseball's Week. Generally this means departure anywhere from 10 to 1; this week, however . . . you will be sweating out the U.S. Open and 3–5 a.m may be more like it. Normally, [assistant managing editor Gilbert] Rogin will stick around until I have completed editing . . . [assistant managing editor Kenneth] Rudeen is the late, late man, reading all the fast-closing offset form copy in the transmission version [to the printer] and consulting with the editor and checker as necessary. This usually keeps him here two or three hours later than Rogin and me . . .

On your desk Thursday mornings, you will probably have a report from Tibby on budget matters, production and delivery reports, ad sales projections, early ad mockups of issues five and six weeks away, momentous events which have transpired over the weekend, etc.

Copy flow: this might be better described orally, but briefly it goes like this. Writer's copy goes to senior editor, who sends it to computer typing when his editing or rewriting is done. Computer printouts are distributed, including a copy to you. After reseacher and copy room have worked it over, top copy goes to Rogin, who edits in blue, then to you (red), then back to typists for changes, back to editors for fit (greening) and to proofreaders. Back upstairs, then back down for final transmission-copy reading by senior editor, checker, and proofreaders again . . .

Picture viewing sessions, layout discussions and layout approval go on throughout the week with, again, Sunday the busiest time. During color projections the conference room gets a bit crowded, with you, the art director, the associate art director, the color quality control man, the production chief, at least one assistant production man, the editor, the researcher, two or three picture department people . . . on hand . . . After viewing pictures or art work, I sometimes make layout suggestions to [art director] Gangel or to Harvey [Harvey Grut, associate art director], but more often I give them a chance to first please me in their own way, making sure they have either read the story, themselves, or understand its implications and highlights. This system seems to produce pleasant surprises and the best results. However, you were the editor of a picture-oriented magazine, and you should feel absolutely free to get into the act as much as you like . . .

The copy flow tends to be light on Thursdays, increasing on Fridays, heavier on Saturdays (particularly when there is a good ballgame on the tube) and quite heavy on Sundays, when from seven to 12 stories and departments of the magazine close . . . This isn't the slowest period of the sporting year—that takes place from mid-July to Labor Day—but isn't exactly pro-football/college football/World Series/beginning of basketball and hockey time, either. Don't hesitate to stir up the staff if the flow of ideas seems to begin and end with suggestions that we cover obvious and regularly-scheduled events.

Hopefully, you will be spared budget reviews, personnel problems, raise recommendations, hirings, firings and memos . . . asking you to write a memo in response to someone else's memo . . .

The liquor cabinet is the third one from the outside wall.

Happy editing.

Terrell's editorshop came to an abrupt end. Just before Christmas, 1978, he informed Donovan that he planned to take early retirement effective the following June. He would then be 56, he had spent 24 years at *SI*, five as managing editor, and "while *SI* had been the most important thing in my life," he explained later, "now I wanted to do something else"—and he meant literally to go fishing. Donovan, disconcerted because he had not expected to name a successor so soon, urged Terrell to stay but hit a stone wall. Announcing Terrell's decision, and the appointment of Gilbert Rogin to succeed him, Donovan expressed a hope: "We will surely be seeing [Terrell's] byline again in *SI*." In this too, Donovan was disappointed.

Retiring to Key West, Terrell never wrote again for the magazine. Like few others in Time Inc., he cut completely.

Rogin, who was as surprised as was Donovan when Terrell quit, was at a ski resort in Utah when Donovan telephoned to offer him the job. Rogin's reaction was to go out on the balcony and give "a tremendous whoop to the snowy mountain."

The reaction suited the personality. Then 49, *SI*'s new managing editor was an intense man—"demonic," Rogin once described himself—who had come up from the bottom at *SI*, rather as Grunwald had at *Time*. In 1955, after a two year stint in the U.S. Army where among other things he had edited the camp newspaper, Rogin came to *SI* as a newsmarker for *SI*'s clip desk, scouring the newspapers and agency wires for sports items. Within a few months he was assigned to the research staff; on the side, he began taking on writing chores no one else would. He proved to be an elegant stylist, with a fascination for the characters who peopled the sports world, boxing's sweaty precincts in particular. But it was for a landlubber's account of a 1961 ocean sailing race from California to Hawaii that he became known. His story, which *SI* published with some trepidation, became a classic; years afterward it was still being delightedly quoted by yachtsmen themselves. "Next time they want to send me to sea," wrote the New York City–bred Rogin, "I'll lock myself in the bathroom for 12 days with canned goods, Sterno, an electric fan and an alarm clock. I'll sit in the tub for four hours, fully dressed, with the fan blowing across me, taking a cold shower. Then I'll get out, eat, undress and go back to the tub to sleep. Four hours later, I'll put on my clothes, take another shower, and so on."

A couple of years later, with mixed feelings about sportswriting as a career ("I was tired of waiting around for 20-year-old second basemen to talk to me") Rogin left the staff to write articles on contract, simultaneously beginning a parallel career as a writer of short stories, mainly for *The New Yorker* (a collection was published, as well as two novels). After a year he returned to *SI*, persuaded by Laguerre to try his hand at editing; his upward progress thereafter was steady. As Rogin took over the managing editorship in June 1979, *SI* edit's veteran utility infielder, assistant managing editor Jeremiah Tax, became executive editor, with senior editor Peter Carry moving up to the vacant assistant managing editorship. Later, senior editor Mark Mulvoy also moved up; in 1984 Mulvoy would succeed Rogin as managing editor.

416

As managing editor, Rogin reminded the staff of Laguerre, in his complete absorption in the magazine. He lived *SI* seven days a week. He was a compulsive editor, with a hand in everything. *SI*'s midweek weekends were the time for him to phone staffers at home to discuss editorial projects; his daily one-mile swims were the time for thinking up more.

SI's basic editorial pattern remained as set by Laguerre and continued by Terrell. But within that pattern the emphasis, both textual and visual, changed. *SI* moved more than ever toward harder sports coverage, pegged more closely to the week's big televised events, where the reader's eye was turned. "I rarely went to a big game. I always watched it on television, because I wanted to know what the reader had seen. What *SI* did for a game was like the review of a play; the pictures were a memento," Rogin said. "No matter how many instant replays you saw, still pictures offered something TV could not provide—what I call the savor factor."

During his editorship, *SI*'s picture displays grew larger; full-page photos and double-trucks multiplied. More than any of his predecessors, Rogin tended to be his own art director and picture editor. "I can't wait to get in and lay out the magazine," he once remarked. With an expanding budget *SI* in 1983 began to use full color illustrations throughout the book—the first national weekly magazine to take this step.

But it was the quality of *SI*'s prose that probably mattered most; it was this, certainly, that was most remarked on by sports buffs. Wrote novelist James Michener in *Sports in America*,* an exhaustive survey of the contemporary sporting scene:

> *SI* has become the bible of the industry, and it has done so because it appreciated from the start the facts that faced printed journalism in the age of television: don't give the scores, give the inside stories behind the scores. And deal openly with those topics which men in saloons talk about in whispers . . .
>
> Its success, after an agonizingly slow start, attests to the high regard in which sportsmen hold it. I have been especially interested in its style, for I judge that much of its acceptance has derived from this. Only *The New Yorker*, among contemporary magazines, has been as effective in sponsoring good writing with a certain wry touch.

*Random House, New York, 1976.

The "whispered" subjects that *SI* wrote openly about, often at length, covered a wide range, from drugs and violence to racism and sexual discrimination—topics that other publications took up later, but which were considered taboo when *SI* first broached them. Jack Olsen's five-part series in 1968, titled *The Black Athlete—A Shameful Story*, was a good example—a searching examination of the exploitation of the black athlete and the reality of racism on and off the field. The author was particularly harsh in his indictment of the college coaches who guided the careers of those "often deprived, frightened, maladjusted and totally unprepared individuals who have come out of intellectual vacuums to make their muddled ways across the country's campuses."

Donovan considered the black athlete series "one of the best pieces of work Time Inc. has been privileged to publish." Reaction was intense—more letters from readers than ever before in the magazine's history. Although most were favorable, there were some readers who were offended by Olsen's thesis. So the following year *SI* published another series, this time by John Underwood, to tell another side of the the story, the plight of the embattled coaches in an age of student revolt. In 1978, Underwood produced a three-part exposé of brutality in football, chilling in its documentation of the physical damage that student and professional athletes were sustaining in a game where the intent to injure was deliberately "being fostered, not quelled." Another early look at a now major scourge was *SI*'s 1969 series on "Drugs in Sport," by Bil Gilbert, who in 1972 together with writer-reporter Nancy Williamson produced a pioneering three-part series on sexist discrimination against women athletes.

The homosexuality of tennis giant Bill Tilden and the public disgrace of Tilden's last, ruined years were the subject of a poignant two-part series in 1975 by Frank Deford. One of the most admired of *SI* staff writers, Deford was hired straight out of Princeton in 1962 and developed into a superb reporter and narrator of major sports events, such as tennis tournaments and basketball playoffs—what he called "deadline stories." But it was his offbeat and satirical pieces that aroused most comment. In one, Deford recounted one man's transcontinental travels with a dead whale named Little Irvy; in another, "The Year of the Great Fan Draft," he described the imaginary crisis in pro football when the fans, preferring to watch the instant replay at home, finally left the stadium standing empty. Deford did not consider himself a sportswriter but rather "a writer who writes sports."

In August 1979, in its 25th anniversary issue, *SI* reviewed a quarter century of sport in the U.S. and permitted itself a bit of praise for the role *SI* had played. Tracing the magazine's fivefold circulation increase to 2,250,000 from 450,000 at launch, *SI* observed:

> It might be said that the interest in and reach of sports in America have increased by about the same degree . . . We believe we have been a major influence in creating a sense of American sport, and in raising the level and quality of sports writing. Moreover, SI has influenced how sports are covered. We obliged fans, the daily press and the networks to consider sport from a national point of view—and as a continuous endeavor.

Certainly, it was a more competitive marketplace *SI* found itself in. Specialty publications, zeroing in on new activities, such as running, were proliferating. Newsweek Inc. also was getting ready to follow Time Inc.'s lead, with a new monthly *Inside Sports* (launched in 1980, it was later sold to another publisher). In the competition for audience, television was offering not only highly sophisticated camera work but more expert commentary, often by former players whom the networks were bringing into the broadcast booths. "They don't parse very well, but they pack in a tremendous amount of information," Gil Rogin conceded.

Still, *SI* looked about as problem free as any division at Time Inc. as the 1980s began. Pretax income, which had more than doubled in the last half of the 1970s, was climbing. In 1981, it passed the $20 million mark on revenues in the $160 million range. Circulation, in particular, was buoyant. Like *Time, SI* had kept its rate base constant throughout most of the 1970s, preferring to raise circulation income through stiff hikes in subscription and newsstand prices. In late 1980, projecting ahead for the years 1981 through 1985, *SI* intended continuing this policy, with no increase over the 2,250,000 rate base. However, it shortly became apparent, as publisher Phil Howlett remarked later, "that there was a [reader] demand out there stronger than we had anticipated—a continuing strong demand we could tap." Accordingly, in 1982, a series of circulation increases began, which by 1985 had upped *SI*'s rate base to 2,725,000.

Helping boost advertising revenues, also, were the special issues that *SI* had instituted outside the regular weekly publishing schedule. The first was an annual review of the sports highlights of the year just past, entitled A Year in Sports. Begun in 1977, the Year in Sports issue ran until 1984; in 1985 it was to be combined with *SI*'s Sportsman of the Year issue, which every December singled out an individual athlete or athletes, man or woman, for distinctive sporting performance or achievement during that year. In 1982, another special issue was added to the schedule, previewing the college and pro football seasons. In 1984 as a one-shot *SI* also previewed the Los Angeles Olympics with a 534-page blockbuster.

The special issues drew well with readers. None, however, could match that standby of *SI*'s publishing schedule that had been introduced in 1964. This was the "sunshine issue" as it was known inside *SI*, better known outside, to millions of *SI* faithfuls, as the "bathing suit issue." Appearing dependably in late January or early February, and identified by its cover photo of a fetching model, minimally clad, disporting herself on some sunny shore, it became *SI*'s biggest newsstand seller by far—a vehicle that propelled more than one cover girl to national fame.

In its inception, the bathing suit issue was a case of pure serendipity. The inspiration for making a regular feature is credited to Laguerre, who was looking for a way to bridge the gap that then existed on the sports calendar between the New Year's Day bowl games and the beginning of the baseball season. The result was a travel story—a 19-page package in the January 20, 1964, issue on swimming and snorkeling in the Caribbean, with a look in passing at swimsuit fashions. That emphasis was later to change. Although there always remained good touristic reasons for *SI*'s choice of locales—the diversions they offered the sports-minded traveler—the swimsuit displays became the attraction.

In 1965, writer-reporter Jule Campbell, later an associate editor, took over the project, finding the models and selecting the suits, choosing the locales (and keeping them secret), scouting the logistics of getting there and back, and seeing everything safely into print. Locales alternated between exotic, faraway places—Bora Bora in the South Pacific, the Seychelles off Africa's east coast—and vacation spots closer to home in Mexico, Hawaii, Puerto Rico. *SI*'s first models were rather modestly attired. But increasingly, as fashion cut away more fabric, the swimsuits became more daring, the poses more provocative. And provoking more reader reaction than any other issue in the year.

Such was the torrent of mail each year that the *SI* letters department prepared a regular series of stock responses: one to thank the readers who liked the issue; another to reply diplomatically to those who felt otherwise ("We are sorry you were offended . . . It is our

420

opinion that the pictures are in good taste"); one to regret the inevitable subscription cancellations (usually from outraged parents); one to rebut the charges of sexism ("We are certainly aware of the many outstanding accomplishments of women athletes"); one to acknowledge requests (presumably from women) that men's swimsuit fashions be included; another to answer the question (most certainly from men): was the model married?

More than an *SI* feature, the bathing suit issue had become, by the 1980s, a national institution—as had *SI* itself.

Inventing Magazines

FOR NEARLY 20 YEARS after the launching of *Sports Illustrated* in 1954, Time Inc. did not start a new magazine. Then, in the early 1970s, the company entered a new creative phase. *Money* and *People* were launched, *Life* was revived as a monthly. Two more new magazines followed in the early 1980s. It was the managerial reorganization of 1969 that helped set the stage for this innovative burst. Under the old corporate structure, the magazine publishers reported directly to Heiskell and Linen; each publisher worried mainly about his own magazine's results and had little reason or time to think about new ventures; top management had enough on its plate too. In the new setup, the publishers reported to the executive vice president in charge of the magazine group, former *Time* publisher Bernie Auer, who had both time and authority to expand his territory by developing new products.

In due course, a magazine development team was organized with former *Time* managing editor Otto Fuerbringer as its captain. The company had lost its enthusiasm for newspaper acquisition, Fuerbringer's previous assignment. And in February 1971, at the invitation of editorial director Lou Banks, he shifted his attention to magazine projects. Two others joined him full-time, Peter Bird Martin, a senior editor of *Time*, and Joe Hazen, who after the suspension of *Architectural Forum* had gone to Time-Life Books and General

Learning. Others were brought on board for specific projects. The assemblage wasn't formally christened the magazine development group until February 1973, but it was no less real in the meantime.

Eventually the team developed guidelines, widely accepted but attributable to no one in particular. Any new magazine should appeal to young adults just starting families who would thus be recruited for the future. An unwritten requirement was that new magazines should not cannibalize advertisers from the existing magazines, which depended heavily on ads for alcoholic beverages, cigarettes and cars, all purchased mainly by men. Therefore, a new candidate ideally should attract advertisers of women's products, health and beauty aids, an enormous category on which Time Inc. was missing out. Any newcomer, of course, would have to be suited to operating on a lean staff, a lesson learned from *Life*. And any new magazine would have to fit in with the company's interests, standards and sense of taste.

The magazine development group was sharply aware of a current trend. Many of the new magazines launched in the late '60s and early '70s appealed to special interests (*Epicure*, *Ms.*, *Psychology Today*, *Rolling Stone*, to name a few), while many of the great general-interest magazines (*Life*, *Look*, the *Saturday Evening Post*) were dead or dying. The message implicit in this fact clashed with another: the fact that high production costs within the Time-Life structure made it very difficult to earn a profit on any magazine that couldn't attract a very large audience.

Auer proposed a solution. The company should explore special-interest magazines, each a monthly, each with a separate editorial staff, but sharing the expenses of publishing, printing and subscription fulfillment. This seemed to offer the best of both worlds. Each magazine might attract just a special-interest-sized audience, but together they would amass sufficient circulation.

Fuerbringer began his search for magazine ideas by reviewing proposals that had been made earlier for single-topic supplements to *Life* (see chapter 17); they inspired three of the four magazines he eventually proposed. *Money* would be a magazine of personal finance, advising people with disposable income how to spend or invest it intelligently. *Well* would address the intensifying interest in health. *View* would speak intelligently about movies and television, reviewing films, profiling the important personalities and taking readers behind the scenes. (In early discussions its name had been *InSight* and, at another point, *See It Now*, the title used by Edward R. Murrow's documentary series on CBS in the 1950s.)

The fourth title, not adapted from a proposed *Life* supplement but clearly owing a debt to that magazine, was *Camera Month*; it would provide technical and aesthetic advice and be a showcase for fine photographs. Inevitably, the four proposals became known around the Time & Life Building as Health, Wealth, Flicks and Pix.

Three of the four were crafted to appeal to younger readers. *Money* was for young people with a little extra income. *View* and *Camera Month* were for the visually oriented generation that had grown up with television. But would these magazines actually appeal to those readers—and to enough of them? To find out, the magazine developers subjected the various concepts to market testing, a procedure the company in its earlier days had tended to shun. By early 1972 the results were in. *Well* and *Money* had done best, *View* hadn't done too badly; *Camera Month* showed the least promise.

For a number of reasons, priority attention went to *Money*. It had been one of Fuerbringer's first favorites. In the troubled economy of 1971 it seemed most likely to interest readers, and it had come out best in testing, albeit by a narrow margin. That fall a promotional brochure for *Money* was circulated among advertisers. It was not a very good brochure. For help in revising it and in putting together a dummy, Fuerbringer sounded out Bill Rukeyser, a member of *Fortune*'s board of editors.

A son of Merryle S. Rukeyser, the author, lecturer and nationally syndicated economics columnist, Rukeyser, then 32, had made his career in financial journalism since graduating from Princeton; he had come to *Fortune* in 1967 from the *Wall Street Journal* and had been promoted to the board of editors four years later. Rukeyser was a bit nervous when Fuerbringer called him. He was relieved to find "this nice, easy-going sort of man talking to me enthusiastically about this new magazine."

The enthusiasm was contagious. In April 1972, Fuerbringer sent a memo to top management, quoting one written by Rukeyser:

An unusual convergence of events makes the present a time of extraordinary public interest in personal economics, and suggests therefore that we would do well to get *Money* onto the market as rapidly as is practical . . . There are signs that consumers are at last emerging from the shocks of the 1970-71 recession and beginning to spend more freely. Interest in the stock market is plainly on the rise. And the interest in nonstock investments (bonds, real estate, syndications of various types) that rose strongly in the wake of the last stock-market break shows no signs of diminishing now that stocks are doing better. The demand for information in this area is particularly intense. Finally, continued inflation is making even relatively affluent families newly receptive to the kind of sophisticated consumer guidance that *Money* will provide.

Management was convinced. Only the name of the new magazine remained to be decided. *Strategy*, *Advantage*, *Ways and Means* and *Money Matters* were among the nominees. Donovan mentioned to Banks that a friend of his had argued that *Money* was an extraordinarily ugly word. Banks replied that if money was an ugly word, then so was sex. Donovan did not argue further. Eight days after Fuerbringer's memo, at the 1972 annual meeting, Heiskell and Donovan announced that *Money* would be a reality, beginning that autumn.

The announcement signified a noteworthy achievement by Fuerbringer. In just over a year he had identified a highly promising idea among dozens of inchoate notions about magazines, and developed it into a proposal persuasive enough to spark Time Inc.'s first magazine launch in 18 years. Only three years from retirement, Fuerbringer was now well embarked on a distinguished second career as a guru of new magazines.

Rukeyser was named managing editor of *Money*. Peter Hanson, also 32, general manager of *Sports Illustrated* when he was asked to help work up financial projections for the prospective *Money*, was named publisher.

The time between announcement and launch was short. The first issue of *Money*, dated October, would have to be ready in August, barely four months away. Rukeyser had to assemble a staff according to the guidelines, a lean group of 16 professionals and four secretaries—and put it immediately to work. Peter Bird Martin signed on as a senior editor. Keith R. Johnson also came from *Time* to edit. The research chief was Marjorie Jack, a 20-year *Fortune* veteran. As advertising director, publisher Hanson recruited Richard B. Thomas from Time Inc.'s subsidiary, Dialogue Marketing Inc.; prior to that he had spent 13 years with *Time* ad sales (where he returned as director in 1984).

The result of these efforts was a substantial inaugural issue: an even 100 pages, nearly half ads. The cover featured blurbs for three stories inside: prescription drug prices, real estate tax shelters, working wives. An unsigned "Introduction to *Money*" advised readers that:

> The task of being responsible about your money rests with you—not your banker, or insurance man or druggist or travel agent. By the same token, the enjoyment of the money you spend is entirely yours.
>
> Responsibility and enjoyment go hand in hand. *Money* will devote itself to enlarging your share of both.

Fuerbringer's contribution to *Money* was explicitly recognized, at Donovan's request, in an unusual line on the masthead crediting him as Editor, Magazine Development. But after the launch Fuerbringer moved on to other projects, and editorial director Banks, at his own request, began overseeing the new publication. In Rukeyser's words, Banks became "the magazine's godfather," keeping a close watch on the enterprise, reviewing story lists and covers, first drafts of articles and, of course, the contents of every issue, after publication.

Money's first issue appeared unsure of itself. The piece on working wives was rather elementary, while an article about real estate syndicates was meaty even for accountants. The magazine had appeal for the middle class and the wealthy, but did not fully satisfy either. It soon became apparent that *Money* would have to speak with a more consistent voice—and in the interest of circulation, one that addressed the concerns of working wives (and their husbands) more than those of wealthy real estate investors.

There were problems on the publishing side as well. The financial projections were proving wrong on several counts. Before launch, Hanson had estimated that *Money*'s annual editorial costs would run about $640 per page, low even by contrast to the company's least expensive existing magazine, *Sports Illustrated*, which cost $2,490 per page; *Time* came in at $7,560 per page. By March 1972, *Money*'s estimated editorial cost had risen by a third. *Money*'s profit and loss projections were also in flux. Few large magazines make a profit in their early years; *Money* was slated to break even in its second year. Six weeks before the magazine's debut, Auer forwarded the latest forecast of *Money*'s finances, noting: "This projection shows it has cost $2,280,000 to launch *Money* and that by 1976 we will earn back all of that. From there on out, *Money* should earn a satisfactory and substantial profit—specifically, slightly over $1 million a year."

One year later, after ten months of operation, the projections had changed dramatically. In the three-year plan for the magazine, Tony

Cox, then general manager of the magazine development group, said frankly:

> The P&L's for *Money*'s plan are not attractive. They show cumulative losses of $7.1 million through 1978. The original projection on which a "go-ahead" was based called for cumulative losses of $2 million with a modest profit in 1974.

Cox was one of the bright young MBAs hired for the controller's office who went on to have a varied Time Inc. career. He had come to magazine development from *Life*, where he had been business manager. In 1975 he would leave to become an assistant to the group vice president for magazines, going on from there to HBO, where he would spend eight years, before becoming a Time Inc. vice president for corporate development.

One important reason for the faulty predictions in 1972 was that Time Inc. had never published a magazine with a business plan quite like *Money*'s, where from the beginning the aim was to shift a greater part of the burden of supporting the magazine from the advertiser to the reader. Subscribers would be charged $15 a year ($12 to charter subscribers), and single copies would be sold on the newsstands for $1.50—high prices at the time, but justified, in the opinion of the magazine developers, because what readers learned in *Money* could save them far more than what they paid for the magazine.

It was sound strategy. But *Money* at first carried it slightly too far. The high cover price and low ad rates actually attracted fewer readers and more advertisers than planned, and unfortunately the first effect swamped the second. Advertising page sales in 1973 ran above expectations, initial response to direct-mail subscription solicitations ran 9 to 13 percent below. Subscription cancellations, also, were 60 percent greater than anticipated. Many charter subscribers, attracted by *Money*'s promotional mailing, felt oversold. The promotion letter had promised such sophisticated financial advice that it attracted an audience older and wealthier than the readership *Money* was actually edited for. The result was a paid circulation of only about 200,000 versus the targeted 225,000. Costs mounted meanwhile, mainly because of unbudgeted extra expenditures on promotion and advertising sales. Thus Tony Cox's big loss projections.

In response, *Money* cut its prices to readers. The annual subscription price fell to as little as $9.75. Newsstand copies were cut from $1.50 to 95 cents. There was one circulation windfall during 1973,

427

following the suspension of *Life*. Millions of *Life* readers held unexpired subscriptions; a remarkably large number chose to receive the balance in the form of *Money* magazine. (A mailing from Time Inc. offered them any of several other magazines or cash; a darkly humorous suspicion around *Money*'s offices was that many of *Life*'s subscribers checked the box labeled "Please send me *Money*" in the belief that they would soon receive a check in the mail.)

At about this time it was becoming evident that some of the fundamental assumptions about *Money* were wrong. Inherently, its circulation potential was larger than was thought at first. While the magazine would have to define its audience more precisely, that audience could be huge. A million was an important threshold, because some advertisers would not consider a magazine with anything less. Accordingly, as it began its second year of publication, a million circulation became *Money*'s new long-term goal.

Progress was unsteady. In February 1974, Henry Grunwald, then managing editor of *Time*, was asked to review the magazine. He reported that he liked it as "remarkably ingenious, authoritative and smooth" but recommended that *Money* become more timely and more service-oriented. Lou Banks continued his detailed critiques. Subscription mailings, aimed at bringing circulation up to predetermined "checkpoints," did well—until the one in the fall of 1974, which drew a response of only 1.26 percent; it was budgeted to draw 2 percent. And a number of subscriptions turned out to be "bad pays." Sandy Steinbreder, who had become publisher in October 1973, called the mailing "completely unsuccessful—it missed its target by 40 percent."

Art Keylor was now the group vice president in charge of magazines. Bernie Auer had given up the job just after *Money*'s launch—and just before *Life*'s closing; he said he did not have the stomach for that decision. (Auer served as assistant to the chairman for about a year, then retired.) In December 1974, Keylor presented a detailed and grim report to the board of directors on *Money*'s future, including plans for a big direct-mail selling effort in the spring of 1975. His conclusion, as summarized in the minutes of the meeting:

> With all of the above in mind, it is my recommendation that we go ahead with our 6 million spring mail. If, in April, however, we are looking at a material deviation from the direct-mail results we are projecting, with no offsetting favorable change in

the other circulation figures you have looked at today, I feel it is a better than 50 percent chance that I would be recommending at that time termination or other disposition of *Money* magazine.

Keylor was doubtful about monthly magazines in general. Having been publisher of *Fortune* (then still a monthly) he knew firsthand the economics of monthly publication: fixed expenses run nearly as high as weeklies but aggregate revenues and profits are considerably lower. If *Money* couldn't turn in a decent financial performance, Keylor felt, it would be a prudent business decision to kill it. Shepley was even more blunt: "When the hell are we going to kill this thing?" he was heard to inquire.

In January 1975, Tony Cox wrote an anguished confidential memo to Steinbreder and Garry Valk, now magazine development publisher. Cox opened by recounting a conversation he had had with a Time Inc. executive: "His comment (not for attribution I'm sure) was that he thinks Art Keylor wonders why we're so actively pursuing new tactics and new approaches when Art's mind is essentially already made up." Cox went on to pour out his own concerns:

I am getting increasingly enthusiastic about our ability to market the product better and thus improve its performance. The programs in the works will make a difference—not by April, but certainly by a year from April. *We must have more time . . .*

Our problem is that the bottom line does not reflect our success. Why? Because in good part we spend too much on staff and quarters; we spend too much on fulfillment—we are part of Time Inc. . . .

Perhaps we can do nothing about it. But management can't have its cake and eat it too. That is, they can't have us endure $1 million or more of unneeded expenses yet still wonder why we can't make profits. Either we act like *Gourmet* or *Psychology Today* and operate with lots of freelancing and a total staff of 35, or else we concede we can't and agree to invest more in *Money* than we'd like. We can't do both—spend à la Time Inc. and turn a profit after four years. One doesn't go with the other . . .

What can we do to get a hearing? The direction this situation is taking is killing me! And, I've got to tell someone. To acquiesce without a fight for what you believe in is the ultimate irresponsibility.

429

Money got its hearing on May 15, 1975, before the board of directors. Two weeks earlier, Steinbreder had sent Rukeyser a memo bluntly outlining the stakes, predicting that the board session would be "the most important presentation *Money* has given since the decision was made to launch the magazine." His plan:

> We are going to ask Time Inc.'s management and the board to give us until December, to invest another $250,000 a month in *Money*. If by that time we have not found the answer to our problems of becoming a viable, profit-making magazine with a potential million circulation by 1979 we will recommend that the magazine be sold or folded.

Considering the large symbolic importance of *Money*—it embodied Time Inc.'s confidence in magazine publishing despite *Life*'s demise—management was not inclined to kill the magazine as long as any hope remained. *Money* got the funds and the time it requested.

By the end of 1975 things were looking up. That July, *Money* had undergone an editorial overhaul; its graphics were revamped, more color introduced. Opening each issue was a new column, Current Accounts, which Rukeyser described in his note to readers as "a series of short, unsolemn reports on the month-by-month interplay between people and money." Two popular features, the Wall Street Letter and the Washington Letter, were expanded, made more timely. In addition, the publisher's office refined its direct-mail selling techniques. Perhaps equally important, if not more so, the U.S. economy began struggling out of recession.

Money still was not making money, but it gave promise of doing so. December came, the reprieve continued. In early 1976, circulation hit 660,000. During that year *Money* began advertising on television, with striking success, and Bill Rukeyser did a series of brief radio programs. By the end of the year the magazine was breaking even on its operations, without taking into account its allocated share of corporate overhead. *Money* was no longer costing the company money out-of-pocket. This was the decisive achievement.

In April of 1977, corporate editor Ralph Graves was able to report to Donovan, with an almost audible sigh of relief, that "the magazine has settled down, not in a stodgy way, to being useful, practical, handy on the great bulk of its stories . . . I think it is now, for the first time, possible to say what the magazine is all about—and pretty consistently. I think it has found its niche and purpose."

Circulation climbed to over 800,000 the following year and ad pages were increasing even faster.

In 1980, *Money* changed editors. Bill Rukeyser, now an experienced managing editor at 40, was named to succeed Bob Lubar as managing editor of *Fortune*. Replacing Rukeyser was Marshall Loeb, 50, economics editor at *Time*. Loeb, super-energetic and brimming with ideas, was one of the company's most experienced economic journalists, an editor who drove himself even harder than his staff. Chicago-born, a graduate of the University of Missouri School of Journalism, Loeb joined *Time* in 1956 after stints with the United Press in Germany and the St. Louis *Globe-Democrat*. At *Time* he wrote or edited over 130 cover stories mainly in the Business section, where he served as both writer and senior editor while also carrying a heavy load as speaker to businessmen's groups. For a time, including part of the Watergate period, Loeb edited Nation. Under Loeb, *Money* would sharpen its editorial focus, lift its circulation from 800,000 to over 1.4 million in 1983 and exceed $12 million in pretax profits.

Of the three other magazine ideas being explored as *Money* was launched, two had been shelved. *Well* looked shaky; health care did not seem to have sufficiently wide appeal. *Camera Month* was designed for too narrow a market. *View*, however, looked promising; like *Money*, it seemed to hold potential for attracting an audience of a million or more. Early in 1973, the magazine development group took on several editors from the recently departed *Life*. One was Dick Stolley, a former assistant managing editor. He had mentioned to Donovan that he wanted "to run something." Donovan assigned him to head the *View* project with an implicit understanding that if a magazine materialized, Stolley would indeed run it.

Stolley set to work on a revised dummy for *View*, based on his assumption that the audience would be young, urban, mainly female, visually oriented, busy and with short attention spans. The result was a magazine combining a number of departments, such as Sports, Children and New Movies with articles on a broad range of subjects—movie stars, the new TV season, the upcoming Watergate hearings, among others. The finished product did not entirely satisfy Stolley; he and most others on the project believed the text should be "racier" in order to attract a wider audience, and that the graphics, a mixture of the stodgy and the avant-garde, needed improvement. There was more work to be done, and Stolley attacked it. Within a few weeks, however, the magazine development group was in possession of a new idea that would transform Stolley's—and the company's—future.

Board chairmen are not usually fonts of editorial ideas, but in this case, as Fuerbringer recalled, "I was walking up to Hedley's office and ran into Heiskell. He was standing in the doorway with his arms stretched up toward the ceiling. He said, 'Hey, Otto, why don't we start a magazine called *People*?' " Heiskell's recollection was slightly different: "Quite obviously, the thing that people are interested in more than anything else is other people. I got the idea that you really could have a look at the world through people, as opposed to the way *Time* does it. I didn't really think about it very much. I walked down to Otto one morning and tried it out on him. To my surprise, he liked it right away. I also remember saying that you've got to call it *People*."

However Fuerbringer heard it, he did indeed like it right away. While neither he nor Heiskell recalled the date of their conversation, it apparently took place in late March or early April of 1973. By April 17, Fuerbringer, in conjunction with a team working under former *Life* assistant managing editor Phil Kunhardt, had composed a brief memo outlining the magazine. While such outlines inevitably evolve as a magazine idea becomes reality, this one changed remarkably little. This is how Fuerbringer described *People* a year before it existed:

> Not slick, but on paper heavy enough for good reproduction, since pictures will be a large part of edit . . . *color cover and color ads*, but *black and white edit* . . .
>
> *Flexible in makeup*; that is, not standard departments in the same place every week. *Standing features*, yes; but only when they can be filled with credit.
>
> *Let each week's topicality dictate the content and flow of the magazine*. Nothing to impede the progress of stories and items of people in action—people in action physically, mentally, socially, artistically.

Plotting the editorial and publishing plans for *People* went fast. Whereas *Money* had been an obviously good idea that had to be slowly and painfully refined, the concept of *People* was something everyone seemed to grasp intuitively. By June there was a rough business plan that, like Fuerbringer's editorial outline, proved remarkably durable: the magazine would contain 51 to 54 editorial pages and initially would sell only at newsstands for 50 cents a copy. A pasted-up (but not printed) dummy, created by the *Camera*

Month team of ex-*Life* editors—Kunhardt, John Loengard, Edward Kern and Janet Mason—won raves. According to an unsigned memo to the files, "Heiskell loved it. Shepley said it was the best thing he'd seen; get it on the newsstands by October." The same group put together a few more pasteups to assure themselves that there were enough pictures available from photo and wire services—and enough people to write about each week.

With those doubts laid to rest, the next step was a full-fledged dummy, produced mainly by the team that had done the pasteups; in addition, Stolley, who was turning *View* over to the business experts for evaluation, wrote and edited some *People* items. The result became known as "the Liz-and-Dick dummy" because it featured the eternally newsworthy Elizabeth Taylor and Richard Burton on the cover. (Their first marriage was breaking up.) But when Donovan asked his other managing editors for comment, he evoked qualified approval only. *Fortune* managing editor Lubar found the writing "sprightly" but criticized the magazine's "somewhat grubby appearance" and its "drearily familiar" cast of characters. Bill Rukeyser, in a well-remembered phrase, called it "journalistic popcorn" and predicted it would succeed. Henry Grunwald found the magazine "potentially very exciting" but concluded that it would require "far more quality, information, variety, and thus money, than are evident in this issue." Jerry Korn, then acting editorial director, reported to Donovan on the weekly managing editors' lunch where, Korn said, "The consensus [on *People*] was powerfully negative . . . The words most often used were 'sleazy' and 'cheap'."

A more upbeat evaluation came from Clare Boothe Luce, in Honolulu. Heiskell had sent her a courtesy copy of the dummy. She had collected the opinions of a hairdresser, a manicurist, a friend, her two maids, her cook, her secretary and her secretary's husband—all of whom liked it. Mrs. Luce for the most part liked it herself. She wrote Heiskell: "Please let me know how you make out with the advertisers. If you make out well, nothing can stop *People*."

Taking prepublication testing beyond informal polls and personal opinions, the company put the Liz-and-Dick dummy on newsstands in 11 cities in numbers sufficient to simulate a national offering of a million copies. In some cities there was a one-day promotional blitz on radio, television and in newspapers; in others, no promotion. In one city where there was no promotion the cover price was set at 50 cents; in the others it was 35 cents. The results were bracing. In the markets where there had been promotion, readers bought 85.2 percent of the available copies. (Because of lost, stolen and ruined copies, 90 percent is considered a sellout.) Even where *People* was not promoted and cost 50 cents it achieved a 38.4 percent sale.

Based on those results the company's circulation experts estimated that within three years *People* could become the fifth largest of the U.S. magazines sold mainly on newsstands (after *TV Guide*, *Playboy*, *Penthouse* and the *National Enquirer*). It was estimated further that the magazine would probably become profitable (before allocation of corporate overhead) in the last half of its second year. Management realized it had a winner with *People*. Among many suddenly urgent tasks was assembling an editorial staff, beginning with a managing editor.

Shortly after the Liz-and-Dick test issue had closed, Stolley had taken a vacation. One day Fuerbringer, with Donovan's blessing, asked Stolley to meet him at a popular saloon in Greenwich, Connecticut, where both lived, and offered him the chance to run *People*. Stolley, then 45, said he would think about it. "With *Life* gone, a lot of us were thinking about a lot of things at that point, reviewing career plans. I thought about going back to Illinois and running for Congress, or going into something else entirely. I was offered a p.r. job with Federated Stores . . . I thought about teaching, even going to law school. Finally I faced up to the fact that I'd really rather be in journalism. I told Hedley that I'd be pleased to do it but that I'd like to do another dummy first."

Stolley's dummy, with Billie Jean King and her husband Larry on the cover, was a magazine strikingly similar to the *People* of a decade later. It contained 53 editorial pages and was divided into 16 sections: In the Money, Jocks, Star Tracks, Up Front, Chatter, Couples, In Her Own Words, Off the Screen, Out of the Pages, Tube, among others. A section called People In the Past was later dropped, and the People Puzzle hadn't yet appeared. The Kings' presence on the cover made the point that *People* wasn't another movie magazine. The writing was generally more self-confident, less giggly than in the first dummy. There were also important cosmetic changes. The text of the first dummy had been set in a widely despised typewriter-like typeface; it was replaced by the sans-serif face that the magazine would use for at least a decade. Overall, *People* looked somewhat crisper and more attractive.

The new magazine needed a publisher; the nod went to Richard J. Durrell, then 48, a former newsstand sales specialist for *Time*, who had been assistant publisher and advertising sales director at *Life* when it folded. When *People* began receiving serious consideration, Valk had asked Durrell to devise a marketing plan. Durrell did, and that plan was included when *People* was presented to the board on October 18, 1973.

That same day it was announced that *People*'s first issue would appear in March 1974. But when the sales staff went out to do business, it soon found that *People* had a serious problem: Madison Avenue's image of the magazine. Like all the Time Inc. magazines at their birth (with the possible later exception of *Discover*), *People* was an original product, out of place in any category. For such publications, acceptance is always a battle. Ad agency executives labored at categorizing *People*—at "positioning"it. Wasn't it really just another *Photoplay*? Or maybe a dressed-up *National Enquirer*? An uptown *Playboy*? Or just an expanded *Time* People section? Another problem, mainly a result of the Liz-and-Dick dummy, was that *People* seemed to lack the sophistication, the polish of other Time Inc. magazines. In ad jargon, it seemed a little "downscale." Faithful advertising clients of the company's other publications needed persuading to invest in *People*. Even Fuerbringer took up the cause, flying to Washington to assure the head of a supermarket chain that *People* would be respectable. Clare Luce's concern about *People* "making it with the advertisers" was justified.

One of the painful lessons from the *Money* experience was that launching a magazine required heavy promotion—which *Money* had not had at first. *People* accordingly scheduled receptions across the country for advertisers and retailers; Stolley appeared at many to explain what the new publication would be like. Dick Thomas, who came from *Money* to be *People*'s advertising sales director, recalled:

> Prospective advertisers were always immensely impressed with Stolley. He never apologized or was defensive. If they thought *People* was garbage, Stolley would just say, "Well, that's your opinion." Since the downscale image was one of the things we were trying to beat, it was terribly helpful to have Dick Stolley talk about the magazine as he saw it. *People* never sounded downscale when he talked about it.

Stolley, Durrell and Thomas—quickly dubbed the Three Richards—were devoted to their task. Fogged in at a Detroit airport one morning, due for a luncheon presentation in Chicago, they checked the yellow pages for charter air services and came upon one they remembered as "Rocket Airways." A hippie-looking aviator, driving a Cadillac that to Stolley resembled a hearse, responded, taking them to a remote corner of the airfield where a four-seater was parked. Thomas remembered "Stolley shouting, 'I've covered three wars and five major disasters for this company and I'll be goddamned if I'm going to die trying to sell ads for you, Thomas!' " They flew through rain and skirted tornadoes but got to Chicago on time.

When he wasn't pitching the magazine, Stolley was busy staffing it. Like *Money*, *People* was supposed to "run lean," relying for its reporting primarily on stringers—journalists, often newspaper employees, who could be called when needed and paid an hourly rate ($7.50 at the time) for services rendered. Hal Wingo, 38, was in charge of recruiting. A *Life* alumnus, Wingo had joined the development group and spent six months working on the prospectus for a magazine he envisioned called *Spirit*, about religion and ethics. "Watergate had happened, and ethics was very much in the air," Wingo said. But *Spirit* was shelved, and soon after Wingo came over to help at *People*, where by the time the first issue appeared, he had assembled a network of 66 stringers, many formerly with *Life*.

The stories sent in by *People*'s stringers were to be heavily rewritten in New York in order to establish the distinctive, consistent style that was so important to the magazine's success. In the interest of running lean, there would be no large research staff either, reporters would check their own work for accuracy. Some Time Inc. veterans suggested that *People* would be a magazine with one writer and ten libel lawyers.

The inaugural issue of *People* was dated March 4, 1974. The cover subject was Mia Farrow, then starring in a new film version of *The Great Gatsby*. Her cover appearance jarred the magazine's ad salesmen, who had assured prospective clients that *People* would not be a movie magazine. The issue carried 20 pages of advertising, slightly below forecast, and sold 978,000 copies, also slightly below forecast, but neither number was worrisome. The editorial staff totaled just 34. Running lean seemed to be working.

It soon became clear, however, that the magazine's editorial plan needed two fundamental changes. *People* could not rely as heavily on outside photo services as originally planned; the magazine would have to assign photographers itself. Stolley enlarged the picture department, not with staff photographers but with staff who could locate and assign photographers to work freelance. *People* also needed researchers. That became clear with the very first issue, which included an article by Sheilah Graham, the former Hollywood columnist, comparing Hollywood and Palm Beach. Buried near the end was a rather sensational line: "The big difference between Palm Beach and Hollywood is that Hollywood is a working city. There you can open every door with talent. You can be illegitimate, as Marilyn Monroe was; a former call girl, as I was . . ." Wingo cleared those last few words with Graham over the phone before publication, but when they appeared in print she threatened to sue. Two weeks later *People* ran an item in the Chatter section explaining that she had meant to say "chorus girl." Graham dropped her threat. The incident emphasized the critical importance of credibility for *People*. If it was to refute the critics who compared it with the supermarket tabloids, it would have to establish a reputation for solid accuracy. Stolley began adding research staff.

In addition to the ordinary travails of any fledgling magazine, *People* was afflicted in its early life by the sort of sneering attitude with which it was regarded. Not many Time Inc. employees were applying for jobs on the new magazine. Stolley recalled, "They thought that for Time Inc. to put out a magazine like this was unseemly. Tacky. You'd be in the elevator and hear cracks like this all the time. Here we'd be, working 80- and 100-hour weeks, and then to get on the elevator and hear someone dump on the magazine—well, it wasn't pleasant. But it was all over the place." Outside the Time & Life Building as well, *People* was often derided as insubstantial, unimportant. Although these charges diminished or disappeared in time, they hurt. The young magazine's staff, sharing the experience of being under attack, developed an extraordinary camaraderie.

Shorthanded, *People*'s top editors found themselves rewriting virtually all copy themselves. Cranston Jones, a former *Time* senior editor who joined *People* soon after its launch, recalled Stolley's elation at reading one just-right piece that Jones had actually redone completely. "God, we've finally got a writer!" Stolley yelled. When Jones winced, Stolley got the message, and returned to his office. An influential contributor to the *People* style of writing was Richard A. Burgheim, a former writer in *Time*'s Show Business and Television sections, who joined *People* when it started, and became the first assistant managing editor. Burgheim proved especially adept at choosing timely cover subjects.

Long hours applied from the top down at *People*. Stolley kept the longest, insisting on editing every item in every issue. Once Wingo found Stolley in his office at 4 o'clock in the morning editing the clues to the People Puzzle. Sleep seemed to be something Stolley could take or leave alone; he became known as the bionic editor.

For all the effort, *People*'s early issues were, perhaps inevitably, uneven and not entirely satisfactory. As with the prepublication dummy, however, Time Inc. editors were being harder on the magazine than were the readers, who seemed most pleased. The Cambridge Marketing Group, hired to study audience attitudes, presented a major report in the fall of 1974. Top management attended the presentation. When Cambridge Marketing's representative rose to address the meeting, his first words were, "Never in my 25 years of research have I seen a product with greater consumer acceptance than *People*." At that, Donovan stood up, took his coat from the back of his chair, said to Heiskell, "Well, Andrew, I've done my part," and left. It was a joke, of course (Donovan quickly returned), but it expressed the prevailing high spirits.

A bit of ribbing, addressed by Donovan to *People*'s editor several months later, gives the flavor of his affectionate regard for this youngest of the Time Inc. magazines. Wrote Donovan:

> Once more *People* seems intent on affronting mature readers like Mr. Heiskell and myself.
> Zsa Zsa—the managing editor should look so good—is called an "aging beauty."
> Omar Sharif, a mere 43, is described as an "aging boulevardier." Actually, beginners-slope training for a boulevardier does not even start until 50.

Not all was smooth sailing, though. From the start, Stolley had figured that *People* would attract a large female readership. Audience testing, once *People* was launched, proved the hunch correct: women readers were outnumbering men, about 60 to 40. But advertising aimed at women was slow in coming; on the whole, ads were thin in *People*'s early issues. Also, on newsstands, *People* was not getting the exposure it needed. The first Time Inc. magazine ever designed for newsstand sale exclusively, *People* was dependent on reaching what were now the most important "newsstands" in the country—the magazine racks in supermarkets, where competition for the best positions was fierce.

With little experience in this area, Time Inc. had been relying on Select Magazines, a distribution cooperative owned jointly by several publishers. After a few months, Durrell concluded that Select was "spread too thin"—unable to get *People* into as many supermarkets as management needed or, once there, assured of displaying it to the best advantage. The outcome was that in October 1974 Time Inc. set up a new organization, Time Distribution Services, to work with Select. TDS's first president was Joseph Corr, a former *Life* promotion director. Corr decided, in contravention of company tradition, to hire outsiders, mainly people who had worked for large merchandisers and knew the retail and supermarket trade. Corr left Time Inc. a year later, but his sales strategy proved correct. TDS improved *People*'s distribution markedly, and in 1978 TDS took over newsstand distribution of all Time Inc. magazines.

By October 1975, *People*'s circulation had risen to well over a million, advertisers were buying pages faster than management had anticipated, and the magazine astonished nearly everyone by turning a profit just 18 months after launch—a virtually unprecedented feat. Equally unexpected was the unsolicited demand for subscriptions—which, at the beginning, were sold at no reduced rate, but simply as a convenience.

Dependence on newsstand sales had, in turn, made *People* especially dependent on the choice of cover subjects—the magazine's most important selling tool. Cover selection is a chancy business at best, defying analysis and often eluding magazine journalism's shrewdest talents. Here, the editors of *People*, different from some on other Time Inc. magazines, had shown no hesitation at commissioning market research. "I know a lot of editors are squeamish about it, but I think that's nuts," Stolley commented, dismissing the objections. On its own, however, the magazine was finding its own guidelines, sometimes proving the research wrong. One accepted rule was that celebrities in music would not draw well, so *People* had avoided them at first. "Then we put Olivia Newton-John on the cover, and pow—it sold like mad. After that, music became a staple for us." Stolley eventually distilled years of experience into his rule of thumb for choosing covers:

> Young is better than old, pretty is better than ugly, television
> is better than music, music is better than movies, movies are
> better than sports, and anything is better than politics.

In the four years from 1976, *People*'s income more than quadrupled, reaching $17 million pretax and putting the magazine on a level with *Sports Illustrated* for profitability. By 1980, *People*'s paid circulation had reached 2.5 million and the magazine had become part of the national consciousness. Without question, it ranked as the preeminent success of the 1970s. Stolley offered four reasons:

> First, it was a great idea. Second, it had no competition. Third,

there weren't any picture magazines around when *People* was born; *Life* and *Look* were both gone, leaving us a vacuum to fill. Finally, there was a sociological, psychological climate that worked for us. This was the real beginning of the Me Decade. We found out that people in the news were quite willing to talk to us about themselves. They'd talk about lots of personal things—their sex lives, their money, their families, religion. They'd talk about things that a few years earlier wouldn't even have been brought up. The counterpart of the Me Decade was the You Decade, and that meant more and more curiosity about other people and their lives.

A lot of American magazines, especially the newsmagazines, had gotten away from the personality story; they'd become more issue-oriented. We intended to reverse that idea with *People*. We'd do issues, of course, but through personalities. I think the formula has worked and certainly has made an impact. More and more magazines and newspapers, and even TV, are now leaning toward personality journalism.

In April 1982, Stolley left *People* to become managing editor of the reborn *Life*, replacing Phil Kunhardt. Stolley's successor at *People* was Patricia Ryan, 39, who thereupon became the second woman ever to become managing editor of a Time Inc. magazine.*

Nine years earlier, Ryan had played an important role in the development of a Time Inc. magazine that never came to be. Then at *Sports Illustrated*, where she had risen from secretary to researcher to writer to senior editor, Ryan had displayed a notably strong news sense, and her proposal to Donovan, in November 1973, was that Time Inc. undertake a magazine reporting the news from the woman's perspective. "A publishing void exists, one I feel Time Inc. could fill with distinction—and to its great profit." She explained:

> *Ms.* is not a magazine but a political tool; *Viva* is schlock; the established women's magazines each have well-defined styles and content that simply are not directed toward the increasingly self-conscious, intelligent female . . . 50 percent of the population does not have a newsmagazine directed toward its interests.

Donovan suggested that Ryan flesh the proposal out. It was, in fact, an idea that had long interested Time Inc. The attractions were

*The first was Ruth Goodhue, managing editor of *Architectural Forum* 1934–43.

obvious: here was undoubtedly the largest group of readers, and associated advertisers, to which Time Inc. was not yet appealing directly. The magazine development group was well aware of the possibilities, although at the time of Ryan's memo it had no women's magazine project under consideration. Early in 1974 *Sports Illustrated* loaned Ryan to Fuerbringer's group where she began working up a more complete proposal, together with a list of story ideas suggesting the magazine's editorial range: Iris Murdoch, Agatha Christie, women police, the first woman rabbi, ski instructors and, as an offbeat, an Iowa feather-duster factory going out of business.

Circumstances dictated a delay on the project. While Ryan was compiling her report, others in the development group were toying with the idea of buying a woman's magazine rather than creating one; *Woman's Day* and *Redbook* came under scrutiny. Then, during the summer of 1974, these proposals were shelved while the development group devoted itself to launching *People* and getting *Money* into the black; Ryan's idea also lay dormant for several months. In March 1975, Fuerbringer returned to it with a long memo proposing a magazine for women: "It should tell women how far out the parameters of their world are, if they want to explore them. It should describe the contemporary woman to herself, and point to what her future might be."

Over that summer the company's top editors assessed the future of consumer magazines and concluded, in the words of Dick Stolley: "The most important single development forecast may be the increase in women who take jobs. Therefore should any new magazine be for women? Should it be called *Working Woman*? [This was before a magazine by that name was actually started by another publisher.] Aimed at those who arrange their lives, their families, their meals, their leisure around jobs."

In September 1975, Fuerbringer retired at 65, and Phil Kunhardt replaced him as editorial chief of the development group. But near the end of the year he took a leave of absence to write a book on his family's historical picture collection centering around Abraham Lincoln.* Pending his return, Kelso Sutton, then corporate circulation director, stepped into the job and sparked an intensive effort to bring a woman's magazine to life. He made a formal proposal to Donovan in April 1976, and two weeks later Pat Ryan began assembling a staff and working on a dummy.

Mathew Brady and His World (Time-Life Books, 1977).

By the end of 1976 it was ready. The title was simply *Woman*. Initial reactions were cool. Time Inc.'s highest-ranking woman, Joan Manley, had a fundamental criticism. Even before the dummy was completed, she wrote to Heiskell: "It did not occur to us to publish something called *Men* and try to cover everything of interest to all intelligent, educated and enlightened men. The formula isn't right for women either."

One more try was in store. In early 1977, Phil Kunhardt asked former *Life* associate editor Eleanor Graves to think about producing a new dummy of *Woman*. She was then developing ideas for Time-Life Films. In June 1977 Mrs. Graves was released from those duties long enough to produce several dummies of a *Woman* that would be weekly, heavier on service articles than the first dummy, and about the size of *TV Guide*, so it would fit easily in a purse. (Because of this last feature the project was sometimes referred to as "Little *Woman*.") The content was a mix of current events, service items, feature articles and columns. In November one of the dummies was test marketed in several cities and did poorly. Further work on *Woman* was set aside as the magazine development group turned its efforts to a new project, one that had never been far out of mind: the revival of *Life*.

Even as the weekly *Life* was being shut down, in December 1972, the possibility of revival was clearly suggested. Donovan said as much; the language of his announcement that *Life* would "suspend publication" not only sustained hope, but served an important legal purpose, blocking competitive use of the *Life* name—a component of numerous Time Inc. enterprises, such as Time-Life Books, Time-Life Records, Time-Life Films.

Calling the closing of *Life* a "suspension" was more than mere legal maneuver, however. Heiskell recalled that plans to relaunch the magazine were being hatched "within days." Within three months there was serious planning for *Life* "specials," each devoted to some topic of the day and produced in the familiar *Life* format. In October 1973, just ten months after suspension, Phil Kunhardt sent Otto Fuerbringer a ten-page description of "*A New Life*" that was to remain a prescient description of the magazine that reappeared five years later:

A revived *Life* should
1) be a monthly
2) have the same large page size as the old *Life*

442

3) cost at least $1.00 a copy ($10 a year for a subscription)
4) be printed on high quality, heavy paper with beautiful reproduction
5) have run-of-the-book color
6) contain advertising
7) be talking to an audience of between 1–2 million readers
8) be able to be produced by a very small editorial staff

The most energetic advocate of reviving *Life*, Kunhardt expressed his passion for the magazine in the closing paragraph of his memo to Fuerbringer:

> America needs *Life* again. Now they haven't got it, people miss it badly. Enough to make an audience for a new *Life* without hardly trying. *Life* should be part of the U.S. decor once more—an elegant, worldly, visually exciting, often passionate, always handsome part of the American home.

Before 1973 was half over, the first *Life* special was out—an issue devoted to Israel, pegged to the country's 25th birthday. Sold only on newsstands, the special issue did moderately well: about half a million copies were bought. The company regarded this initial success cautiously, ascribing it in part to the novelty of *Life*'s first appearance since suspension and to the issue's obviously strong appeal to Jewish readers.

In the spring of 1974, Art Keylor asked Tony Cox, who was working up profit-and-loss projections for *Money* and *People*, to do the same for a possible monthly *Life*. The results were awful, showing the magazine losing about $9 million in each of its first two years. Undeterred, the magazine development group produced a dummy of a monthly *Life*, but with the new *People* magazine demanding attention, *Life* was put on the shelf. *Life* specials continued to appear meanwhile, ten in all, with subjects including One Day in the Life of America, Remarkable American Women, One Hundred Events That Shaped America, and The New Youth, plus five annual Year in Pictures issues. Sales averaged slightly more than 700,000 copies each, priced at $1.50 to $2.

Work resumed on the monthly *Life* in 1977, after the woman's magazine project was stopped. Within a few months, new profit-and-loss projections were ready. Based on a higher assumed cover price and higher circulation—justified by the performance of the *Life* specials—the figures were more promising than earlier estimates. These projections and the prospect of reclaiming *Life*'s photographic franchise sparked considerable topside interest. In December, Grunwald, then corporate editor, wrote Donovan: "I am enthusiastically in favor of the earliest possible attempt to revive *Life*."

Kunhardt and company immediately went to work on a dummy, which they completed in April 1978. It was a hit. Even more encouraging budget projections showed the magazine crossing into the black in its third year and becoming strongly profitable thereafter. On April 24 Time Inc. announced that *Life* would be relaunched as a monthly, beginning with the issue dated October.

If any hesitations remained, they were quickly dispelled. The extraordinary response to the news that *Life* was resuming publication revealed that millions of readers had not merely enjoyed the magazine, but had felt a bond with it and missed it. All three networks put the announcement on the evening news. Every major newspaper carried a story. Bonnie Angelo, chief of *Time*'s London bureau, wrote Donovan:

> Within minutes of the time the announcement ran on the ticker, we had a call from a man asking whether it would be available in Britain. That evening I was at the American embassy for a party, and all kinds of people from Kingman Brewster [then U.S. ambassador] to resident Britishers were jubilant at the return of the magazine they felt had never been replaced.

Phil Kunhardt was appointed managing editor. Noted Donovan, in announcing the appointment: "Phil held practically every other job on the old *Life*: reporter, correspondent, writer, assistant picture editor, senior editor and assistant managing editor." Eleanor Graves was named assistant managing editor. The veteran *Life* photographer John Loengard became picture editor. The new *Life*'s publisher was Charles A. (Chuck) Whittingham, 48, who had spent his 19-year Time Inc. career at *Fortune*, where he rose to assistant publisher. A supersalesman, widely acquainted, Whittingham was known for a phenomenal memory for names (a talent demonstrated one day when a colleague arrived late at a business lunch and Whittingham flawlessly introduced his guests: 20 Japanese businessmen he had met just a few minutes earlier). Another of his talents was ably demonstrated when *Life* took to advertising on television: Whittingham starred in the commercials.

The new *Life*'s first issue did not, as a monthly, have the late-news crackle of the weekly *Life*, but it recalled the old *Life*'s picture flair. The cover, showing brilliant yellow and red passenger-carrying balloons, shouted to be noticed. Inside the photo spreads were reminiscent of the old *Life* but with more liberal use of color: an intimate look inside the Shah of Iran's royal retreat, scenes from the set of a new movie version of *The Wizard of Oz*, panoramic views of Antarctica's cold splendor, a black-and-white picture essay on the rehabilitation of a small boy saved from drowning in a backyard fountain. There were also 56 pages of ads.

Advertisers in the early issues had been guaranteed a 700,000 circulation—a figure that reader demand immediately topped. The October and November issues each sold more than a million on the newsstands, and by mid-November 400,000 subscriptions had been ordered as well. Somewhat conservatively, the magazine raised its circulation guarantee to a million. By 1980 *Life*'s average net paid circulation had reached 1,373,000. It did not become profitable on schedule but was doing steadily better and was meeting the rigorous guidelines set by management.

So, at last, the "other name on the door" at Time Inc. was being successfully published again. Kunhardt would have to step down as managing editor in 1982, for health reasons; Stolley would move from *People* to succeed him.

In the 1980s, Time Inc.'s efforts to invent magazines continued. First to be launched was *Discover*, a monthly newsmagazine of science, developed in less than a year by a small team under *Time* senior editor Leon Jaroff, who became the new magazine's first managing editor. Jaroff had been promoting the idea for a decade, citing the growing reader interest in science, attested by the popularity of Time-Life Books' Nature and Science series, as well as the brisk sales of *Time* cover stories on science, medicine and behavior, many of which Jaroff, as *Time*'s science editor, had shepherded to publication. *Discover* appeared in October 1980, with an initial circulation of 400,000. Although only one of several science magazines created or heavily promoted by competing publishers about that time, *Discover* had, by July 1982, doubled its circulation to 835,000. Advertising, however, was to remain a problem.

Next off the launching pad was *TV-Cable Week*, an extraordinarily ambitious attempt to provide viewers in selected cities, and eventually across the country, with complete, precise listings of everything available on television—cable as well as broadcast. Managing editor Dick Burgheim, who was shifted from *People*, heralded the new magazine as "the most audacious, most watched, most talked about, and inevitably the most exciting journalistic enterprise in

America this year." Dick Munro thought *TV-Cable Week* had "the potential of becoming our largest magazine both in terms of subscribers and revenues." The magazine broke precedent in at least three ways: it was based outside New York City in White Plains; it relied heavily on sophisticated computer technology to produce its core contents, program listings; and it was marketed in a novel way—operators of cable TV systems were supposed to sell subscriptions to people who subscribed to their cable service.

TV-Cable Week was launched to great fanfare in April 1983. By midsummer, severe trouble was evident. The marketing system was proving unworkable, since responsibility for getting and keeping circulation was transferred from publisher to distributor; *TV-Cable Week* was, as one executive observed, "a Time Inc. magazine where Time Inc. had no contact with the customer." Falling far below its circulation targets, *TV-Cable Week* quickly ran through some $40 million of the $100 million investment that was supposed to last four to five years. The future looked impossible. Wasting no time, Time Inc.'s top management announced the end of *TV-Cable Week* on September 15, 1983, only five months after start-up. Munro admitted the corporate miscalculation: "We misjudged the market."

Undeterred by that disaster, Time Inc. made clear that it would keep pursuing new magazine concepts. In 1984, the magazine development group was revived and reconstituted, with an ample budget and a large staff, headed by Marshall Loeb (who also continued as managing editor of *Money*). The move was recognition of magazine publishing's enormous importance to Time Inc.'s future, despite the growth of video as a corporate revenue source. And, there was also recognition that it was inventing magazines—a risky but exhilarating business—that Time Inc. had done best.

A Season of Discontents

"LET ME TELL YOU ABOUT MY JOB," wrote *Time* staff writer Don Morrison in his college alumni magazine* describing his work as the writer of *Time*'s Press section:

I have a wood-paneled office on a high floor with a television set and a three-star view of the Hudson River. I have a blushingly permissive expense account and nearly six weeks of paid holiday a year. In fact, the benefits my employer offers are so generous (medical, dental and psychiatric care, pension and profit-sharing plans—even free meals and taxis home when I work late) that *New York* magazine once did an admiring article about my kind of life at *Time* . . .

My father is very impressed, and I can't wait for another class reunion to tell everyone what a clever fellow I am for having walked into such a classy job.

Or why I walked out on it . . . Matter of fact, I did not even quit. I did something radically more ungrateful toward my corporate benefactors, immensely less romantic in the eyes of my colleagues at other magazines, and, to the father who spent

*Pennsylvania Gazette, University of Pennsylvania, October 1976.

good money educating me out of the laboring classes, vastly more insane. I went on strike.

The strike Morrison joined with ambivalent feelings began on June 2, 1976, and lasted only 18 days. But it was the first walkout by editorial staff members in Time Inc. history, and it tore what one *Time* veteran called "the fabric of civility that was the hallmark of Time Inc.'s corporate culture."

The strike could be viewed as the culmination of a difficult decade in the company's relations with its employees. America had passed through an era of protest, of uninhibited expression of discontents and demands for the correction of inequities and injustices. Time Inc.'s journalists covered those stormy episodes, and not surprisingly some of the passion resounded within the walls of the Time & Life Building. There had been a near strike in 1967, averted only at the last moment. Inflation and improved pay scales elsewhere in the industry had taken some of the luster off Time Inc.'s generous compensation policy, while the nationwide civil rights crusade had drawn management into the task of increasing the number and status of minorities on its employment rolls. And in 1970 the company was confronted with a complaint of sex discrimination brought by a group of women employees before New York State's Human Rights Commission. The women's action and the efforts to improve minority employment opportunities did not cause the strike, but they were background issues in it and were all symptomatic of the mood at Time Inc. during that period.

The women's complaint was founded on a grievance dating back the furthest. From the beginning, women had played an essential role at Time Inc. In 1923, a former *Woman's Home Companion* staffer, Nancy Ford, was hired to supply *Time* writers with information and check finished copy for accuracy. Thus was created a new kind of job, for a while unique in journalism. The *Time* researcher—followed later by the *Fortune* researcher and the *Life* researcher—became an institution figuring in fiction and film. Addressing *Time*'s 20th anniversary dinner in 1943, Henry Luce noted that Time Inc. had made the very word "researcher" a "nationwide symbol of serious endeavor . . . Little did we realize . . . we were inaugurating a modern female priesthood—but behold now the veritable vestal virgins whom levitous writers cajole in vain and managing editors learn humbly to appease."

The flaw in the picture was that the researchers, with few exceptions, were always women; with even fewer exceptions, they were never promoted to writer or editor. This discriminatory sex casting did not escape notice. Quite early on there were polite complaints. In 1944, Mary Fraser and Patricia Divver, legendary "deans of women"—they had served as chiefs of research at *Time, Life* and *Fortune*—discussed the question, "What about women in Time Inc.?" with Louis Gratz, the company's director of staff relations. Divver and Fraser urged that "a consistent policy toward women, their place in the company . . . be devised by the top management." Reflecting later on this and other exchanges with Time Inc. top managers during that time, Divver observed: "They should have thought about women more."

The passage of the Civil Rights Act of 1964 prompted a review of Time Inc. personnel policies in several areas. Under Charlie Gleason, the quiet, reserved Yankee who was named corporate personnel director in January 1965, the status of women employees was seriously examined for the first time. Although the company was probably not in legal trouble, Gleason reported in December 1965, the "paucity of women in important jobs" was, in his view, a management failure. No substantial changes resulted, however.

Progress in minority hiring had likewise been slow. Here, Time Inc.'s personnel practices did not exactly match its editorial positions. Very early on, the young *Time* magazine had taken on the task of reporting every lynching in the U.S.; in 1943, Luce declared *Time* to be "unshakably committed to a pro-civil-rights policy and pro-square-deal policy for Negroes as for every other kind of American." Twenty-five years later, Donovan, as Luce's successor, reaffirmed that pledge, adding a claim that "Time Inc. very possibly had done as much for the cause of civil rights as any private organization in the United States."

But as late as 1961, fewer than 50 employees—about 2 percent of the New York staff—were black; not one held a major editorial job.* In 1961 an assessment ordered by Luce in the wake of mob attacks on the Freedom Riders in Birmingham and Montgomery (where *Life* correspondent Norman Ritter was badly beaten) stated that in the hiring of blacks the company was "vulnerable . . . No Negro is in a meaningful job today." The situation had only marginally improved by the end of 1963, when *Time* named Martin Luther King Jr. its Man of the Year.

Nevertheless, Time Inc. was beginning to move. The year 1963

---

*Life had one black writer, Earl Brown, who left the company in 1961. *Life*'s famous photographer, Gordon Parks, left the staff in 1960 to freelance.

saw the start of a program to seek out minority talent and also the choice of a man to direct the search: William J. Trent Jr., 53, executive director of the United Negro College Fund. Trent was hesitant at first, fearing that as a black he would only be corporate window dressing, but then, he said, "I became convinced that Time Inc. really wanted to do something positive." Targeting his first efforts in the professional field, Trent visited colleges—mainly Southern black schools, where his contacts were excellent, as well as several large urban Midwestern universities—and acted as the company's ambassador to the black community, where doubts about Time Inc.'s intentions still had to be overcome.

Within a year after Trent signed on, he was able to report "cooperation inside this shop"; indeed, the company had added 20 blacks to the staff, including a promotion copywriter, a *Life* reporter and a *Time* correspondent in Washington. Trent also managed to recruit one of Yale's few black graduates, Stanley Thomas, for the executive training program. There was stiff competition among big corporations trying to enlist black Ivy Leaguers; before choosing Time Inc., Thomas had considered offers from Metropolitan Life, TWA, Pan Am and New Jersey Bell.

Not only were a number of large companies reassessing their hiring policies and actively recruiting minorities; the federal government was also weighing in. Title VII of the 1964 Civil Rights Act prohibited discrimination in employment. And an executive order signed by President Johnson a year later required federal contractors to take affirmative action in ensuring equal employment opportunity.

Time Inc.'s reexamination of its practices, guided by Trent, led to four programs dealing with minorities. The first, a concerted effort to hire more blacks at all levels, was an extension of Trent's recruiting activities. A second program involved education: company-supported training programs and scholarships. Technicians from the Hampton Institute in Virginia were trained at Time Inc. TV stations, and some of them were hired, after graduation, by Time-Life Broadcast. Time Inc. also set up an annual scholarship for a black student at the University of Chicago's Graduate School of Business and one at Columbia's Graduate School of Journalism. Another program involved hiring summer replacements from "disadvantaged" areas. These were mainly college students who filled in as copyboys and clerical workers.

The most imaginative of the programs, and the one in which Time Inc. for a while took the most pride, was Program III, as it was designated on the company's chart of affirmative action efforts. This project enlisted unemployed blacks and Hispanics, high school dropouts and ghetto residents, gave them jobs and helped them earn high school equivalency diplomas. A police record was not a bar to entry, nor was past involvement with drugs. Frederick Clarke, a former guidance counselor in New York City's Neighborhood Youth Corps, was recruited to head the project. Under him, some 75 young men went through the program in its first three years, but as in other such efforts to help the hard-core unemployed, results were mixed. "We don't know exactly who the successes and failures were because there was no formal follow-up," Clarke said. "But as a social service effort it was successful. More than half of those people did something positive like going to college or joining the armed forces."

In addition to those programs, there were the "Donovan scholarships," originated by the editor-in-chief in 1961, when he was still editorial director, to attract outside talent. Each magazine was now to take on a black writer, editor or photographer, who would be paid out of corporate funds and not out of regular editorial budgets.

In January 1968, on the occasion of hearings before the federal government's Equal Employment Opportunity Commission, Time Inc. had a chance to publicize its experience in finding (in the commission's language) "relatively large numbers of minorities for white-collar positions." Appearing for the company, Heiskell outlined Time Inc.'s four programs and its other public activities. He furnished a report card: Time Inc. now had 144 black staff in its headquarters alone, 90 percent of them in white-collar jobs—a proportional increase from 2 percent to 5 percent over three years, and on an absolute basis, more than a tripling of black employment.

Heiskell said the company was also trying to do better in hiring Hispanics. He concluded with the observation that Time Inc. had found "one intangible factor" to be most important—"the establishment of an atmosphere within the organization so that each staff member understands his individual responsibility . . . [in] any search for a viable solution to America's most pressing social problem."

Statistics used to measure progress can sometimes be deceiving. While Time Inc. had managed to increase the percentage of minorities on its payroll, few were in writing and reporting jobs. On the publishing side the situation was slightly better, Fred Clarke felt, partly because some schools were providing training in such areas as production and marketing.

Within the company there was no system for training writers, editors, artists, reporters—of any color. "This was a sink-or-swim kind of place," Fred Clarke said. "Time Inc. never really understood the problems minorities face when they join this company. Not only was training pretty much absent, but no network existed to support these people; there was no mentor or 'rabbi' around to listen to their problems."

Moreover, as cultural conflicts bubbled to the surface, some good intentions went awry. A group of volunteers, including several *Time* associate editors, adopted a small black weekly in Harlem, working with its staff both in the Time & Life Building and uptown; but the effort came to be viewed as white do-goodism, and the cooperation soon lapsed. In the spring of 1968, *Time*, wanting to schedule a story on Harlem art, asked a black assistant editor on *Life* to moonlight the assignment. He refused. Nothing, he explained, was more unpopular in the black community than a black reporter who "rents out his color" to the white press. Privately, to his editors on *Life*, he revealed a deeper reason for refusing. He had spent a year and a half working for *f.y.i.*, the company house organ, hoping to be hired by *Time*. He had not made it; now that he was on *Life*, *Time* came to him. Ralph Graves, then senior staff editor, reported the incident to Donovan as evidence that "the Negro in Time Inc. edit is still a very token figure indeed."

Another black edit employee, Marcia Gillespie, recalls that Time Inc. was "a great training ground. But Time Inc. was also an imposing and threatening institution. Blacks who came to work at the company in the '60s were usually handpicked representatives expected to be achievers. The expectation was that we could jump into a predominantly white, Anglo-Saxon world and fit comfortably. In many ways we were expected to walk on water. Problems about editorial perspective were inevitable." Gillespie, on loan from Books, was asked to draw up a list of emerging black American leaders for a *Life* series in November and December 1968 on black history. Shortly after, she was summoned to a meeting in the managing editor's office. "Hell was being raised and I was puzzled about the whole thing. I remember them asking me [about the list], 'Where's Whitney Young? We have to have Whitney.' Young was then Executive Director of the Urban League and was perhaps the black leader best known at Time Inc.'s executive levels, because of the company's own longtime affiliation with the league. But he was hardly a 'new' leader at that stage. I told them that. We had to have a big discussion . . . It was a case of trying to make everybody agree when basically they just do not."

After several similarly frustrating experiences, Gillespie felt she had no future at Time Inc. and left in 1970 to become managing editor of *Essence*, a magazine for black women, which had been founded with the assistance of nearly a dozen major corporations including Time Inc. *Time*, in its August 6, 1979, issue, named Gillespie one of 50 promising young Americans and noted her journalistic achievements in these words: "She took the floundering publication for black women and gave it an audience, ad revenues and an editorial raison d'être."

Further underscoring the problems of dealing with racial questions was *Time*'s experience with its special issue, in 1970, on Black America. On the writing and reportorial team were six blacks. Nevertheless, a recently formed watchdog group of black editorial and publishing staff within Time Inc. called the Black Media Committee, criticized the special issue as a " 'ghettoized' supplement . . . an unfortunate way to emphasize the magazine's interest in Black America." Some earlier criticism had come from a distinguished panel of outside black consultants enlisted by *Time* especially for the occasion.* Arguing that no individual could symbolize black leadership, they had objected "vigorously" (as managing editor Grunwald recalled) to *Time*'s cover choice: Jesse Jackson, then 28, and an emerging activist in the black movement.

The new decade brought in a powerful new cause for agitation at Time Inc. The painful effort to achieve equality for minorities was overshadowed by the suddenly aroused demands of women employees for a broadening of their opportunities. The allegation here was not that the company employed too few women, but that it locked them into relatively low-level jobs and denied them equal chance to advance. In retrospect, what was amazing was that it took so long for the women at Time Inc. to develop a sense of grievance to the point of protesting their status. But when the protest came, it was loud and vehement.

Ironically, a small reference in a New York *Times* story to the

*Attorney Clifford Alexander Jr.; Darwin Bolden of the Interracial Council for Business Opportunity; Lisle Carter, professor of public administration at Cornell; Marian Wright Edelman of Washington Research Project; M. Carl Holman of the National Urban Coalition; James Nabrit III of the N.A.A.C.P. Legal Defense Fund; Austin Scott of the Associated Press; Edward Sylvester Jr. of the Cooperative Assistance Fund; Roger Wilkins of the Ford Foundation.

position of women at *Time* helped trigger the ultimate outburst. In December 1969, in a *Times* staff roundtable mentioning women's liberation as a likely "big issue of the '70s," *Times* critic John Leonard was quoted as saying:

> Take the example of a bright young woman who goes to work for *Time* magazine [with hopes of] becoming an editor of a section . . . This she is unable to do. She will be 'research' for the rest of her life.

Four of *Time*'s researchers clipped the item and sent it to managing editor Grunwald with a notation: "What are *Time*'s plans for the '70s?" Grunwald replied that "John Leonard's statement is nonsense" and promised to write Leonard saying so. Grunwald then went on to tick off the names of the women writers on *Time*'s staff—Piri Halasz, Katie Kelly, Johanna Davis, Ruth Brine—and praised Brine's "excellent piece on the women's liberation movement" which had recently run in *Time*'s Behavior section. As for his plans for the 1970s, Grunwald said:

> I do not intend to make a deliberate attempt to recruit or nurture female writers. Any talented writer, male, female, or otherwise, will be happily considered for employment. There are no limits to careers for women at *Time*, up to and including senior editorships (or managing editorships, for that matter). I must add in candor that I have not met many women who seem to have the physical and mental energy required for *Time* senior editing.* (Of course, I have not met too many men who fill that bill either.)

Grunwald's response ended on the upbeat, urging any researcher who wanted to write to apply for the job and wishing the women a Happy New Year. Marguerite Michaels, one of the four researchers who had sent him the *Times* clipping, remembered her reaction to Grunwald's response: "Fair enough, but we'll see."

In March 1970, *Newsweek* ran a cover story titled "Women in Revolt" and thereby touched off a revolt in its own ranks. *Newsweek*'s editor-in-chief, Osborn Elliott, had commissioned a freelancer to write the cover story—implying that none of the women on the staff were up to the job—and that seems to have been what

---

*Grunwald in effect later disavowed this observation and eventually appointed two women senior editors: Ruth Brine and Martha Duffy.

detonated the explosion. As Elliott related in his memoirs, *The World of Oz,** the "Women in Revolt" issue landed on the desk of Katharine Graham—president of *Newsweek*'s parent Washington Post Company—along with a letter of protest from a large group of women on the editorial staff. Subsequently they filed a complaint of discrimination with the federal Equal Employment Opportunity Commission. *Time*'s Press section recounted the *Newsweek* action, as well as a sit-in at *Ladies' Home Journal*, in two carefully constructed columns that concluded: "The *Journal*'s slogan has long been, 'Never underestimate the power of a woman.' At week's end—to editors everywhere—it had never seemed so apt."

"Editors everywhere" surely included some at Time Inc. Few of them showed any concern. The corporate press office circulated a memo warning management of possible queries and suggesting a response: "There are 50 women who work as editors or writers in Time Incorporated. This group is made up from all our magazines, our book division, and from the corporate staff . . . In addition, there are a number of women at Time Incorporated holding important administrative jobs at the top of research departments, edit reference, and in art departments." Not one, however, ranked high enough to be on the list of recipients of the memo.

The women at Time Inc. watched the *Newsweek* uprising with great interest. A small nucleus from *Fortune* and *Life* began to organize and consider possible forms of action. The catalyst was Marion Buhagiar, a former *Time* researcher, now a *Fortune* staffer, who said she "didn't come to *Time* as a rebel—I was a good Catholic girl." The small nucleus quickly expanded to include women from all the magazines. On the advice of a lawyer in the New York State Attorney General's office, the women rejected the idea of bringing suit in court; instead, they drafted a formal complaint for presentation to the State Division of Human Rights. Eventually, 147 women members of Time Inc.'s editorial staff put their names to this document.

Petitions in support of the action, but addressed to Time Inc. management, also began to circulate, reflecting inevitable divergences in viewpoint—even a generation gap. On *Fortune*, the women displayed more unity of purpose. *Time* researchers were fairly conservative and not given to rocking boats. Some objected to the conspiratorial secrecy surrounding the drafting of the complaint; many regarded the managing editor as a friend and colleague and

*The Viking Press, 1980.

were not inclined to take gratuitous potshots at him, which they felt the complaint was doing. After one acrimonious meeting, some women drafted their own petition. It contained a carefully stated reservation: that the signers "may disagree with some of the particulars in the complaint as regards *Time* magazine." But it also voiced the belief that "the allegations of discrimination in the complaint are largely true and [we] would like to bear witness to that." All but a handful of *Time* women signed.

It was at *Life* that the generation differences were most evident. Some of the older women took the view that their jobs were pretty good, and it was best not to stir up trouble. The younger women tended to have higher expectations. Marian MacPhail, who had been *Life*'s chief of research for 22 years, found herself "both shocked and hurt" by the younger women's impatience. "Of course I appreciated what they were trying to do in the broad sense," she said, "but on the specifics, the *Life* people just didn't have fair gripes."

Filed officially on May 4, 1970, by New York State Attorney General Louis Lefkowitz, the complaint charged *Time*, *Life*, *Fortune*, *Sports Illustrated* and Time-Life Books with sex discrimination by "placing men in writing and managerial positions while placing college-educated women in lower positions where they can expect little or no upward advancement." At a press conference, New York's Civil Rights Bureau chief added that, after a month's investigation, his office "concluded that we had a *prima facie* case without discussing this with [Time Inc.] management." In a press release of their own, Time Inc.'s women complainants listed their demands, declaring: "All we are asking is that women's brains, abilities, writing skills and management capabilities be utilized in the industry."

Time Inc. managers, forewarned, were nonetheless stung. Collectively, their feeling was "hurt," said Daniel Seligman, then senior staff editor. "Their feeling was, 'Why didn't they come to us first?'" To that frequently voiced question there were, then and later, differing answers. Looking back, some women confessed to a fear that management would agree quickly in principle, and then change little in practice; most shared the feeling of *Fortune*'s Evelyn Benjamin: "What did they think a petition was? We *were* going to management first. Time Inc. had so long just ignored the *Newsweek* action . . . If the company had sent around a memo—some, any indication that Time Inc. was aware of its own women and that those women had problems, perhaps so many people wouldn't have signed petitions. I, for one, might not have." *Fortune*'s chief of research, Mary Johnston, was on sabbatical leave when the women's charges were filed, but her deputy, Eleanor Tracy, had signed the complaint. Managing editor Louis Banks was "stunned" and sought Johnston's advice. She gently explained that the women did have legitimate complaints and that the company would be well advised to sit down and deal.

Privately, *Time* research chief Marylois Vega was more blunt. Asked to examine the complaint for management, Vega wrote: "Any fair observer of *Time* over the past 25 years would admit that there has been a prejudice against women in the editorial department of this magazine, and that the discrimination at *Time* has been greater than at *Life* or *Fortune* where female bylines have not been especially infrequent." Many women, she added, believed they were considered "lower level colleagues, if colleagues at all." Referring to a recent trial of adding reporters to the staff at *Time*, Vega observed that "the hiring of some young men right out of college without considering qualified resident researchers started a great deal of unrest."

Two weeks after the complaint was filed, representatives of both sides went before the Human Rights Division for preliminary hearings. In an opening statement for management, Dan Seligman declared: "We do not discriminate at Time Inc. We treat our employees as individuals. We make decisions about hiring and firing, and about promotions and transfers, without referring to an individual's race or sex, but only by referring to his or her present and anticipated future capability to do a job." Seligman added: "I very much doubt that anyone in this room can name any other American company, in any industry, that has so many interesting and high-paying professional jobs held by women."

A firm opponent of affirmative action, and subsequently the author of several *Fortune* articles equating it with reverse discrimination, Seligman believed in the company's stated position, but it turned out to be a position that management would not fight for. "Management viewed the women's actions as extremely unpleasant," Seligman later recalled. "They didn't want to go through any hearings and have these assertions about discrimination aired publicly. There was a lot of resentment on management's part about the hearings." Some managers believed that the women had some legitimate concerns, but they too agreed that the prospect of hearings was undesirable—"the least productive way to arrive at sensible solutions."

In the end, Time Inc. did not have to undergo that public embarrassment. The dispute was put to a series of in-house negotiating

457

meetings, magazine by magazine, aimed at finding practical solutions. Over the next eight months, women staffers were able to confront their editors directly, to air their grievances and propose changes.

No ground was left uncovered. At *Sports Illustrated*, a woman reporter questioned the discrimination—not Time Inc.'s—that barred her from the pit at the Indianapolis Speedway. *SI* should publicly challenge the ban, she maintained; if she could not interview drivers, she could not do her job properly. A transcript of an *SI* meeting records the conversation:

> Assistant Managing Editor: "What do you mean, 'publicly protest'? The Indianapolis rules don't permit women in the pit."
> Reporter: "We're asking our magazine to protest this."
> Executive Editor: "I'm with you. It's OK to have a men's bar at the Oak Room, but not at a public event. A lot of this is the fault of male sportswriters. Perhaps we *should* protest."

In the agreement eventually reached between *SI* and women staffers, managing editor Laguerre noted that "custom has regrettably barred women from some press boxes, press conferences, etc.," and stated that "it is *SI*'s policy to protest and combat the denial of any reasonable press facility to any member of its staff." Seven years later the opportunity to do this arose when *SI* reporter Melissa Ludtke was banned from the locker rooms at Yankee Stadium after World Series games there. Her editor, Peter Carry, urged managing editor Roy Terrell to protest, and on December 29, 1977, a sex discrimination suit was filed in federal court against the Yankees, the American League president, the Commissioner of Baseball (who had decreed the locker-room ban) and the City of New York. The suit was decided in Ludtke's favor the following year, the judge ruling that the exclusion of women sports reporters did put them at a "severe competitive disadvantage."

On many issues during the 1970 meetings, however, Time Inc. editors and the women found it difficult to compromise. When no agreement had been reached by mid-autumn, the State Attorney General's office again raised the threat of public hearings. Under that pressure an agreement was reached in late January and announced by Lefkowitz on February 6. In it Time Inc. stated that it "does not concede or admit . . . that it, or any of its employees, has committed unlawful discrimination in the past." But it formally agreed to "refrain from the commission of unlawful discriminatory practices in the future" and promised that "all job categories" would be "equally open to qualified candidates without regard to sex or marital status." Men would be hired as researchers, efforts would be made to move women into the higher job categories, more consideration would be given to employees seeking promotion. Time Inc. also promised to monitor progress.

For the women at *Life*, where staff cuts had already occurred and more impended, little could change except managerial attitudes— some women later said they detected a greater appreciation for their efforts. At *Fortune*, the improvements were material: for researchers, credit lines on stories to which they had made "a material contribution," and the opening of a writer-trainee category; for some senior researchers, masthead promotion to associate editor. At *Time*, the magazine's research manual was rewritten, in part to redefine and upgrade the job category of researcher, which was retitled "reporter-researcher." Researchers were also to be offered trials as writers and correspondents. At *Fortune* likewise, the reporter-researcher designation was instituted, but later shortened to reporter. As a 1980 memo explained: "In the metamorphosis of the masthead, the title 'reporter-researcher' always had the earmarks of a pupal stage."

Fortune had no trouble "integrating" its previously all-female research department. Before the 1970s ended, more than half of all *Fortune* researchers were men. At *Time* this proved harder. Prior to the complaint, in the late 1960s, research chief Vega interviewed an excellent male candidate for a map researcher position. He accepted her offer, and a salary was agreed upon. But when Vega volunteered the information that he would be the first man ever to hold the job, the young man "paled visibly" and changed his mind. (He would not, in fact, have been the first. During the 1950s, one man was given a six months' trial, which he flunked.) After the complaint was filed and settled, Vega managed to hire two males; each lasted only a few months. It was not until 1973 that *Time* was able to get, and keep, four men for the research staff (by 1980 this number had grown to ten).

Time's progress was not much faster in breaking the male monopoly in editing and writing jobs. In July 1972, Grunwald explored the reasons in a memo to Robert M. Steed, then director of union relations:

> Obviously, we have not done as well as I would have wished. The greatest obstacle remains what I can only describe as the

large-scale indifference of the women at *Time* . . . There have been dishearteningly few women who have come forward wanting to be writers . . . *Time* researchers never were hired for writing ability; . . . the research and writing-editing functions are separate and different, and . . . you cannot turn a researcher into a writer simply by promoting her.

The agreement reached on the women's complaint turned management's attention back to the problem of getting more minority staff members. As Time Inc. entered the 1970s, minorities numbered just under 1,200, out of 11,000 persons on the company's payroll, subsidiaries included. This was significant progress, but a three-man committee from the Time Inc. board of directors found it "uneven," with every part of the company suffering "under-representation of minority groups in the upper levels—officials and managers, professionals, technicians and salesmen." The magazines "should be doing better," the directors suggested. Blacks held only 1 percent of the jobs at *Fortune*, 2.5 percent at *Life* and *SI*, and 4 percent at *Time*.

Adding to the pressures on managers at the divisional level were the companywide 15 percent staff cuts ordered in June 1970 to relieve a cost squeeze and counter a recession slump in advertising revenues. The fears of minority employees that they would be the first to be cut proved unfounded; by mid-1971 only 2 percent of them had been dismissed, as against 9 percent of the whites. Nevertheless, staff turnover among minorities remained high. To help avoid this, the directors' committee suggested training supervisors in the special problems of minority groups, noting that "some of the high turnover could surely be prevented by more imaginative supervision."

The 1970 staff cutbacks had repercussions in another area—union relations. The Time Inc. unit of the New York Newspaper Guild was moving job security higher on the list of its concerns. The union had been growing more militant in its bargaining with management. In early 1967, negotiations had deadlocked after three months of talks, and the Guild had voted to strike. Agreement was reached just five hours before the strike deadline.

That crisis was a testing time for Bob Steed, who was making his debut as Time Inc.'s director of union relations. Then only 30, Steed was a University of Michigan Law School graduate, who for the previous five years had been working on the company's labor contracts as an associate with the law firm of Cravath, Swaine & Moore.

While with the firm he had helped rewrite the company's personnel policy manual. Facing the Guild for the first time, Steed felt very much "the new kid on the block," and his predecessor, Louis Gratz, came out of New Hampshire retirement to lend a helping hand.

Steed had a better time of it in the next round of negotiations, in 1968, which were brisk and businesslike. When the 1971 round of contract talks began, the *Life* staff was again being reduced and the Guild was concentrating on job security. The bargaining resulted, for one thing, in more liberal severance arrangements, which helped ease the pain of *Life*'s demise the following year. Of the 320 *Life* staffers left jobless, about a third were placed elsewhere in the company, the rest given generous settlements. However, the Guild did protest the company policy decreeing that some employees in other divisions should be bumped to make room for *Life* people adjudged more competent.

In normal times most of the well-paid professionals on the magazine staffs felt no need to be collectively represented by a union. Now, in the early 1970s, some of them were finding other forums for voicing their complaints and dissatisfactions. In October 1968, soon after he was appointed managing editor of *Time*, Henry Grunwald had taken his writers to Bermuda for a weekend of uninhibited talk (see chapter 19). A diversity of grievances were aired, ranging from salaries to heavy-handed editing to working conditions. Later, in New York, several writers began meeting in what one called "organized bitching sessions," which revealed, among other things, some rather wide differences in salaries. There was also considerable unhappiness about economies imposed to cut editorial expenses—for example, eliminating copyboys and restricting staffers' subscriptions to newspapers and magazines.

The *Time* writers' group was eventually enlarged to include researchers. In late 1973 it sent a petition to managing editor Grunwald, signed by 33 of 41 writers and 24 out of 40 researchers:

In our opinion the company has been financially strangling the editorial side of *Time* magazine. We believe that the financial officers of the corporation are unaware just how harmful their cutbacks have been,* and we would like you to bring us

*Beginning with the 1970 companywide staff reductions, *Time* had lost 64 of its edit staff of 281, including 11 writers, nine researchers, 13 copyboys and both its newsmarkers; library services had also been reduced. The news service staff, numbering 263 in 1969, was down by 21 correspondents and 43 support staff. Virtually all the last cuts were made in foreign bureaus.

together with them so that we can tell them of our concern for the future of the magazine.

The group's activities had begun to infringe on Guild territory, where bargaining for a new contract was under way. The union newsletter, *On Time*, charged the company with unfair labor practices in "encouraging negotiating sessions with a 'staff association' . . . in clear violation of the National Labor Relations Act and of the [Guild] contract."

Over Guild objections, Heiskell and Donovan went ahead with a scheduled January 1974 meeting with *Time*'s writing and research staff in the company auditorium. Donovan opened his remarks by noting that "we are in negotiations with the Newspaper Guild and so we are under some constraint as to what we can say regarding salaries and other matters . . . We are here to listen and to try to learn, without committing ourselves." What he and Heiskell listened to was a compendium of grievances and questions about corporate priorities. The feeling, expressed by many, was that they were no longer members of a journalistic elite; at Time Inc., they felt, the rewards did not now match their efforts. "There's nothing like watching the sun rise over the Time & Life Building," associate editor Gerald Clarke said, referring to *Time*'s long hours. "It's demanding work physically and demanding mentally. When we came to *Time* we knew the situation and we accepted the hard work because we were rewarded more than other people. That's no longer the case."

Heiskell explained the outside pressures on the company, caught as it was between the Nixon administration's Cost of Living Council, which put constraints on advertising rate increases, and the postal service's impending postage hikes. He added: "Fifteen or 16 years ago, *Time* was a kind of private company presided over by a sort of grandfather who didn't have to justify his decisions to too many people. We are now quite clearly a public corporation and we have to justify what we do every year—indeed practically every month."

Donovan promised that the dialogue would resume after the Guild negotiations were completed. From time to time during the following two years, the *Time* staff committee met with Grunwald for "discussions"—not for "bargaining," it was carefully stipulated—of working conditions, editorial procedures and other staff concerns. Meanwhile, a new Guild contract went into effect, containing for the first time a cost-of-living escalator clause.

In October 1974, *Time*'s editorial closing was moved back a day, from Saturday to Friday. Printing schedules remained unchanged. The purpose was to speed up the copy flow, hold down cost over-runs at the printer's because of late Saturday closings and avoid late deliveries of the magazine the following week. In practice the switch left less time for writers and researchers to get their stories done. Nor did it alleviate the burden of coping with late-breaking news; in fact, the loss of Saturday increased the pressure on Friday. Conse-quently, the editorial staff worked later than ever on closing nights.

Appointed by Grunwald to make a thorough study of the situa-tion, senior editor Jason McManus spent five weeks talking to scores of individuals and examining copy flow in detail. He concluded gloomily that the staff, including the editors, seemed "more and more the prisoners of our deadlines and machines"—closing proce-dures surviving from precomputer days were causing jam-ups in the flow of copy. He warned that there was "an interrelated crisis of morale, of communication, of authority and of organization." McManus gave Grunwald a series of "modest proposals" for improvements, ranging from schedules to staffing, and Grunwald accepted many of them. He also gave McManus a six-month assign-ment as administrative editor "to coordinate these innovations, to seek others, and generally act as a troubleshooter in getting *Time* to print as efficiently and sanely as possible."

The effort was enlarged in September with the appointment of a task force—McManus, news service chief Murray Gart, and former *Life* managing editor Ralph Graves, now associate publisher of *Time*—to study restructuring the magazine's editorial and produc-tion procedures. The task-force report, issued in January 1976 and looking ahead to 1980, was temporarily put aside because of the impending contract talks with the Guild.

The problems at *Time* were but one of several matters that threatened to make the 1976 bargaining round lively and conten-tious. Recent troubles at Time-Life Books had again raised the question of job security. The ongoing book series were approach-ing the end of their life span, and there was a paucity of new series in prospect. In the search for ways to lower costs, staff cutbacks had begun. October 28, 1975—"Black Tuesday," as it came to be called—24 employees were given notice. In December, rumors were confirmed that Books' editorial and publishing operations were to be relocated outside of New York City, destination not yet decided (see chapter 23).

Time Inc. management had some ideas of its own to contribute to the 1976 bargaining agenda. In a shift of corporate responsibilities in 1972, Steed had succeeded Charlie Gleason as personnel director, and his union relations post had been given to Lucy Pullen Werner, previously business manager of *Time* and, as such, a member of the company team in the 1971-72 negotiations. Werner, a University of Washington journalism graduate, later went through the Harvard-Radcliffe Program in Business Administration. She had not sought the union relations job; it was not in line with her previous experience, she felt. Once in the post, however, she prepared herself by reading every negotiating transcript in the Time Inc. files, going back to 1937. Outspoken and articulate, Werner held firm views of her own: "I viewed labor negotiations as a business problem and did not believe in reacting to union demands. I wanted to put forth a position with business objectives."

To determine these objectives, as the 1976 negotiations impended, Steed and Werner solicited the views of both editorial and publishing executives. The operating managers' prime concern, it developed, was the restriction on their authority in salary questions resulting from the company's agreements with the Guild. Since 1942, every Guild contract had specified a "general increase cutoff" or salary ceiling above which the negotiated general increase did not apply, raises instead being given on a discretionary basis. (Discretionary, or merit, raises were sometimes given to employees below the cutoff point as well.) The level of the cutoff point thus became the focus of much of the collective bargaining between Time Inc. and the Guild; the union, quite naturally, wanted the cutoff point set as high as possible, so as to bring the maximum number of employees within the purview of the Guild-negotiated general increase. The company felt otherwise, wishing to keep employee compensation more under managerial control. The various editorial and publishing executives interviewed by Werner and Steed expressed this view, and it was so reported to Donovan, Heiskell and Shepley:

[They] believe that Time Inc. needs a more selective compensation system and that the general increase must be de-emphasized or eliminated to achieve selectivity . . .

The general increase is a massive outpouring of money for which little credit goes to Time Inc., and no credit goes to the department head who is responsible for developing, motivating and rewarding the people who work here . . .

464

Arthur Temple, Time Inc. group vice president 1973-78 and vice chairman 1978-83, chairman Temple-Eastex Inc. 1975-83.

Joe Denman Jr., president Temple-Eastex Inc. 1977-83.

Clifford Grum, treasurer 1973-75, *Fortune* publisher 1975-79, executive vice president 1980-83. On divestiture of Time Inc.'s forest products group, Grum became president and c.e.o. of Temple-Inland Inc.

The Time Inc. video group in 1977. Richard Munro (right foreground), group vice president. Left to right: Gerald Levin (seated), chairman HBO; Nicholas J. Nicholas Jr., president HBO; Thayer Bigelow, president Manhattan Cable Television; Bruce Paisner (seated), president Time-Life Films; Thomas Girocco, vice president and general manager WOTV.

Trygve Myhren, ATC president 1980-82, chairman 1982- , with his predecessor Monroe Rifkin, founder.

James Heyworth, HBO president 1980-83, Time Inc. deputy group vice president—video 1983-84, senior vice president—magazines 1984- .

In charge of programming at HBO since 1979, Michael Fuchs became chairman in 1984.

Winston (Tony) Cox, with *Life* in 1971-73, magazine development 1973-75, HBO 1976-84, vice president – corporate planning 1984- .

...rt-up of the new *Life*, June 1978.
...ing: Philip Kunhardt (behind desk), managing editor; Bob Ciano (at edge of desk), art director; ...anor Graves (sitting), assistant managing editor; John Loengard (in front of desk), picture editor. ...nding: Melvin Scott; Mary Steinbauer; Janet Mason; Lou Valentino; June Goldberg, chief of ...arch; Jeff Wheelwright; Hillary Johnson; Murray Goldwaser; Harriet Heyman; Richard Barrett, ...duction director; Daphne Hurford; Byron Dobell, senior editor; Carla Barr; Mary Simons; David ...nd; Christopher Whipple; Katherine Ryden; Steve Robinson; Loudon Wainwright, senior editor; ...n Morrell; Marie Schumann; Edward Kern; Terry Drucker (kneeling).

...naging editor Philip Kunhardt Jr., with *Life* publisher Charles Whittingham, who was previously ...eral manager of *Fortune*.

Leon Jaroff, managing editor
Discover 1980-84.

Richard Stolley, managing editor
People 1974-82, managing editor *Life*
1982-   , and Patricia Ryan, managing
editor *People* 1982-

Richard Durrell, *People* publisher 1974-83, and his successor, Christopher Meigher III, who had been corporate circulation director 1981-83.

Reginald Brack Jr., associate publisher *Time*
1976-80, publisher *Discover* 1980-82,
president and later chairman Time-Life Books
1982- , group vice president 1984-

Marshall Loeb, *Time* senior editor
1965-78 and economics editor 1978-80,
managing editor *Money* 1980- , editor
magazine development group 1984- .

lliam Rukeyser, the founding managing editor of *Money*
2-80, became managing editor of *Fortune* in 1980.

Board of Directors, 1979.

Front row, seated, left to right: Andrew Heiskell, chairman and c.e.o.;
James Shepley, president; Arthur Temple, board vice chairman and
chairman Temple-Eastex Inc.; Henry Grunwald, editor-in-chief;
Matina Horner, president Radcliffe College; Frank Pace Jr., president
and c.e.o. International Executive Service Corps. Second row,
standing: Charles Bear, group vice president and secretary; Louis
Banks, adjunct professor of management, Alfred P. Sloan School of
Management MIT; Joe Denman Jr., group vice president; Richard
Munro, executive vice president; David Kearns, president Xerox
Corporation; Alexander Heard, chancellor Vanderbilt University; Joan
Manley, group vice president and chairman Time-Life Books; Sol
Linowitz, senior partner Coudert Brothers; Gaylord Freeman Jr.,
honorary chairman of the board The First National Bank of Chicago;
Robert Keeler, partner Taft, Stettinius & Hollister. Third row: Arthur
Keylor, group vice president; Richard McKeough, chief financial
officer; Henry Luce III, vice president; Ralph Graves, editorial
director; Donald Perkins, chairman Jewel Companies, Inc.; Michael
Dingman, president and c.e.o. Wheelabrator-Frye Inc.; Henry
Goodrich, president Southern Natural Resources, Inc.

Henry Grunwald, managing editor *Time* 1968-77, corporate editor 1977-79, editor-in-chief 1979-

Richard Munro, president 1980-   , and Ralph Davidson, chairman 1980-

The risks of such a change are high. We would be asking an employee to exchange a guaranteed increase which has generally outpaced increases in the Consumer Price Index for a chance to prove to himself and to his boss that his individual efforts are worth rewarding and will be rewarded. It is almost inconceivable that the Guild would fail to get authorization for a strike over such a proposal. And such a course, once indicated to the staff and to the Guild, is virtually irreversible. Time Inc.'s credibility is on the line. We cannot afford a last-minute change of heart.

The plan won Heiskell's approval, but he warned Werner, "You will have to be prepared to take a strike."

On the opening day of negotiations, January 6, 1976, a stunned union was informed of management's goal: to get compensation policy under control by reducing the level of the general increase and minimum pay rates while increasing the number of individual merit raises made at the discretion of managers. An announcement to the staff explained: "It is not the purpose . . . to save a single dollar of compensation. We simply want to shift the balance toward individual contribution and away from mathematical formulas." To help achieve the shift, management proposed reserving "a specified pool of merit money" in salary budgets to be spent at its discretion and, by lowering the general increase cutoff point, reducing the number of staffers who received the mandatory percentage raises.

The burden of explaining the new policy and arguing management's case was borne by Lucy Werner. At Donovan's insistence, there were no editorial executives on the company's side of the bargaining table. Group vice president Charley Bear had argued against that policy, and he later commented, "I do believe there would have been better understanding had there been editorial representation."

On the union side, in addition to Jean Davidson, the Guild's longtime local representative for Time Inc., were two members of the Time-Life Books staff, Carol Isenberg Clingan, head of the Guild unit's negotiating committee, and Guild unit chairman Marion Buhagiar, who had come to Books from *Fortune*. Many others weighed in on behalf of the union, including José M. Ferrer III, a *Time* associate editor active in the staff committee talks with Grunwald. An affable, fair-minded Princetonian, Ferrer was trusted by both sides and found himself increasingly in the forefront of negotiations, explaining the particular problems at *Time*.

As the bargaining proceeded, there was a marked rise in Guild membership to more than 60 percent of eligible employees—probably the highest level in Time Inc. history. (Membership usually fluctuated, rising at times of contract negotiations and falling when, for example, the Guild had to increase dues.) This rise reflected, in part, increasing anger over unresolved grievances as well as an influx of relatively senior staff members who previously had had little to do with the Guild. Their reasons were varied: sympathy for their lower-paid colleagues, grievances of their own, frustration over their own impotence in effecting change, coupled with mistrust for how the company's new policy might work. Said Ferrer: "Management was saying, 'Trust us,' when trust for management was at a low level." Steed later considered this a fair statement.

After three months, negotiations reached an impasse over what Steed called "an issue of basic principle" for both the company and the Guild: the extent to which pay raises should be left to the discretion of middle-level managers. On April 15, Guild negotiators won the membership's authorization to call a strike. The vote was 454 to 11. Negotiations resumed, stopped after four days, began again, stopped once more. A federal mediator was called in. While continuing to talk, both sides prepared for a strike. Editors and managers counted heads, prepared lists, sounded out former staffers on their willingness to return to work. Secretaries were trained to operate computer keyboards in the copy room. Guards appeared in the Time Inc. library and on the floors housing machinery. Food and cots were brought in, hotel rooms reserved. The company was determined to keep publishing.

At 6:00 p.m., June 2, its will was put to the test. Some 600 staff members walked off their jobs. A number of others, not Guild members, refused to cross the picket lines; among them was Donovan's son Mark, then an *SI* reporter. Just before the strike, there had also been defections from the union, including several Washington bureau correspondents.

The following day, Heiskell came down to thank the editors, writers and researchers who had remained at work. Spirits were high in the building. But the magazines probably could not have continued publishing without the support services—library, picture collection, wire room, news desk, photo lab, copy processing. All but the picture collection were heavily unionized. As it turned out, though, there were enough supervisors and nonstrikers to keep every operation going. In the centralized copy processing department, serving all the magazines as well as Books, the deskmen—the straw bosses in charge of each shift for each magazine—worked shifts of 16 hours on, eight hours off. Some slept in the building.

Of the magazines, *Fortune*, then still a monthly, was least affected, although more than a third of the research staff was out. "The absence of our very capable chart designer would have hurt in a prolonged strike, but she left her work-in-progress in such good order that there was no hitch," managing editor Bob Lubar reported. "As a matter of fact, all the strikers were outstandingly considerate about handing work over to replacements." In contrast, the monthly *Money*, not yet profitable and thus especially vulnerable to a long walkout, was hit hard. Nearly half the staff, including nine out of ten reporters, struck. At *SI*, most of the 38 strikers came from the research and copy departments. Only four out of 34 writers stayed out. At *People*, where more than two-thirds of reporter-writers and researchers were out, as well as the entire copy, art and production departments, managing editor Dick Stolley cited the "heroic efforts by all hands"—notably "key middle-management staffers"—that were on deck. "Had the strike dragged on for several more weeks, our situation would have become serious," he conceded.

Time-Life Books, with a tradition of union activism, had the largest proportion of its staff on strike: about 70 percent. Books' closing problems were somewhat different from those of the magazines. A missed publishing deadline was expensive, but many of the intermediate deadlines could be ignored without damage; nonstriking staffers concentrated on closing series that were due immediately at the printers. There were fewer strictures on design and style, text and series editors took over writing chores and writers did their own research. As managing editor Jerry Korn reported, "Everybody welcomed the reduction in the amount of editing."

Time, the company's largest editorial operation, was very hard hit. Unhappiness about working conditions was as important as the salary issue in building up strike fervor. Absent were 90 percent of the researchers, more than 80 percent of the writers, one quarter of the domestic correspondents, more than half of the picture researchers, virtually all the copyreaders and proofreaders, about half the production staff. Business office personnel, former employees, spouses and children pitched in to replace the strikers. Retired copy chief Harriet Bachman returned to help her successor, Anne Davis, rally an emergency staff for the copydesk, the nerve center of *Time*'s editorial production system. Senior editors and correspondents became writers. President Shepley, a onetime correspondent, got back into harness to write *Time*'s Law section. Donovan became a writer in the Nation section.

To many staffers, the strike brought a sense of excitement and exhilaration. For the sake of speed, some of the usual layers of editing were eliminated. With discipline more relaxed, old *Time* hands vied to slip cherished puns into print. Senior editor Jesse Birnbaum sneaked by with: "In New York City, nothing is more onerous than debt and taxis." Glitches and errors increased. To ease production, complex layouts were avoided and fewer charts and maps were used.

Marie McCrum, long-time secretary to C.D. Jackson and later to Charlie Gleason, left a memoir of her experience sitting in as a Nation section researcher during the strike:

Looking back . . . the first thing I think of is the gray faces of fatigue—cement gray, puffy dull or pasty pale, relieved occasionally by a bright red splotch on the cheek when tension was high. The second thing I think of is professionalism—a calmness of voice and demeanor, a surface appearance of business-as-usual that made us newcomers unaware of the extent of the readjustments that had taken place . . .

Tuesday morning [of the second week] the managing editor assembled the *Time* staff in the lounge for a review of "how it went last week." Consensus was that it had gone well. Perhaps more manpower was needed at the copydesk, which had been a bit of a bottleneck . . .

Wednesday was quicker paced . . . The typewriters were busier in the writers' offices . . . By late in the day the tension began to build. If copy was on hand, it was checking tension. If there was no copy, it was anticipatory tension, worse for the sure knowledge that the later the text became available, the greater would be the crunch . . .

By the time our third issue rolled around we knew what we were doing . . . But that concentrated period of fatigue at the end of each week seemed to have been cumulative, because we were tiring and there was an element of siege entering the picture. Social life was abandoned from the start . . .

The old stereotype of "lotsa drinks" is a myth. Tired people had a slight libation if they wanted one, then presented meal tickets in return for a dinner tray. The night I left latest (4 a.m.) there was one other researcher just winding up, having checked a sticky lawyered text, and two editors awaited a delayed lay-

468

out. Earlier in the week they had all looked quite pink. That night they were gray again. I wouldn't have missed the experience for anything. I have great respect for the staff and for the way everyone operated who was on *Time* edit in its time of trouble. We survived, and so did the magazine.

On the picket line also, an esprit de corps prevailed. If the strike strained old friendships among the staff, it created new ones; writers, clerks, production assistants, lab technicians, others from different parts of the company, with disparate occupations, got to know each other and each other's problems. "Working for the union was an extraordinary experience," one Guild member recalled. "It was remarkable that a $150-a-week mailroom clerk could sit in the negotiating session and say, 'Yes, I see what the $700-a-week writer wants is right,' and, conversely, that the writer understood the clerk's needs."

For the strikers, the test had been to stop publication of at least one magazine. That possibility faded as the Guild found itself alone. No help came from any of the half a dozen other Time Inc. unions. Notably, the small Teamster unit continued making deliveries across the picket line. With the Democratic and Republican national conventions approaching, the Guild appealed to the candidates of both parties to refuse interviews to Time Inc. correspondents; the request was unheeded. However, a story on the planned consumer boycott of J.P. Stevens & Company had to be postponed because the AFL-CIO notified affiliated unions that any *Time* correspondent seeking information should be turned down.

Defections from the strike began early. Some staff straddled, by working at home. After a few days, when it became apparent that publication of the magazines could not be halted, a group of writers and researchers—mainly senior, mainly from *Time*, mainly recent recruits to the Guild—met in agonized sessions at one writer's East Side apartment. They decided to send a delegation led by associate editor James Atwater to tell the union leadership that if there was not a settlement soon, many would return to work anyway. "We knew the strike was lost. We didn't want to look like damned fools. We didn't want them to pick us off one by one. We wanted to go back together with honor," Atwater said later. Others considered these "weekly waverers" divisive and "elitist," and argued for holding out. But the various pressures to settle were intense. The Guild called the federal mediator back in.

At the June meeting of the Time Inc. board of directors, the strike was a major subject of discussion. Reporting on the Guild's readiness to resume talks, Bear said that management felt nothing was to be gained until the union demands were scaled down. Heiskell complained bitterly of a lengthy *Wall Street Journal* article that gave credence to employee grievances, headlined: "Strike by Staffers at Time Inc. Indicates Decline of Paternalism, Slump in Morale." (Years afterward, Heiskell's rancor remained: "A poison-pen piece. I still remember it with anger.") The directors agreed that, having taken the strike and the initial adverse publicity, management should stand fast on pay policy.

Faced with the prospect of a long strike and escalating defections, the Guild capitulated. At an emotional meeting on June 21 in a Manhattan motel ballroom, union members voted 411 to 31 to accept the contract that had been on the table when the walkout began. It was agreed that they would all meet outside the Time & Life Building the next morning and walk in together.

Three months later, Henry Grunwald wrote a postmortem based on conversations with *Time* writers and researchers and addressed to Donovan. Some excerpts:

> The point that everybody mentioned first and with remarkable unanimity concerns quality. Is the company still concerned with editorial excellence or is it more concerned with profits? . . .
>
> We will have to show that quality and quantity are not the same. And that, for example, reducing the staff in this or that area does not necessarily mean reducing the quality of the magazine. This will take quite a bit of selling. We will also have to find ways to demonstrate the obvious—that a healthy profit margin for *Time* is absolutely essential to quality . . .
>
> There is . . . the feeling that in recent years the majority of employees have not done very well under a merit system. There is a widespread, familiar feeling that inflation is a new fact of life, and that people have not been sufficiently compensated for it.
>
> I tried to find out whether people thought that the outcome of the strike was good or bad for the Guild . . . I think most understand that it was a defeat for the Guild and that another strike is most unlikely for years to come. But there is a contrary feeling that, in a sense, the ice has been broken, that a strike has been shown to be no longer unthinkable, that a certain solidarity was created.

470

Though the strike inevitably left some bitterness, labor relations at Time Inc. subsequently became relatively placid. Guild membership receded toward prestrike levels, and with the normal comings and goings on the various editorial staffs, a new leadership took over. Time-Life Books' move to Alexandria, Virginia, displaced an important union stronghold. The animosity of 1976 subsided, but the union continued to register complaints in negotiating and grievance sessions about the limits on mandatory pay increases and overtime, and on job security. As the 1980s began, the Guild was putting more emphasis on prodding management to strengthen its affirmative action programs to employ more women, blacks and other minorities. On this front, as on others in the past, the prodding was not unwelcome. "The Guild," Charley Bear reflected, "has been instrumental over the years in keeping us attuned to what we should be doing."

By 1980, of Time Inc.'s total staff, there were 4,000 in managerial positions, and within this group, 30 percent were women, 8 percent from minorities, vs. 26 percent and 5 percent respectively only six years earlier. On the editorial and production staffs of Time Inc.'s magazines, 49 percent were women, 9 percent from minority groups. Topping the masthead lists were Eleanor Graves, executive editor of *Life*, and Pat Ryan, an assistant managing editor of *People*. There were also several women senior editors. On the corporate side, two of Time Inc.'s directors were women: Matina S. Horner, president of Radcliffe, and Joan Manley, Time Inc.'s group vice president, books. Time Inc.'s younger enterprises were opening up further opportunities for both minorities and women. By the early 1980s, June Travis and Gayle Greer, a black, were vice presidents at ATC. HBO had three female vice presidents: Gail Sermersheim, Bridget Potter and Iris Dugow. Three blacks—Stan Thomas, Donald Anderson and Nathan W. (Nate) Garner—were senior executives in the video group, and Juanita James, a black woman, was a vice president of Time-Life Books, heading the human resources department. And Fred Clarke, after various tours of duty including two years as director of labor relations in the early 1980s, became director of corporate personnel administration in 1984.

For all the progress, however, it was generally felt that the results were not good enough. The mechanisms for more positive action were in place. In 1972 management had reaffirmed its commitment to equal employment opportunity and afterward set specific numerical goals for hiring and promoting women and minorities. Affirma-

471

tive action officers were designated to identify areas within the company where underrepresentation still existed and develop programs to overcome it. Later, an affirmative action office was added for the handicapped, and for disabled and Vietnam veterans. The officers worked with executives throughout the company, attempting to meet the goals established. Their findings, reported to management periodically, included both successes and shortcomings; as Heiskell observed, "Such statements of policy are reasonably easy, but getting the job done is damned hard."

To discuss the problems and benefits of equal employment, Time Inc. held a three-day conference in January 1980 that was attended by representatives of 18 company divisions and subsidiaries. Executive vice president Dick Munro, soon to become corporate c.e.o., was one of the speakers. "Time Inc. is committed to affirmative action and equal employment opportunity," he declared, "because of a moral choice made years ago . . . The turmoil of the 1960s taught us that one's interest must transcend self and embrace all of society, or we will not have a society, let alone a business to run." Urging the key people assembled to pursue affirmative action with more vigor, Munro concluded: "In the end we will be judged by our efforts and results, and not by the cogency of our excuses for having failed."

Fortune *on*
a Different Frequency

"IT WAS A VERY CIVILIZED DEBATE. Nobody got mad, and people on both sides recognized there was some merit in their opponents' position." So Bob Lubar, who had been managing editor at the time, recalled the controversy that shook *Fortune* in the mid-1970s, dividing most of the editors from most of their colleagues on the publishing staff. The point at issue was one that had been raised just before Luce's death in 1967, as well as in earlier times: whether *Fortune* should be converted from a monthly to a biweekly. The question went beyond publication frequency; it affected the whole character and function of the magazine. In the study of biweekly publication that was getting under way as Luce died, the risks of change—of losing the unique position that *Fortune* had achieved in business journalism—loomed large, and the editorial objections were many. The study continued into 1969 without any action being taken. Those editorial objections remained as the question was posed again, but now the publishing side argued that the greater risk was in inaction, and that without change *Fortune* would be unable to hold its own in the competitive struggle for readers and advertisers.

In February 1970, *Fortune* celebrated its 40th birthday. Donovan spoke at the anniversary dinner, a gala affair at New York's St.

Regis Hotel. He traced the changes in the American economy that *Fortune* had chronicled. First, the decade of the Depression and the New Deal, followed by five years of World War II, and then:

A third era [that] ran all the way from the mid-1940s to the mid-1960s . . . the Age of Eisenhower, the Age of Kennedy and the Age of Truman [which] had more in common with each other than with what went before or with what followed . . . years of relative social stability in this country, high and rising prosperity by any previous standard, and very broad popular support, virtually unquestioning, for the bipartisan foreign policy that had been designed to fight the Cold War.

My own editorship of *Fortune* . . . fell right in the middle of that 20-year period. I suppose in many respects I had the easiest job of all [of *Fortune*'s] managing editors. We had a great big story on our hands: the American business system was working . . . So much [good news] that we had to invent a category of corporation story that we called "the failure story" and try for relief to work one into every issue . . .

That whole era began to come apart in the summer of 1965, with the deepening involvement in Vietnam and the racial violence in Watts. Since then, in my view, we have been living in something approximating a revolutionary age: domestic order in doubt; polarizing tendencies in our politics; some of the best of our youth embittered; most of our major institutions, much of the familiar morality and many of our most cherished ideas about America under skillful and determined attack. This seems in many ways a more formidable challenge to the American system than the Great Depression was.

Donovan recalled *Fortune*'s 25th anniversary, when the magazine ran a year-long series of articles that were, for the most part, confident and hopeful about the next 25 years; they were later published in a book entitled *The Fabulous Future*.* He went on to say:

If we were marking this 40th anniversary with a series of articles looking ahead to the year 2010, I doubt whether it would occur to any *Fortune* editor to call the series "The Fabulous Future" . . . We have, to say the least, turned somewhat wary.

The indications for *Fortune*'s own future were at that point quite uncertain. Donovan was later to describe the magazine's difficulty

*E. P. Dutton & Co., Inc., 1956.

474

as a "high-level packaging problem"—a phrase he did not much like, as applied to a magazine, but which made a point nonetheless.

The package that *Fortune* offered was handsome. Luce's original prospectus had promised that *Fortune* would be "as beautiful a magazine as exists in the United States. If possible, the undisputed most beautiful." If *Fortune*'s cover stock was no longer almost as thick as cardboard, and the magazine no longer weighed over two pounds (as had the first issue), it remained a lavish production. Large pages, with a huge editorial "well" of 40-plus pages uninterrupted by advertising, made for the stunning display of the expansive text pieces and picture spreads in color that distinguished *Fortune* from its rivals. No other business publication was in a position to deal in panoramic fashion with large subjects, such as the three-part series that *Fortune* had run in mid-1969, describing the international cattle-raising, stock-breeding and land-development operations of the Klebergs, owners of the King Ranch in Texas. Nor did *Fortune*'s rivals tackle at comparable depth the major questions of public policy or social development that affected American business: the nation's ailing medical system, dealt with in four related articles in *Fortune*'s January 1970 issue; the environment, the subject of 11 articles and two photographic portfolios in a special issue the following month.

Yet the sheer bulk of this package was daunting. The magazine gave the impression, Lubar conceded, "that there is somehow too much there to pick up and carry around, too much for a reader to plunge into." A survey commissioned by *Fortune* in 1969 indicated that its primary readers, the core group of devoted subscribers, usually read the magazine at home and took three and a half hours to do it—"conjuring up the image," as one of the magazine's publishing executives put it, "of a stuffed armchair and a solid citizen with three and a half hours available." Among a broader, more general business audience, *Fortune* was regarded as editorially authoritative, with interesting advertising. But as a whole, the magazine was perceived as Olympian in tone, rather heavy going for the proverbial tired businessman—a publication often put aside for later perusal, if read at all.

This impression was reflected in the magazine's circulation problems. In April 1968, Hank Luce, who had earlier been *Fortune*'s circulation director, returned as publisher, replacing Art Keylor, who was soon to become group vice president in charge of the magazine division. The next year, *Fortune* had raised its circulation rate base by 40,000 to 515,000, the largest single increase in the magazine's history, and in mid-1969 a further increase of 50,000 was announced for January 1970. But the accelerated growth proved too expensive to be sustained. Circulation costs were rising as the subscription renewal rate fell.

How large was *Fortune*'s potential audience? Periodically, in discussion, the figure of a million came up as the circulation target *Fortune* should be aiming at, but many considered that an unrealistic figure for a magazine with *Fortune*'s specialized reader interest. Within its restricted field, moreover, *Fortune* faced a harder competitive struggle for audience, as Lou Banks, then still managing editor, reported to the Time Inc. board in March 1970: "Whereas *Fortune* once had the corporation crisis, the state of economic thought, the organization man and even the environment all to itself, we now find this kind of coverage thriving in such direct rivals as *Business Week* and the *Wall Street Journal*. Even in *The New Yorker*, the *Saturday Review*. Sometimes in Merrill Lynch's free weekly reader, and *Playboy*," he added.

The rivalry had intensified also for a share of the corporate and industrial advertising "pot" into which *Fortune*, the *Wall Street Journal*, *Business Week*, *Forbes* and other business publications were all dipping. *Fortune* was even facing competition from *Time B*, the newly launched demographic edition of *Time* that offered advertisers an upscale selection of more than a million business executives out of *Time*'s 4 million subscriber list.

In August 1969, *Fortune* had acquired a new publisher—its fourth in five years. Hank Luce moved to fill the *Time* publisher's chair left vacant when Shepley moved up to the corporate presidency. Putney Westerfield, assistant publisher of *Life*, came over to take Luce's place at *Fortune*.

In November 1970 changes followed on the editorial side. Executive editor Bob Lubar became managing editor, succeeding Banks, who moved to the corporate executive ranks as editorial director—Donovan's deputy.

This editorial shuffle had come about in rather unusual circumstances. There was no precedent for a Time Inc. managing editor to declare that he was tempted by the attractions of another career, much less one outside journalism, but Banks had done just that. Taking a sabbatical leave from *Fortune* to spend six months at Harvard as a Nieman Research Fellow, Banks had returned in early 1970 to inform Donovan that he wanted to pursue the academic life full time: "I had seen a whole new vista. I had developed a real fascination for academe." To hold Banks, Donovan offered him the editorial director's post. Banks accepted, but the academic urge remained unassuaged; in February 1973 he left Time Inc. to become a visiting professor at Harvard's Graduate School of Business Administration, subsequently moving to the Massachusetts Institute of Technology as adjunct professor at the Alfred P. Sloan School of Management. He also joined the Time Inc. board of directors.

When Lubar took over as managing editor, he had just turned 50. He had been with the magazine for 12 years; before that, he had spent another 11 as a foreign correspondent for *Time*. A native New Yorker who was a graduate of Columbia College and the Columbia journalism school—and of a summer of hoboing across the country on railroad cars with a friend—Lubar started out in newspaper work on the New York *Times*, then served four years as a Navy officer aboard destroyers in the Pacific in campaigns from Guadalcanal to the shores of Japan. He joined Time Inc. in 1946, covering the United Nations in its early days, afterward working in the New Delhi, London, Mexico City and Bonn bureaus. He came home to join *Fortune* in 1958—attracted, as were many former *Time* correspondents, by the opportunity *Fortune* offered for in-depth reporting—but shortly was moved into an editing slot, taking as one of his provinces the magazine's expanding coverage of international business.

On Lubar's appointment as managing editor, assistant managing editor Dan Seligman stepped up to executive editor. Four years younger than Lubar and like him a native New Yorker (they happened to have attended the same elementary and high schools), Seligman had gone from Rutgers University into the Army and graduated from New York University in 1946. An assistant editor at the *American Mercury*, he had also been writing a labor column for the weekly *New Leader* when he joined *Fortune* in 1950. Seligman established a reputation as a prolific and graceful writer, one of the magazine's best,with a special flair for financial and Wall Street reporting. Among other things, he handled *Fortune*'s annual 500 list and its accompanying feature articles. On the side, Seligman liked to test his mathematical acumen by playing the horses.

Under Lubar and Seligman, *Fortune* displayed a more conservative bent than it had had under Banks, whose editorship coincided with the period of social upheaval in the 1960s. *Fortune* had, as recounted earlier, taken an activist—almost a missionary—approach in directing attention to the developing social forces that the editors believed would affect business. Now, along with the executive changes at the top, came some subtle changes in the magazine's tone

477

and emphasis. Reflecting on *Fortune*'s editorial involvement in public policy questions, Lubar later commented:

> The point was that business should be concerned with these matters, and *Fortune* was obliged to tackle the issues involved. In the early 1970s the magazine stayed with this agenda, but with a difference—we took a skeptical second look at the issues, and quite early adopted a view of measured conservatism.

Fortune's new line took account of the growing disillusionment among some liberals as well as conservatives. "The Social Engineers Retreat Under Fire," by Tom Alexander in October 1972, reported on the growing intellectual dissatisfaction with Great Society programs. In March 1973, Seligman examined "How 'Equal Opportunity' Turned into Employment Quotas." Possibly the most distinguished contribution in this field was an article by sociologist Daniel Bell, a longtime member of *Fortune*'s board of editors, who had left in 1958 to join the Columbia faculty and later had gone on to Harvard. "The Revolution of Rising Entitlements," in *Fortune*'s special Bicentennial issue of April 1975, examined the entitlement problem, pointing out the political crisis that was developing as government was being drawn increasingly into satisfying an ever-growing list of private claims. "We took a dim view," Lubar said, "of the idea that large corporations had an obligation, outside their usual quest for profits, to correct the nation's social ills. All this may look unsurprising now, but the line was not popular, in general, in American journalism at that time."

Fortune also began sounding warnings about the growing government deficits. "The Bad News About the Federal Budget" in the November 1972 issue was the first of several on that subject by Juan Cameron, *Fortune*'s resident Washington editor. "The Pentagon Enters Its Era of Austerity," by Charles Murphy, retired from *Fortune* and freelancing, discussed how the high cost of weapons systems was causing a retrenchment in military procurement.

During this time, new names appeared among *Fortune*'s board of editors. Wyndham Robertson, a former researcher whose reports on corporate malfeasance were becoming a *Fortune* feature, joined Carol Loomis in the ranks of the top writers; eventually Robertson was to become *Fortune*'s first female assistant managing editor.

Despite the rough stretch that Time Inc. went through at the end of the 1960s, *Fortune* had hit a record high in pretax profits in 1969.

Looking ahead, however, publisher Westerfield was cautious, feeling that large corporations could be pulling back into a defensive posture that could hurt advertising sales: "Businesses under attack, whether from government, consumer protection groups, environmentalists or simply profit erosion, tend to stop talking." In 1970, a poor year for magazines generally, *Fortune*'s ad sales fell by 500 pages, to just under 1,350—uncomfortably close to the magazine's breakeven point. By cutting costs, including folding the two annual special issues inaugurated a few years earlier, *Fortune* managed to stem its own profit erosion somewhat. Of further help in *Fortune*'s relatively small economy were earnings from so-called "offshoot products" such as reprints, directories, desk diaries and sponsorship of the *Fortune* Book Club. But by 1971, with advertising sales down further, *Fortune*'s income was only to about half the 1969 level.

It was against this background that in mid-1971 corporate management began to consider several drastic cost-cutting measures for *Fortune*. The one adopted was to cut the very large page size down to more conventional dimensions, not only to save on paper and postage but additionally, to help *Fortune* shed its coffee-table image and make it more enticing to read. There were dangers; some advertisers would not welcome losing the display space they presently enjoyed. In fact, during Hank Luce's days as publisher, he had sounded out the *Fortune* salesmen on the idea and they had advised against it. Another risk was in signaling weakness to the trade; *Esquire* and *McCall's*, neither in robust condition, were cutting their page sizes. The prevailing view, however, was that by shrinking the physical product, *Fortune* could position itself better for the future, when the magazine might want to undertake a large circulation boost. Wrote Westerfield: "We can't afford to be stuck delivering more editorial print order unless we know there will be more advertising to pay the bill . . . a gamble we can't afford today, at $10\frac{1}{4} \times 13$ [inch] page size."

The editors were not wildly excited by the idea of contracting the page size. Seligman, in a memo to Donovan, noted that *Fortune* would lose 10,000 words per issue, a sixth of its editorial content. Lubar, too, worried about losing "some of the sumptuous elegance that makes *Fortune* distinctive in magazine journalism." But, he conceded, "though no one has up to now put it so starkly, some radical reduction in production and distribution costs may be essential to the preservation of *Fortune*'s editorial quality [and] the role we have defined for it."

Announced in April 1972, the new, reduced page size became

effective with the September issue. *Fortune's* pages, 9 by 11 inches, remained wider than those of *Time* and most other magazines— "just so we could be different"—but made for a considerably more portable, convenient package than before. A statement by Lubar, reprinted as an advertisement in the press, explained the change:

> The reduced trim size should once and for all dispose of the question whether *Fortune* can be read in bed. The new *Fortune* *will* be easier to read in bed—and on trains and planes and in limousines. It will be easier to stuff into briefcases.

With the size reduction came design changes by art director Walter Allner. *Fortune* acquired a new cover logo, the seventh since the magazine's founding, stronger and more compact than its immediate predecessor. Inside, *Fortune* now had more extensive use of color and, for the first time, the major text pieces ran continuously, without "jumps" to the back of the book. The spacious editorial well in the middle of the book was retained initially; only later was this modified to allow some interruption by advertising pages.

Reaction from readers to the new smaller size was, on the whole, favorable. From the Ohio farm country one reader wrote, slightly tongue in cheek: "I do like your new format, fits better on the tractor seat."

The worries of the advertising staff also abated as page sales held up. Although the results that year were largely unrelated to the format change, 1972 saw the first improvement in six years. Circulation uncertainties remained, however, and it was decided not to push beyond the existing 580,000 rate base. A subscription price cut from $16 a year to $12 was also announced. Aimed at encouraging a broad sampling of the redesigned magazine, the price cut was later regarded as a mistake, since it increased *Fortune's* dependence on advertising. "The *Fortune* reader simply wasn't paying enough for the product," the magazine's general manager, Lawrence Crutcher, commented later. Savings in physical costs did not come up to expectations either, as prices of paper and printing rose more than anticipated.

At the beginning of 1973, *Fortune* had another change in publishers. Westerfield resigned, to be succeeded by Pat Lenahan, *Fortune's* former business manager and later its advertising director, who had been lending a hand at *Life* for a couple of years as general manager. *Fortune* welcomed Lenahan back happily. One of the publishing staff's favorites, he was a towering, droll Irishman, a gifted raconteur, a Latinist of some note and a fine ad executive; he also got along well with the *Fortune* editors.

Under Lenahan, the question of converting *Fortune* to a biweekly publishing schedule came under serious consideration again. Lenahan himself was a strong advocate of the change, as was advertising director James Hoefer. Both were convinced that *Fortune* as a monthly was not commanding the readership it might attract as a more current, newsier fortnightly; nor was it getting the business it might from advertisers who wanted more frequent exposure than 12 times a year. While circulation had stabilized somewhat, *Fortune* was not maintaining its share of business magazine readers. The Simmons survey figures for 1974–75 showed a disquieting decline in *Fortune* readers among people in the top income bracket, where *Forbes* showed an increase. (*Business Week*'s readership was also off, but only slightly.)

Hoefer took the occasion of a 1974 year-end meeting of the *Fortune* publishing staff with corporate management to plead the case for going biweekly:

> I remember telling Pat that I felt I just had to speak up . . . *Fortune* was not being read by top management. I'd find that out as I went out making calls . . . There was a tremendous burst from the rest of the business press and we seemed to be out of pace . . . I remember asking Heiskell if his friends were reading *Fortune*. I think I hit a chord there—it was one of those moments in any serious conversation when you know you've hit on a bit of truth. Donovan was also watching us. Neither of them responded. But later, Pat asked us to get going with the research [on the effects that change in frequency might have on circulation, ad sales and profits].

The editors remained skeptical. "It is an illusion to suppose that all we need do is split *Fortune* in two," Lubar declared in a note to Lenahan, citing the added staff costs that would take "a big bite out of any profit gain," the necessary reorganization of *Fortune*'s editorial departments and reorientation of its editorial objectives and the conversion of a writing staff "hired and geared to putting out a monthly" to another sort of business journalism. "New magazines, as we are learning in this building right now," Lubar wrote—referring to *Money*, then suffering from early growing pains—"can afford to experiment until they find the right formula, but not a 45-year-old with a reputation to protect."

The debate was temporarily suspended in September 1975, when

481

Fortune got yet another publisher. In a straight trade, Lenahan went upstairs to become corporate treasurer, and treasurer Clifford Grum, who had come to Time Inc. with the Temple merger (see chapter 18), moved down to *Fortune* to take his first line operation job with the company. Grum, who had been a banker before joining Temple Industries, brought special expertise to his job as publisher. Recalled Lubar: "He'd occasionally comment on a piece and keep us from looking like damn fools." The new publisher had been only a casual reader of the magazine: "I cherry-picked it and would pass by a lot of articles." His own experience reinforced his belief that *Fortune* was not being read by its intended audience. Grum became an enthusiastic champion of switching to biweekly publication.

The publisher's study was completed in January 1976 and was unveiled during a three-day conclave of *Fortune* editors, senior writers and reporters at a Glen Cove, Long Island, conference center. The meeting was called to deliberate on the magazine's editorial mission, but the economic projections prepared by Grum's staff stole the show. ("A bolt!" recalled one participant.) *Fortune* appeared pressed against a revenue ceiling while being squeezed from below by rising costs. Grum pictured *Fortune*'s situation three to four years thence:

> By 1979 there is no magazine profit left, with the only gains coming from the sale of T shirts, diaries and reprints! By 1980 it's a loss picture. It's fair to assume that we would not allow such a projection to become fact.

By going biweekly, on the other hand, *Fortune* could break out of the impasse. It could get more money out of more subscribers. It could also offer advertisers exposure 26 times a year and provide a more attractive advertising environment for them, with more pages facing editorial copy and 72 cover spaces (inside front and back, outside back) available.

One outcome of the Glen Cove meeting was the appointment of a committee to study the editorial implications of fortnightly publication; Allan Demaree, soon to be promoted to assistant managing editor, headed the group. The committee's report, submitted in May, did not meet the biweekly question straight on, but suggested that *Fortune*, at whatever frequency, could be made "livelier, more sprightly—more readable and less formidable than it is today."

> We have one thing going for us: the lack of competition on the intellectual front . . . We are a bit like the conservative politi-

cian who, lacking opposition on his right, can safely edge toward the center of the political spectrum without worrying about the loss of his conservative following. Likewise, if we proceed carefully, we can move some distance toward more lively ground without losing the readers who are attracted to *Fortune* because of the depth and breadth of its reporting and the originality of its ideas.

One of the committee's proposals was adopted for the monthly *Fortune*. This was a new column of informal commentary called "Keeping Up," which was introduced that December with immediate success. Seligman, who was slated to edit the column, recalled: "We had thought we'd get columns from all the writers but I volunteered to write the first couple myself . . . It was Hedley who said, 'You keep on writing that column.' So I did." Under Seligman's hand, "Keeping Up" quickly turned from an updating on current business trends, as had been intended, to an intensely personal expression of its author's sometimes quirky but always sharp-edged conservative views—"a kind of curmudgeonly romp . . . opinionated, funny, interesting, outrageous—in short, everything a personal column should be," as one *Fortune* colleague later put it. Over the following years Seligman has continued to turn out his column with record-breaking regularity, never once missing an issue, even for vacation or illness.

Fortune had its best year ever in 1976: pretax earnings of more than $4 million on revenues of nearly $28 million. Advertising exceeded budget, buoyed by a further increase in the consumer categories, which Grum saw as a potential major portion of long-term growth. Grum was itching to make the biweekly move; all that needed to be done was to persuade the editors.

In January 1977 another committee went to work, this one on full-time assignment to dummy up a biweekly *Fortune*. Assistant managing editor Dick Armstrong was chairman, and the group included three non-*Fortune* members—*Time* senior editor Marshall Loeb, freelance writer Paul Lancaster and former book division art director Sheldon Cotler. At a send-off lunch for the committee, Donovan observed that while *Fortune* had been on "a profit roller coaster . . . now, while we are in a period of strength . . . is the ideal time to do something like this." *Fortune* would, though, be taking an irreversible step, Donovan warned: "Once you did it, and if it wasn't successful, you couldn't turn around and tell the reader, 'Well, we're going to give it to you monthly again.' "

The committee had two dummies ready by April, after which Donovan reviewed the whole biweekly argument over lunch with *Fortune*'s board of editors. In his opening remarks Donovan said, "In all frankness, I have come to be attracted to the [biweekly] idea myself. I don't want to pretend to be talking in a neutral way."

But a good many of the editors were still lukewarm, if not hostile, as notes that were kept of the meeting revealed. "I've tried to think of the biweekly decision as a real business problem," Carol Loomis said. "A risk-reward situation in which we're playing double or nothing. The rewards are in the neighborhood of doubling *Fortune*'s profit, the risk is going to zero." Dan Seligman was doubtful: "The editorial concept of the biweekly just seems like a mishmash to me. As we move . . . into the short-article world, what's our selling point?" "My view," said Allan Demaree, "is that we shouldn't make the move . . . We give up part of our monopoly franchise to get into a very competitive swim."

The assembled editors left the luncheon unhappy and unpersuaded. Lubar weighed in afterward with a memo to Donovan, saying he had "moved from a skeptical position to one of firm opposition," maintaining that to make the change would signal to the trade that Time Inc. management had lost confidence in *Fortune*: "Indeed, the mere knowledge that the biweekly task force was at work seems to have convinced a lot of people that we are seeking ways to avert disaster; I am continually being asked polite questions bearing on that suspicion." At one last meeting with Donovan and Heiskell in May, Lubar and Seligman delivered their final arguments for keeping *Fortune* a monthly. They went feeling that Time Inc.'s decision had already been made, as indeed it had.

Announcement of the change, effective in January 1978, followed shortly. Meanwhile, *Fortune* was enjoying another record year, with the May 1977 issue (containing the *Fortune* 500 Directory) alone bringing in an all-time high of $4.5 million in advertising revenues.

With the decision made, the staff buckled down to make the biweekly *Fortune* a success. A new magazine had to be invented and launched while the old one was still being published. Dick Armstrong turned to, with a small task force, on a pilot issue, of which 20,000 copies were printed and distributed for promotional purposes. The editorial ranks had to be quickly expanded by more than a third; research chief Mary Johnston, who did most of the hiring, surpassed herself as a talent hunter, and the staff was quickly enriched by numbers of bright, news-conscious young men and women. As for the veteran staffers, they had to adjust to a quickened pace and a less leisurely approach in their writing. Recalled Lubar:

> It wasn't that the new *Fortune* was intended to be a news-magazine . . . Ours wasn't a duty to cover all the news by departments, like *Time*. We wanted to maintain the maximum opportunity to bring to bear what our magazine offered, which was background analysis; there's still a big gap between our reporting and *Time*'s. But we did have to look at time—small "t"—differently. This was revolutionary for *Fortune*.

The magazine's rather informal editorial procedures were restructured and speeded up. Staffers were assigned "beats" to cover so that they could alert the editors to breaking news stories. In addition to its resident editors stationed in Washington and London (for Europe), *Fortune* established new editorial offices in Chicago, Houston and Los Angeles. Production people quickly adjusted to moving twice as fast: "We no longer could get out the magazine and then enjoy looking at it awhile," recalled production manager Sidney Sklar. Writers and researchers got used to the idea of sometimes being given only a week to report and write a story—as well as having less space in which to tell it.

(Telling *Fortune's* own story in humorous terms, a promotional film portraying the conversion to biweekly publication featured members of the staff parodying hard-nosed journalistic lingo and tactics. Dick Armstrong barked at a writer: "I want that story, Loving—I want it deep and I want it fast!" as Rush Loving jumped on his motorcycle and roared off. A reporter was seen on the phone with Deep Throat, in an underground garage, and another's hands were seen pawing through a file cabinet. The announcer intoned, "Out of the flaming reality of today's burning business journalism, out of the clattering day-by-day drama of tumultuous economic and political events . . . comes new, improved *Fortune!*")

The first regular issue of the biweekly *Fortune*, dated January 16, 1978, went out to subscribers in late December 1977. From the cover—a photo showing an enlarged General Motors car key, heralding a major article on the company—to the last page, the magazine looked distinctly different. Art director Ronald Campbell had done a complete redesign, the most extensive in 25 years.

In its new format *Fortune* was thinner overall—148 pages in the inaugural issue in contrast to the monthly *Fortune's* average of more than 200—but offered readers greater variety: that issue's table of contents listed 11 titles instead of the eight or nine averaged previously. Two ran for six pages each, close to *Fortune*'s traditional length; a few came in at less than 2,000 words. (In the *Fortune* of his day, Donovan liked to observe, a couple of thousand words had hardly sufficed for throat-clearing.) *Fortune*'s Wheel, the capsule summary of the monthly's lengthy contents, was dropped. So was the editorial page. But the other familiar *Fortune* features remained, notably the very popular Business Roundup and Personal Investing department. (Sandy Parker continued to be in charge of Roundup until his death in 1980; he was succeeded by his longtime associate, Todd May Jr.)

Readers' reaction to the biweekly was favorable, allaying the editors' fear that the magazine might lose its audience in the switch. The subscriber who wrote, "Just the beginning of a long and sickening slide to oblivion," was apparently in the minority, though faithful readers sometimes confessed to missing the exhaustive reporting and analysis that had been *Fortune*'s forte. That strong point of long standing—of the old, encyclopedic *Fortune*—was indeed giving ground, and the editors were, at first, groping for a formula to make the magazine "read like a biweekly" with the right combination of timeliness and depth.

Madison Avenue was particularly enthusiastic, giving the biweekly its most resounding vote of approval. Advertising page sales totaled 2,128 in 1978, an all-time high. By the end of the next five years, the total was well over 3,000, and *Fortune* improved by 25 percent its share of advertisers' money spent in the three premier business magazines: *Business Week, Forbes* and *Fortune*. In the process, advertising revenues surpassed $100 million, so that in 1983 *Fortune* found itself among the top ten magazines in both ad pages and revenues.

Over that same five-year period *Fortune*'s income soared. As anticipated, the onetime costs of conversion wiped out profit entirely for 1978. But by 1979 *Fortune*'s pretax earnings of $5.4 million were almost double those of 1977, the last year of monthly publication, even though the biweekly was a more expensive magazine to produce. Indeed, the added editorial outlays, together with higher paper, printing and postage costs, raised *Fortune*'s breakeven point, measured in the number of advertising pages needed to show a profit, by 30 percent. Nonetheless, by 1983 pretax income was topping $14 million.

That success was not entirely due to the change in publishing frequency. *Fortune* was riding a rising tide of advertising expenditure in business publications as a group, which was lifting *Fortune*'s rivals likewise to new highs in ad revenues. The daily press and the radio and television networks were expanding their business coverage also, reflecting the fact, as *Time* phrased it, that "economics has become hot politics and important news."

Accordingly, it was disappointing that *Fortune*'s circulation did not show the same bounce as its advertising. Net paid, which was 628,000 before the switch, rose to 669,000 by 1979, leaving *Fortune* still behind *Forbes* and *Business Week,* although *Fortune*'s circulation growth was marginally better than its competitors'. In 1980 net paid rose to 677,000.

Fortune celebrated its 50th anniversary in 1980. It was an occasion for nostalgia. The sumptuous first issue of February 1930 was reprinted in facsimile as a birthday memento, using similar heavy paper stock and the same large page size and glowing gravure color (reproduced, in this instance, in offset) that had made *Fortune*'s appearance on the publishing scene such a sensation at the time. The anniversary issue, dated February 11, had as its theme "A Phenomenal Half-Century" and featured a sampling of 31 pieces out of the 6,600-odd that had appeared in the 634 issues since *Fortune*'s founding.[*] Also recalling the magazine's earlier days was a book of personal reminiscences by such alumni as Archibald MacLeish, William H. Whyte, Dwight Macdonald, John Chamberlain, John Kenneth Galbraith, Daniel Bell and Charles Silberman.[†]

Two months after *Fortune*'s golden anniversary there was a change in managing editors. Bill Rukeyser, who had left in 1972 to edit *Money,* returned to *Fortune* as managing editor—at 40, the youngest in that job since Donovan. Lubar, after ten years of top-editing, returned to the pleasures and duties of a staff writer as a member of *Fortune*'s board of editors. On the publishing side likewise there had been changes. In April 1979, Pat Lenahan—"the only born-again publisher in Time Inc.," as he called himself—had returned when Grum went back upstairs to corporate management. Hoefer, who remained as advertising director, was later (in 1985) to succeed Lenahan as publisher.

The new management at *Fortune* took over at a time when the publisher's projections for the year from 1981 onward indicated

*The selections, with 39 others, were republished as a book. *For Some The Dream Came True,* Duncan Norton-Taylor, ed., Lyle Stuart, Secaucus, 1981.
†*Writing for Fortune*, Gilbert Burck, ed., Time Inc., New York, 1980.

tougher competitive battles ahead. Biweekly publication had put *Fortune* in better position to attract a busy managerial readership by bringing the magazine closer to the news, and under Rukeyser's editorship *Fortune*'s evolution toward a newsmagazine approach accelerated. Major stories were shortened further; there was more focus on personalities; *Fortune*'s format became more departmentalized. The editorial redefinition of *Fortune* was not over yet.

Living Dangerously
in Cable TV

I F EVER A SUCCESSFUL ENTERPRISE sprang from unpropitious origins, it was Home Box Office, which enabled Time Inc. to become a leading force in cable television. Its direct ancestor was Sterling Information Services, Ltd., the small New York City cable company that Time Inc. bought into in 1965, several months before it received interim rights to wire the lower half of the borough of Manhattan. Time Inc.'s share of Sterling at first was a 20 percent interest—a modest investment of $1,250,000. This was, however, high-risk money, proffered at a time when there was not much confidence in the struggling new communications medium.

Time Inc. must be counted among the pioneers in cable. The company made significant commitments of capital and managerial effort when the industry was still forming and it was by no means clear what shape its evolution would take. There were times when the bet looked like a loser, but the company persevered until cable eventually vied with magazine publishing as Time Inc.'s richest source of profits.

The move into cable, as recounted earlier, reflected the feeling that Time Inc. had already missed its chance in conventional broadcasting. Together, its five stations served too limited a market, and

Time-Life Broadcast's attempt at programming, both for its own stations and for possible network sale, had been a daunting experience. So had been Broadcast's overseas television investments.

Sterling hardly promised more, at the start. It ate money voraciously. Compared with the Midwest localities in which Time-Life Broadcast was seeking out CATV franchises, where wiring for cable was an above-ground operation, Sterling plunged the company into the catacombs under New York City streets. Cables had to be strung through underground ducts, then into apartment buildings and up to the separate apartments, sometimes hundreds of them. Whereas suburban cabling cost perhaps $10,000 per mile, in Manhattan the cost was more like $100,000 and sometimes as high as $300,000. By mid-1967 Sterling had spent $2 million to wire only 34 blocks, and it was serving only 400 subscribers. Without further financing—$10 million was Time Inc.'s estimate of the amount required—Sterling could not finish wiring its franchise area.

Time Inc.'s participation was essential to the rescue of the cable company, which now began. The Chase Manhattan Bank advanced the necessary credit, but only on condition that Sterling Information's individual shareholders guarantee repayment. At this time four shareholders remained: Time Inc.; Sterling Communications Inc., the cable system's parent corporation headed by founder Charles Dolan; and two individual investors who had gone into Sterling earlier, Elroy McCaw and William Lear (see chapter 8). The last two were unwilling to guarantee their share of the bank loan and sold out to Time Inc. and Sterling Communications, with Sterling retaining just over half-ownership. Together, the two remaining owners signed the Chase bank guarantee.

It was an unusual transaction. Of the $10 million, half was available immediately; the other half was untouchable until the cable system had attracted 12,500 subscribers, at which point borrowing could begin at the rate of $100,000 for each 1,000 subscribers until the remaining $5 million was drawn down. By January 1969, Sterling's cable operation had spent the first $5 million but was not yet eligible to begin drawing on the second. The cable system had yet to earn a cent and was requiring some $500,000 monthly for operating expenses. Time Inc. and Sterling began making loans—prorated between them—totaling $2 million.

Finally, in July, the crucial 12,500th subscriber was signed up; Sterling-Manhattan, as Sterling's cable subsidiary was then called, could begin drawing on the second $5 million credit. However, it needed cash even faster than the loan agreement would allow; there

490

were weeks when executives would check the number of subscribers, then run to the bank for another loan installment to meet the payroll. By now the cable system was looking like a rather insidious invention for making huge sums of money vanish. As the months passed, it became clear that even more would be needed. Sterling Communications had exhausted its ability to contribute its proportionate share; the search for a third party investor proved fruitless. By September 1969, Time Inc. had decided to sell out, and the investment banking firm of White, Weld was hired to find a buyer. While the search went on, the drain continued; in addition, Sterling's franchise rights were clouded by the uncertainties of New York City politics. More money was needed. Sterling Communications was still too weak to provide any. Nor was Sterling eager to see Time Inc. add to its contribution, since Time Inc. was now willing to make loans only if convertible to equity. More loans would boost Time Inc.'s potential ownership to more than 50 percent, and that would create problems for both companies. The rules of accounting would force Time Inc. to consolidate Sterling's poor financial results with its own results. And Sterling would become a minority owner of its major asset, which by law would place it under new restrictions.

The solution, developed at a desperate meeting on New Year's Eve 1969, was for Time Inc. to give all its stock in Sterling Information Services to Sterling Communications Inc., the parent company, and in return become its 44.5 percent owner. Time Inc. then made a convertible-to-ownership loan that kept things going for several more months.

Sterling Manhattan was not Time Inc.'s only cable TV worry. In the aftermath of the 1969 management changes, when the company's nonpublishing activities had come up for a general review, the decision was made to sell the five broadcast stations (see chapter 16). That in turn prompted reexamination of the company's commitments to cable. Many of the small operating systems Time-Life Broadcast had bought into were not putting profits onto the corporation's income statement either. Should they be jettisoned as well?

The pros and cons were well summarized in a March 1970 memo to Andrew Heiskell from Edgar Smith, then vice president in charge of cable development under Time-Life Broadcast's new chief, Barry Zorthian. Smith conceded that cable was "a capital intensive, regulated, hardware-type distribution business with debatable near-term earning prospects." But there were reasons for sticking with it:

To ensure Time Inc. a role in the most exciting, changing and hard-to-assess segment of the broadcasting industry, to give Time Inc. an anchor to windward if the drift to electronic communication continues and, finally, to assure access of Time Inc. "software" [programs] to cable TV through control of a significant segment of the "hardware."

Smith noted further that he thought cable would eventually be attractive financially.

Management more than agreed. The conviction now was that cable would grow into a major industry; Time Inc. should hold onto its existing cable investments and use the proceeds from the broadcast station sales to invest in more cable companies. Taking charge of putting the policy into effect was Jim Shepley, then newly installed in the president's office. Later a colleague commented: "Jim Shepley was the believer, he was the godfather. He was not the guy who managed it to be successful, but he was the man with the vision."

In the summer of 1971, an exhaustive internal study called "CATV—A Proposed Strategy for Time Inc." reached completion. Dick Clurman headed the team preparing the study; other members had included Dick Burgheim, then a *Time* writer on loan to the corporate R & D department, and W. Howard Dunn, an assistant to Bear. The study concluded that "investing in CATV systems, for all its financial and managerial *angst*, is a sound long-term investment with little down-side risk"—an encouraging endorsement of the company's television strategy. But another conclusion was that ownership of cable systems was important mainly as a means to an end: "The real interest that Time Inc. should have in CATV is [providing] its content, which will have tremendous impact on American life—and also could ultimately be the largest source of profit from CATV."

Time Inc. was then providing little original "content"—programming—for cable TV. Cable's main selling point was that it offered viewers better reception of commercial television broadcasts. This approach changed shortly, as a result of a memorandum that summer from Sterling Communications' president, Chuck Dolan. Written aboard the *Queen Elizabeth 2*, while Dolan and his family were crossing the Atlantic for a vacation, the memo outlined a scheme that would have enormous future consequences for Time Inc. and become a televised reality under the name of Home Box Office.

492

Dolan's proposal was for a cable network, which he dubbed the Sterling Network, or the Green Channel. The central idea was a service providing nightly entertainment to affiliated cable TV systems, whose subscribers would pay a monthly fee. Monthly fees have since become standard for pay TV, but conventional thinking then held that the future lay in so-called pay-per-view programming: the viewer would pay separately for each show, as at a theater, with a technical device built into the system ensuring that only paying customers could view the program. However, the hardware for this, still in the early stages of development, was complicated, expensive and unreliable. Time Inc. had already had some experience with pay-per-view programming through investment in a small venture called Computer Television Inc., which provided hotel guests with televised movies. (CTI lost money from the beginning, and after spending $3 million, Time Inc. sold out in 1975 to Spectradyne.)

To make clear that he was proposing something different from pay-per-view, Dolan used the unwieldy term "pay cable-per channel." Dolan recognized that the Green Channel would need attractive programming and economical distribution to the participating cable systems, but figured that he had both problems licked. Programming would be only at popular hours and offer viewers "a double feature every night"—usually a movie and a sporting event supplemented by special features. The movie companies, Dolan thought, could be persuaded to sell him film rights. For Sterling Manhattan Cable he had already secured rights to the New York Knicks' basketball games and the New York Rangers' hockey games; Dolan was confident he could get similar rights from the Philadelphia and Boston teams.

The problem of transmission demanded original thinking. Emulating the broadcast networks' relay methods was far too expensive; each network paid the telephone company about $25 million a year to interconnect somewhat more than 100 affiliates. The young Green Channel, which Dolan envisioned linking with scores of cable systems, could not pay such heavy freight. Dolan's scheme was to have the affiliates bear the cost of the hardware, service and marketing. Some entrepreneurs had already established tiny pay-cable "networks" by "bicycling" the programs on film or tape—sending them by mail or air freight from one affiliate to the next. That method precluded mass promotion of the schedule, however, since no affiliate showed the same program at the same time. Moreover, many cable systems did not even have facilities for transmitting tape or film. And of course covering live events was out of the question.

493

Dolan's solution was to distribute via microwave. Some firms had built microwave networks to transmit regular broadcast television to the small cable systems, and Dolan planned to lease those networks.

On November 3, 1971, Sterling's board of directors, which included officers of Time Inc., bought the idea of the Green Channel. As plans for the new network became more specific, memos flew among Time Inc. executives expressing justified doubts about its prospects. Sample comments:

> Can the network obtain movies as anticipated—especially good ones? . . . Will people pay for second-rate sports and old movies when so much is available on commercial TV? . . . Will not the proposed network invoke the wrath of all "free-TV" advocates and at the same time run real risk of failing to arouse much subscriber interest? . . . I suggest that pay-TV entrepreneurs examine introductory offers from sports promoters as cautiously as if they were come-ons from Mephistopheles or a heroin dealer.

To settle some of these questions, surveys of potential customers were conducted in eastern Pennsylvania, New Jersey and New York state. The goal was to get the network running by the fall of 1972— before some competitor launched one first.

In Pennsylvania, one venturesome operator, John Walson, had agreed to try the Green Channel on his Allentown cable system if Sterling decided to go ahead. An experimental attempt to sell the service by direct mail yielded dismal results, however: only 1.2 percent of the prospects said they would buy. (Perhaps nothing more should have been expected, considering that most viewers had never heard of the idea.) Door-to-door solicitation, offering the first month free and a refundable installation charge produced a better response: 50 percent agreed to sign up. There was no assurance that many would not later cancel out.

Before the surveying began, in May 1972, Dolan had hired a young man to help him with the contracts for the Green Channel. Gerald M. Levin, barely 33, was an exceptionally bright lawyer. For four years he had done antitrust work at the Wall Street firm of Simpson, Thacher & Bartlett, under Whitney North Seymour, a noted trial lawyer and civil liberties activist. In 1967 he left to join the Development & Resources Corporation, an international consulting firm, where he gained a new mentor: David Lilienthal, administrator of the Tennessee Valley Authority in its formative New Deal years. From the 68-year-old Lilienthal, Levin recalled, he learned "management as a humanist art." At D & R he found him-self in "a supercharged environment" of engineers working on large-scale public projects; the company was also developing labor-inten-sive, socially useful businesses that the indigenous people could run. In Colombia, Levin set up a carnation-growing company called Flor-America, which employed Indians. Through such experience, said Levin, "I developed an entrepreneurial interest in making things happen." Nelson Rockefeller's International Basic Economy Corpo-ration took over D & R in 1971, after which Levin represented the company in Tehran for a year.

Levin returned home in 1972 ready for a change; in particular, he wanted something to do with motion pictures. In New York law work earlier, he had acquired contacts at Paramount Pictures, Madi-son Square Garden and other entertainment enterprises; through mutual acquaintances at the Garden he met Dolan, then working on the Green Channel—which, as Levin pointed out, was really not such a radical change from his previous work. Both required "engi-neering methods applied to problem solving."

One immediate problem was the new network's name. In place of the original candidate, Sterling Cable Network, which had met with objections, some of the new staff came up with Home Box Office. The term was not original. Used occasionally in the cable industry, it had appeared also in a Time Inc. consultant's memo called "The Problem of the 'Home Box-Office.' " The memo's date: June 7, 1951. Among the Green Channel group, no one much liked Home Box Office, but it was the least bad name proposed so far, and the words "box office" carried the appropriate associations with movies and sports. Anyway, the name could always be changed later.

Sterling and Time Inc. decided to inaugurate HBO service on the night of November 8, 1972. One of the first requirements was some-one to line up programming. The infant enterprise could not prom-ise the job to anyone for longer than two months. So Jerry Levin, whose expertise in movies and sports derived solely from watching them, became HBO's first vice president for programming.

HBO was to debut on John Walson's cable system in Allentown. But a few weeks before launch Walson switched it to his system in Wilkes-Barre. The reasons were several, including easier transmis-sion of the microwave signal to Wilkes-Barre. But more important was geography: with HBO planning to televise National Basketball Association games, the town was safely outside the 75-mile pro-tected zone around Philadelphia where NBA game broadcasts

495

could, under NBA rules, be blacked out at the local team's request. However, there was a problem. Wilkes-Barre had been devastated by Hurricane Agnes several months earlier, and about half the city's 10,000 cable subscribers were still disconnected; the other half had more important things to worry about than an unheard-of new cable channel costing an extra $6 monthly.

Unfazed, Carleton (Tony) Thompson, formerly the Sydney-based South Pacific sales director for Time-Life Books, went to Wilkes-Barre and set up an HBO storefront near the cable system's office, whence he sent out salesmen in search of subscribers. It was testament to the salesmen's ability—and, just as much, to the Americans' astonishing love of television—that 365 people signed up.

In retrospect, HBO's first night was historic. At the time, though, it hardly seemed worthy of notice and in fact was hardly noticed at all. Even a small bit of prearranged publicity fell through. Tony Thompson and Dick Munro, then deputy to group vice president Rhett Austell, were supposed to drive to Wilkes-Barre for a ceremony in which the city manager, along with John Walson, would "inaugurate" HBO while as the local paper photographed the event. But Thompson and Munro became hopelessly trapped in a Manhattan traffic jam during a rainstorm. When they called to explain, they were told it didn't matter; the city manager had decided that the ceremony wasn't worth attending, and the paper had decided that, without him, it wasn't worth covering.

Otherwise, the evening went smoothly. Viewers saw first the face of Jerry Levin, briefly welcoming them to the new network. HBO then took viewers to Madison Square Garden, where Marty Glickman covered a hockey game between the New York Rangers and the Vancouver Canucks. Glickman was a veteran New York sportscaster who had helped Dolan get the rights to Madison Square Garden events. After the game came the second half of the evening's "double feature," the film *Sometimes a Great Notion*. It was not much of a movie, but in light of HBO's later success, many writers have been unable to mention its title without a good deal of verbal organ music. Levin viewed it all in a simulated living room setting at the 23rd Street studio. He wanted to know what the viewer was experiencing. At about midnight the movie ended and HBO signed off.

The new network was off the ground, though barely. Its goal now was to stay aloft. After several months that feat looked easier than anyone had expected. As HBO expanded by microwave connection to more cable systems, it signed up subscribers quickly. By the beginning of June 1973, it had collected 12,500. The staff was jubilant. But then, disconcertingly, the number of subscribers began to decline, continuing steadily downward month after month.

Worried investigation revealed three main causes of the decline. First, it was summer and subscribers were spending less time indoors. Second, HBO had unwisely counted on the cable system operators, who received half the monthly subscription charge, to sell the new service. But they were not experienced at aggressive marketing and were often content to let their systems run quietly with little attention. Third, and most disquieting, subscribers did not feel they were getting their money's worth. No one could blame them. The caliber of HBO's programming was then erratic, and most of the movies the studios were willing to let HBO show were box-office underachievers. Much of the audience interest in HBO movies was generated by the publicity surrounding their theater release, but in its beginning days HBO was stuck with films many people had never heard of.

Hope lingered for years that Time-Life Films might be a source of quality programs for HBO. Early portents were encouraging. As time passed, however, it became obvious that Time-Life Films could not fill HBO's schedule. Even under TLF's most ambitious (and never executed) plans in the late 1970s, it would have had the capacity to produce no more than a dozen or so feature films a year—an insignificant number compared with the 200 to 300 that HBO needed. Nor were Time-Life Films' numerous other programs, including BBC productions, of much interest to HBO. The anticipated cross-feed did not develop.

Sports were generally a better attraction in HBO's first year, but along with basketball and hockey, the Madison Square Garden schedule also included such pseudo sports as roller derby and professional wrestling. The network's occasional specially produced programs were not exactly irresistible: live coverage of the Pennsylvania Polka Festival, for example, probably did not attract many viewers, even in Pennsylvania.

Sterling's situation had worsened meanwhile, and would soon become entirely Time Inc.'s problem—in particular, Jerry Levin's. As the money needs of Sterling and its HBO subsidiary had grown, Time Inc. had filled them, eventually building up such a large investment that management felt Time Inc. ought to be formally in charge. Converting its convertible loans to equity brought the company's share of Sterling to 66 percent by March 1973; by September, 79 percent. As the new majority owner, Time Inc. shuffled management. Dolan left the presidency of Sterling Communications, and was succeeded by Richard Galkin, then president of Sterling-Manhattan.* Levin succeeded Dolan at HBO. (Dolan remained on the Sterling companies' boards.) "We don't know if Jerry can do it," Munro told a visitor on the day of Levin's appointment, "but we're going to give him the ball and find out."

That year saw several other moves affecting Time Inc.'s cable operations. One was the decision to drop an ambitious plan, under discussion with the Hughes Aircraft Company since 1971, for distributing programming nationwide to cable TV systems via an orbiting satellite, which Hughes would build. Recalled Heiskell: "I was petrified by the expense." In another major move, Time Inc. sold off its cable holdings, apart from Sterling-Manhattan and HBO, to the Denver-based American Television and Communications Corp., a major cable systems owner. Time Inc.'s cable properties, then consisting of eight operating systems and three franchises scattered from New Jersey to California, had not, as a group, been producing satisfactory results and their sale to ATC offered obvious advantages. Time Inc. acquired 260,000 shares of ATC stock, plus another 100,000 shares subsequently, giving the company a 9 percent interest in ATC; Shepley went on the ATC board. Nick Nicholas, later HBO president but then a financial officer in the broadcast area, explained: "We decided we should keep a window on the [cable] world by swapping our interest for a minority interest in a large cable company that was well managed."

Sterling had also been on the block; ATC wanted no part of it. Time Inc. proceeded to buy out the remaining Sterling Communications stockholders, dissolve the parent company and make its subsidiaries, HBO and Manhattan Cable, wholly owned subsidiaries of Time Inc. To shed some of the risk, a scheme had been devised under which the network would become a limited partnership, with partnership shares sold to the general public as tax-shelter investments. The investment banking firm of Salomon Brothers began making arrangements. But within weeks Time Inc. was notified that the market for financing of risky venture capital projects had precipitously dried up.

A decision was approaching on HBO. Industry developments made it appear a more dangerous business than ever. Rhett Austell,

---

*Dolan had been president of Sterling Manhattan until William Lamb of the Educational Broadcasting Corporation replaced him in April 1971. Richard Galkin, formerly with Time-Life Broadcast, replaced Lamb in July 1972.

for the broadcast group, summarized them in a memo to Heiskell and Shepley in September, 1973:

1) Increasing evidence [is] that the three television networks and the association of theater owners intend to use their considerable political clout to slow the growth of pay cable . . .

2) Increasing evidence [is] that the "wiring of the nation" may not proceed as rapidly as the consensus forecasts . . .

3) The business formula for HBO has become less attractive as a result of substantially heavier expenditures required for programming. The number of subscribers needed to break even has increased from 175,000 to 225,000.

4) Many of the system owners being courted by HBO are also being wooed by HBO's competitors. The system owners are not sure yet who is for real and who isn't.

HBO, in Austell's phrase, was in a "holding pattern" while its management tried to figure out what to do next. Levin, then on vacation, had already been told what this might be. He was drafting plans for liquidating HBO.

Levin was spared the unpleasant chore. Fortuitous scheduling of a particularly popular movie, *The Poseidon Adventure*, cut HBO's "churn" (subscriber turnover) to 5 percent and in December, a revived marketing drive in Wilkes-Barre netted many new subscribers among households that had been knocked out of cable service by the floods a year earlier. By the end of 1973, HBO had 8,632 subscribers. It was a tiny figure—a few years later HBO would sign up that many in a dull week—but the more important fact was that the total was now increasing. That justified allowing the venture to continue.

But HBO would have to do better, and quickly. In early 1974 Levin wrote his associates: "In a meeting with Jim Shepley today it was made clear to me—again—that we must meet our subscriber goals as of June 30: the magic 20,000. There are no ands, ifs or buts about it." Any faltering and Time Inc. was prepared to shut down HBO.

In the following months, HBO's prospects improved for a number of reasons. It was slowly expanding its microwave network into the Northeast, adding new cable systems. It was accumulating marketing expertise. And as Ralph Graves, then corporate editor watching over cable and film activities, explained in a memo to Hedley Donovan, HBO "has become a much more valuable service chiefly because the movie distributors are now turning loose good movies instead of clinkers." Just barely, HBO met its June 30 target, whereupon Time Inc. management asked HBO to line up 40,000 subscribers before the year was over. That proved easier than anticipated, partly because Manhattan Cable—after much haggling over price, which Munro had to arbitrate—finally began offering HBO to its subscribers. By the end of 1974, HBO had 57,700 paying customers.

In July 1974, Rhett Austell, who was having his differences with top management, took a leave. A year later he returned briefly to work on a magazine project, then left Time Inc. to head American Heritage Publishing Co. Succeeding him as group vice president for television and films was his former deputy, Dick Munro. Video's success under Munro would be an important factor in his elevation to the Time Inc. presidency in 1980. And perhaps the most important decision contributing to that success was one that Munro had to confront immediately upon taking over the video group.

The decision went to the electronic heart of HBO's distribution system. From the start, HBO had used microwave, transmitting the broadcast signal from point to point overland. Subscriber growth projections indicated that with microwave transmission, and with extension of the service as expected—HBO had got up a little momentum at last—the 100,000th subscriber would be signed up sometime in April 1975. And by the end of that year HBO would probably accomplish the impossible: become profitable. Yet that would be a terribly slow and expensive way to become a national network. Levin believed, and convincingly argued, that HBO should therefore take the pioneering step of distributing programs via satellite.

There was nothing new about the idea; it had even been in Dolan's original Green Channel memo. Afterward, there had been Time Inc.'s contemplated satellite venture with Hughes Aircraft, and since 1973 HBO had been consulting with satellite companies. Everyone in the industry could see that satellite distribution was coming. But as of 1975, it had yet to be actually tried.

The advantages were evident. Transmission was nationwide, reception was available to any cable system operator investing in the requisite dish-shaped receiving antenna. Cost of the dishes and their sheer obtrusiveness were thought to be effective security against unauthorized reception. Western Union's Westar satellite was already orbiting and had excess capacity; RCA's Satcom satellite was scheduled to go up later in the year.

To HBO the satellite offered a welcome escape from microwave. But the risks were equally apparent. By FCC standards, the receiving dishes had to be nine meters in diameter; the cost then ran about $75,000. What if not enough cable system operators cared to risk the investment? In that case HBO could be saddled with five years of reserved time on a satellite at a price of $7.5 million.

Nonetheless, it appeared a worthwhile gamble. Strong supporting evidence came from vice president James Heyworth, 32, who had been involved with HBO in various capacities since the beginning (he would eventually become HBO's president). Combining business with vacation in Florida, Heyworth had visited many cable system operators and found enough interest in satellite service in that state alone to justify the expense. In April 1975, HBO announced that UA-Columbia Cablevision, owner of 52 cable systems around the country, would carry HBO programs via satellite on its systems in Fort Pierce and Vero Beach, Florida. Three days later, at the National Cable Television Association convention, ATC announced similar plans for its Jackson, Mississippi, system. The stock market response was immediate. Within five days of the UA-Columbia announcement, Time Inc.'s stock rose 20 percent, from 37½ a share to 44⅞. Stocks of other companies involved with cable rose as well. When Munro went before the Time Inc. board the following month, seeking approval for the satellite contract the task was, he recalled, "a piece of cake."

HBO aimed to begin with a bang: with satellite relay of Muhammad Ali's heavyweight title defense against Joe Frazier—the "thrilla from Manila"—scheduled for September 30, 1975. Over the summer the network rushed frantically to prepare for that date, and barely made it. On the morning of September 30, in Vero Beach, Dick Munro came in from a jog on the beach and, wearing shoes but no socks, joined RCA's representative to sign the satellite contract. RCA's own satellite would not be in orbit for three months, but RCA had solved that by renting a vacant transponder on Western Union's satellite in the meantime.

The big night came off as planned, beginning with welcomes from Andrew Heiskell and FCC Chairman Richard Wiley, followed by two movies, *Brother of the Wind* and *Alice Doesn't Live Here Anymore*, then a repeat of the introduction, then the fight. The picture, relayed from Manila to the U.S. via satellite, then through a welter of land lines and microwave connections and finally via satellite once again to the cable systems in Florida and Mississippi—a 100,000-mile journey in all—came out clear and sharp. The system had been proved.

In the succeeding months, several more cable operators installed receiving dishes and began offering HBO to subscribers. By December 1975, HBO had 287,000 customers—enough to earn a profit under the old distribution system, though not with the satellite. HBO had lost $1 million in 1973, its first full year, and nearly $4 million in 1974; in 1975, with many more subscribers but also three months of satellite costs, HBO's deficit was $3,150,000.

HBO's remarkable lead over its competitors in the next few years has generally been attributed to its early gamble on use of the satellite. The explanation is accurate but incomplete. More important was the failure of HBO's competitors to follow suit for months or even years. Although entrepreneur Ted Turner began satellite distribution from his Atlanta "superstation" WTBS, in December 1976, no other subscription service appeared until Viacom put Showtime on satellite in March 1978, two and a half years after HBO's move. By then, HBO had 1.5 million subscribers in 45 states.

Despite all, 1976 was a crisis year for HBO. The blight that had nearly killed HBO three years earlier hit again: subscribers were canceling—disconnecting—by the thousands. This time, at least, new viewers signed up faster than old viewers canceled, so subscriber totals continued to rise, but at a slower rate. During 1976, a staggering 320,000 subscribers canceled; HBO was left with only 600,000. Losses for the year, HBO's worst ever, were $5.9 million. But from that low point HBO began to ascend rapidly. In the third quarter of 1977, five years after its birth, HBO showed its first profit, and for the full year earned $1,7 million.

To bolster HBO management, Munro in 1976 asked Levin, who had been president and chief executive, to change his title to chairman and chief executive, thus making way for a new president: Nick Nicholas. In 12 years at Time Inc., Nicholas, 36, had held seven jobs, mainly in finance, but also in research and development and in president Shepley's office as an assistant. He had worked out many of the mind-bending financial arrangements that kept Manhattan Cable and HBO alive in its early days, and since January 1974 he had been president of Manhattan Cable.

Now, as president of HBO, Nicholas found an organization that had grown too fast: "I faced the unpleasant task of firing virtually

502

every officer except Jim Heyworth." He brought in Austin Furst, then 32, as programming vice president; Tony Cox, 34, to look after the affiliates; Peter Gross, 30, to handle the networks' many legal matters; Sean McCarthy, 33, as a financial specialist; and Michael Fuchs, 30, as director of special programming. As a young attorney, Fuchs had specialized in show-business law. At HBO he started with sports programming and worked his way up to chief programmer, in the course of which he developed a reputation as a hard-driving dealmaker. Shrewd, witty and aggressive, he became a force both feared and envied in the Hollywood world. By 1984 he would be chief executive officer of HBO.

Furst is credited by Nicholas with having been "singlehandedly responsible for turning HBO around" after the 1976 decline. A former Procter & Gamble man whose Time Inc. career had centered on magazine circulation, Furst introduced an analytical approach at HBO. HBO was already measuring audience size for various programs; Furst put it to gauging also whether audiences liked the shows. A Total Subscriber Satisfaction (TSS) index was devised combining the two measures: if 60 percent of HBO's total audience watched a program, for example, and 50 percent liked it very much, its TSS rating was 30 (50 percent of 60 percent is 30). Entire schedules could be compared by their total TSS ratings. Furst made some changes in HBO's scheduling system to ease subscriber dissatisfactions, and churn also was brought under control, though it remained a problem.

Events finally began to go HBO's way. Late in 1976 the FCC agreed to change the rules affecting satellite transmissions to permit receiving dishes only 4.5 meters in diameter. Recalled Nicholas: "The cost saving, at the time about $60,000 per dish, was important, but not especially significant when amortized over a period of years. The timing, however, was such that it became very important in getting cable operators to make the decision [to buy a receiving antenna] then, instead of later." Subscriber totals began to shoot up.

The following March came another boost for cable. The U.S. Court of Appeals for the District of Columbia handed down a decision invalidating several FCC rules that had tightly restricted cable TV programming. These rules had been founded in fears, encouraged (some said invented) by the commercial broadcasters, that cable would siphon off programs from over-the-air TV and force people to pay for them. Among other things, the FCC kept cable systems from showing movies that were between three and ten years

503

old—the movies most often shown on broadcast channels—and had also imposed complex restrictions on the cable televising of sports. With the FCC rules declared "grossly overbroad" and "arbitrary, capricious and unauthorized by law," HBO was free, finally, to carry the recent movies and major sports events that soon became its strongest attractions.

Abolishing the restrictive rules benefited not only HBO, but also its growing competitors. With the increasing importance of the cable-TV market, the movie companies moved to gain a firm control of distribution. Therefore, HBO began to take a bolder, more creative approach to acquiring movies, not always to the movie producers' pleasure. One approach that Furst used was to pay flat fees instead of a sum based on subscriber totals. Grown large and powerful, HBO could flex its muscles here; grumbling, the producers went along.

Before 1976, HBO had put no money into theatrical films, dealing instead for distribution rights after production. That year, however, Time Inc., in the interest of HBO, put $5 million into Columbia Pictures, for a percentage based on proceeds of "selected pictures"; in the same agreement HBO was licensed to distribute a number of Columbia movies. In 1978, HBO began "prebuying" films—another Furst strategy—in which the network bought pay-TV rights to theatrical movies before the first frame was shot. HBO's first prebuys were *The Bell Jar, Wild Geese* and *Watership Down*. As the prebuying strategy continued under Fuchs, investments were made in such films as *On Golden Pond, Sophie's Choice* and *A Passage to India;* all garnered Academy Awards. With another film, *The Terry Fox Story,* HBO also began making investments in movies to be shown on HBO before theatrical release. Along with investments in productions by others, HBO generated a number of original series and specials. *Standing Room Only,* a showcase for entertainers, was one; a Bette Midler show in this series, in 1977, won the first National Cable Association's pay-TV program award. *Consumer Reports Presents* was an attempt at public service programming, produced in conjunction with *Consumer Reports* magazine. For children, HBO offered *Fraggle Rock,* created by Jim Henson of Muppets fame.

HBO's success was a large factor in the move Time Inc. made in 1977 to reverse its policy of four years earlier, when it had sold off its other cable interests to ATC. With the intent of becoming a major player in the operating and ownership end of cable, Time Inc. now bid for ATC itself.

504

The cable firm had been founded in 1968 by Monroe M. (Monte) Rifkin, then 38. In the early 1950s, as an accountant with Touche, Ross, he had been assigned to the account of TelePrompTer Corp., makers of the devices from which TV performers could read their scripts (without appearing to). Joining TelePrompTer a few years later, Rifkin rose quickly to executive vice president. In 1959 he persuaded the company to get into cable; it eventually became one of the nation's largest system owners. In 1962, Rifkin, an entrepreneur at heart, resigned to team up with Bill Daniels, a Denver-based cable investor and broker. Subsequently going off on his own, Rifkin lined up a group of cable companies to start ATC. ATC grew fast by bidding on new franchises and buying existing systems. Rifkin, a no-nonsense, bottom-line oriented manager, turned his fledgling company into one of the largest and best-managed multiple system operations in the country. By 1973, when it bought Time Inc.'s properties, ATC's annual revenues exceeded $20 million. By 1977 they had risen to $53 million and profits had tripled.

In Time Inc.'s decision to bid for ATC there had been, as Munro described it later, a certain element of chance. Specifically, a freak snowstorm in Florida. In January 1977, Munro and a number of video executives were gathered at the Holiday Inn in Jupiter for a brainstorming session. Sunny weather might have encouraged some tennis playing as well; instead, snow kept everyone indoors, and during the conversation, the idea of acquiring ATC emerged. Putting the proposition to Heiskell and Shepley the following month, Munro cited not only ATC's impressive progress, but also some significant industry trends:

> Cable is evolving into a separate communications medium with its own program originations and is no longer viewed as simply a retransmission carrier of broadcast television signals. Cable's basic subscriber rates have been substantially increased, while costly and unrealistic franchises have been avoided, resulting in improved earnings industry-wide.

The opportunity for suggesting acquisition to ATC arose soon. HBO was taping a Phyllis Diller performance in Denver and Munro asked Nicholas, who would be at the taping, to approach Rifkin. Rifkin was agreeable. Agreement on price was harder to reach; after a few weeks, talks between the two companies broke off. During the summer, Time Inc.'s management decided to increase its existing 11 percent stake in ATC to 20 percent and thus get the benefit of an accounting rule that allows a company owning between

20 percent and 50 percent of another company to add the appropriate fraction of that company's profits to its own.

In December Munro again proposed marriage. Once more, the negotiators gathered in a Time Inc. suite at the Hotel Dorset in New York. Again impasse loomed. The Time Inc. team, led by Munro and Nicholas, was under firm orders from Shepley not to offer more than $46 a share; ATC appeared unwilling to accept less than $52. The difference amounted to about $30 million. After several hours the session ended in apparent failure, and the Time Inc. team returned for a postmortem in Shepley's office. Shepley startled the group by saying, "Well, go ahead and split the difference if you can make the deal." Within an hour, one of the ATC negotiators independently called Nicholas and suggested the same. It turned out that Shepley had been willing from the start to go above $46 a share but had not told his negotiators for fear it would influence the bargaining.

The slightly complicated deal was announced on December 22, 1977. ATC's shareholders would get 1.55 shares of new Time Inc. convertible preferred stock for each of their ATC common shares, putting the total value of the transaction at about $150 million. Nearly a year of FCC and IRS formalities followed. On November 14, 1978, the same day that Time Inc. officially acquired Inland Container Corp. (see chapter 18), ATC became a part of Time Inc.

The merger was a boon to both companies. For ATC, the Time Inc. association offered access to capital; as Trygve Myhren, then vice president at ATC, subsequently explained, "We are an industry of small companies which paradoxically are capital intensive. Small companies that are capital intensive have a tendency to get themselves in trouble at some point . . . so having the kind of financial power that a Time Inc. had was important." For Time Inc., the happy result was an almost immediate rise in ATC profits.

Monte Rifkin, whose continued presence as head of ATC had been a precondition of Time Inc.'s acquisition of the company, stayed on until his contract expired in 1982. Although he had been happy to see ATC join Time Inc., he felt fettered; as he put it later, "it is difficult for an entrepreneur to function within the strictures of a large corporation." The parting was amicable. Rifkin returned to freelance investments in cable systems.

Replacing him as ATC's chief executive was Trygve Myhren, then 45, who would become the architect of ATC's clustering strategy, a tactic adopted after 1980 to escape the punishing battles for new cable franchises in the large city areas. The competition had become so intense, and the cities' demand for a share of the revenues so voracious, that by the time a company won a franchise it could well have promised away any chance of profit (in one case an applicant even promised to plant 20,000 trees along the city's streets). Deciding that such fights were not worth fighting, ATC concentrated instead on buying already functioning systems and consolidating them into clusters, thus achieving economies of scale and decentralizing management.

By the time ATC formally became part of Time Inc. in late 1978, HBO's success was already inspiring competition. First to follow HBO was Showtime, started in 1976 by Viacom, a program syndication and cable company that had been spun off earlier from CBS by FCC order. In itself, Showtime presented no threat to HBO. But in January 1979 the picture changed; TelePrompTer bought half of Showtime, immediately ceased offering HBO programming and switched to Showtime instead. The switch cost HBO 290,000 subscribers—a heavy blow that could have destroyed it two years earlier. Strong enough now to survive, HBO regained the lost subscribers within a few months. More competition materialized in April 1979 when Warner Communications began satellite distribution of a service called forthrightly The Movie Channel. It too nibbled at HBO's market, though not as successfully as Showtime.

HBO, still holding more than 70 percent of the pay-cable business, moved to press its competitive advantage, announcing a new service called Take 2, aimed at the so-called "untouchables" who subscribed to no pay service whatever. On the theory that these nonsubscribers shunned existing services because they were priced too high or scheduled too much "adult" programming, Take 2 offered only the G- and PG-rated films from HBO. (HBO did not offer X-rated movies; it did, however, show R-rated films.) The subscription charge was low: $4 a month, about half as much as HBO. Take 2 was a failure; later research showed its reasoning was wrong. Some people simply did not like the idea of pay TV, nor did they want a slimmed-down version of HBO at a lower price.

As Take 2 faltered, a more promising opportunity for a second pay service was becoming apparent. Experience had taught the industry an unexpected lesson. It had been generally assumed that the competing pay services would take subscribers away from one another. In practice, though, it turned out that many viewers would hungrily subscribe to two services, and quite a few would even take three. If people wanted another service, shouldn't HBO provide it? Extensive research resulted in the launching, in August 1980, of Cinemax, a service planned to complement HBO, showing family and children's movies in the daytime, foreign and R-rated films at night. Within three years Cinemax had 2 million subscribers, virtually all of whom also subscribed to HBO, but it still ranked fourth behind Showtime, The Movie Channel and its parent, HBO. In the 1980s, Time Inc. would begin an urgent effort to strengthen Cinemax by changing its programming mix and building up its subscriber list.

Further bolstering HBO's position was the position taken by the Justice Department. HBO's preeminence in the pay-TV market had given it powerful leverage in bargaining with the studios; the studios complained to the Justice Department that HBO had virtual monopoly power to force film prices down. When the Justice Department did not prosecute, the studios moved to create their own competition to HBO. Getty Oil and four movie companies—Columbia, MCA, 20th Century-Fox and Paramount—combined to form Premiere, a pay-cable service that would show films produced by its owners. The alliance could have damaged HBO gravely; the Justice Department, following complaints by HBO and others, brought action under the antitrust rules. In December 1980 a federal court issued a preliminary injunction against the start-up of Premiere on the grounds that it appeared to be a combination in restraint of trade. Six months later, Premiere was dissolved.

While the studios probed for entry into pay TV, HBO continued exploring ways of getting into moviemaking. Near the end of 1982, with CBS and Columbia Pictures as its partners, HBO formed Tri-Star Pictures. Hollywood's newest film studio, Tri-Star was a logical extension of HBO's system of prebuying films, and offered it a badly needed source of new programming. All three owners shared in the total profits; HBO for its part, acquired pay-TV rights to all of Tri-Star's product. Notable among the films Tri-Star produced were *Places in the Heart, The Natural* and *The Muppets Take Manhattan.* HBO also joined an enterprise called Silver Screen Partners through which stouthearted individual investors could put money into a fund for financing films.

Top management changes at Time Inc. in 1980 had a ripple effect on HBO. With Munro's move upstairs, Levin became head of the video group. When Levin had made his first presentations on behalf of HBO, Heiskell was inclined to refer to him as "a snake-oil salesman." More recently, when Levin's name was mentioned, Heiskell was given to looking off into the distance and saying quietly, "There is *no one* like Jerry Levin."

At HBO, Nicholas, already president, added Levin's old titles of chairman and chief executive. HBO's growth continued. From 4 million-plus subscribers in 1979, it went to more than 6 million in 1980, and in the next few years would add millions more. By its tenth anniversary, in 1982, HBO was recognized, respected and almost as well known as the three commercial networks, or, for that matter, as Time Inc.'s magazines.

With HBO leading the way, all of Time Inc.'s video ventures entered the 1980s in far healthier shape than anyone could have hoped a few years earlier. ATC, strong and profitable, grew impressively more so, ranking either first or second in size among all cable companies in the nation (leadership shifted between ATC and Telecommunications, Inc., a Denver-based competitor). Since turning the corner in 1976, Manhattan Cable also had become a solid money-maker. Thayer Bigelow, 36, Manhattan's executive vice president, who would later become Time Inc.'s chief financial officer, took the cable subsidiary over from Nick Nicholas in 1976. In late 1979 Bigelow was succeeded by John Gault, a senior vice president of ATC.

The rapid growth of the video group's profits, boosted enormously by the ATC acquisition, put it ahead of magazines for the first time in 1980, although with the contribution of Time-Life Books, publishing still led video. That year video earned $72.5 million before taxes; magazines $56.5 million; book publishing $40.3 million.

Magazine profits rebounded the next year, nearly doubling, but the fact that video now challenged publishing's overall position within the company set up an inherent rivalry. Levin termed HBO "a form of video publishing," adding, "and that's something we're comfortable with at Time Inc." He may have been too sanguine. The cultures of magazine publishing and pay television did not easily mix. Magazine executives were uncertain what to make of the brash young newcomers in pay television. "The metabolism is different," explained HBO's Fuchs. "Compared to Time Inc., we're overly aggressive and overly arrogant. It is the rhythm of our business. Publishing is more gentlemanly. This is due to the uncertainty of the creative side of our business. The element of risk is greater in filmmaking than in magazine writing and editing. A magazine article that fails is neither as costly nor as visible as a film that fails." The magazines' editorial staffers tended to think of the people at HBO as "market oriented," as exclusively concerned with making products that sold, while regarding themselves as "creative" and concerned with the quality, integrity and social usefulness of their product. The distinction was at best overdrawn. Constraints applied on both sides. HBO's television programmers operated with the knowledge that well-made movies tended to perform better at the box office; the magazine editors could not, for their part, simply ignore popular taste. In that sense, magazine people had to be market-oriented too. Still, it remained true that there was a vast difference between entertainment and information, and that the numbers reached by television and pay cable were far larger, and therefore dictated a far broader appeal, than was the case with the relatively elite magazines of Time Inc.

Rather ironically, it was HBO's marketing miscalculation that caused a severe setback in the growth of video profits beginning in late 1983. An expected increase in the number of subscribers did not materialize; HBO found itself in a classic squeeze between high fixed costs, in this case expensive long-term contracts for movie rights, and smaller projected audiences, hence smaller revenues. "Management overreached," was the verdict of one high-ranking Time Inc. executive.

HBO's reversals had several causes. Hungry for programming to fill its schedules, HBO had acquired all the films it could lay hands on, contracting expensively for exclusive rights. Exclusivity proved not to be a big draw—subscribers often failed to distinguish between one pay service and another—and the lag in subscriber enrollment worsened. This lag reflected first, tougher competition not only from other cable channels but also from the networks, which fought back with mini-series and other special programs; second, the slowing pace of new cable construction, which could provide new audiences for HBO; and third, the increasing use of video cassettes in the home. Growth slowed and by 1984 video's pretax profits had declined slightly from the previous year's $212 million.

Time Inc. and HBO managements moved swiftly to limit the damage. HBO's chief executive, Frank Biondi, who had been with HBO since 1978 and was one of the architects of a highly expensive, exclusive agreement for rights to Columbia Pictures films, was replaced by Michael Fuchs. Efforts were made to reopen and revise some of the movie contracts. HBO began a process of "down-sizing" its business so as to trim payrolls and other costs.

Even though Time Inc. owned one of the nation's largest cable tele-

510

vision companies and two pay-television networks, it continued to expand its search for new modes of delivering television to the consumer. In 1981 the company purchased a one-third interest in USA Network, an advertiser-supported cable programming service; began also to develop teletext, a system for transmitting information to subscribers in the form of printed words and graphics; and ventured into subscription television, familiarly known as STV. Although the USA Network was not immediately profitable, a turnaround was expected. The teletext experiment was discontinued after three years, but the company continued to be interested in it as a business for the future.

The STV venture was a quick and expensive failure, one of the costliest in Time Inc.'s history, in which $87.4 million was lost over a three-year period. STV involved conventional over-the-air broadcasts but with the signal electronically scrambled; a decoding device was attached to the subscriber's TV set. Time Inc. got into STV via ATC, which had entered joint ventures to provide the service in Boston and Dallas and was operating a wholly owned STV service in Cleveland. Subsequently, the Time Inc. interests were grouped as Preview Subscription Television Inc., with Levin as board chairman and Nate Garner as president. Garner, experienced in marketing for Time Distribution Services, had been introduced to video when he helped with the disbanding of Time-Life Films.

Time Inc. was not alone in its unhappy STV experience; almost all firms venturing into the field lost money. The most frequently mentioned cause of failure was the competition from cable, which offered several channels, whereas STV restricted subscribers to a single broadcast channel. Blame was also put on technical snafus and unexpectedly high start-up costs. The combined subscriber base of Preview STV's three services reached 125,000 in 1981. After that it slid downhill. By the end of 1983, after selling all three, Time Inc. announced that it was getting out of the business.

The STV experience had the effect of reinforcing the company's belief that cable television was "a superior distribution system for information and entertainment." But there would continue to be an accent on flexibility and experimentation. The company planned to continue exploring the possibilities in direct broadcasting by satellite, the old idea of pay-per-view would be reexamined, and there would be new interest in cassettes. One way or another, Time Inc.'s commitment to TV seemed bound to last, but as in the past, it would be difficult at times to predict the directions it would take.

Fallen Star

ARLY IN 1974, Andrew Heiskell had received a telephone
call from James (Scotty) Reston, Washington columnist for
the New York *Times*: Would Time Inc. help in averting a
takeover of Washington's family-owned evening newspaper, the
Star, by an outsider to publishing, an outsider to Washington, a
Texan at that? The bidder in question was Joe L. Allbritton, 49, a
bantam-sized Houston lawyer with boundless energy and proven
financial dexterity, worth over $100 million by his own estimate,
with interests in banking, insurance, stock brokerage, a chain of
mortuaries in California and a hotel group in Europe comprising the
Savoy, the Connaught and Claridge's in London and the Lancaster
in Paris.

Allbritton's reported interest in the *Star* had rekindled Time
Inc.'s. Although the company was no longer searching actively for
newspaper properties, the idea of owning a paper in Washington
and having "a voice in the nation's capital" still held powerful
appeal. Donovan had started his journalistic career there before
World War II; Shepley, as Washington bureau chief during the
1950s, had been an important figure on the local scene.

In the late 1960s, when its newspaper search had been in full
swing, Time Inc. had taken a look at the *Star*. But neither the Kauff-
mann nor the Noyes families, descendants of the two men who had

bought into the *Star* in 1867, 15 years after its founding, was quite ready to sell. After Reston's telephoned alert, however, Heiskell suggested a second look. That March, a group including Time Inc.'s treasurer Clifford Grum, went down to survey the *Star* and its affiliated television and radio stations: WMAL in Washington; WLVA in Lynchburg, Virginia; and WCIV in Charleston, South Carolina. The scouts' conclusions were negative: the money-making possibilities of the broadcasting holdings were canceled out by a money-losing newspaper.

Established as the *Evening Star* in 1852, when Washington was the capital of a nation of 31 states and 23 million inhabitants, the paper had grown with the city. By World War I it was Washington's most powerful daily; by World War II it led all papers in the country in total advertising linage. It was "the paper of establishment Washington, of old Washington, of Chevy Chase Club Washington, of Republican Washington," as one commentator described it.

Then in 1954 the *Star* lost its lead. The Washington *Post* moved ahead by buying out the round-the-clock Washington *Times-Herald*, acquiring circulation leadership and, more valuable, a monopoly in the morning field. Nationwide, morning papers had been gaining on their afternoon rivals. Although their news was always yesterday's, they were delivered when traffic was light, and arrived for breakfast reading. Afternoon papers, trucked through city streets at rush hour, were being forced to go to press earlier and earlier, and were losing their main advantage of timeliness. For most people, evening television was supplanting the afternoon paper as the summary of that day's events. In Washington, where the principal industry was government and a large commuting population traveled mainly by automobile, the morning newspaper readership habit was very strong.

Defensively, in 1972, the *Star* bought out its afternoon competition, the tabloid *Daily News*. Circulation rose to an all-time high of 418,000 vs. the *Post*'s 535,000, then fell back. Ad linage followed circulation down. By 1974 the *Star* had only 32.5 percent of total newspaper advertising in Washington.

Complicating the *Star*'s difficulties were what the Time Inc. survey group considered weak management and unacceptable union featherbedding. Raymond J. Mitchell, an experienced newspaper executive who had headed Time Inc.'s Pioneer Press chain from 1972 to 1974, toured the *Star*'s circulation, advertising and mechanical departments and came away with an estimate that physical production costs were eating up nearly three-fifths of the paper's operating revenues. "They're overstaffed till hell won't have it," Mitchell reported. The *Star* management had been unable to make payroll savings even with automation. Advertising sales and circulation offices were "stacked with low producers with high seniority." Mitchell cited the situation in one mechanical department:

> The press room . . . configuration is excellent but manning is hell. It was hard to get a count of the people in the reel room since most of them were lying around resting on newsprint rolls. The others were sitting on boxes reading magazines and numbered about 20. This, in spite of the fact that they have automatic on all reels. I find, too, that if they run color, rather than just calling in a crew for one unit to wash up the unit, they must call in the entire crew so that if they had color on one unit and ran an eight-unit press, they would have to call in a crew for seven units to watch the crew on the one unit wash up the press.

Time Inc.'s ardor waned. In forwarding Mitchell's memo on the *Star* to Donovan, Heiskell added a note: "In case you thought I was overly pessimistic, glance at this disaster report." On April 8, 1974, Heiskell informed the *Star* management of Time Inc.'s disinclination to buy. The following day came announcement of the paper's sale to Allbritton. The Texan was to pay $25 million for a 37 percent controlling interest in the newspaper and broadcasting properties, with an option to buy more.

The purchase presented Allbritton with one large problem: the FCC's "one to a market" ruling, prohibiting new acquisitions of both newspaper and broadcast properties in the same market area. Allbritton petitioned for a waiver, claiming that profit from the Washington television station—which he subsequently rebaptized with his initials, WJLA—was "critical" to the *Star*'s survival. He won a three-year extension, until February 1979, to dispose of the Washington station. But the prospect of forced divestiture, he later declared in an affidavit to the FCC, provoked "dozens" of inquiries about the broadcast properties, as well as overtures from "a variety of people, including . . . Time Inc." regarding the newspaper.

Stimulating this renewed interest in the *Star* was its apparent improvement under Allbritton's ownership; one who had been watching the situation was Washington attorney and Time Inc. director Sol M. Linowitz, who felt the *Star* offered opportunities for the company. Allbritton had brought in a new editor from the Los

Angeles *Times*, James G. Bellows, formerly editor of the New York
Herald Tribune. Bellows's formula for the *Star* was to dress it up—
get the paper talked about. Front-page features blossomed. Big-
name authors such as Larry King, Jimmy Breslin and Willie Morris
were brought to the *Star* for short stints to write on subjects of their
choice. Pulitzer Prize-winning cartoonist Pat Oliphant was lured
away from the Denver *Post*, and Edwin M. Yoder Jr., a scholarly
North Carolina newspaperman, formerly a history professor at the
University of North Carolina, was put in charge of the *Star*'s editorial page. Most popular of the innovations was a spicy gossip
column, "The Ear" by Diana McLellan, which became an immediate hit—the talk of Washington.

Meanwhile, Allbritton had begun tackling the payroll bloat that
had caused Time Inc. to back off from the *Star* earlier. Explained
Shepley: "Time Inc. didn't want to do the ruthless job that had to
be done, fire all those people." Allbritton did the job, managing to
force substantial wage and manning concessions from the *Star*'s
unions, and also to secure layoffs and early retirement of some 200
editorial and mechanical employees.

Briefly during this period, the *Star* enjoyed a competitive respite.
In October 1975, pressmen at the O.P.—the Other Paper, as the
Star referred to the rival Washington *Post*—went on strike. The
Post, greatly shrunk, was printed outside Washington and trucked
in, but enough *Post* advertising was diverted for the *Star* to show its
first profitable month in five years. Much of that windfall disappeared as the *Post* defeated the strike—breaking the *Post*'s pressmen's union in the process—and resumed printing at its own plant.

At the *Star*, the financial squeeze that Allbritton was applying
eventually provoked Bellows's resignation. The paper's losses were
being slowed, however, and in late 1976, through an intermediary,
Allbritton passed word that, as Shepley recalled, "he felt he
had . . . a marketable property and was willing to sell," since he still
faced the FCC-imposed choice between the *Star* and station WJLA.
At dinner subsequently with Heiskell, Shepley and Donovan in New
York, Allbritton named his price: $35 million in cash or stock, $10
million of which would be Time Inc.'s assumption of a loan.

Two months later Allbritton changed his mind. With the concessions he had won from the unions secured by three-year contracts,
he later told the FCC, "I determined [sic] to keep the *Star*" and
trade away WJLA for a comparable broadcast property in Okla-
homa City, KOCO, owned by the Phoenix-based Combined Communications Corporation. In the cc.avoluted *Star* story, this firm's

president, Karl Eller, was to emerge subsequently as a rival bidder against Time Inc. for purchase of the newspaper. (Eller and Combined had made an offer in 1970 to buy Time Inc.'s broadcasting stations. See chapter 16.)

Since the WJLA-KOCO trade appeared unlikely to win early FCC approval, matters shortly took on a new urgency for Allbritton: "I realized that the value of WJLA-TV or the *Star* would be materially reduced if I were forced to a 'fire sale' situation with either of the properties." By September 1977, Allbritton was dickering seriously with Shepley and by the following January, when the FCC gave only a murky assent to Allbritton's proposed trade of television stations, the sense of urgency heightened. "With great reluctance," Allbritton said, "I decided to sell my interest in the Washington *Star* without determining to whom I would sell it."

The sale of the *Star* was finally consummated in four days of three-way long-distance negotiations involving Allbritton, Shepley and Eller. Shepley and Allbritton lunched in Washington on January 30. Allbritton flew back to Texas; on January 31, Eller arrived in Houston to spend the day at Allbritton's home, talking possible terms. While they were there, Shepley called from New York, also to discuss terms. Allbritton restated his previous cash price. Shepley refused, offering stock, but less. Allbritton refused. Shepley offered to trade Pioneer Press, Time Inc.'s profitable Chicago-area suburban newspaper chain. Allbritton refused, Texas style. "That dog won't hunt," he told Shepley. Eller left for the airport, where Allbritton caught him by phone to say he would give him an answer the next day. Allbritton said the same thing to Shepley in New York. Up early the next morning, Allbritton caught Shepley before he left for the office:

> On the morning of February 1, at approximately 6:45 Houston time, I telephoned Mr. Shepley at his home and said that I had decided to sell the *Star* for cash only, in the amount of $20 million—which was less than the figure I had proposed earlier—if that would be of interest to Time Inc. I asked that Mr. Shepley let me know of his decision that afternoon.

Shepley called back that afternoon. The executive committee of the Time Inc. board had given its approval, he said, and the cash terms were agreed upon in a handshake deal the following day, February 2, when Allbritton flew to New York. Time Inc. would also assume $8 million of *Star* debt, and Allbritton would remain as the *Star*'s publisher "for a period of no less than five years."

516

Filing to *Time*'s Press section the next day, the Washington bureau's Arthur White reported the reaction in the capital:

The Washington *Star*'s Diana McLellan, writer of its best feature, the sassy "Ear" column, came sashaying to work about 10:00 a.m. today through the *Star* lobby and there she was buttonholed by a Washington *Post* reporter . . . "Oh, God, sold to whom?" cried Diana, fearful that [the *Star*] might have gone to some Frisbee manufacturer. When the *Post* reporter told her Time had bought the *Star*, Diana yelled, "Oh, fantastic! Delicious! Divine!" . . . Then, Diana says, she fainted from sheer joy. (She really didn't.)

So you can see what a great secret this whole deal was—if Washington's favorite gossipist was keeled over at the news. To be sure, there had been whispers about town that Allbritton was in a mood to deal . . . But word that Time had bought the *Star* was blockbuster news today at the *Star*, at the *Post*, and everywhere else.

"Somewhere between ebullient and ecstatic"—so *Time*'s Washington bureau assessed the mood at the *Star*. At the rival *Post*, editor Benjamin C. Bradlee declared: "I'm delighted. It's good news for the city, good news for the *Star*, good news for the newspaper business."

Less euphoric comments came from the financial community. There, speculation focused on the risks Time Inc. was running, particularly in entering the afternoon newspaper field where casualties had been heavy; ten afternoon papers in metropolitan areas had folded since the early 1960s (including, as noted earlier, the onetime object of Time Inc.'s attention, the Newark *Evening News*). By ominous coincidence, the same day that the company announced its intended acquisition of the *Star*, the demise of still another afternoon daily was announced: the 102-year-old Chicago *Daily News*, one of the papers most honored for its journalism but no longer able to counter the market trend.

Time Inc.'s entry into the territory of its archrival also invited comment. The obvious symmetry—*Time* and the Washington *Star*, *Newsweek* and the Washington *Post*—provoked the inevitable observation by the *Wall Street Journal* that the transaction "would open a second major competitive front between the publishing empires that control the nation's two leading weekly newsmagazines. . . Time Inc. would reap big psychic rewards from building the *Star* into a formidable competitor of the Washington *Post*.

And *Time* would certainly lose prestige if, with its record of publishing potency, it proves unable to shake the *Post*'s dominance."

On February 16, the full Time Inc. board met to ratify the decision to buy the *Star*. Only a few questions were raised about the wisdom of the purchase. Recalling the session, Radcliffe College president Matina Horner, one of the newer outside directors, remarked later in a Washington *Post* interview:

> Here was a basically philosophical discussion shaping a management decision. I thought decisions were made strictly and only on the bottom line. They had the courage of their convictions. That impress[ed] me.

Shepley described the purchase as a "special situation"—not the prelude to other daily newspaper acquisitions—and deemed the price of the *Star* as low compared with that of other newspapers recently offered for sale. He acknowledged the paper's recent difficulties: "Advertisers were reluctant to purchase space in what was viewed as a sick newspaper." However, with a "good market share"—40 percent—the *Star* could earn between $10 million and $20 million. The corporate secretary's minutes of the board meeting continued:

> [Mr. Shepley] stated that the corporation's group vice presidents and editors were unanimously in favor of the acquisition and asked Mr. Donovan for his comments. Mr. Donovan stated that, from an editorial standpoint, the *Star* was a very attractive proposition. He observed that the proposed acquisition had been well received in the Washington news bureau and in the Time Inc. editorial staff generally, who viewed the acquisition as being professionally stimulating . . . The public opinion climate in the District of Columbia was clearly in favor of the continuation of a newspaper which from time to time would set forth views different from those of the Washington *Post*. He also stated he thought a number of things could be done with the paper to make it better without untoward expense.

Before the vote was taken, Heiskell answered questions:

> Mr. Freeman [Gaylord A. Freeman, First National Bank of Chicago] observed that it was still not certain as to why management wanted to acquire the *Star*. [Mr. Heiskell] stated that if the *Star* were successful, the acquisition would be a great

518

bargain . . . He noted that an important reason why management wanted to acquire the *Star* was in order to obtain a significant editorial voice in the District of Columbia. More and more our fate is being determined in Washington. Mr. Warner [Rawleigh Warner Jr., Mobil Corporation] stated that he concurred . . .

After some further discussion Mr. Watson [Thomas J. Watson Jr., IBM] proposed a resolution approving the acquisition . . . Mr. Warner seconded, observing that in so doing he was operating on the assumption that for the next five years the *Star* would either lose money or barely break even . . . Thereupon, on motion duly made and seconded, the . . . resolution was unanimously adopted.

On March 15, 1978, Time Inc. bought the stock of the Evening Star Newspaper Company from Allbritton's Washington Star Communications, Inc. Company lawyers advised a stock purchase rather than acquisition of assets in order to preserve the wage and manning agreements that Allbritton, as owner of the *Star*, had negotiated with its labor union. There was another change from the agreement originally proposed to the Time Inc. directors; it reflected a closer look at the *Star*'s books. Examination of the *Star*'s financial condition with the "due diligence" customary in such transactions had revealed a discrepancy that Allbritton, to preserve his deal with Time Inc., now offered to make up. The minutes of the March board meeting reported the details:

> As a result of the due diligence investigation, it had been determined that whereas budgetary projections furnished by the *Star* had indicated a breakeven or modest profit for the fiscal year ending September 30, 1978, it now appeared that there would be a loss. [Mr. Shepley] stated that the Washington Star Communications, Inc. had agreed to underwrite any operating loss, from the 12-month period ending September 30, 1978, up to a maximum of $4 million and that accordingly $4 million of the purchase price had been placed in escrow until determination had been effected by the corporation's accountants.

Shortly after this $4 million reduction in the *Star*'s purchase price (the money remained with Time Inc.), there was another development that the company also counted as a gain. In May, after only ten weeks, Allbritton quit as the *Star*'s publisher, thus resolving a situation that had been an awkward one from the beginning. Precip-

519

itating Allbritton's action was the impending deadline he faced under the FCC's order that he divest himself of either WJLA or the *Star*; by the FCC's interpretation, he still retained publishing "control" of the paper despite having sold his stock. Allbritton chose the station over the paper, taking with him an assortment of luxury furnishings from the *Star* building on Virginia Avenue—the inventory noted such items as "48 doilies, white linen, 5½ inches" and "bottle carrier, unusual and rare antique Georgian mahogany with handle"—that were personal property. As befit the *Star*'s circumstances, Time Inc. refurnished the offices in less lavish style.

It was a vastly unequal struggle that the company faced in Washington. The main element in the *Star*'s favor was its position as alternative to the Washington *Post*. The *Post* had a vigorous personality, and its coverage of Watergate had elevated the paper to a status just short of holy writ, in the eyes of some. It was "must" reading for most Washingtonians for its news coverage and for its advertising, especially the classifieds; the *Post* was the place to buy, sell, rent, hire. But its liberal politics and often opinionated reporting aroused strong feelings locally. Many Washingtonians detested the paper. Some merchants regarded the *Post*'s monopoly of local advertising disquieting; the *Star* served as a check on the *Post*'s linage rates.

Whether the *Star*, under Time Inc. ownership, could exploit this feeling and narrow the *Post*'s enormous lead remained to be seen. The corporate record suggests that the difficulties ahead were not fully appreciated before Time Inc. went into the venture. Donovan conceded as much later. "We didn't realize the momentum of the *Post*," he said. "We didn't quite figure on the dynamics of a two-paper market where one paper is so strong."

As the company took over the paper, circulation as reported to the Audit Bureau of Circulations stood at 329,000 daily and 316,000 Sunday, vs. 562,000 and 801,000, respectively, for the Washington *Post*. The *Post*'s share of total advertising linage was 71.9 percent; the *Star*'s 28.1 percent. In the view of newspaper analysts, the critical minimum is about 30 percent; below that, a newspaper loses attraction for advertisers. As it was, much of the *Star*'s advertising was being sold as "add on" to the *Post*. Also, by the *Star*'s own estimate, half of its subscribers took the *Post* as well, further devaluing the *Star*'s advertising appeal.

On the production side, the *Star* had a fairly new plant. But its location, in a decayed and crime-ridden section of southeast Washington, was unfavorable—the building had been sited there as part of a civic redevelopment plan—and Time Inc. eventually had to install a $300,000 security system to protect the building and its surrounding parking area. Newspaper deliveries from the plant were hobbled not only by the normal difficulties of afternoon newspaper distribution but also by the union contracts inherited from the previous management. Unlike the *Post*, which relied on independent distributors with a stake in their own businesses, the *Star* used unionized teamsters, driving *Star*-owned trucks, whose salaries were guaranteed regardless of service, and whose delivery procedures were under the union's control. Subscriber complaints ran abnormally high at the *Star*.

Conversion from afternoon to morning publication, for showdown competition with the *Post*, was considered but rejected as impracticable. It was not a move that could have been taken without considerable advance preparation, starting with reorganization of the paper's entire delivery system. Also, there were the *Star*'s present afternoon readers to consider; in a sudden switch they might not stay with the *Star* against the *Post*, with its greater advertising and news content. "We might have lost in the draw," Shepley said. "Our thinking was that the only way to grapple with that problem of morning publication was to sneak up on it, and get a solid base of readers willing to pay for it." For the moment at least, that could not be risked.

Time Inc.'s editorial options were similarly limited. The feature fare that the *Star* offered under Bellows's editorship—"a sidebar paper," Grunwald called it—had obviously not been attractive enough. The paper's circulation was now some 90,000 below its 1973 peak. It was later suggested that the *Star* might have lowered its sights and gone in more for sensationalism. Shepley conceded that this could have been done: "With Congress, you'd have unlimited opportunities. Put a couple of good reporters to work and you'd have a headline every day. But none of us wanted that kind of paper."

No editorial prospectus of the sort Time Inc. produced in launching a magazine was ever prepared for the *Star*. Donovan said the *Star* was considered to be "a pretty good paper," and the corporate aim was to produce "a somewhat improved version of what was already there." As for management, the usual company practice was followed. The paper was to be run by two co-equal executives, an editor and a publisher, thus preserving the church-state separation that applied on the Time Inc. magazines.

521

Murray Gart, whom Donovan chose to be the editor, had questioned this division of powers. Gart had had seven years of newspaper experience before coming to Time Inc., including stints as city editor of the Wichita *Eagle* and news editor of the Wichita *Beacon,* and shortly after the company's purchase of the *Star*, Heiskell had asked his advice on how to run it. Gart recounted, "I told them I'd find a guy like Jim Shepley, with his mixture of editorial and publishing experience and make him the editor-publisher. You just can't run a paper without one guy in charge. Two days later the roof blew off." Shepley, Donovan and Bear all called him into their offices, Gart recalled, to say that the distinction between the editorial and the business side would be maintained at the *Star*.

In effect, though, Shepley, as chairman of the *Star*'s board, was chief executive. Although as corporate president he could not devote full time to the paper, Shepley remained in an overseer's role, maintaining an office in the *Star* building and making frequent trips to Washington to promote the cause of the paper in the local community, where his contacts were extensive. It was widely assumed around the company that Shepley might return permanently to Washington after retirement from Time Inc. to take over active management of the *Star*; Shepley discounted this speculation.

On the publishing side, Allbritton's sudden resignation had forced Time Inc. to make a quick replacement. Shepley turned to George Hoyt, 41, the *Star*'s general manager. A graduate of the University of Oregon business school, Hoyt had run a chain of four Oregon suburban weeklies before joining Time Inc. in 1971 as publisher at Pioneer Press; in 1974 he followed Ray Mitchell as president. A member of the Time Inc. team that had investigated the *Star*'s finances, he had been general manager only a month before he was named publisher. Hoyt recognized the perils: "It was a high-risk job, sure, but do-able, in my view." To fill the general manager's post, the company brought in John Howard, formerly business manager at *Time*.

Gart arrived at the *Star* in June 1978 to take over from Sidney Epstein, a *Star* veteran from the pre-Allbritton days who had been editing the paper since Bellows's departure. Under Gart, Epstein remained with the paper as executive editor, subsequently as associate publisher. In February 1979, William F. McIlwain, previously editor of Hearst's Boston *Herald-American* and before that editor of *Newsday* on Long Island, was brought in as Gart's deputy and later became executive managing editor. Yoder remained as editorial page editor. Later to join the *Star* as managing editors on the day and night shifts, respectively, were two *Time* men: Ed Jackson, former *Time* international editor, most recently news editor in the magazine's Washington bureau; and Stan Cloud, former White House correspondent.

Inescapably, the advent of new management at any publication arouses some staff turmoil and invites outside press comment. The nature of the *Star-Post* competition invited more than usual. Gart himself suffered rough, even vicious treatment in the press; through him critics hit also at Time Inc. In a city of Democratic leanings there was a backlog of resentment against the Luce publications remaining from their days of Republican identification. Gart considered the *Star*'s position under his editorship to be independent and centrist; as the 1980 presidential elections approached, the *Star* refrained from endorsing either candidate (the *Post* came out for Jimmy Carter).

Gart was a tough operator, and he had been put into an extraordinarily tough job at the *Star*. He kept the paper under tight control, watching his editors closely, personally directing the front-page makeup and play of stories inside. He favored hard news, concisely told, without editorializing; he disliked stories based on anonymous sources. In the *Star* newsroom, there was grumbling that he was toning down investigative reporting; Gart dismissed the accusations with an expletive. "If you have authority and use it, you're going to churn up feelings," he told an interviewer:

> I don't pull my punches . . . Not everybody on this paper gets to do exactly what they want to do. That's part of my style of running something. It's also partly due to the fact that we're shorthanded and have to be deliberate about the things that we try to get done. If I had a nice fat staff and had the luxury of having a lot of talented people sitting around on the bench, as some newspapers do, the atmosphere might be a little different.*

Gart explicitly ruled out any return to the Bellows approach. "I didn't want to settle for a little glamour and a little froth, and do only the things the *Post* wasn't doing . . . You cannot be a major Washington newspaper without playing major-league journalism," he said. The *Star* had been notably weak on foreign news, relying

*Stout, Richard T. and Tinkelman, Joseph, "Is Time Running Out on the Washington Star?" *The Washingtonian*, August, 1981.

mainly on the wire services. The Time-Life News Service, with its correspondents worldwide, offered valuable new resources. News service material, virtually all of it filed to *Time*, was available to *Time*'s editors in New York starting Wednesday or Thursday, yet did not reach the magazine's readers until the following Monday; interim use by the *Star* seemed logical and feasible. It was suggested that the paper could also assign news service reporters on its own, giving the paper coverage tailored to its needs and earning *Time* reporters cherished bylines.

The proposal met with some resistance at *Time* where, as the managing editor wrote Donovan, there were fears that the magazine's Washington readers might feel they were getting "old news because they have read it somewhere—it is demanding too much for them to remember that the source was a *Star* story with a *Time* credit line . . . It might lead to the conclusion that *Newsweek* is a fresher magazine." A compromise was worked out, however, and *Time* correspondents became prolific contributors to the *Star*, which markedly increased the space it devoted to foreign news. Reports credited to the Time-Life News Service began appearing on the front page practically every day.

Still, the *Star*'s staff remained too small for the job it faced. In the last year of Allbritton's regime, the paper's editorial budget was reduced to $8.6 million, vs. $20 million for the *Post*. The staff had been cut 10 percent during the months Time Inc. had been deciding whether to buy the paper, leaving the total number of editorial employees at 225 by midsummer 1978. The *Post*, in contrast, had 490 (and the New York *Times*, also widely read in Washington, more than a thousand). After ten weeks at the *Star*, Gart appealed for funds to add 60 people to the editorial staff. In a confidential memo to Donovan, he explained the mounting staff pressures: "It is difficult or impossible now to require significant [editorial] improvement, when most staffers perform close to their limits simply to keep up with the work load."

Gart got permission to add 20. Although short of what he asked, it was enough to enable him to take his next step—the launching of local editions in the suburbs, where four-fifths of the circulation was located. The *Post* had already begun local sections for Maryland, Virginia and the District inserted into the paper every Thursday. But the *Star*'s plan went further, with special insert sections every day, Monday to Friday, for each of four areas—Fairfax County and the Arlington-Alexandria region of Virginia, Montgomery County and Prince Georges County, Maryland—and a fifth for the District of Columbia itself. These local sections, each with its own logo ("The Fairfax *Star*," "The Montgomery *Star*"), were launched in October 1978. In effect they were small regional dailies, with their own locally based reporters and editors. The *Star* began advertising: "Get a free daily local paper inside your daily paper!"

"Murray is the words man; I'm the numbers man," Hoyt once told a Washington interviewer, explaining the split responsibilities at the *Star*. The numbers Hoyt faced continued to be discouraging—the worst being in circulation. Actual daily sales, as of the month Time Inc. assumed ownership, were only about 308,000 vs. the declared ABC figure of 329,000 representing a six-month average. The first priority had been to stop the circulation slide and recover the hidden loss. Hoyt did not foresee even a tiny profit until 1983. The reasons were many and apparent:

> The staff has been demoralized by the unstable financial situation, rapid succession of managements, lack of monetary incentives, and staff reductions. The middle management is weak resulting from the short tenure of each management group over the last few years. Labor problems and the lack of flexibility and resulting inefficiency permeate almost every department.

Furthermore, Hoyt reported, many capable managers were quitting the paper for better opportunities elsewhere. There were other problems. The *Star*'s advertising sales approach, pitching the paper simply as "add-on" to the *Post*, "is not a viable long-term position." The *Star*'s electronic copy-processing system was old and unable to handle the demands of the proposed local editions. The newspaper delivery system remained unreliable, straitjacketed by union contracts, and more expensive than the *Post*'s. Improvement would prove costly. Time Inc.'s capital investment in the *Star* would ultimately include $400,000 for computerized advertising accounts; $807,000 for new composition equipment to typeset advertising; nearly $900,000 for truck repairs and replacements; $400,000 for computerization in the newspaper mailroom department; nearly $1.2 million in the mechanical departments to upgrade the presses and automate the handling of advertising supplements; more than $600,000 in improvements to the *Star* building, including its new security system.

In October 1978, the company opened negotiations with the paper's ten production and distribution unions and with the Newspaper Guild, representing editorial employees. Initial profit-and-loss forecasts for the *Star*, gloomy as they were, had assumed that these 11 union contracts could be renegotiated in management's favor. Hoyt, reporting to the Time Inc. board that month, outlined the proposed course of action toward the unions in chillingly concise terms:

UNIONS
  Objective
  1. Five-year contracts to accomplish Plan
  2. Flexibility to manage and compete with *Post*
  3. Staff reductions

  Strategy
  —open contracts now
  —feet to fire, close by December 31

  Risk
  —all 11 not signed—don't publish January 1
  —anyone refuse or strike—never reopen

In other words, Time Inc. was presenting the unions with an ultimatum: if all contracts were not signed by December 31, the paper would expire. From the Newspaper Guild, the company wanted a five-year wage freeze and a system of merit raises for upper-level staff. From the other unions, it wanted more flexibility of work rules and the retirement of 80 printers. Little progress was made during the first month of contract talks. Then, in November, Hoyt informed union leaders that the Time Inc. board had approved a $60 million investment in the *Star* over five years—but only on condition of new labor contracts by the December 31 deadline. Without these, Hoyt said, "we are out of business."

Negotiations proceeded slowly, however. In mid-December, Shepley came down to Washington to address a meeting of *Star* union leaders. In some 1,500 words of blunt talk, he reminded them that the *Star*, not the *Post*, was Washington's fully unionized paper: "The Guild, the Teamsters, the Pressmen have no current contracts with the *Post*. If the *Post* achieves a monopoly, what odds do you give the unions of retaining *any* position there?" Nor, he added, was the *Post* now making things easy for the *Star*. "They mean to hold or increase their market share—over our dead bodies if necessary." Shepley then got down to the nub of the situation:

As a matter of plain fact the *Star* requires an infusion of about a million dollars a month of outside cash just to pay its bills, meet its payroll and take the necessary measures to compete with the *Post*. If we continue on our present course—if impasse develops—that million will not be forthcoming for January.

The Washington Star Company will have one and only one option: close down operations, put the real estate on the market and pay off the creditors.

The Time Inc. board has made it clear that the $60 million investment will not be made unless the commitment to this competitive battle with the *Post* is complete, and unless we are given the ability to manage. It would not be responsible of them to authorize the expenditure of Time [Inc.] stockholders' money otherwise, especially when there would be no possibility of succeeding. If there is any doubt in your mind about our resolve, let me assure you that it is firm.

Eight days later the largest of the three Teamsters locals settled on a new contract. Three days after that, the Guild settled, followed by all the others except the printers union, which would lose the most from staff cutbacks. At first the printers doubted the company's resolve, then went to court contending that it would be illegal to close the *Star* because their contract with the paper guaranteed lifetime employment. Hoyt, in response, swore in court that without new contracts from all unions, the *Star* would have to file for bankruptcy. The publisher displayed a bankruptcy petition already prepared. "That was the end for us," the printers' union president declared a few days later. On December 31, just under the wire, the printers and the *Star* reached a new contract, calling for 80 union members to give up their jobs, each to be paid $40,000 in severance.

The contract, however, could not be ratified until 11:00 a.m. on New Year's Day—too late to get an edition out that afternoon. But on January 2 the paper reappeared with a lead editorial declaring: "We're Here to Stay."

It seemed like a reasonable prediction. Labor costs appeared to be coming under control; the foundation had been laid on which to build circulation and advertising growth. In the view of the *Star* staff, Time Inc. had made a promise to keep publishing for five years—an interpretation of the corporate board's commitment that was to cause bitter disagreement between Time Inc. and the staff subsequently.

To promote the *Star*, Time Inc. brought one of its most experienced men in the field, Dick Coffey, who had directed sales promotion for

527

both *Time* and *Life*, out of retirement. An aggressive radio and television advertising campaign was developed, capitalizing on the speed of the *Star*'s afternoon coverage: "Today's News Today." Later, the *Star* began presenting itself as Washington's "unbiased newspaper."

To push the competition harder, Gart maneuvered in May 1979 to capture one of the *Post*'s biggest features. This was the popular comic strip, *Doonesbury*, by Garry Trudeau, whose ribbing of Washington life had made the strip a daily addiction for tens of thousands of readers in the capital. In a complicated deal, Time Inc. bought 20 percent of the Universal Press Syndicate, which distributed *Doonesbury* nationally; in return, UPS took over syndication of columnists such as James J. Kilpatrick, William F. Buckley Jr. and Mary McGrory. The *Star* made sure that every Washingtonian knew of Doonesbury's imminent move. "I'm following Doonesbury to the Washington Star," proclaimed bumper stickers and newsstand and television ads. *Post* editor Ben Bradlee, irked that the *Star* was making hay from a feature currently running in *his* paper, dropped the strip three weeks before the *Star* took it over, leaving the city briefly bereft. Responding to the crisis, local radio and television stations had *Doonesbury* read over the air. The White House added it to President Carter's daily press briefing.

In the midst of the *Doonesbury* hoopla, the *Star* announced bigger news. It would try a morning edition starting July 9. At first it would print only 30,000 copies of the "A.M. Extra" each day, for newsstand sale exclusively. The *Star* made much of the fact that the edition would go to press at 3:30 a.m., an hour after the *Post*'s final edition, and so would include later overseas news. Thus, for the first time, the *Star* would be head to head against the *Post*—a confrontation that Gart had long wanted. More important, it would test the morning market for the *Star*, where initial results were encouraging; after a few months of street sales only, the *Star* began offering delivery to subscribers in selected downtown office buildings.

Despite its limited circulation, the morning edition won favorable comment. "It suggests Time is serious about saving the *Star*," observed John Morton, then a newspaper analyst for the brokerage firm of John Muir & Company. By the publisher's estimate, the A.M. Extra added 12,000 to daily circulation; the acquisition of *Doonesbury*, another 4,000 to 5,000. The impact of the local editions was harder to judge. But for the first time in years, it seemed as though the *Post* might actually feel some heat from its rival.

By November 1979, Shepley was able to paint a fairly favorable picture in a talk before a group of Washington investment analysts. Circulation was up, and "in October national advertising in the *Star* had exceeded $1 million, for an all-time [monthly] record in 127 years of publication."

For the six months ending March 1980, the *Star* reached 346,000 daily circulation, 327,000 on Sunday, the highest ever attained during Time Inc.'s ownership. That month, Gart was able to give Time Inc.'s board of directors a wholly upbeat report on the paper's editorial status. Section by section he described the paper, noting improvements everywhere. Coverage of the arts, the sports pages, as well as national and international news content had been upgraded. The paper had also undergone a complete graphic redesign. Gart called the *Star*'s circulation growth "steady, significant and it comes after a decade or more of almost uninterrupted decline. That's the box office that tells the editors they are doing a lot that is right." The view was not Gart's alone; the New York *Times*'s Scotty Reston felt that the *Star* had become "the finest afternoon newspaper in America."

But the financial drain was not stemmed. In 1979 the paper's loss was $17 million. Not only was income still falling short of expectations, but the paper was hit by two unanticipated items on the cost side: a hike in newsprint prices and the District of Columbia's imposition of workmen's insurance regulations that cost the *Star* $1.1 million in 1980 (and were expected to cost $2 million more in 1981). In early 1980, Charlie Gleason, formerly Bear's deputy, came out of retirement to look at the *Star*'s finances. His prognosis "made Charley Bear blanch," Gleason said. The paper's situation "was somewhere between hopeless and critical." Gleason recalled Shepley's retort: "Yes, but in which direction?"

By midsummer, the *Star*'s upward circulation trend had been reversed. It was selling 20,000 fewer copies per day than it had the year before. There were several reasons. A discount offer with which the paper had sold thousands of subscriptions earlier that year had now expired. A credit squeeze imposed by the Carter administration in order to check inflation affected retail sales and department store advertising budgets in turn; real-estate advertising also shrank as new home construction almost stopped. In addition, the *Star*'s share of the Washington ad market was falling again. The 40 percent market share that Shepley had targeted in discussing the *Star* acquisition with the Time Inc. board of directors was more distant than ever. The lag was particularly apparent in local advertising. Stepping in personally, Shepley wrote letters to several prominent "friends in the business community" asking them, outright, to divert some of their firms' ad dollars to the *Star*.

In the fall of that year came the Time Inc. managerial turnover that made Dick Munro c.e.o. and Ralph Davidson chairman (see chapter 31). Shepley remained as chairman of the Time Inc. board's executive committee and as chairman, also, of the *Star* board.

The new management was specifically committed to improving the company's return on invested capital; inevitably, the investment in the *Star* came up for scrutiny. Munro did not move immediately. Like Shepley, he saw the *Star*'s role in Washington as a serious newspaper, and he agreed with its editorial objectives. He was not for cheapening the paper for survival's sake. "There was no way on God's green earth we were going to do that," he said. But as Munro made plain a few months after assuming the presidency, the company was not going to hang on indefinitely to the *Star* without some sign of improvement. At some point, prudence would have to take over from heroics: "We're not going to march into the sunset with our shoulders squared." A year or so at most was the limit, Munro indicated, before there would have to be a decision.

At the *Star*, meanwhile, the paper's deteriorating condition put added strains on what had been, almost from the outset, a difficult personal and professional relationship between editor and publisher. There were times, associates recalled, when Gart and Hoyt were communicating only through intermediaries. They disagreed on budgets, space allocation in the paper, even news coverage. Gart was putting out a nationally and internationally oriented paper that both Donovan and Grunwald, who succeeded Donovan as editor-in-chief in 1979 (see chapter 31), considered a creditable Time Inc. publication. Any suggestion of interference from the publishing side made Gart bristle. Hoyt would have preferred more of a home-town daily: "The *Star* was a Washington, D.C., newspaper and people didn't buy it to read all about the Middle East. I remember one of our circulation guys complaining, 'I don't have any newsstands in Iran.' "

There was added friction over the installation of a $2,680,000 computerized Logicon copy-processing system which the news staff needed and the publishing side ordered—but which caused problems from the day of its installation in the *Star* newsrooms. It broke down so often that technicians from the manufacturer in California seemed to be flying in constantly to repair it. Text being stored or edited would sometimes just disappear; reporters would have to be called in the middle of the night and asked to remember as much of their vaporized stories as they could. At other times the Logicon system would simply stop operating for hours, adding even more frustration and despair to the situation.

Gart, for his part, was so disheartened that he had already talked with Grunwald that summer of 1980 about taking early retirement (at 55) from Time Inc. It was about then also, in Gart's account of events, that he became convinced that the *Star*'s only chance for survival was to abandon the afternoon field entirely and shift to five-day, morning publication with a weekend edition on Friday taking the place of the former Sunday edition. At least, Gart felt, the funds Time Inc. had committed to the *Star* could be stretched a little further, and the paper preserved as a potentially salable property. Hoyt, with whom Gart discussed the idea, felt otherwise. His retrospective comment:

> It would have been a clear-cut sign of weakness. Advertisers would have folded even more and the *Post* would have moved in for the kill. The buzzards were already flying overhead at that point . . . The newspaper business isn't at all like the magazine business. In the newspaper world, you don't deal with broken wings and hurt animals. You kill them.

In any event, no formal proposal to this effect was presented to Shepley at that time.

The *Star*'s advertising and circulation decline continued into the first months of 1981. To reduce costs, circulation promotion was cut—a move that angered the editorial people and accelerated the decline. "It was at this juncture," Ed Jackson said later, "that the *Post* ad salesmen began using the *Star*'s weakness as a threat to advertisers. 'What are you going to do when the *Star* folds if you don't come with us now?' was their message." By March, the *Star*'s circulation had slipped to 323,000 daily, 294,000 Sunday. The only exception to the trend was in morning edition sales, which were rising. But total advertising linage continued falling to 25.1 percent of the market in May, lower than in 1978.

That month marked the midpoint—in time—in the commitment to the *Star* that Time Inc. had made in negotiating with the *Star*'s labor unions, at the end of 1978. Although the five-year period foreseen then had not yet run out, the money had. Including purchase price, the company had already put some $85 million (unadjusted for taxes) into the *Star*, and no turnaround was in sight.

531

The decision, Munro said later, was "sad"—but not difficult. "When the time came to fish or cut bait, it was a very easy decision. We'd run out of options. You hate to retreat; it's not in our nature. But there was no way we were going to make that thing work. I don't think if we'd had God Almighty down there we could have salvaged it."

One long-shot possibility remained: a joint publishing arrangement with the the Washington *Post* under the Newspaper Preservation Act of 1970. This legislation, permitting agreements between newspapers to share markets and combine production, circulation and certain advertising facilities while retaining their separate editorial identities, had already saved papers in a number of U.S. cities from extinction.* Whether such an agreement could be negotiated in this instance was doubtful. Nonetheless, there was the political aspect to be considered. If the *Post* refused a joint publishing arrangement with the *Star*, it might bear the onus of stilling the last alternative voice in the nation's capital.

Shepley undertook to explore matters with the *Post*'s chairman, Katharine Graham. He entertained few hopes: "Here we were throwing ourselves into their embrace . . . They couldn't possibly accept. But they had to invent grounds. I don't blame them." Discussions with Mrs. Graham and her son Donald, publisher of the *Post*, and with others continued over a period of about two months. During this interval came the June meeting of the Time Inc. board, held in the bracing mountain atmosphere of the A Bar A, a dude ranch in Encampment, Wyoming. There, Shepley went over the *Star*'s financial position at length, describing the company's proposals to the *Post*—essentially, that the *Star* would go to five-day publication, but remain in the afternoon field, leaving the *Post* unchallenged for morning and Sunday readership.

The *Post*'s proposal arrived just before the Time Inc. board's next meeting, a month later in New York. It outlined a complex arrangement which could have kept the *Star* alive a while longer but offered no assurance that its losses would be held within acceptable limits. The *Star* would continue afternoon publication, coexistent with the morning *Post*, but the *Post* would be guaranteed a fixed profit based on monopoly publication. If actual earnings were higher, the *Star* would share them; if lower, the *Star* would reimburse the *Post* for the difference. "A brilliant gimmick," as Shepley described it, the proposal was unacceptable.

After that, Shepley said, he and Grunwald restudied the alterna-

*By mid-1981, joint publishing arrangements were in effect in 23 U.S. cities, including San Francisco, Honolulu, St. Louis, Pittsburgh, and Columbus, Ohio.

tives. Publishing five days a week "would have cut our losses. But Henry and I—and we more than anyone else were for keeping the *Star* alive—both of us, in the end, felt that such a feeble effort wasn't worth it. When it got to the board, I was among those strongly recommending that we close it. Henry was too." Shepley recalled Munro's words that sealed the *Star*'s fate: "Well, I think we'd better get this over with."

Plans for the shutdown were outlined at a meeting Monday, July 20, 1981, with Munro, Davidson, Grunwald, Bear, Grum, Shepley and Hoyt among those present. Two days later at a noon meeting of the Time Inc. board's executive committee, with Gart in attendance, the decision was formally made.

As with *Life* nine years before, the closing of the *Star* required almost military preparations, but on this occasion, it was timed to the dawn hours when activity begins on afternooon newspapers. At 5:30 a.m. the morning of July 23, calls began going out to key *Star* executives. At 7:00 a.m. the *Star*'s outside directors were informed, and, at the same hour, the *Star*'s own story was set in type and locked onto the presses; street sale of that day's morning edition was to begin exactly at 8:30 a.m., by which time a press release had been delivered to AP and UPI. An announcement went up on the *Star*'s bulletin boards: after 128 years, the issue of Friday, August 7, 1981, would be the *Star*'s last.

But unlike those at *Life*, the *Star*'s closing scenes were played out in an atmosphere of recrimination as well as regret. The *Star*'s staff was shaken. Although aware of the paper's problems, most had counted on Time Inc. staying the full five years; they were not aware of the actual losses. Many felt betrayed and vented their anger at Gart, who spent much of that day telephoning other papers, trying to line up jobs for *Star* staffers.

In a *Star* column a couple of days later, Mary McGrory, a veteran of 34 years on the paper and its various escapes from extinction, spilled out her bitterness at Time Inc., "where people we did not know made mysterious decisions about our fate." Wrote McGrory:

> We're sad. But we're mad too . . . Until August 7, we're going to be telling you what goes on in this city and hoping to make you think about the scandal and outrage of it—the capital of the Western World a one-paper town.

The day of the announcement, Munro, Grunwald, Davidson, Shepley and Bear faced the press in a Washington hotel. Munro detailed the *Star*'s losses to date. All but $17 million of the $85 million spent so far had been written off; for that remainder, a reserve was being set up. After taxes, Time Inc. was some $35 million poorer for the *Star* experience (a loss only partially mitigated later by sale of the *Star*'s presses and delivery fleet to the *Post*).

Munro offered no excuses for the *Star*'s failure, except the company's initial misjudgment and overconfidence:

> We were either naive or unrealistic enough to think that we could come in and steal some of the market share from one of the most powerful papers in the country . . . We bought the paper cheap and that coupled with, maybe, our arrogance that we could come down here and make an inroad in this market is what came a cropper.

Added Shepley: "We're not blaming anybody, except our own shortcomings." He said he hoped Time Inc. might yet find a buyer for the paper. In the two weeks that followed, Time Inc. received some 60 feelers about the *Star*, including one, via a third party, from the Reverend Sun Myung Moon's Unification Church interests (who in 1982 launched the Washington *Times* as a morning rival to the *Post*). Shepley rejected the Moon approach outright. Of the others, about a dozen resulted in face-to-face meetings, in which Time Inc. stated its conditions for sale: the buyer must assure continued publication of the *Star* for at least a year, with adequate assurances for the paper's staff—stipulations designed to forestall a buyer from selling off the paper for its physical assets and leaving 1,427 editorial and publishing employees stranded without severance pay or pension rights. It was a responsibility no prospective purchaser was willing to assume. "When we showed them the arithmetic," Shepley recalled, "they ran for cover."

CHAPTER

30

The Flagship Prevails

TIME'S MAN OF THE YEAR for 1976 was Jimmy Carter. He was honored, *Time* explained in its January 3, 1977, issue, "because of his impressive rise to power, because of the new phase he marks in American life, and because of the great anticipations that surround him."

To some extent, Carter owed his rise to power to *Time*. The magazine had spotted him early, picking him in May 1971 out of a group of recently elected, more liberal Southern governors as the face for a cover story on the "new" South. Looking "eerily like John Kennedy from certain angles," as *Time* phrased it, Carter was pictured against a background of the Confederate flag and a cover slash proclaiming, "Dixie Whistles a Different Tune." *Time*'s story gave Carter his first national exposure. Carter proudly framed the cover portrait for his office.

While that 1971 cover story was in preparation, Carter had come to lunch with the editors at the Time & Life Building in New York. The Georgia governor proved to be an impressive conversationalist, and Donovan was attracted by his precise mind. Between them a friendship blossomed, nurtured by a weekend that Donovan and his wife spent as houseguests at the governor's mansion in Atlanta in December 1973.

Donovan acknowledged after the 1976 election that Carter had won his vote—but just barely. "I ended up . . . after a savage debate with myself, voting for Carter," the editor-in-chief told a Time Inc. staff gathering, explaining that it was not until the Sunday before the Tuesday balloting that he finally made up his mind: "I would not have been bothered if [Gerald Ford] had been elected but I concluded there was a wider range of possibilities with Carter. A possibility of greatness even, though certainly no guarantee. It was a somewhat more adventurous vote than a vote for Ford, and I thought the country was probably stable enough to afford some adventure." Donovan did not feel strongly enough to cast the company's vote also. For one thing, *Time* had never endorsed a candidate; *Life* had been the editorial voice of the Time Inc. magazines. Also, as Donovan said: "We didn't see such an overwhelming difference or overwhelming case for one man or the other that we wanted to take on all the inevitable headaches of an editorial endorsement."

During the campaign, this had been a matter of contention. Some media critics charged that *Time*, without actually endorsing Carter, was tilting toward him. He had indeed benefited from sympathetic treatment in *Time* as he emerged from Jimmy Who? obscurity to become a serious contender. His formal declaration of candidacy in December 1974 had rated a column and a half in *Time*, which had not been the case with some other Democratic hopefuls, and the attention that *Time* focused on Carter continued throughout his drive for the nomination. Quite unwittingly, *Time*'s promotion department provided further cause for criticism. In early 1976, full-page advertisements for *Time* appeared that seemed, to some, more like promotion for the candidate than for the magazine. Describing Carter's campaign strategy as reported by *Time*, the ads pictured him looking more like Kennedy than ever—lounging casually in a rocking chair on the porch of the Georgia governor's mansion. Framed by the building's tall white columns, Carter could have been on the White House balcony itself. Two of Carter's rivals for the nomination, Senator Henry Jackson of Washington and Congressman Morris Udall of Arizona, were among those who protested to *Time*.

Concerned about the criticism, Grunwald ordered up an assessment of *Time*'s campaign coverage. The results were not wholly conclusive. The Georgia governor had in fact got more space in *Time* than any other Democratic candidate—but not as much as a challenger on the opposite side, the ex-governor of California, Ronald Reagan. Still, it was a novel position for *Time* to be in, after years of almost automatic identification with the Republican Party, and demonstrated the extent to which *Time*'s politics had evolved under Grunwald's editorship and Donovan's supervision.

Carter's election was the occasion for a cordial exchange of letters between him and Donovan. Recalling an incident during his weekend in Atlanta when he had been out driving with Carter and the governor had personally flagged down a speeding motorist, Donovan wrote:

Dear Jimmy:

For name-dropping purposes, I am now going to claim that I once helped you make a citizen's arrest on a highway near Atlanta.

Please accept my warmest congratulations on the magnificent opportunity you have won.

Carter replied:

To Hedley Donovan:

And I used to think I was name-dropping when I even used your name around my staff members!

I deeply appreciate your congratulations, and I am grateful for your support. With your help, we will have a good administration!

The friendship continued and in 1979, after Donovan retired from Time Inc., he went to Washington at Carter's invitation to serve for a year as a White House senior adviser.

The personal relationship between the two did not inhibit *Time*'s coverage of the Carter administration. Barely eight months into Carter's presidency, coincident with an interview he gave Grunwald and several of the Washington bureau's correspondents in the Oval Office, *Time* was already suggesting "serious questions" about Carter's foreign policy. In January 1978, *Time* appraised Carter's first year and found "his administration . . . strangely out of focus, suggesting that Carter may not be sure what he wants to do." By May, press criticism of Carter was so widespread that Grunwald, in a *Time* Essay, addressed the question: "Are We 'Destroying' Jimmy Carter?" Grunwald rendered a split verdict, faulting the American people for demanding too much of their leaders, faulting Carter for delivering too little. The Essay marked a turning point: if *Time* had tilted toward Carter before the election, it was now leaning away.

When Grunwald wrote that Essay he was deputy to Donovan. He had moved upstairs in October 1977, ending his nine-and-a-half-year tenure as managing editor. Succeeding him at *Time* was Ray Cave, who had been executive editor of *Sports Illustrated* until March 1976, when Donovan, in a surprise move, had brought him over to *Time* as an assistant managing editor.

Seven months after the shift in editors came a change on the publishing side. Ralph Davidson left to assist Shepley in the president's office. Succeeding him as *Time* publisher was the magazine's former advertising sales director, Jack Meyers, who since 1972 had been publisher of *SI*.

The executive appointments came as corporate concern was increasing for *Time*'s competitive position in the newsweekly field. The magazine was not in serious trouble, but it was being pushed.

As the company's flagship publication—a hackneyed description, but more appropriate than ever since the disappearance of the weekly *Life*—*Time* carried a large share of corporate prestige. With a worldwide circulation of more than 5.5 million, it could claim that "more people in more countries get their news from *Time* than from any other single source."

Time's editorial leadership was a tenet of corporate faith likewise, and with it went pride in *Time*'s ability to pull off projects that other newsmagazines simply did not attempt. Two special issues that *Time* had recently produced for the U.S. Bicentennial commemoration were examples—journalistic re-creations of America's founding days, as if *Time* had existed then as a contemporary witness. The first, dated July 4, 1776, covered the events of that week of the Declaration of Independence; Thomas Jefferson was on the cover. Produced in May 1975, outside *Time*'s regular publishing schedule, it sold 6 million copies, of which more than 1.3 million were on the newsstands, about four times the average issue's sales. The second, the following year, took U.S. history forward to September 26, 1789, when President Washington, the cover figure, was forming his first cabinet and Congress was voting on the Bill of Rights. Sales of this issue nearly matched the first.

On the publishing side, the picture was mixed. As it had continuously since 1970, *Time* led all magazines in worldwide advertising revenues; in the U.S. it ranked second only to *TV Guide*. Yet the magazine had been going through a period of declining profitability. Income hit a five-year low in 1976, and in the fall of 1977, group vice president Art Keylor fretted at the prospects: "Mature magazines do not have a high potential for growth." He confessed concern about "the ability of our largest and most mature profit maker—*Time*—to solve the problem of an intensively competitive advertising environment." Keylor warned, "*Time* is subject to enormous built-in cost pressures operating under its current formula which mandate steady and sizable increases in advertising and circulation revenues. Its profit position is subject to possible reversals, especially in a recession year. Cost-cutting is helpful but does not provide the full answer."

In the struggle to maintain its advertising market share among the so-called "5N" group of newsweeklies (the other four were *Newsweek*, *Business Week*, *U.S. News & World Report* and *Sports Illustrated*), *Time* had to overcome two large handicaps. One was the raw price of advertising space in the magazine's pages. *Time*'s ad rates, and its subscription prices as well, reflected a deliberate corporate policy of aggressive pricing to maximize income; as publisher Davidson admitted cheerfully in a talk to the *Time* sales managers, "We haven't been bashful." A onetime insertion of a black-and-white ad page in *Time* cost as much as a half-minute commercial on network TV.

Time was also still plagued by the Madison Avenue concept of "audience efficiency" and the use of total readership rather than paid circulation to measure magazine advertising costs. At a price disadvantage already against *Newsweek* as a result of audience surveys, *Time* was put in a worse position by the 1974–75 figures of the Simmons research organization. Always much watched in the advertising trade, these figures purported to show a sudden, huge gain in *Newsweek*'s total audience and a drop in *Time*'s, making the two magazines virtually equal in perceived overall readership despite *Time*'s commanding lead in paid circulation. Overnight, *Time*'s advertising cost-per-thousand readers jumped 40 percent over *Newsweek*'s.

In January 1975, Time Inc.'s corporate anger exploded in a lawsuit in New York State Supreme Court. The company charged that Simmons employed "invalid and unreliable procedures" for audience measurement and asked the court to rule that Time Inc. need not pay. Simmons countersued; in a settlement reached in June, Time Inc. agreed to resume payments while Simmons agreed to change its survey procedures to distinguish between primary, "in home" readership and secondary or pass-along readership. But *Time*'s total audience was still a touchy subject when, in November 1976, Keylor staged a full-dress review of the question for the Time Inc. board of directors.

Associate publisher Reg Brack gave an overview of the history of audience research and its relation to *Time*'s sales strategy. For years, he pointed out, *Time* had managed to stay above the quantitative fight, preferring instead to sell the magazine's undoubted strengths: quality of circulation and editorial excellence. But now *Time* was being forced to play the numbers game:

> As one general magazine after another left the field, with the demise of *Life* in 1972, the magazine advertising business took a sharp change in the early '70s. All of a sudden *Time* was no longer just a prestigious selective magazine . . . only *TV Guide* and *Reader's Digest* [were] larger in the consumer field. This is a key point. Because of this, *Time* became regarded and even measured in quantitative ways we had always tried to downplay. *Time* also became the largest magazine in ad revenue, and thus the target for every other medium to shoot at. A new generation of media buyers was in place in the advertising agencies, now quite comfortable with the use of not only audience numbers but computer models, and a whole orientation toward quantitative decision-making . . . Selling the editorial qualities of *Time* and discounting audiences was becoming tougher and tougher in ad agency media departments, where the computer reigned supreme.

The settlement with Simmons had produced improvement in one respect, the directors were informed. The new Simmons figures showed *Time* and *Newsweek* with comparable pass-along readership of about 12 million each, but *Time* was shown to be holding an 8-to-5 lead over *Newsweek* in valuable primary readership.

Related to the two newsmagazines' relative audience size was a touchier question, to which Grunwald addressed his comments when his turn came to speak. This was "whether the proposition so often heard in the trade that there isn't much difference between *Time* and *Newsweek* is really true."

The unspoken background to Grunwald's remarks was the change that had taken place in *Time* under his editorship—a greater variety of writing styles, more personalized reporting and more use of outside contributors. *Time*'s reviews of books, music, cinema, theater and art were now signed. Sidey's former *Life* column "The Presidency" had moved to *Time*, and *Life*'s last editor, Tom Griffith, had begun a column of press criticism for *Time*, entitled "Newswatch." A signed sports column had also been launched (it lapsed shortly, however).

Grunwald conceded that *Newsweek*'s improvement tended to blur the distinction between the newsmagazines. But in reporting, writing and editing, he felt, *Time* was superior: "At our very best (need-less to say, we do not reach our very best every time out) *Newsweek* cannot touch us."

> In my opinion, *Time* is a far more distinguished magazine, of far greater quality, scope and depth. But it is true that some of *Time*'s excellence is in areas not necessarily appreciated by the casual reader, which I think includes most ad men.

Grunwald ran down specific areas of comparison:

> *Newsweek* has stronger graphics. I say stronger, not better . . . Some of the layouts are poor and yet the total effect is often gutsier and more inviting . . .
>
> *Newsweek* has a considerable asset in its signed opinion pieces. The introduction of the columnists represents *Newsweek*'s only really major modification of the basic newsmagazine formula. In one sense, of course, this was a reactionary move, because it was an important ingredient of *Time*'s original invention to get away from the babble of confusing and conflicting opinions and to offer a comprehensive, well-organized, consistent package. But today, a majority of readers probably like *Newsweek*'s opinion pieces and those who don't . . . are probably not especially offended . . .
>
> Their news judgment . . . is definitely smart. *Newsweek* is sometimes more willing to jump on a new subject quickly, even without preparation. In short, *Newsweek* does not mind promising more than it delivers if it can make a splash. This impresses some people.

With an editorial budget approximating *Time*'s, Grunwald said, *Newsweek* had moved from being "a second-rate imitator to a very strong challenger." The pressure was on *Time* to maintain its position by improving its "graphics and packaging," by bringing *Time* "more in tune with people's present interests," possibly by adding more opinion features, despite the hazards. One risk was in appearing more like *Newsweek*; the "second . . . more subtle reason" for not doing this before was "the tradition set down by Harry Luce . . . that all opinions expressed in *Time* should more or less represent those of the magazine. However, we did finally make the move toward columnists, and having gone this far, I am convinced that we will have to go somewhat further."

Part of the program outlined by Grunwald was, at that point, already under way. This was in brightening the look of the magazine, an area where Donovan and Davidson also had been pushing for improvement. As editor-in-chief Donovan was far more sensitive to magazine graphics than Luce had ever been; his periodic critiques to his managing editors were as likely to focus on what he considered bad layouts, jarring face-offs and poor picture choices as on substantive points in the text.

Although *Time* had undergone a redesign in 1971, neither Donovan nor Grunwald was entirely satisfied. Nor was *Time* using so-called "fast" color to the extent possible in news coverage. Color pages had first appeared in *Time* as early as 1934, when the magazine published a portfolio of Depression-era paintings, including Grant Wood's classic *American Gothic*. In 1951 Luce had made color a permanent feature, decreeing that there should be at least one such page in every issue. But this was always "slow" or feature color, printed weeks in advance. Color to illustrate current, this-week news coverage was beyond the technology of the times. Color pages could not be closed on the same tight schedule as black-and-white; long preparation was required for the four-color engravings used in the letterpress printing process that most magazines, including *Time* and *Life*, then used. In the mid-1960s, *Sports Illustrated*, forced to compete against color television, broke with the other Time Inc. publications and moved to the faster offset printing process, which used film in preparing color plates. By 1972 *SI* started to run 32 pages of color weekly, two-thirds of its editorial space. In contrast, *Time*, still using letterpress, was running on the average only two to three color pages out of an allocation of 48 or 49 editorial pages per issue. Most of this color was confined to the so-called "early forms" that went to the printer before the late-breaking news pages.

It was thus with a technology transfer in mind that Donovan had brought Ray Cave over from *SI* to *Time*. Cave came, Donovan noted, with experience in "all the phases of *SI*'s demanding schedules, including that magazine's pioneering use of fast color." Long delayed by budgetary considerations—six more color pages per issue, in offset, would add $3 million to *Time*'s $24 million editorial budget for 1977—the expanded color program was finally approved shortly before Christmas 1976. Grunwald put Cave in charge of it.

The program was launched with a flourish in the January 31, 1977, issue covering the Inauguration of Jimmy Carter. It had 12 pages of color, five of them news pictures of the festivities and formalities in Washington on the very day the magazine closed. *Time*'s pages sparkled, but the costs were alarming. Heiskell came down-

stairs to deliver a warning. Recalled Cave: "I looked up, and leaning against my doorjamb was the tallest man in the world, and he
was saying, 'If you use color at this rate you'll be $4 million over
budget.' " Cave reassured him, and *Time*'s course was set: the magazine was committed to a costly color schedule from which there was
no guarantee of financial return. As Grunwald wrote in a memo to
the staff:

> It is obviously quite expensive. It may be hoped that the addi-
> tional excitement and improved appearance that color brings to
> the magazine will eventually be reflected in increased circula-
> tion and advertising. But this is by no means certain.

Added color made a typographical redesign more urgent than ever.
In a fairly speedy four months, Walter Bernard, the former art
director of *New York* magazine, worked one up; he stayed on as
Time's art director to administer its execution. The new design was
unveiled in August. Once again, there was a change in logotype, a
slight thickening and sharpening of the letters in *Time*'s title for better newsstand display. A new feature, much copied later by other
magazines, was the simulated flap at the cover's upper right-hand
corner, suggesting a turned-down page, that was used to bill the
"inside cover" story—a second major article, running at nearly
cover-story length—which had increasingly become part of *Time*'s
editorial package. In the body of the magazine were new headline
typefaces, subheads announcing more directly what the stories were
about, and hairline rules around the text blocks to provide the sim-
pler, more orderly environment that *Time*'s now more numerous
color photographs required. Some on the staff, Cave for one, felt it
looked old-fashioned—and attractive for that very reason, imparting
an established look to the magazine. But the changes, as always with
Time (or, for that matter, with any other magazine), upset many
readers. Some 1,900 letters and telegrams, many quite emotional,
poured in, the largest number on any single subject that year. The
new design proved quite successful, however.

"It's a gamble I wouldn't have taken," Cave said of Donovan's decision to name him managing editor of *Time*. Cave's arrival at the
magazine, after a Time Inc. career spent entirely on *SI*, had shocked
the *Time* staff. In *Time*'s very structured edifice, where editors
started at ground level as writers and worked their way up, a para-
chute landing by an outsider on an upper-story balcony, so to speak,
was unprecedented. Cave himself was only too aware of that. "*Time*

is an institution and it behaves like one. Institutionally, it doesn't like anything different. I was not a *Time* animal. Basically, I'm still not a *Time* animal today," he remarked, years after his appointment. "I'm still an outsider in the sense of the institution."

Being an outsider had not inhibited Cave. He was a strong, self-assured man, with piercing eyes behind heavily bearded cheeks, aloof in his manner and not easy to know. He enforced his own style, a mixture of his newspaper city-desk background and his years at *SI* with Laguerre.

Curiously, Cave's entry into journalism was almost inadvertent. His first ambition had been to follow his stepfather, an Army general, into the military. Taking his stepfather's advice to get a liberal-arts education first, he had gone to St. John's College in Annapolis and had then tried teaching school, unsuccessfully. He ended up taking a job typing the social notes for a Maryland rural weekly. Graduating to the Baltimore *Evening Sun*, he spent almost ten years on the paper (with time out for Korean war service, in military intelligence) doing police and investigative reporting, eventually becoming assistant city editor. On the side, he worked as a stringer for *SI*, which hired him as a full-time writer in August 1959, the same week that he declined a similar job offer from *Time*. At *SI*, Cave climbed the masthead rapidly. Shortly after being named executive editor, in 1974, he had a tour of duty in Donovan's office as acting editorial director. Donovan was impressed and began to think of Cave as having editing potential beyond the sporting confines of *SI*. Donovan was aware that Cave had a reputation for being a tough overseer; from *SI* he brought also a reputation for ambition. The day of Cave's arrival at *Time*, one senior editor typed out a limerick and circulated it in the interoffice mail:

> There once was a new man named Cave,
> Who was neither a fool nor a knave.
>   "Years off I will lop,
>   "If I go straight to the top;
> "Think of the time that will save," said Cave.

Cave's appointment as managing editor was announced in September 1977, effective the following month. With his appointment came other masthead changes. Jim Atwater was named senior editor, and took over administration of *Time*'s color program. Otto Friedrich, who had produced the two hugely successful Bicentennial issues, became Nation editor, succeeding Marshall Loeb, who returned to the Business section and added a signed column, "Executive View," to his responsiblities; subsequently Loeb was named economics editor, a new title. In a later shift, when illness forced Friedrich to give up editing the Nation section, John Elson took over, also with a new title as national editor. In September 1978, Jason McManus was named an executive editor, joining Ed Jamieson in this rank, with senior editor Ronald Kriss moving into McManus's old slot as an assistant managing editor.

On the reportorial side of *Time*, there were also important shifts. With Murray Gart's departure in mid-1978 to become editor of the Washington *Star*, his deputy, Richard Duncan, a 16-year veteran of service in the Washington, Chicago, Ottawa, Miami and Los Angeles bureaus, took over as chief of the Time-Life News Service. Earlier, there had been a change of command in the Washington bureau. When Hugh Sidey stepped aside to devote full time to his column, national political correspondent Robert Ajemian became bureau chief. Strobe Talbott, Washington-based Kremlin watcher, became diplomatic editor; Laurence Barrett, White House correspondent.

Time's new editorial crew meshed well—better, in fact, than might have seemed likely when Cave was first put in. Like Laguerre, his mentor at *SI*, Cave was strict on deadlines and budgets, running a tight, disciplined editorial operation. Like Laguerre, he loaded his deputies with responsibilities, including top editing, or final editorial supervision, of all but the major stories that he watched personally.

As he took over the editorial direction, Cave was aware of his unfamiliarity with *Time*'s main news concerns: "I hadn't spent 17 years on domestic politics, economics, foreign affairs—or anything else but sport." Cave did, however, have the metropolitan newspaperman's feel for what sparked most readers' interest; in a style that Cave himself compared to Fuerbringer's, he kept *Time* quick on the news, with frequent shakeups in the traditional order of *Time*'s news sections to give front-page play, in effect, to cover stories. Cave was to gain a reputation as a shrewd judge of *Time* cover subjects: "Our reader now expects us to stay closer than ever to the news. At the same time we are determined to maintain *Time*'s back-of-the-book franchise."

Cave acknowledged his debt to his two experienced executive editors, McManus and Jamieson, both of whom had sat in as acting managing editor in the Grunwald regime. "From the day I got the job, I felt this strongly: that they would keep me out of trouble. I could depend on those two to keep *Time* working, and free me to do what I think I was brought in to do—help get *Time* to where it should be, especially to get at the looks of the beast."

In getting at the looks of *Time*, Cave brought strong ideas about the interaction of pictures and text. "The best art director *Time* ever had," Grunwald later called him. The graphic changes under Cave's editorship were partly evolutionary, building on the expanded color program and typographical redesign instituted earlier, but revolutionary in their cumulative impact. Picture displays in color grew larger. For greater dramatic effect, two-page spreads opening the major editorial sections became mandatory. More use was made of cartoons and charts to visualize statistics; here, the creations of Nigel Holmes, a British-born designer and chartmaker, who afterward became *Time*'s executive art director, set a new trend in graphic presentation. Catchy little art devices like the illuminated letters of old books were introduced to link together a series of related stories. Use of background tints to set off signed columns, boxes and other self-contained, partial-page editorial features was greatly increased.

Symbolic of the new pictorial emphasis was the rearrangement of *Time*'s editorial floor geography. The layout and picture departments, greatly augmented, moved into the space nearest the managing editor's corner office. While exercising closer personal supervision over *Time*'s graphics, Cave also asserted a greater editorial voice in the magazine's production process, particularly in the juxtaposition of advertising and editorial pages. Makeup editor Charles Jackson, who had been putting together *Time*'s editorial pages, in one capacity or another, longer than almost anyone could remember (he started as a copyboy in 1939) remarked: "Previously, the ad men presented you with a dummy and said, 'Fill it.' Cave would say, 'Oh no, you can't do that with my magazine.' A very convincing man, Ray."

Within the confines of continued tight editorial budgeting, *Time*'s quota of color pages rose slowly, reaching an average of 12 pages per issue in 1979, still less than a quarter of the magazine's total editorial content. Even that much offered a new dimension, Cave felt: "Black-and-white can never, or almost never, command a page or a spread so that it can be the raison d'être for that spread. But color is meant to be looked at, command attention. Its role becomes quite different . . . [to] get the readers' attention, force them into reading the story. *Time* is a text magazine; it is meant to be read."

Time writing changed as the graphics changed. Bolder pictures called for stronger text. McManus described the new demands put on *Time* writers:

546

Against a five-column picture you just couldn't start the usual sort of *Time* story in that tiny space [the remaining single column of the two-page spread]. You needed a tone poem. So this became a new form of address to the reader, a perceptible change in format, in the way stories were presented—a generous picture setting the stage, then a tone poem setting the mood, and after that the traditional *Time* story setting forth the facts.

Of course, you had to have people with the ability to do this—come in and write off the top of a story, and do these tone poems . . . It used to be that writers developed a proprietorial interest in a subject or continuing story and they'd be automatically chosen when something came up [in their area]. Now you'd have a sort of designated hitter who would be sent in . . .

It improved the writing, though. This kind of prose was so exposed that it had to be terrific. It became a showcase for talent, so there was a subsidiary benefit: it gave all the writers a reason to write better.

In November 1978, Cave, speaking to the Time Inc. board, measured the impact of *Time*'s editorial innovations. Most dramatic was the rise in newsstand sales, where in the past 22 months *Time*'s lead over *Newsweek* had doubled. Cave credited aggressive circulation methods as well as the new design, the new emphasis on color. "But what in the end we are achieving," he said, "is to reestablish what was always the fact: that the two newsweeklies are not the same." He outlined plans for maintaining the momentum: speeding up *Time*'s handling of news copy, competing more aggressively for news photos and bidding for serial rights to books that "we feel offer *Time*'s readers significant insights into the events of our era." Just the month before, *Time* had published excerpts from Henry Kissinger's diplomatic memoirs; the practice was maintained in succeeding years with excerpts from books by Watergate figure G. Gordon Liddy, Jimmy Carter and Alexander Haig.

"Finally, just sort of between us," Cave told the directors, "we are going to work at making *Time* more readable." Cave had strong ideas in this area also. Over the years, *Time* stories had been getting longer, and the redesign tended to squeeze out even more of the short items that once dotted *Time*'s pages. Cave had no quarrel with the lengths, as such. During Grunwald's editorship, the stories in *Time*, while getting appreciably longer, had also become "intellectually complete," he felt. But too often, in his opinion, too much information was being crammed in ("sausage stories," as these over-stuffed pieces came to be known around the office). Cave aimed to "loosen up our sense of what a *Time* story is." As he remarked later, in retrospect, "if we've done anything [about *Time* style] it's in having deliberately let it get a little sloppy, relaxed the prose a bit, deliberately left things out in order to help readers get through the piece . . . In my view, a story that isn't read needn't have been written. You may please yourself with such a story, but that's not the business we're in."

One immediate consequence of Cave's announced effort was a search for new writers—a program that resulted, eventually, in one of the most extensive turnovers in editorial staff since the early post-war days. In the process, the average age of *Time* editors and writers came down several years. The recruiting was helped considerably by an upgrading in the *Time* writer's status that had taken place during Grunwald's editorship.

From *Time*'s founding days, the only path to advancement had been the senior editor route, but in 1974, the masthead category of senior writer was established to give comparable status and pay to those who preferred to remain at the typewriter. And with the introduction of bylines, a number of *Time* writers were able to enlarge their individual reputations. These included Theodore E. Kalem, *Time*'s veteran theater critic; the Australian-born art critic Robert Hughes; Michael Demarest, who wrote with wit and elegance about life-styles and fads; and Lance Morrow, the most prolific of *Time*'s essayists, a younger writer of notable grace and erudition who had already developed quite a following among *Time* readers.

Cave recalled his own experience 20 years earlier, when he had first been offered a job at *Time*: he was told he would be assigned to Milestones—"where all our writers start." If that procedure had been relaxed somewhat, promotions were still largely from within. But now Cave started going outside the magazine's own ranks. His *SI* experience was pertinent; a third of the sports magazine's content came from nonstaff contributors, and Cave, who had been in charge of outside text at *SI*, was accustomed to scouting the field. "No one at *Time* ever had to learn to do that," McManus said. "We were uncomfortable at hustling outside talent."

Over the next few years, with more recruiting at the middle and upper levels, there was an infusion of proven talent. From the Washington *Post* came Roger Rosenblatt; from *Horizon* magazine, Stephen Smith; from the New York *Daily News*, assistant managing editor for features William Ewald, who came over to *Time* as a senior editor.

Among the new arrivals, Rosenblatt undoubtedly attracted the most attention. A Harvard-educated New Yorker, he had been an assistant professor of English, director of education for the National Endowment for the Humanities in Washington and literary editor of the *New Republic* before joining the Washington *Post*, where Donovan spotted him as a prospect for *Time*. Hired in 1980, Rosenblatt, then 39, proved himself to be a stylish essayist and versatile cover-story writer, but it was in a journalistic tour de force—a 23-page cover story, produced singlehanded—that he established his extraordinary talents. The story, "Children of War," researched and written in three months, examined the legacy of armed conflict on its young survivors in Northern Ireland, Israel, Lebanon, Cambodia and Vietnam. Rosenblatt's report was one of the most poignant stories *Time* ever published; it was later published as a book.* The impact of Rosenblatt's accomplishment was felt at *Time*, presaging a possible new development in writing and reporting: more solo feats. Commented McManus: "Here you had a superstar writer becoming a superstar reporter. For one man to produce a 23-page story in the magazine—that snapped a lot of heads around here."

In 1980, writers' bylines, hitherto limited to the critical sections, became standard throughout the magazine, with credit also to correspondents and reporter-researchers contributing the major reporting. The development was to bring name recognition to diplomatic editor (and later *Time*'s Washington bureau chief) Strobe Talbott, for his authoritative inside reporting on nuclear arms negotiations between the U.S. and U.S.S.R. He wrote two widely acclaimed books on the subject.

The turn of the decade was a critical period for *Time*. The last years of the Carter administration saw the American economy slide into recession with no abatement of the upward price spiral, which raised *Time*'s physical costs alone—paper, printing, postage—by $21 million in the years 1978 through 1980. *Time*'s up-and-down P & L demonstrated, as the publisher's report to management phrased it, "our leveraged vulnerability in poor economic conditions . . . against steady inflation."

Still, in 1978 ad page sales rebounded, and there was a sizable increase in net circulation income, reflecting higher subscription

*Anchor Press/Doubleday, 1983.

rates. That year also *Time* moved ahead of *TV Guide* to lead all magazines in domestic advertising, with revenues of $199,350,000, as reported by the Publishers Information Bureau (PIB). A fat plum, worth $5 million in ad revenues, was harvested early in 1979 when Gulf & Western Industries ran its entire 64-page annual report as an advertising insert in *Time*'s February 5 issue, the largest single advertisement ever carried by any publication.

But Jack Meyers moved into the publisher's office feeling that the company would have to put more money into the magazine. "The battleship was just staying there. It wasn't moving ahead," he said. "Ray [Cave] and I came to grips with investing in the product in a great big way—but at the same time making sure we got a return."

One investment project was a speedup in *Time*'s production process to get the magazine to subscribers faster—*Time* had lagged behind the competition in this respect. Slow deliveries were bad enough for newsstand sales, especially overseas where delays were the worst, and they were believed to affect subscription sales as well. The trouble centered in Chicago, where editorial and advertising copy for all editions of *Time* was assembled into page forms to be filmed for making printing plates. From Chicago, the film was either flown or trucked to 14 printing plants in the U.S. and abroad. Production hitches when late editorial changes came from New York, as well as weather delays that caused missed plane connections out of Chicago, compounded the woes of the corporate manufacturing and distribution department. Makeshift transportation arrangements were often necessary, such as the chartering of a trio of Learjets at a small suburban airport one harrowing weekend in January 1979 when a sudden severe blizzard grounded all air traffic at Chicago's O'Hare International.

In recounting that incident in the *Time* publisher's letter a couple of weeks later, Meyers announced a technological change that would abolish such occurrences in the future. An electronic transmission system for editorial copy would eliminate air shipments entirely. The new copy transmission system was developed by corporate manufacturing and distribution director James J. McCluskey, and general manager Richard A. Labich, and inaugurated in August 1979. Complete pages with black-and-white pictures, digitalized for reproduction by computer, began going by land lines to eight U.S. printing plants and by undersea cable to a plant in the Netherlands, where copies for Europe, the Mideast and parts of Africa were produced and film relayed by air to South Africa for printing there.

Shortly after the inauguration of electronic transmission for black-

and-white, *Time* began sending four-color pictures by satellite, using a facsimile system, to printers in Chicago, Los Angeles and Hong Kong. As a result, copies of *Time Asia* were on Hong Kong news-stands on Monday, while it was still Sunday in New York. In a bit of pardonable hyperbole, associate publisher Brack declared: "For us, it makes the jet age obsolete."

From the start, electronic transmission made possible some pre-viously unthinkable feats of print journalism. In October 1979, the resignation of Israeli foreign minister Moshe Dayan caught *Time* on a Sunday, a day past normal closing, but a full-page World section story was produced by that evening and caught 92 percent of all U.S. copies and 100 percent of *Time*'s overseas circulation. The extra production cost: a minuscule $1,000.

Even swifter editorial performances became possible when, in January 1982, *Time* moved completely to offset printing, narrowing further the time between closing the magazine in New York and starting up the presses. The ad sales department welcomed the move heartily. It brought *Time* into conformity with the rest of the maga-zine industry; for years it had been standing virtually alone—"like a dinosaur," Meyers remarked—in requiring advertisers to furnish four-color engravings for letterpress printing. Offset printing opened the door to another editorial advance, full fast-color capacity throughout the magazine, which finally came in 1984. Additional flexibility in preparing pictures and text prior to printing was gained when the company began to take into its own hands the electronic copy processing and transmission system formerly operated by the R. R. Donnelley Company, Time Inc.'s longtime contract printers. Using a satellite transponder under lease to Home Box Office, the system aimed to serve all the company's magazines.

In 1981 Meyers drew up a "ten-point integrated action plan" to reposition the magazine and assure its leadership in the newsweekly field. Management backed the plan with an $18 million investment commitment. "We'd been reacting," publisher Meyers recalled. "Now we took the offensive." *Time* boosted its rate base for the domestic edition, which had been held at 4,250,000 throughout the 1970s, to 4.4 million. Two more increases over the next two years brought *Time*'s guarantee to advertisers to 4.6 million. The circula-tion growth was also aimed at forcing *Newsweek* to take expensive steps to keep pace. "It pulls the rubber-band tighter," Meyers explained at a sales management gathering in September 1981.

As it turned out, not all of the $18 million investment was needed.

Time's profits were on the upgrade again; they hit a record high in 1983. And it was in a buoyant mood that *Time*, in 1983, celebrated its 60th anniversary.

That October, a special issue outside the regular publishing schedule sampled the main events of the intervening six decades, reproducing the words, the pictures and the typography that *Time* had originally used in reporting them. To this record of *Time*'s evolution as a newsmagazine, Grunwald added a prefatory editorial declaration, "*Time* at 60: A Letter from the Editor-in-Chief." In it, Grunwald restated the magazine's founding purpose and defined its present role. He recalled the old *Time*, "flip and irreverent" in tone, but carrying with this "a certain solemnity about American—and Western—values." Grunwald continued:

Today we like to think that some of the old irreverence is still there. As for American and Western values, *Time* very consciously maintains its faith in them. We believe in freedom, including freedom of conscience and enterprise; in democracy, however imperfect; in a strong and beneficial American role in the world, however difficult.

In 1963, in a 40th anniversary greeting, President John Kennedy thought he detected in a maturing *Time* "an occasional hint of fallibility." Well, yes. But *Time* still knows what it knows. We are still in the business of making judgments and we still do not claim objectivity, which from the start we considered impossible and undesirable. Instead we aim for fairness and balance . . .

Sixty years ago, the universe of knowledge, it appeared, was manageable . . . Brevity and simplification were the goals . . . The basic form of *Time* journalism was the narrative—chronological narrative when possible. And so it remains. But increasingly, exposition and analysis had to supplement narration . . .

Time always practiced "personality journalism" and still does. But events made it ever harder to uphold Carlyle's dictum that history is but the biography of great men. At 60 . . . *Time* is less likely than it used to be to explain events through people; roughly half its covers are about trends and events rather than individuals . . .

Occasionally, the enormity of these past 60 years has exploded the familiar framework of *Time* . . . and the physical appearance of the magazine changed dramatically. Yet the structure always reasserted and reassembled itself, the departmental structure that is the organizing principle and essence of *Time*. It is a form that not long ago some people proclaimed obsolete in a world of instant and random electronic communications [but which] in today's chaotic world . . . seems more useful than ever . . .

Journalism can never be silent: that is its greatest virtue and its greatest fault. It must speak and speak immediately, while the echoes of wonder, the claims of triumph and the signs of horror are still in the air. *Time* has spoken once a week for 60 years and, in so doing, has often been wrong—but, we hope, more often right.

A Corporation for the 80's

NO COMPANY RULE decreed a managerial change to mark the turn of each decade, but circumstances had made that a pattern. In 1959 and 1960 had come Luce's designation of Donovan as his successor and the accession of Heiskell and Linen to the chairmanship and presidency; in 1969, the managerial reorganization that brought in Shepley as president and made Heiskell chief executive officer. In 1979, the machinery was set in motion again. Donovan retired at 65; Henry Grunwald took over as editor-in-chief, with Ralph Graves as editorial director. The following year, Heiskell reached retirement age; Shepley, two years younger, likewise stepped down. Dick Munro was named president and chief executive officer; Ralph Davidson, chairman; and Clifford Grum, executive vice president. During this time also, in September 1979, vice chairman Roy Larsen, the last active member of the small group who had launched the enterprise nearly 60 years earlier, died at age 80.

These appointments marked a sharp break with the past, perhaps the sharpest yet in nearly 60 years of Time Inc.'s corporate existence. Heiskell's 20 years as chairman—the last ten as chief executive—and Donovan's long tenure—five years as Luce's deputy, then 15 years on his own as editorial chief—had given great continuity to the previous management. Also, that management had been

554

appointed by Luce, together with Larsen, and had worked intimately with both. Although Grunwald's editorial associations with Luce were close, Davidson had dealt with him mainly overseas, in Europe, and Munro admitted frankly that while on *Time* and *Sports Illustrated* he had barely glimpsed Luce: "I can't recall ever shaking his hand."

Differences between the new generation and the old went beyond this, however, and were especially marked on the business side among the younger executives Munro brought into position after his own appointment. To make a somewhat facile distinction, the earlier generation had proved themselves first as publishers, while their successors came in more widely experienced, and probably better trained, as managers. In this, they reflected their times: during the 1960s and 1970s, when they joined the company—often, but not always, from graduate business school backgrounds—management had come to be seen as a skill nearly abstract from the specific businesses to which it was applied.

For all his success as chairman, Heiskell never hesitated to admit that he had felt ill prepared to run Time Inc. "When I became chairman, I didn't know what a balance sheet was," he claimed, with slight hyperbole. He was determined that his successor would bring broader business experience to the job. Several years before his own retirement, therefore, Heiskell began shuffling likely managerial candidates among various assignments in the company.

Munro was one who had shown promise early. He had been with the company just two years when in 1959 *Time* promotion director Nicholas Samstag wrote in a prescient memo that he had "never known a man anywhere near Dick's age [28] to pick up the threads of a complicated new job so quickly and so well . . . would be a top executive for Time Inc. if we can hold him."

Dick Munro was 26 when he came to Time Inc., a crew-cut ex-Marine Corps rifle instructor, a thrice-wounded combat veteran of the Korean War. Born in upstate New York in 1931, Munro had moved to Florida with his mother after his parents' divorce, then had gone to Colgate University (the 26th member of his family to attend the school), majoring in English and psychology. He left after a semester to enlist in the Marines, ending up in trench warfare along the 38th parallel, sleeping all day and fighting all night against the Chinese troops entrenched at the other side of Korea's demilitarized zone: "We would get up toward nightfall, blacken our faces and set off single file across the DMZ looking for them." One night Munro felt a bayonet go through his leg. "Then I heard a grenade

555

hit and roll . . . fortunately, it hit my legs, not my head." Munro spent a year in the hospital. He emerged with skin grafts and missing a metatarsal bone in his left foot; he also had a 30 percent disability pension.

It was while he was back at Colgate, a big man on campus—president of the inter-fraternity council—that he was recruited for *Time*. After three years there, mainly in promotion, Munro moved to *SI* as assistant business manager, a job which, Munro conceded, he would not have been qualified for in later years. "Very few men in the corporate departments then had been to business school . . . It was a very simple company. Nobody looked at the balance sheets— they were all liberal arts people. Only the people in the controller's office understood bookkeeping." In 1962 he became *SI*'s business manager and in 1965, general manager. In 1969, when *SI* publisher Garry Valk was moved to *Life,* Munro was his obvious successor. But at the 34th (executive) floor meeting where the new appointments were being worked out, it was noted that Munro had just been sent to Chicago, to head Pioneer Press, and was not available. "What do you mean?" Valk retorted. "He's the most qualified, and he ought to have the job." Valk convinced Heiskell and Shepley, who called Munro back to New York. "If Garry Valk hadn't been there just then to speak up," Munro said later, "I wouldn't have become chief executive of Time Inc."

At *SI,* Munro was remembered by his colleagues as a publisher who "got his hands dirty, who paid attention to details and was involved in every aspect of the business." For his own part, Munro remembered the exhilaration of seeing the magazine which for so long had been a drag on corporate profits at last off and running.

As *SI*'s publisher, Munro continued to impress. In 1973, he was called in to Heiskell's office to receive a new assignment. "So far you've been very lucky," Heiskell told him. "Now I'm going to give you some cats and dogs." He meant the company's video operations, then quite unpromising ventures, which under Munro's supervision were to improve dramatically. By 1979 the video operations were on the road to rivaling publishing as a source of corporate income. ATC, which Time Inc. had acquired on Munro's recommendation, was well managed and profitable. HBO was minting money and growing astonishingly fast, though Munro disclaimed credit for its success. "My only contribution," he insisted, "was believing in Jerry Levin, who persuaded me that HBO had a future. For example, I am given credit for putting HBO on the satellite. I just approved it. Levin was the guy who believed." Credit clung to

Munro nevertheless, making him obviously a formidable contender for the job of running Time Inc.

Ralph Davidson was similarly being marked out for advancement. Davidson's abilities as a corporate ambassador had been demonstrated during his years abroad, with Time-Life International. Then, as publisher of *Time*, from 1972 to 1978, he had guided the magazine through a difficult competitive period. In May 1978 Shepley announced that Davidson was joining him in the president's office to "share my duties . . . and familiarize himself with all of Time Inc.'s major lines of business."

Clifford Grum was the exception to the rule of home-grown talent at Time Inc. He was so immediately impressive upon his arrival from Temple Industries in 1973 that Heiskell and Shepley soon set a larger role for him. As corporate treasurer, Grum displayed not only financial acumen but great skill as a negotiator, and his stint as publisher of *Fortune* from 1975 to early 1979 gave him a measure of magazine experience to complement the knowledge he brought of forest-products operations.

The selections represented joint recommendations to the board, by Heiskell and Shepley, in which Donovan had been involved before his retirement. "A sort of church-state collaboration," Donovan called it, in which "we were consulting each other in terms of how individuals would get along with each other"—particularly important in Time Inc.'s system of dual editorial and business hierarchies. Also applying in the selection process was what Heiskell described as "the Watson rule"—for the former IBM chairman who had sat on Time Inc.'s board—that the successors "be young enough to serve for ten years or so, giving them time enough to set their own course, to shape and implement their own policies." Formal preparation for the managerial transition began in January 1978, when Munro, then still heading the video group, was elected to the board of directors. In August 1979, a year before their retirement, Heiskell and Shepley created a corporate operations office consisting of Munro, Davidson and Grum, along with chief financial officer Dick McKeough and group vice president Bear. Munro, appointed as executive vice president of Time Inc., was named chairman of the new operations office. There he, in essence, performed the functions of a chief executive, reviewing operations, planning and policy—but without final decision-making authority. It was probably the closest thing to on-the-job training that a future chief executive could get.

In April 1980, six months before the transfer of power, Davidson and Grum were also elected to the board of directors. This briefly puzzled Time Inc.-watchers. The New York *Times* groped for an explanation: "Expectations had been that J. Richard Munro, executive vice president of Time and a director since 1978, would become the next chairman and chief executive officer and Mr. Davidson the next president. But with Mr. Grum's election to the board along with Mr. Davidson, some questions have arisen as to which of them might succeed to the presidency."

Since 1969, the company's hierarchical structure had conformed to a pattern common among large corporations, with the chairman serving as chief executive officer, the second in command as president and chief operating officer. Heiskell felt the arrangement was not quite right for Time Inc., however. As chief executive he held ultimate responsibility for running the company, while as chairman he had to manage Time Inc.'s unusually large board, which now numbered more than 20, of whom seven were outside directors named in the five previous years.* To lighten the burden on his successor, Heiskell proposed splitting these duties. "The board was dubious," Heiskell later remarked, "but with my typical lack of concern I bowled it through."

In June 1980, the executive choices were announced. Munro would be chief executive officer with the title of president. Davidson would be chairman of the board, representing Time Inc. to local and foreign governments and business groups—"all those outside forces that impinge on us," in Heiskell's phrase at the time. Grum would be executive vice president, with the group vice presidents reporting to him; he and Davidson would report to Munro.

As for the drama of the annunciation—there was very little. There was no remembered moment when Heiskell told Munro he had been chosen. In fact, Munro said, "I'm not sure Andrew ever told me." As Heiskell's retirement approached, Munro began to wonder. "I used to think, am I the crown prince or not? I started having lunches with him about two years earlier. I would come from those lunches thinking, What did he say? I think I went to the 'corporate rabbi,' Charley Bear, and asked him, and he told me that I would be c.e.o. Each time Andrew and I had a meeting it became

*Matina S. Horner and Robert T. Keeler (1975); James F. Beré, Michael D. Dingman, Henry C. Goodrich and David T. Kearns (1978); Donald S. Perkins (1979).

a little more obvious." Finally, Munro recalled, "one day I came in and he said, 'Well, I guess it's all set.' "

The new chief executive was a contrast to his predecessor. Aside from the physical difference—at 5 feet 8 inches Munro was a head shorter than Heiskell—there was a difference of manner and style. It became a cliché to describe Heiskell as "urbane" and "courtly" but only because those adjectives were so obviously correct. Heiskell made a point of living well and enjoying it. He appreciated fine food and wine; Grunwald, at the dinner marking the executive transition, likened Heiskell to "one of those great Bordeaux which he distinctly appreciates—suave, mellow, engaging but with an unmistakable air of authority." Munro's predominant qualities were energy, ebullience, enthusiasm; he was the all-American go-getter. He usually arrived at the office at 7:15, had working breakfasts, and was out by 5:30, often including six or seven miles of running in his schedule. He drank rarely, did not smoke and was more of a meat-and-potatoes man at mealtime. Munro maintained that he "never ate fish in my life," and at least once, on a foreign tour, brought a jar of peanut butter along as an emergency ration, in case the local cuisine proved too exotic.

Munro also brought to his job a particular zeal for two of Heiskell's and Donovan's long-running concerns: corporate philanthropy and the assurance of equal opportunity for all those who work or might work at Time Inc. Munro addressed dozens of different audiences on corporate social responsibility and declared that it was as important to Time Inc. as the company's financial results. Time Inc. had long been a major corporate giver; when Munro took over, it was donating only about 1 percent of its pretax profit to charitable causes. Munro quickly raised that to 2.4 percent and set a new goal of 5 percent.

Among the people with whom Munro would surround himself as chief executive was a trio of young executives who seemed headed for greater things: Jerry Levin, Nick Nicholas and Kelso Sutton. Born within a few months of each other in the northeast U.S., these three had independently made outstanding records for themselves, and clearly held Munro's confidence. In 1983 all three were elected to the board as directors, and by 1984 each was made an executive vice president reporting directly to Munro. Sutton, who had been publisher of *Sports Illustrated*, was named group vice president for magazines the same day Munro was made president; while his appointment was technically an action of the outgoing management, it was of course made with Munro's approval. Nicholas would later be named Time Inc.'s chief financial officer and in 1984, with his elevation to an executive vice presidency, Nicholas was put in charge of all video operations. Simultaneously, Levin, the man Munro had believed in at HBO, moved out of the video area to become the company's chief strategist and planner. These three men were to be Munro's most trusted lieutenants; they were as much a part of the new generation of management as Munro and Davidson themselves.

On the editorial side, the clock had ticked over a year earlier, with Donovan coming up to age 65 in May 1979. The two candidates for editor-in-chief, corporate editors Ralph Graves and Henry Grunwald, were already in position, both of them possessors of the requisite background. Graves, after *Life* suspended weekly publication, had been acting editorial director, had then spent a while dealing with films and cable TV, going on to *Time* as associate publisher before moving up as Donovan's deputy in April 1976. Grunwald had come up from *Time* 18 months later. Donovan explained that he wanted to set up the choice well in advance. But unlike the situation Heiskell faced on the business side, Donovan felt it necessary first to assure the status of the job he was passing on. "I having been personally anointed by Harry Luce," there had been no question about his own appointment, Donovan observed. "But legitimacy was hard to give to my successor, not being the founder of the company."

It was often remarked around the company that Donovan's great contribution as editor-in-chief was precisely this: in preserving the position itself. There was no disparagement in the remark. That the editor-in-chief's office as it existed in Time Inc. would survive him was not a foregone conclusion. To the office Donovan brought an immense presence, different from Luce's but commanding nonetheless; Donovan personally radiated vast authority and rectitude. Events, however, had threatened to erode the importance of the job within the corporate structure. When Time Inc. had been primarily a publisher, it had been quite logical for the editor-in-chief to be on an equal level with the company's chief executive. But as the company expanded and publishing operations, while also growing, came to comprise less than half the company's business, some board members, as related earlier, had raised questions.

In August 1977, Shepley as president had proposed that Time Inc. consider reorganizing itself in the form of a holding company and a number of subsidiaries. The company's disparate components had so little in common, his reasoning went, that they would operate more efficiently as independent units. Each subsidiary would have its own board of directors and its own chairman, who would report to the c.e.o. of the parent company. One subsidiary, embracing all publishing operations, would have an editor-in-chief, who would continue to report directly to the parent company's board of directors. While on paper this would have left the editor-in-chief with as much authority as before—he would still be in charge of all editorial matters and would answer only to the board—in practice it would have inevitably diminished his role: it would have broken up the triumvirate at the top. Henry Grunwald, newly in position as corporate editor, wrote Donovan that December, describing his objections to the reorganization proposal:

> Time Inc. is a force in the idea business, among other reasons, because it is in that business all across the board, from various kinds of publishing to broadcasting. The trouble with substituting a number of wholly owned subsidiaries for the present structure may not be only that it would seem to downgrade magazines, but that it might dissipate the overall impact and presence of Time Inc. in the idea business . . . The proposed reorganization runs the risk of diffusing—balkanizing—the component parts of Time Inc. It would leave the top management (noneditorial) of the parent company as the only body capable of directing and speaking for the company's idea enterprise *as a whole* . . . I assume from our conversations that in your view, the editor-in-chief should still exercise editorial judgment and "conscience" for the entire company, and that this fact should be made explicit. But can he exercise this constitutional function if, structurally, he is to be the editor-in-chief of only one or two subsidiaries? Despite his membership on the parent board, he would inevitably seem to have been transferred to a lower level of authority.

Donovan did not immediately oppose the reorganization plan, although he came to do so. And in the face of widespread in-house opposition, it slid from serious consideration as the year ended. But this did not settle the question entirely. There followed other suggestions, which never became formal proposals, that the editor-in-chief should report to the company's chief executive officer rather than directly to the board. These Donovan instantly opposed. Any such change, he felt, would inevitably compromise the editorial independence of Time Inc.'s magazines and books. He also recognized that another critical period of transition—his own retirement—was approaching, a period when his successor would be most susceptible to pressure for change. He therefore set out to get the editor-in-chief's functions concretely defined and officially recorded before turning them over to the next man.

The result was a statement presented to the board of directors, setting forth explicitly where Time Inc.'s chief editorial executive was to stand. In magazine publishing he was the final authority, answerable only to the board. That authority did extend to book and newspaper publishing (as the company was then engaged in), but with the recognition that his immediate editorial involvement here would be of a lesser degree. In the company's nonpublishing affairs, he was to be the editorial guardian, charged with alerting corporate management or the board itself to any activity that could adversely affect the Time Inc. publications. The status of the editorial director, as deputy, was made explicit also. The statement in full:

The Role of the Editor-in-Chief

The board of directors has the final responsibility for the editorial quality of Time Inc. publications, as it does for all other aspects of Time Inc. operations. The board exercises its responsibility for Time Inc. editorial quality through its appointment of the editor-in-chief, who serves at the pleasure of the board, and is responsible solely to the board for editorial content.

The board recognizes that Time Inc. as a corporation has been built upon the editorial quality of its publications, and that these publications have been intended, from the founding of the company, to advance the public interest as well as pay a competitive return on investment.

The board, recognizing the special character of the editorial process, does not undertake to pass upon editorial content or positions, and delegates to the editor-in-chief the continuing appraisal and direction of the company's editorial work. If the board finds editorial performance generally unsatisfactory over a significant period of time, it will appoint a new editor-in-chief, but it does not seek to supervise him month by month. The editor-in-chief is a member of the board and of its executive committee.

* * *

The board recognizes that Time-Life Books and the Washington *Star* are quite different in their editorial operations from

562

the magazines (and from each other), and benefit from a considerable autonomy. The board does not expect the editor-in-chief to maintain the same immediate authority over the editorial work of Books and the *Star* as he does over the magazines. He will, however, appoint the managing editor of Books and the editor of the *Star*, with the concurrence of the chairmen of those subsidiary companies; he will serve on the boards of directors of both companies; and their senior editorial executives will have direct access to him.

* * *

The chief executive officer of Time Inc., by delegation of the board, is responsible for the financial health of the company's publications. He is inevitably concerned with the quality of editorial performance, as the editor-in-chief must be concerned with the financial boundaries and consequences of the editorial effort. Where their responsibilities intersect, the c.e.o. and editor-in-chief are jointly responsible to the board.

* * *

In nonpublishing affairs of Time Inc., the editor-in-chief has the standing of a Time Inc. board member. He has further responsibilities that may apply if nonpublishing activities of Time Inc. seem to be in conflict with editorial positions of the company's publications; all board members value the integrity of the Time Inc. publications; the editor-in-chief is not assumed to have special virtue in this regard, but he does have a full-time responsibility for editorial quality. Thus he has a specific obligation to the board to express his concern, when such exists, to the c.e.o. and if necessary the board, as to whether the good name of Time Inc. publications might be affected unfavorably by some nonpublishing activity of the company.

* * *

The editorial director of Time Inc. is appointed by the board of directors, on recommendation of the editor-in-chief, and is the senior deputy to the editor-in-chief. He is available to report to the board and its committees, and the board in its discretion may invite him also to serve as a director.

Donovan's statement was formally adopted by the directors, as company policy, on December 21, 1978. At the same board meeting, on Donovan's recommendation, Henry Grunwald was appointed editor-in-chief, effective the following June 1, 1979, with Ralph Graves as his deputy. In comment later, Donovan said he had felt

it "extremely important to have Henry and Ralph set up as a team
... I'm grateful they worked together so well, for those several
years." (In 1984, at age 60, Graves retired; Jason McManus, then
executive editor of *Time*, succeeded him with the title of corporate
editor.)

On the evening of May 30, 1979, two days before the official transition, some 500 Time Incers gathered at the Plaza Hotel for dinner,
dancing and speeches marking what was, counting from 1928 when
Luce took over from Hadden, only the third change in Time Inc.'s
editorial leadership in over half a century. Correspondents were
flown in from around the world. The evening was in large measure
a salute to Donovan, to the integrity—the word echoed throughout
the tributes—and to the style that had imbued his 15-year editorial
stewardship. Observed Grunwald:

> I never really managed to acquire his uncanny knack for keep-
> ing his temper, nor have I mastered his restrained vocabulary.
> There is, you see, a special language—Donovanese. To give
> you only one example, when Hedley really disliked a story, he
> would say: "I have quite a few bothers with this." I will never
> be able to hear the word bother again without a kind of sinking
> sensation in my thorax.
>
> Nor could I ever emulate his massive calm. When I was man-
> aging editor of *Time* I often speculated what it would be like if
> we received the news of a second coming. I imagined that the
> phone would ring—not right away, but perhaps 25 minutes or
> so after the first flash. Trudi Lanz [Donovan's secretary] would
> say: "Would you come up to see Mr. Donovan please." I would
> grasp my usual tranquilizing cigar, and, braving the angry peo-
> ple in the elevator who hate cigars, would ride to the 34th floor.
> Hedley looks up from some useful reading, his face serene,
> while the sound of distant prayer rises from Sixth Avenue,
> along with lots of the prescribed wailing and gnashing of teeth.
> Hedley leans back in his chair and asks: "Well, what are the
> plans? Do you think it's worth a cover?"

Donovan's remarks about Grunwald were brief and unequivocating:

> The other day I came across an 18-page memo on the American
> press that Henry Grunwald had written to Harry Luce back in
> 1963, while Henry was a senior editor on *Time*. Luce had
> shown the memo to me, and I returned it with a three-word

note: "Thanks. Brilliant memo." You will notice the vanity of the old writer; here I am tonight quoting my own comment in full and not a word from Henry's memo. But brilliant was the word for Henry in 1963, it is the right word for him today, and I am confident that he will do a brilliant job as editor-in-chief. I am very proud to entrust my job to him.

Then, with a quote from a relative newcomer to Time Inc., Donovan added: "Arthur Temple once said to me: 'We have to keep the *magic* around here.' I like that word 'magic.' Henry, you are Magician-in-Chief."

Despite their marked personality differences as people, Grunwald and Donovan were close in their political views and editorial philosophy; both acknowledged their debt to Luce. In managerial style, Grunwald was more intense, volatile, inclined to move more quickly. His first few years would see the editorial shifts noted already: Bill Rukeyser from managing editor of *Money* to managing editor of *Fortune*; Marshall Loeb, to take over at *Money*; *People* managing editor Dick Stolley as managing editor of *Life*; executive editor Pat Ryan to the top job at *People*. Grunwald would authorize (in conjunction with Munro and the board) the launch of two new magazines, *Discover* and the short-lived *TV-Cable Week*. He also launched the "American Renewal" project of early 1981, in which all seven Time Inc. magazines published articles on how America could renew its sense of hope and pride. "It was a bit more theatrical than Hedley might have liked," Grunwald conceded, "but editing requires a little bit of show biz." Overall, however, "I didn't want to change things too much. At the outset there was no reason to want to do things differently."

On the business side the new management felt a strong urge for change. Munro, for his own part, declared his intent to limit his own tenure and to retire after ten years, at 60. Even this, he worried, might be stretching it; in his view, most managers should spend no more than six to eight years in a job. While admiring of Heiskell, he said flatly: "Andrew ran this place very well for 20 years. Too long. Nobody should run a company that long."

As was soon evident, Munro also intended more important changes, in the size and shape of Time Inc., and in its corporate performance.

Between 1970 and 1980 Time Inc.'s revenues more than quadrupled, to $2.9 billion, and through expansion and acquisition the company climbed from No. 187 to No. 137 on the *Fortune* 500. It ranked 100th in total return to shareholders over the decade. The new management wanted to improve on this performance. It therefore set a number of financial performance targets, including a return-on-equity goal of 20 percent—a substantial increase; Time Inc.'s average return during the 1970s had been 13.7 percent. There were strong arguments for measuring corporate performance by return on equity since it showed how well the company was investing the shareholders' money; Time Inc. was just one of many companies to make this its principal gauge of success. (Heiskell had tended to downplay return-on-equity targets, worried that they could discourage creativity. From retirement, he commented bluntly: "Yardsticks don't invent magazines; people invent magazines.")

More pressing decisions faced the new management as a result of the company's growing capital requirements. Partly because of the demands of the nonpublishing ventures—forest products for mill expansion and plant renovation, and video for cable installations and more recently, for movie production—Time Inc.'s capital needs had multiplied eightfold over the decade, to $400 million annually. Faced with the problem of allocating funds to areas offering the largest and surest returns, and shucking cash-hungry ventures earning relatively poor returns, management began undoing some of the expansion of the 1970s.

"It sounds like we were critical of our predecessors," Munro said later, "but the world had changed. We had grown *very* big and *very* capital-intensive. We did what we did because we had to. We had been handed one of the most prestigious companies in America, and didn't want to foul it up."

The shrinking process began in February 1981, four months after the managerial change, with the abrupt halt of Time-Life Films' plans for expansion (see chapter 22). Six months later, the Washington *Star* was closed (see chapter 29). In 1982, the planning began for the biggest contraction of all—a spin-off of Temple Eastex and Inland Container.

The proposal had been informally on the table for several years. Heiskell and Arthur Temple had discussed it as early as 1978, and there had been what Heiskell described as a "substantial nibble," in the $1.5 billion range, from another major forest products company. But Time Inc. saw "no urgent need" for divestiture at that point. ATC had just been acquired, HBO and Manhattan Cable had gone into the black and, additionally, Temple-Eastex's forest holdings had greatly increased the asset value of Time Inc.

The picture had changed subsequently. The sudden surge in video profits—they soared from $6.1 million in 1978 to $72.5 million in 1980—contrasted with the lackluster performance of the forest-products group, reflecting the difficulties in the building industry. During that period, moreover, forest products operations were demanding large capital infusions; from 1976 to 1981, the capital invested in these operations more than tripled, rising by nearly $600 million. In 1981, video pulled even with publishing in profitability and in 1982 video was well ahead, while forest products lagged further behind. Video's capital requirements nearly doubled but were justified by the group's stunning profits—two-thirds of Time Inc.'s pretax income that year.

Clearly, a reexamination was called for. In mid-1981, a nine-month study of the company's financial performance over recent years began, aimed at formulating, in Munro's words, "new directions for the future." Munro had put Nicholas in charge, and all members of senior management participated. The resulting report went to the Time Inc. board in March 1982.

The study made a strong case for bringing the company back to two main areas of interest, information and entertainment, through two main lines of business, publishing and video; forest products were out of place in Time Inc. The dictum of Luce's will—that Time Inc. should remain "principally a journalistic enterprise . . . operated in the public interest"—was recalled. In the enlargement of the company since then, Nicholas wrote, "much was accomplished . . . of which Time Inc. management can be proud." These included the greatly strengthened competitive position of the Time Inc. magazines which constituted "the historic heart of the company"; the development, "from a relatively small capital base," of such important new profit centers as HBO, *People* and *Money*; and the creation of "substantial, though hidden, asset value" in timber and timberlands. Over the past ten years, moreover, returns to Time Inc. shareholders were double the market average. But the corporate portfolio needed restructuring, Nicholas argued. There was enormous growth potential in video; magazines, although a "mature" business, produced "extraordinary" cash flows; books were less promising. Forest products had "low strategic potential" while consuming almost exactly half—49 percent—of all Time Inc.'s invested capital. "It must follow that timely divestiture of forest products is a strategic imperative for Time Inc.," he wrote.

The corporate decision was announced at the 1983 annual meeting of shareholders, in May. Management's plan called for creation of a new company, headquartered in Diboll, of which Clifford Grum would be chief executive. "Whether we like it or not," Munro declared then, "image is important. Currently ours has an element of corporate sprawl." In October the spinoff proposal for the new company, now named Temple-Inland Inc., was presented to the stockholders and in December it was approved. Under the spinoff plan 90 percent of Temple-Inland's stock was distributed to Time Inc. shareholders; Time Inc. itself retained 10 percent (with the proviso that this block would be disposed of within five years).

With the separation, Time Inc. returned to its structure of a decade earlier, with two main component parts—publishing and video. The enormous difference was in the scope of its operations. The company was publishing seven magazines instead of four. Time-Life Books had been reorganized and was regaining profitability. Instead of a few small cable operations, Time Inc. owned ATC, one of the two largest cable companies, as well as HBO, the nation's largest pay-TV network, and Cinemax.

In a letter to shareholders accompanying the 1983 annual report, Munro described the implications for the future of this "pivotal year for Time Inc.":

The result [is] a new Time Inc., turned solely toward the business of communications . . .

The forest products spin-off enabled us to begin 1984 with several major new advantages. First, we now have a clear-cut identity, both within the company and outside it. Second, cash flow and reserves are sufficient to satisfy the foreseeable capital needs of our current information and entertainment businesses. And third, for the first time in three decades, management can give its undivided attention to the growth areas where Time Inc. has carved out profitable consumer franchises . . . Notably new is our ability to move faster toward the company's primary financial goal—a solid increase in the value of Time Inc. to those who own it . . .

Operationally, our primary goal is to achieve profitable growth in Time Inc.'s two principal businesses . . . A second goal, scarcely less important, is to develop and acquire compatible new businesses . . .

We have two criteria for such new businesses. Any we choose must fit comfortably under our information and entertainment umbrella. Any we pursue must offer the potential for a high return on our investment.

In developing compatible new businesses or extending current ones, Time Inc. will be guided by a deep devotion to quality. That certainly is not new, but it will be newly strengthened . . . Achieving quality, we well know, is far more than a matter of philosophy and devotion. It also requires reinvestment . . . Reinvestments, when they can add perceptibly to our margin of quality, will be increased.

Unchanged in the new Time Inc. is the recognition that we must continue to take risks, though at improved odds. We're convinced, however, that the worst risk of all would be not taking any.

Index

579

586

CURTIS PRENDERGAST was with Time Inc. for 24 years, serving as news bureau chief in Tokyo, Johannesburg, Paris and London. He also spent brief tours as an editorial writer for *Life* and as associate editor of the European edition of *Time*, and has written two books for Time-Life Books.

GEOFFREY COLVIN, a member of *Fortune*'s board of editors, joined the magazine in 1978, after working in radio and television in the Boston area. Before coming to Time Inc., Colvin helped produce the memoirs of CBS founder William S. Paley.

ROBERT LUBAR began his 39-year career with Time Inc. as a foreign news writer. After ten years abroad as a *Time-Life* correspondent in the London, New Delhi, Bonn and Mexico City bureaus, he returned in 1958 to join *Fortune*, where he served as associate editor, assistant managing editor, executive editor and, from 1970 to 1980, as managing editor.

MARTA FITZGERALD DORION was head editorial researcher for the Canadian edition of *Time*, in Montreal, before rejoining *Time*'s New York staff as a senior researcher, later becoming deputy chief of research. She was also on the staff of *Fortune*.

RAISSA SILVERMAN, a senior editorial researcher for *Time*, was for five years head researcher for the magazine's Nation section, including the years of Vietnam and Watergate. She served also as researcher for *Time*'s Essay and Law sections.

JANE FURTH, formerly a researcher for Time-Life Books and Time-Life Records, is a second generation Time Incer, her father, the late Albert L. (Bill) Furth, having been executive editor of *Fortune*.

LEO McCARTHY is associate art director of *Fortune*.